MW01119861

How Television
Shapes Our Worldview

How Television Shapes Our Worldview

Media Representations of Social Trends and Change

Edited by Deborah A. Macey,
Kathleen M. Ryan, and
Noah J. Springer

LEXINGTON BOOKS
Lanham • Boulder • New York • Toronto • Plymouth, UK

Published by Lexington Books
A wholly owned subsidiary of Rowman & Littlefield
4501 Forbes Boulevard, Suite 200, Lanham, Maryland 20706
www.rowman.com

10 Thornbury Road, Plymouth PL6 7PP, United Kingdom

British Library Cataloguing in Publication Information Available

Library of Congress Cataloging-in-Publication Data
How television shapes our worldview : media representations of social trends and
change / edited by Deborah A. Macey, Kathleen M. Ryan, and Noah J. Springer.
    pages cm
  Includes bibliographical references and index.
  ISBN 978-0-7391-8704-3 (cloth : alk. paper) — ISBN 978-0-7391-8705-0 (electronic)
1. Television broadcasting—Social aspects. 2. Television broadcasting—Political
aspects. 3. Television programs—Influence. I. Macey, Deborah A., 1970- editor of
compilation. II. Ryan, Kathleen M., 1962- editor of compilation. III. Springer, Noah J.,
1986- editor of compilation.
  PN1992.6.H68 2014
  791.43'655—dc23
                                                                        2014004898

♾™ The paper used in this publication meets the minimum requirements of American
National Standard for Information Sciences—Permanence of Paper for Printed Library
Materials, ANSI/NISO Z39.48-1992.

Printed in the United States of America

This book is dedicated to Dr. Jack A. Barwind, who passed away during the editing process.

Contents

Acknowledgments

The editors would like to thank Ji Yoon Ru for her work as an editorial assistant on this book. They would also like to thank Alison Pavan and the team at Lexington Books and Rowman & Littlefield Publishers, Inc. for their help in bringing this edition to publication.

Chapter One

Introduction

Deborah A. Macey,
Kathleen M. Ryan, and
Noah J. Springer

On September 29, 2013, *CBS Sunday Morning* welcomed viewers to what they called "TV's Second Golden Age,"[1] claiming that while television is more vast than ever, programming is better than ever. Television and its increased choices and fragmentation created spaces where producers took risks and pushed the boundaries of what could be done on television. With cable channels and on-demand Internet streaming media like Netflix developing their own original series, viewers can choose from a variety of quality and niche programming. We see complex, detailed storytelling featuring people and situations not traditionally seen on the small screen: the political intrigue of a costume drama steeped in sex, gore, and mysterious white walkers (*Game of Thrones*, 2011–present); an ethically riddled emergency room nurse dealing with a little addiction problem (*Nurse Jackie*, 2009–present); a "modern" spin on the family comedy, including a same-sex family and a May-December romance (*Modern Family*, 2009–present); a tense spy thriller for the post-9/11 era, where the brilliant lead agent's battles with mental health issues threaten both her sanity and national security (*Homeland*, 2011–present). However, by referencing Newton Minow's now-infamous claim that television is a "vast wasteland," the CBS producers acknowledged that not all of our television landscape reflects the quality character dramas of *Breaking Bad* (2008–2013) and *Downton Abbey* (2010–present). Despite this proclaimed new golden age, reality TV still seeks the greatest profit for the lowest amount of capital (*The Real Housewives* franchise, 2006–present; *Jersey Shore*, 2009–2012)[2] and advertising continues to be the dominant funding model, promoting programming that focuses on the lowest common denominator for content.

While CBS celebrated television's second golden age, we were editing these chapters about television's vast impact on how we understand our place in the world and suddenly, the world intruded upon our editing process.[3] Two of our co-editors live in Boulder County, Colorado, where torrential rains caused what has been described as a thousand-year flood, drenching the Front Range of Colorado's Rocky Mountains in early September. In early November 2013, the most devastating cyclone to ever make landfall slammed into the Philippines; the human toll and physical damage from Typhoon Haiyan was still being dealt with at this writing, but at least 5,100 people were killed and millions displaced. Two weeks later, a late season outbreak of more than one hundred tornados and funnel clouds spread across a swath of the Midwestern United States from Milwaukee, Wisconsin, to St. Louis, Missouri (the home of our third editor). Personal experience and mediated experience collided; we found ourselves relying on television to understand what was happening across the globe and to know when it was safe to travel outside our homes (or when we needed to seek shelter). Since its entrance into our homes, television has been the predominant means of information distribution, and cultural storytelling; it is a medium through which the public accesses information about most everything. However, those programs that CBS and media scholars deem as a "quality" are not the only ones that teach us about world affairs and other cultures. Those series with seemingly little redeeming value also teach us a vast amount of information and expectations about history, politics, and social values of our own and others' cultures.

In fact, journalists, bloggers, and scholars have argued about the representations of family values in programs like *Here Comes Honey Boo Boo* (2012–present) and *Keeping Up with the Kardashians* (2007–present).[4] Through news, situation comedies, police dramas, and reality TV we learn about the world around us, and our role within it. These genres, narratives, and cultural forms are not simply entertainment, but powerful socializing agents that show the world as we might never see it in real life.

While our first book looked specifically at how television influenced perceptions of the self and identity, the current collection, *How Television Shapes Our Worldview: Media Representations of Social Trends and Change*, interrogates the ways through which television molds our vision of the outside world and informs our socialization within it. The editors have brought together a diverse set of scholars, methodologies, and theoretical frameworks that help explain television's powerful influence over how we learn about what is going on in the world, and conventional social norms and expectations about cultural interactions and institutions, even if these representations are incomplete and/or incorrect.

Scholars have long debated television's influence as well as its ability to accurately portray these societal conventions. In 1999, The History Channel released a documentary in its *Modern Marvels* (1994–present) series called, *Television: Window to the World.*[5] The documentary summarizes the history of television and its relation to society as a whole. However, this "window" metaphor had already been challenged by a variety of scholars who see it as disguising the true political and economic interests behind television, and limiting the potential discourse concerning the medium.[6] The other traditional metaphor for television is that of a mirror, reflecting contemporary society into our homes. Likewise, this conception of television has run into various critics arguing that television actually reflects the television owner's "perception of a symbolic universe that supports advertising"[7] or nostalgically presents the "least objectionable programming" as if it were fact.[8] The world represented by *Leave It to Beaver* (1957–1963) did not in fact reflect the racial composition of the United States in the 1950s. Nor did it reflect the political turmoil over civil rights, changing demographics, or the economic disparities of the time. The same could be said about the racial makeup of New York City at the turn of the century when programs such as *Friends* (1994–2004), *Sex and the City* (1998–2004), and *Will & Grace* (1998–2006) presented a "whitewashed" and economically inaccurate portrayal of life in the city. Rather, as Jason Mittell states, through narrative structures, news gathering strategies, editing techniques, and selective presentation, television acts as a "funhouse mirror that alters and distorts images: some elements are enlarged and highlighted, while others shrink or disappear altogether."[9]

Nevertheless, television has changed dramatically in the last fifty years. The big three (ABC, CBS, NBC) no longer dominate the television landscape; we no longer have the most trusted man in America, Walter Cronkite, who could turn the political tide against the Vietnam War with one out-of-character and unconventional news editorial.[10] Instead, television viewers chose from Fox News Channel's Sean Hannity and Bill O'Reilly or MS-NBC's Rachel Maddow and Chris Matthews, receiving a fragmented and fractured version of the news. The editors and authors of this collection agree upon television's vast power to shape our understanding of the world and the need to critically analyze contemporary television representations. Mittell's notion that it is the individual television viewer's perception that is reflected back and reinforced, possibly amplifying the distortions, typifies our current fragmented media landscape. Jack A. Barwind, Philip J. Salem, and Robert D. Gratz provide an enlightened view of the implications of this kind of selected narrowcasting in this edition, claiming that we have lost an understanding of the commons. In addition, this book examines how many aspects of our past and current social worlds are formed through television. While acknowledging the distortions, selectivity, and social constructions that skew and alter the content we receive in our homes, the authors investigate the pedagogical role of television and interrogate the ways that television teaches audiences about the world at large.

Despite its nostalgia and focus on identity, our first edited collection hinted at this second golden age and pointed to the increasingly fragmented television landscape.[11] This edited collection expands the discussion of how selective and fragmented viewing choices impact our notion of community, providing a framework for the book that is divided into six sections. The first section, "Not Necessarily the News," focuses on the role of television in current affairs, particularly news and politics. In "A Bigger Screen for a Narrower View," Barwin, Salem, and Gratz describe how people in the United States have sorted themselves into segregated and homogenized communities and how these lifestyle choices are also reflected in their homogenized, although fragmented, media choices. In particular they argue that these choices at best create an individualist view of the world but also contribute to creating a polarized understanding of our social world, "making it increasingly difficult to identify our common interests and to promote the general welfare." In the third chapter, Kathleen M. Ryan, Lane Clegg, and Joy C. Mapaye probe the oft-heard critique (from both the left and right sides of the political spectrum) of bias in the news media. The chapter investigates structural and partisan bias in televised news by examining the presentation and tone of news stories and interviews on cable channels and broadcast networks during the 2008 presidential election for political bias. In the final chapter in this section, "Television, Islam, and the Invisible: Narratives on Terrorism and Immigration," Tim Karis explores subjectivity and the terrorism narrative surrounding the German media coverage of the death of Osama bin Laden.

The second section of this book, "Boy (and Girl) Meets World," demonstrates how television intersects with individual lives and social trends. In chapter five, "Your Dreams Were Your Ticket Out: How Mass Media's Teachers Constructed One Educator's Identity," Edward A. Janak explores his decision to become a teacher juxtaposed with an examination of the trends in the US education system and mediated portrayals of teachers. Janak conducts an auto-ethnographic analysis of how televised depictions of teachers informed his own identification as an educator, particularly the influence of his favorite television teacher, Gabe Kotter of *Welcome Back, Kotter* (1975–1979). Janak finds himself, and now his students, at the intersections of various social identities. Katherine J. Lehman argues in "Defying Gravity: Fox's *Glee* Provides a Forum for Queer Teen Representation," that *Glee* (2009–present) is a place where queer teens can find visual comforts in knowing that they are not alone, as "it gets better."[12] In addition, Lehman asserts that other teens, allies, teachers, and parents can find various roles of acceptance of non-heteronormative sexualities through the range of situations and characters on *Glee*. As the series raises complex questions about gender and sexual identity, it empowers viewers to become advocates for acceptance in their own lives. Audiences are prompted to respond to anti-gay slurs, to advocate for same-sex relationships, and to develop greater compassion toward GLBTQ youth. Finally, Cindy Conaway and Peggy Tally long for the good old days, where their pioneering television single girls taught them about friendship, independence, and feminism, while riding the second wave of the women's movement and paving the way for all single girls, televised or otherwise.

Section three, "America's Most Wanted," explores the notions of good and evil and television's role in perpetuating these frames and their real-life implications. Chandler Harris and Lauren Lemley explore the notions of good and evil through two baseball episodes, asserting that the very different outcomes resulted not only from the individuals' responses to the incidents, but also from television's ability to frame and concretize these events in our national, historical, and cultural consciousness. In chapter 9, Susan H. Sarapin and Glenn G. Sparks expand on the idea that television cultivates our understanding of real life through a distorted and dramatic lens. In particular, the authors quantitatively assess perceptions of the US criminal justice system and find that there is indeed a "CSI effect" that influences individuals' beliefs and expectations. The last chapter in this section investigates our understanding of heroism, patriotism, and gender through two Cold War television series, *The A-Team* (NBC, 1983–1987) and *Airwolf* (CBS, 1984–1986; USA, 1987). Charity Fox argues that while conventional and traditional notions of these concepts are in constant flux, these two shows exhibit the paternalistic white hero's struggle to re-secure his dominant role within the social hierarchy.

The fourth section, "The More You Know," draws its title from a public service campaign airing on NBC for more than two decades, that "focuses on some of the country's most important social issues in the core areas of education, diversity, health and the environment" and provides information on creating positive social change.[13] Likewise, authors in this section emphasize the relationship between television and environmental and social change as represented on television. Carrie Packwood Freeman, an animal rights activist and scholar, writes about the representations of the two most prominent and enduring vegetarians on television: Lisa from *The Simpsons* (1989–present) and Phoebe Buffay of *Friends*. Freeman argues that through humor these representations challenge the "carnonormativity" of mainstream culture, but within the limits of broadcast television, ultimately providing a more morally relativistic view of eating animals, and at times, reinforcing stereotypes. Both Freeman and Jennifer Ellen Good connect consumption to environmental issues. Good expands the focus on the environment arguing that with "more screen" there is "less green." Through the lens of cultivation theory, Good explains that the more time we spend with television, the less time we have for other pursuits, specifically being out in nature. In addition Good argues that the more time spent with television, the more we are cultivated into a consumer culture, and ultimately this consumer culture is damaging to the environment. In the final chapter of this section, Katherine A. Foss explores how television medical dramas influence our expectations about health care on personal and systemic levels. This chapter examines the static and changing television portrayals of doctors over the past sixty years, while considering the roles of the patient and doctor/patient interactions. Ultimately Foss argues that a "disconnect exists between the current status of American health care and its images in entertainment television," despite this genre's dominance and diversity.

The following section, "The Voice" speaks to the ideas of power and authenticity in having a voice in the creation and/or the reception of television productions. Chapter 14, "Made Impossible by Viewers Like You: The Politics and Poetics of Native American Voices in US Public Television," interrogates PBS's production and editorial roles in perpetuating Native American stereotypes on television documentaries. In particular Leighton C. Peterson argues that "public television has been complicit in the erasure and misrepresentation of Native voices." While there is more support for Native American content, "old paradigms, tropes, and expectations continue." Peterson argues that by incorporating more Native voices in the production and editing processes and by allowing authentic Native languages on screen, Native Americans can challenge these misrepresentations. In chapter 15, "He Who Has the Gold Makes the Rules: Tyler Perry Presents the 'Tyler Perry Way'" Danielle E. Williams conducts a star text of Tyler Perry to discuss how Perry, as a public creative figure, uses his voice, vision, and power to reach and represent underserved African American audiences, while opening up opportunities for other Black television professionals. In "'Real' Black, 'Real' Money," Gretta Moody examines audiences' perception of "Blackness" in the reality series *Real Housewives of Atlanta* (2008–present). Her African American viewers discuss the limits of Black elite authenticity through the narrative and editorial construction of the *Real Housewives* franchise. The final chapter in this section, "Viewing 90210 from 12203: Affluent TV Teens Inspire a Cohort of Middle-Class Women" explores how the original *Beverly Hills 90210* (1990–2000) gave voice to a cohort of young women, now in their forties, to discuss relevant social issues at a time of transition, to explore and laugh about their changing attitudes and fashions as parents, all the while maintaining the strong bonds of friendship, like the characters in the series.

The final section of the book looks to the future. Stylés I. Akira and Larry Ossei-Mensah discuss how television series dictate the aesthetics of contemporary interior design. The authors argue that "trends in interior décor have depended heavily on television programming" and that these status symbols have displaced the real with artifice and contributed "to the meltdown of the global economy." The penultimate chapter, "Bordertown: Manufacturing Mexicanness in Reality Television," expands on Gloria E. Anzaldúa's notion of "Borderlands/La Frontera," by exploring both the physical and psychic borders between Mexico and the United States. Ariadne Alejandra Gonzalez argues that even with the changing demographics of the US population, misrepresentations of old world versus new world, outsider versus insider, and Mexican versus American endure in A&E's *Bordertown: Laredo* (2011), justifying historical and current racial inequities that systemically persist in these bordertowns. In the final chapter, "Cyborgs in the Newsroom: Databases, Cynicism, and Political Irony in *The Daily Show*," Noah J. Springer argues that previous accusations of political cynicism and apathy against *The Daily Show with Jon Stewart* (1999–present) prove problematic if the program is considered under Donna Haraway's "cyborg politic." Drawing on the text itself, Springer examines the underlying problems between comparing the ironic politics of Stewart and company with more traditional modes of journalism. Rather, Springer argues *The Daily Show* is better understood as thinking like a cyborg, drawing on an Internet as a database to construct political and media criticism.

How Television Shapes Our Worldview: Media Representations of Social Trends and Change offers a valuable addition to television and cultural studies. This book incorporates multiple theoretical frameworks and methodologies while keeping the pedagogical possibilities of television in view. The authors expose the continuing influence of television on how audiences view the world, while acknowledging the increasing fragmentation and distortion of the medium. Whether or not you think television is in its second golden age or a vaster wasteland than Minow predicted, for better or worse one thing remains true: television content, despite its various forms and genres, its changing screens and outlets, as well as audiences, shifting viewing patterns, produces the dominant cultural narratives and shapes the way we understand the world around us.

NOTES

1. *CBS Sunday Morning*, "Welcome to TV's Second 'Golden Age,'" reported by Lee Cowan, first broadcast September 29, 2013, by CBS.

2. *The Real Housewives* franchise started in Orange County in 2006 and has successfully branched out to Beverly Hills, New Jersey, New York, Atlanta, and Miami. *Jersey Shore* (2009–2012) produced six seasons, spinning off *The Pauly D Project* (2012), *Snooki and JWOWW* (2012–2013), and *The Show with Vinny* (2013).

3. Kathleen M. Ryan and Deborah A. Macey (eds.), *Television and Self: Knowledge, Identity, and Media Representation* (Lanham, MD: Lexington Books, 2012).

4. Kevin Tustin, "Journalist's Notebook: Honey Boo Boo and Family Values," published January 23, 2013; Lauren Palazzo, "Family Values from Honey Boo Boo Child," published January 19, 2013; Amanda S. McClain, "Keeping Up with Contradictory Family Values: The Voice of the Kardashians," in *Television and Self: Knowledge, Identity, and Media Representation*, eds, Kathleen M. Ryan and Deborah A. Macey, (Lanham, MD: Lexington Books, 2012), 575–585.

5. *Modern Marvels*, "Television: Window to the World," created by Bruce Nash, History.

6. Todd Gitlin, *The Whole World Is Watching: Mass Media in the Making and Unmaking of the New Left* (Berkeley: The University of California Press, 1980); Gaye Tuchman, *Making News* (New York: Free Press, 1978); Herbert J. Gans, *Deciding What's News: A Study of* CBS Evening News, NBC Nightly News, Newsweek *and* Time (New York: Pantheon, 1979); Edward S. Herman and Noam Chomsky, *Manufacturing Consent* (New York: Pantheon, 1988); Eileen R. Meehan, *Why TV Is Not Our Fault: Television Programming, Viewers, and Who's Really in Control* (Lanham, MD: Rowman & Littlefield Publishers, 2005).

7. Meehan, *Why TV Is Not Our Fault*, 5.

8. Stephanie Coontz, *The Way We Never Were: American Families and the Nostalgia Trap* (New York: Basic Books, 1992), 30.

9. Jason Mittell, *Television and American Culture* (New York: Oxford University Press, 2010), 270.

10. "Who, What, When, Where, Why: Report from Vietnam by Walter Cronkite," *CBS Evening News*. February 27, 1968.

11. Ryan and Macey, *Television and Self*, 3.

12. It Gets Better Project, http://www.itgetsbetter.org.

13. The More You Know, http://www.themoreyouknow.com/about/.

Section I

NOT NECESSARILY
THE NEWS

Chapter Two

A Bigger Screen for a Narrower View

Jack A. Barwind,
Philip J. Salem, and Robert D. Gratz

In *The Big Sort*, Bill Bishop argues that in recent years people in the United States have increasingly clustered into like-minded groups.[1] He documents how changes in area and regional neighborhood grouping have been reflective of political preferences, leading to polarized communities with divisions that are deeper and more irreconcilable than in previous eras. This geographic, economic, and political clustering is mirrored in a similar clustering in our media environments. Fragmentation of the media, including television, spawned niche genres. In turn, these specific segments of mass media produced audiences that can more easily remain within their own sphere of comfort. Television's evolution, including the development of cable and satellite, has contributed to a withering notion of the "commons," or the common good, and its replacement with social isolation primarily based on interests of the individual. Television has, to a significant degree, moved from promoting the commonalities among us to reinforcing our disagreements by targeting smaller groups and differing interests. This transition discourages the recognition of common problems or collective action, posing a fundamental threat to a democratic society.

THE DEVOLVING COMMONS

Throughout our nation's history, Americans have walked a tightrope, balanced between a quest for independence, individual freedom and liberty, and support for an interdependent system characterized by shared values, community resources (such as elaborate mechanisms for national defense and for public education), and overlapping interests. Visible examples of these interdependent systems range from the Boston Common, America's oldest park, founded in 1634, where Colonial militia mustered for the Revolution, to an interstate highway system linking communities and interests across the nation, to a comprehensive public school system that produced the best education generation in history, to a Congress that over the years has attempted to balance diverse interests and develop policies that pursue the common good and promote the general welfare. Our nation's history is characterized by a broad-based recognition that national success requires, in the midst of great diversity and occasional traumatic disruptions (such as the Civil War), that the national interest is best served by maintaining a central core of what we value in common. Increasingly, over the past half-century, political dialogue in this nation has undergone a fundamental transition away from any kind of focus on our commonalities. In 2003, historian Lizbeth Cohen described an earlier time when politicians such as Franklin Roosevelt, Harry Truman, and Dwight Eisenhower worked hard to persuade citizens of some common good.[2] She portrayed a future political climate in which politicians employing marketing segmentation techniques "at best construct a composite vision out of the specialized interests of their distinct constituencies, and at worst avoid discussing any common good at all."[3]

As politicians employed market segmentation analyses and techniques, they increasingly focused on the differences between specific segments of the population rather than on the common good. "When politicians began to apply one-to-one marketing methods to elections, they abandoned the possibility of a common good."[4] The consequences of this focus on segmentation were significant, contributing to an important change that pollsters detected in public opinion polls conducted in the 1990s. Bishop, whose own research relied on personal interviews with media researchers, noted the following:

> . . . people had grown intolerant of advertising's intrusiveness, but that impatience was just part of the deeper distress. Americans were developing a generalized discomfort with differing points of view. It was a deepening anger that encompassed politics, culture, entertainment, religion, and commerce. In the summer of 2004, J. Walker Smith told me that his polling for Yankelovich Partners detected this rancorous turn in public opinion beginning in the 1990s. People became "increasingly uncomfortable with tolerating trade-offs," Smith said. "So it makes it difficult for people to compromise or to listen to other people's opinions."[5]

One consequence of this increasing segmentation and deepening division of political differences has been a steady increase in irreconcilable differences within our political system. Far from focusing on seeking solutions based on the common good or the general welfare, our political discourse is increasingly characterized as a stalemate. Congressional scholar Nelson Polsby analyzed the institutional history of the federal government and identified the late 1960s as the time when the continuing deadlock began.[6] Polsby wrote, "In important respects the US population resembles the population that attempted to build the Tower of Babel."[7] It was as if Americans had lost the ability to speak a common civic tongue.[8]

In this political environment incivility leads to stagnation, confusion, and polarization. This in turn fosters more incivility reinforcing a destructive cycle. While politics has been viewed with a "suspicious eye" throughout American history, mutually agreed-upon protocols by politicians have traditionally constrained the type of behaviors cited above. No more! Politicians perpetuating lies, demonstrating rude behaviors during a Presidential address, and encouraging protestors who are performing vulgar and offensive acts on fellow members of Congress serve as prime examples.[9]

MEDIA FRAGMENTATION

At the same time these political changes were occurring, parallel changes were underway within media outlets. The network equivalent of the commons existed for the decades during the emergence of the television generation with the dominance of three major networks: CBS, NBC, and ABC. National evening newscasts included dominant personalities such as Walter Cronkite (CBS), Chet Huntley/David Brinkley (NBC), and Howard K. Smith (ABC) presenting the nightly news to families who often gathered together for this daily event. Whatever your position is on a liberal or conservative media bias, the dominance of these three networks for an extended period of time provided a common lens through which the vast majority of Americans viewed their nation, their world, and a wide range of issues. As these networks faced increasing competition for media attention, the screen through which Americans got their information and upon which they built their opinions grew bigger, both literally and figuratively.

Although cable television began in 1948 as an innovation bringing service to a rural area, the growth of cable television systems greatly enhanced the number and diversity of available information channels. This accelerating growth began in the 1960s as this rural innovation moved into more communities. By 1970, the number of subscribers had increased at an annual rate of about 21 percent, and the number of cable systems had grown by 14 percent per year.[10] As this growth continued and expanded, other changes in media resources also flourished. Satellite providers offered a similar diverse range of channels, and a still more diverse information universe arrived via the Internet. As the range of available media resources expanded, the opportunity for increasing fragmentation of media viewers also grew. The apparent inconsistency between having a broader range of media choices available for consumption yet selecting a narrower range of media outlets for utilization is similar to the self-sorting observed in housing preferences. Bishop summarized the situation as follows:

> Even if Americans don't live among those from another party as much as they did a generation ago, they certainly have increasing access through the media and the Internet to all manner of opinions and points of view. The choice is there, but there is a media corollary to the phenomenon of assortative mating. *Given unprecedented media choices, people self-segregate into their own gated media communities.* In cities (most outside the United States) where a variety of newspapers reflect an array of political points of view, people don't buy several newspapers to learn what others are thinking. Instead they buy the one that best fits their political proclivities. "They read one newspaper or the other based on what they agree with," University of Pennsylvania political scientist Diana Mutz told me. "It's one of the main problems with choice; we choose to be with people similar to ourselves."[11]

Some estimates of subscription television saturation are as high as 91 percent.[12] Peter Svensson noted a downturn in subscribers that he thought related to the current economic crisis.[13] However, he speculated that more people might be getting information from Internet sources. This point is critical, and in the last section, we detail how the Internet fragments and polarizes media consumption even more.

How extensive is media saturation? Thomas Mann and Norman Orenstein reported Adam Thierer's data from a Knight Foundation/AEI workshop on the "Information Needs of Communities in a Digital Age" as follows:

> In 2010 there were almost 600 cable television channels, over 2,200 broadcast television stations, more than 13,000 over the air radio stations, over 20,000 magazines, and over 276,000 books published annually. As of December 2010, there were 255 million websites, and over 110 million domain names ending in .com, .net, and .org, and there were over 266 million Internet users in North America alone.[14]

They continue:

> There are an estimated 26 million blogs on the Internet. YouTube reports that 20 hours of video are uploaded to the site every minute, and 1 billion videos are served up daily by YouTube, or 12.2 billion videos viewed per month. For video hosting site Hulu, as of Nov. 2009, 924 million videos were viewed per month in the U.S. Developers have created over 140,000 Apps for the Apple iPhone and iPod and iPad and made them available in the Apple App Store. Customers in 77 countries can choose Apps in 20 categories, and users have downloaded over three billion apps since its [the iPhone's] inception in July 2008.[15]

One might think the extreme amount of choices available would provide a diverse knowledge base. However, fragmentation led to the opposite outcome. We have previously commented on the plethora of media sources and the changes in the media that reinforced the narrowing of media choices.[16] The Internet with its ability to customize information to individual tastes fostered the creation of an information bubble in which individuals seek out and/or are presented with information that conforms to their existing beliefs.[17] This same argument can be made for the fragmented television offerings found on cable and satellite systems. In fact, current media audiences tend to stay within the bubble of their primary beliefs, not becoming exposed to arguments that challenge their belief systems.[18] Thus, talk-radio, Fox News Channel (FNC), CNN, and MSNBC, among others including the new media outlets of the Internet, iPad, iPod, smartphones, and the like, express extreme political views often passed on to the public under the guise of news to an audience predisposed to accept their message as the truth, thus potentially yielding an audience that is homogeneous and frequently "dogmatic," ripe for anxiety, fear, and anger. Mann and Ornstein observed the following: "With the increased competition for eyeballs and readers, all media have become more focused on sensationalism and extremism, on infotainment over information, and in the process, the culture has coarsened. No lie is too extreme to be published, aired, and repeated, with little or no repercussion for its perpetrator."[19]

In a news marketplace based on targeting and size of audience and governed by what Richard Latham calls "The Economics of Attention," the 24/7 news cycle provokes and demands programming that produces an audience to consume advertised products, though profit may not be the only motive for these media outlets.[20] The Internet and the ever-expanding blogosphere add more and more opinion to the mix. Eli Pariser observed that mostly like-minded souls follow blogs, creating a "filter bubble" in which more and more people know less and less.[21]

The American press has changed over the nation's history, making a transition from the partisan press of the 1700s, through a period emphasizing media ethics and responsibility lasting into the twentieth century, to the market-driven, niche-focused contemporary media we see today.[22] Media competition often leads to a sensationalized media product. Fringe views produce a large audience. Fear builds the size of audience, particularly an audience made vulnerable by its own ignorance and sense of economic trepidation that exists today. While a "free" media is an inherent and essential aspect of a democracy, functioning as a "watch-dog" representative of the people, "for-profit media" frequently yield social anxieties in an effort to build audience share. The media simultaneously informs and protects as well as produces anxiety, fear, and anger. FNC developed a business model that became a standard and other outlets copied. FNC discovered success by identifying a loyal group of like-minded followers (in this case conservatives) who like hearing the same message repeated over and over again but in different ways by different commentators who provide support for basic fears (MSNBC and the old Current TV copied the same model to a lesser degree with liberals). Simultaneously, FNC assured their viewers that their messages represented "Fair and Balanced" news. It is interesting to note that FNC profits were greater than the combined profits of NBC, CBS, and ABC even though the size of viewership was less.[23] The major networks cut their news budgets and drastically reduced personnel with the result being an "agenda setter" with little depth in terms of hard news and more attention to soft news about lifestyles and entertainment.[24]

Network news today reminds one of the original Headline News Network (HLN) when cable first started. HLN broadcast thirty-minute news reports only interrupted by breaking news. Each program mostly consisted of summaries of stories with live reports of breaking news from CNN, an affiliate of HLN, and there were occasional feature segments on slow news days. One thirty-minute program followed another with each consequent program updating the headlines and stories from the previous broadcast.

Today, people present different levels of reality as if all ideas about reality are equivalent. An uncritical public and a media trying to sell its products cannot differentiate descriptions from inferences from evaluations. Events, reports, meta-reports, editorials, and entertainment are equally "real." Media presents them as real and an uncritical public consumes the products as real. Whatever we construct is real in its consequences.

CHOOSING REALITY

Today's audiences are not passive consumers of information. Individuals select the content and how to process it. The interactive nature of the new technologies also provides the opportunities to actively engage in the construction of the content we consume. Self is the source.[25] We construct the technological milieu we inhabit.

In the contemporary media environment, a significant number of people either fail to see the subjective nature of news reporting or simply prefer a "talking head" who reinforces their point of view. This latter position is supported in a Pew Research Center report that 40 percent of Republicans regularly watch FNC while only 12 percent regularly view CNN and just 6 percent regularly view MSNBC.[26] Democrats demonstrated some diversity with 25 percent watching CNN, 16 percent watching MSNBC, and 15 percent tuning into FNC.[27] Associate this data with the housing patterns and the growing intolerance of those with different opinions cited at the start of this chapter and a picture emerges of a reflexive relationship between a specified media outlet and a specified audience. It could be argued that the media and the audience feed each other and, by so doing, create a "wishful" world-view.

In two recent columns, Leonard Pitts offered observations related to these issues. His first column commented on the state of critical thinking today. Pitts noted that an acceptable contemporary strategy appears to be to "ignore any inconvenient truth, any unsettling information that might force you to think or even look with new eyes upon, say, the edifice of justice. Accept only those "facts" that support what you already believe." He concluded that, "when people are determined to believe a lie, there is nothing more futile than the truth."[28]

In his second column, Pitts discussed a statement made by Arizona Senator Jon Kyl. Kyl claimed that if you want an abortion, you go to Planned Parenthood, and "that's well over 90 percent of what Planned Parenthood does."[29] Politifact, the organization that routinely checks the claims of political figures, confirmed estimates close to Planned Parenthood's own report that only 3 percent of its services were related to abortion, and Politifact rated Kyl's statement as false.[30] Pitts quoted a later clarification from Sen. Kyl's office indicating that Kyl's statistical claim "was not intended to be a factual statement." Pitts observed this incident typified a pattern characterized by "audacious lies . . . repeated ad nauseam until people mistake them for truth . . . [with] the most absolute contempt for the facts and for the necessity of honest debate." He concluded that situations such as this one are not so much cases of liberals or conservatives as they are cases of "true believers so rigidly committed to their ideological crusades that they feel justified in vandalizing reason and sacrificing integrity in furtherance of their cause. The end justifies any means. . . . If you can't prove your points with the facts at hand, make up some facts and prove it with those."[31] Additionally, as advocates employ this strategy, media frequently report on both the made up "facts" themselves and the reactions that others have to these invented news items, thereby creating an echo chamber that reinforces what were originally invented "facts." As far back as 1944 Ernst Cassier suggested the following:

> Physical reality seems to recede in proportion as man's symbolic activity advances. Instead of dealing with the things themselves man is in a sense constantly conversing with himself. He has so enveloped himself in linguistic forms, in artistic images, in mythical symbols or religious rites that he cannot see or know anything except by the interposition of (an) artificial medium.[32]

Neil Postman adds, "What is peculiar about such interpositions of media is that their role in directing what we will see or know is so rarely noticed."[33]

Postman goes so far as to consider media as epistemology—media as knowledge, not just a source of knowledge. In a way the media invent the reality they later report as "truth."

Dealing with the differences has always been difficult with just two parties, but public figures must also deal with constituents, sponsors, and observers. These third parties will hold public figures accountable for their actions. However, in the past, many of these constituents et al. did not witness the actual confrontations and negotiations that are central to making policy. When they are present to observe conflict between others, the nature of the conflict changes. The presence of these third parties and any audience increases the likelihood that face issues will dominate, and the social actors will make more dramatic efforts to support their preferred images and attack the images of others.[34] They will become more animated and express more polarized views as communication yields to performance for an audience.[35] Technology diminishes the likelihood that public figures can find a backstage as live coverage and dissemination of their communication has moved from C-SPAN to YouTube to Twitter. It is difficult to distinguish political drama from governance. Indeed, it has become difficult to distinguish authentic events from staged performances.[36]

As recently as 2000, the most pervasive news and the mass media outlets were local and network television news, newspapers, cable, radio, and magazines. A significant development in the equation above is the advent and proliferation of cable. As more and more of American society became wired, "news" outlets became fragmented, moving to serve niche audiences. Cable and satellite news are to over-the-air network news as magazines are to newspapers. Fragmentation developed simultaneously with the ubiquitous, 24/7 news cycle and its voracious demand for information. The Internet joined the fray and along with TiVo moved electronic news from synchrony to asynchrony, increasing audience along the way. John Tooby observed, "The Internet also releases monsters from the Id—our evolved mental programs are far more easily triggered by images than by propositions, a reality that jihadi websites are exploiting in our new round of religious wars."[37]

E-mail can also reinforce information and invented "news" collected from the news media and the Internet. After conducting a national telephone survey immediately after the 2008 presidential election, R. Kelly Garrett noted that e-mail usage, by fostering "informal political communication within existing social networks, poses a unique threat to factual political knowledge" and that "the data demonstrate rumors e-mailed to friends/ family are more likely to be believed and shared with others and that these patterns of circulation and belief exhibit strong political biases."[38] In 2012, 19 percent of people saw news on social network sites, and about 15 percent of US adults (25 percent for 18- to 29-year-olds) report that they receive most of their news from family and friends through social networking, with over three-quarters then following links to full news stories.[39] The result of all this is an audience which self-selects exposure to reflect and reinforce its strongly held opinions. David Frum noted that catastrophic events such as the Boston Marathon bombings or the Sandy Hook shootings are unlikely to change perceptions since, even after such horrific events, people will select sources that confirm already established attitudes and beliefs.[40] The more educated and informed are also better equipped to challenge anything they might encounter that might challenge their perceptions. In the end, social change may only be possible through generational change, a process of attrition.[41]

With a plethora of news sources reflecting the bias of the audience, the problem becomes one of attention. How does one compete for the same audience knowing that size does matter? The issue is economic. Latham points out that we have moved from a world defined by "stuff" to a world defined by "fluff."[42] In an economy of attention, where information is abundant and not in short supply, the competition is for "eyeballs and ears." Fluff sells, packaging is more important than the package. Thomas Davenport and John Beck identify an interesting trend in the print news market that illustrates the fight for attention:

> In general, the newspapers requiring the most attention to be digested (and not coincidentally, those supplying the most and highest-quality information) such as the *Wall Street Journal*, *New York Times*, and *Washington Post*, have a declining circulation, whereas easier-to-attend-to papers such as *USA Today* have had long upward trends in circulation.[43]

In television, this trend is also evident. In an earlier piece, we noted the tendencies for consumers *and* the producers of public discourse to confuse various forms available to them.[44] A *news report* attempts a description of the event, and the criteria for such a report is accuracy or at least as confirmable a report as possible. *Meta-news* consists of reports of other reports, and the criteria for any synthesis and analysis of other reports are similar to the original reports themselves. How accurate is the newscast or web news compiler? An editorial is an evaluation of an event and often involves statements about what should be done about events. Criteria for such a format are similar to good argument and involve accuracy, logic, and good evidence. Finally, entertainment is a dramatic media performance. What happens in such a performance is intended to be exaggerated and to challenge an audience's sense of perspective. Problems develop when opinion in the form of an editorial or entertainment becomes the "news." It should come as no surprise that the "news networks" such CNN, FNC, and MSNBC have steadily increased the amount of opinion and decreased the amount of news.[45] An MSNBC executive recently declared that his network was not the place to come for breaking news.[46] A content analysis of *The Daily Show*, an admitted source for entertainment and fake news, revealed the show rivaled national sources for presenting traditional news.[47]

Additionally, information communication technology has enabled anyone to become a reporter. Law enforcement officials and traditional media obtained photos and messages from people at the recent bombing at the Boston Marathon and other tragedies. The people at the event extended their participation with the authorities, and these same people became stringers for news bureaus. Local television stations frequently encourage their viewers to upload the videos they have taken to expand their capacity for on-the-spot news coverage. These bits and pieces of "speed journalism" are not enough to "make the news," since someone must connect them into a sensible narrative.[48] The story can be wrong—inaccurate—as when the *New York Daily News* continued to run pictures of the wrong people as the Boston Police Department's primary suspects.[49] One of the men in the pictures reported over 200 hundred aggressive phone messages within the day of the publication of the pictures, described people following and harassing him, and received advice from the Boston Police to take down his Facebook account.[50] The interactions of a tragic event; a panicked public; multiple amateur sources of data; pressured reports at a newspaper, station, or website; and management and owners competing for readership have led to cyberbullying and stalking.

In the past, there were expectations that an editorial opinion would conform to standards for good argument and rhetoric. The public provides little reasoned discourse online. The messages in discussion boards or forums exhibit three characteristics: (a) negative emotions, (b) polarization, and (c) flaming.[51] Arguments are stunted with little development or structure.[52] Many are afraid to voice a different opinion.[53] Those professionals hired to post opinions admit that the pressure to express something immediately leads to superficiality and bad grammar.[54] Furthermore, there is the temptation to dramatize and to entertain.[55]

The most viable options are for mindful and critical uses of information and communication technology, processes that require those who use these technologies to become more deliberate and involved. Although people are more active in accessing data, too much of the processing of that data into information and knowledge has been passive and reflexive. Reversing the big sort requires a conscious effort at trying to understand different points of view and evaluating our own ideas and values as well.

WE HAVE MET THE ENEMY

Media are merely a part of a self-organizing process that includes our participation. Media executives learn what we value and they reinforce the values by broadcasting and publishing what we want to hear. The final product will be an amplified message that may bear little resemblance to what happened. "When the facts contradict the legend, print the legend" the publisher noted in John Ford's classic film *The Man Who Shot Liberty Valance*. After selecting and consuming from what media offer, we express our values in more polarizing terms. Media executives pay attention to these expressions and the cycle continues.

In this analysis, we suggested that even as the opportunities for access to an ever widening supply of information have grown steadily and at an accelerating rate, a general response has been to narrow the channels on which individuals rely. Even though the screen and the information available through that screen have grown bigger, the view collected from that screen has frequently grown narrower. Focusing primarily on what has happened in the national political environment, Bishop offers this summary of the last quarter century:

> Beginning nearly 30 years ago, the people of this country unwittingly began a social experiment. Finding cultural comfort in "people like us," we have migrated into ever narrower communities and churches and political groups. We have created, and are creating, new institutions distinguished by their isolation and single-mindedness. We have replaced a belief in a nation with a trust in ourselves and our carefully chosen surroundings. And we worked quietly and hard to remove any trace of the "constant clashing of opinions" from daily life. It was a social revolution, one that was both profound and, because it consists of people simply going about their lives, entirely unnoticed. In this time, we have reshaped our economies, transformed our businesses, both created and decimated our cities, and altered institutions of faith and fellowship that have withstood centuries. Now more isolated than ever in our private lives, cocooned with our fellows, we approach public life with the sensibility of customers who are always right.[56]

We suggest the narrowing described by Bishop is based to a significant degree on the way that we interact with the mass media and other electronic sources of information, on our self-imposed restriction of our sources of information, on our increasing tendency to act in a self-reflexive manner by choosing sources that reinforce our pre-existing point of view, and our unwillingness to engage in genuine dialogue and argument. Robert Reich noted the following:

> . . . we increasingly live in hermetically sealed ideological zones that are almost immune to compromise or nuance. Internet algorithms and the proliferation of

media have let us surround ourselves with opinions that confirm our biases. We're also segregating geographically into red or blue territories; chances are that our neighbors share our views, and magnify them. So when we come across someone outside these zones, whose views have been summarily dismissed or vilified, our minds are closed.[57]

Through this narrowing of our view, we have created a fundamental risk for our nation *by making it* increasingly difficult to identify our common interests and to promote the general welfare.

In the quest for "eyeballs," the producers of the news construct dramatic narratives rife with conflict, whether or not that drama overstates the reality it portends to report. Dealing at a high level of abstraction (opinions of opinions) is far more interesting than the event itself. In this way the news reinvents reality and we are left with "all the 'news' that's fit to invent." We participate in the invention by selective exposure to various outlets, and we use our online activity to construct our own inventions and to propagate the inventions we find comforting. We are left with Walt Kelley's admonition expressed in the first Earth Day poster: "We have met the enemy, and he is us."[58]

NOTES

1. Bill Bishop, *The Big Sort: Why the Clustering of Like-minded America Is Tearing Us Apart* (Boston: Houghton Mifflin, 2008).

2. Lizbeth Cohen, *A Consumers' Republic: The Politics of Mass Consumption in Post-War America* (New York: Knopf, 2003).

3. Cohen, *A Consumers' Republic*, 342.

4. Bishop, *The Big Sort*, 194.

5. Bishop, *The Big Sort*, 189.

6. Nelson W. Polsby, *How Congress Evolves: Social Bases of Institutional Change* (New York: Oxford University Press, 2004).

7. Polsby, *How Congress Evolves*, 147.

8. Bishop, *The Big Sort*, 236.

9. Recent examples include events such as those reported in Carl Hulse, "In Lawmakers Outburst, a Rare Breach of Protocol," *The New York Times*, September 10, 2009, A26; Paul Kane,"'Tea Party' Protestors Accused of Spitting on Lawmaker, Using Slurs," *Washington Post,* March 20, 2010, http://www.washingtonpost.com/wpdyn/content/article/2010/03/20/AR2010032002556.html.

10. Rolla E. Park, "The Growth of Cable TV and Its Probable Impact on Over-the-Air Broadcasting," *The America Economic Review*, 61, no. 2 (1971), 69.

11. Bishop, *The Big Sort*, 74; italics added.

12. "Percent of Households with Cable and Satellite Television, " Free By 50, accessed February 14, 2010, http://www.freeby50.com/2010/02/percent-of-households-with-cable-and.html.

13. Peter Svensson, "Pay TV Industry Loses Record Number of Subscribers," *ABC-News*, August 10, 2011, http://abcnews.go.com/Technology/wireStory?id=14271831#. T7ub247v3v9.

14. Thomas E. Mann and Norman J. Ornstein, *It's Even Worse Than It Looks: How the American Constitutional System Collided with the New Politics of Extremism* (New York: Basic Books, 2012), 59.

15. Mann and Ornstein, *It's Even Worse Than It Looks*, 59.

16. Jack A. Barwind, Philip J. Salem, and Robert D. Gratz, "All the News That's Fit to Invent," Paper presented to the Popular/American Culture Associations, SWTX PCA/ACA Joint Conference. San Antonio, TX. April 23, 2011.

17. Eli Pariser, *The Filter Bubble: What the Internet Is Hiding from You* (New York: The Penguin Press, 2011).

18. "Americans Spending More Time Following the News, Ideological News Sources: Who Watches the News and Why," Pew Research Center for People & the Press, accessed September 12, 2010, http://www.people-press.org/2010/09/12/section-1–watching-reading-and-listening-to-the-news.

19. Mann and Ornstein, *It's Even Worse Than It Looks*, 62.

20. Richard A. Latham, *The Economics of Attention: Style and Substance in the Age of Information* (Chicago: The University of Chicago Press, 2006).

21. Pariser, *The Filter Bubble*.

22. Eric Burns, *Infamous Scribblers: The Founding Fathers and the Rowdy Beginnings of American Journalism* (New York: PublicAffairs, 2006); W. James Potter, *Media Literacy*, 5th ed. (Los Angeles: Sage, 2011).

23. David Carr and Tim Arango, "A Fox Chief at the Pinnacle of Media and Politics," *The New York Times*, January 10, 2010; "Americans Spending More Time Following the News," Pew Research Center for People & the Press.

24. See: Kathleen M. Ryan and Joy Chavez Mapaye, "Beyond 'Anchorman': A Comparative Analysis of Race, Gender, and Correspondent Roles in Network News," *Electronic News* June: 4 (2010), 97–117.

25. S. Shyam Sundar, "Self as Source: Agency and Customization in Interactive Media," in *Mediated Interpersonal Communication*, ed. Elly A. Konijin, Sonjia Utz, Martin Tanis, and Susan B. Barnes (New York: Routledge, 2008), 58–74.

26. "Americans Spending More Time Following the News."

27. Ibid.

28. Leonard Pitts Jr., "Facts Might Be Stupid Things, But They Are Still Facts," *Austin American-Statesman*, March 21, 2011, A9.

29. Leonard Pitts Jr., "Lies, Lies and More Lies," *Austin American-Statesman*, April 14, 2011, A7.

30. Pitts Jr., "Lies, Lies and More Lies."

31. Ibid.

32. Ernst Cassirer, *An Essay on Man* (New Haven: Yale University Press), 25.

33. Neil Postman, *Amusing Ourselves to Death* (New York: Penguin Books, 1985), 11.

34. Joseph. P. Folger, Marshall Scott Poole, and Randall. K. Stutman, *Working Through Conflict: Strategies, Relationships, Groups, and Organizations*, 6th ed. (New York: Pearson, Allyn and Bacon, 2009).

35. Roy. J. Lewicki, David. M. Saunders, John. W. Minton, and Bruce Barry, *Negotiation*, 5th ed. (Boston, MA: McGraw-Hill Irwin, 2006).

36. Kenneth Gergen, *The Saturated Self: Dilemmas of Identity in Contemporary Life* (New York: Basic Books, 1991).

37. John Tooby, "Rivaling Gutenberg," in *Is the Internet Changing the Way You Think?*, ed. John Brockman (New York: Harper Perennial, 2012), 64.

38. R. Kelly Garrett, "Troubling Consequences of Online Political Rumoring," *Human Communication Research*, 37, (2011), 255–274.

39. "State of the News Media 2013." *Pew Research Center's Project for Excellence in Journalism, accessed March 18, 2013,* http://stateofthemedia.org.

40. David Frum, "After Boston, Nothing Will Change," *CNN*, April 23, 2013, http://www.cnn.com/2013/04/23/opinion/frum-boston-change; David Frum and Celeste Headlee. "Why Can't Traumatic Events Bring Politicians Together?" *NPR*, April 26, 2013, http://www.npr.org/2013/04/26/179240478/why-cant-traumatic-events-bring-politicians-together.

41. Frum and Headlee, "Why Can't Traumatic Events Bring Politicians Together?"

42. Latham, *The Economics of Attention*.

43. Thomas. H. Davenport and John C. Beck, *The Attention Economy: Understanding the New Currency of Business* (Boston: Harvard Business School Press, 2001), 95.

44. Barwind, Salem and Gratz, "All the News That's Fit to Invent."

45. "State of the News Media 2013."

46. Bill Carter, "Devoted to Politics, MSNBC Slips on Breaking News," *New York Times*, June 2, 2013, http://www.nytimes.com/2013/06/03/business/media/devoted-to-politics-msnbc-slips-on-breaking-news.html?hp&_r=4&pagewanted=all&.

47. Pew Research Center's Journalism Project Staff, *"Journalism, Satire, or Just Laughs: 'The Daily Show with John Stewart' Examined."* Pew Research Journalism Project, accessed May 8, 2008, http://www.journalism.org/files/Daily%20Show%20PDF_3.pdf.

48. Trevor Butterworth, "Speed Journalism: Some Stories Need Just a Tweet—Some Need Real Thought," *The Daily*, June 13, 2011.

49. Mark Morales and Bev Ford, "Boston Marathon Spectator Salah Barhoum, Who Was Interviewed by Authorities Following the Bombings, Swears He 'Didn't Do It,'" *New York Daily News*, April 18, 2013, http://www.nydailynews.com/news/national/hs-track-star-speaks-didn-article-1.1320766?print.

50. Morales and Ford, "Boston Marathon Spectator."

51. Dirk Oegema, Jan Kleinnijenhuis, Koos Anderson, and Anita van Hoof, "Flaming and Blaming: The Influence of Mass Media Content on Interactions in Online Discussions," in *Mediated Interpersonal Communication*, eds, Elly A. Konijin, Sonjia Utz, Martin Tanis, and Susan B. Barnes (New York: Routledge, 2008), 331–358.

52. Donald Ellis and Ifat Maoz, "Online Argument Between Palestinians and Jews,." *Human Communication Research*, 33, no. 3 (2007), 291–309.

53. Angela C. S. Marques and Rousley C. M. Maia, "Everyday Conversations in the Deliberative Process: An Analysis of Communication Exchanges in Discussion

Groups and Their Contributions to Civic Discourse." *Journal of Communication*, 60, no. 4 (2011), 611–635.

54. Justin Green, "A Brief Mediation on Blogging," *Daily Beast*, May 21, 2013, http://www.thedailybeast.com/articles/2013/05/21/a-brief-meditation-on-blogging.html.

55. Frum, and Headlee, "Why Can't Traumatic Events Bring Politicians Together?"

56. Bishop, *The Big Sort*, 302–303.

57. Robert Reich, "American Bile," *The New York Times*, September 23, 2013, http://opinionator.blogs.nytimes.com/2013/09/21/american-bile.

58. Walt Kelly, *Pogo: We Have Met the Enemy and He Is Us* (New York: Simon & Schuster, 1987).

Chapter Three

Measuring the Messenger: Analyzing Bias in Presidential Election Return Coverage

Kathleen M. Ryan,
Lane Clegg, and Joy C. Mapaye

Media bias has long been discussed in relation to the presentation of political news and information to media consumers. Bias is defined as "a concept used to account for perceived inaccuracies to be found within media representations"[1] and is usually used in reference to both broadcast and print news reporting. According to John Hartley, accusations of bias imply that one viewpoint has been favored over the other in a story, a concept that inadvertently leads to the idea that "there are only two sides to a story."[2]

In the United States, journalistic professional organizations offer reporting standards to benefit the public: news is to be bias-free, objective and factual, and not laced with opinion or other persuasive devices. These guidelines are tied to ethical codes. The Society of Professional Journalists (SPJ) urges journalists to investigate the accuracy of all of their information, identify their sources whenever possible, question a source's motive if they ask to remain anonymous, and to examine their own cultural values and to avoid imposing them on others.[3] Electronic journalists are encouraged by the Radio Television Digital News Association (RTDNA) to "present analytical reporting based on professional perspective, not personal bias."[4]

But in the eyes of the public, these standards seem to be ignored, especially in regards to political reporting. A 2008 survey by the Pew Research Center for the People & the Press found that 70 percent of voters believed the media wanted Barack Obama to win the presidential election, with only 9 percent saying McCain was favored. When respondents were grouped by political affiliation, the divide became even more striking: 90 percent of Republican, compared to 62 percent each of Democratic and Independent, voters said the media was backing Obama.[5] Even in non-election news, political affiliation can influence the perception of bias: 70 percent of Republicans felt that the press was politically biased in reporting, contrasted with 39 percent of Democrats and 61 percent of Independents.[6]

The question then becomes: does this perceived media bias truly exist? Are certain networks prone to inadvertently (or purposefully) favoring one candidate over the other in their supposedly objective news coverage? This chapter determines if the public perception is, in fact, reality. It analyzes television and cable news coverage of 2008 election returns and identifies if the coverage is biased or not.[7] While the election coverage in this study was skewed in favor of the winner (Barack Obama) and the Democratic Party, the results also demonstrate that overall each network offered analysis from partisans across the political spectrum.

LITERATURE REVIEW

The Perception of Bias

Historically in the United States, bias in news coverage was not considered something to be avoided. Instead, America's founders and political leaders (such as Alexander Hamilton, Thomas Jefferson, and George Washington) embraced bias, utilizing print media to publicize their thoughts and opinions through persuasive writing in self-funded newspapers and other documents.[8] Debates became particularly heated during the time of the Federalist and Anti-Federalist papers, when newspapers were notorious for publicizing a single viewpoint through poignant writing and persuasion. Historian Eric Burns, who calls Hamilton a writer whose "abilities matched his zeal,"[9] says Hamilton didn't shy from highly opinionated pieces on issues—and individuals like Jefferson. But Hamilton wasn't the only founder who refused to hide his bias. Burns notes that Sam Adams (*Boston Gazette*), James Rivington (*New York Gazetteer*), and John Fenno (*Gazette of the United States*) were all part of what he dubs the "gutter age" of news reporting, with the press "conceived as weapons, not chronicles of daily events . . . masthead to masthead, firing at each other, without ceasing, without blinking, without acknowledging the limitations of veracity."[10] Jefferson himself argued that the competing opinions in a free press, would leave readers "open to . . . all the avenues of truth."[11]

Bias may have been accepted—and expected—in reporting during America's foundation, but in the modern era ideological bias in the news is one of the more discussed yet least understood concepts for those studying contemporary politics and reporting.[12] Edward S. Herman and Noam Chomsky claim that while the news media are supposed to be both obstinate and ubiquitous in their attempts to be true and just, they in actuality only serve the economic, political, and social needs of privileged groups that dominated domestic society; propaganda—and bias—fuel US media reporting.[13] However, Matthew

A. Baum and Tim Groeling found traditional news sources, such as those cited by Herman and Chomsky, are less likely to provide slanted or biased coverage than overtly partisan sites. The results, they argue, indicate that "the increased reliance of many politically attentive Americans on partisan (web) sites such as Daily Kos and Free Republic could potentially pose a significant challenge to American democracy."[14]

Hostile Media Perception

It may be that bias, like truth, is often in the eye of the beholder. Hostile media perception argues that "two groups surrounding a single issue . . . tend to believe the media unfairly favor the other side."[15] Hostile media perception has been used for a variety of topics—religious conflicts, social issues, labor disputes—and researchers have found that audience members favoring one side of an issue think the bias is particularly prevalent if they have been told (by partisans or researchers) that the media source opposes their beliefs.[16] Tien-Tsung Lee argues that cynicism, either personal or political, is one of the best predictors of perceived media bias by individuals.[17]

Hostile media perception has been used to investigate bias in televised news coverage of election and politics. Joel Turner looked at the bias that viewers attach to the television channel *before* they even consider the program. He focuses on viewer perceptions of CNN and Fox News Channel (FNC) and found that attaching the CNN or FNC label to a story or program sends an "ideological cue" to the viewer regarding the content of that story or program. Turner's experiment manipulated network attributions; i.e., identical stories were identified to subjects as airing on either CNN or FNC. He found that individuals could watch virtually identical stories yet derive different partisan signals depending upon which network with which the story was identified: CNN stories were perceived as having a liberal slant, FNC stories as conservative, and those with no network affiliation as neutral.[18]

In a study of the 2004 election campaign, researchers looked at the link between the influx of soft news programming (including satirical "fake" news on Comedy Central) and the rise in perceived partisanship of news organizations. The first part of the study used national survey data to find the factors that led political partisans to choose certain cable news networks and programs. The second part of the study employed experimental methods to reveal how a viewer's partisan feelings influenced their perceptions of cable television shows and channels including CNN, FNC, and *The Daily Show*. The study found that partisan participants perceived more bias in programs that did not align with their own personal political beliefs than programming which did align with their beliefs. The authors argued the results suggested that partisanship is a driving force behind cable news and programming.[19]

Jonathan Morris compiled surveys from the Pew Research Center, gathered during the 2004 Presidential election, that considered the political consequences of audience fragmentation as well as the polarization of American television audiences. Of all networks, Morris found that FNC has been the biggest beneficiary of audience fragmentation, picking up the individuals who feel disillusioned by what they perceive to be a liberally biased media. The results of the study showed that those who watch FNC have distinct voting patterns and hold a different perception of political reality when compared to others. The study concluded the television news audience is divided and that fact will likely continue to contribute to the further polarization of our news media.[20]

Election Cycle Bias

Election year reporting has long been a specific focus of studies seeking to understand how—or if—media organizations slant election news.[21] Studies include how an anchor's facial expressions can influence voting,[22] the use of election exit poll data to determine a winner before polls closed and its impact on voting,[23] and the partisan-based agenda-setting function of bloggers and political pundits.[24] The problem is that the studies, far from developing a consensus, seem to instead contradict one another.[25] For instance, Frederick Fico and Eric Freedman found that most newspaper stories favored the Democratic or more liberal candidate. However, newsrooms with a higher proportion of female editors were more balanced in terms of total stories favoring conservative and liberal candidates, and stories covering open races as well as stories from newsrooms with a bigger proportion of women reporters tended to provide more evenly balanced treatment of candidate platforms.[26]

By contrast, Tawnya Adkins Covert and Philo C. Wasburn investigated the supposed bias of partisan publications; they concluded that the mainstream media in the United States tend to present a narrow, homogenous, and centrist conservative view of political life. They found that the view was often presented in such a way because of the heavy media reliance on government officials, large bureaucratic organizations, and other large political organizations as the standard and predictable sources. However, in their analysis of the liberal *Progressive* and the conservative *National Review*, they also found that how information is used is more indicative of bias as opposed to who is quoted.[27] Other studies have found either pervasive liberal bias in news coverage,[28] a conservative bias,[29] or little evidence of ideological bias at all.[30]

Kenneth Dautrich and Thomas M. Hartley surveyed reporters and found that while the reporters have ideological tendencies, there is little evidence that those tendencies slip into news content.[31] They note the reasons for conflicting results in measuring bias may be found in the style of political, and specifically election-year, coverage: "the news media tend to focus on the horse race and insider issues such as the quality of campaign organizations and strategies . . . *Winning is often attributed to effective campaign strategies.*[32] In this view, bias may be less a lapse of reportorial ethics than a result of looking at politics in terms of winners and losers: while winners do get criticized, they face less criticism than those who lag in the polls.

Television's election coverage has been critiqued for focusing on the "horse race" elements of the campaign, but a study of the 2000 and 2004 elections found that this sort of coverage didn't necessarily result in biases amongst the major television networks.[33] The study looked not only at what news was covered, but who was interviewed within the story and the order which those interviews were placed. When comparing the 2000 to 2004 presidential election, the latter was found to be fairly "even handed" in terms of stories covered, which partisans were interviewed, and which side was heard from first in the story.[34] Within these findings, CBS showed a correlation figure (indicating their bias) three times as that of the two other networks. That being said, the correlation statistic was still remarkably low, indicating that even though CBS slanted to the left, the tilt was so small (i.e., statistically insignificant) that overall little bias was present in the news coverage. Instead, the stories were either fairly well balanced (representing both sides within one story) or stories in favor of one side were countered with similar stories favoring the other.[35]

During the 2008 election, however, evidence emerged indicating a slant within news organizations' coverage of the election, which coincided with a predominance of "horse race" coverage. The Center for Media and Public Affairs reported "the Democratic ticket won the race for good press even more handily than Barack Obama won the election,"[36] with only FNC offering more positive portrayals of the Republican presidential ticket than any other news organization. Fifty-four percent of stories focused on either strategy/tactics or the campaign "horse race."[37] Meanwhile, the Project for Excellence in Journalism (PEJ) found that overall Obama received more positive coverage than McCain, except on FNC, which had an equal percentage of positive and negative stories for each candidate.[38] The study also found that NBC's coverage of Sarah Palin was the most positive of any of the networks or cable channels, including Fox.[39] However, stories of the campaign were most frequently presented as a "horse race": 53 percent of all campaign coverage focused on tactics, strategy, and polling[40]—areas where Obama was leading.

A Holistic View

It is important to note that the CMPA and PEJ studies only discussed "positive" and "negative" coverage of the candidates, their campaign standing, and their policies; it is a leap to assume, as the conservative website Newsbusters did, that reporting on McCain's trailing in the polls translates into a "pro-Obama, anti-McCain bias" at every news organization but FNC.[41] In order to do that, one would have to look at not only the topics covered, but also who was speaking within each story. Was a McCain partisan the first voice heard in a story on Obama campaign finances? Did an Obama supporter speak in a story on McCain's foreign policy? Without looking at these details within stories, any claim of bias risks being seen as hostile media perception, i.e., the audience member (in this case the researcher) finding evidence of bias in coverage which goes against one's personal views.

Consider one of the minor story lines from the 2008 election season: MS-NBC's use of partisan political analysts (Keith Olbermann and Chris Matthews) as the lead anchors of the network's election coverage. The two were abruptly removed in early September, in favor of political correspondent David Gregory, after months of accusations that the network was biased. The change came as "a direct result of tensions associated with the channel's perceived shift to the political left," as seen through the frequent critiques of the Bush administration by Olbermann and Matthews on their non-election programs.[42] In this intensified environment, stories by MSNBC about a Republican candidate's dropping poll numbers could be interpreted as "biased" simply because the cable channel was perceived as "liberal."

The PEJ and CMPA coverage illustrates a limitation of most studies that study bias: the studies look solely at news coverage approaching Election Day (in the case of PEJ, the sample ended in late October) while ignoring the coverage of election returns. Previous studies similarly only looked at news coverage approaching an election. While this focus on pre-election coverage is laudable, no previous studies have tried to ascertain if bias infringes upon coverage as and after the results are reported. Who is commenting on election night and post-election news? Are there attempts to undermine the victor/victor's party—or dismiss the losing party—as the results are filing in? This study fills that gap, looking at coverage in the day before, day of, and day after the 2008 Presidential election. There is one hypothesis:

Hypothesis: A bias existed in the election night coverage because of the overwhelming national victory of Barack Obama and Democratic candidates.

The study also seeks to answer two research questions:

Research Question 1: Was bias more prominent within the segments featuring political party partisans than within segments strictly reporting election results?

Research Question 2: Was there a distinct difference between the networks and cable channels in the bias (if there was any) presented?

The study analyzed the topics of the stories covered, which candidate was the focus of the reports, and the presence of political partisans within the news report.

METHODOLOGY

A content analysis was conducted on a constructed sample of data from the day before Election Day, Election Day, and the day after Election Day (November 3–5, 2008). The dates were selected to determine if any changes in coverage as election results became known. The evening newscasts were recorded from the broadcast networks (ABC's *World News*, CBS's *Evening News*, NBC's *Nightly News*, and PBS's *Newshour*) as well as the cable news channels (CNN's *The Situation Room*, FNC's *The Fox Report*, and MSNBC's *Race to the White House*) on the day before and after Election Day. In addition, a randomly generated daytime hour was selected and recorded from each news organization for the day before and day after Election Day. A randomly selected daytime (7 a.m.–6 p.m.) and evening hour (6 p.m.–2 a.m.) was recorded from each on Election Day; Fox's on-air broadcast network, which does not offer weekday newscasts, was recorded on Election Day only. As previous studies had only looked at the network evening newscasts, this is an expansion of the news universe to compare both cable and broadcast outlets and consider programming outside of the traditional news window.

The methodology followed guidelines set forth by Zeldes et al., assigning numerical values to various situations that occurred during a newscast.[43] The situations included the following:

1. Whether the Republican or Democratic candidate was mentioned first in the story.
2. Which candidate (Republican or Democratic) received more total time within the story (this would include analysis favoring a candidate).
3. Whether or not video was presented featuring Republican or Democratic campaign activities.
4. Whether or not audio clips/sound bites featuring Republican or Democratic partisans were present.

Values assigned to these situations were configured in two different ways, reflecting both a "partisan balance" value and a "structural balance" value. The partisan balance value was configured through subtracting the number of components within a news story or broadcast that favored the Democratic from the number favoring the Republican candidate. The result of that equation (the positive or negative value) indicates which party the broadcast or particular story favored. The structural balance is then found by figuring the absolute value of the partisan balance score to determine how evenly or unevenly the parties were represented within the news story, with a score of more than 0 implying that a story was imbalanced.[44] The following example demonstrates the coding matrix:

- If Senator Barack Obama (or an "Obama partisan") was mentioned first in the analytical segment (featuring pundits) during the 2008 presidential election coverage then that component will be said to favor Obama: value = 1.
- If both Senator Obama and Senator McCain were featured in visual and audio clips then this component is said to be balanced: value = 0 (balanced).
- If Senator Obama's partisans or views were given more total time within the story, that component would favor Obama: value = 1.
- Republican value total Democratic value total (0–2) = -2.
- The value of -2 shows that this particular story favors the Democratic candidate (partisan bias).
- Figuring the absolute value of that partisan balance yields the structural balance of 2.

The data was coded by one of the authors and a student worker. Three networks (MSNBC, CNN, and ABC) were used as our sample for reliability purposes. For each question, the inter-coder reliability was between .90 and 1.00.

A "story" was defined the following ways:

1. Anchor Introduction: when the anchor introduces a pre-produced reporter package, a reporter live in the field, or another anchor at a different studio or field location.
2. Correspondent Package: Packages are defined as when a network-employed correspondent, different from the anchor, reports on a story in-depth. The story may be produced on tape, it may include a correspondent live in the studio wrapping the pre-produced segment, or it may include the reporter live in the field reporting on an ongoing event, including interviews with outside people, with or without a pre-produced segment.
3. Q&A: An anchor directs questions to various guests, who may give long answers. Guests may include correspondents, consultants hired by the network or cable channel for election coverage, and outside people.

After each story was coded, its partisan and structural balance were calculated.

Partisan balance scores ranged from 0 to +/-4, structural balance ranged from 0 to 4. A story with only Democratic presence would have a partisan balance ranking of -4 while one with only Republican presence would be ranked +4; both stories would have a structural balance ranking of 4, indicating extreme bias. Stories with presence of the opposition (or opposition partisans) would be ranked from +/-3 to +/-1 for partisan balance and 3 to 1 for structural balance, with the lower number indicating less bias. A ranking of 0 indicates a neutral story.

To explain observed imbalance a correlation was conducted of the partisan and structural balance of stories, again using the negative/positive associations described in the previous paragraph.[45] A moderate to large correlation in a positive direction would indicate a partisan balance favoring Republicans, with a moderate to large negative correlation favoring Democrats. However, a correlation nearer to 0 indicated a balance in the stories, either by presenting both sides within an individual story or by presenting a similar number of stories favoring each candidate/side of an issue. This would indicate that structural rather than partisan bias was the cause of an imbalance.

RESULTS

In total, the study found 485 stories from eight networks. Of the 485 stories, 374 (77 percent) were about the election (see Table 3.1). The stories regarding the election were then used in the analysis of this study. Multiple questions on the coding sheets asked about the presence or absence of video or audio pertaining to the Republican or Democratic candidate. For the purposes of this study, the Republican and Democratic candidate referred to anyone running on the party's ticket—not just the presidential race.

H1–The Existence of Bias

H1 assumed that an overall bias would be present in election coverage in favor of Democratic Party candidates, because of the victory of Barack Obama and other Democrats for state and regional offices. To measure this, we looked at the overall partisan rating for the networks and cable channels; a negative rating would indicate a bias for the Democratic Party candidates and a positive rating for the Republican Party. We found that the majority of stories, as expected, favored the Democratic Party (see Table 3.2). H1 was proved.

There was a striking, and significant, difference between coverage about the presidential election and that of other political races. The vast majority of stories were about the presidential race, and those stories were far

Table 3.1.   **Election Stories Across Networks**

Network	Total Election Stories
ABC	41
CBS	51
Fox	15
NBC	64
PBS	39
CNN	55
FNC	53
MSNBC	56

Table 3.2.   Overall Partisan Bias

Favor Democrats	57%
Favor Republicans	25%
Neutral	18%

N=374

more likely to be biased in favor of the Democrats than in favor of the Republicans or neutral (see Table 3.3). Stories about other political races were more balanced, with almost equal percentages of those favoring the Democrats and neutral stories. It is interesting to note that stories favoring Republicans made up almost the same percentage (though not number) of stories in both stories about the presidential race and those about other political races.

As the election approached, coverage favoring the Democratic Party candidates gradually gained more traction, moving from just under half of all stories to nearly two-thirds (see Table 3.4). Stories favoring Republican candidates made up about a quarter of all stories through election night. By the day after the election, coverage overwhelmingly favored the Democratic candidates, with three quarters of all stories tilting to the Democratic Party and just 10 percent favoring the Republican.

RQ1–Partisans' Effect on Bias

RQ1 asked whether or not there was more of a bias present in segments that featured political partisans. To measure this, we assessed the partisan bias and structural bias scores against the presence, or absence, of a party partisan in the story. Party partisans were counted as those identified by the network or news channel as having a relationship to the party, such as by being a strategist or consultant for a specific political party.

The question had mixed results. While it wasn't surprising that stories with a presence of a party partisan (or absence of the opposition) would favor that party over another, what was surprising was that the *absence* of a Democratic

Table 3.3.   Partisan Bias by Topic

	Presidential Race	*Other Political Races*
Favor Democrats	60%	39%
Favor Republicans	25%	24%
Neutral	15%	37%

*Significance .001 (Pearson's Chi Square)
N=374.

Table 3.4. Partisan Bias by Day

	Mon. p.m.	Tues. p.m.	Tues. p.m.	Wed. p.m.
Favor Democrats	48%	49%	63%	73%
Favor Republicans	25%	23%	27%	10%
Neutral	23%	28%	10%	16%

Significance .001 (Pearson's Chi Square)
N=374

Party partisan didn't necessarily indicate that a story would be unfavorable to that party (see Table 3.5). Forty-seven percent of stories which favored Democrats had no party partisans present; by contrast, only 18 percent of stories without a Republican partisan favored the GOP. Just 8 percent of stories with Democratic partisan presence favored the Republican candidates, in contrast to 37 percent of those with Republican partisan presence favoring Democrats. Stories with a Democratic partisan were also less likely to be neutral. The results are significant to .000.

There was also a significant difference in the degree of bias in the stories, depending upon the presence, or lack of, a party partisan (see Table 3.6). Stories featuring a Democratic partisan were more likely to be highly biased (bias rankings 3–4) than slightly biased (bias rankings 1–2) or neutral; by contrast, those with a Republican partisan or without partisans of either party were likely to be slightly biased over the other categories. In fact, for the presence or absence of a Republican partisan produced the same percentage of slightly biased stories (50 percent); similarly 22 percent of stories without a partisan, Democratic or Republican, were neutral.

At best, the answers to RQ1 are mixed. For the overall election victor (in 2008, the Democratic Party), stories will be more highly biased in favor of the Democratic Party if a political partisan is present. However, for the overall loser (the Republican Party), the presence of a party partisan didn't lead to any more story bias than those without partisans of either party.

Table 3.5. Partisan Bias by Party Partisan

	Democratic Partisan Present	Democratic Partisan Absent	Republican Partisan Present	Republican Partisan Absent
Favor Democrats	82%	47%	37%	62%
Favor Republicans	8%	31%	49%	18%
Neutral	10%	22%	14%	20%

Significance .000 (Pearson's Chi Square)
N=374

Table 3.6. Structural Bias by Party Partisan

	Democratic Partisan Present	Democratic Partisan Absent	Republican Partisan Present	Republican Partisan Absent
Bias Rankings 3–4	57%	18%	36%	29%
Bias Rankings 1–2	33%	61%	50%	50%
Neutral	10%	22%	14%	22%

Significance .000 (Pearson's Chi Square)
N=374

RQ2–Bias across Networks

RQ2 asked whether or not there was a difference between the networks and cable channels in the presentation of bias. To measure this we looked at two things. First we analyzed the partisan and structural bias scores of each news outlet. Second, we conducted a zero order correlation between the networks, comparing partisan and structural bias. Recall, structural bias would indicate overall bias in storytelling, and not necessarily bias in favor of one political party (or candidate) or the other.

The study found that there was no significant difference between network news and the cable news channels, but there were some interesting trends (see Table 3.7). PBS, CBS, and NBC were the three news operations which more consistently favored the Democratic Party, with approximately two-thirds of election stories each being pro-Democratic. Stories on the Fox broadcast network were more likely to favor the Republican Party than any other channel, including FNC (40 percent of the Fox network stories favored the Republican Party, in contrast to 33 percent on FNC). A similar situation occurred with NBC and MSNBC; with 61 percent of NBC's stories showing a tilt toward the Democratic candidate, and 59 percent at MSNBC. Of the broadcast networks, even though Fox had a higher percentage of stories favoring Republicans than

Table 3.7. Partisan Bias by Network

	ABC	CBS	Fox	NBC	PBS	CNN	FNC	MSNBC
Favor Democratic	54%	63%	33%	61%	67%	51%	49%	59%
Favor Republican	28%	17%	40%	20%	15%	30%	33%	25%
Neutral	18%	20%	27%	19%	18%	19%	18%	16%

Significance .047
N=374

any other network, *overall* it was the most balanced in its coverage, including the highest percentage of neutral stories of any channel. On cable, CNN and FNC were virtually indistinguishable from one another in terms of stories favoring either party, but FNC had the lowest percentage of neutral stories of any channel by a large margin.

The structural balance looks at the degree of tilt at each network and cable news channel. Again, the results were not significant but demonstrated interesting trends (see Table 3.8). CNN emerged as the news operation with the largest percentage of stories with the highest bias ranking, and also the lowest percentage of neutral stories. For every channel, stories tended to fall into rankings which indicated an attempt at presenting some views of the opposition (Bias Rankings 1–2), with Fox and PBS having the highest percentage of stories in this category and CNN and FNC the lowest. Fox had the highest percentage of neutral stories, at 27 percent.

The zero order correlation demonstrates if the structural or the partisan measures are a better predictor of biased coverage at network news organization and cable channels. A Pearson's Correlation closer to zero would indicate a lack of bias with positive figures indicating a Republican favoring and negative Democratic. The overall negative result and high significance indicates news organizations' storytelling was biased in favor in the Democratic Party due to a greater presence of the various partisan factors, i.e. who was mentioned first, presence of party partisans, video of candidate, and more total time for one side over the other (see Table 3.9). However, none of the network and cable channel correlations approached significance. Given that we had eight variables, significance would be achieved only at .006 and lower; the lowest figure we had was for MSNBC at .011.

The weak correlation shows that despite the *overall* partisan bias in news outlets, when it came to *individual* outlets, stories more or less were balanced. Instead, it was structural bias that determined any perceived imbalance in reporting. Though the correlation between news outlets is weak, nonetheless interesting trends emerge. MSNBC, which as mentioned earlier had an internal

Table 3.8.   Structural Bias by Network

	ABC	CBS	Fox	NBC	PBS	CNN	FNC	MSNBC
Bias Ranking 3–4	29%	27%	13%	30%	18%	36%	30%	27%
Bias Ranking 1–2	54%	53%	60%	52%	64%	47%	49%	57%
Neutral	17%	20%	27%	18%	18%	17%	21%	16%

Significance .047
N=374

Table 3.9. Zero Order Correlation of Partisan and Structural Bias Measures

	Total	ABC	CBS	Fox	NBC	PBS	CNN	FNC	MSNBC
Pearson's	-.22	-.02	-.10	.09	-.10	-.10	-.01	.07	-.13
Significance	.000	.692	.052	.074	.068	.044	.786	.159	.011

controversy due to perceived bias of its anchors, during the election period was the one outlet which most favored Democratic candidates. FNC and Fox, meanwhile, were the only two outlets with a positive Pearson's Correlation, indicating a favoring of Republican candidates. CNN and ABC were the two outlets with the least amount of favoritism, both showing a slight imbalance toward the Democrats.

DISCUSSION

Zeldes et al. found that in election years with a Republican presidential victory (the highly contested 2000 election and the 2004 election), network television had a slight imbalance in favor of the Democratic Party (a structural bias) and 45 percent of stories favored Democrats (indicated by who spoke first, the presence/absence of sound or pictures from both parties, the presence/absence of party partisans).[46] So while the results found in H1 were not necessarily expected to the degree found in this study, they were not, in fact, extraordinary. After all, the 2008 election saw a rejection of Republican candidates in national, state, and local elections. In addition, and perhaps more importantly, it was an historic event: the first time an African American had been elected President. It makes sense that the news outlets would cover this issue. These results also account for why the coverage gradually became more favorable to the President's party: as the election results were known and digested the stories shifted to covering how the victory had occurred. A legitimate question remains: if stories during this period that inserted Republican pundits, especially after the polls had closed and results were confirmed, had more of a slant than those which simply reported the returns and post-election celebrations. Are those Republican partisan-laden stories reporting the news or distorting reality through a false sense of parity (and if the victory were overwhelmingly Republican, could a similar question be raised of Democratic partisans)? Or are these partisans simply offering suggestions of how to govern within an administration by the opposition?

It's also not surprising that the percentage of stories at every network (with the exception of Fox) tilted to the Democratic Party. What is interesting is that when the presidential race was removed from the equation, stories were more evenly balanced (54 total stories with 20 neutral, 11 favoring the Republican and 21 favoring the Democratic). Most of the unbalanced stories (10 for the Republican and 17 for the Democratic) came from the "slightly imbalanced" category (ratings 1–2). This shows that even with the Democratic Party dominance in Congressional, gubernatorial, and local races, most of the news outlets nonetheless attempted to present a balanced approach (i.e., having pundits from both sides of the table) and avoid partisanship in their reporting.

The use of "most" is telling. FNC and CNN—more frequently than any other network—used what we would dub moderate-to-high partisan stories favoring the Republican Party (each had 8 stories ranking either a 3 or 4 on the scale, indicating a lack of Democratic presence). FNC, meanwhile, was the only network where neutral stories (those favoring neither Republicans nor Democrats) made up a *single*-digit percentage of stories covered, though the number (11) was higher than any other news outlet but NBC (12). By contrast, when reporting on Democrats, all of the networks tended to be more centrist in their reporting, with the vast majority of stories ranking -1 or -2 on our scale, indicating some attempts at presenting either the Republican candidate or a Republican Party partisan (142 of the 212 Democratically biased stories). NBC, the network which tilted most toward the Democrats, had 13 stories ranking -3 or -4, with 26 ranking -1 or -2.

This can help to explain the mixed results for the structural and partisan bias, as looked at in RQ2. When considering systematic measures, we found that even the networks or news channels which tilted toward one party still offered equally slanted stories favoring the other party. FNC had 16 stories which ranked 3 or 4 on our systematic scale, but *half* of its highly slanted stories favored the Democratic Party. CNN had the highest percentage of highly slanted stories of any news organization, but their overall correlation between structural and partisan measures was the closest to zero. This indicates that though individual stories may have been highly biased for the Democratic Party, those stories were nearly balanced out by equally biased stories in favor of the Republican Party. Following close behind in terms of highly biased stories were NBC and FNC (each had 30 percent of stories in the 3 or 4 category), but unlike CNN, these channels each showed evidence of a partisan tilt, either in favor of the Democrats (NBC) or the Republicans (FNC). And a full four outlets favored the Democrats, twice as many as favored the Republicans or were neutral. As a result, *overall* the zero order correlation is at -.22, a Democrat-leaning tilt higher than a shift at any individual outlet.

This demonstrates that the claim of a news media favoring the left is complicated; it may be valid in some cases, but it shouldn't be accepted uncritically. However, it certainly shouldn't be dismissed outright. Watching the coverage, it was apparent that many networks and programs had carefully constructed their commentary panels to include a Republican analyst, a Democratic analyst, someone who was neutral, and often correspondents who reported for the network. The same panel formula appeared on network after network and program after program. In an effort to appear balanced, our news has become a calculated and staged production. Adding a qualitative component to the study would be useful to understand the context of the news story; i.e., if a segment discusses a candidate or issue but takes a negative tone despite the appearance of balance due to the panel "casting." For example, just moments after the polls closed, MSNBC had commentators from across the political spectrum speculating as to the reasons behind McCain's failing campaign. That discussion may have lasted two minutes and helped MSNBC appear balanced or even biased to the Republican by the study's terms (it featured only the Republican candidate, and had commentators from both sides), while in reality the story was unfavorable to McCain. Textual analysis, when used alongside the content analysis, could help to further flesh out these complexities.

It's important to note that the study didn't consider what arguably are the most opinionated shows on the cable news channels: nightly talk shows like *The O'Reilly Factor* on FNC or *Countdown with Keith Olbermann* on MSNBC.[47] In future elections it would be important to include these types of programs in the sample set. While not traditional newscasts, the programs nonetheless air on news channels, and could skew each channel toward significance in favor of one side or another. While the news may not be biased, the talk shows could be the programs which give the networks the reputation of leaning to one side or the other—a hostile media perception which could lead viewers to assume bias exists in news coverage as well, even if the stories are covered in the same way as a competitor. On the networks, the Sunday morning talk programs were also eliminated; these shows could similarly offer insight to the "op-ed" slant of the network overall—and how viewers might perceive news stories as biased based on the network's reputation.

The study was limited by the lack of daily news programming on Fox. Every other network has a weeknight evening newscast as well as daytime news programming; Fox only offered election night coverage, so it was impossible to track how stories changed or get a sample which approached the numbers of the other outlets. Including *Fox News Sunday* (as well as other Sunday talk programs) would expand the sample size and allow researchers to see if Fox programming changed as results became evident. It would also be advantageous to look at programming from a larger selection of days. A sample from across the election season would offer researchers evidence if bias was prevalent throughout the campaign, and could demonstrate if outlets shift their coverage as voter preferences become evident. It would also show if the coverage shifts (or doesn't shift) as election results are revealed.

It is important to remember that the scope of the differences—regardless of the tilt of the news outlet—is also quite narrow. Even the most partisan outlets (Fox, MSNBC) had a correlation ranking of less than +/-1. This demonstrates that the news outlets are presenting both Democratic and Republican candidates, viewpoints, pundits, etc., within most stories. There is an attempt at presenting, at least on the surface, both points of view in election debates.

While there may be no statistically significant differences between the news outlets, the study nonetheless offers evidence which should concern both news scholars and consumers. The pervasive tilt to the Democratic Party by four of the US networks and cable outlets is worrisome (including two that have shared corporate ownership and news operations), even when taking into account the overall Democratic Party victory in 2008. It is beyond the notion that the victor is getting more positive coverage simply because the results were historic (i.e., the election of first African American president, who ran on the Democratic Party ticket), the campaign was better run, or the candidate(s) covered issues deemed more salient to the voters. Instead, the tilt indicates a similar approach to issues across news organizations and perhaps an inability by those organization to see how their stories are slanted. In the case of PBS, a tilt to the Democrats, however slight, can add fuel to the argument that a publicly funded news organization has a news agenda which is unfriendly to Republican or conservative viewpoints. For CBS, the results echo those found in 2000 and 2004; but for NBC the results are a shift from the results found in the earlier study.[48] This could indicate an influx of the progressive agenda from its sister cable channel (MSNBC) into the broadcast network.

So are we seeing in this political reporting the beginnings of a return to the highly partisan free-for-all common in the news media of the founding fathers? Perhaps not. What is more troubling to us is not the existence of a slight tilt at individual outlets in favor of one party or the other, but rather that the tilt isn't acknowledged by the news outlets in question. Instead, each continues with the pretense that news reported is, in the words of FNC, "fair and balanced." Recognition of the tilt would be more honest to viewers, allowing them to better judge the information they are receiving, and better participate in the political process. This, we would argue, allows viewers to move from a hostile media perception to an understanding that news is subject to interpretations based upon various viewpoints of the world: an important contribution by news organizations to the public sphere.

NOTES

1. John Hartley, *Communication, Cultural and Media Studies: The Key Concepts* (London: Routledge, Taylor & Francis Group, 2002), 17.

2. Hartley, 18.

3. "Code of Ethics," Society of Professional Journalists, accessed October 29, 2011, http://www.spj.org/ethicscode.asp.

4. "RTNDA Code of Ethics and Professional Conduct," Radio Television Digital News Association, accessed August 31, 2010, http://www.rtdna.org/pages/media_items/code-of-ethics-and-professional-conduct48.php.

5. "Most Voters Say News Media Wants Obama to Win," Pew Research Center for People & the Press, accessed August 31, 2010, http://pewresearch.org/pubs/1003/joe-the-plumber.

6. "Internet News Audience Highly Critical of News Organizations." Pew Research Center for People & the Press, accessed August 31, 2010, http://people-press.org/report/348/internet-news-audience-highly-critical-of-news-organizations.

7. The study uses methodology developed to compare bias in election coverage across broadcast networks in 2000 and 2004. See: Geri Alumit Zeldes, Frederick Fico, Serena Carpenter, and Arvind Diddi, "Partisan Balance and Bias in Network Coverage of the 2000 and 2004 Presidential Elections," *Journal of Broadcasting & Electronic Media* 52 (2008), 563–580.

8. Eric Burns, *Infamous Scribblers: The Founding Fathers and the Rowdy Beginnings of American Journalism* (New York: PublicAffairs, 2007).

9. Burns, *Infamous Scribblers*, 265.

10. Burns, *Infamous Scribblers,* 3.

11. Thomas Jefferson, *Master Thoughts of Thomas Jefferson*, ed. Benjamin S. Catchings (New York: The Nation Press, 1907), 27.

12. Joel Turner, "The Messenger Overwhelming the Message: Ideological Cues and Perceptions of Bias in Television News," *Political Behavior* 29 (2007), 441–464.

13. Edward S. Herman and Noam Chomsky, *Manufacturing Consent: The Political Economy of the Mass Media* (New York: Pantheon, 2002).

14. Matthew A. Baum and Tim Groeling, "New Media and the Polarization of American Political Discourse," *Political Communication* 25 (2008), 359.

15. Tien-Tsung Lee, "The Liberal Media Myth Revisited: An Examination of Factors Influencing Perceptions of Media Bias," *Journal of Broadcasting and Electronic Media* 49–1 (2005), 45.

16. See: Amarina Ariyanto, Matthew J. Hornsey, and Cindy Gallois, "Group Allegiances and Perceptions of Media Bias: Taking Into Account Both the Perceiver and the Source," *Group Processes and Intergroup Relations* 10–2 (2007), 266–279; Kyun Soo Kim and Yorgo Pasadeos, "Study of Partisan News Readers Reveals Hostile Media Perceptions of Balanced Stories," *Newspaper Research Journal* 28–2 (2007), 99–106; Cindy T. Christen, Prathana Kannaovakun, and Albert C. Gunther, "Hostile Media Perceptions: Partisan Assessment of the Press and Public During the 1997 United Parcel Service Strike," *Political Communication* 19–4 (2002), 423–436.

17. Lee, "The Liberal Media Myth Revisited."

18. Turner, "The Messenger," 451.

19. Kevin Coe, David Tewksbury, Bradley J. Bond, Kristin L. Drogos, Robert W. Porter, AshleyYahn, and Yuanyuan Zhang. "Hostile News: Partisan Use and Perceptions of Cable News Programming," *Journal of Communication* 58–2 (2008), 215.

20. Jonathan Morris, "Slanted Objectivity? Perceived Media Bias, Cable News Exposure and Political Attitudes," *Social Science Quarterly* 88–3 (2007), 707–728.

21. See: Yue Tan and David H. Weaver, "Media Bias, Public Opinion, and Policy Liberalism from 1956 to 2004: A Second-Level Agenda Setting Study," *Mass Communication and Society* 13–4 (2007), 412–434; Dave D'Alessio and Mike Allen, "Media Bias in Presidential Elections: A Meta-Analysis," *Journal of Communication*. 50–4 (2000), 133–157; Doris Graber, *Mass Media and American Politics*, 4th Edition (Washington, DC: CQ Press, 1993); Peter M. Sandman, David M. Rubin, and David B. Sachsman, *Media: An Introductory Analysis of American Mass Communications* (Englewood Cliffs, NJ: Prentice-Hall, 1976).

22. Brian Mullen, David Futrell, Debbie Stairs, Dianne M. Tice, Roy F. Baumeister, Kathryn E. Dawson, Catherine A. Riordan, Christine E. Radloff, George R. Goethals, John G. Kennedy, and Paul Rosenfeld, "Newscasters' Facial Expressions and Voting Behavior of Viewers. Can a Smile Elect a President?" *Journal of Personality and Social Psychology* 51–2 (1986), 291–295.

23. Michael S. Lewis-Beck, "Election Forecasts in 1984: How accurate were they?" *PS: Political Science and Politics* 18–1 (1985), 53–62.

24. D. Travers Scott, "Pundits in Muckrakers' Clothing: Political Blogs and the 2004 Presidential Election," in *Blogging, Citizenship and the Future of Media*, ed. Mark Tremayne (New York: Routledge, 2006), 39–58.

25. Kenneth Dautrich and Thomas M. Hartley, *How the News Media Fail American Voters* (New York: Columbia University Press, 1999).

26. Frederick Fico and Eric Freedman, "Biasing Influence on Balance in Election News Coverage: An Assessment of Newspaper Coverage of the 2006 U.S. Senate Elections," *Journalism & Mass Communication Quarterly* 85 (2008), 499–514.

27. Tawnya Adkins Covert and Philo C. Wasburn, "Information Sources and the Coverage of Social Issues in Partisan Publications: A Content Analysis of 25 Years of the *Progressive* and the *National Review*," *Mass Communication and Society* 10 (2007), 67–94.

28. See: Daniel Sutter, "Can the Media be so Liberal? The Economics of Media Bias," *Cato Journal* 20–3 (2001), 431–451; S. Robert Lichter, and Richard Noyes, *Good Intentions Make Bad News. Why Americans Hate Campaign Journalism*, Second Edition (New York: Rowman & Littlefield, 1988).

29. See: Daniel M. Butler and Emily Schofield, "Were Newspapers More Interested in Pro-Obama Letters to the Editor in 2008? Evidence From a Field Experiment," *American Politics Research* 38–2 (2010), 356–371; Eric Alterman, *What Liberal Media? The Truth About Bias and the News* (New York: Basic Books, 2003).

30. See: Robert M. Eisinger, Loring R. Veenstra, and John P. Koehn, "What Media Bias? Conservative and Liberal Labeling in Major U.S. Newspapers," *Harvard International Journal of Press/Politics* 12–1 (2007), 17–36; Michael J. T. Robinson and Margaret A. Sheehan, *Over the Wire and on TV: CBS and UPI in Campaign '80* (New York: Russell Sage, 1983); Robert G. Meadow, "Cross-Media Comparison of Coverage of the 1972 Presidential Campaign," *Journalism Quarterly* 50 (1973), 482–488.

31. Dautrich and Hartley, *How the News Media*, 100.

32. Dautrich and Hartley, *How the News Media*, 94, emphasis added.

33. Zeldes et al., "Partisan Balance and Bias."

34. Zeldes et al., "Partisan Balance and Bias," 576.

35. Zeldes et al., "Partisan Balance and Bias," 577.

36. S. Robert Lichter, "Election Watch: Campaign 2008 Final: How TV News Covered the General Election," *Media Monitor* XXIII–1 (2009), 3.

37. Lichter, "Election Watch," 2.

38. Pew Research Center's Journalism Project Staff, "Winning the Media Campaign," *Pew Research Center's* Project for Excellence in Journalism, accessed September 6, 2010, http://www.journalism.org/node/13312.

39. Pew, "Winning,"

40. Pew Research Center's Journalism Project Staff, "The Color of News: How Different Media Have Covered the General Election," *Pew Research Center's* Project for Excellence in Journalism, accessed 6 September 2010 http://www.journalism.org/node/13436.

41. Richard Noyes, "No Doubt About It: All but Fox News Tipping Obama's Way." *Newsbusters,* accessed September 6, 2010, http://newsbusters.org/blogs/rich-noyes/2008/11/01/no-doubt-about-it-all-fox-news-tipping-obama-s-way.

42. Brian Stelter, "Media Decoder: The End of MSNBC's Experiment," *New York Times*, September 7, 2008, http://mediadecoder.blogs.nytimes.com/2008/09/07/the-end-of-msnbcs-experiment/.

43. Zeldes et al., "Partisan Balance and Bias."

44. Zeldes et al., "Partisan Balance and Bias."

45. This follows methodology developed by Zeldes et al.; see "Partisan Balance and Bias."

46. Zeldes et al., "Partisan Balance and Bias."

47. *The O'Reilly Factor* is still on the air at FNC; *Countdown with Keith Olbermann* is no longer aired by MSNBC.

48. Zeldes et al., "Partisan Balance and Bias."

Chapter Four

Television, Islam, and the Invisible: Narratives on Terrorism and Immigration

Tim Karis

During the first hours and days after the killing of Osama bin Laden had been announced, the Obama administration had to face a lot of questions. Had the operation been carried out in accordance with international law? Was the codename *Geronimo* offensive to Native Americans? Had Islamic laws been breached by burying the body at sea? And most importantly: was it really him? The latter question often came alongside the public demand to make pictures of bin Laden's dead body available to the public. These pictures, it was argued, would prove to the world that the story of the chase down and killing of the world's most wanted terrorist was actually true. President Barack Obama, however, decided that the pictures would not be released. When asked about this policy on *60 Minutes*, he answered: "It is important for us to make sure that very graphic photos of somebody who was shot in the head are not floating around as an incitement to additional violence." When asked about his reaction when he saw the pictures, he briefly added: "It was him."[1]

To this day, the Obama administration has not released any pictures showing a dead Osama bin Laden. In a visual culture such as ours, this is highly remarkable. And yet, it is important to realize that the administration did not altogether refrain from providing the public with visual material regarding bin Laden's killing. Instead, on May 7, five days after the killing, the US Department of Defense released five clips of video footage that had been secured by US Special Forces at bin Laden's last refuge in Abbottabad, Pakistan.[2] In four of the five videos, bin Laden can be seen giving statements. Only one of these four appears to have been produced for release with the remaining three appearing to be rehearsal material. Bin Laden gives his statements in sparse and unimpressive surroundings and, at one point, misses a cue. Although the videos were released with their soundtracks erased, it is apparent just by looking at the visual material that these videos would have destroyed bin Laden's larger-than-life appearance had they been released by Al-Qaeda. It was, however, a fifth video that by far gained most of the attention. The media called it "most revealing,"[3] "extraordinary" and "astonishing."[4] One journalist wrote: "In the most candid scenes, bin Laden can be seen watching news coverage of himself on television."[5]

In the following, I will take the video of bin Laden's channel surfing through television news programs as a starting point for an analysis of how television creates public images and narratives. These images and narratives can change over time in a complex and often ambiguous media discourse. Taking the leading German television news magazine *Tagesthemen* (1978–present) as an example and focusing on the media narrative on Islamic terrorism, I will briefly trace that developing narrative from the Beirut attacks of 1983 to the prevented attacks on Times Square in 2010, sketch out its component parts, and end with some reflections as to whether this narrative may have been dissolved in the context of the release of the bin Laden videos. Most importantly, I will point out how the terrorism narrative got entangled with a different media narrative revolving around Muslim immigration to Germany and other European countries. The link between the two narratives, I argue, is based on a notion of "invisibility" that is applied both to terrorists hiding from criminal prosecution and immigrants allegedly creating so called "parallel societies" that have but little contact with the rest of the country. My main argument is that since television creates what is visible and what is invisible in a society, it is of major importance to re-evaluate its role in creating public images of Islam, to take seriously the complexities and ambiguities of media discourse and, thereby, to go beyond the notions of "bias" and "Islamophobia" that have for a long time dominated academic research on Islam in the media.[6]

THE VIDEO: BIN LADEN CHANNEL SURFING

I want to start by describing the famous video of bin Laden's channel surfing in a bit more detail. For the first minute of the 4:14-long video, all we see is a television set displaying a list of television channels, apparently an on-screen menu. As we learn from an information box at the bottom of the screen, Al Jazeera is then selected and watched for a few seconds. At this time, Al Jazeera is broadcasting some footage showing Osama bin Laden calmly walking around in a mountainous region with a companion. Shortly before the on-screen-menu is displayed again, bin Laden can be seen shouldering a machine gun. Next, there is a camera panning from the upper left to the lower right, away from the television set and on to Osama bin Laden holding a remote control in his hands and apparently watching the footage of himself on Al Jazeera. After that, the camera zooms out so that both the television set and bin Laden huddling in front of it can be seen. He wears a ski-cap and is covered in a brown blanket. During the rest of the video, the camera sometimes zooms on to the television set again, but otherwise stays in the same position. On the television, various images of Osama bin Laden are shown as well as an image of the burning Twin Towers of New York's World Trade Center.

A quick review of media reporting on the video reveals what was found most remarkable about the video was its extraordinary *ordinariness*. In the video, bin Laden does not appear as a "gun-toting rebel or the scholarly sheikh dictating messages to the outside world"[7] but rather "aged and frail,"[8] "haggard,"[9] or simply "like an elderly grandfather."[10] Commentators found the footage to be evidence of bin Laden's vanity and obsession with his own public image or, in a rather different nuance of the same argument, his strategic will to create a particular image of himself in the public mind. In an interview with *ABC News*, Lawrence Wright, author of an acclaimed Al-Qaeda history, put it like this: "He's always been very careful about controlling his image and he was nurturing his image, watching himself on television in what was the most revealing, most human, least controlled moment of his entire career. [This is] just a guy who wants to be seen, who wants to be known . . . Very pathetic in a way."[11]

A lot more has been said about this video and even more could be added, but I want to focus on two aspects here. First, it is important to realize that the footage of an old man watching television can only be of impact in the context of a larger discourse, in which this particular old man, Osama bin Laden, is widely known and commonly associated with a particular style of visual appearance. Seeing bin Laden in a different visual context has an eye-opening effect for viewers, which is further enhanced by the juxtaposition of the aged bin Laden in front of the television set with the agile bin Laden on the television screen. Second, the video creates confusion about the roles of the observer and the observed. In the discourse so far, distinctions have been quite clear: a Western recipient of a newscast would be "the observer" and Osama bin Laden would be "the observed." But now, all of sudden, bin Laden himself becomes a recipient of a newscast, thus identical with "the observer" and therefore necessarily different from "the observed." This has a major effect on the believability of bin Laden's former media image: if Bin-Laden-on-television is not identical with Bin-Laden-outside-television, then the Bin-Laden-on-television becomes less believable. The powerful symbol of Islamic terrorism becomes a media invention, a hoax, a chimera. Thus, the whole media discourse centering on Osama bin Laden, or rather, as pointed out in the following, the media narrative on Islamic terrorism is substantially called into question. Had a picture of bin Laden's dead body been released, this would have been a clear proof of his demise, but with the release of the video of bin Laden watching television something much more important happened—bin Laden died as a discursive symbol.

In short, the video quite uniquely demonstrates that television images are not copies of the real world, but contingent symbols that are created and shaped in media discourse. These symbols can become very powerful for a time, as the example of Osama bin Laden plainly proves, but they are at the same time very fragile elements of a media discourse that is itself ever-changing and full of ambiguity.

ISLAM AND THE MEDIA

In the following, I will sketch out the media discourse in which the symbol "Osama bin Laden" has played a significant part for more than ten years after the 9/11 attacks. In order to do that, I draw on a larger research project, in which I analyzed news coverage on Islam in the 1979–2010 time period.[12] This research is centered on the German television news magazine *Tagesthemen*, which is one of the most popular, most influential, and most trusted news programs of the country. For the study, I conducted 80 in-depth-analyses of the 3–5-minutes reports that are characteristic for the format, concentrating on the visual material used in the television reports.

Research on the portrayal of Islam in Western media has been conducted for a rather long time, starting with Edward Said's renowned study *Covering Islam*[13] in which he applied the critical stance toward Western notions of Islam first developed in *Orientalism*[14] onto contemporary media reporting. Today, research on Islam and the media is an interdisciplinary endeavor bringing together expertise from media studies, religious studies, sociology, political sciences, Islamic studies, and other disciplines. This research tradition has produced a lot of important and sometimes disturbing insights into the way Western media portray Islam in an often uninformed and, at times, hostile way.[15] However, I argue in my work that too many studies are confined to the identification of a rather homogenous set of stereotypes. Researchers commonly assume that this set of stereotypes has been passed on in the West for generations. Its widespread use in media reporting is interpreted by researchers as an indication of a one-dimensional Western perception of Islam, variously called "Orientalism," "Islamophobia," or, in the German context, "*Feindbild Islam*." By basing their research on these concepts, too many studies fail to get a deeper understanding of the fine nuances and

ambiguities that are characteristic for the discourse. For example, most studies miss that a lot of media coverage actually revolves around the fact that
many Muslims are victims of various discriminations—and that the reporting
journalists unanimously condemn these discriminations. These reports, I argue, should not be considered to be exceptions to a media discourse that is, in
essence, islamophobic. Rather, they should be considered to be a distinct part
of a complex discourse in which various, and sometimes opposing, elements
are in many ways entangled.[16]

DISCOURSE AND NARRATIVE

In order to analyze such a complex discourse, it is helpful to turn to the understanding of mass media as producers of contingent and dynamic orders of
knowledge, as it is put forward by the British Cultural Studies. It is these orders of knowledge that I call media discourses. For the purpose of analysis, it
is expedient to distinguish a number of individual media discourses with each
media discourse centered on a different subject matter: "the climate change
discourse," "the financial crisis discourse," "the Islam discourse." Within the
Islam discourse, as Cultural Studies would argue, all public knowledge of
Islam is produced, distributed, and continuously altered over time.[17]

Discourse Analysis is a heterogeneous field encompassing lots of individual approaches, which are for the most part drawing from the works of
Michel Foucault. In my research, I developed a narrative approach to discourse analysis that starts with Foucault and then takes its cues from British
media scholar John Fiske, British Anglicist David Herman, German sociologist Willy Viehöver, and German media scholar Knut Hickethier.[18] In short,
this approach proceeds on the assumption that public knowledge, which is
produced in media discourses, is ordered in narratives. Thus, what we know
about Islam, we know from the stories the media tell—shorter stories in
individual reports and larger stories developing over time. The telling and
constant re-telling of these larger stories is what makes the media, and particularly television, in the words of John Fiske, "our own culture's bard."[19] It
is by way of storytelling that the media are constantly "constructing meaningful totalities out of scattered events."[20]

In a *longue durée* perspective, the larger narratives are of particular interest. Thus, the aim of my research on the coverage of Islam on *Tagesthemen*
between 1979 and 2010 was to identify a repertoire of Islam narratives that
journalists have drawn on in that time period, to describe the narrative's relationships to each other and to call into question the taken-for-grantedness
with which they are told. In order to do that, a qualitative research method

was developed. The interpretive work centered on the question, in which way individual journalistic statements from the *Tagesthemen* reports and individual images used in these reports reflected larger narratives on Islam and, at the same time, contributed to the further development of these narratives. As a result of this research, the following narratives were identified: (1) The Rise of Fundamentalism, (2) The Decline of the Old Orient, (3) The Clash of Civilizations, (4) The Islamic Terrorism, (5) The Problem of Integration, and (6) The Discrimination of Muslims. In the following, I will focus on the fourth of these narratives and briefly discuss its special relationship with the fifth.[21]

THE TERRORISM NARRATIVE

According to the narrative approach developed in my research, a narrative is comprised of five elements. It starts with a state of equilibrium (1), which is then disrupted by the action of a villain (2), creating disequilibrium. The narrative then charts the course of this disequilibrium (3), particularly the ways in which this disruption is harmful for people, who are presented as the victims in the narrative (4). Media narratives usually do not have final resolutions. Instead, several different versions of possible resolutions (5) are inscribed into the narrative.[22]

Thus, the first question that needs to be asked about the terrorism narrative is: which is the state of equilibrium that is assumed to have been disrupted by the emergence of terrorism? In one word, this state of equilibrium can be called "security." This concept, however, has several meanings. First, terrorism clearly endangers the operational safety of buildings and other infrastructure and the physical integrity of humans. In that sense, the concept of security is ever-present in *Tagesthemen* reports. More importantly, however, references to security are also made in a more general sense. Security is then understood as an overall normalcy, as the basic condition for everyday life. For example, this can be seen in a *Tagesthemen* report from 1983 that was broadcast on the occasion of terrorist attacks on French and American soldiers in Beirut. In the words of the reporting journalists, the attack had to be understood as an "assault on peace."[23] According to this statement, the attacks should not be understood as an attempt to accomplish strategic goals within a military conflict, but as an end in itself. Thus, a disruption of equilibrium is assumed to be not only the result of terrorist activity, but also its actual aim—a feature of the narrative that sharply differentiates it from the other narratives of the Islam discourse. Another example of this notion of terrorism can be found in a *Tagesthemen* report from February 27, 1993, which was broadcast one day after the first terror attacks on the World Trade Center in New York

City. In this report, Mario Cuomo, then governor of the State of New York, is quoted as follows: "Fear is the weapon they use against you. And that's what terrorists are all about. . . . What they're trying to do is deny you normalcy."[24] This idea of terrorism aiming at the destruction of normalcy as such is the true beginning of the terrorism narrative. It does not start with terror attacks in the West, but with the insight that Western security might, from one moment to the other, prove a false security.

1993 AND BEYOND: ASSOCIATIONS

This leads to the question as to when this narrative was first established in media discourse. When was the notion of terrorism as an ultimate threat to Western normalcy first introduced in the media? Drawing on a sample of eighty reports from a singular news magazine, this question can hardly be answered with any certainty. However, it is striking to see how *Tagesthemen* reports from 1993 on the World Trade Center bombings differ a lot from reports on the Oklahoma City bombings of 1995. In 1993, journalists were very reluctant to speculate on the question whether the explosions in the World Trade Center had, in fact, been caused by a bomb and, if so, whether this might suggest a terrorist background. Ever since the events of 1993, however, journalists were quickly jumping to conclusions and speculated excessively on the alleged probability of a terrorist background and on the likely villains in that scenario: Muslims. This is particularly evident in the context of the Oklahoma City bombings from 1995. On April 20, 1995, the day after the bombing, that day's edition of *Tagesthemen* is full of references to the events of two years earlier. "Then, too," it is stated in one report, "America had considered itself to be safe."[25] Right after that statement, images of those responsible for the attacks on the World Trade Center are displayed. In another report from the same day, Oklahoma City is coined "one of the largest centers of Islamic fundamentalism." Furthermore, *Tagesthemen* reporters talk about a "growing suspicion of the responsibility of Arab terrorists" for the Oklahoma City bombings. In that same report, a terrorism expert is interviewed, according to whom the attack "appears to have a connection to the Middle East" and has been conducted due to the "hatred different Islamic organizations nourish against the United States."[26]

These assumptions are of particular interest because, as was revealed in breaking news during the same edition of *Tagesthemen*, Muslims were, in fact, not responsible for the Oklahoma City bombings. Rather, the attack was executed by Timothy McVeigh, a non-Muslim American. Thus, while journalists in 1993 apparently lacked the possibility to bring the event in line with an established interpretive pattern, in 1995 they prematurely invoked the Islamic-terrorism narrative. By 1995, thus, this narrative was an integral part of the journalistic repertoire and an obvious choice when it came to interpreting bombing attacks.

In the following years, whenever a terrorist attack occurred, *Tagesthemen* journalists would look back at earlier attacks and draw comparisons. For example, a report that was broadcast on September 11, 2001, actually starts with footage from 1993 in which a fireman strides across a scene of devastation not unlike the ones emerging in New York City at the time of broadcasting. These visual similarities are verbalized in the report: "February 26, 1993, the images are much alike: an attack on the World Trade Center in New York. Ramzi Ahmed Yousef, one of the captured bombers, stated in his interrogation that if he had had more explosives, he would have been able to cause the collapse of both towers."[27] The reference to and use of similar images show that the narrative is essentially based on an associative rather than a causal structure. Within the logic of the narrative, terrorist attacks occur not *because* a different terrorist attack occurred before, but rather both attacks *independently* give evidence of the existence of Islamic terrorism. It is by way of linking events to each other that narrative coherence is produced and it is this coherence that allows journalists to talk about what is unwrapping before them in a meaningful way. Even on September 11, 2001, a day often cited to have been an enormous challenge for journalists due to its unexpectedness, the media, after an initial phase of confusion, were actually very quick to invoke the Islamic terrorism narrative.[28] Just hours after the attack, *Tagesthemen* showed the aforementioned images from 1993 and proceeded by portraying a "bloody trace of terror" from 1993 via the Nairobi and Darussalam attacks of 1998 to the present day.[29] After 9/11, the attacks from that day became the central point of reference in *Tagesthemen*, as is the case, for example, in *Tagesthemen* reports on the bombings in Madrid in 2004 and the *Tagesthemen* report on the prevented bombings on New York's Times Square in May 2010: "The bomb was supposed to hit the heart of New York. Today, many people think of when, back then, two airplanes brought the terror into the city."[30] This associative narrative structure has one important effect—It gives rise to the disturbing expectation that one terrorist attack will certainly be followed by another.

VILLAINS: OSAMA BIN LADEN AND
THE INVISIBILITY OF TERRORISM

On September 11, 2001, *Tagesthemen* did not fail to mention who they held responsible for the attacks: "Terror is given a face: Osama bin Laden. The Saudi multi-millionaire becomes the world's most wanted man."[31] Based on my research sample, it appears that the focus on bin Laden as the major villain of the narrative really begins with the 9/11 attacks. Before that, Islamic terrorists were hardly ever mentioned by name. Instead, narrative coherence was produced by frequent reference to a number of alleged common features of Islamic terrorists—features that after 9/11 would, in part, also be applied to bin Laden. The first of these features is the terrorist's presumed irrationality. This notion is in line with the basic idea of the narrative outlined above: terrorists do not act out of strategic considerations, but out of sheer hatred. In the context of the Oklahoma City bombings, which *Tagesthemen* considered to be an attack executed by Islamic terrorists, this idea of terrorism as an end in itself is evoked several times. This is one example: "[The attack] shows that there are terrorists—religious or other kinds of fanatics—who, unlike politically motivated perpetrators, do not waste any thought on who they are killing or how many people. Mass murder seems to be factored in, or rather, it seems to be the point."[32] This notion of the religiously fanatic terrorist can also be found much earlier in the material. In a *Tagesthemen* report on the Beirut attacks from October 1983, these attacks are commented upon as follows: "The members of this militant group have proven their hatred against Americans several times during the past weeks. . . . Americans and Frenchmen are foreign devils, that is the position of this militant group. . . . They consider it their divine mission to humiliate the foreign devils and to kill them. In order to execute this mission, they are even willing to give their lives."[33] It is striking how these notions are echoed in more recent *Tagesthemen* reports concerned with Al-Qaeda. As is stated on *Tagesthemen* on September 11, 2001, "[Al-Qaeda's] terror is not directed against representatives of the United States alone, but increasingly becomes a compulsion to the mass killing of innocent people."[34] In these examples, terrorism does not appear as a political strategy, but as pure hatred or even—as is implied by the word "compulsion"—as a mental deficiency. Thus, the question, that is repeatedly asked with regards to Islamic terrorists is not "What do they want?," but "Where does the hatred come from that causes terrorists to do things like that?"[35]

At the same time, when it comes to Al-Qaeda, the notion of terrorist irrationality, while never completely dismissed, is sometimes eclipsed by a notion of terrorist professionalism. Throughout the reports, Al-Qaeda is depicted not as a fanatic mob, but as a highly regulated organization. For example, referring to the attack in Madrid in 2004, it is said that "the range of the attack and the coordination necessary to have ten bombs explode at different places at the same time"[36] indicated the likeliness of Al-Qaeda's responsibility. Osama bin Laden embodies this professional terrorism. In the footage shown of him, he never appears fanatic, outraged or hateful, but—while the West is seized with panic and fear—relaxed and reflective, calm and confident.

The second feature Islamic terrorists share, according to the terrorism narrative, is their invisibility. Again, the *Tagesthemen* reports on the Oklahoma City bombings provide some good examples. The alleged decision of Muslims to make Oklahoma City "one of the largest centers of Islamic fundamentalism" is explained with reference to the fact that Oklahoma is located in the Midwest where, for the Muslims, it would be "easy to escape public attention."[37] The notion of an anti-Western Muslim conspiracy is further evoked in the report by showing amateur footage of a Muslim conference held in Oklahoma City in 1992. Unlike other footage, these unprofessional recordings with poor image quality give the impression that this footage was not meant to be released to the public. Audience members are led to believe that by showing this amateur footage, *Tagesthemen* is providing an exclusive look behind the curtain of the secret terrorist underground. To give another example, in a report on the situation in Algeria, which was broadcast on January 6, 1993, the existence of a "terrorist underground," an "Islamist underground," or an "armed Islamist underground" is mentioned.[38] Twelve years later, again referring to Algeria, the notion of terrorist invisibility is evoked again: "It is in the mountains behind the village that the fanatic Muslims had their hiding place."[39]

Most notably, the notion of terrorist invisibility is evoked with reference to Osama bin Laden and Al-Qaeda. Bin Laden and the "worldwide web of terrorist cells [he is] supposed to have woven"[40] can be regarded as an embodiment of the notion of terrorist invisibility. The notion of an invisible terrorist network comprised of cells "just waiting to be called to action"[41] perfectly fits a narrative, in which the story of an invisible, yet ever-present menace is told. Bin Laden's invisibility is pointed out on *Tagesthemen* when there is mention of the way he only communicates with the West by way of "messages on an audio tape"[42] or when it is stated that he "found shelter in Afghanistan with the holy warriors of the Taliban"[43] At the time of this statement, again, low quality, low light amateur footage is used, showing bin Laden in midst of mummed companions in a small tent.

Remarkably, just after this footage of the "invisible" bin Laden is shown, the report proceeds by showing footage of Afghan women wearing burqas. At this point in the report, the burqas are quite likely symbolizing Taliban rule in Afghanistan. But it is also tempting to think about the burqa as a symbol oscillating between visibility and invisibility. On the one hand, the burqa as such is highly visible. In fact, it is so visible that in some European countries, attempts have been made to ban the burqa from public spaces although only a few Muslim immigrants in these countries actually wear burqas.[44] Apparently the burqa exceeds the visibility of other garments in such a way that it can hardly be ignored. On the other hand, what is most striking about the burqa is the invisibility of the person wearing it. In the scene described above, this is impressively captured in a camera shot which starts with a total view of several women in burqas, then zooms in and ends on a close-up of one of the women's veiled faces.[45] Normally, a close-up of a person's face is expected to reveal not only what a person looks like, but also that person's inner emotions, thoughts and subjectivity. Since this is clearly not possible in case of the veiled face of the woman wearing a burqa, the shot creates confusion and fundamentally disappoints standard viewing habits.

THE INVISIBILITY OF THE "PARALLEL SOCIETY"

The burqa, in short, is an ambiguous if not paradox symbol. As such it can also be found in *Tagesthemen* reports dealing with matters of immigration of Muslims into European countries. In those cases, the burqa becomes a symbol of what, in Germany, has been called the "parallel society."[46] This term is used to describe the fact that in some European countries, large Muslim communities emerged who have but little contact with the so-called "majority society." In these communities, Muslim immigrants were able to build a widely independent infrastructure (shops, clubs, restaurants, etc.) thereby creating an environment in which it became possible for Muslims living in Germany to hardly get in contact with traditional German culture and, most importantly, the German language. While similar communities have existed for a long time in other countries, such as the United States, Germany for a long time did not consider itself to be an *Einwanderungsgesellschaft* (immigration society). Migrants who came to Germany were—and for the most part still are—expected to seamlessly blend into German society—to "integrate." It is due to their presumed lack of contact with non-Muslims that Muslims living in the "parallel society" are perceived as invisible to the rest of the country and it is precisely for this reason that the burqa is used as a symbol for the "parallel society." Furthermore, this notion of migrant invisibility creates a highly problematic connection between the terrorism narrative and the integration narrative.

The notion of a parallel Muslim society emerging in Germany can be found in *Tagesthemen* reports as early as 1980, thus long before the term "parallel society" was first used. In a report from March 13, 1980, focusing on an Islamic school, the notion of a willful segregation of Muslims from German society is expressed as follows: "Because they fear Western influence on their children, many Turks send even their youngest children to the Imam in order to have them cram the Qur'an. In Turkey, religious education for young children is prohibited. Whereas in Germany, it is a vehicle for political agitation and a cordon against the integration of young Turks into Germany."[47]

However, in the 1980s, the "parallel society" is not considered to be a security threat for German society. In later years, especially after 9/11, this changes significantly. For example, in a report about the Madrid attacks from March 2004, Spain is called a "refuge" for terrorists and a "safe place for bin Laden's fighters, since many Arabian immigrants live here, which makes it easy to keep a low profile if wary authorities start asking around."[48] The invisible "parallel society" of Muslims is thus depicted as a safe haven for terrorists who want to remain invisible. Similarly, on September 19, 2001, *Tagesthemen* reported: "These days, time and time again, the Federal Republic of Germany is being referred to as a refuge for Islamic terrorists."[49] The illustration used for this statement is highly problematic, because an image of Muslims kneeling in prayer is displayed. Terrorism is thereby suggested to be a characteristic of the Muslim citizens of Germany or of Islam as such. Likewise, in a report broadcast in November 2004, days after a radical Muslim assassinated Dutch film-maker Theo van Gogh in Amsterdam, the Netherlands is portrayed as follows: "The country is thrown out of joint. What happened? The former model country for an open, multi-cultural society has failed in the matter of integration, has let it happen that a dangerous parallel society could emerge. A minority, arguably, but it despises the values of the West and considers Islam to be a superior culture."[50] Again, this statement is illustrated with imagery derived from an Islamic religious context: the camera is positioned in a mosque and pointed to the entrance to the prayer room. The door to the prayer room is open, but one Muslim stands in the doorway as if it was his job to keep the camera out of the prayer room. This particular imagery not only suggests an equivalence of radical Muslims capable of murdering Dutch citizens on grounds of religion, but also it conveys the impression that the Muslims are trying to keep the media from taking a good look at this "parallel society."

The notion of Muslim migrants trying to prevent reporting is quite common in *Tagesthemen* reports. For example, a report broadcast on October 15, 2001, starts with footage showing a scuffle between *Tagesthemen* reporters and members of a radical Muslim group operating in Germany. One Muslim covers up the camera lens with his hand and another one can be heard shouting "We don't want to talk, damn it!"[51] In the context of a narrative, in which invisibility is the villains' most important strategy, this is highly remarkable—By taking the role of investigative reporter, by addressing itself to make visible that which wants to remain invisible, *Tagesthemen*, the story's narrator, virtually becomes the story's hero.

To some extent, this can also be seen in reports in which *Tagesthemen* reporters are actually invited by Muslim migrants to report on their lifestyle. One example can be found in a report from October 3, 2001. In Germany,

October 3 is a national holiday and in 1997 the Muslim community chose this day to create an annual "Day of the Open Mosque" inviting non-Muslims to visit their places of prayer. *Tagesthemen*, it should be noted, did not take notice of this event until 2001, a few weeks after 9/11, when their report projected an image of the allegedly strange life going on in the "parallel society": "Many visitors—and there are a lot more than in the last five years—learn for the first time how things are done in a mosque. In socks, they follow the prayers of the Muslims. They wonder at the strange sounds, the rhythmic movements . . ."[52] In this example, *Tagesthemen* reporting style almost resembles the tone of an anthropological study.[53] This suggests that *Tagesthemen* reporters consider it their mission to enlighten the public on what goes on in an allegedly alien and usually invisible "parallel society." This is even more evident in a report from July 26, 2005, in which reporters—at the instance of the conviction of Theo van Gogh's murderer—visit a mosque in Amsterdam. In this report, the reporting journalists note that they were "allowed to shoot without constraints" in the mosque, suggesting that their report was a rare and particularly authentic insight into the "parallel society." At the end of the report it is stated in conclusion: "More openness—a first step has been made."[54] *Tagesthemen*'s "expedition" into the "parallel society" is thus considered to have been a successful (or even heroic) endeavor as it has increased the Muslim's visibility in the eyes of non-Muslims.

My main argument here is that by applying the notion of invisibility to both terrorists and Muslim migrants the ominous equation of Muslims and terrorists becomes plausible for viewers in a very subtle and complex way. Research focusing on clear-cut stereotypes that are assumed to have been passed on through Western notions of Islam for decades cannot capture this complexity and therefore misses aspects of the discourse that should be taken into account when it comes to critically reviewing media portrayals of Islam.

WHO IS THE VICTIM?

As mentioned above, my research is based on the assumption that narratives are composed of five elements. At this point, it has yet to be answered who, in the terrorism narrative, is considered to be the victim. In order to point out the exceptionality of the terrorism narrative in this respect, a side glance to the other narratives of the media discourse on Islam is in order. In the narrative on Islamic fundamentalism, for instance, it is Muslim women and children who are depicted as the victims of strict fundamentalist regimes in Islamic countries. In the integration narrative, too, women and children are considered to be the major victims—in that case, the victims of their husbands' or parents' failure to provide them with the opportunity to integrate into Western society. In the infamous clash of civilizations narrative, obviously, the West as an abstract entity falls victim to Islamic culture. In the terrorism narrative, however, virtually everyone—that is to say, each and every individual in the West—is the victim of this story. In accordance with the notion that terrorism's goal is to threaten the everyday life of individuals, *Tagesthemen* reports are full of references to people, who, due to terrorist activities, are abruptly being torn out of their routines and their normalcy. One example can be found in a report from March 11, 2004, describing the situation after the Madrid bombings: "It happened this morning around 8 a.m., when, in Madrid, the devastating attack unexpectedly struck down many innocent people. The explosives detonated amidst the morning's rush hour traffic . . . In this train alone, 59 passengers, who were on their way to work like every other day, died because of the bombs."[55] Similarly, in a report covering the prevented bombings on Times Square in April 2010, *Tagesthemen*'s focus is on the effect the attack would have had on ordinary people: "It could have ended in a catastrophe. Thousands of people were on their way to have a nice evening in the restaurants and theaters on Broadway and on Times Square."[56] In one of the reports revolving around the Oklahoma bombing, a female passerby—herself symbolizing the everyday person—is asked about her emotions after the attack. Her answer encapsulates the notion described above: "We are all in danger."[57]

The word "we" in that last statement is of major importance because it reveals that, if everybody is a victim in this story, the television viewer is a victim too. As is stated in the same edition of *Tagesthemen*: "The attack on Oklahoma City has put the fear of God into America. The nation is sitting in front of their television screens and is taken in by that glaring hole in that high-rise building."[58] In a way, rather unexpectedly, the television viewer becomes a participant in the terrorism narrative, becomes involved in it in a much more immediate way than is usually the case. It is safe to assume that this intrusive nature of the narrative is one of the major reasons why it became, for a time, virtually dominant within the Islam discourse.

DISSOLUTIONS

This leads back to my introductory remarks about the bin-Laden video. If the television viewer is the victim in this narrative, how can Osama bin Laden, the narrative's most prominent villain, be watching television? If bin Laden's terror organization Al-Qaeda is renowned for its professionalism, how is it possible that these videos appear amateur-like or even trashy? And most importantly: How can it be that in these videos, bin Laden—who for a long time has been a symbol of terrorist invisibility—is not only visible, but virtually exposed, particularly in the video of him channel surfing?

Undoubtedly, after the release of the videos, journalists could not continue to tell the story of Islamic terrorism the way they used to. This does not mean, however, that they stopped telling this story altogether. For example, a few weeks after bin Laden was killed, when bombs went off in the Norwegian capital and sixty-nine people were shot on a nearby island, many journalists speculated the perpetrator had an Islamist background before it was revealed that the person was actually a non-Muslim Norwegian pursuing a racial and anti-Muslim agenda. Media narratives, thus, do not simply disappear whenever something happens that calls its leading assumptions into question. However, it is important to note that media narratives always inherently include notions of possible endings to the story they are telling. The media narratives actually depend on ideas as to how the equilibrium that was disrupted—with this disruption causing the whole story to come into existence in the first place—can be restored. For example, part of the narrative on Islamic fundamentalism is the strong notion that fundamentalists might, at some point in the future, become more moderate or else, the people in the countries they rule might rise up against them.

In the case of the terrorism narrative, the idea that terrorism can be defeated by increasing security measures at home or by military action overseas does exist in *Tagesthemen* reports, but is eclipsed by the notion that in so doing, Westerners would betray the very values that terrorism is fighting against, adding a tragic note to the narrative. There is, however, a different notion as to how this story might end. It is as simple as it is surprising: the story might end because it just does. In order to understand this, it is important to remember how the terrorism narrative begins. It begins with the disruption of an equilibrium, the equilibrium being the overall normalcy of everyday life. This equilibrium, thus, is effectively restored when everyday life unspectacularly returns. In *Tagesthemen* reports, this notion is frequently invoked. One example can be found in a report dating from February 27, 1993, the day after the World Trade Center bombings. While on the preceding day, the *Tagesthemen* report is filled with blurry images of chaotic scenery, the report from February 27 starts with a long and harmonious shot of a man slowly jogging past the World Trade Center. This shot is accompanied by the following statement: "Already, the site of catastrophe has been re-opened for workouts. Everyday life returns."[59] Much more than all police measures, political programs, or military actions frequently demanded to be put into place in order to defeat terrorism, it is this scenery that really captures what a "happy ending" of this story might look like. On September 11, 2002, one year after the 9/11 attacks, a *Tagesthemen* journalists reports from Manhattan, Kansas, a small village chosen to symbolize the heartland of America due to the fact that it shares its name with New York City's most famous borough. While on this day of commemoration, television screens around the world were once again filled with the airplanes crashing into the Twin Towers and the scenes of devastation that followed, this other Manhattan is portrayed as a small-town paradise: blue skies, people strolling along quiet streets, a cheerful and bright farmer's market, and finally, a loose and lighthearted atmosphere at a rock concert.[60] The "serenity of the countryside," as this setting is called in the report, becomes a metaphor for an America that might just find a way back to normalcy.

Television reports like the one just described are hardly ever put on the agenda of academic research, precisely because of their everyday character. However, by taking a thorough look at these reports, there is a lot to learn about the way media narratives are structured and media discourses are ordered. Thus, it is important for research on Islam and the media to go beyond notions of "bias" and "Islamophobia" and to acknowledge the complexities of the discourse while holding on to, or even deepening, its critical stance toward media reporting. In this chapter, I could only sketch out one media narrative within a larger media discourse drawing from material derived from only one television news magazine. Of the many ways in which this research could and should be extended, adding an internationally comparative perspective seems paramount. German media discourse on Islam undoubtedly features a lot of elements similar to the French, British, or American discourses, but at the same time, when researchers go beyond the simple identification of stereotypes and inaccuracies, they are sure to find a well of rich differences in the ways narratives are construed and entangled with each other.

Crucially, when it comes to media research on Islam, researchers have to remain open for the possibility of change in the way Islam is depicted in media discourse. The release of the bin Laden videos and the reactions to them made it quite clear that this discourse is highly dynamic. The current events in the Arabic world that have somewhat prematurely been called the "Arab Spring" provide another example of this. Interestingly, when these events first developed, journalists and politicians alike expected them to become a possible foundation for the development of a new story the media could tell about Islam. For example, a commentary for the online edition of the *Washington Post* from May 19, 2011, was titled "Writing the Middle East's New Narrative."[61] In this commentary, author David Ignatius analyzes a speech given by President Obama on that same day. In his speech, Obama had called the Arab Spring a developing "story of self-determination."[62] This story, the "new narrative of hope and self-reliance," in Ignatius's words, was supposed to replace an old story: "the old narrative of rage that was Osama bin Laden."

NOTES

1. "Obama: Bin Laden will not walk this Earth again," interview by Steve Kroft, *60 Minutes*, CBS News, May 4, 2011, accessed October 14, 2013, http://www.cbsnews.com/stories/2011/05/04/60minutes/main20059768.shtml.

2. The five videos and a protocol of the press conference, in which their release was announced, can be found on the website of the US Department of Defense: "Background Briefing with Senior Intelligence Official at the Pentagon on Intelligence Aspects of the U.S. Operation Involving Osama bin Laden," the U.S Department of Defense, accessed October 14, 2013, http://www.defense.gov/transcripts/transcript.aspx?transcriptid=4820.

3. Bob Orr, "Videos Demystify the Osama bin Laden Legend," *CBS News*, May 7, 2011, accessed October 14, 2013, http://www.cbsnews.com/stories/ 2011/05/07/eveningnews/main20060808.shtml.

4. "He's Coming to Get You: The Day Osama bin Laden Sat Glued Watching TV of Barack Obama, the Man Who Had Him Killed," *Daily Mail*, May 8, 2011, accessed October 14, 2013, http://www.dailymail.co.uk/news/article-1384573/Osama-Bin-Laden-sat-glued-watching-TV-pictures-Barack-Obama.html.

5. Elisabeth Bumiller, "Videos From bin Laden's Hide-Out Released," *New York Times*, May 7, 2011, accessed October 14, 2013, http://www.nytimes.com/2011/05/08/world/asia/08intel.html?_r=1.

6. To name but a few of a large number of studies conducted in an interdisciplinary and international research field, see the essays in *Muslims and the News Media*, ed. Elizabeth Poole and John E. Richardson (London, New York: Tauris, 2006); Kai Hafez, *Die politische Dimension der Auslandsberichterstattung*; (Baden-Baden: Nomos, 2002); and Thomas Deltombe, *L'islam imaginaire. La construction médiatique de l'islamophobie en France: 1975–2005* (Paris: La Découverte, 2005).

7. Paul Harris, "Bin Laden Videos Give a Remarkable Insight into Life in His Lair," *The Guardian*, May 7, 2011, accessed October 14, 2013, http://www.guardian.co.uk/world/2011/may/07/bin-laden-video-abbottobad-seals-death.

8. Frank Gardner, "Osama bin Laden's Abbottabad House 'Was Al-Qaeda-Hub,'" *BBC*, May 8, 2011, accessed October 14, 2013, http://www.bbc.co.uk/news/world-us-canada-13325595.

9. Orr, "Videos."

10. Harris, "Bin Laden."

11. Brian Ross and Avni Patel, "Bin Laden Tapes Show 'Pathetic' Side of Al Qaeda Leader," *ABC News*, May 9, 2011, accessed October 14, 2013, http://abcnews.go.com/Blotter/osama-bin-laden-tapes-show-pathetic-side- al/story?id=13559652#.TtZbjfKVpdO. For the Al-Qaeda-biography by the interviewee, see Lawrence Wright, *The Looming Tower: Al-Qaeda and the Road to 9/11* (New York: Knopf, 2006).

12. Tim Karis, *Mediendiskurs Islam: Narrative in der Berichterstattung der Tagesthemen 1979–2010* (Wiesbaden: Springer VS, 2013).

13. Edward Said, *Covering Islam: How the Media and the Experts Determine How We See the Rest of the World* (New York: Vintage Books, 1997).

14. Edward Said, *Orientalism: 25th Anniversary Edition* (New York: Vintage Books, 2003).

15. For a literature review with a focus on research conducted in the United States, see Dina Ibrahim, "The Middle East in American Media. A 20th-Century Overview," *The International Communication Gazette* 71 (2009): 511–524. For research conducted in Germany, see Susan Schenk, *Das Islambild im internationalen Fernsehen. Ein Vergleich der Nachrichtensender* Al Jazeera English, BBC World *und* CNN International (Berlin: Frank & Timme, 2009): 34–55.

16. I explained this argument in further detail in Tim Karis, "Postmodernes Feindbild und aufgeklärte Islamophobie? Grenzen der Analysekategorie, Feindbild in der Islambildforschung," in *Vom Ketzer bis zum Terroristen: Interdisziplinäre Studien zur Konstruktion und Rezeption von Feindbildern*, ed. Alfons Fürst et al. (Münster: Aschendorff Verlag, 2012): 179–190. For a critical stance on the prevalent methods of analyzing media reporting on Islam, see also Joris Luyendijk, "Beyond Orientalism," *The International Communication Gazette* 72 (2010): 9–20.

17. For a detailed discussion of this approach, see Karis, *Mediendiskurs Islam*, 59–76.

18. Both Fiske and Herman borrow from the works of Bulgarian philosopher Tzvetan Todorov. See John Fiske, *Television Culture* (London, New York: Routledge, 1987), 138–48; David Herman, "Introduction" in *The Cambridge Companion to Narrative*, edited by David Herman (Cambridge: Cambridge University Press, 2007); Willy Viehöver, "Diskurse als Narrationen," in *Handbuch Sozialwissenschaftliche Diskursanalyse Bd. I: Theorien und Methoden*, ed. Reiner Keller et al. (Wiesbaden: VS Verlag für Sozialwissenschaften, 2006), 179–208; Knut Hickethier, "Narrative Navigation durchs Weltgeschehen. Erzählstrukturen in Fernsehnachrichten," in *Fernsehnachrichten. Prozesse, Strukturen, Funktionen*, ed. Klaus Kamps and Miriam Meckel (Wiesbaden: Westdeutscher Verlag, 1998), 185–202.

19. John Fiske and John Hartley, *Reading Television* (London, New York: Routledge, 1996), 64.

20. Elizabeth S. Bird and Robert W. Dardenne, "Myth, Chronicle, and Story. Exploring the Narrative Quality of News," in *Media, Myths, and Narratives. Television and the Press*, ed. James W. Carey (Newbury Park, CA: Sage, 1988), 70.

21. All narratives are particularized in Karis, *Mediendiskurs Islam*, 159–307.

22. A detailed discussion of my understanding of media narratives and their component parts can be found in Karis, *Mediendiskurs Islam*, 88–99.

23. *Tagesthemen*, "Anschlag in Beirut und Reaktionen aus dem Ausland," first broadcast October 23, 1983 by ARD. All translations from *Tagesthemen* reports are my own unless otherwise noted. If available, the titles of the reports are given according to the archival entries of the broadcasting network, *Arbeitsgemeinschaft der öffentlich-rechtlichen Rundfunkanstalten der Bundesrepublik Deutschland (ARD)*.

24. *Tagesthemen*, "Anschlag auf das World Trade Center New York," first broadcast February 27, 1993, by ARD. The quote given is Cuomo's original statement (not translated).

25. *Tagesthemen*, "Sicherheitsmaßnahmen in New York," first broadcast April 20, 1995, by ARD.

26. *Tagesthemen*, "Wie Washington auf den Anschlag reagiert," first broadcast April 20, 1995, by ARD.

27. *Tagesthemen*, "Bin Laden," first broadcast September 11, 2001, by ARD.

28. James W. Carey notes that, whilst hesitant at first, as the day progressed, American reporters speculated intensively about the question as to who was responsible for the attacks, thereby prominently evoking the notion of Islamic terrorism. See James W. Carey, "American Journalism on, before, and after September 11," in *Journalism after September 11,* ed. Barbie Zelizer and Stuart Allan (London, New York: Routledge, 2003): 71–74. For a comprehensive overview of worldwide media reactions to 9/11, see the special issue of the *Journal of Media Sociology* edited by Tomasz Pludowski and titled "How the World's News Media Reacted to 9/11. Essays from around the Globe" (Spokane: Marquette Books, 2010).

29. *Tagesthemen*, "Bin Laden," first broadcast September 11, 2001, by ARD.

30. *Tagesthemen*, untitled report on the prevented terror attacks on Times Square, first broadcast May 2, 2010, by ARD.

31. *Tagesthemen*, "Bin Laden," first broadcast September 11, 2001, by ARD.

32. *Tagesthemen*, "Wie Washington auf den Anschlag reagiert," first broadcast April 20, 1995, by ARD.

33. *Tagesthemen*, "Anschlag in Beirut und Reaktionen aus dem Ausland," first broadcast October 23, 1983, by ARD.

34. *Tagesthemen*, "Bin Laden," first broadcast September 11, 2001, by ARD.

35. *Tagesthemen*, untitled interview with Dan Shiftan, University of Haifa, first broadcast September 11, 2001, by ARD.

36. *Tagesthemen*, "Al Kaida und Spanien," first broadcast March 11, 2004, by ARD.

37. *Tagesthemen*, "Wie Washington auf den Anschlag reagiert," first broadcast April 20, 1995, by ARD.

38. *Tagesthemen*, "Algerien als Polizeistaat und Gottesstaat," first broadcast January 6, 1993, by ARD.

39. *Tagesthemen*, "Algerien: Volksabstimmung über Islamisten-Amnestie," first broadcast September 29, 2005, by ARD.

40. *Tagesthemen*, "Bin Laden," first broadcast September 11, 2001, by ARD.

41. *Tagesthemen*, "Bin Laden," first broadcast September 11, 2001, by ARD.

42. *Tagesthemen*, "Al Kaida und Spanien," first broadcast March 11, 2004, by ARD.

43. *Tagesthemen*, "Bin Laden," first broadcast September 11, 2001, by ARD.

44. For a thorough analysis of these policies in several European states see Bijan Fateh-Moghadam, "Religiös-weltanschauliche Neutralität und Geschlechterordnung: Strafrechtliche Burka-Verbote zwischen Paternalismus und Moralismus," in *Als Mann und Frau schuf er sie. Religion und Geschlecht*, ed. Barbara Stollberg-Rilinger (Würzburg: Ergon Verlag, forthcoming).

45. *Tagesthemen*, "Bin Laden," first broadcast September 11, 2001, by ARD.

46. The term "Parallelgesellschaft" ("parallel society") was first used by German sociologist Wilhelm Heitmeyer in a study concerned with young Turkish immigrants living in Germany and their attitudes towards the Islamic religion, the use of violence,

and democracy. Heitmeyer wrote about this study in the popular German weekly newspaper *Die Zeit* as early as 1996: Wilhelm Heitmeyer, "Für türkische Jugendliche in Deutschland spielt der Islam eine wichtige Rolle," *Die Zeit*, August 23, 1996, accessed October 25, 2013, http://www.zeit.de/1996/35/heitmey.txt.19960823.xml. However, the term did not gain much prominence until after the 9/11 attacks, when the discussion on Muslim migration into European countries got much more attention. For an overview of the academic and public discussion of the term see the essays in *Was heißt hier Parallelgesellschaft? Zum Umgang mit Differenzen*, ed. Wolf-Dietrich Bukow et al. (Wiesbaden: VS Verlag für Sozialwissenschaften, 2007).

47. *Tagesthemen*, "Islam in the Federal Republic," first broadcast March 13, 1980, by ARD.

48. *Tagesthemen*, "Al Kaida und Spanien," first broadcast March 11, 2004, by ARD.

49. *Tagesthemen*, "Islamgruppen in Deutschland," first broadcast September 19, 2001, by ARD.

50. *Tagesthemen*, "Niederlande: Rassismus statt Liberalismus," first broadcast November 13, 2004, by ARD.

51. *Tagesthemen*, "Kaplan-Sekte: Die heimlichen Anwerber," first broadcast October 15, 2001, by ARD.

52. *Tagesthemen*, "Tag der offenen Moschee," first broadcast October 3, 2001, by ARD.

53. Stanislawa Paulus makes a similar argument with reference to her research on TV-documentaries on Islam. See Stanislawa Paulus, "Einblicke in fremde Welten. Orientalische Selbst/Fremdkonstruktionen in TV-Dokumentationen über Muslime in Deutschland," in *Orient- und IslamBilder. Interdisziplinäre Beiträge zu Orientalismus und antimuslimischem Rassismus*, ed. Iman Attia (Münster: Unrast, 2007), 283.

54. *Tagesthemen,* "Van-Gogh-Mord: Die Niederlande danach," first broadcast July 26, 2005, by ARD.

55. *Tagesthemen*, "Spanien: Anschlag im Urlaubsland," first broadcast March 11, 2004, by ARD.

56. *Tagesthemen*, untitled report on the prevented terror attacks on Times Square, first broadcast May 2, 2010, by ARD.

57. *Tagesthemen*, "Wie Washington auf den Anschlag reagiert," first broadcast April 20, 1995, by ARD.

58. *Tagesthemen*, untitled segment about the Oklahoma City bombings, first broadcast April 20, 1995, by ARD.

59. *Tagesthemen*, "Anschlag auf das World Trade Center New York," first broadcast, February 27, 1993, by ARD.

60. *Tagesthemen*, "USA. Stimmung im Land," first broadcast September 11, 2002, by ARD.

61. David Ignatius, "Writing the Middle East's New Narrative," *Washington Post*, May 19, 2011, accessed October 14, 2013, http://www.washingtonpost.com/opinions/writing-the-middle-easts-new-narrative/2011/05/17/AFTmAm6G_story.html.

62. "Remarks by the President on the Middle East and North Africa," the White House, accessed October 14, 2013, http://www.whitehouse.gov/the-press-office/2011/05/19/remarks-president-middle-east-and-north-africa.

Section II

BOY (AND GIRL) MEETS WORLD

Chapter Five

"Your Dreams Were Your Ticket Out": How Mass Media's Teachers Constructed One Educator's Identity

Edward A. Janak

"BUT WHY DO *YOU* WANT TO BECOME A TEACHER?"

It was one of the most common questions I heard in the years leading up to my career in the public school classroom, and even throughout my time spent teaching on all levels. Whether I was a classroom teacher exploring Shakespeare with freshmen or a university professor training the next generation of educators, I have always considered myself a teacher first and foremost. The answer to that question has evolved over time, but typically comes back to what is both a simple, yet complex, response: because it is who I am. Being a teacher is core to my identity, and the underlying assumptions of the question tend to flout the teaching profession's status. It was a question laden in cultural assumptions about the validity of the nation's school system, about perceptions of teachers, and even about socially constructed gender roles.

To understand teacher identity is to understand any other form of social identity. To fully explore this concept, this chapter relies upon fairly standard definitions of the concepts of social group and social identity. At its most simple level, a social group is the group into which a person is born: for example, a person's ethnicity, sex, socioeconomic status, affectional orientation, faith system, or ability/disability/area of giftedness. A social identity, on the other hand, is the characteristics and boundaries of those groups as set forth by the society in which they exist, as well as the group(s) with whom a person *chooses* to identify. This becomes much more problematic and complicated, as social identities can come from biological factors, social factors, political factors, or occupational factors.

"You're a teacher?"

In the decade I spent in the public school classroom, the topic of my profession of choice was frequently greeted with disbelief. While understandable when it came from those who knew me during my misspent youth, all too often it came as a result of the simple fact that I didn't look the part. Just as we ocularize identity in this country—citizens of the United States like to be able to identify people's social identity with a glance, whether accurate or not—we also ocularize professions, and I definitely did not look like the teachers people remembered from television and the movies.

Throughout my profession, I came to realize that there most definitely exists a "teacher culture" in the United States, complete with its own "teacher identity." People talk about so-called "chick flicks" and "bromances." The underlying assumption behind both somewhat offensive terms is that a person's sex defines their taste in entertainment—indeed, that their sex defines their identity. In the case of teachers, this is true in regards to our profession: what we do shapes to no small degree who we are and what we enjoy. For many people, Arnold Schwarzenegger's 1990 film *Kindergarten Cop* was just another forgettable comedy in his oeuvre in which he plays a police detective who has to go undercover as a kindergarten teacher in order to bust some local drug dealers; teachers, particularly those in early childhood education, recognized it as a primer and documentary. Just as any other social identity is a construct of the society in which it incubates, so too is teacher identity; and just as social identity is impacted by media norms, particularly those of television, so too has teacher identity been shaped by media norms.

"Funny, you don't look like a professor."
 "Why thank you for noticing the dearth of
 tweed and elbow pads in my wardrobe."

At this stage in my career, I am able to connect some of my development as a teacher to the historic context in which I worked and the media to which I was exposed at the time. This is due in no small part to my study of the foundations of education in the United States—the historical, sociological, and philosophical roots that produced the nation's schools and teachers—which allows me to see how my career followed national trends in many cases or bucked trends in others. While my knowledge of the field has shifted over time, the role of the media on my identity has been constant: as I left the public schools for the university, my viewing has become more politicized and aware—to use current vernacular, more *meta*. I have come to realize how much of my identity is folded into my role as a teacher, and how much that has been shaped by both my viewing habits as well as those of the society in which I worked.

This chapter explores how all of these intersections—media culture, teacher identity, and social identity—went into shaping both the academic I have become and also (and more significantly) the person I have become. There is a long history of teacher autobiography/auto-ethnography for social commentary—from Pat Conroy reflecting on his days teaching at Daufuskie Island in 1977's *The Water Is Wide* to Jonathan Kozol using his classroom experiences to paint stinging social satire in 1991's *Savage Inequalities* to Gregory Michie reflecting on social perceptions of minority youth in 1999's *Holler if You Hear Me*. Teacher voice has often served to reflect on the classroom as a sort of bell jar for analyzing society at large. While those authors do admirable work, this chapter cannot aspire to achieve such results; instead, it uses autobiography as a stepping stone for an analysis of social perceptions of teaching from the 1970s to the present, as bent through the media prism. It contextualizes my experiences as a teacher and my exposure to teachers in the media with the greater socio-educational trends impacting teachers in public schools.

In order to examine this intersectionality, the chapter selects five stages of my life and development as an educator as snapshots to examine—five acts in the drama that is my teacher life, if you will. For each stage, it examines the greater social context regarding the public perception of the public schools, how this was reflected or shaped by the then-current teachers on television, and how these were impacting my professional development. Interestingly, the chapter is bookended by what was once, and has become again, a seminal influence on my teacher identity and that of the future teachers whom I train: Gabe Kaplan's Mr. Kotter.

PROLOGUE: *WELCOME BACK, KOTTER* IN IDENTITY FORMATION

"What do you mean, you don't want to be a Sweathog?"

The 1970s were an unusual time to grow up. As a child, what stands out the most are memories of plaid and polyester, Saturday morning cartoons and weekend variety shows, feathered hai,r and a general sense of *laissez-faire* that permeated all aspects of society. And Kotter. *Welcome Back, Kotter* (1975–1979) was one of the few "adult" television shows that my mother, a single parent trying to raise a son on a heavily feminist diet of Helen Reddy's "I am Woman" and pro-ERA messages, allowed me to watch. This might be due to the fact that for as long as I can remember, I wanted to be a teacher; as a very young child, I would line up my stuffed animals in rows and play school. Or, this might have been my mother's attempt to expose me to a man working in what was considered a feminized profession at the time. Regardless of reason, I became an avid viewer of the show.

For those unfamiliar, the show revolved around a teacher, Gabe Kotter (played by Gabe Kaplan), who grew up in a tough Brooklyn neighborhood, got out to attend college, then was placed back at his high school alma

mater, James Buchanan High, by the New York City school board. His ad-
ministrative nemesis, Mr. Woodman, was still principal—and remembered
Kotter as a youthful troublemaker rather than seeing him as the responsible
educator he had become. In youth, Kotter and his friends dubbed themselves
"Sweathogs"—a nod to a gang name, while remaining innocuous enough
for 1970s prime time—and Kotter was introduced to the new generation of
Sweathogs that Woodman felt Kotter should teach.[1]

The Sweathogs became Kotter's homeroom and first-period class. There
was an ever-evolving group of background students that often remained
nameless and voiceless. Whether this was an accurate depiction of the high
turnaround in students in inner-city schools or just a way to avoid paying
scale to the actors is unknown. However, the core group of Sweathogs remained, characters that both reinforced and rebutted stereotypes of urban
students that remain today. The enforcer of the group was the self-proclaimed
"Puerto Rican Jew" named Juan Luis Pedro Phillipo de Huevos Epstein,
a student voted "most likely to take a life" in the yearbook. The athletic,
popular member was Freddie "Boom Boom" Washington, one of the few
Sweathogs who both had a steady relationship and abided by school policies
in order to play basketball. The group's pet was the quiet, diminutive Arnold
Horschack, known for his outlandish laugh and demands for attention in a
classroom where nobody else participated, raising his hand and yelling "Ooo!
Ooo ooo!" The group's leader was the muscular, attractive, popular Vinnie
Babarino, a role that would become breakout for the young John Travolta.
Kotter used a variety of progressive, innovative teaching methods both in the
classroom and in his apartment (where the Sweathogs consistently broke in
to spend time with their favorite teacher), and hijinks ensued.

Like many boys of my generation, I allowed what I watched on television
to shape my imaginative play. To many of my friends, this meant playing in
stereotypical roles: cops and robbers, Bugs and Elmer. To me, it meant playing school. When I could convince the boys I knew at the time into playing
Kotter, they fought to be the Sweathogs; I, on the other hand, insisted on
being Mr. Kotter. This was likely due to the fact that 1970s portrayals of
teachers were still overwhelmingly positive—for example, *Room 222* (1969–
1974), *The Paper Chase* (1978–1986), and *The White Shadow* (1978–1981).

From the viewpoint of educational history, portrayals of teachers in mass
media followed the socially accepted view that teachers were figures worthy
of respect. There were a number of teachers on television and in the movies,
even if they were rarely, if ever, shown in their classrooms. As explained by
Mary Dalton and Laura Linder in the 1970s, "[w]ith so many teacher characters and so little teaching, it becomes clear that the occupation of teacher
is convenient shorthand for intelligence and respectability."[2] The nation was
still in the throes of launching Lyndon Johnson's "War on Poverty," and the
public schools became perceived as integral in that war. The passage of the
1965 Elementary and Secondary Education Act (reauthorized since, most

recently in 2002 but renamed No Child Left Behind) was emblematic of this belief: learn more, earn more. While the public schools had been considered an integral part of achieving the American Dream since the 1840s, this belief was finally *de jure* codified in that act.[3]

Indeed, teachers on small and silver screens were portrayed as intellectual and upright figures to be revered. The 1950s epochal Mr. Chips and Miss Dove had been supplanted by the more cutting-edge 1960s figures of Sidney Poitier's *To Sir with Love* and Sandy Dennis's *Up the Down Staircase* in many minds, showing teachers overcoming social obstacles to become respected amongst students and faculty alike. By the 1970s, Americans were shown figures that were able to use teaching as a metaphor for a larger struggle on the small and silver screens. While there were some teachers depicted as addressing social upheaval on the small screen, most notably in *The White Shadow*,[4] the upheaval of the 1960s was still fresh in many people's minds, impacting the onscreen portrayals of teachers. Americans were seeking escapism, not reminders of reality as the nation's schools dominated headlines as flash points for controversy and struggle, from the Orangeburg Massacre and Kent State at the university level to the busing controversy culminating in the US Supreme Court Decision of *Swann vs. Charlotte-Mecklenburg Board of Education* (1970) that mandated racially-motivated busing, Americans did not want to be reminded of the problems with schools. As explained by Dalton and Linder:

> Social relevancy programs . . . sidestepped classroom settings, perhaps because students provided so much impetus to social movements in real life that it was a subject TV producers wished to avoid. A few shows . . . tried to approach some of the troubling issues facing educators at the time, such as integration or race relations. For the most part, however, the retreat from reality was abject.[5]

If Americans had lost faith in their government and politics, they still had faith in their public schools and believed teaching was a noble calling. Because and beyond what I saw on television, to the child born into a blue-collar family being a teacher was a profession of respect, a way to enter the white collar world. As such, when I entered university in 1988, I knew that teaching was the profession for me, education the major.

ACT 1: UNIVERSITY YEARS

"But why do you want to become a teacher?"

In the field of educational history, the period from the 1950s through the 1980s is referred to as the period of the five Es. One of these Es is emancipation from local control; as the period progressed, educationally we moved inexorably closer and closer to our current neoliberal state of centralized control over our public schools. The US Supreme Court heard educational cases more and more frequently, Congress passed more and more pieces of legislation, and the Secretary of Education was carved out as a separate cabinet position (16th in line of succession to the president, for the record).[6]

The general population wanted more centralized control of their public schools. In 1983, the report *A Nation at Risk* was released. Just as the Watergate scandal created a sense of disillusionment amongst Americans, this widely read and reported document altered perceptions regarding public schools.[7] Nothing, it seemed, was sacrosanct any more. This report changed the national conversation regarding schooling in two substantive ways: first, it was the first expression that Americans had lost faith in its public schools; second, in a marked departure from policies and beliefs of years past, it ushered in the desire among the general population for more federal control, culminating in 2002's No Child Left Behind. The report linked educational success with national success in militaristic terms. It's opening paragraph read, in part:

> Our nation is at risk. Our once unchallenged preeminence in commerce, industry, science, and technological innovation is being overtaken by competitors throughout the world . . . the educational foundations of our society are presently being eroded by a rising tide of mediocrity that threatens our very future as a Nation and a people . . . If an unfriendly foreign power had attempted to impose on America the mediocre educational performance that exists today, we might well have viewed it an act of war. As it stands we have allowed this to happen to ourselves . . . We have in effect been committing an act of unthinking, unilateral educational disarmament.[8]

That same year, Rudolf Flesch published *Why Johnny Still Can't Read*, a scathing attack on the approaches to teaching reading in the public schools that topped bestseller lists.[9] This doubt was reinforced by the portrayal of teachers in the media. As early as the 1970s, there were some teachers in film that were not portrayed as the moral, upstanding pillars of their community.[10] However, after the publication of *A Nation at Risk*, it became cool to include teacher characters who were buffoons, openly antagonistic, sexually promiscuous (particularly with students), and/or otherwise generally incompetent. To most of my generation, asking about teachers in '80s movies instantly conjures up two images: Mr. Hand from *Fast Times at Ridgemont High* (1982) and Ben Stein's nameless economics teacher from 1986's *Ferris Bueller's Day Off* ("Bueller? Bueller?").[11]

As the nation turned its attention to its public schools, there was a surge in teacher characters on television. Admittedly, most of these were in short-lived series—does anyone remember *Making the Grade* (1984), *Fast Times* (1996), *Pursuit of Happiness* (1987), *Homeroom* (1989), *Mr. Sunshine* (1986), *Spencer/Under One Roof* (1984), *Teachers Only* (1982), or Yakov Smirnoff as a teacher in *What a Country!* (1986)—but two of the decade's more popular sitcoms, *The Facts of Life* (1979–1988) and *Saved by the Bell* (1983–1993), both revolved around schooling and teaching.

As the nation reeled from the report and began shedding a more critical eye toward its schools, I began my training toward becoming a teacher. Admittedly I was not influenced by either Mrs. Garrett from *The Facts of Life* or Mr. Belding from *Saved by the Bell* when I began my first course in education. This course, similar to that in universities across the country then and now, was a generic "introduction to education." In the lecture hall for this course was myself, about ninety-seven women, and two other men. On the first day of class, the professor of the course called the three of us with penises to the front of the room and handed us course drop slips. "You don't want to become teachers," he intoned, "you'll never be able to support a family on a teacher's salary."

Thus I was introduced to two concepts surrounding public perception of teaching at the time: how the profession was viewed as feminized and how performing gender impacted that.

As described by John Richardson and Brenda Wooden Hatcher, teaching had become feminized as a profession due to two social forces: the spread of compulsory education, creating concurrent demands for teachers that were economically advantageous; and the limits on what society believed women were capable professionally.[12] In short, as the demand for more teachers arose, school districts realized that women, who typically earned less than men for the same work, would be the most economical route to staffing the schools; and women, due to a dearth of other opportunities, accepted this.

Second, as teaching was feminized—or otherwise thought of as "women's work"—at the time, the professor of this class believed that only women should engage in it as a profession. In a sense, he was fulfilling Judith Butler's notion of performativity of gender as a social temporality:

> Gender ought not to be construed as a stable identity or locus of agency from which various acts follow; rather, gender is an identity tenuously constituted in time, instituted in an exterior space through a *stylized repetition of acts* [emphasis in original]. The effect of gender is produced through the stylization of the body and, hence, must be understood as the mundane way in which bodily gestures, movements, and styles of various kinds constitute the illusion of an abiding gendered self. This formulation moves the conception of gender off the ground of a substantial model of identity to one that requires a conception of gender as a constituted *social temporality*.[13]

Luckily for me, I was a proud rebel throughout high school and college; in typical adolescent angst mode, the minute a professor told me not to do something, it made me desire it all the more. As if my identity as a future teacher hadn't been cemented by my late night viewings of *Kotter* as a child, this made my future profession concrete.

ACT 2: PUBLIC SCHOOL TEACHING

"But why do you want to become a teacher?"

It was the summer of 1992 that I earned my initial teaching credential from
the state of New York. That was the summer that defined Generation X:
musically, Cameron Crowe's *Singles* documented the rise of grunge, Lol-
lapalooza was still travelling around the country before settling in Chicago
and giving rise to the new dawn of music festivals. Hip-hop music gained
credibility, and "college music" became "alternative rock."[14] As a result of
these movements, issues of social justice—racism, poverty, sexism—were
becoming topics of conversation, laying the bedrock for first multicultural
schooling and now education for social justice.

Throughout my decade as a public school teacher, public schooling had
rebounded a bit in the public perception from the sociopolitical attacks of
1983. This restored faith in the public schools was demonstrated politically. Both of the major pieces of federal legislation that came out during
this period—1991's America 2000, proposed by President George H. W.
Bush,[15] and 1994's Goals 2000: Educate America Act signed by President
Bill Clinton—set forth stringent standards for American schools, and made
them voluntary for schools to meet.[16] The exception to this is 1993's School-
to-Work Opportunities Act, which mandated more vocational education and
career exploration opportunities for all American school children via appren-
ticeships and similar opportunities.[17] However, that act didn't last past initial
reauthorization as the nation began listening to the rhetoric that all American
youth deserved a chance to earn a four-year degree, in spite of the fact that
the majority of American jobs require a two-year degree or less.[18]

This emphasis on college being essential for happiness became more and
more reflected in the teacher films of the period. Starting with 1995's *Dangerous Minds*, teacher flicks became troublingly formulaic; take one white
middle-class teacher, place in an inner city and surround with brown lower-
class children, have said teacher sacrifice personal life to teach well, have
said students become inspired by teacher sacrifice and all pass, graduate, and
go on to college.[19] The covertly racist and classist tones of these films are
troubling in and of themselves, the underlying messages sent to the general
public even more so. College was the only measure of success, and teachers
had to become messiahs to ensure this. After all, the movies showed that any
teacher can be 100 percent successful if they just sacrifice enough. Just watch
Meryl Streep in 1999's *Music of the Heart* or Hillary Swank in 2007's *Freedom Writers.* Sometimes there are minor variations—the teacher is minority,
for example. However, even then it's typically not a teacher but a coach,
such as Samuel L. Jackson in 2005's *Coach Carter*, reinforcing stereotype

even more. Or, for another variation, white teacher and white students: Julia Roberts teaching "feminism" in 2005's *Mona Lisa Smile*, all the while courting a potential new husband and learning that girls becoming housewives is okay. This became such a trope it was even lampooned in 1996's Jon Lovitz vehicle, *High School High*.

I knew I was not messiah material. As a teacher, my identity was forged by early exposure to Gabe Kaplan's Kotter, Sidney Poitier's "Sir," and Nick Nolte's Alex Jurel. All had the same characteristic trait: they did what was right by the students in spite of external pressure from administration or society. And, for doing such, all were deemed rebellious, outsiders. However, outsider status is almost essential to being a good teacher within the increasingly neoliberal system that is American public schooling. Indeed, outsider status is one of the essential traits of what Mary Dalton refers to as the "Hollywood model" of being a good teacher: the teacher is an outsider, is personally involved with students, learns from her or his students, exhibits tension between themselves and their administrators, and follows a personalized curriculum.[20] It is amazing how, in retrospect, I see that my public school teacher identity hewed to this model.

Throughout my public school career, I modeled my teacher identity on this Hollywood model—and always wondered, "what would Kotter do?" It was easy to perpetuate outsider status—as a long-haired rebel from New York state teaching in conservative, rural South Carolina, this was assured from my date of hire. To this date, I have taught—and thoroughly enjoyed—populations opposed politically and socially to many of my core beliefs. However, this tension and exposure is valuable—if not me, then who? If not now, then when? While I didn't realize it at the time, by challenging my students' ways of thinking, I was merely putting into practice one aspect of teaching for diversity: recognizing that intellectual strength comes from hearing a variety of opinions, not from surrounding yourself with like-minded individuals. As Michele Moses and Mitchell Chang point out, this is a belief that is philosophically grounded in the works of thinkers such as Aristotle, John Stuart Mill, John Dewey, and Martha Nussbaum.[21] It was when I read Dewey's *How We Think* (1910) that I found the most eloquent defense of the necessity of making students confront their beliefs and hear oppositional, problematizing points of view, as Dewey quoted John Locke:

> There is nothing more ordinary than children's receiving into their minds propositions . . . from their parents, nurses, or those about them; which being insinuated in their unwary as well as unbiased understandings, and fastened by degrees, are at last (and this whether true or false) riveted there by long custom and education, beyond all possibility of being pulled out again. For men, when they are grown up, reflecting upon their opinions and finding those of this sort to be

as ancient in their minds as their very memories, not having observed their early insinuation, nor by what means they got them, they are apt to reverence them as sacred things, and not to suffer them to be profaned, touched, or questioned. They take them as standards to be the great and unerring deciders of truth and falsehood, and the judges to which they appeal in all manner of controversies.[22]

I became personally involved with students; I would attend block parties and got to know their families and backgrounds. Just as the Sweathogs would arrive unannounced and uninvited at Kotter's apartment, so too throughout my career would I have a carload of students show up at my door, and I would treat them as Kotter treated his. I'd pour them a glass of southern sweet tea, and we'd sit outside and chat about music, literature, or life—whatever they needed. I never knew the impact this had until almost twenty years later when I received an e-mail from one of the more frequent attendees/guests. He informed me he had just passed the bar exam in Tennessee, and had me to thank for it. It seems his stepfather was extremely violent; whenever the abuse would get too much, this student would head to my place for a respite. In some ways, according to the student, I kept him alive and showed him not all men were violent. To say I wept upon reading this is an understatement.

I have always been open to learning from my students. This took many forms, some expected, some unexpected. I would learn about their culture and community, their values and mores, and allow these to help shape and influence my curriculum and pedagogy. Often even their side comments and under-breath mumblings revealed much about how a lesson is being perceived. I learned this on my first day of teaching. There I was, a white—alt-Gen X guy ready to connect with a student population that was 85 percent African American with my extensive knowledge of hip-hop music and Spike Lee films. Yes, even I laugh at this thought today. I went into my first day, ready to play some Red Hot Chili Peppers and "really reach" them when I heard one student make the comment (expletives deleted) "Look at that man . . . bet he plays us some Red Hot Chili Peppers and expects to reach us with that nonsense." That crashing noise was all my expectations crumbling around me.

Throughout most of my career, even as a white male, I have had tension between my methods and those favored by my administration. Whether questioning a particular curriculum item, handling a complaint about the noise emanating from my room, or wondering why I was taking a junior-level English course outside to read Walt Whitman and Henry David Thoreau, administrators often looked askance at my approaches. I learned that they would not argue with results—and my students were successful. And over time I learned that it is easier to be proactive and get administration on my side than to be reactive and occasionally apologetic.

Finally, throughout the entirety of my teaching career, I followed a personalized curriculum. In the "standard" English courses that I taught I used the textbook as a guide and tool, but not an absolute; I would supplement with my own favorite poems, short stories, or excerpts from comics and graphic novels such as 1991's *Maus*. Beyond that, every year I taught I was empowered to teach a course strictly of my own design. While many teachers, particularly early career teachers, would view this with nervousness and trepidation ("What do you mean you want me to teach a class for which there is no syllabus or textbook or scope and sequence guide?"), for me it was a challenge to be embraced. I taught writers' workshops, literature from around the world, media history, and public speaking—all my own design, all to my own standards, all which allowed me to tap into my outsider status and provide materials not typically used in traditional curricula in order to not just reach my students, but try to change their lives.

ACT 3: HIGHER EDUCATION

"I know why I am a teacher, but why do you *want to be a teacher?"*

If the Hollywood model taught me to be a good teacher, then when I made the transition into higher education—I became a teacher of teachers—that its converse would directly shape my curriculum. As a teacher, I still pattern my classroom persona on the Hollywood model; however, in my practice, I also use it as characteristics of what not to do. As Dalton explains:

> I have described the good teacher as an outsider, one who is not well-liked by other teachers. The bad teacher is generally presented as neither liked nor disliked (by other teachers) but as part of the system embedded so deeply into the structure of the school as institution that he or she must be accepted or at least tolerated. While good teachers get involved with students on a personal level and seem to genuinely like them, bad teachers are typically bored by students, afraid of students, or eager to dominate students. The good teacher often has an antagonistic relationship with administrators while the bad teacher fits into the administration's plan for controlling students. Finally, as good teachers personalize the curriculum to meet everyday needs in students' lives, bad teachers follow the standardized curriculum, which they adhere to in order to avoid personal contact with the students.[23]

This issue of following the curriculum is one of the most substantive I have to deal with in terms of preparing new teachers—and something I did not have to cope with as a public school teacher. Indeed, we have moved back to the 1980s in terms of lost faith in our teachers. In media portrayals, teachers are becoming less and less intellectual, more and more rife for satire. Teachers are highly sexualized, incompetent, or both, as exemplified by Cameron Diaz's Elizabeth Halsey in *Bad Teacher* (or the 2013 CBS television series it spawned).[24] The school system is ripe for overhaul, as demonstrated in the 2010 documentary *Waiting for Superman* or the 2012 film, *Won't Back Down*.[25] This is exemplified not only on the silver screen but also on the small screen from series focusing on teacher's struggles within the system such as *Boston Public* (2000–2004), to series which allow this theme to enter temporarily such as the highly regarded fourth season of *The Wire* (2002–2008), to one-time specials "celebrating" teachers such as CBS' *Teachers Rock!* (2012).[26] Again, art reflects reality, as the films are simply depicting the public's general mistrust of public schools as reflected in 2002's No Child Left Behind (NCLB) and the Common Core (CC) standards movement.

In 2001, the Elementary and Secondary Education Act was due for reauthorization; Congress, led by Senators Ted Kennedy and John Kerry, decided to take the formerly voluntary standards of America 2000 and Goals 2000 and codify them into law.[27] As such NCLB mandated minimum criteria for teacher certification ("highly qualified"), disaggregated how schools reported student data (breaking out by race, class, and sex), and held schools (but not students) accountable for how students did on standardized tests in literacy and math. In a marked break with previous acts federal and state, the law even "suggested" particular curricula be followed, thanks to the generosity of the corporations publishing those curricula and their lobbyists.[28]

NCLB linked accountability to funding, a pattern not unique to that particular law. However, while it encouraged particular prescriptive curricula, it didn't mandate those—there were no national standards. The National Governors Association brought a variety of groups together and, in 2010, released the Common Core standards. To date (2013), forty-five states, four territories, Washington, D.C., and the Department of Defense Schools have all adopted the CC as their baseline.[29] There are two primary areas—reading and math—and a third area focusing on Grades 6–12 Literacy in History/ Social Studies, Sciences, and Technical Subjects. In short, US students in the elementary schools are no longer being taught science, social studies, art, music, health, or any other subject other than reading or math. Instead, students spend up to three hours a day sitting in a proscriptive, sometimes online, "literacy block" followed by up to three hours in a proscriptive, sometimes online, "math block."[30]

As an educator who has spent a lifetime defined by the Hollywood model of being a good teacher, this cannot be. I actively teach preservice teachers to subvert, in the best sense of the word.[31] The rebellious part of my teacher identity has moved to the fore and I continue to prepare teachers to think for themselves, to prepare their own curriculum, and to look for ways to subvert the existing curriculum that allows them to put their voice into things but doesn't necessarily run the risk of getting them fired. It is a fine line to tread, to be sure.

In addition to the political/curricular challenges that I encounter as I transitioned from public school teacher to university teacher, there was one other challenge to my identity: getting old. One of the additional keys to success I had throughout my career was maintaining a certain level of pop culture hipness—I kept akin on what my students were watching and listening to in order to make relevant connections in my teaching. However, with the transition into higher education came the transition into middle age; I knew I was getting old when one day I was flipping through the radio dial and heard some of that amazing, rebellious, cutting-edge "college music" of my youth—The Cult followed by REM followed by the Replacements. I turned it up, jammed along, and felt wonderful about myself until I heard the radio station's call sign: "Thank you for listening to Classic Rock 102.7."

That "classic rock" moment made many things come clear to me as I made the transition from teaching high school to university; I couldn't be hip, so I had to find my own shade of cool. As I rewatched the first season of *Kotter*, one theme came through that I had missed in earlier viewings. He made no bones about his age or the toll that being middle-aged had on him. It was in part because he acknowledged his age that his students accepted him, not because he was one of them or was able to identify with them; in fact, on the first episode, he tries to relate to the students with disastrous consequences. On a personal level, I learned that I could only be myself in all my 20th century glory. On a professional level, this became transcendent; how could I convince my students to be the "good teachers" of the Hollywood model when they were entering the profession at a time that they were almost coerced into doing the things that I defined as being a "bad teacher"? How could I convince them that there was still a place for being an outsider, rebelling against the administration, and choosing their own curriculum in today's world? And it would be Kotter that I turned to once again.

EPILOGUE: *KOTTER* IN CURRENT PRACTICE

"This is my place. And these . . . these are my people."[32]

So goes one of the first lines of the character Vincent Barbarino, by way of introduction of himself to Mr. Kotter. It's interesting to note that while many teachers portrayed on television are outsiders moving into an alien environment, Gabe Kaplan's Kotter is an insider—a graduate of the school in which he is returning to teach—yet is an outsider, as someone who left to further his education. This outsider status is cemented in Barbarino's comment—it is no longer Kotter's world, but the new generation's.

My degree is in the foundations of education; I examine how teaching and our public schools have developed historically, sociologically, and philosophically; discuss current practices and policies in their foundational contexts; and make predictions of future trends. My work is largely theoretical, though it does have some broad implications for practice. For five years I almost exclusively taught courses that relied on my foundational expertise at the university, and then my teaching load changed.

Due to shifting personnel, my assignment was changed radically in the 2011–2012 academic year; I moved from a course in foundations to a course in pre-methods. I was now going to teach almost exclusively the practical aspects of the job: lesson planning, classroom management, instructional strategies, and the like. Also, my classes would continue to be comprised of both future elementary and secondary teachers, so I couldn't rely upon my teaching background for assistance. Finally, the course is six credits; it would be me and a group of thirty preservice teachers in the same room for three-hour lecture periods twice a week.

As I was sitting down to plan the course, my stress level was elevated, visions of the end of my career danced in my mind. I was sharing this with a colleague, who provided some helpful advice: "Why don't you talk to them about why you became a teacher and what you learned over time?" And thus, I returned to Kotter.

With the magic of YouTube and DVD, I infused my course with examples of the teachers in the media that inspired me—and led conversations about how to recognize those who perpetuate the messianic tradition of teaching. In spite of its dated wardrobe and vaudevillian references (I never thought I'd have to pause and explain who Groucho Marx was), *Kotter* is the one that resonates most strongly with students.

Watching the episodes from the first season allows us to engage in conversation regarding a wide variety of issues facing teachers, from choices of instructional strategies to dealing with administration to maintaining a private life. It affords opportunities to discuss the shifting legalities of the public schools, exploring how much of what was portrayed on the screen was questionable, if not illegal, today. The world of *Kotter*'s Buchanan High was a world prior to special education law, so there were no accommodations for disabilities, learning or otherwise. The ways that Kotter and Woodman referred to students—Kotter in jest, Woodman in earnest—would get either sued in today's litigious society.[33] Kotter's hosting an overnight sit-in for his students to protest the poor cafeteria food, while appropriate at the time, would get any teacher fired in today's world.[34]

However, even Kotter's mistakes became teachable moments: students learn that sometimes the best lessons come from watching what not to do, rather than what to do. And thus, in addition to Kotter, I returned to my cinematic idols: Nick Nolte fighting with a parent about what is really important in *Teachers* (1984), Sandy Dennis having a horrible first day of school in *Up the Down Staircase* (1967), or Sidney Poitier struggling to come to know his students as people in *To Sir, With Love* (1967). I would show a roughly ten-minute clip from a film or a Kotter episode in its entirety to spur conversation about a topic and off the class would go.

As anyone who uses popular culture in their classes will attest, I knew this could be an effective tool, and a good way for me to break up that 180-minute class, but I didn't realize the impact I was having until I received an e-mail in late May, a couple of weeks after the semester ended, from a former student. It read, in part, "So I'm finding myself with more time on my hands than I thought this summer and was hoping you could recommend some good teacher flicks for me to watch to help with my professional preparation . . ."

"Who *made you want to become a teacher?*"

I hope my students find their own Kotter. To many of my students, its *Harry Potter*'s Dumbledore or *Buffy*'s Giles; to others, it's *How I Met Your Mother*'s Lily or *New Girl*'s Jess. In light of the recent television shows' fairly realistic portrayals of teachers in various settings, from *Boston Public* to season four of *The Wire*, opportunities for more contemporary examples abound. I continue to ask my students what teachers influenced them and how, encouraging them to find the kind of affirmation of their best practice, encouragement to become a "good teacher" regardless of what's going on externally to them and be aware of the unrealistic expectations of the messianic images of certain films or the negative images in certain shows. I teach them to be critical examiners of media portrayals of teachers, resisting the "bad teachers" portrayed while embracing the positive role models. I urge them to use self-reflection to become aware of their identity as a teacher, how it is impacted intersectionally by social identity factors, and recognize the influences that are impacting it daily. I want them to become empowered in their teacher identity before hearing their favorite songs on classic rock radio someday.

NOTES

1. "Welcome Back (Pilot)." *Welcome Back, Kotter*, directed by Bob LaHendro (1975; Burbank, CA: Warner Home Video, 2007), DVD.

2. Mary Dalton and Laura R. Linder, *Teacher TV: Sixty Years of Teachers on Television* (New York: Peter Lang, 2008), 58.

3. Public Law 107–110, The No Child Left Behind Act of 2001. Accessed October 9, 2013, http://www2.ed.gov/policy/elsec/leg/esea02/index.html.

4. *The White Shadow*, which aired for three seasons from 1978–1981, starred Ken Howard as Ken Reeves, a white retired National Basketball Association player who began coaching in a predominantly black high school. The show was set at the fictional Carver High School, located in Los Angeles, and while similar thematically to *Kotter*, tended to be more dramatic. The show tackled topics such as alcoholism, teenage pregnancy, sports gambling, and child abuse.

5. Dalton and Linder, *Teacher TV: Sixty Years of Teachers on Television*, 54.

6. Michael W. Kirst, "Who's in Charge? Federal, State, and Local Control," in *Learning From the Past: What History Teaches Us About School Reform*, ed. Diane Ravitch and Maris Vinovskis (Baltimore: Johns Hopkins University Press, 1995), 47–51.

7. David C. Berliner and Bruce J. Biddle, *The Manufactured Crisis: Myths, Fraud, and the Attack on America's Public Schools* (Cambridge, MA: Perseus Books, 1995), 3–4.

8. *A Nation at Risk.* (Washington, D.C.: U.S.A. Research, 1984), 6.

9. Rudolf Flesch, *Why Johnny Can't Read and What You Can Do About It* (New York: Perrennial Books, 1966).

10. As early as the 1970s, there were some teachers in film that were not portrayed as the moral, upstanding pillars of their community—most famously Diane Keaton's elementary school teacher by day, barfly by night in *Looking for Mr. Goodbar*.

11. *Ferris Bueller's Day Off*, directed by John Hughes (1986; Los Angeles, Paramount Home Video, 2000), DVD.

12. John G. Richardson and Brenda Wooden Hatcher, "The Feminization of Public School Teaching: 1890–1920," *Work and Occupations* 10, no. 1 (1983): 82.

13. Judith Butler, *Gender Trouble: Tenth Anniversary Edition* (London: Routledge, 1999), 214.

14. For a history of the era, see Mark Oxoby, *The 1990s* (Westport, CT: Greenwood Press, 2003). This work is part of an excellent larger series, *American Popular Culture Through History*.

15. Kevin Kosar, *Failing Grades: The Federal Politics of Education Standards* (Boulder, CO: Lynee Reinner Publishers, 2005), 98–100.

16. Kosar, *Failing Grades*, 117–121.

17. "School to Work Opportunities Act," *United States Department of Education.* Accessed August 12, 2013, http://www2.ed.gov/pubs/Biennial/95–96/eval/410–97.pdf.

18. The United States Department of Labor keeps data on the fastest-growing occupations, which can be organized to include amount of education. "Selected Occupational Projections Data: Search by Education," *United States Department of Labor—Bureau of Labor Statistics*, Accessed August 13, 2013, http://data.bls.gov/oep/noeted.

19. Robert Lowe, "Teachers as Saviors, Teachers Who Care," in *Images of Schoolteachers in America*, ed. Pamela Bolotin Joseph and Gail E. Burnaford (Mahwah, NJ: Lawrence Erlbaum Associates, 2001) 211–228.

20. These elements are explained in detail in Mary Dalton, "The Hollywood Model: Who is the Good Teacher?," *The Hollywood Curriculum: Teachers in the Movies* (New York: Peter Lang, 2010), 23–43.

21. Michele Moses and Mitchell J. Chang, "Toward a Deeper Understanding of the Diversity Rationale," *Educational Researcher* 35, no. 1: 7–9.

22. John Dewey, *How We Think.* (Boston: D.C. Heath and Company, 1910), 24.

23. Dalton, *The Hollywood Curriculum: Teachers in the Movies*, 63.

24. For further discussion on the sexualization of teachers, see Dale M. Bauer, "Indecent Proposals: Teachers in the Movies," *College English* 60, no. 3, (1998).

25. *Waiting for Superman* is, at best, suspect in its motives and, at worst, guilty of perpetuating the poor opinion of not just public schools, but teaching as a profession, to the point of negatively influencing some preservice teachers. For a thorough discussion on the questionable motives of the director and producers, see the website put together by Rethinking Schools, www.notwaitingforsuperman.org; specifically, Barbara Miner, "Ultimate $uperpower: Supersized Dollars Drive Waiting for Superman Agenda," *Not Waiting for Superman*. Accessed August 14, 2013, http://www .notwaitingforsuperman.org/ Articles/20101020–MinerUltimateSuperpower. For an examination of the effects of the documentary on preservice teachers, see Aaron Jensen, Edward Janak, and Timothy Slater, "Changing Course: Exploring Impacts of *Waiting for Superman* on Future Teachers' Perspectives on the State of Education," *Contemporary Issues in Educational Research* 5, no. 1 (2012).

26. *Boston Legal* depicted the struggles of a group of teachers and administrators working in an inner-city Boston high school; the characters ranged from lampoonish to serious. In the fourth season of *The Wire*, the character of detective Roland "Prez" Pryzbylewski becomes a middle school math teacher in inner-city Baltimore after being involved with an accidental shooting of another officer. Through the eyes of this outsider, the flaws of the system become discussed in depth. CBS's special, *Teachers Rock!* is particularly problematic. While billed as a celebration of teachers when it aired in August 2012, in fact it actually undermined the public schools in a myriad of ways. It promoted heavily the film *Won't Back Down*, which was a celebration of the Parent Trigger Law movement, calling for parents around the nation to take over their community's public schools and fire all administrators and teachers. In addition, it was a charity event funding the controversial Teach For America program, which replaces American teachers with untrained college graduates. The program was actively protested by groups such as Parents Across America, Save Our Schools, the Daily Kos, and Democratic Underground.com. A telling satire of the program came on the site "Students Last," ostensibly satirizing the "Students First" movement, in which the program was billed as allowing audience members to take the title literally and throw rocks at teachers in a stoning booth. See Students Last, "Stoning Teachers Raises Some Eyebrows," Accessed October 9, 2013, http://studentslast.blogspot. com/2012/08/stoning-teachers-raises-some-eyebrows.html?spref=fb.

27. Kosar, *Failing Grades*, 186–195.

28. Diane Ravitch, *The Death and Life of the Great American School System* (New York: Perseus Books, 2010), 97–99, 101, & 200–222.

29. "In the States," *Common Core State Standards Initiative*. Accessed August 14, 2013, http://www.corestandards.org/in-the-states.

30. Samples of these blocks are a simple online search away. For example, the literacy block posted by Methuen Public Schools of Methuen, MA: "Balanced Literacy Model," *English Language Arts Mapping Model*. Accessed August 14, 2013, http://www.methuen .k12.ma.us/images/ela_mapping/balanced%20literacy%20model.pdf. For a math example, see "Sample Math Block Schedules," *Palm Beach Schools*. Accessed August 14, 2013, http://www.palmbeachschools.org/qa/documents/Sample-MathBlockSchedules.pdf.

31. The notion of teaching to subvert is not new in the slightest—it has been around since the early 1970s. See Neil Postman and Charles Weingartner, *Teaching as a Subversive Activity* (New York: Delta Books, 1971).

32. "Welcome Back (Pilot)." *Welcome Back, Kotter,* directed by Bob LaHendro (1975; Burbank, CA: Warner Home Video, 2007), DVD.

33. The name of the group of students, "Sweathogs," is an abbreviated form of the term that Woodman used to describe them: "Remedial Sweathogs." In the show's pilot episode, Woodman takes great glee in making Kotter teach this group of students, assuming that Kotter is being set up for failure. In a later episode, "Arreviderci, Arnold," the character of Horschack actually earns grades high enough to be removed from Kotter's class; however, while Kotter calls the student "proof of my success as a teacher," Horschack struggles with mainstream education and soon makes his way back to the familiar confines of Kotter's group. "Arreviderci, Arnold," *Welcome Back, Kotter*, directed by Bob LaHendro (1975; Burbank, CA: Warner Home Video, 2007), DVD.

34. In this episode, students are frustrated by the cafeteria's insistence on serving liver for lunch; Kotter talks to them about various forms of social protest and finds himself leading a sit-in in his own classroom that carries on overnight. "The Sit-In." *Welcome Back, Kotter,* directed by Bob LaHendro (1975; Burbank, CA: Warner Home Video, 2007), DVD.

Chapter Six

Defying Gravity: Fox's *Glee* Provides a Bold Forum for Queer Teen Representation

Katherine J. Lehman

When Fox's hit show *Glee* debuted in 2009, it opened new possibilities for queer teen representation on television. The series introduced Kurt (Chris Colfer), a feminine and fashionable gay teen from a working-class family, struggling to find himself in small-town Lima, Ohio. Joining a high school show choir of other misfits gave Kurt the courage to embrace his identity and come out to his family and friends. But his problems weren't resolved in a single episode: Over multiple seasons, Kurt has challenged discrimination, talked back to bullies, brought his boyfriend to the prom, and forged a closer relationship with his father. Kurt has also been joined by other queer characters, including a lesbian cheerleader and a transgendered diva. The series has boosted queer visibility on television and attracted both praise and criticism. While groups such as the Gay & Lesbian Alliance Against Defamation (GLAAD) have applauded *Glee*'s gay-affirmative plotlines, some viewers and critics complain that the feminine, fashion-obsessed, shrill-voiced Kurt, and his relationship with the more masculine Blaine, represent a limiting stereotype of gay men.[1]

Glee (2009–present) is one of many recent programs to depict the lives and loves of queer youth.[2] However, the program is exceptional given several things: its inclusion of multiple gay, lesbian, bisexual, and transgendered characters and actors; its outspoken gay producer, Ryan Murphy; and its direct references to social concerns such as bullying and the movement for gay marriage. *Glee*'s popularity—drawing up to 14 million viewers and $2 million in advertising per half hour at its peak—as well as its vibrant fan culture have inspired cultural debate about GLBTQ politics and representation.[3] *Glee* has defied the conventions of network television, proving that a program with queer characters can be commercially successful and attract a diverse audience. This chapter will analyze *Glee*'s representation of relationships, sexuality, and identity among queer youth, as well as its mixed reception by audiences and critics.

QUEER TEENS ON TV: WHY *GLEE* MATTERS

Recent scholarship attests to the importance of queer representations in building viewers' self-esteem and shaping their political leanings. Characters such as Kurt and Santana, the cheerleader who came out in *Glee*'s third season, can serve as role models for youth who might otherwise feel isolated and marginalized. A recent viewer study found that *Glee* offers queer teenagers "potential raw material" for starting conversations with friends and family about their struggles and desires.[4] Actress Naya Rivera says high school girls have credited her character, Santana, with giving them the courage to come out.[5] Additionally, the Trevor Project hotline, which aims to prevent suicide among queer and questioning youth, has reported increased call volume since *Glee* began addressing queer themes—with many callers making direct references to the series.[6] As Murphy himself told *Out* Magazine: "The gay characters do transmit a certain message: You are not alone. You don't have to harm or hate yourself. . . . I wish I'd had this show growing up. I think if I had, I would be a lot less fearful and a lot braver."[7]

Glee also gives parents and teachers insight on how to address teens' struggles with sexual identity. In episodes about bullying, the show's creators strategically addressed teachers' responsibility to end harassment and school policies on the issue.[8] Furthermore, shows like *Glee* have the potential to shape collective politics simply by providing relatable characters and provoking debate.[9] Demographers have found that straight Americans are more likely to support legalization of gay marriage if they know someone who is gay. Furthermore, communication research suggests that television characters can provide that point of personal connection. During one 2004 experiment, straight viewers demonstrated fewer prejudiced attitudes after watching programs with gay and lesbian characters (*Newsweek* dubbed the phenomenon "The *Will & Grace* Effect," after the long-running NBC sitcom).[10] Given that *Glee* debuted in 2009 as same-sex marriage became central to political debate, the series may help to advance public support for marriage equality.

While premium cable networks such as HBO and Showtime have provided strong venues for GLBTQ representation, network television has traditionally been more cautious for fear of losing audience interest and sponsor support. Historically gays and lesbians have been featured as short-lived characters, tragic tales, or comedic sidekicks. When *Glee*'s producer Ryan Murphy took the helm of the teen series *Popular* on the WB network in 1999–2001, network executives warned him that even his straight characters were "too gay" and would alienate audiences unless he toned them down.[11] Ellen DeGeneres made headlines in 1997 when both the actress and her character came out as a lesbian on her sitcom *Ellen* (1994–1998); however, the series failed to thrive after the transition. *Will & Grace* (1998–2006) subsequently had a successful eight seasons on NBC, but it centered on a marriage-like friendship between a gay man and straight woman. Some critics and viewers felt that the vain, histrionic supporting character Jack promoted a harmful stereotype of gay men, and noted that affection between men was rarely depicted on this supposedly gay-affirmative series.[12]

Gay and lesbian teens are hardly new to television. Prominent characters of the 1990s and early 2000s included: Billy (Ryan Phillipe) from 1992–1993 on the soap opera *One Life to Live* (1968–present), Rickie (Wilson Cruz) on *My So-Called Life* (1994–1995), Jack (Kerr Smith) on *Dawson's Creek* (1998–2003), and wiccan lesbian Willow (Alyson Hannigan) on *Buffy the Vampire Slayer* (1997–2003).[13] In recent years queer teenage characters have increased in prominence and complexity, assuming roles on *Ugly Betty* (2006–2010), *Pretty Little Liars* (2010–present), *United States of Tara* (2009–2011), and *Desperate Housewives* (2004–2012), among many other programs. An *Entertainment Weekly* cover story reported that homosexuality was an "expected part of teen-centric television" with more than two dozen regular or recurring queer teen characters on the air. *EW* credited the trend to the growth of activism in high schools—45 percent of high schools boasted a gay-straight alliance club in 2011, compared to only 25 percent a decade earlier—and the increasing visibility of queer youth, who are coming out at earlier ages (the average coming-out age is now 16, compared to 19–23 in the 1980s.)[14] Reality television has also played a role in normalizing GLBTQ representation, as *The Real World* (1992–present), *Big Brother* (2000–present), *American Idol* (2002–present), *Queer Eye for the Straight Guy* (2003–2007), and *Dancing with the Stars* (2005–present), among others, have included GLBTQ cast members.

Although *Glee* is not alone in representing queer lives, the series is unique in its reach and popularity across diverse age groups. The series features a Midwestern high school glee club that becomes a haven for outsiders. Each hour-long episode incorporates old and new pop songs, as the group prepares for competitions and uses music as a means for connection, grappling with identity, and working through conflicts. *Glee*'s musical format and irreverent humor distinguish it from the average comedy; furthermore, the series provides multiple points of identification, from the high school students themselves to the teachers, coaches, counselors, and parents who populate McKinley High. The inclusion of songs from previous generations—one episode featured Stevie Wonder classics, for example[15]—ensures that viewers of different ages can connect to the series.

Glee's engagement with multiple forms of media has strengthened its popularity and appeal. Communication researchers have deemed *Glee* a "transmedia" text; viewers engage with the series not only through the aired program itself, but also music videos and soundtracks that are easily shared online. Fans can interact with the show's stars via Facebook or Twitter, see them perform in the "*Glee* Live! In Concert!" tour, or watch the companion reality show, *The Glee Project*, in which producers search for new cast members. Online forums provide a venue where viewers engage with the meaning of the series and petition for even greater inclusion of gay and lesbian themes.[16] The impact of the series extends far beyond the weekly episodes, as these multiple media venues bring *Glee* into viewers' everyday lives.

COMING OUT AND CHALLENGING GENDER NORMS

Many *Glee* plotlines center on the importance of coming out to one's family and the broader community. Kurt's coming-out process was central to *Glee*'s debut season, and established the show as sympathetic to GLBTQ concerns. Later plotlines centered on Santana, a Latina cheerleader who falls in love with her bisexual best friend; Dave Karofsky, a football player whose same-sex desires drive him to bullying and despair; and Wade, an African American transgendered teen.[17] In comparison to earlier network TV—which might have featured the coming-out process in a single episode and smoothed over the consequences—*Glee* presents coming out as a continuous, sometimes painful, but ultimately worthwhile process.

The process isn't without humorous moments, either. In an early episode, Kurt's father, Burt (Mike O'Malley), walks in on his son wearing a sparkly bodysuit and dancing to Beyoncé's "Single Ladies (Put a Ring on It)." Searching for a plausible explanation, Kurt explains he's warming up for his role on the football team—and then uses his connections to finagle a position as kicker. In a televisual twist, Kurt leads the football team to victory by teaching them his dance moves—thus enhancing their confidence—and scoring the winning field goal. He decides to tell his father the truth anyway, and Burt reacts calmly. "I've known since you were three," he admits. "If that's who you are, there's nothing I can do about it. I love you just as much."[18]

Burt is a working-class single father, an average guy who wears flannel and watches football. His acceptance of Kurt provides a model for other viewers to follow, and reflects Murphy's own relationship with his father.[19] The men's bond is made more poignant by the absence of Kurt's mother, who died when he was a child. This family structure strategically counters the stereotypical notion that an overbearing mother creates an effeminate son;

the fact that Kurt developed his distinctive style in a male-headed household implies that his gender identity is innate and authentic.

Still, some critics have complained that *Glee* makes Kurt too feminine; as scholar Taylor Cole Miller argues, "The show continues to rely on his clothing, speech, mannerisms, and song choice to code his queerness, a practice of stereotyping bemoaned by gay men."[20] Indeed, many plotlines center on Kurt's non-normative gender identity as much as his sexual orientation. In an early episode, Kurt asserts his right to sing the song "Defying Gravity" from the musical *Wicked*—traditionally a woman's solo. Teacher Will Schuester (Matthew Morrison) denies his request, insisting that Kurt is incapable of reaching the song's high notes, but agrees to let him audition when his father complains of discrimination. The story was based on barriers that actor Chris Colfer himself had faced in his high school choir.[21] As Kurt prepares for a flawless audition against a female soloist, his father receives an anonymous phone call deriding Kurt as a "fag." Kurt sees the fear in his father's eyes and decides to bomb the audition to prevent further harassment. "That phone call yesterday was just the beginning, especially if I get up in front of a thousand people to sing a girl's song," he tells his dad. "I love you more than I love being a star."[22] The episode emphasizes the importance of questioning boundaries, but also the personal costs of challenging convention.

Glee also features women in gender-transgressive roles. Miller's research suggests that these characters' strength and sass appeal to *Glee*'s gay male viewers.[23] Among them are Sue Sylvester (played by lesbian actress Jane Lynch), the cheerleading coach who antagonizes the glee club with her megaphone and ruthless competitive streak. Her short hair and tracksuit mark her as masculine, and she jokes about being mistaken as a lesbian. *Glee*'s second season introduced Coach Beiste, a muscular, deep-voiced football coach played by lesbian bodybuilder Dot-Marie Jones. Among the teens, Lauren Zizes (Ashley Fink) brings heft and attitude to the wrestling arena. *Glee* cleverly challenges expectation by making these women definitively heterosexual—in one episode, Coach Beiste and Sue even fight over the same man.[24] *Glee* therefore challenges the association of athleticism with lesbianism but also fails to provide butch lesbian visibility. *Glee*'s primary lesbian romance occurs between svelte cheerleaders Brittany and Santana—although Santana's sharp tongue, tough persona, and promiscuous tendencies make her somewhat androgynous, her appearance conforms to gender norms.

Santana's journey is less linear and predictable than Kurt's. A cheerleader perpetually wearing a miniskirt uniform and heavy makeup, she pursues promiscuous relationships with boys and is skilled at seduction; in one episode she takes football player Finn's virginity.[25] She has an affectionate relationship with fellow cheerleader Brittany (Heather Morris), often holding her hand and sharing back rubs, and referring to her as "my girl." In an early episode, the naïve Brittany casually tells friends that she and Santana have had sex, but aren't dating.[26] Her offhand remark evolves into an onscreen relationship, as Santana becomes sexually involved with Brittany but is unable to express emotions or make any commitment. "It's better when it doesn't involve feelings," she insists. "I'm not interested in any labels." A visiting sex education teacher intervenes, asking Santana if she might be a lesbian. "Who knows?" Santana sighs. "I'm attracted to girls, I'm attracted to guys." She decides to sing a romantic duet with Brittany that expresses her fear and desire and ends in an embrace. She later apologizes to Brittany, confessing, "I'm a bitch because I'm angry. . . . I have all of these feelings for you that I'm afraid of dealing with because I'm afraid of the consequences. I want to be with you, but I'm afraid of the talk and the looks. . . . I love you."[27]

While Brittany accepts her friend's disclosure, she refuses to be in an exclusive relationship with Santana because she is already dating a male glee-club member. Feeling trapped in her secret, and in love with someone who doesn't share the same devotion, Santana unleashes her fury on her other friends. Stung by her barrage of insults, straight white football player Finn (Cory Monteith) yells back at Santana in the school hallway, calling her a coward for hiding her desires. "You can't admit to everyone that you're in love with Brittany," he tells her. "Why don't you just come out of the closet?" In a cruel twist of fate, Finn's words are overheard and broadcast in a public forum—essentially forcing Santana out of the closet. Santana is traumatized, channeling her vulnerability into a rendition of Adele's "Rumour Has It" and striking Finn with her fists.[28]

The following episode focuses on healing, as the glee club serenades Santana with songs "for ladies, by ladies"—including hits by lesbian icons Melissa Etheridge and k.d. lang. Strangely enough, the men sing the bulk of the songs, with Finn taking a protective stance toward Santana. "You deal with your anxiety surrounding this stuff by attacking other people. Someday that's not going to be enough and you're going to start attacking yourself," Finn says, then references their shared sexual history. "You were my first—that means something to me." When Santana is taunted by a guy who vows to set her straight, the girls of *Glee* retaliate with a group rendition of Katy Perry's "I Kissed a Girl." The song is meant to provide playful solidarity, but their saucy performance titillates the men and the lyrics seem to describe a one-time sexual experiment rather than the life-altering identity Santana must embrace. In the closing scenes, Santana croons k.d. lang's melancholy "Constant Craving"—a truer expression of her undeniable and contradictory desires.[29]

Santana's plotline came partly in response to outspoken fans, who pressured the show's creators to include more lesbian content and bring the cheerleaders together. As the *Los Angeles Times* reported, "Fans of 'Glee' have long suspected that there was something special going on between Santana and Brittany. . . . The relationship might have been just another inside joke on a show full of inside jokes, but fans wanted more. They dubbed the pair 'Brittana,' and tweeted and blogged endlessly about how great it would be if the two became a real couple." Actress Rivera said fans should "take credit" for Santana's transformation: "Who knows if the writers would have taken that relationship so seriously if there hadn't been such an outpouring for them to get together."[30]

Glee is distinctive in taking Santana's desires seriously, rather than treating her romance as an ephemeral crush. This is not the one-time kiss or experimental relationship that comprises the bulk of "lesbian" romance on mainstream television. As GLAAD's president said, "The story line with Santana struggling with her affection for another teenage girl, calling herself a lesbian but not knowing how to say that out loud yet, is one that hasn't been told on a prime-time network television show at that level, particularly by an LGBT teen of color."[31] However, some critics complained that Santana is essentially forced out of the closet, and her seemingly bisexual orientation is erased in the process. While her friends' supportive reaction is heartening, it is primarily the straight glee members who serenade her with lesbian-friendly songs. Finn's chivalrous attitude toward Santana (and his protective attitude toward Kurt) struck some viewers as demeaning—especially given that he never really apologizes for broadcasting her secret.[32]

In subsequent seasons, *Glee* introduced a transgendered character, Wade (played by Alex Newell, who auditioned via *The Glee Project* reality series). Initially a member of a competing glee club, Wade is a timid young man whose personality and talent come alive when he dons a wig, sparkly dress, and high heels and becomes a diva named "Unique" onstage. Although Wade finds an ally in Kurt, the show distinguishes their identities. Kurt initially tries to protect Wade by discouraging his desire to cross-dress. "I've worn some flamboyant outfits, but I've never dressed up as a woman," Kurt says. Wade replies, "That's because you identify yourself as a man. I thought you, of all people, would understand."[33] Bloggers applauded *Glee*'s effort to address trans issues and hoped that Newell, initially slated for a two-episode appearance, would become a regular cast member.[34]

The following season, Wade transfers to McKinley High and becomes Unique in everyday life, assuming a female identity and feminine mannerisms even when not in full feminine garb. While Unique finds acceptance within the glee club, much like Kurt, she must battle traditional conceptions of gender. In one episode, fellow glee-club member Ryder (Blake Jenner) refuses to see Unique as female; she accuses him of prejudice and challenges him to a musical duel. Ryder finally relents, conceding: "I'm not going to pretend that I understand everything that's going on with you. But you have a truth. And as your friend I need to support that truth. So, you're a girl, dude."[35] While the episode ultimately celebrates friendship and values Unique's self-identity, some viewers were unhappy with the resolution. Transgendered blogger Michelle Wolf felt the conflict was true to life: "No matter how we educate those around us, and no matter how we appear, attempting to overcome that lingering mindset that we are 'really a . . .' is both heartbreaking and infuriating." However, she felt that the "personal truth" approach was a cop-out: "The inherent danger of taking this position is that it all becomes very subjective. Sure you feel you are female, but I feel you are not, and therefore my opinion is equally valid. . . . I would have been much happier if *Glee* addressed this by pointing to the validation [of trans identities] provided by the medical, psychological, and psychiatric communities."[36]

In another episode, Unique auditions to play the female role of Rizzo in McKinley's production of *Grease*—over the objections of other students and coach Sue Sylvester. When the director grants her the part, we learn that Rizzo is far more than just a role for her. Unique explains: "I don't feel right in the men's locker room, but I can't go into the girls.' And I don't feel right in men's clothing, but I can't wear dresses every day. It sucks to never know your place. It's just nice, for once, to feel like I've found one." When the director warns her that her stage performance may attract negative attention, she responds gravely: "Dreams aren't free."[37]

NEGOTIATING FAMILY RELATIONSHIPS

While the glee club serves as a basis for acceptance and identity formation within an often-hostile high school, the teens have more mixed relationships with their families. Kurt's working-class dad accepts his son's orientation, and seeks to communicate with him across their differences. In the episode "Sexy," Burt even talks with his son about sex, bringing him brochures on gay sexuality from a health clinic. Although both men are visibly uncomfortable with the conversation, it shows that Burt can provide guidance and support even in unfamiliar territory. "When you're ready [for sex] . . . I want you to able to use it as a way to connect to another person. Don't throw yourself around like you don't matter," Burt tells his son.[38] Kurt stands by his dad through health crises and a successful political campaign, and their bond is moving, and made even more powerful by the absence of Kurt's mother.

However, their relationship is not without tensions. When Burt remarries, taking Kurt's friend Finn as a stepson, Kurt becomes jealous of the bond they share over football and masculine pursuits. To regain his father's attention, he dons a flannel shirt and hunting vest, assumes a twangy accent, and gruffly sings a cover of a John Mellencamp song. He even brings a girl home and flirts with her in front of his dad, pretending that he's not gay. When his dad figures out why Kurt is upset, he admits that it's sometimes easier to relate to Finn. However, he firmly tells Kurt not to change for his sake. "Your job is to be yourself, and my job is to love you no matter what."[39]

Santana's parents are reportedly "fine" with her lesbian identity, but we don't see the conversation happen onscreen. Santana's grandmother, on the other hand, is aghast at her disclosure. Santana gently broaches the topic at the kitchen table, explaining: "I love girls the way I'm supposed to feel about boys. . . . I want you to know me, who I really am." Her grandmother calls Santana's desires shameful and asks her to leave the house.[40] This scene conflates an older Latina woman with intolerance, and hints at the reason why Santana was initially hesitant to come out. Her familial conflict reflects the experiences of queer youth of color, who are less likely to be out to their parents than white teens, and often feel compelled to choose between their sexual identity and their ethnic heritage.[41] Unfortunately, unlike Kurt's deepening relationship with his dad, Santana's grandmother has not been given more screen time to evolve.

Unique's parents, who rarely appear onscreen, are also concerned with her desire to dress in female clothing. When they learn she has been bullied, they ask her to give up her hard-won role of Rizzo in the *Grease* production. Unique follows their wishes about the play, but later returns to wearing dresses. Actor Newell explains that Unique's parents are motivated by love rather than prejudice: "It's not that they're not supportive, they're more worried about my safety."[42]

The show also addresses queer family issues in less predictable ways. In the pilot, we learn that the talented and straight Rachel (Lea Michele) is the daughter of an interracial same-sex couple. Her two dads are rarely shown onscreen but play a pivotal role in helping her to avoid a hasty marriage and instead pursue her dreams of stardom in New York. Rachel's "gay dads" often serve as a punchline, and she does long for a relationship with her birth mother, but over the course of multiple seasons her fathers help to normalize gay parenting.

PURSUING SEXUAL DESIRE

Traditionally, same-sex affection has been scarce on network television or used as a way to heighten viewer ratings, as with the one-time same-sex kisses on shows like *Friends* (1994–2004). *Glee* slowly but surely builds up to sexual relationships among its queer characters, even though its depiction is not as frequent or daring as some viewers would like. While Santana's identity emerges through sexual experimentation, Kurt comes out, develops crushes on straight friends, then pursues a more classic romance. Disheartened by anti-gay hostility at his school, Kurt visits the all-male Dalton Academy where diversity is celebrated and the glee club is revered. Kurt is clearly smitten with the dark, handsome stranger who takes his hand, leads him to where glee club "The Warblers" are rehearsing, and serenades him with Katy Perry's romantic "Teenage Dream."[43] Although Blaine (Darren Criss) was intended to be merely a platonic mentor for Kurt, talking him through a tough bullying situation, Blaine became his steady boyfriend due to overwhelming fan response.[44] The two create a classic couple, singing a jazzy duet by the fireplace in *Glee*'s Christmas special and ice-skating at Rockefeller Center when Kurt relocates to New York City.[45] The episode featuring the couple's first kiss drew nearly 11 million viewers, becoming the night's most-watched show among eighteen- to forty-nine-year-old viewers.[46] While the episode sparked backlash from a few conservative critics, the kiss was motivated by somewhat innocuous circumstances: Blaine comforting Kurt over the loss of a pet bird. Missing from their romance is sexual desire—while other *Glee* characters indulge their lusts, Kurt and Blaine initially never venture beyond a soulful kiss. "I don't know anything about sex," Kurt tells Blaine early in their friendship. "I like romance."[47] This personality trait makes Kurt less threatening to viewers who would fear gay sexuality, but also counters the stereotype of gay men as promiscuous.

Blaine later pressures Kurt to have sex in the parking lot of a gay bar but Kurt refuses; their relationship is finally consummated in a bedroom as a fireplace blazes and the love theme from *West Side Story*, "One Hand, One Heart," plays. This scene is presented tastefully. The boys embrace, fully clothed, on the bed, a scene juxtaposed with straight leads Finn and Rachel in a similarly intimate position.[48] This pairing is strategic; gay sex may indeed be too cautious or overly romanticized in *Glee*, but Murphy is also working against stereotypes that would place Kurt and Blaine in a different category from their heterosexual peers. As Murphy explained, "Everybody has seen a straight couple losing their virginity, but has anyone dovetailed the gay and straight stories together and given them equal weight? That seemed like an exciting choice and a new thing."[49] Many critics praised the episode's sensitive, "delicate" tone even as conservative groups blasted *Glee* for "celebrating teen sex."[50]

Although the boys eventually break up due to Blaine's infidelity and the difficulty of maintaining a long-distance relationship, the fourth season deepens their friendship and closes with Blaine planning to propose marriage.[51] In the season five premiere, the couple quickly reunites and Kurt accepts Blaine's deeply romantic proposal, set to The Beatles' "All You Need is Love." Blaine considers the proposal a "cultural statement" as well as a private declaration of commitment, and recruits several rival show choirs to serenade Kurt.[52] Murphy feels the relationship on the whole conveys a message: "I think what it says to a lot of young gay people who are confused and ashamed is that you can get love and are worthy of love."[53]

Santana and Brittany's relationship begins with friendship and sexual experimentation, but later evolves into a more classic romance. After they start dating, Santana publicly expresses affection for Brittany, insisting on their right to kiss in the high school hallways when the principal objects. She frequently serenades Brittany and, in one Valentine's Day episode, orders a singing telegram for her from a campus Christian group called the "God Squad." The Christian students deliberate at length—including a debate on the meaning of Biblical passages about homosexuality—before deciding that "love is love" and delivering the song to Brittany.[54]

However, Brittany and Santana's eventual breakup after Santana leaves for college is less emotional and drawn out than Kurt and Blaine's separation. Although Santana develops feelings for other women at college, the bisexual Brittany immediately begins dating a boy from the glee club, and the prospect of her dating women other than Santana is not explored. For some fans, this reflected an all-too-familiar media formula in which women briefly "go gay" then return to dating men. One blogger complained that "the sum amount of screen time that Brittany and Santana got through their whole relationship was less than what they have shown for Brittany and [her new boyfriend] Sam in one episode."[55] Bloggers and readers on the site AfterEllen.com fretted over the abrupt breakup and Murphy's dismissive response to fans, asking whether *Glee*'s creator even respected lesbians.[56] Bloggers on the Glee Equality Project site demanded the series treat its lesbian and gay relationships with the same candor as straight ones; critics also cited the lack of screen time given to Santana and Brittany as a couple, and the fact that Kurt and Blaine rarely kiss.[57] To be fair, Season Four does emphasize the lifelong connection between Brittany and Santana, as Santana returns from New York to help Brittany through a personal crisis in the season finale.[58]

Although she has close friendships, Unique has yet to find romance on *Glee*. Throughout Season Four she hides behind a screen name—pretending to be a blonde white girl named Katie—to get close to fellow glee-club member Ryder through instant messaging. When Ryder discovers the deception and angrily confronts her, Unique explains, "I know I'm not your vision of beauty." The ruse, she confesses, was her way to get close to someone without her transgendered body "getting in the way."[59] Unique's insecurity seems warranted for a teen newly discovering her gender identity, but actor Newell hopes that Unique will be granted a romance like *Glee*'s other cast members. "I think she needs someone who would support her no matter what. When you look at Unique, she doesn't have too many people who support her and accept everything she's going through on the inside."[60]

ADDRESSING BULLYING AND TEEN SUICIDE

When *Glee* debuted, the media was rife with tragic stories of teen bullying. In six prominent cases, anti-gay harassment drove teens to suicide, prompting cultural debates about schools' policies and the vulnerability of queer youth. Celebrities and public figures participated in the "It Gets Better" project, telling their own stories of surviving bullying and urging teens to look beyond the pain to their bright future ahead.[61] *Glee* addresses bullying from multiple angles, probing causes and prevention, but also promoting hope. *Glee* actors Chris Colfer and Max Adler (who played closeted gay football player Dave Karofsky) also provided videos for the "It Gets Better" site, strengthening the connection between the series and political activism.[62]

Anti-gay harassment is rampant in American schools. According to 2010 survey data compiled by Advocates for Youth, "84.6 percent of GLBTQ students reported being verbally harassed, 40.1 percent reported being physically harassed and 19 percent reported being physically assaulted at school in the past year because of their sexual orientation."[63] Queer high school students surveyed in 2003 reported that in many instances, school authorities overheard verbal harassment but failed to intervene. Other studies suggest that GLBTQ youth have higher-than-average absentee and dropout rates and are prone to depression and substance abuse because they don't feel safe at school.[64]

Harassment is a rite of passage at McKinley High, as glee-club members are routinely mocked and doused with cold slushies by the popular crowd. However, in a continuing plotline, Kurt experiences bullying on a different level, when he is harangued and body-slammed into a locker by football player Dave Karofsky. Teacher Will Schuester witnesses the violence and expresses his sympathy to Kurt, but seems powerless to stop the assault. After meeting Blaine and gaining greater courage, Kurt confronts his bully, who forcefully kisses him then threatens to kill him if he discloses the secret.[65] Kurt opts to change schools, joining Blaine's Dalton Academy, which has a strict anti-bullying policy and seems more tolerant of diverse gender expression. (That Kurt has both the option and financial means to join a private school gives him an escape that many bullying victims lack.)

Kurt eventually transfers back to McKinley when his bully apologizes for his behavior. Karofsky, along with Santana, becomes a "Bully Whip" that patrols the halls in uniform protecting vulnerable kids from harassment. The program is a clever ploy by Santana to boost her popularity, but it also presents a creative peer-directed strategy for reducing bullying.[66] *Glee* presents other moments of peer solidarity, as when the glee club dons outlandish Lady Gaga–inspired costumes to defend Kurt's fashion choices, and when candidates for class president speak out against bullying. When Unique is chased by a group of girls calling her a "freak," her glee-club friends offer to walk her home from school every day.[67]

While violent encounters in the hallway may be the most visible form of bullying, *Glee* also addresses how anti-gay attitudes are endemic to high school culture. After Kurt transfers back to McKinley High, he and Blaine take the bold step of attending their junior prom as a couple. The two enter arm in arm, the flamboyant Kurt wearing a kilted ensemble that a friend calls "gay *Braveheart.*" Kurt is heartened that his classmates don't even seem to notice. His revelry ends abruptly, however, when he learns he has been elected prom queen. He leaves the room in tears, telling Blaine it's just the latest joke at his expense. "We thought that because no one was teasing us or beating us up that no one cared, like some kind of progress had been made," he says. "It's still the same. All that hate—they were just afraid to say it out loud. So they did it by secret ballot." However, he decides to take the crown to prove he can't be shaken.[68] When the prom king refuses to dance with him, he slow-dances with Blaine instead. In the closing scene the couple embrace in their prom picture, Kurt wielding a scepter and a crown.[69] The episode speaks to real-life queer teens who are excluded from rituals like proms and pressured to wear gender-normative clothing, and suggests that name-calling can be as hurtful as physical violence. Kurt's resilience saves the day, and his regality is apparent amid the ignorance of his classmates.

In the third season, Karofsky—as his classmates call him—has transferred to a new school, and his football buddies find out that he is secretly gay. As mournful music plays, Karofsky is mocked and pushed around the locker room, the word "fag" spray-painted on his locker. Back at home, he goes online for solace, finding that cyberbullies have posted hateful words on his Facebook wall. He somberly puts on a suit and attempts to hang himself, and is cut down just in time by his father.[70]

The episode emphasizes the community's responsibility for preventing youth bullying and suicide. Teachers and counselors regret not doing more to ease Karofsky's suffering. Kurt, who had earlier ignored Karofsky's phone messages, makes plans to visit him in the hospital. The glee club dedicates its winning regional competition performance to Karofsky, singing uplifting songs about survival and resilience (with Santana at the helm).

The "It Gets Better" theme is evident in this episode, as Mr. Schuester asks the teens to reflect on what they have to look forward to in life. Blaine answers, "I'm looking forward to marriage equality in all 50 states." Santana admits, "I'm looking forward to the day when my grandmother loves me again." When Kurt visits Karofsky in the hospital, he is dreading going back to school and explains that being gay has cost him his friends and his mother's trust. Kurt tells him to close his eyes and imagine the future: A successful career with a partner and family in a bigger, more progressive city. The episode makes a powerful statement about bullying and resilience, but perhaps would be even more consequential if a more central character attempted suicide.[71]

Critics initially felt that *Glee* presented bullies as one-sided, irredeemable characters. As a *Newsweek* columnist wrote in 2010: "Viewers might learn something from bullies drawn with depth, too. Who would see themselves in the slushie-chucking meathead jocks on *Glee*? Sure, we root for their comeuppance—they're predators who lack any compassion or remorse. But life is more complex than that."[72] With Dave Karofsky's example, *Glee* suggests that bullies can change and that their behavior often stems from deeper insecurities.

While Karofsky's case is most striking, *Glee* addresses less dramatic, but still painful, moments of everyday bullying. In one episode Finn and Kurt—soon to be stepbrothers—decorate Finn's bedroom together. Aware that Kurt has a crush on him and uncomfortable with their close living quarters, Finn angrily calls Kurt's tastes "faggy." The slur is quickly shut down by Kurt's father, who kicks Finn out of the house. Finn apologizes, later backing up Kurt when he is bullied in the hallway.[73] In the following season, he sings an affectionate song to Kurt at their parents' wedding reception.[74] In another episode, the football team apologizes to Coach Beiste for making fun of her masculine appearance.[75] As Murphy explains, "there are different forms of cruelty that people get away with. . . . If you can change any young impressionable minds and make them aware of the consequences of their actions and all different forms of cruelty, I think that's a great, great gift."[76]

Prior to introducing Wade/Unique, however, *Glee* did not have the best track record for sensitivity to transgendered issues. In one episode the glee club reprises *The Rocky Horror Picture Show*, and Mike (Harry Shum, Jr.) refers to the play's main character as a "tranny" when explaining his parents' opposition to *Rocky Horror*.[77] Critics slammed *Glee* for casually using this term after it had painstakingly addressed the problems with using the word "fag." As GLAAD wrote about the episode:

The show's inclusion of the word "tra**y" [sic] was made all the more confusing by the decision to change the word "transsexual" to "sensational" in the song "Sweet Transvestite." As many commentators have pointed out, it seems strange that Fox would want the word "transsexual" cut from a well known song, but find "tra**y" acceptable. Unfortunately the larger problem here is that the word "tra**y" has become an easy punch line in popular culture, and many still don't realize that using the term is hurtful, dehumanizing and associated with violence, hatred and derision against transgender people—a community that is nearly invisible in media today.[78]

Although other critics defended the episode, calling GLAAD oversensitive and heavy-handed, *Glee*'s producers did not respond publicly to the criticism. The song lyrics may have been changed as a concession to the network, or in recognition of the fact that gendered female singer Mercedes (Amber Riley) was performing the song. The introduction of Unique may not make up for past transgressions, but it does demonstrate that *Glee* is capable of growth.

ENVISIONING HAPPY ENDINGS

Glee's creators claim that, despite the often-heavy subject matter, the show ultimately aims to uplift viewers. Murphy explains: "It's about happy endings and optimism and the power of your personal journey and making you feel that 'the weird thing about me is the great thing about me.' I've done other shows with gay characters, and I will say that in many of those cases, the gay characters didn't have a happy ending. And I thought 'You know what? Enough.'"[79]

In fact, *Glee*'s characters might be candidates for the "It Gets Better" project. Upon graduation, Kurt and Rachel share a warehouse apartment in New York City, even welcoming Santana to crash at their loft. While Rachel pursues her dreams of stardom, Kurt scores an internship with *Vogue* under the tutelage of editor Isabelle (Sarah Jessica Parker) and later joins Rachel at the elite performing-arts academy. The traits that once made Kurt different are now assets, and in one joyful scene Isabelle and her friends—some of them drag queens—invade Kurt and Rachel's apartment for an impromptu dance party.[80] Other characters on this comedic musical series have even more improbable outcomes: cheerleader Brittany, who typically seems to lack intelligence, is revealed to be a math genius and receives early admission to MIT.[81] These plotlines breathe new life into the series as the characters graduate, but they may work against Murphy's earlier attempts to depict the uglier realities of high school.

The characters seem to live most authentically when they leave Lima. However, even this small town is changing for the better, if the Season Four finale is any indication. Back in Ohio, Blaine buys an engagement ring for Kurt, emboldened by the same-sex marriage initiatives happening across the country. An older lesbian couple (played by queer icons Patty Duke and Meredith Baxter) just happen to sell him the ring and offer to serve as mentors.

Over dinner with Kurt and Blaine, they reminisce about a time when queer lives were less visible. "There were no gay clubs at school. Nobody talked about it. We had no representation," says Baxter.

"Do you remember when we couldn't even do *this* in public?" Duke's character asks, holding her partner's hand. She later surprises and delights her partner by proposing marriage, asserting that it's only a matter of time before their union is legal in Ohio.[82] As the women publicly kiss and exchange the ring, other patrons at the restaurant Breadstix give them a standing ovation. Some critics astutely wondered if this was the same small town in which Kurt received death threats and harassing phone calls for merely being himself. Other critics perceive *Glee*'s population of openly gay characters as uncharacteristic for rural Ohio.[83] At times, Murphy's eagerness to depict happy endings and to further political progress hinders the series from accurately depicting the prejudices that still exist in the heartland.[84]

Despite Murphy's best efforts, the complications of real life can intrude upon *Glee*'s cast and audience. The recent death of *Glee* actor Cory Monteith to a drug overdose also puts the series' optimism in sharp relief. While it's true that some teens, like Kurt and Karofsky, bounce back from their high school struggles, others battle their inner demons well into adulthood. Producers' decision to memorialize Monteith by having his character Finn die on the show in the 2013–2014 season blurs the line between fiction and reality, making the actor's death even more consequential to viewers. This plotline may also provide an opportunity for *Glee* to address issues of addiction, loss, and heartbreak as well as triumph.[85]

Glee is a television fiction, of course, but it offers a welcome change to the short-lived and tragic tales of the past. Rather than being tokens or empty stereotypes, *Glee*'s queer characters are endearing and evolve over multiple seasons. *Glee*'s musical and multimedia formats speak to viewers outside the confines of a structured episode. As the series raises complex questions about gender and sexual identity, it empowers viewers to become advocates for acceptance in their own lives. Audiences are prompted to respond to anti-gay slurs, to advocate for same-sex relationships, and to develop greater compassion toward GLBTQ youth. And, while a Broadway role may be out of reach for the average teen, *Glee* reminds queer viewers that the future can be fabulous—and that they can achieve greatness despite, and through, their trials.

NOTES

1. Matt Kane, "*Glee* Gives Fans the Kiss They've Been Waiting For," GLAAD, March 16, 2011, http://www.glaad.org/2011/03/16/glee-gives-fans-the-kiss-theyve-been-waiting-for; Taylor Cole Miller, "Performing *Glee*: Gay Resistance to Gay Representations and a New Slumpy Class," *Flow*, July 6, 2011, http://flowtv.org/2011/07/

performing-glee/; Christopher Kelley, "*Will & Grace* Changed Nothing," *Salon*, October 2, 2012, http://www.salon.com/2012/10/03/will_grace_changed_nothing/.

2. In this article I use the terms "GLBTQ" and "queer" interchangeably to refer to characters who are not heterosexual or disgendered.

3. Dorothy Pomerantz, "TV's Biggest Moneymakers," *Forbes*, April 10, 2012, http://www.forbes.com/pictures/mfl45jigd/tvs-top-moneymakers/; Bill Gorman, "Broadcast Finals Tuesday: Dancing, Lost Adjusted Up; V Adjusted Down," *TV by the Numbers*, April 14, 2010, http://tvbythenumbers.zap2it.com/2010/04/14/broad-cast-finals-tuesday-dancing-lost-adjusted-up-v-adjusted-down/48563/.

4. Alice Marwick, Mary L. Gray, and Mike Ananny, "'Dolphins Are Just Gay Sharks': *Glee* and the Queer Case of Transmedia as Text and Object," *Television and New Media 20* (2013):11, doi: 10.1177/1527476413478493.

5. Robert Ito, "'Glee' Actress Naya Rivera's Santana Comes out to Applause," *Los Angeles Times*, May 24, 2011, http://articles.latimes.com/2011/may/24/entertain-ment/la-et-naya-rivera-20110524.

6. Jennifer Armstrong, "Gay Teens on TV," *Entertainment Weekly*, September 1, 2011, http://www.ew.com/ew/article/0,,20361194_20524710,00.html.

7. Natasha Vargas-Cooper, "Murphy's Honor," *Out*, April 11, 2013, http://www.out.com/entertainment/television/2013/04/11/ryan-murphy-glee-american-horror-story?page=full.

8. Armstrong, "Gay Teens on TV"; Dave Itzkoff, "Teenage Dreams and Nightmares," *The New York Times Arts Beat*, November 11, 2010, http://artsbeat.blogs.nytimes.com/2010/11/10/teenage-dreams-and-nightmares-talking-never-been-kissed-with-ryan-murphy-of-glee/.

9. Larry Gross, *Up from Invisibility: Lesbians, Gay Men, and the Media in America* (New York: Columbia, 2001).

10. Debra Rosenberg, "The 'Will & Grace' Effect," *Newsweek*, May 23, 2004, http://www.thedailybeast.com/newsweek/2004/05/23/the-will-amp-grace-effect.html; Edward Schiappa, Peter B. Gregg, and Dean E. Hewes, "Can One TV Show Make a Difference? *Will & Grace* and the Parasocial Contact Hypothesis," *Journal of Homosexuality* 51 (2006): 15–37. doi:10.1300/J082v51n04_02.

11. Vargas-Cooper, "Murphy's Honor."

12. Kelley, "*Will & Grace* Changed Nothing."

13. Armstrong, "Gay Teens on TV."

14. Armstrong, "Gay Teens on TV."

15. *Glee*, "Wonder-ful," directed by Wendy Stanzler, first broadcast May 2, 2013, by Fox.

16. Marwick, Gray, and Ananny, "Dolphins Are Just Gay Sharks."

17. Throughout this chapter, I am using the characters' first names with the excep-tion of Dave Karofsky, who, as an athlete, most often goes by his last name.

18. *Glee*, "Preggers," directed by Brad Falchuk, first broadcast September 23, 2009 by Fox.

19. Maria Elena Fernandez, "Chris Colfer's Journey from Small Town to 'Glee.'" *Los Angeles Times*, September 8, 2009, http://latimesblogs.latimes.com/showtracker/2009/09/glee-creator-and-executive-producer-ryan-murphy-discovered-chris-colfer-but-dont-tell-the-young-actor-that-it-makes-him-feel.html.

20. Miller, "Performing *Glee*."

21. Sarah Kuhn, "Life Stages," *Backstage*, September 3, 2009, http://www.backstage.com/interview/life-stages/.

22. *Glee*, "Wheels," directed by Paris Barclay, first broadcast November 11, 2009, by Fox.

23. Miller, "Performing *Glee*."

24. *Glee*, "I Kissed a Girl," directed by Tate Donovan, first broadcast November 29, 2011, by Fox.

25. *Glee*, "The Power of Madonna," directed by Ryan Murphy, first broadcast April 20, 2010, by Fox.

26. *Glee*, "Sectionals," directed by Brad Falchuk, first broadcast December 9, 2009, by Fox.

27. *Glee*, "Sexy," directed by Ryan Murphy, first broadcast March 8, 2011, by Fox.

28. *Glee*, "Mash Off," directed by Eric Stoltz, first broadcast November 15, 2011, by Fox.

29. *Glee*, "I Kissed a Girl," directed by Tate Donovan, first broadcast November 29, 2011, by Fox.

30. Ito, "*Glee* Actress Naya Rivera's Santana."

31. Armstrong, "Gay Teens on TV"; Ito, "'Glee' Actress Naya Rivera's Santana."

32. Katherine J. Wolfenden, "Challenging Stereotypes in Glee, Or Not?" *Student Pulse* 5 (2013), http://www.studentpulse.com/articles/724/challenging-stereotypes-in-glee-or-not-exploring-masculinity-and-neoliberal-flexibility.

33. Glee, "Saturday Night Glee-ver," directed by Bradley Buecker, first broadcast April 17, 2012, by Fox.

34. Cael, "Exploring Gender: Trans Character on Glee," *Lezbelib*, May 6, 2012, http://www.lezbelib.com/tv-movies/exploring-gender-trans-character-on-glee.

35. *Glee*, "Feud," directed by Bradley Buecker, first broadcast March 14, 2013, by Fox.

36. Michelle Wolf, "Trans as 'Personal Truth'? Thanks for the Screw Over, *Glee*," *Pinkessence Transgender Social Network*, March 24, 2013, http://pinkessence.com/profiles/blogs/trans-as-personal-truth-thanks-for-the-screw-over-glee.

37. *Glee*, "The Role You Were Born to Play," directed by Brad Falchuk, first broadcast November 8, 2012, by Fox.

38. *Glee*, "Sexy."

39. Glee, "Laryngitis," directed by Alfonso Gomez-Rejon, first broadcast May 11, 2010, by Fox.

40. *Glee*, "I Kissed a Girl."

41. Durryle Brooks, "Gay, Lesbian, Bisexual, Transgender and Questioning (GLBTQ) Youth: A Population in Need of Understanding and Support," Advocates for Youth, last modified 2010, http://www.advocates foryouth.org/storage/advfy/documents/glbtq_youth%202010.pdf.

42. *Glee*, "Glease," directed by Michael Uppendahl, first broadcast November 15, 2012, by Fox; Rae Votta, "'Glee' Q&A: Alex Newell on Unique's Future," *Billboard*, November 21, 2012, http://www.billboard.com/articles/columns/pop-shop/474063/glee-qa-alex-newell-on-uniques-future-his-beyonce-obsession-frank.

43. *Glee*, "Never Been Kissed," directed by Bradley Buecker, first broadcast November 9, 2010, by Fox.

44. Armstrong, "Gay Teens on TV"; Michael Ausiello, "Scoop: Darren Criss Joins 'Glee,'" *Entertainment Weekly*, September 26, 2010, http://insidetv.ew.com/2010/09/26/darren-criss-glee-kurt-boyfriend/.

45. *Glee*, "Extraordinary Merry Christmas," directed by Matthew Morrison, first broadcast December 13, 2011, by Fox; *Glee*, "Glee, Actually," directed by Adam Shankman, first broadcast December 13, 2012, by Fox.

46. Kane, "*Glee* Gives Fans the Kiss They've Been Waiting For."

47. *Glee*, "Sexy."

48. *Glee*, "The First Time," directed by Bradley Buecker, first broadcast November 8, 2011, by Fox.

49. Tim Stack, "'Glee': Ryan Murphy Defends Tonight's Controversial Teen Sex Episode," *Entertainment Weekly*, November 8, 2011, http://insidetv.ew.com/2011/11/08/glee-ryan-murphy-the-first-time-exclusive/.

50. Luchina Fisher, "'Glee' Sparks Controversy with First Time Episode," *ABC News*, November 9, 2011, http://abcnews.go.com/blogs/entertainment/2011/11/glee-sparks-controversy-with-first-time-episode/.

51. *Glee*, "All or Nothing," directed by Brad Buecker, first broadcast May 9, 2013, by Fox.

52. *Glee*, "Love, Love, Love," directed by Bradley Buecker, first broadcast September 26, 2013, by Fox.

53. Stack, "'Glee': Ryan Murphy Defends Tonight's Controversial Teen Sex Episode."

54. *Glee*, "Heart," directed by Brad Falchuk, first broadcast February 14, 2012, by Fox.

55. Steph Mineart, "Ryan Murphy Does Hate Lesbians, Apparently," *Commonplacebook*, December 7, 2012, http://commonplacebook.com/current-events/glbt-issues/ryan-murphy-does-hate-lesbians-apparently/.

56. Heather Hogan, "Is Ryan Murphy Trolling 'Glee's' Lesbian Fandom?" *AfterEllen.com*, November 7, 2012, http://www.afterellen.com/is-ryan-murphy-trolling-glees-lesbian-fandom/11/2012/.

57. "GEP Mission Statement," Glee Equality Project, accessed July 1, 2013, http://glee-equality-project.tumblr.com/missionstatement.

58. *Glee*, "All or Nothing."

59. *Glee*, "All or Nothing."

60. Votta, "'Glee' Q&A: Alex Newell on Unique's Future."

61. It Gets Better Project, accessed July 1, 2013, http://www.itgetsbetter.org/.

62. "Chris Colfer for the Trevor Project," It Gets Better, accessed July 1, 2013. http://www.itgetsbetter.org/video/entry/733/; "Glee's Max Adler," It Gets Better, accessed July 1, 2013, http://www.itgetsbetter.org/video/entry/ahfm_iv-554/.

63. "GLBTQ Youth." Advocate for Youth.

64. "GLBTQ Youth." Advocate for Youth.

65. *Glee*, "Never Been Kissed"; *Glee*, "The Substitute," directed by Ryan Murphy, first broadcast November 16, 2010, by Fox.

66. *Glee*, "Prom Queen," directed by Eric Stoltz, first broadcast May 10, 2011, by Fox.

67. *Glee*, "Theatricality," directed by Ryan Murphy, first broadcast May 25, 2010, by Fox; *Glee*, "Mash Off"; *Glee*, "Feud."

68. *Glee*, "Prom Queen."

69. *Glee*, "Prom Queen."

70. *Glee*, "On My Way," directed by Bradley Buecker, first broadcast Feburary 21, 2012, by Fox.

71. *Glee*, "On My Way."

72. Joshua Alston, "The Bully Pulpit," *Newsweek*, October 21, 2010, http://www.thedailybeast.com/newsweek/2010/10/21/tv-isn-t-exactly-hurting-for-gay-teen-role-models.html.

73. *Glee*, "Theatricality."

74. Glee, "Furt," directed by Carol Banker, first broadcast November 23, 2010, by Fox.

75. *Glee*, "Never Been Kissed."

76. Itzkoff, "Teenage Dreams and Nightmares."

77. *Glee*, "The Rocky Horror Glee Show," directed by Adam Shankman, first broadcast October 26, 2010, by Fox.

78. Matt Kane, "*Glee* Episode Hits the Wrong Note," *GLAAD*, October 29, 2010, http://www.glaad.org/2010/10/29/glee-episode-hits-the-wrong-note/.

79. Fernandez, "Chris Colfer's Journey from Small Town to 'Glee.'"

80. *Glee*, "Thanksgiving," directed by Bradley Buecker, first broadcast November 29, 2012, by Fox.

81. *Glee*, "All or Nothing."

82. *Glee*, "All or Nothing."

83. Ray Votta, "Glee Season Finale," Billboard.com, May 10, 2013, http://www.billboard.com/articles/news/1561269/glee-season-finale-all-or-nothing-delivers-regionals-a-surprise-wedding-and/; Dan Kimple, "A Gift of 'Glee' from Lima, Ohio," *The Huffington Post*, April 23, 2012, http://www.huffingtonpost.com/dan-kimpel/a-gift-of-glee-from-lima-ohio_b_1447646.html.

84. In one recent hate crime, two gay Miami University students were violently assaulted outside a bar when they attended an LGBTQ benefit in Oxford, Ohio, in 2010. Eric Resnik, "Two Miami U. Students Beaten in Possible Hate Crime," Gay People's Chronicle.com, June 4, 2010, http://www.gaypeopleschronicle.com/stories10/june/0604104.htm.

85. The actor died at age 31 but reportedly battled substance abuse in his teens. Steve Almasy, "'Glee' Star Cory Monteith Found Dead," CNN.com, July 15, 2013, http://www.cnn.com/2013/07/14/showbiz/glee-star-dead; Jocelyn Vena, "Will Cory Monteith's Finn Die from 'Accidental Drug Overdose' on 'Glee'?" MTV.com, August 15, 2013, http://www.mtv.com/news/articles/1712413/cory-monteith-glee-death-ryan-murphy.jhtml\.

Chapter Seven

Friendship and the Single Girl: What We Learned about Feminism and Friendship from Sitcom Women in the 1960s and 1970s

Cindy Conaway and Peggy Tally

For those of us who viewed pioneering Sixties and Seventies television and learned about relationships from programs like *That Girl* (1966–1971), *The Mary Tyler Moore Show* (1970–1977), and *Rhoda* (1974–1978), the innocence of that era may be more illuminating and healthy than what young women learn about relationships on today's TV shows featuring single women. We may not have learned as much about sex from our sitcoms as girl viewers learn from today's shows, but we learned fundamental lessons about women's friendships and about independence. This chapter describes how these shows, which pioneered the role of the "single girl" on television, approached friendship and also considers how demonstrations of ethnicity changed over time. We grew up with these shows. Peggy, age 53, grew up watching *That Girl* and idolizing Ann Marie's glamorous single life as she played with her similarly carefree Barbie Dolls. Cindy, age 46, watched *The Mary Tyler Moore Show (MTM)* and *Rhoda* with her feminist working mother. These shows were foundational to how we saw the world. For both of us, as Jewish viewers, the Jewish character of Rhoda was particularly influential.

Until 1966, there were few unmarried women playing lead roles on television—and few models for girls who might have questioned or dismissed the 1950s stereotype of the American housewife who married young, started raising a family, and didn't aspire to a professional career. Change was coming. Young girls in the late 1960s and 1970s had role models their older sisters did not. They watched television programs where women struck out on their own and chose their own nontraditional careers, instead of getting married and "settling down" in their early twenties. They saw women who were arbiters of style. They saw women separate from the nuclear family and, in lieu of marriage, make up their own "families" of neighbors and workmates. These characters reflected the pioneering feminism of the day and offered girls a view that being single was a better option than marriage at a young age to the wrong man and that an artsy career might beat the life of a homemaker. At the same time, while these shows gave superficial nods to feminism and social progressivism, they also reflected the culture of the times, and often took a more traditional turn in how they actually portrayed the characters.

Despite their mixed messages, these programs exerted considerable influence on female viewers, especially girls and younger women, when it came to their own feminist awakening and friendship. Demonstrations of ethnicity changed. Explicit references to ethnicity went from hidden to featured and then coded (only seen by those "in the know").

This chapter begins with Ann Marie, the main character of *That Girl*, who, despite her seeming independence, was really quite reliant on her father and boyfriend, and who hid any sense of ethnicity. It then goes on to the more competent and self-sufficient, but still docile and very WASPy Mary Richards. From there, we will see how Mary can in turn be contrasted with her friend, the far more brazen and Jewish character of Rhoda Morgenstern. While on *MTM*, Mary's discomfort with assertiveness is in opposition to Rhoda's seeming toughness, on the spinoff, the character of Rhoda is often indecisive, relies on her family, and minimizes her ethnicity. These changes offer some not-so-subtle messages about what it means to be single (and Jewish) in this seemingly progressive era of the Seventies. Rhoda also transforms as she is married, then separated, then divorced. Each show, in different ways, tries to offer a portrait of the single woman of its time. Each program reflects the changes occurring in the larger culture, but also tries to allay the audience's fears about what will happen to these women. Each woman offers a different conception of how to relate not only to the men in her life, but also to her nuclear family, and her created "family" made up of co-workers, friends, and neighbors.

WHO WAS "THE SINGLE GIRL?"

That Girl was not the first single woman character on a sitcom. For example, *My Friend Irma* (radio 1947–1954, TV 1952–1954) was about a "dumb blonde" with a steady boyfriend and perpetually infuriated boss. Gerard Jones in *Honey, I'm Home!: Sitcoms: Selling the American Dream*, writes that similar series like *Private Secretary* (1953–1957) and *My Little Margie* (1952–1955) followed this theme of the "nutty" woman who is constantly getting into trouble or making trouble for her bosses.[1] Because the main characters were so non-threatening and non-assertive, male viewers could enjoy these characters while women could see themselves as helpers.[2]

For example, *Our Miss Brooks* (radio 1948–1957, TV 1952–1956) starred Eve Arden as a sarcastic English teacher, Connie Brooks. While Brooks was more competent than the previously mentioned characters, her story often revolved around husband hunting. Mary Dalton writes that, although at first glance Miss Brooks seemed unhappy about being single, in reality the character had a kind of independence she wouldn't have had if she were married. Miss Brooks is similar to Sally Rodgers of *The Dick Van Dyke Show* (1961–1966) who often complains about lousy boyfriends but whose fun job as a comedy writer looks pretty fulfilling and not worth giving up for just anyone.[3] As Katherine Lehman has noted, another group of shows, including *The Patty Duke Show* (1963–1966) and *Gidget* (1965–1966), expressly targeted young female audiences and tried to capitalize on sweeping societal changes, including the earliest stirrings of the women's movement.[4] However, those shows featured teens living at home. The primary shows in this chapter are different because these characters became role models for young women seeking their independence from their nuclear homes.

The "single girl" was a new and important figure in postwar popular culture; she allowed viewers to make sense of and negotiate larger social changes around gender roles and acceptable social behavior. The single girl was a liberated woman whose career ambitions were represented through media in different formats, including situation comedies. There were constant efforts to tame her, and the resulting images of single women that producers ultimately allowed reflected these compromises.[5]

On *That Girl*, aspiring actress Ann Marie, played by Marlo Thomas, represented the new breed of independent single women. For girls and young women in the late 1960s, Ann showed that a young woman could live alone in a New York City apartment and thrive, both in her career and her personal life. Lynn Spangler points out in *Television Women from Lucy to Friends: Fifty Years of Sitcoms and Feminism*, that this was the first show in which a female protagonist voiced a wish to be independent.[6] There were limits to this independence, though, as a series of temporary jobs often meant that Ann was dependent on her father and her boyfriend, Donald.

That Girl arguably helped to negotiate the larger cultural changes by minimizing them in the fictional character of Ann Marie. Lehman observes, "Popular TV series placed tight constraints on the single woman's independence and sexuality. Sitcoms, in particular, commonly situated single characters within a workplace "family," tempered their professional ambitions, and failed to represent their sex lives onscreen."[7] Just as today there are limits to what the network executives would feel comfortable showing, even within a vastly broader range of cultural mores and sensibilities, so too in these early shows there existed a kind of constant negotiation between what was occurring in the larger society, and the effort to somehow contain those changing lifestyles within a more conservative format.

At the same time, however, by pushing the envelope slightly, there was the possibility of attracting the younger viewer, who wanted to see more openness on television. By contrast, older viewers were thought to be reluctant to relate to or find comfort in these changing images of women, so the push-pull between the older and younger tastes of television viewing audiences were often played out within the storylines about the single woman.[8] It may seem quaint that older viewers were considered important, given today's effort to routinely court the eighteen- to thirty-four-year-old viewer; however during that era, when the mass audience still truly meant that shows were being created for the largest audience possible, including younger and older viewers, these efforts to play to the middle, so to speak, was a powerful dynamic.[9] In this way, a realistic portrayal of single women on these shows was always thought to be potentially alienating to the wide swath of viewers whose cultural attitudes were still rooted in earlier stereotypes about women's proper roles.[10]

The term "single girl" itself reflects some of these compromises. The term offers a new and appealing alternative to the earlier term "spinster," which conjures up a lonely and unloved woman who can't find a man. At the same time, "girl" has connotations of not being a grown woman. It signals a kind of time in between girlhood and marriage. Interestingly enough, during this period there were not a significant number of women in this age cohort who were actually single, although there were increasing examples of them being created as screen and television characters.[11] It was not so much that people were witnessing a wide-scale trend of women who were not married and living on their own in American society during this period as much as the fact that this kind of lifestyle was gradually becoming part of the cultural Zeitgeist, through radical books such as Betty Friedan's *The Feminine Mystique*, released in 1963.[12] At the same time, by cultivating these new images of women in shows like *That Girl*, television networks could also begin to attract younger, female audiences, who were just beginning to be seriously treated as a potential audience cohort in their own right. These portrayals of single women drew on the new push toward appealing to younger audiences, including women who were starting to enter the workforce.[13] By the time the 1970s offered such programs as *MTM* and *Rhoda*, these portrayals began to reflect the women's movement that was already in full swing.

That Girl offers an important theoretical counterpoint to what would occur later in the 1970s: she is the "before" image of the "single girl," offering anxious viewers a comforting image of a young woman who is still part of the nuclear family. *MTM*, by contrast, is the "after" image, and the single women characters on this show reflect the revolution in women's roles that had occurred by that time. *Rhoda* goes on to reincorporate the nuclear family, yet in a space in which independence and sexuality are acknowledged. The single girl in these programs offers a moving snapshot of how the larger culture was processing these social changes around women's roles. They also represent an important site for studying how women viewers derived pleasure from these representations. Authors such as Lehman, Bonnie Dow, and Susan Douglas have noted how shows like these could be simultaneously feminist and anti-feminist and potentially inspire social change, but also allow for the multiple pleasures and seemingly "apolitical" sources of vicarious enjoyment.[14]

THAT GIRL

Ann Marie was a glamorous heroine: innocent, single, and leaving her family for the first time. She was a liminal figure in many ways, representing the transition from earlier young women on TV who lived at home but dated, to a woman in her early twenties who moved to an apartment in the city. Although Ann (Marie is her last name, leading to confusion in some episodes) leaves small-town Brewster, New York, to live in New York City alone, she is still squarely placed within her nuclear family.[15] She wasn't just "thrown into the world," in Marlo Thomas's words.[16] For Thomas, this kind of "soft landing" into being a single woman in the city was a true representation of how young women made the transition to the big city and it remained a core piece of the series in all five seasons.

There are many examples of how Ann draws on her family of origin, as well as her boyfriend, Donald, to support her through the situations that come up in her quest to be independent. Ann's parents, especially her father, Lou, frequently show up at her apartment to help her solve problems or simply to fret about corruption by the big city, particularly when it comes to her virginity. She was sometimes shown as daffily naïve, especially when it came to issues around money or work. For example, in "Many Happy Returns" Ann receives a personal visit from Leon Cobb, an IRS auditor, because she didn't answer several letters from the IRS. He tells her that she owes $2,600 in back taxes, which Donald doesn't understand, because she didn't earn enough money to warrant that kind of bill. Although she has been scrupulous about pasting newspaper items about her acting work into a scrapbook, she is clueless about where any of her receipts or W2 forms are located. It turns out that she overstated her earnings, so that her father would think she was able to support herself as an actress in the city.[17]

The episode was economical in its ability to symbolically portray Ann as both naïve when it came to understanding how overstating her earnings would require her to pay more in taxes, while at the same time it reveals that the source of her overstating her income was to allow her to remain independent from her father. The episode also revealed that she was both inept and disorganized in tending to her money and receipts, and in need of rescuing by another male in her life. In this way, she remains childlike, even in her attempts to find a modicum of freedom, by dissembling about her true earnings. This seeming ignorance around managing money stands in direct contrast to the real actress, Marlo Thomas, who created the character of Ann Marie. Far from being ditzy, Thomas, the daughter of veteran actor Danny Thomas, was a creative and powerful professional. Thomas herself became the head of Daisy Productions, the production company that created *That Girl*, and she revolutionized the television industry by becoming one of the first female owners of her own production company.[18]

In terms of the original genesis of the show, Thomas was originally approached by Clairol, the women's hair color company; they wanted to create a vehicle for her talents by offering her a lead in a TV series. Rather than trade on earlier stereotypes of women who were playing traditional gender roles, such as Barbara Billingsley (June Cleaver) or Lucille Ball (Lucy Ricardo), Thomas instead proposed to ABC that they allow her to develop a character who was expressly moving away from these conventional roles for women. She offered up herself as an example of a potential television character, a woman who would be somewhat like herself, independent and college educated. In interviews about the genesis of the program, Thomas explained that she worked hard to convince the ABC executives that young women were hungry for new images of women, who were expressly not like their mothers. They weren't racing to get married but wanted to pursue lives outside of the nuclear family; they wanted to develop their own identity apart from that of mother or wife. In short, they wanted an education and a career in the big city. In her view, television needed to listen more closely to what the culture was saying, and cited Friedan's popular bestseller, *The Feminine Mystique*, as a necessary precursor for understanding why she wanted to make this kind of show for young women.[19]

Interestingly enough, Thomas's vision of the show was that it was a kind of extended reflection on changing relationships for women, rather than simply being a comedy that only went for the laughs, or as she put it, *That Girl* was created as a "relationship" show, not a "fall down funny show."[20] For example, the character of Ann is in a long-term relationship with Donald Hollinger, played by Ted Bessell, and, as we will show, in many episodes, there was a constant negotiation between Ann's desire for independence and parity within their relationship with Donald's need to somehow tamp down or control Ann's supposedly unrealistic or "daffy" desires or expectations. Donald was both figuratively and literally the "straight man," trying to tame the unruly woman, and at the same time, preserve some shred of his own heterosexual masculinity. Their relationship was a classic battle of the sexes, where Ann would challenge Donald, and Donald would protest, but eventually give in, while at the same time asserting, at least on a superficial level, that he was still in control. Rather than being a sexist man, however, Donald too was a kind of liminal figure, both traditional in his attitudes but also struggling with these very assumptions as he also wanted to be supportive of Ann's fledgling career and higher aspirations for freedom and independence from her nuclear family.[21]

In terms of the specific dynamics of their relationship, an ongoing dilemma occurred around their relative sexual engagement with one another. Though they are clearly boyfriend and girlfriend, by today's standards their relationship looks almost as if they are somehow permanently chaste. In other words, though they are committed to one another, the relationship is never consummated, even implicitly. In one episode, for example, titled "Rain, Snow and Rice," Ann and Donald are attending a wedding in Connecticut.[22] Because of a snowstorm, they are stranded at the hotel, but there is only one room available. This causes a comic situation in the form of a crisis, because it is understood that they are not sexually active with each other, yet will have to share a room. In another episode titled "Odpdypahimcalfss," it is Donald's mother who takes on the role of the shocked visitor, when she finds a pair of Donald's pants in Ann's closet.[23] Again, the comedic possibilities precisely exist in this situation because it is somehow assumed initially that Ann and Donald aren't sleeping together, so there would be no reason for Ann to have Donald's clothes in her closet.

Whereas the episode with the pants in Ann's closet at least implicitly suggests a kind of Oedipal crisis where Donald's mother tries to come to terms with Donald and Ann's relationship, in "The Rivals," the relationship between Ann and Donald becomes an open source of jealousy for Ann's father Lou.[24] Interestingly enough, it is not so much because Ann and Donald are sexually active, though whether they are or not is often the source of comedic confusion on the show; what really resonates in these shows is the emotional intensity between Donald and Ann that the father finds threatening. Even as the show makes it clear that the couple isn't engaging in sex before marriage, this doesn't lessen the ways in which the father and boyfriend are somehow in competition for Ann's affection.

More generally, these episodes which focus on the dynamics of Ann and Donald's relationship and the Oedipal tensions they arouse are also meant to signal the ways in which young women were trying to move away from these family dynamics altogether by living alone in the big city. At the same time, there was clearly a sense that the city was dangerous for young women, and many of the episodes deal with the comedic possibilities of living alone in the midst of these potentially dangerous situations. For example, in the second episode of the first season of *That Girl*, Ann moves from Brewster to her own apartment in New York City.[25] Her father is very upset about this, and worries that she won't be safe. Though the move is supposed to mark her transition to an independent life, she soon meets her next-door neighbor, with whom she forms a kind of sisterly familial bond. Later in the same episode, Ann's mother moves in with her because she is angry at Ann's father. Though her mother eventually returns to her father, it is clear that the so-called "move" away from home is filled with counter-examples of Ann still being tied to her family, hence the episode's title "Hello, Goodbye, Hello."

In another episode entitled "Leaving the Nest Is for the Birds," Ann tries to demonstrate her independence by inviting her family to dinner, only to have a Peeping Tom intrude on the meal.[26] Each of these episodes invariably has Ann explain to her father or boyfriend that while she acknowledges that there are scary and difficult things that will occur when she is on her own, she will be fine and will still need the people who love her in her life, including them. She reassures the people she loves that she will always be the same person inside, and still love them, even as she gains new experiences. In this way, *That Girl* arguably offers a kind of working through of the anxieties that older viewers might have in seeing a younger woman leave home to be on her own. At the same time, the show worked hard to ultimately allay those fears by showing how Ann still has the support of not only neighbors and her boyfriend, but her parents as well, who make periodic appearances in many of the episodes.

It may be difficult, if not impossible, from our current historical vantage point to realize just how revolutionary *That Girl* was for its time. Watching the "backlash" that was to occur in 1980s television, as authors such as Susan Faludi note, it is even more striking how the tropes about women being single and outside the mainstream still remain part of the cultural discourse to this day and how *That Girl* tried to move beyond them by making a living on one's own for women an appealing and upbeat possibility.[27] The end of the series was progressive in the sense that although Ann and Donald became engaged, no wedding ever took place on the show, and in fact, Ann did not get married. Though in reality, the network wanted Ann to get married on the show, Thomas fought hard to keep her character's fate ambiguous. It is also notable that the final episode titled "The Elevated Woman," shows Ann and Donald arguing over the way that men treat women.[28] Ann believes that

Donald used her as a character in an article he wrote about women's liberation, and the argument that ensues is over their disagreement about whether men treat women as the lesser sex. Donald protests that he has always treated women with respect and Ann convinces him to attend a women's lib meeting. However, on the way there they get stuck in an elevator with a newlywed couple and the rest of the episode re-visits old scenes they had together over the years and whether they were evidence of Donald's sexism toward her.

That Girl was a transitional show for women because while Ann remains closely tied to her family and boyfriend, the final episode offered a clear indication of what was to come for women more generally. The act of not getting married, for a show that was a "relationship show" and also a romantic comedy, marks a significant change for young women during this period in American history. And, by having both Donald and Ann debate sexism, the implication is that changes were coming soon, and that Donald could be a part of that transition. Thomas was able, by way of a provisional conclusion, to take single women up to a certain point in a television show, but it would remain for her televisual sisters, including Mary and Rhoda, to lead the way to the next iteration of single women on TV.

THE MARY TYLER MOORE SHOW

Mary Richards, played by Mary Tyler Moore, differed from Ann by being significantly more independent and competent, although more concerned than Ann about "doing things wrong" or embarrassing herself. Lisa Schwarzbaum of *Entertainment Weekly* wrote that Mary, "the first great grown-up single working woman on TV, was endowed by her creators . . . with an inalienable right to life, love, and the nerve-racking pursuit of happiness. We adored her because she was so nerve-racked."[29] Fleeing from a broken engagement, she first appears applying for a secretarial job at the WJM newsroom where she doesn't get the job because it is already filled. However, there is a lower-paying associate producer job that the boss, Lou Grant, gives her despite the fact that he would prefer a man.[30]

She appears to do her job nearly flawlessly, making up for Lou's hard-drinking gruffness, writer Murray's lack of confidence in his looks and his paycheck, and anchorman Ted's near-total idiocy and childishness. Mary's seeming perfection in looks contrasts with her frequent discomfort. Susan Crozier writes, "Those moments in which Mary seems to shrink and lose the power to speak as she tries to remove her leggy body from the gracelessness of uncomfortable social situations are defining. These are precisely the moments in which she becomes endeared to the viewer, for they reveal her capacity to make embarrassment into a virtue and an enlivening force."[31] That, and her terrible parties, make her relatable, despite her being gorgeous and looking so good in her clothes.

Unlike Ann, who seems to have friends as pretty much an afterthought while having close ties to family and Donald, Mary relies on her friends, and rarely sees her family or depends on a boyfriend. Along with Mary's sisterly relationship with neighbors Rhoda and Phyllis (Phyllis's preteen daughter Bess calls her "Aunt Mary"), she creates a "work family" that includes her daughterly relationship with Lou, her sisterly relationship with Murray, Ted as the dim uncle, and "Happy Homemaker" Sue Ann as the sex-obsessed aunt she might not otherwise socialize with, but whom she often defends against the outside world as one would members of one's own family. Unlike earlier sitcoms that primarily concentrated on the home and family lives of characters, such as *I Love Lucy* (1951–1957) or *Leave It to Beaver* (1957–1963), *MTM* emphasized Mary's workplace as equal in importance to her home life. This split focus between home and workplace echoes that of Moore's earlier series *The Dick Van Dyke Show*. Similarly, *The Bob Newhart Show* (1972–1978) followed Bob Hartley in his home and in his psychiatry practice and was produced by production company MTM soon after *MTM*. The split focus allowed for two mostly separate settings for the protagonists, which allowed for Mary to be seen as competent but subservient at work, while being far more confident with friends and suitors at home, much as Bob Hartley was seemingly an excellent therapist at his office, but often seemed baffled by the antics of wife Emily and neighbor Howard at home. The work family as primary focus (with little attention to home lives,) would later be a staple of many sitcoms including *WKRP in Cincinnati* (1978–1982), *Newsradio* (1995–1999), and *The Office* (2005–2013). In her study, *Prime Time Families*, Ella Taylor explains, "With families perceived as deeply troubled, the hopes and fantasies of a sustaining community turned to work relations and professional allegiances."[32] The work family took the place of the nuclear family, but added the shared mission of doing a job together. This replaced family values themes, and the shows rarely had children as major characters, which allowed for more sophisticated storylines.

While Mary is deferential to most at the office (she's seemingly the only one who can make coffee, run errands for Lou, and help everyone with personal problems), at home she is much more in charge. In contrast to Ann's taxes, Mary's returns in "1040 or Fight" are 100 percent perfect—she has even saved a Popsicle stick from when she bought a business-related treat.[33] In that case, the only reason her audit goes on for so long is that the auditor is in love with her. This is not unusual. Unlike Ann with her stable relationship, Mary frequently gets involved with male co-stars, and never gets "tied down." She frequently has dates for just an episode or two, and seems only wistful about this, not depressed or bitter. Even when she does have a recurring boyfriend, she considers marriage or commitment only a few times.[34] Although Mary's co-workers seem to think of her as innocent, there are subtle references to the idea that she is sexually active with at least some of the men she dates. For example when she arrives home fully dressed at 5 a.m., or when her visiting father reminds her mother to not to forget to "take her pill" and Mary and her mother chorus, "I won't."[35] Unlike shows today, which tend to have longer relationship arcs, Mary's love life was simply not foregrounded.

Also unlike Ann and earlier single heroines, Mary's friendships were consistent and important. While Ann has a few friends we see in some episodes, for example married neighbor Judy and the tomboyish Pete Peterson (played by Ruth Buzzi), most episodes focus on her, Donald, and sometimes Mr. or Mrs. Marie. Although Mary was always the main character on *MTM*, episodes would be centered around workmates Ted, Lou, Murray, and in later episodes, Sue Ann or Ted's girlfriend, and later wife, Georgette. Episodes could also be devoted to her "home friends" Phyllis and her daughter Bess, or most importantly, Rhoda. As Jennifer Keishin Armstrong points out in her book, *Mary and Lou and Rhoda and Ted*, it was unusual for shows not to have every episode centered around a "star," which was one of the ways the show was innovative and set the tone for future situation comedies.[36]

Mary and Rhoda's friendship begins with a rivalry over who will get the apartment Mary eventually takes.[37] Its large size, dressing area, sunken living room, small but complete kitchen, and balcony, but dull décor contrasts with Rhoda's dark, cramped, garret, complete with garment rack and hot plate but a lot of flair, beads, and peacock feathers. The apartments are just one of the ways the two are put in opposition. Mary is tall, thin, and classy and has a lot of self-confidence with men. Rhoda, on the other hand, wears frumpy and later "artsy" clothes, but constantly laments her lack of success at dating. At work although she is very competent, Mary respects authority. Rhoda has complete confidence in her work as a window dresser and a total lack of deference to authority. Niceness is Mary's trademark.

After this initial standoff, however, the two quickly bond. Mary tries to talk Rhoda out of her feelings of unattractiveness, although this is hard when men invariably fall for Mary, sometimes even those Rhoda meets first. They are sometimes partners in schemes worthy of Lucy and Ethel, such as when Mary and Rhoda join the "Better Luck Next Time" club for divorced people to qualify for a cheap trip to Mexico, or when Mary has to stay up all night writing obituaries, and she and Rhoda make up fake and funny ones.[38] They sometimes are at odds, as when Rhoda, jealous when her boyfriend prefers

Mary, tells Mary she's won a "Teddy" broadcasting award, which Mary hu-
miliatingly discovers in front of a crowd she has not.[39]

Frequently, however, they socialize, and spend their time debriefing bad
dates with, as Rhoda once called losers, "feebs" or stressful workdays.[40] Their
companionship taught a generation of women what women's friendships
could be like. Unlike earlier friendships like Lucy and Ethel, in which Lucy
was always the ringleader and Ethel the sidekick, it's a real, equal, friendship,
one that Mary no longer seems to have once Rhoda leaves for her eponymous
spinoff. It is clear that Mary sometimes worries about the future, as she was
brought up to be a traditional wife and mother. Allyson Jule writes that the
show "reveals the emerging paradox in American culture: the growing freedom for women and men to shape their own lives that is accompanied by a
new sense of loss and uncertainty. Something important could be gained but
something important could be lost as well."[41] It is unclear when the show ends
where Mary, fired from WJM along with everyone but Ted, will go, or if she
will ever be married. Yet it doesn't seem disastrous, only sad, since it's clear
she has made "a family" out of her workmates and others who made her feel,
as she says, "less alone."[42]

Women and girl viewers could find role models in either Mary or Rhoda.
New Yorker Rhoda was initially seen as unsympathetically hostile by the
original test audiences that saw the pilot episode of *MTM* until the writers
had Phyllis's daughter Bess say she liked her.[43] That allowed both Mary and
the audience to find things to like in Rhoda, especially her sense of humor
and contrast to Minnesota-raised Mary. While Mary was in a sorority, Rhoda
was a "Sharkette."[44] Although many working women found inspiration in
Mary for her independence, competence, and increasing confidence, her past
as a member of the pompom squad, her success with men, and her impeccably fitting wardrobe made her a mostly unattainable type. Rhoda, however,
consistently talked about herself as chubby (even if Valerie Harper actually
wasn't) and dressed in an "artsy" manner, including flowy clothing and lots
of scarves. Most importantly for us, and for many viewers who had only seen
themselves in guest characters, often unsavory ones, Rhoda was Jewish.[45]
After four seasons on *MTM*, Rhoda was "spun off" into her own show to
become a lead character.

RHODA

It was surprising that a Jewish character, much less one with a New York accent and attitude, could even be a major character on a 1970s network sitcom,
and that the spinoff could include multiple Jewish characters. David Zurawik

writes in *The Jews of Prime Time* that CBS claimed to have done research before *MTM* was greenlighted, saying that Americans did not want to see divorced people or "people from New York, men with mustaches, and Jews" on their screens.[46] However, *Rhoda* was an instant hit.

It's not clear whether audiences would have accepted the character as a lead if Valerie Harper, who played Rhoda, had been more like her. Although while on *MTM* Rhoda had weight issues and saw herself as unattractive to men, Harper was actually thin, attractive, and married. Rhoda was originally dressed in oversized sweatshirts and was later allowed to "lose weight" and win a beauty contest at her department store. An article in *Time* magazine stated,

> When she heard that MTM was auditioning for the part of a Bronx Jewish girl, she tried out without much hope: "I'm not Jewish, not from New York, and I have a small shiksa nose." She was, in fact, a lapsed Catholic, but she had a flawless ear for intonation. After considering more than 50 actresses for the part, Mary beamed at Valerie and said the magic words: "That's Rhoda."[47]

It is interesting how much the culture had to change in order to make Rhoda a viable heroine. America was only ready for a Jewish main character if she wasn't too Jewish. Mary Tyler Moore was turned down for the role of Danny Thomas's daughter in *Make Room for Daddy* because as Thomas (Marlo's father) said her nose was too small and she clearly could not be related to someone so ethnic. Marlo Thomas herself had plastic surgery to reduce her "Lebanese nose" (photos on the Internet are the best proof of this) and other marks of ethnicity before she could be the "adorable" Ann Marie. Therefore, perhaps Rhoda could really only play lip service to "looking Jewish" by the time she got her own show.[48] Judaism on *Rhoda* was no longer talked about the way it was on *MTM*, but rather was coded, reduced to Ida (her mother) making an occasional brisket or attending "sisterhood," or "Hava Nagila" being played at an anniversary party.[49] It didn't really matter, though. Rhoda was "one of us." We knew she was Jewish, and what it felt like to "look Jewish" in a culture that valued blonde girls with delicate features. One Jewish viewer, Elizabeth Gold, wrote in *The Forward*, "I loved that many of Rhoda's jokes centered around subjects about which I felt particularly insecure: weight, food, parental relationships, difficulty in finding a romantic partner, the ironical curse of being a smart, funny, ambitious and, yes, Jewish woman."[50] This represented much of the appeal of *Rhoda* for Jewish viewers who could see past the fact Judaism was never explicitly mentioned, and understand that all the Morgensterns, and other friends like Gary Levy (Ron Silver), were Jewish.

On her own show, Rhoda is married to Joe early in the first season. They are mostly happy for the first two seasons, but are separated in the third,

and divorced by the beginning of the fourth. Rhoda actually comes off as
much more comfortable with herself than she was on *MTM*, even during her
separation and after her divorce. She is more approachable than she was on
MTM, perhaps because she was "chosen" once, even though didn't work out.
It is up to her sister, the chubby Brenda (played by the actually Jewish and
chubby Julie Kavner) to make self-effacing comments about her appearance
and dating prospects, even as multiple men are interested in her. Yet the show
takes back some of the independence Rhoda had on *MTM*, in part because the
producers seemed to have trouble making the show audiences wanted to see,
and so kept trying experiments.

Rhoda first lives with Brenda in her creatively decorated studio, and then in
the same building in an apartment with Joe, then post-divorce in another less
expensive apartment in the same building. They frequently spend time with
their parents, Ida and Martin, which brings Rhoda back into the nuclear family. Although Rhoda and an old high school friend start a business in the early
seasons, for the last two seasons she gives up her autonomy and works for a
man very much like Lou Grant, but the few other ill-defined characters who
work there hardly make it a workplace family. Rhoda is clearly best friends
with sister Brenda, and Carlton the drunken doorman is a consistent (if never
seen) presence. However, since "friend" characters came and went in various seasons without ever being referred to again, friendship seems somewhat
minimized in favor of family.

New York, which on *That Girl* often seems like a glamorous playground,
is a much scarier place on *Rhoda*. Ann seems to have few concerns about
safety in New York. She locks her door but seems unworried, and nearly
everyone she meets is well dressed, and seemingly civilized. However,
just a few years later, Rhoda (who while in Minneapolis was sometimes
mocked for her New York paranoia) and Brenda not only live in a doorman
building (as useless as he often is), but have a "secret knock" each time
they enter each other's apartments, and visitors announce themselves at
the door, even when Carlton manages to rise from his stupor to announce
them. This seems to go along with the perceived (and real) seaminess of
much of Manhattan at that time and reinforces the importance of family
and close friends as security.[51]

LIFE AFTER ANN, MARY, AND RHODA: *GIRLS* AND
THE DILEMMA OF POST-FEMINIST SINGLEHOOD

For those of us who lived through the Sixties, Seventies, Eighties and to more
recent times, the picture of the carefree single woman has been in a state of
continual transformation, and not always for the better. Today, if a young
woman turns on her television or computer, she sees a range of images of sin-

gle women, but the dominant theme is that, somehow, the relations between men and women have gone awry. The theme of friendship and its importance to the single woman has also changed. Friendship was, of course, important to subsequent single sitcom women on workplace sitcoms, such as single mother Elaine Nardo of *Taxi* (1978–1983), *Murphy Brown* (1988–1998), and the characters on *Designing Women* (1986–1993). Another strain of situation comedies focused on friendships between co-ed characters who were friends, for whom family and work were sidelined, such as *Seinfeld* (1989–1998), *Friends* (1994–2004), and *How I Met Your Mother* (2005–2014). In both workplace and "hangout" sitcoms, the single women on those shows had a group of male and female friends who they relied on for emotional support as well as social life. In sitcoms about friends, however, whenever there were chances for the single woman to have romantic relationships with male co-stars, storylines tended to focus more on romance and sex, and there was less of a focus on family—for instance we saw parents on *Friends* only occasionally (no one from Phoebe's family even attended her wedding), and Elaine's father on *Seinfeld* only once while the characters had dates or storylines around longer relationships in nearly every episode.[52] It's also important to note that although many of the actresses on these shows were Jewish, or some characters seemed to be, there were very few references to their Judaism and this was also mostly coded. Take *Friends* for example. Ross Gellar, played by the Jewish David Schwimmer, seems to identify as Jewish, as when he wants his son to meet the "Hanukkah Armadillo" instead of Santa Claus.[53] His sister Monica (played by the non-Jewish Courteney Cox), on the other hand, is only referred to as Jewish once (when she pretends to be a minister to impress a young woman whose baby she and Chandler want to adopt).[54] Although "Rachel Green" is clearly a Jewish name, Rachel, is the spoiled Long Island "princess." Her father, played by Jewish actor Ron Leibman, never refers to a Jewish heritage, perhaps because Jennifer Aniston is not Jewish, and Marlo Thomas plays her mother.[55]

Following up on the influential *Sex and the City* (1998–2004), which featured four women who prized friendship with each other while looking for romance, HBO now airs a wryly funny show called *Girls* (2012–present), in which the single twenty-something young women are also strongly bonded to one another as they live away from their families after college; they often have failed romantic encounters. In both these shows, women's friendships are tied to their status of being single, and are shown to be a positive source of support in a culture that hasn't figured out how to make relationships between the sexes more stable and lasting.

And, whereas "women's lib" was beginning to be discussed on shows like *That Girl*, which spoke optimistically about the possibilities for young women to strike out on their own, more contemporary images, from recent situation comedies, romantic comedies, and books, instead show how difficult this has been, precisely in terms of finding a meaningful romantic relationship. These stories and articles in popular media cite reduced opportunities for marriage due to demographic realities such as young women being more educated than men in their age cohort, lowered chances for having children as a result of delaying childbirth, and dilemmas for young women in an age of speedy "hook-ups." Popular books such as *The End of Men* and *Marry Him: The Case for Settling for Mr. Good Enough,* offer a much more grim assessment of what it means to be a single woman in today's society.[56] In this sense, these "retro-retro" images recall the earlier negative equation of being single with having reduced life opportunities.

In more recent television shows about single women, by contrast, friendship with other women and even men is portrayed as a positive source of support and nurturance. These images of friendship for single women, which began in earnest with the character of Mary, and took on even more urgency with Rhoda, is a lasting legacy from this earlier period of television history. In these ways, then, these earlier shows have much to tell us about the "history of the present," to use Foucault's phrase.[57] They explain to us that while sex is something that must constantly be re-negotiated in every era, the bonds of friendship can be an enduring legacy. The innocence of the earlier shows may contrast vividly with the raunchy and explicit sexuality of the later single women comedies, but the lessons they taught us about the need for social bonds and social connections, even as women live outside of traditional marriages, was incredibly important. In this way, we would do well to re-visit some of these earlier women, to honor their struggles, which are eerily reminiscent of our own.

NOTES

1. Gerard Jones, *Honey, I'm Home: Sitcoms: Selling the American Dream* (New York: St. Martin's, 1993).

2. Ashley Dykes, "Situation Comedies and the Single Woman on Television" (unpublished PhD diss., Louisiana State University, 2011).

3. For instance, as when the man who owns the deli where the writers get their lunch reveals his love for Sally, and she turns him down in *The Dick Van Dyke Show,* "Romance, Roses, and Rye Bread," directed by Jerry Paris, first broadcast October 28, 1964, by CBS.

4. Katherine Lehman, *Those Girls: Single Women in Sixties and Seventies Popular Culture* (Lawrence: University Press of Kansas, 2011).

5. Lehman, *Those Girls.*

6. Lynn C. Spangler, *Television Women from Lucy to Friends: Fifty Years of Sitcoms and Feminism* (Westport, CT: Praeger, 2003).

7. Spangler, *Television Women*, 6.

8. Lehman, *Those Girls*.

9. Bonnie Dow, *Prime-Time Feminism: Television, Media Culture, and the Women's Movement Since 1970* (Philadelphia: University of Pennsylvania Press, 1996).

10. "The Ugly Truth About the TV Ratings Game," TheTVAddict.com, accessed January 4, 2011, http://www.thetvaddict.com/2011/01/04/one-program-executive-attempts-to-use-jedi-mind-manipulation-to-convince-us-that-these-are-not-the-tv-shows-we-are-looking-for/.

11. Lehman, *Those Girls*.

12. Betty Friedan, *The Feminine Mystique* (New York: Dell, 1964).

13. Lehman, *Those Girls*.

14. Lehman, *Those Girls*; Dow, *Prime-Time Feminism*; Susan J. Douglas, *Enlightened Sexism: The Seductive Message that Feminism's Work is Done* (New York: Henry Holt and Company, 2010).

15. *That Girl*, "What's in a Name?" directed by Jerry Paris, first broadcast 1966 by ABC. In this episode (based on the unaired pilot), Ann's agent wants her to change her name to forestall the inevitable "Ann Marie what?" but she will not when her father disapproves.

16. "The Making of That Girl," *That Girl*, directed by Marlo Thomas (1966: Los Angeles, CA: Shout Factory, 2006), DVD.

17. *That Girl*, "Many Happy Returns," directed by Jay Sandrich, first broadcast January 30, 1969, by ABC.

18. "The Making of That Girl."

19. "The Making of That Girl."

20. "The Making of That Girl."

21. "The Making of That Girl."

22. *That Girl*, "Rain, Snow and Rice," directed by John Erman, first broadcast February 2, 1967, by ABC.

23. *That Girl*, "Odpdypahimcaifss." directed by Hal Cooper, first broadcast February 22, 1968, by ABC.

24. *That Girl*, "The Rivals," directed by Hal Cooper, first broadcast January 11, 1968, by ABC.

25. *That Girl*, "Goodbye, Hello, Goodbye," directed by Bob Sweeney, first broadcast September 15, 1966, by ABC.

26. *That Girl*, "Leaving the Nest Is for the Birds," directed by Hal Cooper, first broadcast March 2, 1967, by ABC.

27. Susan Faludi, *Backlash: The Undeclared War Against American Women* (New York: Crown Publishers, 1991).

28. *That Girl*, "The Elevated Woman," directed by Roger Duchowny, first broadcast March 19, 1971, by ABC.

29. Lisa Schwartzbaum, "Love Is on the Air," *Entertainment Weekly*, February 14, 1992.

30. *The Mary Tyler Moore Show*, "Love Is All Around," directed by Jay Sandrich, first broadcast September 19, 1970, by CBS.

31. Susan Crozier, "Making It After All: A Reparative Reading of *The Mary Tyler Moore Show*," *International Journal of Cultural Studies* 11 (2008), 51–67.

32. Ella Taylor, *Prime-Time Families: Television Culture in Post-War America* (Berkeley: University of California Press, 1989), 139.

33. *Mary Tyler Moore*, "1040 or Fight," directed by Jay Sandrich, first broadcast November 28, 1970, by MTM.

34. *The Mary Tyler Moore Show*, "One Boyfriend Too Many," directed by Jay Sandrich, first broadcast December 13, 1975, by CBS. In this episode, she chooses between ex-boyfriend Dan who she "almost married" and current boyfriend Joe (Ted Bessell), who committed in his previous episode, *The Mary Tyler Moore Show*, "Mary Richards Falls in Love," directed by Jay Sandrich, first broadcast November 22, 1975, by CBS; but neither man is seen or mentioned in future episodes.

35. *The Mary Tyler Moore Show*, "Just Around the Corner," directed by Jay Sandrich, first broadcast October 28, 1972, by CBS; *The Mary Tyler Moore Show*, "You've Got a Friend," directed by Jerry Belson, first broadcast November 25, 1972, by CBS.

36. Jennifer Keishin Armstrong, *Mary and Lou and Rhoda and Ted: And All the Brilliant Minds Who Made* The Mary Tyler Moore Show *a Classic* (New York: Simon and Schuster, 2013).

37. "Love Is All Around."

38. *The Mary Tyler Moore Show*, "Better Late . . . That's a Pun . . . Than Never," directed by John C. Chulay, first broadcast February 2, 1974, by CBS.

39. *The Mary Tyler Moore Show*, "Bob and Rhoda and Teddy and Mary," directed by Peter Baldwin, first broadcast November 14, 1970, by CBS.

40. *The Mary Tyler Moore Show*, "Love Blooms at Hemples," directed by Jay Sandrich, first broadcast November 10, 1973, by CBS.

41. Allyson Jule, "Using *The Mary Tyler Moore Show* as a Feminist Teaching Tool." *Gender & Education,* 22.1 (2010): 123–130.

42. *The Mary Tyler Moore Show*, "The Last Show," directed by Jay Sandrich first broadcast March 19, 1977, by CBS.

43. Armstrong, *Mary and Lou and Rhoda and Ted.*

44. *The Mary Tyler Moore Show*, "Some of My Best Friends Are Rhoda," directed by Peter Baldwin, first broadcast February 26, 1972, by CBS.

45. "Love Is All Around."

46. David Zurawik, *The Jews of Primetime. Brandeis Series in American Jewish History, Culture, and Life* (Hanover: University Press of New England, 2003).

47. "Rhoda and Mary: Love and Laughs." *Time,* October 28, 1974, 68.

48. Vince Waldron and Dick Van Dyke, *The Official* Dick Van Dyke Show *Book: The Definitive History and Ultimate Viewer's Guide to Television's Most Enduring Comedy* (New York: Applause, 2001).

49. Vincent Brook, *Something Ain't Kosher Here: The Rise of the "Jewish" Sitcom* (Rutgers University Press, 2003).

50. Elizabeth Gold, "Headwraps and All, Rhoda Morgenstern Is a Misfit Girl's Dream: A Lonely Teenager Discovers Mary Tyler Moore's Wise-Cracking, Insecure Sidekick and Derives Inspiration," *Forward*, February 2, 2000, 18.

51. David Kirby, "Making It Work; Sitcom City," *The New York Times*, October 26, 1997. This article describes various sitcom locations in New York City and says that Rhoda's post-divorce apartment (a different unit than the same building she lived with Joe) was, "at 332 West 46th Street, not a particularly safe or likely neighborhood for a single woman in the mid-1970's."

52. *Friends*, "The One with Phoebe's Wedding," directed by Kevin Bright, first broadcast February 12, 2004, by NBC; *Seinfeld*, "The Jacket," directed by Tom Cherones, first broadcast February 6, 1991, by NBC.

53. *Friends*, "The One with the Holiday Armadillo," directed by Gary Halvorson, first broadcast December 14, 2000, by NBC.

54. *Friends*, "The One with the Birth Mother," directed by David Schwimmer, first broadcast January 8, 2004, by NBC.

55. *Friends*, "The One with the Two Parties," directed by Michael Lembeck, first broadcast May 2, 1996, by NBC.

56. Lori Gottleib, "Marry Him!: The Case for Settling for Mr. Good Enough," *The Atlantic Monthly*, March 1, 2008; Hanna Rosin, "The End of Men," *The Atlantic Monthly*, July 2010.

57. Michel Foucault, *Discipline and Punish: The Birth of the Prison* (New York: Vintage, 2nd edition, 1995).

Section III

AMERICA'S MOST WANTED

Chapter Eight

Epic Failures: Media Framing and the Ethics of Scapegoating in Baseball

Chandler Harris and Lauren Lemley

With reasoning ranging from the historical to the psychological, hundreds of individuals have argued that baseball is more than just a game, in the words of Ken Burns, a microcosm of America which "follows the seasons, beginning each year with the fond expectancy of springtime, and ending with the hard facts of autumn. . . . Most of all, it is about time and timelessness. Speed and grace. Failure and loss. Imperishable hope. And coming home."[1] Craig Muder, Director of Communication for the National Baseball Hall of Fame and Museum, added an historical perspective to Burns's claim, writing that "baseball, it seems, grew up with America. From its origins as a New York City-area club game in the 1820s to the powerful healing it provided after the September 11 attacks of 2001, the sport has time and again demonstrated its link to patriotism and other all-American values."[2]

But baseball fans have not been the only people to notice this connection between sport and life. It's been a familiar topic of fictional television and film; in the Hollywood blockbuster *Field of Dreams* (1989), one character articulates this well, arguing that "the one constant through all the years, Ray, has been baseball. . . . It reminds us of all that once was good, and that could be good again."[3] Academics from a diversity of disciplines have also noted this connection. Media scholar Neil Blain claimed that "sport is strongly connected with real life. It is understood not as an equivalent of real life, but as continuous with real life,"[4] and psychologists Lynn McCutcheon and her colleagues wrote that while "we may disagree about politics, religion, or how to provide the best public education for our tax dollars, we can unite behind our favorite baseball team. The act of rooting for the team that represents our city or region promotes a feeling of unity and social solidarity."[5]

Thus, if baseball has served a fundamental role in American life, Burns's claim that the history of baseball is not merely a series of success stories, but also includes narratives of "failure and loss" should come as no surprise. Although there have undoubtedly been countless moments of failure and loss in the thousands of baseball games played in the sport's nearly 200-year history, two stories stand out above the rest as examples of failure on a monumental scale—drastic falls from the height of success to the depths of failure. Yet, surprisingly, neither of these moments resulted from an error made by a baseball player or manager. In both cases the otherwise well-meaning actions of a fan and an umpire quickly transported an individual from obscurity to infamy.

THE FINAL ANONYMOUS DAY OF STEVE BARTMAN

It was October 14, 2003, and the jubilant crowd of 39,577 at Wrigley Field was certain they were about to achieve what was for many a lifelong dream.[6] The Cubs were just six outs away from the World Series and a chance to win a championship, a plateau they had not reached since 1908. They could envision the imminent celebration, mostly because they had dreamt about it their whole lives, as had their fathers, and their fathers' fathers for that matter. The Cubs had their young ace, Mark Prior, on the hill, and he was pitching a masterpiece. As he took the mound to start the top of the eighth inning, the Cubs bullpen was dormant. There would be no need for them tonight. Prior would lead them to the promised land. Marlins shortstop Mike Mordecai lifted a fly ball out to left field, which Cubs outfielder Moisés Alou secured. The Cubs were five outs away.

The crowd began holding up five fingers as if to countdown how few obstacles now stood in the way of their dream. Television cameras showed crowds of people milling around outside Wrigley Field on Waveland Avenue, ready to celebrate in the streets. One fan was seen holding a sign stating, "We Can Do This!" "We," it stated, because this was not just about the players, the coaches, and the owners. This was, more than anything, about the Cubs fans. They had suffered long before any of the current players, coaches, and owners had arrived on the scene. Marlins second baseman, Luis Castillo fouled a ball down the left field line, and Alou gave chase. As he reached up into the stands to make the second out of the inning, a Cubs fan reached for the ball and unintentionally knocked it away from Alou's open glove. Alou was irate, and with good reason. The players pleaded with the umpires for a fan interference call, but replays showed that because Alou reached into the stands, no such call was justified. Suddenly, the fans' positive energy turned into a mixture of anger and anxious nervousness. Castillo walked, followed by consecutive hits by Ivan "Pudge" Rodriguez and Derrek Lee, and in minutes the game was tied. The fan who had prevented Alou from making the catch for the crucial second out sat in stunned silence, Cubs hat and radio headphones in place. The now perturbed crowd began pelting the guilty fan with concession items, and security guards felt it was in his best interest to escort him out of the ballpark. Fans continued to hurl beer and insults at him as he made his way through the concourse, where "a tight ring of security guards whisked Bartman, his sweatshirt pulled over his face, into an office, hiding him there until after the waiting mob outside the ballpark had dispersed hours later."[7] Ultimately, the Marlins scored eight runs in that eighth inning to put Chicago's celebration on hold.

TWICE PERFECT—JIM JOYCE AND ARMANDO GALARRAGA

On June 2, 2010, something happened in a baseball game in Detroit, Michigan, that seems to happen in almost every game in every sport, ever played: a mistake was made by an umpire.[8] Yet, this mistake proved to be bigger than the game itself. Detroit Tigers pitcher Armando Galarraga was pitching a perfect game into the ninth inning against the Cleveland Indians. In other words, he had not allowed a runner to reach base safely in any way (e.g., hit, walk, or error). Indians rookie Jason Donald hit a ground ball to the right side, which Miguel Cabrera fielded and threw to Galarraga, covering first base for the final out and sealing the perfect game—or so it seemed. Just as the crowd began to roar with excitement for the history they had witnessed, umpire Jim Joyce called Donald safe. Replays clearly showed that this call was incorrect. It seemed as if everyone—players, coaches, and fans, alike—reacted in anger toward Joyce. Everyone, that is, except for Galarraga. He simply put his hands on his head in sheer disbelief of what had happened. Joyce told *Sports Illustrated* writer Tom Verducci that he remembered exactly how Galarraga smiled at him, and was enthralled by how the player reacted.[9] Galarraga simply walked back to the mound and retired the next Indians batter to end the game, a starkly different reaction than Cubs fans had seen from Alou.

TELEVISION'S BLAME GAME

Despite their unique characteristics, these two events would not have intensified as they did had the games not been nationally televised. Scholars in a number of fields, namely communication, media studies, journalism, and political science, have established the important role the news media play in crafting public opinion.[10] Indeed, Jared Rutecki and Gregory Rutecki wrote that "media determine which subjects are presented to their audience, how content is placed into context through cultural 'frames,' and ultimately, whether topics are affirmed or rejected by the public."[11] The present chapter builds on this work, examining these frames from a rhetorical perspective as what Kenneth Burke called terministic screens, or ways in which language symbolically acts to "color" the way audiences "perceive, record, and interpret" an event.[12] Burke viewed all language as symbolic action, contending that "we *must* use terministic screens, since we can't say anything without the use of terms; . . . and any such screen necessarily directs the [audience's] attention."[13] In this chapter we argue that, while media coverage of failure on the baseball field undoubtedly constructs such screens to "structure messages in ways that resonate with schema already embedded in cognition," societal cognitions are not inherently unchangeable.[14] By juxtaposing the media's framing of the Bartman and Joyce episodes, we contend that communicators can learn valuable lessons from the way failure narratives are communicated through televised sports broadcasting. To set the stage for this analysis, we will overview the role that identification, media framing, and scapegoating play in sports. With these theoretical frameworks in mind, we will then examine the Bartman and the Joyce/Galarraga games independently to determine how scapegoating and media framing figured in each episode of failure, before finally drawing some conclusions about television's role in translating and communicating life lessons from the field to a TV screen near you.

Researchers in a variety of disciplines have investigated the role of attribution in sports.[15] Indeed, the cross-disciplinary team of Ro'i Zultan, Tobias Gerstenberg, and David A. Lagnado, drawing on their diverse backgrounds in economics and brain sciences, argued that "team sports is a commonplace context in which blame (and credit) is attributed to individuals for their team's outcome."[16] A number of studies have specifically investigated the role of a fan's identification with his or her team as a determining factor for the attributions he or she makes during times of perceived success or failure. These studies largely supported the conclusion that "high-identification persons may be expected to exhibit the most intense reactions to the team's performances," and therefore, for these individuals, "the team's performances are relevant to their feelings of self-worth."[17] But, as sports psychology scholars Tim Rees, David K. Ingledew, and Lew Hardy reminded us, "people do not engage in attributional thought in a vacuum. Invariably, attributions are made in a social context, and social factors influence attributions."[18] These social factors have always been present when a group of highly invested fans gather to watch a key game or match, and when mounting expectations of success rapidly descend into failure, attribution theory's conception of the self-serving bias suggests that the spectators will look for an external agent or factor to blame so that they need not blame themselves, or by extension, their team.[19]

One tactic for projecting this blame externally is scapegoating, which Kenneth Burke discussed in *Permanence and Change* as a means by which people have assigned blame for millennia, noting that "the scapegoat mechanism in its purest form, [involved] the use of a sacrificial receptacle for the ritual unburdening of one's sins."[20] This ritual derived from the ancient Israelite practice of casting burdens onto the back of an animal and then beating or killing the animal to release the people of these burdens. Leviticus 16:21 specifically commanded that "[Aaron] shall lay both his hands on the head of the live goat, and confess over it all the iniquities of the people of Israel, and all their transgressions, all their sins, putting them on the head of the goat, and sending it away into the wilderness."[21] Rabbi Howard Cooper argued that individuals today still long for a sense of atonement, which they attempt to find by scapegoating the other.

> For we think we understand how certain "unacceptable" feelings in ourselves—feelings like greed, violence, lust, envy, jealousy, rage, aggression, possessiveness, vanity, murderousness—can become unconsciously disowned, or displaced, and then end up being projected outside of ourselves onto others, whom we will then feel are threatening us in a malign fashion with these very same impulses.[22]

More pejoratively, psychologist Krauple Taylor classified these projections as "displaced aggression," rhetorical acts capable of creating victims in every office building, school, church, battlefield, and even on every field or court of play.[23]

But as psychologist Gordon W. Russell noted, regardless of the source of the scapegoating, "it typically falls to a reporter or someone in the newsroom to define and attach a label to unruly crowd behaviors."[24] This rhetorical construction on the part of the media has been studied by scholars in both journalism and communication through the concept of framing, defined by one of the theorists to coin the term, Robert M. Entman, as a tactic of "selection and salience. To frame is to select some aspects of a perceived reality and make them more salient in a communicating text."[25] This is of particular importance to our present analysis as it relates to the role television news and sports media outlets play in framing and reframing an event "by emphasizing different attributes of the event—consciously or unconsciously—in order to keep the story alive and fresh."[26] Although these frames have often proved informative and entertaining for the viewer, such symbolic action can also have powerful negative consequences. In his examination of rioting at sporting events, Russell argued that "media hyperbole frequently has the effect of unwittingly orchestrating conflict through priming of aggressive schema."[27] With this potential for media framing to create both positive and negative outcomes in mind, we turn to an examination of the ways in which failure was rhetorically framed during these two infamous moments in baseball history.

FAILURE ON THE FIELD

Our analysis focuses on the events detailed earlier: Steve Bartman's October 14, 2003, interference from the stands that prevented Cubs outfielder Moisés Alou from making a crucial out in the eighth inning of Game 6 in the 2003 National League Championship Series, and Jim Joyce's June 2, 2010, "blown" call, which kept Tigers pitcher Armando Galarraga from entering the record books as the twenty-first person in baseball history to pitch a perfect game. At some point in the moments, days, and even years following these failures, the media consciously framed Bartman and Joyce as scapegoats. But this is where the similarity between these two episodes ends. Ten years after that fateful night at Wrigley Field, Bartman is still so widely held responsible for keeping the Cubs from the World Series that he remains in seclusion, intentionally keeping himself out of the public eye for fear of what fans might *still* do to punish him for interfering with that foul ball.[28] But Joyce, on the other hand, continues to umpire games, and in a 2011 poll conducted by *Sports Illustrated* and ESPN, was voted the best umpire in the Major Leagues by current players.[29] This analysis seeks to understand why these differences have occurred and draw conclusions about the lessons baseball and media framing can offer society.

Bartman's Failure

As the shocking events unfolded in Chicago on that October night in 2003, the media's portrayal of the Bartman narrative had a clear impact on the fans in and around Wrigley. Thom Brennaman and Steve Lyons were broadcasting for Fox that night, and their producer was Jeff Gowen. All three men knew the enormity of the situation and the virtually unprecedented difficulties they would face in deciding how to communicate the episode to their viewers. Gowen described his initial reactions to the play in Alex Gibney's 2011 television documentary, *Catching Hell*: "When it first happened and I saw Moisés react that way, time stood still for a brief moment there. I don't know if that happens in history making events, but I had to register, 'Did I just see that?' . . . I probably got on my feet and screamed, 'I need to see everything we have on this.'"[30] The first word from either of the announcers was Brennaman's call as the play happened: "In the air down the left field line, Alou reaching into the stands and he couldn't get it and he's livid with a fan."[31] In this brief statement, not unlike thousands of other play-by-play calls, the media rhetorically established a framework for scapegoating Bartman that remains powerful and accurate for many today. After seven seconds of complete silence, the announcers aired the first replay, trying to make sense of the situation and arriving at the question on everyone's mind:

> Brennamen: And that's a Cubs fan who tried to make that catch.
>
> Lyons: Why?[32]

To Cubs fans, the fact that Bartman had not reached out over the field did not matter. It mattered only that he had impeded Alou. But Lyons, known for his witty commentary, may have taken it a little too far in the moment: "Here at Wrigley, when the opposing team hits a home run, they throw the ball back onto the field. I'm surprised someone hasn't thrown that fan onto the field."[33] Rabbi Cooper's discussion of scapegoating described the symbolism of the "throwing the ball back" ritual in his claim that "certain 'unacceptable' feelings in ourselves . . . can become unconsciously disowned, or displaced, and then end up being projected outside of ourselves onto others."[34] When fans throw the ball back, they are doing just that, projecting the negative feelings onto the ball, outside their community, and onto the field so they could be taken away by another. Likely without intending to do so, Lyons's assertion provided the initial justification the crowd needed to cast Bartman as scapegoat.

Wrigley Field is a unique ballpark for many reasons, one of which being that just beyond the small section of outfield bleachers lies Waveland Avenue, so close to the field that players regularly hit home runs onto the street. Fans who cannot obtain tickets to the game commonly gather on Waveland to get as close to the action as possible, listening to live radio broadcasts or watching small antenna televisions to fill in the details they cannot see for themselves. Matt Liston, a Cubs fan and filmmaker, was standing at the back of the bleacher section that night where he could both watch the game and turn around to watch the reaction of the crowd standing on Waveland Avenue. He recounted what he experienced in *Catching Hell*.

> Now keep in mind, Wrigley Field is the only stadium without a JumboTron. There's no big screen for replays . . . [so] if you're not sitting right around Bartman, you don't really know what the heck happened. But the fans outside the park were listening to radio except for one guy was standing out there with a television on his head. And what's happening with the telecast at that point is they keep on replaying the Bartman incident, over and over. Now this famous "asshole, asshole" chant starts.[35]

Thus, in the absence of any way to review the events and reach a conclusion on their own, television viewers in the crowd outside Wrigley began to reinforce the media's framing of Bartman as scapegoat.

But in the minutes following the incident, fans *inside* the ballpark were not sure who to blame because another fan, unaware of what had just occurred, retrieved the ball Bartman had deflected and lifted it proudly into the air. From Josh Doust's perspective in the upper deck, that was the person who had interfered. Doust and a few other fans began angrily yelling at the man holding the ball until someone received a phone call from a friend at home who said the Fox broadcast was casting blame on a fan in a green turtleneck and blue sweatshirt—Steve Bartman. Doust joined in the chorus of fans berating Bartman, and can be seen in a video, shot by another fan and memorialized in *Catching Hell*, yelling, "Rot in hell. Everyone in Chicago hates you. You suck."[36] In this way, the media's framing of Bartman as scapegoat actually superseded the accounts of eyewitnesses and served to magnify the frenzy of the crowd by providing them with verified evidence of Bartman's guilt.

The next day, the *Chicago Sun-Times* identified Bartman by name, revealing his identity as a twenty-six-year-old computer consultant who coached youth baseball. Although reporters camped outside Bartman's Northbrook, Illinois, home, he remained in hiding, only responding through a written statement read by his brother-in-law. While Bartman did show remorse and accept blame for the Cubs' loss, his statement supported the media's scapegoating, and ultimately encouraged them to continue. Later that afternoon on ESPN's *Pardon The Interruption*, the co-hosts discussed the Cubs' loss by ranking those who held any degree of responsibility in a segment entitled, "Food Chain." Tony Kornheiser, one of the co-hosts, condemned Bartman, proclaiming "this kid is meat. Right now, this kid is meat."[37] It was through powerful terministic screens, such as casting Bartman as meat at the "bottom of the food chain," that he went from simply being known as "the fan" or "headset man" to Steve Bartman: the fan who cost the Cubs a shot at the World Series. It was a judgment he would never escape.

Indeed, the televised image of Bartman being led out of Wrigley by security is the image most people remember him by, and Reverend Kathleen Rolenz argued that this image directly paralleled the Biblical scapegoating narrative:

> On the Day of Atonement, a goat was chosen. The priest then would take the goat into the temple, would pray over the goat, lay his hands on the goat, and that was to confer the sins of the people onto that animal. And then the animal was led out of town, and the people of the community would then jeer and insult and throw their sins onto the goat. And then they would lead the goat outside the city, shut the gates so that the goat could never again return to the fold. . . . And then of

course the whole idea of Bartman being led out of the stadium amidst jeers and boos and people throwing stuff at him. It reminded me of what happens with the scapegoat. The goat is innocent. The whole idea of the scapegoat is you take an innocent thing and you put your sins upon it. Scapegoats are solitary and vulnerable. So in that sense, he was the perfect scapegoat.[38]

Rolenz's analysis raises an important question about the morality of Bartman's role as scapegoat. Although his action did interfere with a play, it was not the only opportunity the Cubs received that night, or in game seven the following evening, to advance to the World Series. So was the media actually justified in casting Bartman as the solitary scapegoat? To that end, Gibney concludes *Catching Hell* with an important thought: "as time passes, the city is haunted more by what it did to Bartman than what Bartman did to Chicago. There are many who say the city should forgive Bartman, but it's really up to Bartman to forgive Chicago."[39]

Joyce and Galarraga's Triumph Over Failure

Following the final out of the *almost* perfect game, both Joyce and Galarraga returned to their respective clubhouses, traditionally separated from one another to avoid a conflict of interest. Joyce was fairly confident he had made the correct call and thought the fans were just mad he did not give them the call they wanted. He would later provide this description of how they treated him:

> Somehow, they get the next batter to ground out to end the game and I'm thinking this'll finally be the end of it. But then, soon as the game is over, everything kicks up a notch. The yelling. The booing. Even the small sliver of doubt I have on the field, it starts to grow as I make for the clubhouse. It moves from the back of my mind to the front and center, from a doubt to a worry because I have never heard anything like this before. Folks are really letting me have it. The rest of the crew, they've never heard anything like it either. We leave the field together, and it's only later that I realize they're helping me run a gauntlet.[40]

Joyce referred to this experience as a "gauntlet," imagery that was very similar to the experience Bartman had at Wrigley Field. It also resembled Reverend Rolenz's description the treatment of scapegoats in the Biblical narrative: "And then the animal was led out of town and the people of the community would then jeer and insult and throw their sins onto the goat."[41]

In the Detroit locker room, the Tigers showered Galarraga with beer as he entered the clubhouse. This was a time for celebration, not despair. The media gathered around Galarraga's locker to get his take on what had just transpired. They were looking for the player to contribute to a scapegoating narrative that would frame Joyce's failure similarly to Bartman's. But instead of blaming

Joyce, as would have been all too easy for him to do, Galarraga took blame away from the umpire, telling reporters, "he probably feels more bad than me. Nobody's perfect. Everybody's human."[42] While the rest of the world began to paint a negative image of Joyce as the scapegoat, Galarraga, the man who had more right than anyone to blame Joyce, forgave him.

Unlike players, Major League Baseball umpires are not required to meet with the media after the game. So technically, Joyce could have ducked questions about the call, but in this scenario, he believed it was best to face the issue head on. The reporters, twenty to thirty of them according to Joyce, flooded into the small umpires' locker room, crowded around Joyce, and the exchange began:

> Reporter: Have you seen the replay?
>
> Joyce: Yep.
>
> Reporter: So what do you think?
>
> Joyce: I kicked the shit out of it, that's what I think.
>
> Reporter: How do you feel about it?
>
> Joyce: I feel like hell. This is a history call, and I kicked the shit out of it. And there's nobody who feels worse than I do. . . . . I feel like I took something away from that kid, and I don't know how to give it back.[43]

Joyce began crying in front of the group of reporters, finally excusing himself from the room. While it was likely not enacted for this purpose, Joyce's transparency was perhaps the most important action he could have taken to avoid his own scapegoating. Rather than have the media cast guilt onto him, he met the blame head on, owned it, and showed he truly cared about his mistake and understood the magnitude of the moment. Because there are no challenges or use of instant replay in baseball, an umpire's call is simply not questioned, and MLB umpires rarely, if ever, apologize for blown calls. Yet, Joyce felt so terrible that he owned his mistake and showed humility.

The Tigers' manager, Jim Leyland, and the Tigers' general manager, Dave Dombrowski, caught wind of Joyce's reaction to the situation and went to console him in the umpires' locker room—an unprecedented action in a community where separation between officials and teams is considered essential to preventing bias on the field. Although Dombrowski tried his best to soften the mood, he was little help. Joyce only asked for one favor—to bring Galarraga over so he could speak with him in person. Dombrowski summoned Galarraga, who seemed puzzled at first, but did not question his general manager's request. Galarraga described the scene upon approaching Joyce:

When he sees me, he starts to cry. It is not a screaming cry, like for a child. It is a gentle cry, like for a man. He says, "My God." That is all. Just, "My God." Like he cannot believe it. Like he is heartbroken. Then he shakes his head back and forth and says, "I am so sorry, Armando. I do not know what else to say." I do not know what to do about this, so I go to where Jim Joyce is sitting and I give him a hug. "It is all right," I say. "Mr. Joyce, this stuff, it just happens."[44]

Galarraga then repeated to Joyce what he had said to the crowd of reporters only minutes earlier: "Nobody's perfect."

The next day, the Tigers were set to play the Indians again. Joyce was scheduled to be the home plate umpire and had been given the option to take the day off, but refused. In keeping with baseball tradition, each team would send a representative to home plate before the game to exchange lineup cards with the home plate umpire. It is a ceremony that usually goes unnoticed. But it was the center of national attention on June 3, 2010. The Tigers sent Galarraga as their representative, offering the two men an opportunity to publically display their reaction to the events of the previous day. Galarraga waited at home plate as Joyce emerged from the umpires' tunnel, and the tears began streaming down Joyce's face. The men shook hands, and Galarraga handed Joyce the lineup card. As Joyce's name was announced, the crowd booed. But when Galarraga patted Joyce on the back, and Joyce returned the gesture before Galarraga walked back to the dugout, the crowd gave the men a standing ovation. Their "boos" quickly transitioned into applause. The humility and grace shown by both men over the course of the twenty-four hours that culminated in this exchange established a narrative that countered any thoughts of permanently casting Joyce as a scapegoat. Media framing of the event shifted as dramatically as the crowd's behavior, turning from narratives of blame to narratives of grace.

The story quickly became national news. There was more to this event than any headline about a perfect game could have delivered, and the media covered every angle. Amy K. Nelson's ESPN piece entitled, "A Perfect Storm," chronicled the days after the game and how the public reacted to the story. In it, Joyce said that "everybody talks about how I handled it, but Armando . . . you talk about handling a situation, you talk about sportsmanship. It was perfect. Imagine that: me saying perfect."[45] Nelson concluded her piece by asking Joyce what the word perfect meant. His reply was poignant: "what does the word perfect mean? Sometimes the word perfect means being able to accept imperfection."[46] And this gracious framing of the situation extended far beyond the reach of sports-centric networks. In a segment for ABC's *World News with Diane Sawyer*, John Berman gave a detailed account of all that transpired during the series in Detroit, concluding that "you might say that one man missed the chance to be perfect. But two men seized the chance to be good. And being good in life trumps being perfect in baseball."[47]

Ultimately, although the media could have chosen to frame Joyce as a scapegoat, replaying him "running the gauntlet" of angry fans again and again, as they did following the Bartman episode, they elected to emphasize a different narrative of events. But what accounts for such a difference? The primary answer is located in the actions taken by the story's cast of characters. Less than a year after the game that brought them together, Galarraga and Joyce co-authored a book, appropriately titled *Nobody's Perfect*. In it, Joyce wrote about how this event touched the lives of many in a positive manner:

> For a long time, it doesn't go away. I start to hear from people all over the country . . . all over the world, even. Seems we've struck some kind of chord, me and Armando. Me, for the way I copped to my mistake and apologized and took my lumps. Armando, for so graciously accepting my apology and for carrying his disappointment with such dignity and cheer.[48]

In the aftermath of that now-infamous June 2nd game, the media framed a morality narrative, one that claimed forgiveness and humility were more powerful than blame and scapegoating. George Will, a renowned baseball writer, appeared on ABC's *This Week* a few days after the game and gave his opinion on perfection, saying, "the perfect is the enemy of the good. You strive for perfection in anything, in baseball [or] anything else, and you're going to destroy the rhythm of the game and the human element that we love in the game."[49]

BOTTOM OF THE NINTH

Renowned sportswriter Jeremy Schaap argued that singular moments have the potential to make a lasting impact, claiming that "it is not the content of our character or the essence of our souls that typically defines us. Men [sic] are more often measured by their deeds; sometimes, just one deed."[50] This was certainly the case for the individuals whose failures and responses to failure lie at this heart of this chapter. Of course, as is the case for anyone living under the scrutiny of press attention, professional athletes and officials are never completely in control of the stories told about their actions. For as our analysis has shown, "a story's meaningful context is the frame that shapes the news story."[51] Indeed, it is the combination of these two factors—the individual's actions and the context provided by media framing—that ultimately determines the legacy of a failure. Without a doubt, Joyce employed a more successful response to his error, and in doing so was able to avoid the scape-goating that still haunts Bartman today. In fact, the two men's responses were opposite in virtually every respect. While Bartman sat alone in the stands, was escorted into hiding, had another read a statement of apology on his be-half, and remains in seclusion ten years later, Joyce immediately faced report-ers to apologize quickly and publicly, returned to work the next day, and has been willing to discuss his experience on screen and in print ever since. Our analysis of the televised media framing of each event shows that the tenor of each man's choices played a key role in the way the public remembers the him: Bartman shielding his face while running from an angry crowd and Joyce and Galarraga shaking hands at home plate the day after the umpire's blown call. James Briggs of the *Oakland Press* also compared these two situ-ations in a column published a few days after Joyce's error. He argued that

> in less than 24 hours, Bartman became a symbol for everything that was wrong with baseball and the Cubs. To this day, Bartman keeps a low profile, and must fend off reporters tracking him down at his home and work. When he dies, news organizations will run stories reminding us all over again of that fall evening in Chicago. It is his defining moment. That could have been Joyce's curse. And, in truth, he's not completely off the hook. Joyce's blown call almost certainly will be the largest footnote on his career. But it won't be his defining moment. He will be remembered as a good umpire who made a mistake, but also as a man who stood tall and owned that mistake.[52]

Indeed, our analysis shows that, while media framing is a powerful phenom-enon, these frames are only as strong as the actions they narrate.

Additionally, these two baseball games remind fans, viewers, and ulti-mately the public at large that scapegoating is a high-stakes strategy for coping with failure. Reverend Rolenz articulates this powerfully when she suggests that "we need to look at what damage the idea of scapegoating does and not only to the person that becomes the scapegoat but to those people that are jeering and berating the scapegoat. It diminishes our humanity."[53] We need look no further than the scenes, described earlier, of Bartman and Joyce running a gauntlet on national television to know the weight of her argument. It is a powerful lesson, reinforced vividly through the medium of television.

In a 2010 article, Pulitzer-prize-winning author Jon Meacham claimed that, "of all sports, I think, baseball most resembles life. The seasons are long; defeat is familiar; repetition often, but not always, makes you better. And it is not necessarily fun all the time."[54] Unlike failures in politics and business that result in televised hearings and protests, failures on the baseball field are often experienced more personally because of a fan's identification with his or her team. Rather than feeling that the error was committed by a "giant unfeeling corporation," or "some politician I never voted for anyway," failures in baseball spark questions such as: "How could he do that to *my* team?" This personal connection adds a critical human element to the lessons taught though baseball as fans gather around televisions to watch their teams play. Meacham went on to consider Joyce's failure in light of another story unfolding that summer, the BP oil crisis. He concluded that

> There is no comparison between a baseball game and the nation's worst environmental disaster, but there is a lesson to be learned from how Jim Joyce and Armando Galarraga handled what was, in their world, an epic event. Be honest, admit mistakes, and keep moving. That is perhaps the only way to cope with tragedy of any scale.[55]

Unexpectedly, Joyce's story, one that was unprecedented in almost every aspect, set a new precedent for how individuals should react to failure, not only in the game of baseball, but in life. It was fitting that such a story took place on the baseball diamond—the setting for America's pastime and a mirror of America's story.

NOTES

1. "1st Inning: Our Game," *Baseball*, directed by Ken Burns (1994; Arlington, VA: Public Broadcasting Service, 2004), Videocassette (VHS).

2. Craig Muder, "Baseball Doubles as a Symbol of the Country," *Phi Kappa Phi Forum* 89, no. 2 (2009): 17.

3. *Field of Dreams*, directed by Phil Alden Robinson (1989; New York: NBC Universal, 1989), Videocassette (VHS).

4. Neil Blain, "Beyond 'Media Culture': Sport as Dispersed Symbolic Activity," in *Sport, Media, Culture: Global and Local Dimensions*, ed. Alina Bernstein and Neil Blain (New York: Routledge, 2003), 251.

5. Lynn E. McCutcheon, Mara Aruguete, Jennifer S. Parker, John A. Calicchia, F. Stephen Bridges, and D. D. Ashe, "Nearly the Greatest: Psychological Profiles of Professional Baseball Players Who Almost Became Famous," special issue, *North American Journal of Psychology* (2007): 22.

6. Many of these details were remembered by one of the authors, but for more information on this game, see "Cubs will have to wait another year," ESPN, accessed August 15, 2013, http://scores.espn.go.com/mlb/recap?gameId=231015116.

7. Daniel G. Habib, "You Gotta Believe," *Sports Illustrated*, October 31, 2003, 46.

8. Many of these details were remembered by one of the authors, but for more information on this game, see "Umpire: 'I just cost that kid a perfect game,'" ESPN, accessed August 15, 2013, http://scores.espn.go.com/mlb/recap?gameId=300602106.

9. Melissa Segura and Tom Verducci, "A Different Kind of Perfect," *Sports Illustrated,* June 14, 2010, 44.

10. For examples of this work, see: Maxwell E. McCombs and Donald R. Shaw, "The Agenda-Setting Function of the Mass Media," *Public Opinion Quarterly* 36 (1972): 176–187; Robert Entman, "Framing: Toward Clarification of a Fractured Paradigm," *Journal of Communication* 43 (1993): 51–60; James N. Druckman, "The Implications of Framing Effects for Citizen Competence," *Political Behavior* 23, no. 3 (September 2001): 225–256; and Anita Atwell Seate, Jake Harwood, and Erin Blecha, "'He was Framed!' Framing Criminal Behavior in Sports News," *Communication Research Reports* 27, no. 4 (October/December 2010): 343–354.

11. Jared W. Rutecki and Gregory W. Rutecki, "A Study of Media Impact on Public Opinion Regarding Performance Enhancement in Major League Baseball," *The Open Sports Sciences Journal* 3 (2010): 140.

12. Kenneth Burke, "Language as Action: Terministic Screens," in *On Symbols and Society*, ed. Joseph R. Gusfield (Chicago, IL: University of Chicago Press, 1989), 116.

13. Burke, "Language as Action," 121.

14. Stephen W. Littlejohn and Karen A. Foss, *Theories of Human Communication, Tenth Edition* (Long Grove, IL: Waveland Press, Inc., 2011), 344.

15. For a review of such studies, see Mark S. Allen, "A Systematic Review of Content Themes in Sport Attribution Research: 1954–2011," *International Journal of Sport and Exercise Psychology* 10, no. 1 (March 2012): 1–8.

16. Ro'i Zultan, Tobias Gerstenberg, and David A. Lagnado, "Finding Fault: Causality and Counterfactuals in Group Attributions," *Cognition* 125 (2012): 429.

17. Daniel L. Wann and Michael P. Schrader, "Controllability and Stability in the Self-Serving Attributions of Sport Spectators," *The Journal of Social Psychology* 140, no. 2 (2000): 161.

18. Tim Rees, David K. Ingledew, and Lew Hardy, "Attribution in Sport Psychology: Seeking Congruence Between Theory, Research, and Practice," *Psychology of Sport and Exercise* 6 (2005): 198.

19. For early research on this idea, see: Miron Zuckerman, "Attribution of Success and Failure Revisited, or The Motivational Bias Is Alive and Well in Attribution Theory," *Journal of Personality* 47, no. 2 (June 1979): 245–287. For its application to groups, see: Jack A. Goncalo and Michelle M. Duguid, "Hidden Consequences of the Group-Serving Bias: Causal Attributions and the Quality of Group Decision Making," *Organizational Behavior and Human Decision Processes* 107 (2008): 219–233.

20. Kenneth Burke, *Permanence and Change* (Berkley and Los Angeles: University of California Press, 1954), 16.

21. Leviticus 16:21 (New Revised Standard Version).

22. Howard Cooper, "Some Thoughts on 'Scapegoating' and Its Origins in Leviticus 16," *European Judaism* 41, no. 2 (October 2008): 112.

23. Hazel Davis, "The Process of Scapegoating," *Journal of Analytical Psychology* 32, no. 3 (July 1987): 286.

24. Gordon W. Russell, "Sport Riots: A Social-Psychological Review," *Aggression and Violent Behavior* 9 (2004): 354.

25. Robert M. Entman, "Framing: Toward Clarification of a Fractured Paradigm," *Journal of Communication* 43, no. 4 (Autumn 1993): 52.

26. Hsiang Iris Chyi and Maxwell McCombs, "Media Salience and the Process of Framing: Coverage of the Columbine School Shootings," *Journalism & Mass Communication Quarterly* 81, no. 1 (Spring 2004): 22.

27. Russell, "Sport Riots," 369.

28. *Catching Hell*, directed by Alex Gibney (2011; Bristol, CT: ESPN Films, 2011) DVD.

29. Joey Nowak, "Players Tab Joyce MLB's Best Umpire," MLB.com, August 18, 2011, http://mlb.mlb.com/news/article.jsp?ymd=20110818&content_id=23386260&vkey=news_mlb&c_id=mlb.

30. *Catching Hell*.

31. *Catching Hell*.

32. *Catching Hell*.

33. *Catching Hell*.

34. Cooper, "Some Thoughts on 'Scapegoating' and Its Origins in Leviticus 16," 112.

35. *Catching Hell*.

36. *Catching Hell*.

37. *Catching Hell*.

38. *Catching Hell*.

39. *Catching Hell*.

40. Armando Galarraga, Jim Joyce, and Daniel Paisner, *Nobody's Perfect: Two Men, One Call, and a Game for Baseball History* (New York: Atlantic Monthly Press, 2011), 213.

41. *Catching Hell*.

42. Jim Hawkins, "Nobody's Perfect," *The Oakland Press* (Pontiac, MI), June 3, 2010.

43. Galarraga, Joyce, and Paisner, *Nobody's Perfect*, 217.

44. Galarraga, Joyce, and Paisner, *Nobody's Perfect*, 228.

45. Amy K. Nelson, "A Perfect Storm," January 3, 2011, http://espn.go.com/video/clip?id=5985349.

46. Nelson, "A Perfect Storm."

47. John Berman, "Blown Call," *World News with Diane Sawyer,* ABC, originally aired June 3, 2010.

48. Galarraga, Joyce, and Paisner, *Nobody's Perfect*, 237.

49. George Will, "This Week," ABC, originally aired June 8, 2010.

50. Jeremy Schaap, "Bill Buckner: Behind the Bag," ESPN, originally aired October 25, 2011.

51. Thimios Zaharopoulos, "The News Framing of the 2004 Olympic Games," *Mass Communication & Society* 10, no. 2 (2007): 236.

52. James Briggs, "Detroit Tigers Pitcher Armando Galarraga Saves Jim Joyce from Steve Bartman's Curse," *The Oakland Press,* (Pontiac, MI), June 6, 2010.

53. *Catching Hell*.

54. Jon Meacham, "What an Umpire Could Teach BP," *Newsweek*, June 14, 2010, 2.

55. Meacham, "What an Umpire Could Teach BP," 2.

Chapter Nine

Eyewitnesses to TV Versions of Reality: The Relationship between Exposure to TV Crime Dramas and Perceptions of the Criminal Justice System

Susan H. Sarapin and Glenn G. Sparks

The "CSI effect" is one of the most frequently mentioned yet least understood media effects of the twenty-first century. Despite popular belief in this general media effect, most media scholars continue to refer to the phenomenon as anecdotal. The "CSI effect" is actually a misnomer because it implies the existence of a single effect that results from exposure to a single subgenre of crime-oriented television—forensics-oriented TV programs. The literature reveals that there are, in fact, numerous alleged "CSI effects." A variety of perspectives on this media phenomenon include the following purported consequences of heavy or frequent crime-oriented television (COTV) viewing:

- a heightened expectation of seeing hard, scientific evidence at trial[1]
- a greatly increased interest in forensic science as a career choice and subsequent increase in forensic science academic programs[2]
- an overburdening of actual forensic laboratories' personnel and financial assets around the United States, fueled by the need to run unnecessary and expensive tests to satisfy jurors' unrealistic expectations[3]
- an increase in acquittals due to the jurors' heightened levels of reasonable doubt[4]
- an increase in convictions due to jurors' beliefs in scientific evidence (especially DNA) offered by the prosecution as absolute and indisputable[5]
- the bestowing of the greatest credibility on expert witnesses specializing in forensic science[6]
- an increase in juror confidence in the ability to properly evaluate forensic evidence because of greater knowledge learned from TV[7]
- an overestimation of the accuracy of scientific evidence[8]

- an overestimation of real-world, crime-oriented facts, such as the prevalence of particular crimes or the frequency of murders committed by females[9]
- the adoption by criminals of countervailing steps to take to avoid leaving forensic evidence through which identification of them can be made, such as when a criminal cleans up the bloody scene of a crime with bleach, a rapist wears a condom to avoid leaving seminal fluid, a burglar wears gloves to avoid leaving fingerprints, and a murderer removes a victim's teeth to prevent identification of the corpse[10]

Media wonks, reality crime television talking heads, police and forensic investigators,[11] and characters in dramatic COTV programs speak about the CSI effect with reverence, apprehension, and sincere belief in its existence. Even real-world practicing attorneys give implicit credence to a widespread awareness of it by occasionally invoking the CSI effect in opening and closing arguments.[12] In this chapter, we use the term to refer quite specifically to the ostensible influence of fictional, crime-oriented TV viewing on viewers' estimations of the frequency of various "facts" and events within the world of criminal justice that are commonly represented on television as happening disproportionately more frequently than their actual occurrence.[13] These facts would include, but not be limited to, impressions about the frequency of particular crimes (e.g., murder), the frequency of crimes committed in a particular manner or place (e.g., murders committed by gun or rapes committed in a parking garage), the proportion of the work force consisting of attorneys and police, the percentage of kidnapped children who are murdered, the frequency of court trials in which forensic evidence is presented, and more. Testing these perceptions between infrequent (light) and frequent (heavy) viewers of COTV should offer insights into the plausibility of a demonstrable CSI effect.

This study is an attempt to quantify the CSI effect by gathering evidence to aid in determining whether frequent viewers of COTV would estimate the frequency of crime facts any differently from those who seldom or never view such programs. It would be difficult to imagine an environment in which such an effect could have a more consequential influence than the courtroom. It behooves us to look at the manner in which heavy viewing of COTV could translate into beliefs and behavior during an actual trial.

REAL-WORLD COURTROOMS: JURORS AND VIEWERS

In the American court system, jurors serve as fact finders. They are instructed and reminded repeatedly throughout the trial as to their obligations to listen to and look at evidence, that is, the facts of the case. While jurors are usually unaware of the real-world percentage of criminal cases that involve physical forensic evidence, tending to overestimate this statistic, they have learned from TV to expect to see at least some hard, scientific evidence.[14] According to Brent E. Turvey, a forensics investigation consultant/trainer, "A literature review conducted by [Frank] Horvath and [Robert T.] Meesig determined that physical evidence is used in less than 25 percent of the cases prosecuted in the United States, with the percentage in some regions dipping to less than 5 percent,"[15] and, on the basis of anecdotal reports from attorneys, forensic evidence is available on average in only 10–15 percent of criminal cases.[16]

For those who watch crime drama frequently as opposed to those who watch it rarely, there might be a measurably higher expectation of seeing incontrovertible hard, scientific evidence in support of a guilty or not-guilty verdict. In a real trial, the absence of forensic proof can have devastating consequences for those jurors whose consumption of TV crime drama is high and the amount of this type of proof does not comport with their expectations.

In addition, frequent COTV-viewing jurors' expectations might be related to the types of evidence they anticipate seeing. Jacqueline Connor and Anne Endress Skove explained that confusion could result when dramatic television portrayals of criminal scenarios deviate from the actual courtroom experience, which they routinely do.[17] Most notably, the authors claimed, the success of fictional dramas depends on showing certain inappropriate and unprofessional behavior during trial, such as the proffering of manifestly prejudicial, cumulative, or immaterial evidence, to intensify the emotion between the TV courtroom actors. This technique maintains the viewer's arousal, attentiveness, and involvement at high levels and obviates a switch to a competing channel. In the actual courtroom, this kind of evidence would be deemed inadmissible, oftentimes long before the jury takes its place in the jury box. Connor and Skove noted, "The reality is that the rules of evidence are complex and take months, if not years, to learn. Moreover, many procedures are derived from protections to the parties and to the cause of justice that have been developed over centuries. Conveying this level of complexity to an audience in under an hour, while maintaining the excitement and pace the audience has come to expect, is difficult."[18]

Therefore, one of the chief assumptions that gives rise to postulating about CSI effects is that those people who regularly watch crime-oriented dramatic television programs expect to see fingerprint, ballistics, gunshot residue, DNA, and other types of hard, scientific evidence significantly more often than do those who are infrequent or non-viewers of COTV because that tends to be the norm for this genre of television programming.[19] For example, if viewers' TV consumption had led them to believe that in most suicides, a suicide note is left at the scene, this appraisal could render frequent crime-drama-viewing jurors particularly vulnerable to certain arguments regarding the likely cause of a victim's death. In other words, if no suicide note had been discovered, then they might believe that the cause of death was not suicide. In short, jurors' expectations, attitudes, and other assessments about criminal events and proceedings must be anchored in some sort of essential belief about the real-world frequencies of events related to crime, no matter the source of those beliefs. However, when one examines the current literature pertaining to CSI effects, few studies focus on how COTV viewing might affect this knowledge.

Most of the several dozen peer-reviewed journal articles written about the CSI effect have been theoretical or speculative. Numerous magazine and newspaper articles have concentrated on the mere entertainment value of such a concept as TV shows having a potential influence on people's real lives. In comparison, only a small number of these many articles have been empirical. These investigations include studying the effect of COTV viewing on:

- participants' reasons for acquitting the defendant[20]
- participants' tendency to require forensic evidence as a condition for rendering a guilty verdict[21]
- participants' attitudes toward forensic evidence[22]
- participants' assessments of the reliability of forensic science expert testimony[23]
- the beliefs of law enforcement personnel and forensic scientists toward the existence of some sort of CSI effect[24]
- participants' verdicts in a circumstantial murder-case scenario.[25]

All of these potential effects are interesting and important, but seem to us to presume some media influence on more basic beliefs that have not yet been thoroughly documented. This study seeks to explore the evidence for a relationship between media exposure and some of these essential beliefs about the real-world facts pertaining to criminal justice.

George Gerbner and Larry Gross's media cultivation theory,[26] Albert Bandura's social cognitive theory (SCT),[27] and other studies of learning from fiction provide the theoretical underpinnings for this study. These lines of research assert the notion that television depictions serve as vicarious models of attitudes and behavior for viewers. Furthermore, the more frequently people attend to these television representations, the more closely their perceptions of real-world behavior mirror what they are exposed to on TV.

Television makes the most salient contributions, through the stories it tells, to viewer constructions of social reality.[28] Founding theorists summarized it concisely when they asserted, "The most general hypothesis of cultivation analysis is that those who spend more time 'living' in the world of television are more likely to see the 'real world' in terms of the images, values, portrayals, and ideologies that emerge through the lens of television."[29] Gerbner and Gross further explained, "The substance of the consciousness cultivated by TV is not so much specific attitudes and opinions as more basic assumptions about the 'facts' of life and standards of judgment on which conclusions are based."[30] Researchers founding their investigations on media cultivation must look at this fundamental assumption of the theory in which Gerbner posits that heavier TV viewers will overestimate the facts of life because television shows tend to exaggerate and embellish the facts, especially those related to crime and violence. Recently, scholars have devoted more attention to the specific mechanisms that may operate to produce any cultivation effect. Larry J. Shrum relies on the *accessibility principle* to explain cultivation effects.[31] According to this principle, people tend to make judgments about the world around them by drawing upon the information that comes to mind most quickly. Heavy TV viewers may find that this sort of information is the information derived from their TV viewing. Given this possibility, are the viewers of COTV significantly overestimating the facts about criminal activity and the criminal justice system? Are their perceptions of the facts significantly different from those of infrequent viewers of crime-oriented TV programming?

The well-known Bobo doll experiments with children contributed to Bandura's conceptualization of vicarious learning—learning by observing and imitating.[32] The stimulus was a televised movie, and the results confirmed Bandura's contention that positively reinforced aggressive acts can be learned even when the stimulus material is mediated through the television screen, and the observer does not actually receive the reward for the behavior. Bandura et al. stated, "In most televised programs, the 'bad guy' . . . amasses considerable social and material rewards through a series of aggressive maneuvers, whereas his punishment is generally delayed until just before the last commercial."[33] Considering the hundreds of daily opportunities children have to witness antisocial behavior vicariously, which frequently represent lessons in how crime occasionally does pay, "the terminal punishment of the villain may have a relatively weak inhibitory effect on the viewer."[34] Media cultivation theory adheres to certain assumptions about what are called "first-order effects." Shrum has defined first-order judgments concisely as "a person's perceptions about the prevalence of things"[35] and more fully as conclusions, which

> . . . require people to provide some sort of quantitative estimate regarding the prevalence of particular objects, people, or behaviors. Most often, these judgments require percentage estimates, such as the prevalence of particular occupations (e.g., percentage of the workforce employed as lawyers or police officers),

the prevalence of crime (e.g., percentage of the population that will be involved in a violent crime), or the assessment of personal risk (e.g., percentage estimate of one's own chances of being involved in a violent crime).[36]

Heavy and frequent exposure to this type of television programming could lead viewers to hold beliefs that emerge as first-order determinations, such as the belief that certain criminal acts occur more frequently than they actually do in the real world or the belief that too many criminals are insufficiently punished.

This essential principle regarding first-order effects has not yet been studied as the primary subject of interest in regard to the CSI effect. With so many different approaches taken in previous investigations, the CSI effect has proved itself to be a rather elusive phenomenon. This study asserts as its predominant warrant the potential impact of a heavy diet of televised crime-drama fare on the judgments of jurors in criminal trials. That is, how might these fundamental first-order beliefs about the prevalence of things in the real world derived from this genre of fictional TV programming manifest themselves in actual juror decision making.

LITERATURE ON MEDIA EXPOSURE AND ITS EFFECTS ON MOCK JURORS

American citizens, most of whom lack direct experience inside a courtroom,[37] obtain the bulk of their information about our justice system from a wide array of media channels and programming genres. It is on the basis of this content that they form their impressions of, and ultimately attitudes toward, the civil and criminal legal processes to which they have been exposed. Julian V. Roberts and Anthony N. Doob[38] reported a significant link between the reading of newspaper accounts of sentences in criminal trials and harsher attitudes toward sentencing due to an audience perception of judicial leniency. During *voir dire*, the process of questioning and selecting jurors, a defense attorney could become aware of a likely negative outcome for his or her client if a person being interviewed were to admit to being a frequent reader of newspapers. A juror like this could be expected to argue for recommending a stiffer sentence for a convicted defendant. For more than thirty years, pretrial publicity (PTP) has been a frequent focus of academic inquiry. Its effects have shown up as a source of unique patterns of behavior in the jury room.[39] Christine L. Ruva and Cathy McEvoy exposed sample groups to one of several versions of a trial, including a control-group report irrelevant to the stimulus trial account.[40] The authors found the mock jurors to be biased in their verdicts in the direction of the PTP. The researchers summarized their findings, reporting:

Even though the jurors in this study were admonished not to use information contained in the PTP when making decisions about the defendant's guilt, jurors who were exposed to negative PTP had nearly twice the conviction rates as did nonexposed jurors. These results are consistent with previous research demonstrating that PTP can bias juror decision-making by impeding jurors' ability to reach a verdict solely on the basis of evidence presented at trial.[41]

Perhaps more illuminating in regard to how media exposure actually works on its audiences to produce its effects, Ruva and McEvoy's mock jurors were unable to recall which information, or evidence, was presented through pretrial publicity and which was presented at trial.[42] This confounding of information that may or may not be factual, plus confusion surrounding the source and reliability of "evidence," could be a consequence of watching a steady diet of crime drama on television. A network and cable staple, the *Law & Order* franchise even advertises its stories as being "ripped from the headlines." Frequently, very little time elapses between an actual crime, the headline story sensationalized in print and on TV, and a one-hour, thinly veiled dramatic adaptation of it on television. Criminal and complicated civil cases can take years to come to trial. One can imagine the potential for juror bias and source-memory errors creeping into trial deliberations of those highly publicized cases.

Frequent viewing of crime-oriented television can affect potential jurors in many ways that impinge on the efficacy of our system of justice. Even some forty years ago, sociologists and psychologists were lamenting the state of the TV-viewing public's understanding of the structure and functioning of the nation's courts and jury system. Richard L. Henshel and Robert A. Silverman remarked, "Fictional drama about crime and criminal justice is ridden with formula and stereotype, its primary purpose being the satisfaction of the emotional needs of the viewing audience rather than the portrayal of crime in an authentic way. . . . All of which leads to pervasive and impressive ignorance among laymen . . ."[43] For those whose criminal-justice-system knowledge void is filled with fictional COTV fare, distorted perceptions of legal actors and procedures can be persuasive enough to exert a more consequential and disturbing power, that of influencing one's very trust in the system itself. Referring to some of the anticipated repercussions of the presumed CSI effect, political psychologist Tom Tyler reasoned, "[C]hanges in juror behavior may also reflect . . . increased mistrust of the government and the law."[44] Tyler pointed to a precipitous decline in Americans' confidence in our legal system with a concomitant increase in the proportion of adult US citizens who believe that the courts are too lenient on criminals.[45] In fact, a historical index of polls conducted by Gallup revealed a steep drop in public confidence in the US Supreme Court, from a high of 25 percent in the middle of 1997 reporting a "great deal" of confidence to just 14 percent by the middle of 2007.[46] In one decade, public trust in this institution fell almost 50 percent. Today, that figure sits at 13 percent, with a high of 21 percent of Americans reporting very little confidence in the Supreme Court. Tyler identified what he considered to be one of the most troubling possible consequences of frequent exposure to crime drama—a decreasing trust in legal authorities.[47] The lower level of trust and confidence in the justice system and its actors, including lawyers and judges, has resulted primarily in the restricted latitude of discretion for judges performing their sentencing function. Three-strikes legislation and sentencing guidelines have greatly constrained independent judicial pragmatism and wisdom. Tyler pointed to a secondary focus on the police, which has arisen from public perceptions of a greater propensity for police officers to engage in racial profiling, planting of evidence, unnecessary use of force, and other questionable and even illegal behavior often presented in fictional crime drama on television.[48]

Specifically addressing the importance of this study's findings about the public's perceptions of crime and the criminal justice system, Tyler opined: "People need to feel comfortable with the verdict reached, even when the 'truth' of the case cannot be known. The processes of the trial build trust and confidence in the state and the prosecution, leading the community to feel comfortable with the uncertainty inherent in the verdict."[49] People with no direct experience with the justice system form impressions of crime, criminals, crime investigation, justice, the courts, and their legal actors from television. These perceptions then shape attitudes and beliefs about certain crimes and penalties, the police, lawyers, judges, and juries, all of which form the basis of public confidence in or distrust of these entities. These same attitudes also shape the public's willingness to serve on juries, to perform other civic activities such as voting, and even to obey the laws of the land. Unfortunately, what we see on television is a distorted picture of our institutions and agents of justice and those who are brought to justice—both in the frequency of and motivation for certain behavior.[50] This is not to say that everything we see about crime on television is inaccurate. However, when we see a distinctly disproportionate number of rapes by strangers on the small screen than what is the case in real life, it would likely make it more difficult for a juror who is a frequent viewer of COTV to believe that a woman was raped by a male she had known for a long time. This is the type of first-order effect that can emerge from a skewed representation of the real world on TV. The attitudes and beliefs of frequent viewers of fictional crime drama on television would tend to mirror the TV world.

THE CURRENT STUDY

Examples such as the one above about stranger rape and predictions of other potential juror behavior arise from the assumptions incorporated in Gerbner's media cultivation concept. Originally, cultivation theory presumed effects based upon overall TV viewing and not viewing of specific genres; however, over the past decade or so, media cultivation has been extended to apply to niche genres of programming, such as crime drama and soap opera. Helena Bilandzic and Patrick Rössler reviewed this new approach, and found that not all of the genre-specific studies of cultivation effects adhered to the fundamental cultivation hypothesis, which posits the hyperbolized inferences about the real world "cultivated" by the long-term viewing of fictional television.[51] Nevertheless, our initial presumption was that with respect to COTV, we would find evidence that was congruent with the media cultivation hypothesis.

> H1: In contrast to those who seldom view COTV, frequent viewers will tend to provide overestimations of statistics pertaining to the world of criminal justice.

Another variable of interest comes from the findings of studies of juror characteristics that may be predictive of verdict in a trial, that is, the variable of gender. Carol J. Mills wrote that a "juror's sex is the variable most often correlated with his or her verdict."[52] Furthermore, she reported that females are commonly considered more empathic and lenient, and thus less likely than males to render verdicts of conviction.[53] In a similar vein, John K. Cochran and Beth A. Sanders searched the literature on gender differences as they related to attitudes toward the death penalty.[54] The numerous studies they examined consistently showed that men were significantly more likely than women to favor the death penalty. The authors noted:

> [F]emale proponents of capital punishment tended to be white, married, political conservatives, had high incomes, came from middle- and upper-class backgrounds, and perceived that the courts were too lenient with criminals. When the influences of these common and gender-specific correlates of death penalty support were controlled, the gender effect remained robust and statistically significant.[55]

Cochran and Sanders measured a broad array of potential determinants of an individual's perspective on the death penalty and examined sex differences for each variable, including

- value orientations
- socialization practices
- traditional social norms and roles
- status inequalities
- feminist consciousness
- life experiences/life chances[56]

Of particular relevance to the current study is the last variable on the authors' list, life experiences/life chances. As part of their assessment of this possible discrepancy between males and females, Cochran and Sanders measured their respondents' "levels of exposure to the mass media, specifi-cally, the average number of hours per week that they watched television."[57] Cochran and Sanders found a significant effect of mass media exposure on women's lack of support for the death penalty. In other words, the more fe-males were exposed to television, the greater was their opposition to the death penalty. So, with the gender effect shown to be so enduring after controlling for dozens of variables, as was the case in the Cochran and Sanders study,[58] we found it reasonable to pose the following research question:

> RQ1: Will gender interact with COTV viewing such that one gender will be significantly more likely to overestimate statistics pertaining to the world of criminal justice than the other gender at a higher level of COTV viewing?

METHOD

Over the course of two months during the summer of 2009, a total of 709 randomly selected residential phone numbers were dialed in a cross-sectional, random-sample survey design. A total of 103 jury-eligible adults from a small, Midwestern college town agreed to be interviewed as subjects in this study. The interviews posed questions about perceptions of the world of criminal justice as well as questions about exposure to various TV programs. Not all respondents answered every question, which explains the varying N in some analyses. There were sixty-nine females and thirty-four males, ranging in age from twenty to ninety-seven with a median age of sixty-three years and a mean age of 62.28 years. From 2000 to 2010, the median age of the Ameri-can population rose to 37.2 years.[59] Obviously, the age of our sample skewed older than that of the general population. This is most likely due to the trend toward giving up landline telephony, which was used in this study, in favor of wireless connections. This change in communication technology use is more common among the younger generations.[60] Additionally, it is more likely that older, retired people would be at home to answer the telephone. In the current study, age was significantly associated with only income, political leanings, and the frequency of general-TV viewing, all three of which were controlled in the regression that examined the contribution of COTV viewing in over-estimates of crime-related facts. None of these was a significant predictor of overestimating the real-world statistics about crime.

The stimulus instrument in this study was a questionnaire consisting of six-teen questions, some of which pertained to perceptions of criminal behavior, the percentage of the work force composed of lawyers, and the percentage of the work force composed of police. Answers were recorded in percentage fig-ures on a scale ranging from 0 to 100. This 100-point scale did not constrain responses to merely a 5- or 7-level scale. Another section of the questionnaire was a list of questions asking for demographic information (gender, age, level of education, crime victimization experience, etc.). Finally, participants were queried about the amount of their overall television viewing and the amount of their fictional and nonfictional crime-TV viewing. The questionnaire took from twelve–twenty-five minutes to complete over the telephone. Media use and political leanings were measured in the following ways.

MAJOR MEASURES

Crime-Oriented TV Viewing (COTV)

To quantify the respondents' levels of fictional crime-oriented TV viewing, the names of several television programs were recited one by one. Programs such as *Law & Order*, *CSI*, *Cold Case*, and *NCIS* represented this category. Participants indicated for each show the number of times per week they normally watch it. Next, the respondents were asked if there were any other crime-drama shows they watched and the total number of times those were watched in a typical week. Following the tenet of media cultivation theory that specifies effects for exposure to "fiction" programming, the number of weekly instances of dramatic or fictional COTV viewing was the only measure represented by the COTV variable. The scores on this continuous quantitative variable ranged from 0 times a week to fifty-eight times a week. Crime reality programming was *not* included in the COTV variable.

Crime-Reality TV Viewing

To date, this is a category that has not been parceled out of the crime-TV viewing variable in previous studies of the CSI effect. Crime reality is a genre characterized by dramatizations of real crime scenarios, and, as such, is inconsistent with the assumptions of media cultivation, which calls for fictional representations. Even the production values of crime-reality programs are distinctly different from crime fiction. In her analysis of crime-reality TV content, Kathleen Curry called it "a voyeuristic, video-cam perspective" of crime in the streets.[61] Although this genre is not what Gerbner had in mind, it is about crime and it is dramatic, qualities that could invite academics to deem it persuasive about the "facts" of crime and the criminal justice system through a form of mediated socialization. When this type of program content is not considered a distinct mediated format, it could manifest a confounding influence during the process of teasing out potential effects from fictional COTV. Analogous to the COTV measure, the crime-reality viewing variable was represented by programs such as *Forensic Files*, *48 Hours Mystery*, *Crime 360*, and *The First 48*. Consumption of this TV genre was measured in the same manner as the COTV variable.

General-TV Viewing

The overall TV-viewing measure was drawn from the respondents' self-reported amount of viewing of all genres of programming, in hours and fractions of hours, on average weekdays added to their reports of total Saturday and Sunday routine hourly viewing. The general-TV viewing measure was calculated by subtracting the amount of COTV viewing and crime-reality viewing from the overall viewing measure.

Politics

Americans' political views often have been found to correlate with certain attitudes toward the criminal justice system, such as support of or opposition to longer and harsher sentences for specific crimes,[62] advocacy of or opposition to the death penalty,[63] and more. Where their political leanings fall on the liberal-to-conservative continuum could have an impact on their judgments and sentence recommendations as jurors. Gerbner, Gross, Michael Morgan, and Nancy Signorielli examined the relationships between respondents' self-designated political views and their amount of television viewing.[64] Finding support for their "contention that television is fundamentally different from other media,"[65] their results showed "heavy viewers are consistently more likely to present themselves as moderate,"[66] and, "heavy viewers are generally less likely to choose either the liberal or the conservative label."[67] Of course, it is important to remember that Gerbner et al. were exploring overall television content—not the genre-specific programming that this study investigated. Considering that the authors concluded, "the amount of time people spend watching television relates systematically and consistently to how they position themselves along the liberal-moderate-conservative political continuum,"[68] a test of political views and COTV consumption within the framework of perceptions of criminal justice facts would be highly recommended. Participants' political leanings were assessed on a 5-point, Likert-type scale from 0 to 4, ranging from "very liberal," coded as 0, to "very conservative," coded as 4.

RESULTS

Upon review of the mean estimates of the sixteen questions about the facts of crime, a scale reliability test was run on all of the items to examine them for their usefulness as a composite index. Ultimately, a thirteen-item index was constructed to maximize internal consistency and reliability. The correlations between the individual items on the index and the composite index ranged from .344 to .607. Cronbach's alpha for the index was .74. For convenience, we refer to the thirteen-item measure as the index of Estimated Crime-Oriented Statistics, the *ECOS* index.

Hypothesis 1 predicted that, in contrast to those who seldom view COTV, frequent viewers would tend to provide overestimations of statistics pertaining to the world of criminal justice. Upon review of the raw-data descriptives (see Table 9.1), it was obvious that this was the case. The mean figures for the entire sample were higher than the real-world statistics for all but three items on the ECOS Index:

- the percentage of murder trials ending in a guilty verdict
- the percentage of murders in which a gun was used
- the percentage of rapes reported to the police.

Estimations for the latter two crimes were, in fact, quite close to the actual statistic. When attention is focused on the two separate COTV viewing groups, there is one set of estimates that stands out among all others—the averages for the respondents' perception of the percentage of all deaths (for any reason whatsoever) in the US due to murder. This index item exhibited the greatest disparity between the infrequent viewers and frequent viewers of COTV, a result that is consistent with the fact that portrayals of violence

Table 9.1. COTV Viewers Statistics

Scale Item	Real-World†	Entire Sample (Mean)	COTV Non-Viewers (N = 33) (Mean)	COTV Viewers (N = 70) (Mean)
% Work Force Made up of Lawyers	0.45	14.75	10.28	16.82
% Work Force Made up of Police	0.64	16.27	12.16	18.18
% Kidnapped Children Murdered	<1.00	36.49	24.75	42.03
% All Deaths Due to Murder	0.80	19.79	10.38	24.23
% All Murder Victims Who Are Females	21.70	43.96	36.73	47.37
% Murder Trials with Guilty Verdict	80.00	57.52	56.15	58.17
% Murder Trials with Scientific Evidence	20.00	65.49	61.36	67.43
% Murders in which a Gun Is Used	66.90	64.79	67.97	63.29
% Rapes Reported to Police	40.00	38.72	36.38	39.79
% Rapes Committed by Stranger to Victim	27.00	37.25	28.85	41.21
% Rapes in which a Weapon Is Used	11.00	56.88	52.36	59.04
% Rapes that Occur at Night	67.00	71.50	73.18	70.71
% Rapes that Occur in a Parking Garage	8.00	23.01	19.88	24.45

† Sources of real-world statistics include the US Department of Labor Bureau of Labor Statistics, National Vital Statistics Report, Federal Bureau of Investigation, and the US Department of Justice Bureau of Justice Statistics.

on television—and particularly depictions of murder—are ubiquitous.[69] The frequent viewers of COTV estimated this statistic at close to 2.5 times the response of the infrequent viewers. A two–tailed, independent samples *t*-test was conducted to check for significance of the difference on this one item. The results showed that heavy COTV viewers were significantly more likely than light viewers to overestimate the percent of all US deaths due to murder, $t(90.13) = -3.655, p < .001$.

As seen in Table 9.2, which shows the correlation matrix for all study variables, including the ECOS Index, the Pearson correlation between COTV viewing and the index was .242, $r^2 = .059, p = .008$. This means that COTV viewing accounted for 5.9 percent of the variance in the dependent variable, the index of perceptions of crime and the criminal justice system, a small-to-medium-sized effect. Hypothesis 1 was supported.

Research Question 1 asked whether gender would interact with COTV viewing such that one gender would be significantly more likely than the other to overestimate statistics pertaining to criminal events at a higher frequency of COTV viewing. The influence of gender on the results is indisputable. For the entire sample, females' mean estimates on the thirteen index items were higher than those of the males in every case but one (see Table 9.3).

When the sample of males (Table 9.4) and females (Table 9.5) was broken down to show frequent and infrequent COTV viewers in each group, it became clear that differences between the two viewing groups were more likely to show up for the female viewers. Table 9.6 reports the descriptives for the variables used in the analysis of Research Question 1. A two-tailed, independent samples *t*-test was run between the male scores and the female scores on the ECOS Index. Females scored significantly higher than males, $t(96) = 4.05, p < 0.001$, indicating that females were significantly more likely than males to overestimate crime-related statistics. Looking specifically at the interaction, two more two-tailed, independent samples *t*-tests were run between male frequent and infrequent COTV viewers and between female frequent and infrequent COTV viewers on the ECOS Index. For males, there was no significant difference between the perceptions of heavy and light COTV viewers, $t(29) = -.540, p = .593$. For females, however, heavy COTV viewers were significantly more likely than light viewers to overestimate statistics associated with crime and the criminal justice system, $t(65) = -2.659$, $p = .010$. The results for Research Question 1 reinforced the findings of the extant literature and confirmed the authors' expectations that gender would have an influence on first-order perceptions and that heavy or frequent viewing of fictional crime drama would further accentuate the gender differences, as it did here for females.

Table 9.2. Correlation Matrix for Study Variables*

	Education	Sex	Income	Age	Politics	Neigh. Crime	Gen. TV	Crime-Reality TV	COTV
1. Education	—								
2. Sex	-.257**	—							
3. Income	.457****	-.138	—						
4. Age	-.188	-.004	-.271**	—					
5. Politics	-.065	-.027	.015	.213*	—				
6. Neigh. Crime	-.246*	.126	-.240**	.001	-.013	—			
7. General TV	-.296***	.134	-.295***	.291***	-.035	-.112	—		
8. Crime-Reality TV	-.264**	-.071	-.314***	-.071	-.110	.172	.006	—	
9. COTV	-.321***	-.089	-.280**	.076	-.005	.024	.078	.547****	—
10. ECOS Index	-.421****	.382****	-.283**	.025	-.053	.342***	.201	.111	.242*

* $p < .05$ for every variable
** $p < .01$
*** $p < .005$
**** $p < .001$

Table 9.3.   Means for ECOS Index

Scale Item	Entire Sample, Males			Entire Sample, Females		
	N	M	SD	N	M	SD
% Work Force Made up of Lawyers	33	7.17	8.06	68	18.43	14.65
% Work Force Made up of Police	33	7.17	5.91	68	20.69	15.98
% Kidnapped Children Murdered	34	18.09	21.97	69	45.56	31.39
% All Deaths Due to Murder	34	9.29	14.66	69	24.96	22.70
% All Murder Victims that Are Females	34	39.21	18.07	69	46.30	22.15
% Murder Trials with Guilty Verdict	34	60.12	23.94	69	56.25	21.41
% Murder Trials with Scientific Evidence	34	62.00	25.47	69	67.20	24.94
% Murders in which a Gun Is Used	34	62.00	20.99	69	66.16	19.22
% Rapes Reported to Police	33	36.03	18.80	69	40.00	18.54
% Rapes Committed by Stranger to Victim	34	36.15	18.73	69	37.80	21.40
% Rapes in which a Weapon Is Used	34	48.91	25.62	68	60.87	23.46
% Rapes that Occur at Night	34	71.03	18.74	69	71.74	17.06
% Rapes that Occur in a Parking Garage	33	20.77	19.85	69	24.09	15.81

In order to explore the possibilities of third-variable explanations in the present study, multiple linear regression analysis was conducted to determine whether crime-drama TV viewing continued to be related to the overestimation of the items of crime-related facts—even after controlling for a host of other possible contributing variables. Table 9.7 shows the results of the regression that examined the contribution of COTV viewing in overestimation of crime-related facts after controlling for a number of other independent variables, which are reported in their order of entry into the regression. After the influence of seven other independent variables was considered, COTV viewing, the independent variable of interest, was still a statistically significant predictor of the dependent variable, $b = 2.810$, $t(81) = 1.981$, $p = .05$. The R^2-*change* for COTV viewing was .029, indicating that COTV viewing accounted for an extra 2.9 percent of the variance in the estimation of crime-oriented statistics after controlling for the influence of seven other variables.

General-TV viewing was not a statistically significant predictor of the dependent variable, $b = .407$, $t(82) = .389$, $p = .70$. Similarly, crime-reality viewing had no significant effect on the ECOS Index, $b = -1.740$, $t(82) = -.483$, $p = .63$. The interaction of general-TV viewing and sex also had no effect on perceptions of crime and the criminal justice system. However, the interaction of COTV viewing and gender, a variable entered in the last block of the regression, did show up as a significant predictor of the

Table 9.4. ECOS Index Items by COTV Viewing for Male Respondents

Scale Item	Actual Statist. (%)	COTV Non-Viewers, Males			COTV Viewers, Males		
		N	M	SD	N	M	SD
% Lawyers in Work Force	0.45	14	8.00	8.05	19	6.55	8.23
% Police in Work Force	0.64	14	7.57	6.70	19	6.87	5.44
% Kidnapped Children Murdered	<1.00	14	18.22	24.03	20	18.00	21.05
% All Deaths Due to Murder	0.80	14	5.71	5.77	20	11.80	18.29
% All Murder Victims Who Are Females	21.70	14	33.79	18.53	20	43.00	17.20
% Murder Trials Ending in Guilty Verdict	80.00	14	58.43	27.65	20	61.30	21.65
% Murder Trials with Scientific, Forensic Evidence	20.00	14	55.36	26.05	20	66.65	24.64
% Murders in which a Gun Is Used	66.90	14	61.64	23.63	20	62.25	19.57
% Rapes Reported to Police	40.00	13	36.23	20.83	20	35.90	17.91
% Rapes Committed by Stranger to Victim	27.00	14	31.93	20.58	20	39.10	17.24
% Rapes in which a Weapon Is Used	11.00	14	50.21	28.70	20	48.00	23.97
% Rapes that Occur at Night	67.00	14	72.86	23.51	20	69.75	15.09
% Rapes that Occur in a Parking Garage	8.00	13	15.15	15.92	20	24.43	21.63

Table 9.5. ECOS Index Items by COTV Viewing for Female Respondents

Scale Item	Actual Statist. (%)	COTV Non-Viewers, Females			COTV Viewers, Females		
		N	M	SD	N	M	SD
% Lawyers in Work Force	0.45	18	12.06	11.72	50	20.72	15.01
% Police in Work Force	0.64	18	15.72	15.04	50	22.48	16.07
% Kidnapped Children Murdered	<1.00	19	29.55	31.07	50	51.64	29.59
% All Deaths Due to Murder	0.80	19	13.82	18.70	50	29.20	22.81
% All Murder Victims Who Are Females	21.70	19	38.89	20.60	50	49.12	22.26
% Murder Trials Ending in Guilty Verdict	80.00	19	54.47	17.63	50	56.92	22.80
% Murder Trials with Scientific, Forensic Evidence	20.00	19	65.79	25.78	50	67.74	24.85
% Murders in which a Gun Is Used	66.90	19	72.63	16.95	50	63.70	19.61
% Rapes Reported to Police	40.00	19	36.47	17.97	50	41.34	18.75
% Rapes Committed by Stranger to Victim	27.00	19	26.58	15.00	50	42.06	22.03
% Rapes in which a Weapon Is Used	11.00	19	53.95	23.90	50	63.55	22.97
% Rapes that Occur at Night	67.00	19	73.42	16.75	50	71.10	17.30
% Rapes that Occur in a Parking Garage	8.00	19	23.11	15.17	50	24.46	16.18

Table 9.6. Study Variables Related to Gender

Statistic	Frequent COTV for Entire Sample	Infrequent COTV for Entire Sample	All Males on ECOS Index	All Females on ECOS Index	Male Frequent COTV Viewers on ECOS Index	Male Infrequent COTV Viewers on ECOS Index	Female Frequent COTV Viewers on ECOS Index	Female Infrequent COTV Viewers on ECOS Index
M	24.23	10.38	470.25	580.33	478.87	456.59	605.06	513.00
SD	22.90	15.06	110.59	131.28	86.03	144.61	127.71	119.59
N	70	33	31	67	19	12	49	18

Table 9.7.   Hierarchical Regression of the ECOS Index‡

Dependent Variable: Estimated Crime-Oriented Statistics (ECOS) Index					
	B	*SE(B)*	*ß*	*t*	*Sig.*	*R²Δ*
Block 1						.278
Education	-7.913	9.301	-.096	-.851	.40	
Sex	92.154	27.525	.323	3.348	.00	
Income	-10.754	10.050	-.115	-1.070	.29	
Politics	-8.874	11.569	-.067	-.767	.45	
Block 2						.066
Neighborhood Crime Level	46.344	14.376	.299	3.224	ᵃ.00	
Block 3						.009
General-TV Viewing	.407	1.046	.048	.389	.70	
Crime-Reality Viewing	-1.740	3.603	-.050	-.483	.63	
Block 4						.029
COTV Viewing	2.810	1.419	.194	1.981	.05†	
Block 5						.000
General-TV X Sex Interaction	.444	2.579	.020	.172	.86	
Block 6						.044
COTV X Sex Interaction	7.173	2.918	.237	2.458	.02	

‡ 2-tailed *p* values: †*p* = .05, all other *p* < .05; A correlation was computed between frequency levels (on a 5-point scale of 0–4) of participants' estimates of crime in their neighborhoods and scores on the ECOS Index. Results indicate that respondents who estimated higher crime levels in their neighborhoods were also more likely to overestimate crime-oriented statistics, *r* = .342, *p* < 0.005. A correlation between neighborhood crime levels and COTV was not significant, *r* = .024, *p* = .810.

overestimation of crime-related statistics, $b = 7.173$, $t(79) = 2.458$, $p = .02$, and it was responsible for an additional 4.4 percent of the variance in the dependent variable. The results support the notion that it is COTV viewing alone and not general-TV viewing or crime-reality TV that is related to overestimates of crime-related facts.

THE PROBLEM OF CONFOUNDING VARIABLES IN CULTIVATION ANALYSIS

In cultivation analyses, relationships between a given dependent variable and TV viewing often have been shown to be a function of third variables. That is to say, demographic, or naturally occurring[70] variables like gender, education, place of residence, etc. are frequently associated with both TV viewing and the dependent variable under study. Consequently, relationships that are initially construed as evidence of a cultivation effect can sometimes be best explained by third variables. In other words, these variables can be seen as "confounding" the relationships. Furthermore, the independent variables, themselves, may be interrelated. These possible problems are always present in cultivation analysis because the tradition in this research is to embrace the survey method over the experimental method. While this methodological choice follows logically from the theory's thesis that cultivation processes occur over a long period of time and cannot be detected by experiments, it also makes it virtually impossible to arrive at unequivocal conclusions about the causal process between variables.

L. J. Shrum, Robert S. Wyer, and Thomas C. O'Guinn sought to address the issues of causality and the correlational nature of cultivation studies by employing priming techniques in two experiments.[71] Shrum et al. posited the notion that television is a "natural prime."[72] The authors stated that their procedures were informed by the assumptions advanced by Amos Tversky and Daniel Kahneman as encompassed in their availability heuristic. Shrum et al. explained: "[T]elevision viewing can increase the accessibility of instances of those things that are often encountered in television programs (e.g., crime and violence). Accessibility may be enhanced by the frequency and recency of viewing these instances, as well as the vividness and detail in which the instances are encoded into memory."[73] The researchers' experiments dealt with source- and relation-priming conditions. They expected to discover whether making source details salient would be sufficient to lead respondents to discount the information they obtained from television and thus adjust their perceptions to account for the influence of television content. Shrum et al. predicted, "The priming conditions should have an effect only if the primed concept (television) is one that persons normally use as a basis for judgments."[74] The results supported the fundamental assumption of media cultivation, that television viewing exerts a causal influence on social reality judgments rather than serving as a mere correlate of social perceptions.

DISCUSSION

The primary purpose of this study was to explore one of the many different CSI effects. In this case, we investigated the notion that regular viewing of crime-oriented programs might be associated with overestimates of facts pertaining to real crime. Cultivation theory would interpret such an association as evidence of a first-order media effect.

Overall, the data supported the hypothesis that heavy COTV viewing was associated with the tendency to overestimate facts about the world of criminal justice. Of course, one problem always present in a survey investigation is the problem of interpreting statistical associations as evidence for causal relationships. Rather than heavier COTV-viewing cultivating a tendency to overestimate real-world crime facts, it could be the case that, for whatever reason, those who already have a tendency to overestimate real-world crime are consequently motivated to watch more crime-oriented TV programming. While the method employed here cannot determine a causal direction between the two variables, we did attempt to address the third-variable problem by introducing seven other possible third variables that might play a role in the relationship of interest. The regression analysis that tested the impact of these seven variables revealed that even after considering their collective impact (explaining 35 percent of the variance in the dependent variable), a positive relationship persisted between COTV and the tendency to overestimate facts about crime. While it is always possible that some unmeasured variable could account for this relationship, until such a variable is identified in future research, it appears as if the relationship posited in Hypothesis 1 is supported. The best way to address this limitation in future studies is to employ a longitudinal survey design that is capable of examining the causal direction between the two variables.

This investigation into the CSI effect had other limitations as well. Our sample was drawn from a small Midwestern city with a relatively low crime rate. Had a more cosmopolitan sample been used, results might have differed. In addition, the town's population of people of color is small and not demographically congruent with national norms. This fact made testing the influence of race or ethnicity problematic. A larger random sample or one drawn randomly from a city with a more nationally representative number of non-white residents might attenuate this particular limitation. Another limitation of this study to be considered is the decreasing use of telephone landlines in homes and apartments occupied by younger residents as cell phones and less expensive voice-over Internet protocol applications replace them. Age did not play a significant role in this study; however, if a larger number of younger respondents had been included, perhaps the results would have been different.

CONCLUSION

Henshel and Silverman suggested that social researchers could learn so much more about criminality and justice in society were we to simply recognize that most people are completely unaware of the official, hard facts of crime.[75] They called for a shift in the analysis of things criminal "away from 'what *is*' toward 'what the relevant actors *think* is.'"[76] Although Henshel and Silverman believed that individuals certainly engage in purposeful, rational, and meaningful behavior, they appreciated the fact that people also succumb, at times, to the influence of social stimuli, which can elicit a less realistically grounded, less informed, perhaps even irrational, type of behavior. In addition to this concept, they wrote, "The 'Thomas theorem,' as Merton has called it, the idea that 'situations defined as real are real in their consequences,' is pregnant with intimations of later elaborations on the significance of individual and socially mediated perception."[77] For example, a juror's decision could be made on the basis of what his or her own *picture* of reality is, no matter where that picture came from and irrespective of the objective reality, and yet the verdict itself is real and has real repercussions. That is precisely why we should seek to discover what the public's perceptions are, where they originate, and which processes shape them.

The findings of this study support the possible existence of a particular CSI effect involving an impact of viewing on overestimations of facts about the world of criminal justice. Additional studies are certainly warranted in order to shed more light on what sorts of CSI effects might really exist—and which ones might be only illusory or mythical. By first adhering to the principles of media cultivation and social cognitive theory, further research into the CSI effect can lead to improved explication of the mechanism(s) by which crime-oriented programming is posited to impose its influence. In this way, researchers may be able to find evidence pertaining to crime-drama viewing's ultimate hypothesized effect on jury verdicts.

NOTES

1. N. J. Schweitzer and Michael J. Saks, "The CSI Effect: Popular Fiction About Forensic Science Affects the Public's Expectations About Real Forensic Science," *Jurimetrics* 47 (2006), 357–364.

2. Stefan Lovgren, "'CSI Effect' Is Mixed Blessing for Real Crime Labs," *National Geographic News*, September 23, 2004, accessed December 16, 2013, http://news.nationalgeographic.com/news/2004/09/0923_040923_csi.html

3. Sheila L. Stephens, "The CSI Effect on Real Crime Labs." *New England Law Review* 41 (2006), 591.

4. Simon Cole and Rachel Dioso-Villa, "CSI and Its Effects: Media, Juries, and the Burden of Proof," *New England Law Review* 41, no. 3 (2007); Simon A. Cole and Rachel Dioso-Villa, "Should Judges Worry about the 'CSI effect'?" *Court Review* 47 (2011), 20–102.

5. Cole and Dioso-Villa, "CSI and Its effect"; Cole and Dioso-Villa. "Should Judges Worry"; Mark Godsey and Marie Alou, "She Blinded Me with Science: Wrongful Convictions and the 'Reverse CSI-Effect,'" *Texas Wesleyan Law Review* 17, no. 4 (2011), 481–498.

6. Godsey and Alou, "She Blinded Me with Science."

7. Laura Huey. "'I've Seen this on CSI': Criminal Investigators' Perceptions About the Management of Public Expectations in the Field," *Crime, Media, Culture* 6, no. 1 (2010), 49–68; J. Herbie DiFonzo and Ruth C. Stern, "Devil in a White Coat: The

Temptation of Forensic Evidence in the Age of CSI," *New England Law Review* 41 (2007), 503–532.

8. Tom R. Tyler, "Viewing CSI and the Threshold of Guilt: Managing Truth and Justice in Reality and Fiction," *The Yale Law Journal* (2006), 1076.

9. Christopher J. Ferguson, "Violent Crime Research," in *Violent Crime: Clinical and Social Implications,* ed. Christopher J. Ferguson (London: Sage Publications, 2010), 3–18.

10. Ferguson. "Violent Crime Research;" Rowan Hooper, "Television Shows Scramble Forensic Evidence," *New Scientist* (2005), 1; Joe Milicia, "Criminals Taking Tips from TV Crime Shows," *USA Today*, January 30, 2006.

11. Veronica Stinson, Marc W. Patry, and Steven M. Smith, "The CSI Effect: Reflections from Police and Forensic Investigators," *The Canadian Journal of Police and Security Services* 5, no. 3 (2007), 1–9.

12. Kit R. Roane and Dan Morrison, "The CSI Effect," *US News & World Report* 138 (2005), 48–54.

13. Mary Beth Oliver, "Portrayals of Crime, Race, and Aggression in 'Reality-Based' Police Shows: A Content Analysis," *Journal of Broadcasting & Electronic Media* 38, no. 2 (1994), 179–192.

14. Brent E. Turvey, "The Role of Criminal Profiling in the Development of Trial Strategy," *Knowledge Solutions Library,* November, 1997, accessed December 16, 2013, http://www.corpus-delicti.com/Trial_Strategy.html.

15. Turvey, "The Role of Criminal Profiling."

16. Turvey, "The Role of Criminal Profiling."

17. Jacqueline Connor and Anne Endress Skove, "Dial 'M' for Misconduct: The Effect of Mass Media and Pop Culture on Juror Expectations," in *Future Trends in State Courts* (Williamsburg, VA: National Center for State Courts, 2004).

18. Connor and Skove, "Dial 'M' for Misconduct," 2.

19. Schweitzer and Saks, "The CSI Effect."

20. Kimberlianne Podla, "CSI Effect: Exposing the Media Myth," *Fordham Intellectual Property, Media & Entertainment Law Journal* 16 (2005), 429–65.

21. Honorable Donald E. Shelton, Gregg Barak, and Young S. Kim, "A Study of Juror Expectations and Demands Concerning Scientific Evidence: Does the 'CSI Effect' Exist?" *Vanderbilt Journal of Entertainment & Technology Law* 9, no. 2 (2007), 331–68.

22. Stinson, Patry, and Smith, "The CSI Effect."

23. Schweitzer and Saks. "The CSI Effect."

24. Stinson, Patry, and Smith, "The CSI Effect."

25. Susan H. Sarapin and Glenn G. Sparks, "The Viewing of TV Crime Drama and the 'CSI Effect': There's a Verdict Hanging in the Balance," paper presented at the National Communication Association Annual Convention, San Francisco, CA, November 13, 2010.

26. George Gerbner and Larry Gross, "Living with Television: The Violence Profile," *Journal of Communication* 26, no. 2 (1976), 172–94.

27. Albert Bandura, "Social Cognitive Theory of Mass Communication," *Media Psychology* 3, no. 3 (2001), 265–299.

28. Helena Bilandzic, "The Perception of Distance in the Cultivation Process: A Theoretical Consideration of the Relationship Between Television Content, Process-

ing Experience, and Perceived Distance," *Communication Theory* 16, no. 3 (2006), 333–355.

29. Gerbner and Gross, "Living with Television," 175.

30. Gerbner and Gross, "Living with Television," 175.

31. Larry J. Shrum, "Media Consumption and Perceptions of Social Reality: Effects and Underlying Processes," *Media Effects: Advances in Theory and Research* 2 (2002), 69–95.

32. Albert Bandura, Dorothea Ross, and Sheila A. Ross, "Vicarious Reinforcement and Imitative Learning," *The Journal of Abnormal and Social Psychology* 67, no. 6 (1963), 601–07.

33. Bandura et al., "Vicarious Reinforcement," 606.

34. Bandura et al., "Vicarious Reinforcement," 606.

35. Larry J. Shrum, "Assessing the Social Influence of Television: A Social Cognition Perspective on Cultivation Effects," *Communication Research* 22, no. 4 (1995), 404.

36. Shrum, "Assessing the Social Influence of Television," 404.

37. Valerie P. Hans and Juliet L. Dee, "Media Coverage of Law: Its Impact on Juries and the Public," *American Behavioral Scientist* (1991), 136–149.

38. Julian V. Roberts and Anthony N. Doob, "News Media Influences on Public Views of Sentencing," *Law and Human Behavior* 14, no. 5 (1990), 451–468.

39. Hans and Dee, "Media coverage of Law," 136–149.

40. Christine L. Ruva and Cathy McEvoy, "Negative and Positive Pretrial Publicity Affect Juror Memory and Decision Making," *Journal of Experimental Psychology: Applied* 14, no. 3 (2008), 226–235.

41. Ruva and McEvoy, "Negative and Positive Pretrial Publicity," 232.

42. Ruva and McEvoy, "Negative and Positive Pretrial Publicity," 226–235.

43. Richard L. Henshel and Robert A. Silverman. "Perception and Criminal Process." *Canadian Journal of Sociology/Cahiers canadiens de sociologie* (1975), 39.

44. Tyler, "Viewing CSI," 1076.

45. Tyler, "Viewing CSI," 1050–1085.

46. Gallup, "Supreme Court: Gallup Historical Trends," accessed May 22, 2012, http://www.gal lup.com/poll/4732/supreme-court.aspx.

47. Tyler, "Viewing CSI," 1050–1085.

48. Tyler, "Viewing CSI," 1050–1085.

49. Tyler, "Viewing CSI," 1083.

50. Robert S. Lichter, Linda S. Lichter, and Stanley Rothman, *Prime Time: How TV Portrays American Culture* (Washington, DC: Regnery Pub., 1994).

51. Helena Bilandzic and Patrick Rössler, "Life According to Television, Implications of Genre-Specific Cultivation Effects: The Gratification/Cultivation Model." *COMMUNICATIONS-SANKT AUGUSTIN THEN BERLIN-* 29 (2004), 295–326.

52. Carol J. Mills, "Juror Characteristics: To What Extent Are They Related to Jury Verdicts?" *Judicature* 8, no. 22 (1980), 23.

53. Mills, "Juror Characteristics," 22–31.

54. John K. Cochran and Beth A. Sanders, "The Gender Gap in Death Penalty Support: An Exploratory Study," *Journal of Criminal Justice* 37, no. 6 (2009), 525–533.

55. Cochran and Sanders, "The Gender Gap," 525.

56. Cochran and Sanders, "The Gender Gap," 525–533.

57. Cochran and Sanders, "The Gender Gap," 529.

58. Cochran and Sanders, "The Gender Gap," 525–533.

59. Lindsay M. Howden and Julie A. Meyer, "Age and Sex Composition: 2010." *2010 Census Briefs* (2011), 1–15.

60. Michael W. Link and Jennie W. Lai, "Cell-Phone-Only Households and Problems of Differential Nonresponse Using an Address-Based Sampling Design," *Public Opinion Quarterly* 75, no. 4 (2011), 613–635.

61. Kathleen Curry, "Mediating COPS: An Analysis of Viewer Reaction to Reality TV," *Journal of Criminal Justice and Popular Culture*, 8, no. 3 (2001), 169–185.

62. James D. Unnever, Francis T. Cullen, and Bonnie S. Fisher, "'A Liberal Is Someone Who Has Not been Mugged": Criminal Victimization and Political Beliefs," *Justice Quarterly* 24, no. 2 (2007), 309–334; Mark Mauer, "Why Are Tough on Crime Policies so Popular?" *Stanford Law & Policy Review*, 11 (1999), 9–17.

63. Cochran and Sanders, "The Gender Gap," 525–533.

64. George Gerbner, Larry Gross, Michael Morgan, and Nancy Signorielli, "Political Correlates of Television Viewing," *Public Opinion Quarterly* 48, no. 1B (1984), 283–300.

65. Gerbner et al., "Political Correlates," 293.

66. Gerbner et al., "Political Correlates," 295.

67. Gerbner et al., "Political Correlates," 296.

68. Gerbner et al., "Political Correlates," 297.

69. Danielle M. Soulliere, "Prime-Time Murder: Presentations of Murder on Popular Television Justice Programs," *Journal of Criminal Justice and Popular Culture* 10, no. 1 (2003), 12–38; Lichter, Lichter, and Rothman, *Prime Time.*

70. Jacob Cohen, Patricia Cohen, G. W. Stephen, and S. A. Leona, *Applied Multiple Regression/Correlation Analysis for the Behavioral Sciences* (Mahwah: Lawrence Erlbaum Assoc. Incorporated, 2003).

71. L. J. Shrum, Robert S. Wyer, Jr, and Thomas C. O'Guinn, "The Effects of Television Consumption on Social Perceptions: The Use of Priming Procedures to Investigate Psychological Processes," *Journal of Consumer Research* 24, no. 4 (1998), 447–458.

72. Shrum et al., "The Effects of Television Consumption," 448.

73. Shrum et al., "The Effects of Television Consumption," 448.

74. Shrum et al., "The Effects of Television Consumption," 449.

75. Henshel and Silverman, "Perception and Criminal Process," 33–47.

76. Henshel and Silverman, "Perception and Criminal Process," 34.

77. Henshel and Silverman, "Perception and Criminal Process," 40.

Chapter Ten

Paramilitary Patriots of the Cold War: Women, Weapons, and Private Warriors in *The A-Team* and *Airwolf*

Charity Fox

Popular culture in the Reagan era of the Cold War explored contradictions in changing gender roles, issues of privatization, and the lingering effects of cultural changes from the 1970s. Popular 1980s television series focused on "mercenary"-type characters that captured the contradictions of the era, as they featured patriotic mercenaries and interchangeable "independent" women working in the day-to-day battlefields of the Cold War. Unlike the boorish mercenaries of the Middle Ages, American mercenary figures throughout Cold War–era popular culture were represented as benevolent heroes, connecting idealized displays of masculinity, rugged individualism, and patriarchal capitalism within fun, action-packed, romantic mercenary narratives. Appearing across television series, films, and novels during the Cold War, popular culture mercenary narratives communicated stories of successful individual outcomes from pursuing strategies like containment, cultural export, and privatization. Over a half-century, these portrayals created a collective cultural heuristic; they formed a learned framework for understanding privatized warriors in the Cold War as American heroes.[1]

By highlighting heroic individuals and small teams implementing order outside of traditional state authority structures, these popular culture mercenaries shaped consumers' worldview by creating a cultural framework for accepting and glorifying private warriors as quintessentially heroic "American" figures. This chapter will explore how the television series *The A-Team* (NBC, 1983–1987) and *Airwolf* (CBS 1984–1986; USA 1987) presented their mercenary characters as heroic private warriors successfully controlling women, weapons, and battlefields in the later years of the Cold War. Action-adventure dramas produced by Universal Television, *The A-Team* and *Airwolf* presented a worldview that lauded private benevolent warriors avoiding persecution by their government and judgmental civilians. These paramilitary patriots made a living helping restore order on small and large scales through their mastery of people and weaponry. By narratively cleaning up the leftover remnants of Vietnam and the various crises of confidence in the 1970s through a temporary retreat to the battlefield, mercenary narratives in the late Cold War demonstrated new ways to prove masculinity, competency, and superiority in local and international affairs, and regain the spot at the top of social and cultural hierarchies.

NEW WARS, HARD BODIES, AND SMALL SCREENS

In the social milieu of the early 1980s, white male patriarchy faced a shrinking sphere of influence over domestic concerns, as cultural faith in traditional power structures and institutions had faced a number of challenges through the 1970s. Women and minorities were changing social institutions at home, while Americans were in danger in many parts of the world, and the Soviet Union appeared to be "winning" the Cold War. The energy crisis of 1973 laid bare an American dependence on foreign-owned oil reserves subject to political and economic whims. President Richard Nixon resigned in 1974 after his administration was disgraced in the Watergate scandal; his misconduct raised suspicion of government leaders in areas where there had been little doubt before. American involvement in the Vietnam War was a contentious and difficult issue at home and abroad. United States military forces backed out of Vietnam in disgrace after the Fall of Saigon in 1975, breaking promises and leaving behind allies. The domestic economy was in recession, with stagnant growth amid rampant inflation, or stagflation. Within American society, feminist and civil rights activists vocally pushed for legal and political enforcement antidiscrimination laws and policies; each step toward equality under the law represented hard-fought legal and cultural battles and hardened beliefs on all sides.[2]

In July 1979, President Carter spoke directly about the perceived sense of "malaise" in American society. Carter explicitly asked Americans to recognize that the nation was undergoing a "crisis of confidence" that was sowing discord, doubt, and affecting the unity of Americans.[3] He urged conservation and moderation instead of indulgence and conspicuous consumption as a way to weather the energy crisis as well as shore up national security and unity. It was a difficult sell.

The détente phase of the Cold War came to a close in 1979 as well, with overt and covert hostilities resuming with actions such as the Soviet invasion of Afghanistan and the Iranian Revolution. The Iran Hostage Crisis that began in November 1979 seemed to be the final nail in the coffin of American Exceptionalism; not only were Americans captured by revolutionaries in the overthrow of the American-backed Shah, but the rescue mission mounted by the US military in early 1980 failed miserably.[4] Military prowess seemed to be gone, and expressing patriotism through mass consumption—dogmatic to civil religion since the end of WWII—had been officially discouraged by a president urging mass conservation practices instead.[5]

The neoconservative reaction to this crisis of confidence was the Reagan Revolution, a conservative turn in American politics that reflected both a shift in demographics in the US (as whites and the wealthy moved to the suburbs, the south, and the west, thus shifting political control away from previous strongholds of the urban north and east) and a shift in political rhetoric that aimed to "get back" the power and dominance of "real" Americans. Ronald Reagan's election as president in 1980 marked the power of the suburban demographic, the end of the Great Society with the collapse of New Deal political alliances, and a renewed commitment to hawkish foreign policy. Reagan and other neoconservatives pushed for an end to détente, labeling it a weak strategy of appeasing enemies. Instead, they advocated for a stronger, more militant stance and unilateral US movement against small communist countries (particularly those in Latin America). Reagan reversed previous rhetorical gestures of détente through his belligerent rhetorical attacks on the Soviet Union, labeling it an "evil empire." In the early 1980s under Reagan, tensions between the United States and the Soviet Union were at the highest point they had been since the nuclear crises of the early 1960s.[6]

Popular culture of the 1980s reflected this milieu through narratives in which characters defeated the crisis of confidence through militaristic tactics, framing their victory as a quest to reclaim lost power and status within the context of a crisis of (white) masculinity. In *Warrior Dreams: Paramilitary Culture in Post-Vietnam America*, James William Gibson identifies a mythology of paramilitary warriors found on the fringes of popular culture.[7] Gibson argues that perceptions of post-Vietnam social crises of race, sex, economics, and personal and national failure had severe consequences for white American men, whose cultural and imaginary responses constituted fantasies of a "New War." In the New War fantasies, traditional "heroic American warriors of legend" could be "unleashed . . . [to] do what was necessary to win victory and thus affirm the fundamental truths of America's virtue and martial prowess."[8] As a balm for crises of masculinity, cultural products containing New War fantasies provided narratives of psychological retreat to an archaic paramilitary warrior mythos, giving consumers an outlet to fight and "right" all the wrongs that they felt in their regular lives.[9]

In his genre study, Gibson finds that New War fantasies feature a violent male warrior isolated from interpersonal contact and deprived of love, stability, and family. Freed of any responsibility other than destroying the current (corrupt) world order, the warrior regresses to a state of infantile rage that enhances his ability to continue fighting without regard for anything outside his mission. Women in these New War fantasies are limited to either mother/sister/virgin figures or sadistic femme fatales; all woman cause softness or weakness in the warrior and are quickly eliminated by his enemies. New War fantasies employ a "diffuse" racism rather than a strict color code of heroes and enemies. Enemies are ideological others, with race being a secondary characteristic; "in the telling of the tale, it emerges that most of the enemies are not white. Hence the heroes fight drug dealers [or other enemies] who *just happen* to be black."[10] Filled with vengeance and violence, New War fantasies provide graphic "ways of arguing about what is wrong with the modern world and what needs to be done to make society well again," up to and including apocalyptic destruction of the world order.[11]

While much of the harsh New War fantasy that Gibson found stayed on the fringes of popular culture, the gendered language arguing that "soft-ness"/femininity will lead to tragedy and "hardness"/masculinity will lead to success pervaded mainstream popular culture as well. In *Hard Bodies: Hollywood Masculinity in the Reagan Era*, Susan Jeffords examines the interconnections between political rhetoric and policies and popular culture depictions of masculine, heroic, individualized white men.[12] Jeffords notes the gendered language used to critique Carter and praise Reagan; Carter was critiqued as feminized—soft, mushy, gentle, paralyzed (i.e., castrated), wavering, uncertain—as while Reagan was praised as masculinized—steely, strong, willful, aggressive, decisive, domineering. Similarly hypermasculine traits graced the indestructible heroes of iconic Hollywood action-adventure film franchises begun in the 1980s, including the *Indiana Jones* (*Raiders of the Lost* Ark, 1981), *Rambo* (*First Blood*, 1982), *Terminator* (1984), and *Die Hard* (1988) franchises. For Jeffords, these popular culture products argued for "a rearticulation of masculine strength and power through internal, per-sonal, and family-oriented values" throughout their depictions of characters' invincibility and resistance to injury.[13]

As we move from Gibson's fringes to Jeffords's popular films we can see how mainstream popular culture began to incorporate watered-down versions of New War warrior mythos, hard-body machismo, and Reaganesque family values, even in the mass-mediated, family-friendly forms produced for network television series of the 1980s. The three major broadcast television networks in the 1980s—ABC, CBS, and NBC—provided free broadcast programming through a series of local affiliates, which were the main choices for television viewers in the early-mid 1980s.[14] In *Seeing Through the Eighties: Television and Reaganism*, Jane Feuer argues that "television and Reaganism formed mutually reinforcing and interpenetrating imaginary worlds," as network television programming was full of programs "used [by audiences] to *avoid* dealing with the economic and social realities of the times . . . [as well as per-petuating] a contradiction in Reaganite ideology . . . [through] 'a curious mix of populism and elitism.'"[15] Feuer sees television in the 1980s as a postmodern art form, where "its postmodernity correlates to the development of the Rea-ganite cultural formation, while its specific 'artistic' products can be viewed as symptomatic of that formation, yet at the same time critical of it . . . [a] 'complicitous critique' [that] now reemerges as a characteristic of certain forms of so-called neoconservative culture."[16] Feuer sees serial (melo)dramas like *Dynasty* (1981–1989) and yuppie spectacles like *thirtysomething* (1987–1991) as part of this complicitous cultural critique of Reaganism through their curious mix of populism and elitism. Recognizing the importance of melodrama and conspicuous consumption in 1980s television programming adds interpretive nuance, as the same melodramatic, soap-operatic qualities that made *Dynasty* and *thirtysomething* popular pervaded *The A-Team* and *Airwolf* as well. The plot scenarios and twists of *The A-Team* and *Airwolf* are just as outrageous and unbelievable as soap opera melodrama, especially when boiled down to a one-sentence plot summary; and the characters and narratives are equally compelling for fans when followed over the course of a long television season.

Delving deeper into *The A-Team* and *Airwolf*, we can tease out the ways that the anger behind the New War fringe, and the boasting of "hard bodies" masculinity, combined with melodramatic, soap-operatic qualities of Reagan-era television culture. The private warriors in *The A-Team* and *Airwolf* offer a combination of likeable, alienated, isolated characters that fight in Cold War battlefield situations. The generic pattern of the episodes allowed a weekly rehash of the characters' ingenuity, resourcefulness, superiority over their enemies, and ability to escape any sticky situation. They operate in world of maleness with little room for women, and their bodies and their weapons—both the physical weapons they create and utilize as well as their ability to use strategy and mental acuity as a weapon—are invincible, unstoppable, and hardened. These private warriors are framed as paramilitary patriots; they believe in the American project—life, liberty, pursuit of happiness—and embody a benevolent, ambitious "American spirit" even while they enforce their patriotic beliefs through violence or threats of violence outside the authority of the state.

THE A-TEAM (1983–1987)

The A-Team begins every episode with a voiceover explaining the diagetic world of the show:

> In 1972,[17] a crack commando unit was sent to prison by a military court for a crime they didn't commit. These men promptly escaped from a maximum security stockade to the Los Angeles underground. Today, still wanted by the government, they survive as soldiers of fortune. If you have a problem, if no one else can help, and if you can find them, maybe you can hire—The A-Team.[18]

The opening statement explains the overarching series narrative and provides a preview of the structure of the episodic stories—the members of the A-Team are talented, resourceful, helpful members of the Los Angeles underground community who use their specialized military training to help the downtrodden. And, while they are technically fugitives on the wrong side of a dispute with the government, a situation which could make them villains in another type of narrative, they are framed as heroic, innocent men rather than as dangers to society; their pursuit by government officials is an example of government overreach rather than a reflection on the main characters.

The core members of the A-Team, in order of military rank, are: Colonel John "Hannibal" Smith (George Peppard), the roguishly handsome, white-haired team leader whose outrageous strategies bring success; Captain H. M. "Howling Mad" Murdock (Dwight Schultz), the mild-to-moderately insane ace pilot who "cracked up" after his time in Vietnam and resides in a VA psych ward; Lieutenant Templeton "Faceman" Peck (Dirk Benedict), the attractive, wily acquisitions officer capable of obtaining anything he wants; and Sergeant Bosco "B. A." (for "Bad Attitude") Baracus (Mr. T), the brutally strong, somewhat child-like muscle of the team and its mechanical genius.

While serving in Vietnam, Hannibal, Face, and B. A. were ordered on a secret mission to rob the Bank of Hanoi in order to weaken the North Vietnamese, but their commanding officer was killed and their orders were destroyed while they were on the mission. They were arrested by the US military and accused of plotting the heist for their own gain—hence "the crime they didn't commit." Hannibal breaks the team out of military prison, and they escape to the underground world of Los Angeles, where they are constantly pursued by military police.[19] Early in the series, the team often worked with investigative reporter Amy Allen (Melinda Culea), who protected their whereabouts from the MPs and touted their heroism in her newspaper columns after missions had been completed.

The A-Team typifies the banality of the New War, Hard Body genre when mass-mediated for network television in the 1980s. The family-friendly violence is almost cartoonish—cars flip wildly through the air from conveniently spaced obstacles, thousands of rounds of ammunition shot by "crack commandos" fail to produce any blood or kill anyone, and no one is ever seriously hurt or endangered on screen. In a typical episode, the A-Team is approached by a client who is having some sort of difficulty with the bad guys. Hannibal devises a plan to send a warning to the bad guys on behalf of the client. This warning upsets the bad guys, so they redouble their bad guy efforts, often cornering the members of the A-Team in a (not-so-) "inescapable" situation, such as locking them in a garage full of welding equipment and spare parts. After a "working" montage scene that combines close-up shots of hands working and battle preparations set to *The A-Team* theme song, the members of the A-Team fight back against the bad guys. They subdue and chasten them, restoring the order that they promised to their client amid car chases, machine gun fire, fisticuffs, and wisecracks, all under the looming specter of the military police.[20] The series had a fun, adventurous feel to it—a combination of tense situations with predictable outcomes, amusing and sometimes goofy dialogue (especially from crazy Murdock), and a sense that the main characters balance extreme capability with a roguish, likeable arrogance.

The high ratings for *The A-Team* fell by the fourth season, which was awash with cameo appearances—including Rick James, Hulk Hogan, the game show *Wheel of Fortune*, and Boy George of the English pop band Culture Club—but to no avail.[21] To revive ratings and audience interest, the series was narratively reworked for the fifth season, beginning with a three-part episode resolving the overarching series narrative. Hannibal, Face, and B. A. are finally caught by the military police, put on trial for bank robbery and murder, convicted, and sentenced to death by firing squad. With the help of Murdock and newcomer Frankie Santana (Eddie Velez), blank rifle shells, and some special pills, Hannibal, Face, and B. A. survive the firing squad and escape. However, the capture, prosecution, and escape were all orchestrated by the secretive and powerful General Hunt Stockwell (Robert Vaughn) with the help of Murdock and Frankie. In order to finally clear their names and be free of government persecution, the A-Team agrees to perform suicide missions for Stockwell's secret government agency in return for a full presidential pardon.[22] For the rest of Season 5, the A-Team was transplanted to Northern Virginia, kept under close surveillance in a luxurious house, and sent out on missions of Stockwell's choosing.

This attempt to resolve and yet still continue the overarching series narrative changes the feel of the show completely. Once the A-Team members' independence is curtailed, their ingenuity becomes a necessary trait exploited by Stockwell to get out of impossible, locked-door situations of international intrigue, rather than a celebration of the team's creative problem-solving and unorthodox approaches in helping ordinary people who have run out of options against local thugs. In this final season, the A-Team becomes an unfortunate tool of an uncaring government that only seeks to use them until their usefulness (or their lives) is depleted. The series ended abruptly, without a finale resolving the fate of the A-Team.

AIRWOLF (1984–1986; 1987)

In the pilot episode of *Airwolf*, "Shadow of the Hawke," Michael Coldsmith-Briggs III, codename "Archangel" (Alex Cord), has lost control of the newest and most impressive piece of machinery ever developed by his super-secret pseudo-governmental agency The Firm: a state-of-the-art helicopter capable

of super-sonic speed named Airwolf.[23] Airwolf's designer has absconded
with the helicopter to Libya, where he is being fêted by Muammar Gaddafi's
military elites in exchange for revealing the technology behind Airwolf.
Archangel must convince Stringfellow Hawke (Jan-Michael Vincent), a
reclusive Vietnam veteran and a phenomenal test pilot, to complete another
mission for The Firm—sneak into Libya, steal Airwolf, and return it to Archangel and The Firm. With the help of his best friend and father figure, Domi-
nic Santini (Ernest Borgnine), String successfully steals Airwolf and brings
it back to the United States, but he does not return it to The Firm. Instead, he
hides it inside a mountain, refusing to deliver Airwolf until The Firm finds his
brother St. John, who has been missing in action/a prisoner of war in Vietnam
for over a decade. Archangel and Hawke strike a deal—as long as String has
Airwolf hidden, The Firm agrees to look for St. John. String will in turn fly
Airwolf on missions for The Firm, or else they will allow the full weight of
the US government to fall on Stringfellow Hawke.

Even from this first episode, viewers can sense the difference in the tone,
narrative, and characterization between *Airwolf* and *The A-Team*. *Airwolf* is a
much more serious show on all levels, and episodes featured more convoluted
plot lines. The acting is melodramatic instead of tongue-in-cheek; the episodic
plot lines deal with high-stakes espionage, nuclear threats, attempted *coups
d'etat*, and destructive scientific breakthroughs; and the overarching series
narrative involves ransoming advanced military technology to a secret division of the United States' intelligence agencies in exchange for information
on one POW/MIA soldier from Vietnam. Instead of car chases and fisticuffs,
action scenes in *Airwolf* consist of aerial dogfights between Airwolf and enemy fighters (particularly other souped-up helicopters or Russian-made MIG
fighter jets). In practice, this means that "action scenes" are edited pieces of
aerial footage interspersed with shots from "inside the cockpit"—where the
pilots sit nearly still in uniforms and full-face helmets among flashing plastic
lights, switches, toggles, inscrutable controls and dials, and the latest computer screens combined in a static but apparently impressive display of "fu-
turistic" 1980s technology. Given the leaps in technology since 1984, these
action sequences look quite dated, giving *Airwolf* the feel of a period piece.

String lives in a well-appointed log cabin on a lake in an extremely remote
area accessible only by helicopter, desiring only isolation after the tragedies
of his life and traumas from his experiences in Vietnam. Dom is the opposite
of String—loud, cheerful, opinionated—the antidote to String's brooding
demeanor. Practically family, Dom was String's father's best friend, and
he has looked after String ever since his parents were killed in an accident.
His business, Santini Air, supplies helicopters, airplanes, and stunt pilots for
private charter use, particularly for use in films and other Hollywood-type

productions. String only leaves his sanctuary to work a job for Dom or take Airwolf on a mission for The Firm.

The Firm is a super-secret, black ops division of the intelligence branch of the US government, the kind of operation that is hidden from Congress and possibly even from the president. Archangel is in charge of the section that developed Airwolf and manages Hawke as an asset. Archangel is always clothed in impeccably tailored, head-to-toe blindingly white suits with either a black or a white eye patch (covering an injury suffered when Airwolf was first stolen). He is always assisted by a beautiful, extremely intelligent woman—interchangeable females apparently drawn from a deep well of talent—who is also always in head-to-toe white. Archangel and Hawke have a friendly working relationship that develops across the first three seasons.

The producers of *Airwolf* introduced new elements in each season in an effort to keep the series fresh and respond to declining ratings. In the second season, String and Dom were joined by Caitlin O'Shannessy (Jean Bruce Scott), a former Texas Highway Patrol helicopter pilot. She becomes a junior member of both the Airwolf team and Dom's charter business.[24] In the third season, String discovers that his brother St. John has an "Amerasian" son, a boy named Le that String decides to adopt.[25] By the end of Season 3 in 1986, CBS cancelled the series. Universal Television produced a fourth season for the USA network, using an entirely different cast, crew, location, writers, and budget.

In the opening scene of the first episode of Season 4, "Blackjack," an explosion at Santini Air kills Dom and critically injures String. Meanwhile, The Company (nee The Firm) has located String's brother St. John (Barry Van Dyke) in a POW camp in North Vietnam, where he is being displayed as bait for String to fly Airwolf into an ambush. New Company agent Jason Locke (Anthony Sherwood), pilot Major Mike Rivers (Geraint Wyn Davies), and Dom's niece, Jo Santini (Michele Scarabelli), locate Airwolf and extract St. John from Vietnam. Apparently perfectly healthy and of sound mind after 15 years in a POW camp, St. John takes over the task of flying Airwolf on missions for The Company while String recovers in an undisclosed location.[26]

Airwolf Season 4 is generally considered to be a completely separate series that continues the name and the same basic premise the original.[27] Because of its shoestring budget, Season 4 was produced without any new aerial shots. Instead, "new" aerial battle scenes combined new and recycled footage; cockpit scenes with the new actors were filmed in a mock-up of Airwolf and edited into old stock footage of Airwolf and other aircraft flying, fighting, and exploding from the first three seasons.[28] The changes in Season 4 resolve the overarching series narrative of Seasons 1–3, but, much like the final season of *The A-Team*, this resolution probably should have ended the series rather than begun a new season. What internal logic existed in the diagetic universe of *Airwolf* was thrown off completely by the series reboot. Combined with the underfunded production and complete elimination of all of the original characters, *Airwolf* Season 4 is a dreary, cheap, campy imitation of the first three seasons.

WOMEN AND WEAPONS IN THE BATTLEFIELD

In the wake of the Vietnam War, social upheavals, and cultural crises of confidence of the 1970s, the mercenary characters in these series chose to live their lives in a primarily male world. They retreated from the domestic sphere, which had become a site representing crises in confidence and loss of social power, heading for the familiar arena of the paramilitary Cold War battlefield, where others sought protection rather than concessions from the heroes. In both series, there is a revolving door of female characters presented as pretty objects to be protected, romanced, or exchanged. While there are frequently female actors playing *characters/caricatures* within these series, there are very few differentiated or recognizable female *roles* within the homosocial world of the mercenary's battlefield. Clients and missions changed with each episode on *The A-Team* and *Airwolf*, and the barely sketched female characters were quickly discarded when the mission was over. Instead, weapons take the place of women, feminized through their production, usage, and pet names such as "my baby" and "The Lady," indicating a gendered level to the sustained relationship between the mercenary and the equipment that he obsessively protects and possesses.

The main recurring female characters in these series are Amy Allen in *The A-Team* Seasons 1–2 and Caitlin O'Shannessy in *Airwolf* Seasons 2–3. Both are slightly tomboyish, independent truth-seekers, and they are depicted as sisterly figures rather than as potential romantic interests. Amy Allen is an investigative journalist who attaches herself to the A-Team to secure headlines and bylines for her own career, and she is written out of the series at the beginning of Season 2. In the episode "When You Comin' Back, Range Rider?," the A-Team is hired by a Native American, Daniel Running Bear, to protect the wild mustangs on his tribe's reservation from Carter, a local rancher who has been capturing and selling them to a glue factory.[29] The A-Team narrowly misses being captured by the ruthless Colonel Decker, and Hannibal warns Amy that Decker will begin targeting her, making it unsafe for her to continue working with them. Amy has developed a romantic interest in Daniel, so she decides to stay on the reservation with him, to "see where this [relationship] goes." In choosing to pursue a (hetero)sexual relationship

in a domestic sphere, Amy must opt out of the male private warrior environment. In a watered-down version of Gibson's New War, the battlefield sphere
that the A-Team inhabits cannot coexist with female sexuality or feminized
domesticity, and she will endanger them all—including herself—if she remains part of the team.

Caitlin O'Shannessy is introduced in the Season 2 premiere episode of
Airwolf, "Sweet Britches."[30] A Texas Highway Patrol helicopter pilot, Caitlin
pushes a local sheriff too far. In retaliation, he arranges two different situations for his redneck thugs to gang rape Caitlin to "take the feistiness out of
her"—the first on a lonely stretch of highway at night, and the second when
the sheriff arrests Caitlin and hands over the keys to the jail to his thugs.
String thwarts both of these attacks, using Airwolf to flatten the (empty) jail
after the sheriff refuses to surrender himself. Caitlin tracks down String and
Dom at Santini Air a few episodes later, and Dom gives her a job.[31] Soon,
Caitlin is brought into the Airwolf fold and becomes a supporting member of
the team, even learning to fly Airwolf herself. Caitlin has an innocent school-
girl admiration for String and is characterized as a heterosexual woman, but
as a sisterly character, she does not express any female sexuality or drive to
have her own domestic sphere.

Rather than including well-developed female characters as part of the mercenary's battlefield sphere, the most consistently gendered "she" in these series involves the sexualization and gendering of weaponry for the mercenary
figures. Other scholars have discussed the ways that large weapons can act
as a substitute phallus reinforcing the hyper-masculinity of action-adventure
heroes in film and novels of the 1980s.[32] However, in the watered-down realm
of television, I would argue that instead of a substitute phallus, weaponry
functions as a substitute female character that reinforces masculine hetero-
sexuality within the homosocial world of the mercenary's battlefield, even in
the absence of overt (sexual) expressions of male heterosexuality.

In *The A-Team*, this substitution of weapons for women is often seen in
throwaway lines of dialogue, such as when B. A. refers to his van as his
"baby," or Hannibal refers to his machine gun with a phrase like "Isn't she
beautiful?" More important than dialogue, is the weekly "working montage"
scene in episodes of *The A-Team*, which visually reinforces the sensuality of
constructing a weapon by hand. These montages are full of close-up shots of
hands interacting with machinery, of flesh intricately shaping and manipulat-
ing metal and wood, reinforcing the intimacy between man and machine in
the construction process. These working montages mimic the shots found in a
PG-13–rated sex scene, where closely cropped shots of flesh on barely identifiable bits of flesh indicate sensual or sexual contact without revealing the
whole image. In *The A-Team*'s working montages, these visual techniques are

applied instead to closely cropped shots of flesh on barely identifiable bits of weaponry. In keeping with the theme of disposable female characters in *The A-Team*, these weapons are used for very specific, mission-related purposes. As temporary weapons used to facilitate an immediate escape from the bad guys, these sensually produced weapons are quickly discarded at the conclusion of the mission, when their immediate usefulness is depleted.

The gendering of weaponry is both more direct and more long-term in *Airwolf*, because, unlike the A-Team's weekly creation of disposable weapons, the Airwolf helicopter is an indispensable, reusable tool that forms the basis of all missions. Because of this, Airwolf itself becomes a feminized object. In the beginning of the series, Dom refers to Airwolf as a "beast" while he is learning to fly it, because Airwolf is a scary, powerful weapon that he can barely control. As he becomes more comfortable and more in control, though, Dom begins referring to Airwolf as "my baby" and urges String to "take her out more often" on "maintenance flights" just to "make sure she's ok."[33] By Season 3, Airwolf has become known primarily as "The Lady" to the Airwolf team, with the nickname (i.e., "Dom, go get The Lady ready" or "I'm going to go pick up The Lady, you stay here") peppered throughout the dialogue.[34]

This evolution from *A Beast* to *My Baby* to *The Lady* draws on literary traditions about taming and domesticating beasts/women as well as long military traditions of referring to ships, planes, and other vessels as "she." However, there is also a very strong dialogic emphasis on Airwolf's long-term femininity within Dom's constant admonitions to String. Dom complains that Airwolf needs "regular tending" and should be "taken out, just for fun" to "keep her happy," complaints that recall the type of language often used in advice columns for men (or women) interested in maintaining happiness and faithfulness in a long-term (sexual) relationship. The idea conveyed through this language is that regular pampering, frequent but gentle "use," and at least a minimum level of special attention will keep The Lady (and, in turn, other long-term ladies) happy and willing to perform all of the tasks that the mercenary might ask of her.

In the homosocial world of the battlefield the mercenary figures in these narratives have replaced most short- and long-term heterosexual relationships with short- and long-term relationships with their weapons. Much like the military chant immortalized in Stanley Kubrick's 1987 film *Full Metal Jacket* distinguished between the uses of a weapon and a penis—"This is my rifle, this is my gun. This is for fighting, this is for fun"—the line between obtaining pleasure from weaponry and pleasure from female companionship is slippery and indistinct in these mercenary narratives.[35] The mercenary figures' weapons are just as feminine, sensual, one- or two-dimensional, and silent as most of the female characters in the series. They can be impressive, intelligent, and downright scary if not properly controlled and directed by the mercenary figures. But, properly "maintained," both the lady and the weapon will continue to serve the needs of the mercenary in the realm of the battlefield, and perhaps even beyond the battlefield when the mercenary figure returns to the top of domestic social hierarchies. For these paramilitary warriors, weapons replace women in relationships in the same way that the battlefield replaces the domestic sphere as a comfortable, reassuring home.

PATERNALISTIC WARRIORS AND PARAMILITARY PATRIOTS

Mercenary figures in 1980s narratives were taking a temporary retreat from domestic society, replacing women with weapons and regular social interactions with those of the battlefield, but they still took responsibility for providing protection and asserting paternalistic control. This warrior group was damaged and fundamentally altered by the crises of the Cold War; as a response to that damage, *The A-Team* and *Airwolf* showed independent white men successfully asserting authority and control over willing dependents using whatever means necessary—violence, paternalism, rhetoric, separate gendered spheres, and technological superiority. The mercenaries in *The A-Team* and *Airwolf* embody aspects of a paramilitary patriotism, a term I use to capture the dissonant contradictions between their mercenary and paramilitary actions against the state as well as their expressions of love for American ideals. The characters in these narratives have been betrayed by their government on some level; they are haunted by that betrayal, but they profess a deep patriotic love of their country and a deep sense of paternalistic responsibility to protect even those who betrayed them. Their retreat to the battlefield sphere is temporary, supported by a sense of optimism, of regrouping and preparing for a return to (benevolent) dominance and security; diminished benevolent paternalistic power is depicted as a short-term problem. The incompetence of those still working within the system drove them to retreat; if the system was so broken as to make them leave and perpetuate incompetence, then working outside it is the most patriotic thing they can do.

Despite the trauma he suffered from Vietnam, String continues to work with The Firm for personal and political reasons. His given reason for flying Airwolf is to keep pressure on The Firm to search for his brother; but, his unique position in the intelligence world also gives him knowledge of vast dangers that could ruin the world (such as an impending nuclear strike) as well as access to a piece of weaponry that can literally save the world (by exploding the missiles before they strike). In the urgency of these situations (only five minutes until nuclear holocaust!), everyday shades of gray coalesce into stark black and white contrast. While he may have issues with his own and his brother's treatment at the hands of the US government, those problems pale in comparison to the trauma and responsibility that would be on his shoulders if he refused to use Airwolf to fly the missions asked of him. By eliminating nuance within the narrative, the range of String's possible responses is limited; of course he will continue to help the government that hurt him, out of a sense of decency as well as patriotism.

The personal motivations of the members of the A-Team are not quite as high-stakes, but they speak to a deeper pride in a particular view of Americanism. When Amy Allen asks Hannibal why they stay in the United States even though they are being chased by the government, Hannibal sets her straight on their patriotism:

> *Amy*: What I can't understand is why you all aren't just living in Switzerland where it's safe for you.
>
> *Hannibal*: We aren't living in Switzerland, Miss Allen, because we aren't Swiss. . . . We're Americans. We have a little problem now, but we'll work our way out of it somehow, some year. In the meantime, we stick together and do what we know best. If we help you, we need to know you'll protect us—not sell us out. It's hard enough the way it is, without more trouble.[36]

Here, Hannibal is expressing a broad sense of optimism and patriotism. The A-Team will work their way out of their temporary injustice, because their "little problem" is individualized, not related to traditional institutions or unjust power, social, or economic structures. Recalling deep puritanical roots of Americanism, Hannibal invokes a protestant work ethic as the source of his patriotism as well as the solution to his "little problem."

Part of the guiding philosophy that holds the A-Team together as they work through their "little problem" is "The Jazz." As B. A. explains their group's dynamics to Amy in the pilot episode:

> *B. A.*: [laughing] You talking about Hannibal? He ain't afraid of nothing.
>
> *Amy*: Then what? Do you think he has a death wish or something?
>
> *B. A.*: No, he's just got the jazz that's all. Hannibal got the jazz.
>
> *Amy*: The "Jazz?"
>
> *B. A.*: Yep, he's been living on the edge ever since I known him. He's one crazy hooked together dude. That's what kept him alive through Nam. Kept me and the others alive also.
>
> *Amy*: Then why do *you* do it?

B. A.: [smiling] For the jazz baby. It's like walking into a casino in Vegas, laying down your money on the crap table and winning on the first roll. You can't walk away. You just can't. You know you can beat 'em, 'cause you just done it.

Amy: [laughing and shaking her head "no"] It's not the same thing.

B .A.: Sure it is. You want this guy Valdez bad enough, and we get him, you'll feel it. Wait and see.[37]

For the members of the A-Team, "The Jazz" is code for the reasoning behind their often reckless decisions. The code transforms this word for a quintessential American music form into a broader worldview on the powers of improvisation, ingenuity, creativity, and excitement. This version of "the jazz" includes the surge of adrenaline that accompanies the unknown factors of battle and adventure as well as the satisfaction of confronting and overcoming danger and completing your mission. But, "the jazz" is also about controlling the outcomes of situations and participation of others in those situations. It is about confidence that can border on arrogance, and reveling in the actions taken to prove superiority in a situation. In the world of the A-Team, "the jazz" becomes about winning, establishing dominance, making others lose, and enforcing your worldview on another group that had been trying to assert their worldview on you. In short, "the jazz" banishes the idea that participating in the Vietnam War would cause Americans like the members of the A-Team to have any regrets or experience the crisis of confidence, self-pity, or general malaise that supposedly infected the rest of America after in the 1970s. By dominating others and being in control, "the jazz" erases regret and encourages progress, renewed strength, and working together to get through this "little problem right now." Dealing with diminished benevolent paternalistic power is pictured as a short-term problem for the paramilitary patriots of *The A-Team* and *Airwolf*. Within these narratives dealing with betrayal, isolation, and retreating to the battlefield sphere, there is also a strong sense of underlying optimism, of regrouping and preparing for a return to (benevolent) dominance and security. Instead of fussing over "little problems," the members of the A-Team and Stringfellow Hawke focus on extending their paternalistic protections.

   Television in the late Cold War era provides a fascinating ground for examining the flow between worldviews and popular culture amid individual, cultural, and international tensions. The 1980s are marked by contradictions between public and private, male and female, and individual and group progress. In the popular culture of the late Cold War, mercenary narratives featured characters balancing isolation and rejection from society with a deep nationalistic patriotism, metaphorically highlighting paths for recovery for both "regular" (white male) Americans and the nation as a whole from the crises of confidence and culture of the 1970s. In a metaphor for ideal nation-building in the late Cold War, these mercenary figures constructed social groups appropriate to the sphere of the battlefield by assembling all-male, multi-faceted teams organized in hierarchical paramilitary patterns. Instead of including well-developed female characters as part of the mercenary's domestic/battlefield sphere, the most consistently gendered "women" in *The A-Team* and *Airwolf* involved the sexualization and gendering of weaponry for the mercenary figures. Weapons were constructed and disposed of on a weekly basis in *The A-Team*, much like their revolving list of interchangeable clients, while the helicopter in *Airwolf* became "The Lady" of the show. The private warriors' weapons replaced women as a way to show their hetero-sexuality in the homosocial environment of the battlefield.

As paramilitary patriots, the mercenary characters in *The A-Team* and *Airwolf* are willing to sacrifice all for their country and for those in need. They might be reluctant to act, but desire to act is less important than honoring the responsibility to protect and provide for those ostensibly under their care that impels their action. During their retreat to the battlefield, these white male mercenary figures are constructing a need and a role for themselves within regular society, hoping that the created need for paternalism, hierarchy, and "benevolent" social control will cause them to be invited back to the top spot that they lost through the crises of the Cold War. These mercenary narratives show the benevolent, paternalistic, white mercenary trying to recapture a secured, ascendant place at the top of American social hierarchies, reaching back through generations of mercenary narratives for that elusive confident feeling. It is a nostalgic grasp for a place that never was assured, confident, or the least bit secure. These television series offer viewers a glimpse into contemporary understandings of the possible, thinkable, idealized, and heroic, at a particular moment in the Cold War, providing a way to make sense of shifting understandings of race, gender, class, and family as constructed through a lens of benevolent dominance and control.

NOTES

1. Charity Fox, "Manifest Mercenaries: Mercenary Narratives in American Popular Culture, 1850–1990" (PhD diss., The George Washington University, 2010).

2. For more detail on changes in American culture in the 1970s, see: Beth Bailey and David Farber, *America in the Seventies* (Lawrence: University Press of Kansas, 2004); Jefferson Cowie, *Stayin' Alive: The 1970s and the Last Days of the Working Class* (New York: The New Press, 2010); Bruce J. Schulman and Julian E. Zelizer, eds., *Rightward Bound: Making America Conservative in the 1970s* (Cambridge: Harvard University Press, 2008); and Bruce J. Schulman, *The Seventies: The Great Shift in American Culture, Society, and Politics* (New York: Free Press, 2001).

3. Daniel Horowitz, *Jimmy Carter and the Energy Crisis of the 1970s: The "Crisis of Confidence" Speech of July 15, 1979*, 1st ed. (New York: Bedford/St. Martin's, 2004).

4. Melani McAlister, *Epic Encounters: Culture, Media, and U.S. Interests in the Middle East since 1945* (Berkeley: University of California Press, 2001).

5. For Carter's urging on mass conservation, see Horowitz, *Jimmy Carter and the Energy Crisis of the 1970s*. For discussion of consumerism as Americanism, see Lizbeth Cohen, *A Consumer's Republic: The Politics of Mass Consumption in Postwar America* (New York: Vintage Books, 2004) and Victoria de Grazia, *Irresistible Empire: America's Advance through Twentieth-Century Europe* (Cambridge: Belknap Press of Harvard University Press, 2006).

6. For more on the cultural shift to conservatism from the 1970s to the 1980s, see: Bailey and Farber, eds., *America in the Seventies*; Cowie, *Stayin' Alive*; and Schulman and Zelizer, *Rightward Bound*.

7. James William Gibson, *Warrior Dreams: Paramilitary Culture in Post-Vietnam America* (New York: Hill and Wang, 1994).

8. Gibson, *Warrior Dreams*, 27.

9. Gibson builds on a number of themes found across cultural studies. Others have also explored similar themes, including Douglas Kellner, *Media Culture: Cultural Studies, Identity and Politics between the Modern and the Postmodern* (New York: Routledge, 1995) and Richard Slotkin, *Gunfighter Nation: The Myth of the Frontier in Twentieth-Century America* (Norman: University of Oklahoma Press, 1998).

10. Gibson, *Warrior Dreams*, 72–73; Emphasis added.

11. Gibson, *Warrior Dreams*, 13.

12. Susan Jeffords, *Hard Bodies: Hollywood Masculinity in the Reagan Era* (New Brunswick: Rutgers University Press, 1994).

13. Jeffords, *Hard Bodies*, 13.

14. The Fox Broadcasting Company did not launch their television network until 1986, and cable, which began in the 1970s as a subscription service for wider television choices, was just beginning to offer 24-hour programming and original programming in the early 1980s. For example, HBO first began offering 24-hour cable programming in late 1981.

15. Jane Feuer, *Seeing Through the Eighties: Television and Reaganism*, Consoleing passions series (Durham: Duke University Press, 1995), 12. Emphasis in original.

16. Feuer, *Seeing Through the Eighties*, 7.

17. For the first season, the opening credits began with the phrase "Ten years ago," which was replaced by "In 1972" for Seasons 2–4. Mirroring the changes to the overarching narrative in Season 5, the voiceover was eliminated in the final season and the theme music was "updated" with a more synthetic sound (electric drums, synthesizers, and a slightly New-Wave-ish take on the martial theme).

18. All five seasons of *The A-Team* are available on DVD from Universal Studios. All episodes are also currently available on Hulu Plus for Internet streaming: "The A-Team–Hulu," Hulu.com, accessed July 5, 2013. http://www.hulu.com/the-a-team.

19. The A-Team's crime is addressed particularly in the pilot "Mexican Slayride: Part 1 and 2," *The A-Team*. Season 1, episode 1 and 2, directed by Rod Holcomb, aired January 23, 1983 (Los Angeles: Universal Studio, 2010), DVD; and in their

trial in Season 5: "Trial by Fire," *The A-Team*. Season 5, episode 2, directed by Les Sheldon, aired October 3, 1986 (Los Angeles: Universal Studios, 2006), DVD.

20. The series pilot, "Mexican Slayride," shows this typical pattern. It opens with a near capture of Hannibal and B. A. by Colonel Lynch from the film set where Hannibal is playing a Godzilla-like monster, then chronicles the path that journalist Amy Allen takes to hire the A-Team to find her friend Al Massey, who has disappeared in Mexico. The team finds that Massey has been kidnapped by a gang leader. In the course of their rescue, the team is cornered by the gang, builds an armored car out of spare parts in the village, and escapes while rallying the village to their side. "Mexican Slayride: Part 1 and 2," *The A-Team* Season 1, Episode 1 and 2, directed by Rod Holcomb, aired January 23, 1983 (Los Angeles: Universal Studio, 2010), DVD.

21. A short list of notable cameos in *The A-Team* Season 4 includes: Rick James in "The Heart of Rock and Roll," *The A-Team*, Season 4, Episode 6, directed by Tony Mordente, aired November 5, 1985 (Los Angeles, CA: Universal Studio, 2006), DVD; Hulk Hogan in "Body Slam," *The A-Team*, Season 4, Episode 7, directed by Craig R. Baxley, aired November 12, 1985 (Los Angeles, CA: Universal Studio, 2006), DVD; Wheel of Fortune (the game show) in "Wheel of Fortune," *The A-Team*, Season 4, Episode 13, directed by David Hemmings, aired January 14, 1986 (Los Angeles: Universal Studio, 2006), DVD; and Boy George in "Cowboy George," *The A-Team*, Season 4, Episode 16, directed by Tony Mordente, aired Feburary 11, 1986 (Los Angeles: Universal Studio, 2006), DVD.

22. "Dishpan Man," *The A-Team* Season 5, Episode 1, directed by Tony Mordente, aired September 26, 1986 (Los Angeles: Universal Studio, 2006), DVD; "Trial by Fire," *The A-Team*, Season 5, Episode 2, directed by Les Sheldon, aired October 3, 1986 (Los Angeles, CA: Universal Studio, 2006), DVD; "Firing Line," *The A-Team*, Season 5, Episode 3, directed by Michael O'Herlihy, aired October 10, 1986 (Los Angeles: Universal Studio, 2006), DVD.

23. "Shadow of the Hawke: Part 1 and 2," *Airwolf*, Season 1, Episode 1, directed by Donald P. Bellisario, aired January 22, 1984 (Los Angeles: Universal Studios, 2005), DVD. All four seasons of *Airwolf* are available on DVD from Universal Studios. All episodes are also currently available on Hulu Plus for internet streaming: "Airwolf–Hulu," Hulu.com, accessed July 5, 2013. http://www.hulu.com/airwolf

24. "Sweet Britches," *Airwolf*, Season 2, Episode 1, directed by Alan J. Levi, aired September 22, 1984 (Los Angeles: Universal Studios, 2006), DVD.

25. "Half-Pint," *Airwolf*, Season 3, Episode 12, directed by Bernard McEveety, aired December 21, 1985 (Los Angeles: Universal Studios, 2007), DVD.

26. "Blackjack," *Airwolf*, Season 4, Episode 1, directed by Alan Simmonds, aired January 23, 1987 (Los Angeles: Universal Studios, 2011), DVD.

27. Because it is so different, the fourth season is alternately referred to as *Airwolf* (1987), *Airwolf II*, and *Airwolf* Season 4 in print and online sources. For the sake of continuity, I refer to it as *Airwolf* Season 4 in this chapter.

28. The use of stock footage is often very noticeable, especially when watching the episodes in close proximity with each other. For example, the exact same shot of Airwolf flying over the ocean is used in the final episode of Season 3, Episode 22, "Birds of Paradise" and in Season 4, Episode 1, "Blackjack." This was probably not

as noticeable when the episodes were separated by months, networks, and production companies, but for a DVD or online viewer, it is jarring, uncanny, and a little hilarious to see the same visual shots used over and over. It adds a ridiculous, campy feel to otherwise overly serious situations. "Birds of Paradise," *Airwolf*, Season 3, Episode 22, directed by Bernard L. Kowalski, aired March 29, 1986 (Los Angeles, CA: Universal Studios, 2007), DVD; "Blackjack," *Airwolf*, Season 4, Episode 1, directed by Alan Simmonds, aired January 23, 1987 (Los Angeles: Universal Studios, 2011), DVD.

29. "When You Comin' Back, Range Rider?: Part 1 and 2," *The A-Team*, Season 2, Episode 5, directed by Christian Nyby, aired October 25, 1983 (Los Angeles: Universal Studios, 2005), DVD.

30. "Sweet Britches," *Airwolf*, Season 2, Episode 1, directed by Alan J. Levi, aired September 22, 1984 (Los Angeles: Universal Studios, 2006), DVD.

"Sweet Britches" is the predatory nickname that the head thug/wannabe rapist continually uses when cornering Caitlin and professing his manhood in front of his fellow thugs.

31. "The Truth About Holly," *Airwolf*, Season 2, Episode 4, directed by Alan J. Levi, aired October 13, 1984 (Los Angeles: Universal Studios, 2006), DVD.

32. For example, Gibson, *Warrior Dreams*; Jeffords, *Hard Bodies*; Kellner, *Media Culture*.

33. "Firestorm," *Airwolf*, Season 2, Episode 2, directed by Ray Austin, aired September 29, 1984 (Los Angeles: Universal Studios, 2006), DVD.

34. References to the Airwolf helicopter by variations of the nickname "The Lady" are frequent throughout the series, with the transition to the nickname completed throughout Season 3.

35. *Full Metal Jacket*. Directed by Stanley Kubrick (1987; Burbank, CA: Warner Home Video, 2001), DVD.

36. "Mexican Slayride: Part 1 and 2," *The A-Team*, Season 1, Episode 1, directed by Rod Holcomb, aired January 23, 1983 (Los Angeles: Universal Studios, 2010), DVD.

37. "Mexican Slayride: Part 1 and 2," *The A-Team*, Season 1, Episode 1, directed by Rod Holcomb, aired January 23, 1983 (Los Angeles: Universal Studios, 2010), DVD.

Section IV

THE MORE YOU KNOW

Chapter Eleven

Lisa and Phoebe, Lone Vegetarian Icons: At Odds with Television's Carnonormativity

Carrie Packwood Freeman

The best thing the animal rights movement has going on American television is Lisa Simpson, at least from my perspective as a vegan and animal rights activist for over fifteen years, a critical animal studies media scholar, and a frequent viewer of American TV since the 1970s. Lisa's character has been advocating for progressive causes (to help human and nonhuman animals) since *The Simpsons'* premier in 1989. And since she decided to stop eating animals in 1995, she's the longest-running and most prominent vegetarian character in American TV history.[1] And I would count Phoebe Buffay (played by actress Lisa Kudrow) on the hit NBC sitcom *Friends* as the second-most prominent vegetarian character, as she avoided animal meat for the bulk of the decade that series aired, from 1994–2004.[2] These clever, independent, and progressive female TV characters stand out as they stand up for animals in a sea of carnonormativity.

For vegetarians and anyone who cares about the rights and interests of nonhuman animals, watching television can be a frustrating and alienating experience, reminding you how at odds your beliefs are with mainstream cultural practice. You see frequent commercials for seafood restaurant buffets and family-size buckets of fried chickens, body parts being fileted and sauteed on cooking shows, leather bags and jackets for sale on QVC, deer being bagged on outdoor channels, gastronomes reveling in eating grotesque parts and exotic species on reality TV, and news stories that largely ignore nonhuman animal issues, discussing farmed animals primarily as economic commodities or public health concerns.[3]

Television is reflecting (and reinforcing) the routineness of animal oppression in American society, as agribusiness breeds and slaughters over nine billion land animals every year (not counting the millions who die at hatcheries, factory farms, and in transit due to being ill, injured, or discarded), and the fishing industry captures and kills double that amount of sea creatures (plus many more "by catch" accidentally killed in nets but not meant for consumption).[4] For most Americans, eating these animals is a cultural choice and habit rather than a biological requirement, as plant-based diets have been shown to be nutritionally adequate and often healthier in terms of disease prevention and longevity.[5] Yet current polling estimates only 3 percent of the US population is actually vegetarian (abstaining from animal flesh) and 1 percent is vegan (abstaining from all animal products), equating to somewhere between six and twelve million vegans and vegetarians.[6] But up to a third of Americans, while not strict vegetarians, say they are eating meatless meals a significant amount of the time.[7] This is a hopeful trend not just for animals and human health, but also for the environment, as the earth cannot continue to sustain a growing human population of animal-eaters, since raising animals for flesh, dairy, and eggs is significantly more resource-intensive and polluting than growing plant-based crops.[8] In an era of climate change, peak energy, freshwater shortages, and mass extinction of species, a paradigm shift to a plant-based diet has become an ecological imperative.

This raises the question as to how much television programming is aiding this socially and ecologically responsible shift toward vegetarianism. Yet studies of television, like the programming itself, are anthropocentric, often emphasizing gender, race, and class bias while ignoring species bias.[9] This suggests a need to study the media's portrayal of nonhuman animals and their relationship with humans, especially scholarship critical of humanity's systematic oppression of nonhuman animals. In this chapter, I examine how human privilege operates by studying the characterization of ethical vegetarianism as an alternative lifestyle and comedic fodder in primetime television. The rebellious dietary choices of Lisa on *The Simpsons* and Phoebe on *Friends* provide an opportunity to analyze the construction of animal rights identities and how that is perceived and negotiated by the meat-eating mainstream. I articulate how, and to what extent, these smart and strong[10] vegetarian females serve as a challenge to the hegemony of carnism, an ideology that normalizes the practice of using and consuming certain animal others.[11]

To set the context for this critical television analysis of carnism, I begin by explaining ethical philosophy on why nonhuman animals matter, why that means we shouldn't farm or kill them, and why we still do, despite our psychological discomfort with causing them harm. I establish the cultural importance of television as a site of cultivation and social learning, especially what it teaches us about ourselves in relation to food and farmed animals. Then I share the findings of my analysis of how comedic themes around vegetarians in *The Simpsons* and *Friends* function to both reinforce and challenge carnism. I end with suggestions for ways that television programming can be fairer to fellow animals and less carnonormative.

LITERATURE REVIEW: ANIMAL ETHICS, VEGETARIANISM, AND TELEVISION

In the 1970s, ethics philosophers began to articulate the moral relevancy of nonhuman animals based on their sentience, consciousness, and subjectivity.[12] If other animals are also feeling, thinking, social beings with a desire to live, this calls into question the basis of human entitlement to discriminate against them as "inferiors." Peter Singer labeled that bias "speciesism," an oppressive system comparable to sexism and racism.[13] As it is unfair to objectify human subjects by enslaving or using them as mere resources, animal rights philosophy asks for moral consistency in applying this logic to respect other sentient animals. According to this logic, breeding and farming anyone for food items is an unjust, objectifying practice, as is hunting/fishing/killing anyone (unless done for sheer survival).[14] Yet American society has largely accepted the practice of mass farming and fishing of certain nonhuman animal species (e.g., pigs not dogs, tuna not dolphins), and an entrenched animal industrial complex has legally and economically integrated the habitual sale and consumption of animal products firmly into American culture.[15]

Psychologist Melanie Joy examined *why* humans do not tend to ethically question this unnecessary violence against fellow sentient beings.[16] While most people might like to perceive meat-eating as merely a dietary *behavior*, Joy coined the term "carnism" to foreground and label the entrenched *ideology* that perpetuates and excuses this violent behavior. She calls meat-eaters *carnists* rather than *carnivores* or *omnivores* because, for most of us in America, eating animals is a "philosophical choice" based on an accepted belief system, not primarily a "biological constitution" or necessity.[17] Society justifies carnism through its construction of meat-eating as "normal, natural, and necessary."[18] Eating animals becomes a taken-for granted, naturalized social norm as the majority of society puts it into daily practice. Social norms are constructed prescriptions that show us how our culture expects us to behave: "norms keep us in line by rewarding conformity and punishing us if we stray off course."[19] The social, psychological, and physical *invisibility* of violence (in this case farmed animal cruelty and killing) is key to its social acceptance as a norm.

Joy explained that this violent carnistic system is on shaky moral ground as it is "riddled with absurdities, inconsistencies, and paradox" and thus requires a "complex network of defenses."[20] These psychological defenses include a cognitive trio: (1) *objectifying* sentient farmed animals as things, (2) *deindividualizing* the animals whom we eat so they aren't known as unique individuals or friends, and (3) *dichotomizing* animals into categories such as inedible/edible or sensitive/senseless to justify eating certain species and sparing others (including ourselves). The media (particularly the news media) are one of the main institutions that legitimizes carnism. Joy claimed, "media fail to challenge the system and support carnistic defenses: they maintain the invisibility of the system and reinforce the justifications for eating meat."[21]

Considering the pervasiveness of television in Americans' daily lives, it is an influential and predominant source of cultural production rather than being merely just a source of entertainment. Cultivation analysis reveals that, over time, television, as a "common symbolic environment,"[22] has a mainstreaming effect on heavy viewers, nudging their beliefs closer to the cultural norm and television's version of social reality—a view that tends to conform to status quo power structures, fostering acquiescence rather than resistance. And social cognitive theory also supports television's influence, as viewers may model behaviors they often see rewarded and reinforced on television and begin to identify with favorite characters. While television should be socially responsible, considering its impact, corporate-owned media are beholden to commercial interests more so than ethical or social imperatives.[23] That doesn't lend itself to a heavy support of environmental and animal rights values and issues, which could be viewed as threatening to "free-market" capitalistic growth and pursuit of profit, especially restaurant and food advertisers. Pro-environmental and pro-animal topics are therefore more likely to be symbolically annihilated in a commercial media system, giving viewers the impression they are a low sociopolitical priority.[24]

The dominant way of viewing animals and food is through an anthropocentric and carnistic lens, so television generally reflects this carnonormativity.[25] Likewise, most people portrayed on television are assumed to be carnists by default unless proven otherwise. A cursory view of the television menu reveals that carnism is normalized through meat's emphasis without controversy or apology in popular genres, such as meat-centric cooking and culinary shows, hunting and fishing shows, and ubiquitous food and restaurant advertisements selling meat, egg, and dairy products. In particular, meat is associated with hedonistic pleasure and heterosexual masculine identity in fast-food advertising.[26] Ecofeminists parallel the commercial objectification of nonhuman "food" animals with that of human female bodies—both as pleasurable objects of male consumption.[27] Generally, commercial meat messages visually emphasize animals as objects disassociated from their former existence as a living subject.[28] Objectification of farmed animals is also common in American news coverage, as reporting tends to focus on farmed animals as economic commodities, considering them en masse rather than as individuals, and without considering their perspective and interests in stories that affect them. While some news stories supported farmed animal welfare reform ("happy meats"), a focus on animal rights (a vegan stance) was more infrequent.[29] A UK study found the news failed to frame veganism as a legitimate challenge to speciesism, describing the news as "vegaphobic" in its tendency to represent vegans in more derogatory ways as ascetic, sentimental, or extreme.[30]

METHODOLOGY: SAMPLING VEGETARIANISM
A LA LISA & PHOEBE

Television is too vast a text to do a comprehensive examination of an ideology as pervasive as carnism, so as a qualitative researcher who goes for depth not breadth, I am focusing on a less common representation—vegetarianism—as a vehicle for revealing carnistic norms. Vegetarianism could be examined in a variety of television formats—those rare vegetarian cooking shows, soy product advertisements, or vegetarian reality show participants (whose diet is useful as a dramatic tool for conflict building), but I thought it would be most productive to examine recurring vegetarian characters in fictional entertainment. There is a small cadre of these characters, primarily women, including Darlene from *Roseanne* (1988–1997), Angela from *The Office* (2005–2013), Rachel from *Glee* (2009–present), and Spock from *Star Trek* (1966–1969). But keeping significance and manageability in mind, I chose to study the most prominent long-time vegetarian characters in popular primetime shows, Lisa from *The Simpsons* and Phoebe from *Friends*, as these animal-inspired vegetarian icons have been in America's living rooms for almost two decades (especially considering the shows' syndication).

The Simpsons (1989–present), winner of a Peabody Award and over twenty-five Emmy awards, is a Fox animated half-hour situation comedy created by Matt Groening that is now the longest-running scripted TV show in history.[31] Its subversive humor centers on a "dysfunctional" American family of five living in the fictional town of Springfield. The brainy eight-year-old daughter, Lisa Simpson, is voiced by Emmy-winner Yeardley Smith. *Friends* (1994–2004), winner of six Emmy awards and six People's Choice Awards for "Favorite Television Comedy Series," is a popular NBC half-hour situation comedy developed by Marta Crane and David Kauffman starring six friends (in their mid-20s through mid-30s) living and working in New York City.[32] Lisa Kudrow won an Emmy and an American Comedy Award for her portrayal as Phoebe.[33] As a fan I have watched many seasons of these

shows over the years, but to create a more focused and manageable sample
for study, I selected only the episodes where food, particularly the characters'
vegetarianism, was either a major or minor theme (seven episodes of *The
Simpsons* and six episodes of *Friends*). Among my sample, vegetarianism
usually turned out to be a minor theme consisting of a conversation or just a
one-liner. But it became a major theme once on *Friends*, in the 1998 episode,
"The One with the Fake Party" in which Phoebe's pregnancy has her craving
and eventually eating meat,[34] and three times on *The Simpsons*, in the following episodes: "Lisa the Vegetarian" (when a petting zoo lamb inspires her to
go vegetarian in 1995),[35] "Apocalypse Cow" (when the family rescues Bart's
4-H cow in 2008),[36] and "Penny-Wiseguys" (when anemic Lisa temporarily adds insects to her diet in 2012).[37] As it is the richest episode, "Lisa the
Vegetarian" will get significant attention in my analysis. This episode won
a Genesis Award from the Humane Society of the US and an Environmental
Media Award and is the favorite episode of executive producer David Mirkin,
an animal advocate and vegetarian, who had to promise Paul McCartney to
make Lisa a permanent vegetarian character, as part of McCartney's agree-
ment to star in the episode.[38]

My main research question is: In what ways does the presence of vegetarians on these comedy shows serve to challenge and/or to reinforce carnism? I
will examine this through comparing and contrasting the comic portrayals of:

- Vegetarian characters versus carnistic characters in their food-based interactions,
- Plant-based versus animal-based foods/diets, and
- Similarities and distinctions between Lisa and Phoebe in the social dynamic of each respective show.

Because I am studying the television genre of situation comedies, the philosopher Henri Bergson's theory of laughter is useful, particularly two of his
primary concepts.[39] First, he viewed laughter as a form of social corrective,
used to nudge an eccentric person back into conformity. If people are out of
line, yet not in illegal ways that justify imprisonment, laughter is used as a
social tool of isolation to nudge the outsider to voluntarily rejoin the group.
Second, difference itself is amusing, especially if it puts a character at an
extreme, such as too rigid and inflexible (in body or mind) at one end of the
spectrum, and too loose and elastic (in body or mind) at the other end. For
example, a "rigid" person with uptight morals or mechanical movements is
funny, as is a "loose" person with lax morals or clumsy movements.

This critical discourse analysis is informed by my critical perspective on
speciesism, and is more specifically guided by the theoretical frameworks of

Bergson's theory of laughter, Joy's psychological theory of carnism, and, to a lesser extent, the media's social cognitive theory. This means I'll highlight concepts such as use of comic extremes to contrast character traits, laughter/ ridicule as a social corrective, the pressure to conform with social norms, psychological defense mechanisms and justifications for meat-eating, and audience identification with characters.

TASTING THE SAMPLE: ANALYSIS & FINDINGS

Use of Comic Extremes

Both Lisa and Phoebe possess similar likeable traits, making them admirable characters in some senses (e.g., they are ethical, smart, strong, caring, reliable, honest, independent, feminist, and musical). But their animal-rights inspired vegetarianism is something that places them at a potentially amusing dietary and ideological extreme from a mainstream carnistic society. Despite some similarities between these two committed vegetarians, I don't actually see them on the same end of Bergson's comic elasticity spectrum; Lisa is portrayed at the *rigid* extreme (as her righteous indignation, uptight over-achieving tendencies, and strident advocacy for causes make her a goody-goody) and Phoebe is portrayed more at the *loose* extreme (as her new-age beliefs make her more free-spirited and open and often make her appear flaky, goofy, weird, or naively idealistic). While both vegetarian characters are seen as idealistic, Phoebe's idealism is portrayed as cultural to who she is as a "hippie" type (it's more personal, almost an essentialized personality based on her unorthodox upbringing), while Lisa's idealism is portrayed as progressive and activist (it's more public—a political choice). Some sense of moral judgment toward carnism is implied by Phoebe, who will gladly explain her principled personal choice not to eat animals ("no food with a face"[40] and "meat is murder"[41]), but she doesn't campaign for vegetarianism nor seem to expect any friends to go veg, unlike Lisa. Principal Skinner called Lisa an "agitator" after her criticism of meat-based school lunches and worm dissection set off the school's "independent thought alarm."[42] Lisa actively tries to convert people to causes, like vegetarianism. For example, in "Lisa the Vegetarian" she told everyone how she realized that killing and eating animals is wrong and expects others, especially her family, to be similarly enlightened (an amusing naivety that soon fades). In the "Apocalypse Cow" episode she tries to convert Bart to vegetarianism by hiding a CD of cow mooing sounds in his bedroom to make him think his 4-H pet cow, Lou, who he raised but reluctantly had to send to slaughter, was talking to him in his sleep.

Lisa's conversion tactics face resistance, serving as comic fodder. In the episode where Lisa went vegetarian,[43] she tries to bring Springfield residents along with her, but the community uses ridicule and laughter to try to embarrass Lisa back into conformity, which is how Bergson says laughter works as a social corrective.[44] But what *The Simpsons'* producers meant to be humorous here isn't so much Lisa's different behavior/ideas (although her initial optimism is amusing) as much as the town's ignorant and unreasonable resistance to her reasonable ideas. In this way, *The Simpsons'* producers are using laughter as a way to ridicule morally inconsistent *social norms* rather than just encourage continued carnistic conformity. For example, Lisa's classmates laughed at her vegetarianism on two occasions using childish taunts such as "are you gonna marry a carrot?" and also repeating back the insults verbatim that they learned in a meat council marketing film that Principal Skinner showed to combat Lisa's dissent (there, her classmates called her "crazy" and a "grade A moron"). These particular examples make Lisa appear smarter and more of a critical-thinker than the other children as they prove her point that they have been "brainwashed by corporate propaganda." While the adults don't tend to take the juvenile approach of outright laughing at Lisa, except when she suggests friends and neighbors eat tomato soup at the BBQ, all authority figures in her life and meat marketing messages pervasive around town demonstrate overwhelming resistance or at least a lack of support for her ideological stance. For example, her dad gave her the silent treatment the next day after she ruined his BBQ. Considering the Bergsonian notion of amusing extremes,[45] both Lisa as vegetarian and other characters as carnists can be viewed as extremely *rigid*, but in different senses—Lisa in her strident indignation and everyone else in their close-minded defense of their dietary habits. The community's pressuring tactics worked to make Lisa feel isolated in her vegetarianism; exasperated, she finally exclaimed "The whole world wants me to eat meat! I can't fight it anymore!" and deliberately, yet reluctantly, bites into a hotdog. But just then, vegans Apu and Paul and Linda McCartney become the adult mentors and role models she needed to remain consistent to her cause. In addition Lisa finds out Apu's hotdogs at Kwik-E-Mart are tofu-dogs, unbeknownst to any carnistic customers who eat them.

When it comes to laughter as a social corrective in *Friends*, laughter is often used to keep *the audience* conforming to carnism. Phoebe's circle of friends does not attempt to ridicule *her* into carnistic conformity, probably because Phoebe is not actively trying to convert them (so she doesn't face the resistance that activist Lisa does). Phoebe's main group (with the possible exception of dim-witted Joey) are portrayed as normal, respectable, mainstream characters who affectionately laugh (along with the largely carnistic audience) at her quaint eccentricities; her friends snicker behind her back or through gestures to each other, such as eye rolling, meant to reinforce to themselves (and hence to the audience) that it's obvious to everyone except Phoebe that carnism is legitimate and her ideology is weird. We tolerate Phoebe's eccentricities because she's just being her uniquely authentic self. She can't help it; it's somewhat endearing and amusing. But in this way, I would say the audience is not encouraged to emulate Phoebe (unless they want to identify as "hippie") because she is not often socially rewarded for her vegetarianism and it is part of what makes her somewhat odd. So overall, laughter fails to function in *Friends* like it often does in *The Simpsons* to ethically critique social norms of meat-eating, as *Friends* could be seen as ethically legitimizing carnism by emphasizing its normalcy among good people, which highlights the unorthodoxy of Phoebe's Bohemian choice to eschew meat.

The contrast created by extremes in *The Simpsons* helps make Lisa's vegetarianism more overtly ethical or "right" than the way Phoebe's vegetarianism is more neutrally presented in *Friends* as the personal or cultural choice of a flower child. Because Phoebe's friends are more tolerant of her vegetarianism, and they themselves (while each possessing their own quirks/vices) aren't buffoons or fatally flawed, the diets and beliefs of the carnistic characters on *Friends* do not come across as wrong-headed, foolish, or ethically hypocritical. Consider the fact that, once in an early episode, during a fight with Phoebe, Monica gloated that she had lied to Phoebe about the pâté being vegetarian. Although Monica displayed blatant disrespect for Phoebe's ethical beliefs, the show's producers framed it so that we, like Monica, find this trick more amusing than reprehensible, indicating eating animals really isn't the serious offense, or unappetizing experience, Phoebe believes it is.[46]

When it comes to the *The Simpsons*, however, Homer and almost all the authority figures are generally self-centered, somewhat idiotic, and largely ineffectual. Because the social dynamic represents such a strong contrast between Lisa as the smart, committed, caring vegetarian and almost everyone else as somewhat shallow and unreflective meat-eaters, it makes Lisa's animal-friendly stance seem *right* and ethically preferable (even if we might make fun of her activism). Her moral wisdom is especially apparent when contrasted with Homer, as an extreme example of moral apathy. For instance, in Lisa's moment of vegetarian epiphany, when she realizes she can't eat the lambchops at dinner because she envisions them falling off the body of the lamb she met at the petting zoo, Homer ignorantly reassures her "This is lamb, not *a* lamb"—nonsensically disassociating the meat product from the living species. A few sentences later he further proves his ignorance about animals used for food, as Lisa has to inform him that bacon, ham, and porkchops all come from the same animal. He laughs "Yeah, right, Lisa, a wonderful 'magical' animal."[47]

In Ann Marie Todd's eco-focused rhetorical analysis of *The Simpsons*, she agreed that Lisa and Homer represent "extremes of dietary conflict" with both being equally intolerant of the other (until the resolution of the "Lisa the Vegetarian" episode).[48] Lisa's character represents the "environmental ethic of caring for non-human creatures"[49] as opposed to Homer's character who represents humanity's self-centered and thoughtless exploitation of others. Similar to my assessment, Todd agreed that Lisa's vegetarian stance is meant to appear as morally right, saying "she represents a moral center to the show, which enables her to reveal the irony of her father's anthropocentric actions."[50]

The Moderate Lacto-Ovo Vegetarian

There are times when Lisa and Phoebe are portrayed as less extreme, and thus more sympathetic, relatable characters. They can appear more moderate because they *do* eat some animal products (dairy and eggs) and haven't ventured as far as veganism. The vegan comparison isn't highlighted in *Friends*, but in *The Simpsons*, veganism is shown as more hard-core. For example, Lisa's crush, Jesse, a teen eco-activist, condescendingly tells her vegetarianism is "a start" making her a "poser," whereas he is a Level 5 Vegan and "won't eat anything that casts a shadow."[51] His nonsensical position (which in theory would include not even eating plants) makes the audience sympathize with Lisa's meat-free diet as a reasonable compromise for an animal advocate. Hyperbole is again used to express the extremism of vegan ideology when Lisa compared herself to another vegan, Apu, and said he must think she's a "monster" because she eats cheese. Apu admits he does think that, but his tolerance keeps him from "badgering" people.[52]

Phoebe's moderate side is seen not so much in comparison to veganism, but in her flexibility to be a team-player with carnists. Not only does she not mind being around animal flesh while hanging out with her friends, once she is shown eagerly partaking in the turkey "wishbone" ritual of breaking the bird's bone, saying of vegetarians, "Just because we don't eat the meat doesn't mean we don't like to play with the carcasses."[53] And once Phoebe was even willing to eat meat to fit in with her boyfriend's snobby, disapproving parents who were serving veal at the group's first introduction.[54] This demonstrates that Phoebe was "reasonable" enough to rank love (or at least social conformity) above her unconventional principles in this one significant instance. But *Friends'* producers characterize her veal-eating as a big compromise when Phoebe's overly obliging, sarcastic commentary highlights the ethical controversy that *should* reasonably exist over eating babies: "That's okay. I am a vegetarian except for veal. Yeah, no, veal I love. It's any baby animals—kittens, fish babies, especially veal!" But Phoebe gets to remain meat-free in the end because, after only one bite, her nausea forces her to throw it up.

You Don't Win Friends with Salad: Portrayal of Meat Versus Vegetarian Foods

Neither *Friends* nor *The Simpsons* is for or against meat completely. Overall, meat-based diets and plant-based diets are portrayed in ways that are both positive and negative (see Table 11.1). Meat is definitely portrayed as pervasive and central to the average American's diet, and quite essential to celebrate special occasions. For example, to celebrate Ross's birthday, Monica brought "five steaks and an eggplant for Phoebe," which highlights vegetarians as different from the group norm.[55] And to celebrate Monica's promotion, the *Friends* characters, besides Phoebe, all order various meat-based dishes when they go out to dinner (except a financially strapped Rachel who ordered a side salad because it was cheaper, so this vegetarian option appears less preferable),[56] and Phoebe's friends don't order vegetarian dishes even for her own birthday celebration.[57] Dinnertime at the Simpsons' house appears to be meat-centered with plant-based side dishes, and when Homer threw a party (in the "Lisa the Vegetarian" episode), he made it a BBQ. When Lisa objected, he informed her that "all normal people love meat . . . I'm trying to impress people." And then he and the family conducted a conga line dance in front of Lisa, repeatedly chanting "you don't win friends with salad. You don't win friends with salad . . ." When Lisa then tried to interrupt Homer's meat-grilling at the BBQ by announcing "Good news everyone! You don't have to eat meat! I made enough gazpacho for all!" she was laughed out of the yard, with one guy yelling "Go back to Russia"—the ridiculousness of which indicates that labeling vegetarians as un-American is hyperbolic. Relegating meat-free entrees to a lower status, the party-goers let the dog eat the gazpacho.

Table 11.1. Diet Portrayals

Diets	Positive Portrayal	Negative Portrayal
Plant-Based	More ethical Healthier in many respects	Lacking in taste Lacking in some nutrients (potentially protein and iron)
Meat-Based	More impressive in taste and stature Contains protein and iron Popular and normal to American culture	Based on violence/suffering Can be gross Often unhealthy

Part of why meat "impresses people" is because it is portrayed as being *tastier* food, especially on *The Simpsons*. Homer is always salivating over bacon, and Bart, when once considering vegetarianism, said "it's not my fault there's nothing good to eat on this planet except meat!"[58] Homer described a portabella mushroom he was eating as a "rubbery fungus-like steak,"[59] and Chandler told Phoebe that "soyburgers suck."[60] Even Lisa once admitted her diet was "bland."[61] Veggie options can be seen as deficient, such as when the school lunch lady served Lisa an empty hotdog bun as her entree, sarcastically saying it was "filled with bunly goodness."[62] On the other hand, sometimes producers portray certain animal meats as grotesque and unappetizing, such as the gray intestine-shaped tripe served once at Springfield Elementary[63] and the insect smorgasbord at the "Springfield Insectivorian Society" (maggot stew, mug 'o slugs, and windshield casserole).[64]

The healthfulness of meat-based diets is called into question at times when *The Simpsons'* characters are shown gluttonously stuffing themselves, such as at Homer's BBQ (especially the overweight, bloated, and immobilized police chief).[65] And when Marge surprisingly concluded that the family would be healthier if they moved vegetables from side dish to main entree, the whole family, besides Lisa, ironically got sick off of the vegetarian meal Marge made from organic local produce.[66] Lisa blamed their poor immune systems, explaining "your bodies are so used to processed food. It's a shock when you eat vegetables full of vitamins, minerals, and trace amounts of bug feces."

Yet there are times that a *plant-based* diet is implied to be nutritionally insufficient, and these health issues caused identity crises for Lisa and Phoebe when they both made the hard decision to go back to eating animals for a limited time. For Lisa it was when she fainted due to anemia.[67] Marge was hoping she'd have to stop being vegetarian, but the doctor conceded that Lisa could just take humongous iron supplement pills. Lisa hated the pills and was talked into eating insects by the lunch lady who reasoned that we all already end up eating spiders in our sleep and bug parts in our peanut butter, therefore some vegetarians decided it was morally acceptable to eat insects (and Lisa herself wondered if they were really animals). Soon Lisa realized that was a slippery moral slope when she considered eating shrimp too. And when grasshoppers in her dreams told her they feel pain, she knew she couldn't eat bugs anymore, so she was a vegetarian again by the end of the episode (without any more references to anemia).

Phoebe started eating animals to succumb to her pregnancy cravings and was thus able to blame it on someone else—the baby—saying "the baby wants me to eat meat."[68] She couldn't trick the baby with a soyburger, so she started eating Chandler's meat sandwich, claiming "I can't help it. I need the meat. The baby needs the meat!" After downing a whole steak off the bone, she frustratingly told Joey that if she eats meat for the next six months of her pregnancy she'd be eating "like a million cows." So Joey makes a sacrifice for a friend and offers to stop eating meat during her pregnancy "so no extra animals would die. You'd be eating *my* animals." Phoebe gladly takes him up on the offer and eats all types of meats with gusto during her pregnancy, giving the impression that meat-free diets don't provide enough prenatal nutrients and that vegetarians would relish eating animal flesh if they could find a moral justification for it.

Taking a Stab at Beef: Carnistic Doubts

But moral issues arise for carnist characters on the shows too, as they occasionally acknowledge that meat involves suffering, or at least, death. It appears these characters are conflicted when it comes to meat, as they want to eat it but do not want to know the individual who it's from (especially if they are friends) or to see the slaughtering. For example, Joey does not think about *who* he is eating, as he is fine eating chicken but not "birds." When he finds out emu are birds, he ignorantly says "people don't eat birds?! What, would they fly into our mouths?! What, would you order a big bucket of fried birds or their wings? (Pause). Wait. Oh!"[69] Our feathered friends get more attention on *Friends* with the recurring theme of Chandler and Joey keeping a duck and a chicken for pets. The guys never consider eating these particular birds since they become part of the family, yet they do still eat other ducks and chickens as "poultry." The Simpsons don't eat their pets either, but dogs and cats are not seen as "edible" species in American carnistic culture. As mentioned earlier, Bart briefly considered going vegetarian once.[70] He said he'd never eat meat again if he could save his 4-H cow, Lou, from slaughter, but then a few sentences later admitted the death of unknown animals was a lower priority by saying "Sorry, Lisa. I can't be vegetarian. I love the taste of death. But please help me get my cow back." During Lou's rescue, some hippie animal rights activists used the secret signals "Milk is murder" and "Cheese is genocide" to emphasize killing in the dairy industry. Later in the same episode, Homer heroically disguised himself in a cow costume to impersonate Lou, and he himself ended up getting taken to the slaughterhouse. Homer was shaken up by his near-death experience and came to this nonsensical revelation: "The things I saw! It makes me never want to eat meat again! (Pause) Just fish, chicken, burgers, veal on Fridays, deer, but only in season, and, if necessary, the sweetest meat of all—human." Lisa patronizingly considered this a victory where her dad was concerned. Homer *did* express an animal rights sentiment in the "Lisa the Treehugger" episode, conceding that animals want to control and retain ownership of their own bodies by exclaiming, "I knew this day would come. The cows are taking back what's theirs!" This was his initial concerned response to seeing "cows" holding the protest sign "Krusty Burger = Earth Murder," before he realized they were actually human activists in costume.

Probably the best satirical critique on meat's violence comes during the meat council propaganda video that Principal Skinner shows the class to try to get Lisa from forcing vegetarian lunch options on the school.[71] In it cowboy Troy McClure takes little Jimmy on an educational trip from the "high density cattle feedlot" to "the killing floor" to show him how meat goes from ranch to stomach. The audience can't see the killing and butchering, we just hear the screams and stunning and thuds repeatedly and then steaks fall onto a truck at the other end. Jimmy comes out shocked, shivering, and nauseated while Troy obliviously asks "Getting hungry, Jimmy?" The humor here emphasizes that slaughter is obviously an *un*appetizing experience. Jimmy then asks (on behalf of a "crazy friend") if it is wrong to eat meat, and Troy informs him that his crazy friend is ignorant of the food chain (a chart where all nonhuman animals point to a human man in the middle). Then he scares Jimmy with more absurd science by dramatically claiming, "If a cow ever got the chance, he'd eat you and everyone you ever cared about." It ends with Jimmy realizing you are a "grade A moron" if you question eating meat (with the pun further trivializing the seriousness of the killing). Because the film's rationales for meat-eating were so poor and the violence too scary to stomach, *The Simpsons'* producers made a clear statement that the ethical controversy over meat is warranted yet silenced by those in power.

CONCLUSIONS ABOUT CARNONORMATIVITY

Lisa and Phoebe live in a carnonormative social world where their ethical vegetarian stance represents a nonconformity that is tolerated by the community but not emulated or encouraged. Going against the grain puts these herbivores at comic extremes, exposing them to ridicule by the group at times. While Lisa and Phoebe are generally strong enough to withstand this peer pressure, the lesson viewers may take away is that vegetarianism is ultimately more isolating or socially challenging than it is rewarding, living up to Homer's contention that "you don't win friends with salad." This is especially true with Phoebe's character, as her vegetarianism is one of the traits that brands her as kooky and laughable, allowing the audience to dismiss her political stances. Naomi R. Rockler's feminist analysis of *Friends* noted: "When *Friends* does present political issues, it does so through its most marginalized character [Phoebe], and in ways that mock and undercut these issues. Although she seems to believe that the personal is political, Phoebe's function is not to raise consciousness about issues, but rather to encourage viewers to laugh at them."[72] Lisa's character, on the other hand, is less often the butt of the jokes (based on her vegetarianism, at least) and more often a vehicle for revealing the paradoxes of carnism, making the apathy, hypocrisy, or hedonism of carnists appear humorous. I also find it productive that Lisa's and Phoebe's rationales for vegetarianism are based on a prohibition against killing animals rather than just a protest against the poor welfare conditions on modern farms, as this resists the temptation for vegetarians to start eating so-called "happy meats" and shows a respect for an animal's right to life.

While the treatment of vegetarianism on *Friends* and *The Simpsons* does challenge carnism in some ways, I believe that, ultimately, carnism is more often reinforced. The shows reinforce Joy's three tenets of carnism by portraying meat as "normal, natural, and necessary."[73] The first two traits are the most prominent, as, based on the shows' limited number of vegetarian characters, this dietary choice is clearly portrayed as an *alternative* to the norm and not necessarily a growing trend or ideal goal for everyone. The shows reflect the reality that the typical American vegetarian is likely to be a young, white, middle-class, atheist female,[74] but this portrayal risks stereotyping vegetarians and limiting the ideology's appeal to a diverse audience, especially males. The meat-masculinity connection is largely upheld,[75] as the one vegetarian male on either show, Apu, an Indian Hindu, is a minor "outsider" character overshadowed by the main male characters' hedonistic adoration of meat.

Related to Joy's[76] third carnistic tenet, the shows don't frequently emphasize meat as nutritionally "necessary" because Phoebe and Lisa prove you can generally thrive without it, but there are times where their meat-free diet is portrayed as insufficient. In this way, a vegetarian diet is implied to be more *emotionally* satisfying to Lisa and Phoebe (by living their values) than it is *physically* satisfying (especially considering their cravings for meat and flavor at times).

The Simpsons and *Friends* do sometimes break through Joy's "cognitive trio"[77] of psychological defenses when they show farmed animal subjectivity and individuality. Lisa tends to envision the animals talking to her and actually sees the meat as belonging to someone—as animated portions of individuals' bodies. And even carnist characters individualize certain farmed animals with whom they have bonded, wanting to spare them from slaughter, even though these same carnists will routinely and willingly eat the body parts of other members of those species. Because the violence toward these other animals is widely accepted as a social norm, and their identities and suffering is concealed, carnism's moral inconsistency remains unexamined and its hypocrisy unspoken by the majority. In this way the shows do perpetuate

Joy's last psychological defense, dichotomization, as the carnist characters view humans as separate from (and more important than) other animals and put certain species in categories of edible/inedible based on cultural norms (e.g., eat pigs and fish but don't eat cats and dogs, nor anyone you know personally).[78] This exemplifies the carnistic paradox Joy discussed, where carnists *know* their meat was someone but can avoid acknowledging this uncomfortable truth by maintaining a mental and physical distance from the live animals and the slaughterhouse. Vegetarians like Lisa and Phoebe disrupt this distance, not only through verbalizing that meat is murder, but also through visibly eschewing meat products, making every meal serve as both dietary protest and evidence of vegetarianism's viability.

Ultimately, the shows promote a moral relativism where a pluralistic society "agrees to disagree" and tolerates a diversity of dietary practices. In some sense, this cultural harmony sounds ideal, but it serves to excuse carnism by portraying it as a popular and democratic cultural choice rather than as an oppressive system that warrants moral justifications. Instead, it is the (mainly female) characters who reject this complicity toward animal violence and must defend their nonconformity and be tolerated by the mainstream, similar to how vegetarianism is tolerated in pluralistic American society. But in many ways, the carnist characters reveal they share many of the same compassionate values toward nonhuman animal life, and it's only the invisibility, ignorance, and normalcy of this systemic violence that enables their continued complicity.

For television to be a less carnonormative environment in the future, the programming would need to portray a wider range of vegetarian and vegan characters, especially males, who remain contently animal-free for life and serve as role models who inspire their friends and family to reduce and eliminate flesh, eggs, and animal milk in their daily meals. If television incorporated more vegan characters and living animals commonly used for human food, it could provoke themes where the community acknowledges or debates the moral inconsistencies around breeding, killing, and eating other sentient beings. And if vegans were shown to be more common and mainstream and not at comic extremes of militancy or goofiness, it would make their ethical stance more appetizing and keep them from being perceived as the odd (wo) man out.

Vegan-friendly television programming seems more economically viable, and therefore more feasible, airing on public or non-commercial entertainment venues, as they are not dependent on animal industrial complex advertising revenues. New media outlets available through the Internet and consumer-driven content may also offer innovative opportunities to overcome the hegemony of carnonormative culture. One could argue that as long as carnism is the mainstream ideology and practice in American culture, television is bound to reflect this reality; this provokes "chicken and egg" (pun intended) questions about whether our society is ever going to overcome its sense of separation from (and superiority over) the animal kingdom if we do not see a more humble and respectful humanity modeled on television—our main cultural storyteller. I think directional influence cannot be all chicken or all egg, so animal and environmental advocates must continue to push for legal and cultural reform to make veganism more socially viable and popular, while media consumers must urge media producers to see nonhuman animals as worthy of socially responsible representation. I'd like to envision a television culture where only characters who don't at least question our moral right to consume fellow animals come across as "grade A morons."

NOTES

1. "The Simpsons (TV Series 1989–present)," IMDb, accessed July 20, 2013, http://www.imdb.com/title/tt0096697/.

2. "Friends (TV Series 1994–2004)," IMDb, accessed July 20, 2013, http://www.imdb.com/title/tt0108778/?ref_=sr_1.

3. Carrie Packwood Freeman, "This Little Piggy Went to Press: The American News Media's Construction of Animals in Agriculture," *Communication Review* 12, no. 1 (March 2009): 78–103, doi:10.1080/10714420902717764.

4. "Farmed Animal Indicators: HumaneTrends.com," *Humane Research Council,* August 15, 2011, http://www.humanetrends.org/farmed-animal-indicators/; Peter Singer and Jim Mason, *The Ethics of What We Eat: Why Our Food Choices Matter* (New York: Rodale, 2006).

5. "Position Paper on Vegetarian Diets," Academy of Nutrition & Dietetics, July 2009, http://www.eatright.org/about/content.aspx?id=8357.

6. Singer and Mason, *The Ethics of What We Eat*; Charles Stahler, "How Often Do Americans Eat Vegetarian Meals?," *The Vegetarian Resource Group*, 2011, http://www.vrg.org/journal/vj2011issue4/vj2011issue4poll.php.

7. Stahler, "How Often Do Americans Eat Vegetarian Meals?"

8. "Livestock a Major Threat to Environment," *Food and Agriculture Organization of the United Nations*, November 29, 2006, http://www.fao.org/newsroom/en/news/2006/1000448/index.html; "Protecting Life in the Sea," Pew Enviornmental Group, 2007, http://www.pewtrusts.org/uploadedFiles/wwwpewtrustsorg/TaxonomyCopy/Environment/oceans_final_web.pdf.

9. While no comprehensive studies prove this, a cursory review of television and media studies' textbooks and academic journals reveals the focus is on human social justice rather than on fairness toward nonhuman animals in representation/content.

10. As a Mensa member and A student, Lisa is more clearly portrayed as intelligent and brainy, while Phoebe may not be perceived as intelligent by all viewers

(although smarter than *Friends* co-stars Joey and perhaps Rachel). Phoebe is more street smart, while Lisa is more book smart. I argue that, although Phoebe is spacey and silly much of the time, she is also a confident, problem-solving survivalist who is headstrong in her beliefs, displaying an underlying sense of cleverness and strength.

11. Melanie Joy, *Why We Love Dogs, Eat Pigs, and Wear Cows: An Introduction to Carnism* (San Francisco: Conari Press, 2010).

12. Tom Regan, *The Case for Animal Rights* (Berkeley: University of California Press, 1983); Peter Singer, *Animal Liberation*, 2nd ed. (New York: Random House, 1990).

13. Singer, *Animal Liberation*.

14. Gary L. Francione, *Rain Without Thunder: The Ideology of the Animal Rights Movement* (Philadelphia: Temple University Press, 1996); Regan, *The Case for Animal Rights*.

15. Barbara Noske, *Humans and Other Animals: Beyond the Boundaries of Anthropology* (London: Pluto Press, 1989); Bob Torres, *Making a Killing: The Political Economy of Animal Rights* (Oakland: AK Press, 2008).

16. Joy, *An Introduction to Carnism*.

17. Joy, *An Introduction to Carnism*, 30.

18. Joy, *An Introduction to Carnism*, 96.

19. Joy, *An Introduction to Carnism*, 106.

20. Joy, *An Introduction to Carnism*, 133.

21. Joy, *An Introduction to Carnism*, 103.

22. George Gerbner et al., "Living with Television: The Dynamics of the Cultivation Process," in *Perspectives on Media Effects*, ed. Jennings Bryant and Dolf Zillmann (Hillsdale: L. Erlbaum Associates, 1986), 17.

23. See Edward S. Herman and Noam Chomsky, *Manufacturing Consent: The Political Economy of the Mass Media* (New York: Pantheon Books, 1988); Robert Waterman McChesney, *Rich Media, Poor Democracy: Communication Politics in Dubious Times* (Urbana: University of Illinois Press, 1999).

24. John Bellamy Foster, *Ecology Against Capitalism* (New York: Monthly Review Press, 2002); Jennifer Ellen Good, *Television and the Earth: Not a Love Story* (Halifax: Fernwood, 2013); James Shanahan and Katherine McComas, *Nature Stories: Depictions of the Environment and Their Effects*, (Cresskill: Hampton Press, 1999).

25. I use the term "carnonormative" similar to how the term "heteronormative" describes the television environment in which heterosexuality is the dominant, default, or normalized sexual orientation. Dustin Bradley Goltz, *Queer Temporalities in Gay Male Representation: Tragedy, Normativity, and Futurity* (New York: Routledge, 2010).

26. Carrie Packwood Freeman and Debra Merskin, "Having It His Way: The Construction of Masculinity in Fast Food TV Advertising," in *Food for Thought: Essays on Eating and Culture*, ed. Lawrence C. Rubin (Jefferson: McFarland, 2008), 277–293; Richard A. Rogers, "Beasts, Burgers, and Hummers: Meat and the Crisis of Masculinity in Contemporary Television Advertisements," *Environmental Communication* 2, no. 3 (November 2008): 281–301.

27. Carol J. Adams, *The Sexual Politics of Meat: A Feminist-Vegetarian Critical Theory* (New York: Continuum, 1990).

28. Carol J. Adams, *The Pornography of Meat* (New York: Continuum, 2003); Liz Grauerholz, "Cute Enough to Eat: The Transformation of Animals into Meat for Human Consumption in Commercialized Images," *Humanity & Society* 31, no. 4 (November 2007): 334–354.

29. Freeman, "This Little Piggy Went to Press."

30. Matthew Cole and Karen Morgan, "Vegaphobia: Derogatory Discourses of Veganism and the Reproduction of Speciesism in UK National Newspapers," *The British Journal of Sociology* 62, no. 1 (2011): 134–153. There isn't a comparable study of US news.

31. "The Simpsons on FOX–Official Site," The Simpsons, accessed July 20, 2013, http://www.thesimpsons.com/#/about.

32. "Friends (TV Series 1994–2004)." IMDb, accessed July 20, 2013, http://www.imdb.com/title/tt0108778/?ref_=sr_1.

33. "Lisa Kudrow - Awards," IMDb, accessed July 20, 2013, http://www.imdb.com/name/nm0001435/awards.

34. *Friends,* "The One with the Fake Party," directed by Michael Lembeck, first broadcast March 19, 1998, by NBC.

35. *The Simpsons*, "Lisa the Vegetarian," directed by Mark Kirkland, first broadcast October 15, 1995, by Fox.

36. *The Simpsons*, "Apocalypse Cow," directed by Nancy Kruse, first broadcast April 27, 2008, by Fox.

37. *The Simpsons*, "Penny-Wiseguys," directed by Mark Kirkland, first broadcast November 18, 2012, by Fox.

38. The Simpsons, "Lisa the Vegetarian," directed by Mark Kirkland, first broadcast October 15, 1995, by Fox (see the director's commentary on DVD).

39. Henri Bergson, "On Laughter," in *Comedy*, ed. Wylie Sypher (Baltimore: Johns Hopkins University Press, 1956), 61–103.

40. *Friends*, "The one with the two parties." directed by Michael Lembeck, first broadcast May 2, 1996 by NBC.

41. *Friends*, "The One with the Fake Party."

42. *The Simpsons*, "Lisa the Vegetarian."

43. *The Simpsons*, "Lisa the Vegetarian."

44. Bergson, "On Laughter."

45. Bergson, "On Laughter."

46. *Friends*, "The One with George Stephanopoulos," directed by James Burrows, first broadcast October, 13, 1994, by NBC.

47. *The Simpsons*, "Lisa the Vegetarian."

48. Anne Marie Todd, "Prime-time Subversion: The Environmental Rhetoric of 'The Simpsons,'" in *Environmental Sociology: From Analysis to Action*, ed. Leslie King, 2nd ed. (Lanham: Rowman & Littlefield, 2009), 238.

49. Todd, "Prime-time Subversion," 241.

50. Todd, "Prime-time Subversion," 241.

51. *The Simpsons*, "Lisa the Tree Hugger," directed by Steven Dean Moore, first broadcast November 19, 2000, by Fox.

52. The Simpsons, "Lisa the Vegetarian."

53. *Friends*, "The One with The Lottery," directed by Gary Halvorson, first broadcast April 3, 2003, by NBC.

54. *Friends,* "The One with Ross's Inappropriate Song," directed by Gary Halvorson, first broadcast November 14, 2002, by NBC.

55. *Friends*, "The One with Five Steaks and an Eggplant," directed by Ellen Gittelsohn, first broadcast October 19, 1995, by NBC.

56. Friends, "The One with Five Steaks and an Eggplant." While Rachel orders vegetarian to save money, Joey tries to save money by asking the waiter to leave some veggies (nuts and leeks) off his Thai Chicken Pizza.

57. *Friends,* "The One with Phoebe's Birthday Dinner," directed by David Schwimmer, first broadcast October, 31, 2002, by NBC.

58. The Simpsons, "Apocalypse Cow.

59. *The Simpsons*, "A Star Is Torn," directed by Nancy Kruse, first broadcast May 8, 2005, by Fox.

60. *Friends*, "The One with the Fake Party."

61. *The Simpsons*, "The Real Housewives of Fat Tony," directed by Lance Kramer, first broadcast May 1, 2011, by Fox.

62. *The Simpsons*, "Lisa the Vegetarian."

63. *The Simpsons*, "Lisa the Vegetarian."

64. *The Simpsons*, "Penny-Wiseguys."

65. *The Simpsons*, "Lisa the Vegetarian."

66. *The Simpsons*, "A Star Is Torn."

67. *The Simpsons*, "Penny-Wiseguys."

68. *Friends*, "The One with the Fake Party."

69. *Friends*, "The One with Ross's Inappropriate Song."

70. *The Simpsons*, "Apocalypse Cow."

71. *The Simpsons*, "Lisa the Vegetarian."

72. Naomi R. Rockler, "'Be Your Own Windkeeper': 'Friends,' Feminism, and Rhetorical Strategies of Depoliticization," *Women's Studies in Communication* 29, no. 2 (2006): 260.

73. Joy, *An Introduction to Carnism*, 96.

74. Donna Maurer, *Vegetarianism: Movement or Moment?* (Philadelphia: Temple University Press, 2002).

75. Adams, *The Sexual Politics of Meat.*

76. Joy, *An Introduction to Carnism.*

77. Joy, *An Introduction to Carnism*, 133.

78. Joy, *An Introduction to Carnism.*

Chapter Twelve

Television and the Environment: More Screen–Less Green

Jennifer Ellen Good

Throughout most of human history we knew the environment extensively and intimately because we were immersed in it. The environment was us and we were the environment. Arguably it was not until the Industrial Revolution that, as a species, we finally left the land en masse and huddled together in increasingly dense urban centers. When we left the land, we also left daily interaction with the land to a diminishing number of farmers. And later as mediated communication changed how we gathered to share our stories, we increasingly gathered around flickering screens; television came to be the primary storyteller about our relationship with the environment.

Researchers tell us that day-to-day time spent in the environment, in the outdoors, is increasingly rare, a phenomenon researcher and author Richard Louv calls "nature deficit disorder."[1] Indeed, we do not have much time for outdoor pursuits. The three things that occupy most of our time are sleep, work/school, and television. For example, according to mediated communication research company Nielsen, we spend 157 hours and 32 minutes per month, or just over five hours a day of traditional television watching—a number that does not include over thirteen hours a month of time-shifted viewing or viewing of television shows on other screens.[2] When all types of viewing are calculated, average viewership per day in the United States sits at over eight hours—a number that has steadily increased over the past sixty years.[3] Sleep, work/school, and television: these are the activities that occupy our time and sit at the core of most people's lives.

In the past few decades, television effects research has been able to establish clear links between the quantity of television viewing and various value and attitudinal outcomes.[4] In what follows I will make the case that television, more than any other aspect of our lives, explains not only our relationship with

213

the environment but also explains the current environmental crisis in which we
find ourselves.

MAKING SENSE OF TELEVISION'S EFFECTS

We have always believed that television affects us. Some of the effects were
immediately obvious. Where we once were civically involved—volunteering,
organizing, playing—television's arrival brought families into their living
rooms and gathered them around TV's glow. As Robert Putnam points out in
Bowling Alone: The Collapse and Revival of American Community: "More
television watching means less of virtually every form of civic participation
and social involvement."[5]

Time use studies (of the type that Putnam draws upon) have been a fairly
straightforward way to conceptualize and research television's effects on how
we spend our days and nights. One need only look at historical trends for
various kinds of activities and to see whether and in what ways those trends
changed with the introduction of television. Theories and studies of how television's *content* affects us have been harder to put together. Early massive
effects theories were intuitively appealing. These early theories proposed that
because humans had evolved to believe that what we saw was real (and to react with alacrity if we sensed threat), television would similarly be perceived
as reality—and reacted to accordingly.[6]

It did not take long, however, for researchers to realize that television's effects were subtler than this. Indeed, in his classic study of how radio listeners
responded to the dramatization of the H. G. Wells story *War of the Worlds*,
Hadley Cantril and colleagues conducted research with people who had heard
the broadcast. The researchers found "no simple observable variable consistently related to the reaction [to the supposed invasion], although a lack of
critical ability seemed particularly conducive to fear in a large proportion of
the population."[7] For example, those with more formal education were more
likely to follow up hearing about the Martians' arrival with further investigation such as tuning in other radio stations for corroboration of the invasion.

Rather than mediated communication being some kind of "magic bullet"
or "hypodermic needle" that would affect all audience members immediately,
identically, and profoundly, researchers began to investigate more subtle effects.[8] Television's effects did not have to be immediate and universal in order
to be significant. Like all socializing forces, researchers came to understand
that television affects us by its sheer omnipresence. For example, Albert Bandura's famous Bobo doll experiments explored whether children would model
adults' interactions with a Bobo doll (a blow-up doll that can be knocked over

but it stands back up). Bandura's research showed that children did mimic the adult behavior they saw in person and the adult behavior that they saw on a television screen. In fact, the screen seemed to provide an even better behavioral modeling opportunity. As Bandura and his co-investigators offered, "The available data suggest that, of the three experimental conditions [human in the same room, human on television, cartoon cat on television], exposure to humans on film portraying aggression was *the most influential in eliciting and shaping aggressive behavior.*"[9] Bandura's social learning research was based on his sense that learning can happen vicariously. "Traditional theories of learning generally depict behavior as the product of directly experienced response consequences. In actuality, virtually all learning phenomena resulting from direct experiences can occur on a vicarious basis through observation of other people's behavior and its consequences for them."[10] In other words, it didn't matter that we were observing people via a screen, we still learn. Social learning theory therefore provided, and continues to provide, a fundamental way of making sense of how television affects us. In the same ways that our families, friends, schools, jobs, clubs, sports teams, religious institutions, etc., shape us and our world, so too does television.

CULTIVATION THEORY

Cultivation theory, like social learning theory, is predicated on the notion that we learn from what is around us—and if television is prominent in our lives, then we will learn from it. One aspect of cultivation theory that differentiates it from social learning theory is cultivation theory's measurement of the relationship between quantity of viewing and our understanding of the world.

Cultivation theory, originally conceptualized by George Gerbner, proposes that the more television we watch, the more like television our understanding of the world becomes. As Gerbner offers, "We have used the concept of 'cultivation' to describe the independent contributions television viewing makes to viewer conceptions of social reality. The 'cultivation differential' is the margin of difference in conceptions of reality between light and heavy viewers in the same demographic subgroups."[11] Television, in other words, "reveal[s] how things work . . . describe[s] what things are...tell[s] us what to do about them."[12]

A typical cultivation study begins with an analysis of some aspect of television's prime-time fictional content. For example, a cultivation study on the impact of violent television (undoubtedly the most studied cultivation topic) might measure such things as the frequency of violence, the duration of violent episodes, the types of violence, the demographic attributes of who undertakes violent acts, who solves violent crimes, etc. One general finding of such studies has been (not surprisingly) that television depicts the world as a meaner and more dangerous place than it actually is. As Gerbner points out, "Consider how likely television characters are to encounter violence compared to the rest of us. Well over half of all major characters on television are involved each week in some kind of violent action. While the FBI statistics have clear limitations, they indicate that in any year less than 1 percent of people in the United States are victims of criminal violence."[13]

In the second stage of a cultivation study, researchers survey people to find out if heavier viewers of television are more likely to answer questions about the real world—for example the likelihood of certain kinds of violent crimes happening to them—with answers based on television's world (a world that can be defined by the content analysis). For example, cultivation researchers have consistently found that heavy viewers cultivate "exaggerated perceptions of the number of people involved in violence in any given week . . . as well as numerous other inaccurate beliefs about crime and law enforcement."[14] These findings led Gerbner and his colleagues to develop the concept of the Mean World Syndrome—a "complex of outlooks which includes an exaggerated sense of victimization, gloom, apprehension, insecurity, anxiety and mistrust."[15]

Cultivation researchers have looked at the differences between heavy and light television viewers related to a variety of topics in addition to violence, such as sexism, racism, homophobia, materialism, and the environment. It is the relationship between television viewing and the environment to which I now turn.

ENVIRONMENTAL CULTIVATION

Given the fact that Americans spend so much time watching television, it is not surprising that television affects our understanding of the world around us. As highlighted above, we learn from television (in the same way we learn from other socializing forces in our lives). Television also affects our understanding of the world because the hours that we spend with television are hours that we don't have available to do other things—such as being outdoors engaged in the environment. Scholars call this "time displacement." The fact that many hours each day are displaced by television and we don't have time to be in the outdoors is important because the research indicates that the more we are in the environment, the more we care about it. As Randy White and Vicki Stoecklin explain, "Research has substantiated that an empathy with and love of nature, along with later positive environmental behaviors and attitudes, grow out of children's regular contact with and play in the natural world."[16] However, the research also indicates that we are spending less time in the environment. Louv states, "In the space of a century, the American experience of nature has gone from direct utilitarianism to romantic attachment to electronic detachment."[17]

Time displacement helps us to understand one aspect of why television affects our relationship with the environment. But time displacement does not speak to the content we consume when we watch television. In a first step toward exploring this, cultivation researchers have undertaken content analyses to study how the environment is portrayed on television. In a study of 317 hours of prime-time fictional network television (ABC, CBS, NBC) content from the early 1990s, researchers found that "environmental episodes" (a section of the show in which the environment was an explicit theme) were few and far between. Indeed, for the most part the environment was absent. In only 1.7 percent of the programming was the environment an "outstanding theme" (i.e., the focus of the program). As the researchers point out, "compared to other themes such as entertainment, family, personal relationships, and financial success, nature as a theme is very infrequent."[18]

When a similar study was conducted that broadened the years to include the years 1991–1997, and added the Fox network to ABC, CBS, and NBC, the findings were similar. Indeed, in the 410-hour sample of non-news entertainment and fictional television the time allotted to the environment was approximately 2 hours 22 minutes, or about half of 1 percent of the total hours that were watched. As the researchers highlight, in six years of fiction/entertainment programming there wasn't enough environmental programming to outrun one Monday night football game.[19]

A more recent content analysis of 140 hours of fiction and non-fiction television programming on four "free-to-air" channels (TV One, TV2, TV3, and Maori TV) in New Zealand similarly found that while nature was unlikely to be a theme in urban-based stories (nature was at least a minor theme in less than 17 percent of the episodes), the likelihood of an environmental theme increased with the distance from a city. Nature was at least a minor theme in just over 35 percent of rural stories and at least a minor theme in almost 67 percent of stories taking place in uninhabited areas.[20] Overall, however, in forty-seven of the seventy-seven programs analyzed, nature was entirely absent—and nature was the focus of the program in less than 10 percent of the programs.[21]

The content analysis is the first step in a cultivation theory investigation of the relationship between television viewing and how we think about the environment. The next step is to determine whether attitudes about the environment are different for heavy and light viewers of television (i.e., whether heavy viewers' attitudes about the environment have been cultivated by television). Several studies have undertaken this analysis.[22] As with all cultivation studies, the core of what study participants were asked fell into three fundamental categories: what the participants believed about certain aspects of the real world (in this case, the environment), participants' television viewing habits, and participants' demographics.

One of the ways that researchers have measured environmental attitudes is with the New Environmental Paradigm (NEP) scale. The scale measures perceptions related to the environment's limits to growth, the fragility of nature's balance, the possibility of an environmental crisis, the degree to which humans are isolated from the rest of the environment, and the likelihood that a respondent applies anthropomorphic thinking to the nonhuman world. In other words, the NEP's fifteen statements (listed in the endnotes) measure "ecological worldview."[23]

Television viewing habits are usually measured by simply asking survey participants how much television they watch each day while specifying average weekday and average weekend viewing. Some environmental cultivation studies have also made use of a television viewing scale developed by L. J. Shrum and colleagues in 2011, which consists of six Likert statements such as "I spend time watching television almost every day" (the full scale can be found in the endnotes).[24]

What these environmental cultivation studies have found, after controlling for demographic variables, is that there is a relationship between quantity of television viewing and scores on the NEP scale: on average, the more television watched, the lower the scores on the environmental attitude scale.[25] Heavy television viewers (often calculated based on four or more hours of television viewing each day) score lower on the NEP, indicating that they are less likely to see the environment's limits to growth, the fragility of nature's balance, and the possibility of environmental crisis. Heavier viewers of television are also more likely than lighter viewers to feel that humans are isolated from the rest of the environment and apply anthropomorphic thinking to other species, valuing human needs above those of others and giving animals human-like attributes.

One explanation for why heavy viewing has this effect has already been offered above: time displacement.[26] Environmental cultivation researchers have offered a second possibility: symbolic annihilation. Symbolic annihilation proposes that television has an impact on us not only because of what television tells us, but also because of what television *doesn't* tell us. As Hugh Klein and Kenneth Shiffman highlight,

> The basic idea is that groups that are valued in a particular culture tend to be shown frequently in the media, and viewers/readers come to learn about these groups' purported characteristics and their implied value to the culture-at-large

by virtue of their media exposure. But when certain groups are not valued in that same culture, the media tend not to include them in their storylines and, in the process, cast them aside and disenfranchise them by not showing them.[27]

In the context of environmental cultivation, the premise is that because of television's lack of environmental content, heavier viewers are less likely to be concerned about the environment because the environment is "cast aside" and "disenfranchised" on television.

Time displacement therefore provides an example of television's environmental effects by highlighting how television deprives us of time for exploration and play in the environment. Symbolic annihilation highlights the fact that television can affect us by not telling environmental stories. What remains is a question about how the stories *we do regularly consume* on television affect our relationship with the environment.

TELEVISION AND MATERIALISM

At the most fundamental level, television exists to sell audiences to advertisers. As Gerbner points out, "Given the tight links among the various industries involved in the production and distribution of electronic media content, and the fact that most of them are trying to attract the largest and most heterogeneous audience, the most popular program materials present consistent and complementary messages, often reproducing what has already proven to be profitable."[28] The fact that we receive "free" television in return for exposure to advertising is an arrangement that television viewers consented to long ago—and it is a deal that we, by and large, find unremarkable. The assumption that we are being affected by this bombardment of advertising is similarly unremarkable, if somewhat startling when we are reminded of the sheer magnitude of what we are being hit with. As Neil Postman offers in his ground-breaking book *Amusing Ourselves to Death: Public Discourse in the Age of Show Business*, "An American who has reached the age of forty will have seen well over one million television commercials in his or her lifetime. We may safely assume, therefore, that the television commercial has profoundly influenced American habits of thought."[29]

Yes, there are now various ways to avoid overt advertising, but product placement (advertisers paying to place their products in the scenes of television programming) and product integration (the actual discussion of products by people in television programs) highlight the fact that such advertising avoidance misses the subtlety with which we are reached. Indeed, Gerbner's thoughts from 1998 continue to resoundingly resonate: "Formula-driven, assembly-line produced programs increasingly dominate the airwaves. The formulas themselves reflect the structure of power that produces them and function to preserve and enhance that structure of power."[30] In fact, television's formulaic content is so steeped in materialism—affluent characters/celebrities, storylines that celebrate consumption, contestants vying for money and prizes—that the entire viewing experience is a celebration of that which advertisers covet: a belief that we are what we buy and a belief that we should ever-increasingly consume.

Surprisingly, perhaps, while the case can be made that the essence of television is a celebration of materialism, there have been relatively few cultivation studies that have explored the relationship between television and materialistic attitudes. As Shrum has highlighted, "Television's role in the cultivation of material values [is] a construct that has received little attention in cultivation research."[31] Mark Harmon has similarly commented that "[f]ew researchers... have taken the path that the most consistent and significant message of commercial television is commercialism and that the place to look for long-term, subtle, and pervasive effects is in materialism among heavy [television] viewers."[32] That said, some cultivation researchers have explored the relationship between television viewing and materialistic attitudes and have found that heavier viewers are more materialistic.[33] Indeed, Shrum and his colleagues go so far as to call the effect that television has on materialistic attitudes "robust."[34]

In order to measure levels of materialism, several of these studies[35] made use of Marsha Richins and Scott Dawson's eighteen statement materialism Likert scale (or a modified fifteen statement version of the scale) that contains statements such as "I admire people who own expensive homes, cars and clothes" and "Some of the most important achievements in life include acquiring material possessions" (for a full list of the statements that comprise the scale, see the endnote).[36]

Intuitively we know the way in which our "stuff" and the environment are related. As the aforementioned scale highlights, materialism celebrates our association between who we are and the stuff that we own. The environment happens to contain the raw materials to create the stuff. When materialism is the priority, the environment cannot be. As E. F. Schumacher succinctly offers in *Small Is Beautiful: Economics as if People Mattered*, "An attitude of life which seeks fulfillment in the single-minded pursuit of wealth—in short materialism—does not fit into this world, because it contains within itself no limiting principle, while the environment in which it is placed is strictly limited."[37]

Cultivation researchers have also statistically explored the relationship between television, materialism, and attitudes about the environment (or, in the language of statistics, researchers have explored whether materialism mediates the relationship between television and attitudes about the environment). The results of that analysis support the intuition that the three elements of television, materialism, and environmentalism are related: as television viewing increases, materialism increases and environmentalism decreases.[38]

Therefore, the effects of television viewing on environmental attitudes are threefold. First, when we watch hours of television viewing each day we displace time available to do other things—such as be in the environment. Second, the environment is symbolically annihilated by television such that significant stories involving the environment are largely absent. Thus when we aren't encouraged to think and care about the environment, we tend not to think and care about it. Third, the stories that television does tell are saturated in materialistic messages: messages that tell us that we are what we buy—and we should buy endlessly.

MORE VIEWING, MORE MATERIALISM, AND LESS ENVIRONMENTALISM: THE NEED FOR MEDIA LITERACY

Anyone who has ever watched television (that's pretty much all of us) has opinions on what constitutes great television and horrible television. And increasingly we have control over the television that we watch: there are hundreds of channels we can access via "traditional television" and we can add timeshifting/PVR, online streaming, downloaded shows, etc., to the ways that we watch. But while the number of channels and screens on which we can access television may have increased, television's meta-message of the celebration of materialism hasn't changed. The number and types of things we can do with our screens has increased exponentially, and research indicates that our television viewing is at all-time highs.[39]

So it would seem that new information and communication technologies are not sounding the death knell for television. Far from it. If anything, it would seem that new screens and new software are allowing people to access television in larger quantities, in more places, and with greater engagement than ever before. Therefore, if we have concerns about the relationship between these large quantities of television and the state of the environment (and I would suggest that we have reason to be concerned), then perhaps media literacy offers a way forward. As Postman offers at the end of *Amusing Ourselves to Death*,

> It is the acknowledged task of the schools to assist the young in learning how to interpret the symbols of their culture. That this task should now require that they learn how to distance themselves from their forms of information is not so bizarre an enterprise that we cannot hope for its inclusion in the curriculum; even hope that it will be placed at the center of education.[40]

The Association for Media Literacy (AML) started in Canada almost forty years ago. The AML's goals include "helping students develop an informed and critical understanding of the nature of the mass media, the techniques used by media industries, and the impact of these techniques. [The AML] also aims to provide students with the ability to create their own media products."[41]

It is this creative aspect of the AML's mission that is particularly compelling. The ability to create and share television has, until recently, been extremely limited. Now the tools for such productions are readily available and creating such alternative messages and stories has become an important part of media literacy. As the Media Literacy Project highlights, "Just as literacy is the ability both to read and write, media literacy involves both understanding media messages and creating media. [. . .] Becoming an active agent for change in our media culture is a natural result of being media literate."[42]

And creating change has never been more important. In 2005 the Millennium Ecosystem Assessment—a study conducted by 1,300 scientists and social scientists (the largest group of scientists ever assembled to assess human impact on the environment)—concluded that, "human activity is putting such a strain on the natural function of Earth that the ability of the planet's ecosystems to sustain future generations can no longer be taken for granted."[43] Recently an article asked, "Has the Earth's Sixth Mass Extinction Already Arrived?" A dozen scientists answered this question, proposing that the indicators "now suggest that a sixth mass extinction may be under way, given the known species losses over the past few centuries and millennia."[44]

The fact that there is a relationship between television viewing and how we understand our relationship with the environment has not always been clear. However research over the years has made clear that in the same ways television affects our understanding of other aspects of our lives, television affects our understanding of, and relationship with, the environment. When we watch television's stories for hours each day, we are not doing other things; in particular we are not outdoors, engaged with nature. And television's materialistic tales encourage increased consumption. All of which take a toll on the planet: more screen means less green.

NOTES

1. Richard Louv, *Last Child in the Woods: Saving our Children from Nature-Deficit Disorder*. (Chapel Hill: Algonquin Books, 2005).

2. "New Cross Platform Report says fewer people have multichannel subscriptions," *Broadcasting & Cable*, August 10, 2013, http://www.broadcastingcable.com/article/print/493938–Nielsen_Time_Spent_Watching_Traditional_TV_Up.php.

3. "The Nielsen Company Historical Daily Viewing Activity Among Households and Persons 2+," *Nielsen*, August 10, 2013, http://www.nielsen.com/content/dam/corporate/us/en/newswire/uploads/2009/11/historicalviewing.pdf.

4. For example Michael Morgan, James Shanahan, and Nancy Signorielli, *Living with Television Now: Advances in Cultivation Theory and Research* (New York: Peter Lang, 2012).

5. Robert Putnam, *Bowling Alone: The Collapse and Revival of American Community* (New York: Touchstone, 2001), 228.

6. Sandra Ball-Rokeach and Melvin DeFleur, *Theories of Mass Communication* 5th ed. (White Plains: Longman, 1989).

7. Hadley Cantril, Hazel Gaudet, and Herta Herzog,. *The Invasion from Mars: A Study in the Psychology of Panic* (Princeton: Princeton University Press, 1940), 189.

8. Ball-Rokeach and DeFleur, *Theories of Mass Communication.*

9. Albert Bandura, Dorthea Ross, and Sheila Ross, "Imitation of Film-Mediated Aggressive Models," *Journal of Abnormal and Social Psychology* 66, (1963), 3–11 (italics added).

10. Albert Bandura, *Social Learning Theory* (New York: General Learning Press, 1971), 2.

11. George Gerbner, "Cultivation Analysis: An Overview," *Mass Communication & Society* 3/4 (1998,), 180.

12. James Shanahan and Michael Morgan Shanahan, *Television and its viewers: Cultivation Theory and Research* (Cambridge: Cambridge University Press, 1999), ix.

13. Gerbner, "Cultivation," 185.

14. Gerbner, "Cultivation," 185.

15. Shanahan and Morgan, *Television*, 55.

16. Randy White and Vicki Stoecklin, "Nurturing Children's Biophilia: Developmentally Appropriate Environmental Education for Young Children." *White Hutinson Learning and Leisure Group*, 2008, accessed July 2, 2013, http://www.whitehutchinson.com/children/articles/nurturing.shtml.

17. Louv, *Last Child*, 16.

18. James Shanahan and Katherine McComas, *Nature Stories: Depictions of the Environment and Their Effects* (Cresskill: Hampton Press Inc., 1999), 86.

19. Katherine McComas, James Shanahan, and Jessica Butler, "Environmental Content in Prime-Time Network and TV's Non-news Entertainment and Fictional Programs," *Society and Natural Resources* 14 (2001), 533–542.

20. Rowan Howard-Williams, "Consumers, Crazies and Killer Whales: The Environment on New Zealand Television," *International Communication Gazette* 73 (2011), 27–43.

21. Howard-Williams, "Consumers."

22. For an overview, see: Jennifer Good. *Television and the Earth: Not a Love Story* (Black Point: Fernwood Publishing, 2013).

23. Riley Dunlap, Kent VanLiere, Angela Mertig, and Robert Jones, "Measuring Endorsement of the New Ecological Paradigm: A Revised NEP Scale," *Journal of Social Issues* 56, 3 (2000), 425–442. The revised scale included the following statements for the survey instrument:

1. We are approaching the limit of the number of people the earth can support.
2. Humans have the right to modify the natural environment to suit their needs.
3. When humans interfere with nature it often produces disastrous consequences.
4. Human ingenuity will ensure that we do NOT make the earth unlivable.
5. Humans are severely abusing the environment.

6. The earth has plenty of natural resources if we just learn how to develop them.
7. Plants and animals have as much right as humans to exist.
8. The balance of nature is strong enough to cope with the impacts of modern industrial nations.
9. Despite our special abilities, humans are still subject to the laws of nature.
10. The so-called "ecological crisis" facing humankind has been greatly exaggerated.
11. The earth is like a spaceship with very limited room and resources.
12. Humans were meant to rule over the rest of nature.
13. The balance of nature is very delicate and easily upset.
14. Humans will eventually learn enough about how nature works to be able to control it.
15. If things continue on their present course, we will soon experience a major ecological catastrophe.

24. L. J. Shrum, Jaehoon Lee, James Burroughs, and Aric Rindfleisch, "An Online Process Model of Second-Order Cultivation Effects: How Television Cultivates Materialism and Its Consequences for Life Satisfaction," *Human Communication Research* 37, (2011), 34–57. The questionnaire asked respondents to rate how/if they agreed with the following statements:

1. I watch less television than most people I know.
2. I often watch television on weekends.
3. I spend time watching television almost every day.
4. One of the first things I do in the evening is turn on the television.
5. I hardly ever watch television.
6. I have to admit, I watch a lot of television.

25. For example: Jennifer Good, "The Cultivation, Mainstreaming and Cognitive Processing of Environmentalists Watching Television," *Environmental Communication: The Journal of Nature and Culture* 3, no. 3 (2009), 279–297; Jennifer Good, "Shop 'til We Drop?: Television, Materialism and Attitudes About the Natural Environment," *Mass Communication and Society* 10, no. (2007), 365–383; Shanahan and McComas, "Environmental Content"; James Shanahan, Michael Morgan, and Mads Stenbjerre, "Green or Brown? Television and the Cultivation of Environmental Concern," *Journal of Broadcasting & Electronic Media* 41, no. 3 (1997), 305–323.
26. For example: Good, "Shop"; Good, "Cognitive."
27. Hugh Klein and Kenneth Shiffman, "Underrepresentation and Symbolic Annihilation of Socially Disenfranchised Groups ('Out Groups') in Animated Cartoons," *The Howard Journal of Communications* 20 (2009):55–72.
28. Gerbner, "Cultivation," 178.
29. Neil Postman, *Amusing Ourselves to Death: Public Discourse in the Age of Show Business* (New York: Penguin Books, 1985), 126.
30. Gerbner, "Cultivation," 176.
31. Shrum et al., "Process," 35.
32. Mark Harmon, "Affluenza: Television Use and Cultivation of Materialism," *Mass Communication & Society* 4, no. 4 (2001), 405–418.

33. For example: Good, "Shop"; Shrum, et al., "Process"; Harmon, "Affluenza"; Sirgy et al., "Does Television Viewership."

34. Shrum et al., "Process," 47.

35. For example: Shrum, et al. "Process"; Good "Shop."

36. Marsha Richins and Scott Dawson, "A Consumer Values Orientation for Materialism and its Measurement: Scale Development and Validation," *Journal of Consumer Research* 19 (1992), 303–316. The questionnaire included the following statements, which respondents were asked to rate:

1. I admire people who own expensive homes, cars and clothes.
2. Some of the most important achievements in life include acquiring material possessions.
3. I don't place much emphasis on the amount of material objects people own as a sign of success.
4. I usually buy only the things I need.
5. I enjoy spending money on things that aren't practical.
6. I try to keep my life simple, as far as possessions are concerned.
7. I have all the things I really need to enjoy life.
8. My life would be better if I owned certain things I don't have.
9. The things I own say a lot about how well I'm doing in life.
10. I like to own things that impress people.
11. I don't pay much attention to the material objects other people own.
12. The things I own aren't all that important to me.
13. Buying things gives me a lot of pleasure.
14. I like a lot of luxury in my life.
15. I put less emphasis on material things than most people I know.
16. I wouldn't be any happier if I owned nicer things.
17. I'd be happier if I could afford to buy more things.
18. It sometimes bothers me quite a bit that I can't afford to buy all the things I'd like.

37. E. F. Schumacher, *Small is Beautiful: Economics as if People Mattered.* (New York: Harper & Row, 1975), 30.

38. Good, "Shop."

39. "New Cross Platform Report says fewer people have multichannel subscriptions." *Broadcasting & Cable.* 2013, accessed August 10, 2013, http://www.broadcastingcable.com/article/print/493938–Nielsen_Time_Spent_Watching_Traditional_TV_Up.php.

40. Postman, *Amusing*, 163.

41. Association for Media Literacy, accessed August 10, 2013, http://www.aml.ca/.

42. Media Literacy Project. accessed August 10, 2013, http://medialiteracyproject.org/.

43. The Board of the Millennium Ecosystem Assessment, *Living Beyond Our Means: Natural Assets and Human Well-being* (Washington: Millennium Ecosystem Assessment, 2005).

44. Anthony Barnosky, Nicholas Matzke, Susumu Tomiya, Guinevere Wogan, Brian Swartz, Tiago Quental Tiago, Charles Marshall, Jenny McGuire, Emily Lindsey, Kaitlin Maguire, Ben Mersey, and Elizabeth Ferrer, "Has the Earth's Sixth Mass Extinction Already Arrived?" *Nature* 471 (2011), 51.

Chapter Thirteen

From Welby to McDreamy: What TV Teaches Us about Doctors, Patients, and the Health Care System

Katherine A. Foss

You're at home slicing a bagel for a late-night snack. As your honey-wheat bagel turns crimson, you realize that the knife has sliced a good chunk of your thumb. Feeling light-headed, you rinse the wound, coming to the conclusion that a Hello Kitty Band-Aid won't suffice. You wrap a dishtowel around your hand, alert your spouse (who by now is wondering where her half of the bagel is), and the two of you reluctantly drive to the emergency room.

Your emergency room experience is nothing like you expected. You anticipate a whirl of activity, with bloodied gurneys, shouts of "The pulse-ox is dropping!" and a witty and lovable receptionist who comforts you in your self-inflicted condition. Instead, the waiting room is quiet as you check in with the humorless receptionist. During your forty–minute wait, you see two other patients in the waiting room: a toddler sleeping across the lap of her tired parents and an overweight bearded fellow reading a sports magazine (you never do figure out what his deal is). There are no chemical spills forcing evacuation, rogue ambulances crashing through the walls, or beloved elderly women with Alzheimer's who bestows her wisdom upon you and then bursts into song.

Finally, your name is called and you head back. The nurse inquires about drug allergies, takes your blood pressure, and washes your bloody thumb. Then you wait, making jokes about needing a transfusion to your spouse. The doctor enters. You're hoping for McDreamy, but this guy looks like any Target patron. He injects some Lidocaine into your hand, and then stitches you up. Five hours after your ordeal began, you return home in one piece. Two months later, you get a bill for $458.73, most of which is paid for by your insurance.

Most hospital experiences are like the mundane scenario above—ordinary, time-consuming, and expensive. Yet, television paints a very different picture of the typical hospital visit. Non-stop activity, graphic scenes, unforgettable patients, unlimited diagnostic tests, and the absence of health care cost

227

discussions characterize fictional depictions of health care. And, of course, the "typical" TV doctor is far from average: Marcus Welby, Kelly Brackett, Hawkeye Pierce, Gonzo Gates, Peter Benton, Cristina Yang, Greg House. In nearly sixty years, the definition of the television doctor has expanded from the old and wise white male to include physician characters of different sexes, ethnicities, ages, religions, sexual orientations, and countries of origin. And yet, many of the characteristics of the TV doctor are the same: sexy, confident, skilled heroes who risk anything to save their patients. Using examples from fictional medical programs of the 1960s through the 2000s, this chapter explores television's messages about doctors, patients, the hospital experience, and the health care system.

THE USE OF TELEVISION TO INFLUENCE HEALTH

However distorted, idealized, or inaccurate, fictional medical programs play a fundamental role in our knowledge of health issues, health behaviors, and perceptions of health professionals and the health care system. Viewers learn about disease, treatments, terminology, and medical practices from watching television.[1] In fact, educators have even used these programs to deliberately teach students about medicine.[2] And, as network news audiences have declined, entertainment media have become an important tool in disseminating health information.[3] Formal campaigns have used entertainment media to effectively promote designated driving and immunizations and create awareness of HPV, emergency contraception, and date rape and other health issues in popular television programs.[4]

Fictional television also heavily influences viewers' perceptions of doctors and the health care profession. George Gerbner and colleagues found a strong cultivation effect between television consumption and perceptions of doctors.[5] Heavy television viewership has been positively correlated with perceptions of doctors, especially at a time in which fictional doctors were overwhelmingly heroic and compassionate.[6] As television portrayals shifted to include more fallible physicians, recent cultivation studies noted a shift in the perceptions of heavy viewers.[7]

Given that the TV doctor has been a staple part of television since *The Medic* (1954–1956), it is likely that fictional messages about medicine will continue to influence viewers. Therefore, to explore the messages in fictional programs is to gain a better understanding of potential public perceptions of the doctor-patient relationship and health care as a whole—even though real-life physicians would hardly keep their licenses if they performed a double amputation at a dimly lit accident scene with little surgical training (*ER*), repeatedly broke into their patients' houses (*House, M.D.*), or other unbeliev-able feats we accept from our favorite on-screen heroes.

CHANGING DEPICTIONS OF MEDICINE

In the last 100 years, the medical profession has evolved from the country doctor who performed crude operations on the kitchen table to a billion-dollar health care industry. At least in developed countries like the United States, drastically improved sanitation and immunizations have eradicated cholera, diphtheria, polio, and other top killers from a century ago. Diagnostic testing has advanced dramatically since the stethoscope and the blood pressure cuff of the 1800s, as disease is caught much earlier through the imaging tools of CAT, PET, and MRI scans.[8] As American medicine has changed, so has its mediated representations.

From the 1930s to the 1960s, affordable insurance and numerous techno-logical innovations meant that many health conditions could be successfully treated and that this treatment was readily accessible.[9] Most people held the medical profession in high regard, believing it and other institutions were "engines of social good" that worked in the public's best interest.[10] Media representations reflected this optimism, conveying images of caring and com-passionate doctors who skillfully used medical technology to perform com-plex procedures.[11] Fictional depictions of physicians, like those in the film and TV series *Doctor Kildare* (1961–1966), and the television dramas *The Medic, Ben Casey* (1961–1966), and *Medical Center* (1969–1976), featured heroic fictional doctors who seldom failed to cure their patients.[12] Members of the American Medical Association (AMA) heavily influenced the content of these shows, routinely reviewing, advising, and approving the scripts.[13]

In the 1970s, new medical innovations made diagnosis and treatment more expensive, causing health care costs to rise dramatically.[14] At the same time, the doctor-patient relationship began to change as more people were encour-aged to question authority, including medical authority, and to become more active in their health care.[15] Medicine became more focused on preventing disease, as health policy experts and health professionals began to educate consumers on healthy lifestyle choices to reduce their risk of disease: an approach called the personal responsibility model.[16] In the 1980s, budget cuts eliminated many institutional programs to improve health, as health maintenance organizations (HMOs) became more prevalent, eroding public confidence in the health care system.[17]

Television content of the 1970s and 1980s reflected the changes in at-titudes toward health care providers and the medical profession. While scholars label *Medical Center* (1969) and *Marcus Welby, M.D.* (1969–1976) as traditional medical dramas, the program *M*A*S*H* (1972–1983) deviated from generic conventions, portraying doctors and nurses with personal and often humorous problems.[18] At the same time, the health professionals in *M*A*S*H* were skilled surgeons who cared about their patients.[19] Despite this program's conflicting portrayals, as a whole, television featured (usually white) male characters who acted as "powerful, almost omnipotent, healer(s), while largely ignoring the constraints of the healthcare system, including the rise of HMOs."[20] The 1980s continued to offer conflicting portrayals, with the spin-off of *M*A*S*H*, *Trapper John, M.D.* (1979–1986), depicting physicians as compassionate skilled doctors, while *St. Elsewhere* (1982–1988) portrayed doctors as cynical and flawed people, many of whom had more problems than their patients.[21]

In the 1990s, the Institute of Medicine released a report on medical mistakes, bringing the issue into public discourse.[22] The authors estimated that between 44,000 and 98,000 people died each year from medical errors—more than the number of deaths from traffic accidents, breast cancer, or AIDS.[23] This report received extensive media attention. Numerous media stories addressed the prevalence of pharmaceutical and hospital mistakes, accompanied by popular literature that cautioned people of the dangers of the health profession, with books titled *How to Get out of the Hospital Alive*, *Take Charge of Your Hospital Stay*, and *Protect Yourself in the Hospital*.[24] Such attention to medical errors increased already rising skepticism of the medical profession and prompted health officials to examine patient safety procedures.

The vast improvements in technology over the last two decades have helped facilitate the personal responsibility model. Internet usage has helped many people to feel more informed about their health and better understand their medical conditions or illnesses.[25] Patients who use the Internet for health information have reported feeling more engaged in their health and more confident about conversing with their physicians.[26] And yet, many doctors dislike Internet information, believing that it confuses patients, wastes time, and leads to a questioning of their authority as care providers.[27]

With new technology, the emphasis of patient responsibility and advocacy, paired with the Affordable Care Act and other insurance reform, today's health care industry is radically different than even twenty years ago. In the midst of this change, four medical dramas emerged in television, spanning this time period. *Chicago Hope*, which ran for six seasons (1994–2000), featured an elite hospital, full of the best surgeons in their specialties.[28] Debuting at the same time, *ER* (1994–2009), on the other hand, focused on medical residents and students in a public emergency room.[29] This fast-paced show contained several story arcs per episode, with graphic close-ups that would set the tone for future medical dramas and health-related reality programs.[30] Ten years after these programs premiered, *House, M.D.* (2004–2012) began, revolving around a flawed, yet brilliant, diagnostician (based on Sherlock Holmes) and his team of specialists, which ran for eight seasons.[31] Finally, in 2005, *Grey's Anatomy* (2005–present) came on the air, which, like *Chicago Hope*, featured surgeons.[32] Unlike its predecessor, though, the surgeons began the program as interns, at the beginning of their careers. As the original characters progressed through the ranks, new interns began. While scholars have noted similarities in these programs to older medical dramas, the camera work, diversity in characters, storylines, and pace distinguish these shows as a new era of this staple genre in television history.[33]

CONTEMPORARY REPRESENTATIONS

What do these medical dramas teach us about doctors and other health professionals? We can think about characteristics of these latest medical drama docs, many of which challenge the stereotype of the physician as a white, able-bodied, man. We can explore the doctor-patient relationship as it is modeled in television, keeping in mind that these programs use actual physicians as script advisors. Furthermore, as viewers, we see our roles as patients fictionalized on the small screen, with health behaviors and conditions carried out. Finally, we can ponder the overall utopic depiction of the health care system, as a world in which everyone is treated, regardless of his or her insurance status.

The Sexy Superheroes of Medicine

A major shift occurred with the 1980s medical drama *St. Elsewhere*. For the first time, women and people of color played doctors on television—and not just a peripheral physician character, as seen with the 1970s paramedic drama *Emergency!*, in which an African American doctor, referred to as "Mike," dressed like an orderly and constantly made mistakes. With *St. Elsewhere*, Dr. Phillip Chandler (actor Denzel Washington) pioneered the competent and confident African American physician, accompanied by a blend of other characters that included both men and women. While this program began to challenge the physician stereotype with a few characters, *ER* introduced a diversity that would change all future medical dramas. In the course of the show (again fifteen seasons), characters represented numerous people of color and women in powerful roles, including a female chief of staff who was gay and had a physical disability (the character Dr. Kerry Weaver, portrayed by able-bodied actress Laura Innes). Although *Chicago Hope* was not quite as diverse, the show still contained new roles for women and African Americans, as did the program *House, M.D.* Such diversity in these dramas paved the way for *Grey's Anatomy*, a show that features Dr. Meredith Grey, a female surgeon, and includes gender and racial diversity in its cast.

St. Elsewhere also introduced viewers to the promiscuity of the fictional hospital. In contemporary medical dramas, health professionals routinely engage in relationships with each other. Everyone pairs up with each other in the insular world of the hospital. For example, nurse Camille Schutt is involved with three doctors within the first season of *Chicago Hope*. In *ER*, Dr. Doug Ross has an on and off-again relationship with nurse Carol Hathaway, as well as pairing up with a med student, numerous patients, and others he meets, mostly through the hospital. Likewise, nurse-turned-physician Abby Lockhart bounces between Drs. John Carter and Luka Kovac. On *House, M.D.*, Dr. James Wilson dates a nurse, then another doctor. House and his supervisor, Dr. Lisa Cuddy, have a tumultuous relationship. *Grey's Anatomy* contains so many inter-hospital relationships that one could hardly keep track, as demonstrated by the syphilis outbreak among the nurses and doctors in the first season. Not only are the doctors promiscuous, but they often engage in sexual activity at work. In the *House, M.D.* episode, "Airborne," Drs. Allison Cameron and Robert Chase break into the patient's home and have intercourse on the patient's bed.[34] And yet, few consequences come of the rampant promiscuity, other than a treatable sexually transmitted infection, pregnancy scares, and a few kids, who are rarely shown in the program. While TV doctors' flirtatious behavior is certainly not new (think of Hawkeye Pierce of *M*A*S*H*), the extent to which characters participate in such relationships has grown dramatically.

On the other hand, in some ways, the health professionals of contemporary television have not changed much since the days of Marcus Welby, Hawkeye Pierce, and other characters from the 1960s and 1970s. Even with the increased diversity, some characteristics of the TV doctor remain constant. As Joseph Turow has observed, we still have attractive, heroic, skilled professionals featured in television.[35] Fictional mortality rates are so low that doctors rarely lose patients. For example, no patients die in *House, M.D.* until the end of the second season in "Euphoria, Part 1."[36] Even when patients are given low chances of survival, they usually pull through, without complications. The skill of these health professionals is especially exemplified when they save patients, despite their own abundant personal problems. Doctors successfully treat patients while experiencing an aneurysm, terminal cancer, mental illness, limb amputation, and violent assaults inside the hospital, as well as divorce, custody battles, and the deaths of loved ones. Such heroism is exemplified in the eighth season finale of *Grey's Anatomy* after a plane crash in the wilderness jeopardizes the lives of five physicians.[37] In the first few minutes of the episode, surgeon Meredith Grey loses her sister. She mourns for thirty seconds. In the next scene, she is back in "doctor mode," using a safety pin as a surgical tool to save the hand of her husband. Likewise, Dr. Arizona Robbins panics when she sees her femur sticking out of her skin.[38] Yet, she immediately calms down when she realizes that the pilot needs medical attention and briefs another doctor on his condition. Dr. Mark Sloan ignores his own injuries (which eventually become fatal) at the crash site, as he attends to other survivors.[39] We see similar skill in the wake of disaster during hospital shootings in *ER*, *Chicago Hope*, *Grey's Anatomy*, and *House, M.D.*, during outbreaks (and subsequent quarantines), chemical spills, and other situations that one would think might impede medical care. Without hesitation, characters like Dr. Grey, Dr. Kovac, Dr. House, and others handle a live bomb, enter a building that is about to collapse, or deliberately expose themselves to dangerous infection for the sake of their patients.

Physicians like Dr. Greene, Dr. Diane Grad, Dr. Allison Cameron, and Dr. Izzie Stevens are not just providers, but mentors, parental figures, and friends. For example, in the *ER* episode "John Carter, M.D.," John Carter skips his own graduation to comfort a young girl awaiting surgery.[40] Similarly, in the episode "The Crossing," after working for two days straight, Dr. Kovac spends his night off comforting a dying bishop in the Intensive Care Unit.[41] And in "The Parent Rap" episode of *Chicago Hope*, surgeon Jeffrey Geiger dresses as a clown to entertain a group of injured children.[42] Throughout these shows, doctors repeatedly go above and beyond to comfort their patients.

TV's health professionals are willing to do anything for their patients, jeopardizing their careers or even their lives. Without consent, Dr. Ross detoxes a heroin-addicted baby.[43] Dr. Elizabeth Corday (*ER*) performs an illegal organ transplant to help an HIV-positive patient live longer[44] and Dr. Izzie Stevens, of *Grey's Anatomy*, severs the cord of her patient's LVAD (a temporary heart device) to boost his position on the transplant list.[45] And in nearly every episode of *House, M.D.*, Dr. House and his team violate hospital protocol to save their patients.

Health professionals in television serve as advocates for their patients, protecting them against hospital bureaucracy or the villainous HMO enterprises. Doctors stand up for their patients so that they can receive the best possible care. In the second episode of *Chicago Hope*, neurosurgeon Dr. Aaron Schutt fights the HMO representative so that Schutt can perform a sight-saving surgery on a patient with a tumor on her optic nerve.[46] Schutt tells the representative, "Given the difficulty and risk of the procedure, I want Mrs. White to have every conceivable advantage," implying that he can give her that advantage.[47] The HMO representative allows Schutt to operate and he successfully removes the tumor, allowing the woman to see again. Likewise, in other episodes of the four dramas, physicians ignore hospital protocol, use experimental procedures, and risk their careers for their patients. In this way, physicians protect their patients from the unseen authorities that focus on the bottom line, not patient care. These physicians care little about rules, protocol, threats of disciplinary action, or other components of bureaucracy that threaten their patient care. And yet, these attitudes are unique to fictional television. Surveys of real-life physicians suggest that most doctors practice "defensive medicine," in that they are overly cautious in administering care to protect themselves from litigation.[48] Television paints doctors and other health professionals as providers first, ignoring their roles as employees or regular people.

Patients

Television patients are flawed, irresponsible, and, often, amusingly quirky— characteristics that help bolster the heroic doctor image. As in older dramas, patients exist to support the doctors in the storylines, making them look like heroes, therapists, friends, and mentors; reinforcing their exceptional skill; and teaching them important lessons. Contrary to real life, television patients rarely have mundane conditions, like urinary tract infections. On TV, patients seek treatment after tumbling into a polar bear pit, falling through a plate glass window, and inhaling fumes in a chemistry explosion.[49] All patients have unique stories that help them to connect to the audience, as illustrated by the impoverished mother who cannot afford her daughter's asthma medication (later prompting Dr. Ross to buy it and deliver it to her); the architect with the degenerative eye disease, causing him to go blind (Dr. Lewis gives him a puppy), and the teenage patient in *House, M.D.* who loses her arm to cancer just as she is about to embark on a solo-sailing adventure.[50] Through the dialogue and overall narrative, these programs teach us about responsible health choices and how to best behave in hospital.

As long as fictional patients follow their physicians' advice, they are encouraged to take responsibility for their health, especially in terms of illness prevention. TV doctors praise fictional "responsible" patients—those who live healthy lifestyles and criticize patients who do not. Physicians also lecture patients who lie or omit important details of their medical history or seek medical treatment when they believe that it is not needed.

Storylines convey the dangers of unhealthy eating, substance abuse, and other "risky" behaviors. Fictional doctors connect unhealthy eating to patients' ill health. For example, when an overweight woman complains of abdominal pain to Dr. Carter, in the episode "Faith" of *ER*, the conversation negatively reflects on her diet choices:

Carter: What'd you have for breakfast this morning?

Woman: The usual. Three fried eggs, bacon, glass of buttermilk, toast with jam.

Carter: Ah, the American Heart Association breakfast.

Woman: Don't lecture me doctor. My mother had the exact same breakfast every day of her life. Died last year at 96. Car accident.[51]

Carter's response to the woman's description of her breakfast indicated the widespread cultural knowledge that a diet high in fat and cholesterol is unhealthy. The episode "Que Sera, Sera?" of *House, M.D.* focuses on the extreme size of a morbidly obese man, beginning with the image of fire-fighters sawing a large hole in the wall of a house in order to get the patient out.[52] While House determines that the patient's ill health is not related to his weight, the endless jokes and quips about the patient's size suggest the nature of his poor choices.

As viewers, we also learn about the dangers of using tobacco and other substances. Along with the numerous fictional patients that die of lung cancer, smokers face other consequences. In the *Grey's Anatomy* episode titled "Tell Me Sweet Little Lies," surgeons tell a guitar player that his newly reattached fingers will likely turn necrotic due to poor circulation if he does not quit smoking.[53] And in another episode of *Grey's Anatomy*, a patient's desire to smoke is so intense that he lights a cigarette while he is on oxygen.[54] The room explodes and the patient is badly burned. The patient's responsibility for his burns is further underscored when, in response to the patient's actions, Chief of Surgery Dr. Richard Webber says to another doctor, "What kind of idiot lights a cigarette in a hospital?"[55] Alcoholics and other drug abusers also experience ill health for their choices, including the need for liver transplants and even death.

People who tried to treat themselves were portrayed as foolish and often needed medical treatment for their choices. In *House*, a teenager develops neurological problems after taking anti-smoking remedies purchased online.[56] Another patient mixes fertility drugs with birth control, causing a stroke and a liver tumor.[57] Diet also causes health problems for patients. While patients are expected to eat healthy, extreme diets and dietary supplements cause patients health distress, including heart failure from diet drugs and scurvy due to an all-protein diet.[58] These storylines convey the dangers of self-treatment, conveying to viewers to consult their doctors, rather than search the Internet.

On the lighter side, "bad" patients are also quirky, providing the comic relief for the shows. In the *ER* episode "Mars Attacks," a man deliberately

cuts his ears with kitchen shears in order to look like a *Star Trek* character
for a science-fiction convention.[59] In another episode, two men cut off their
fingertips as they lifted a lawnmower up to trim the hedges.[60] A frustrated
writer in *Grey's Anatomy* needs surgery after he eats his novel and the pages
become wedged in his intestinal tract.[61] People also suffer injuries from self-
circumcision and objects inserted during sex.[62] Similarly, in "Oh the Guilt" of
Grey's Anatomy, two people get caught having an extra-marital affair when
they become intertwined during intercourse and cannot free themselves. And
in the *House, M.D.* episode "Deception," a young woman complains to Dr.
House of vaginal discomfort and tells him that she is "on the jelly."

> House: You have an infection. Gonna need a sample.
>
> Woman: I brought the jar.
>
> House: No, I meant a sample of your—
>
> *House looks up and sees the patient holding a jar of strawberry jelly.*
>
> House: Okay, we have a neurological problem here.
>
> Woman: There's something wrong with my brain?
>
> House: Oh yeah. You can cover yourself up, got what I need. [63]

Later in the episode, House hands the woman a prescription for antibiotics
and advises her to abstain from sex. The woman asks, "How long?" House
replies, "On an evolutionary basis, I'd recommend forever." House's comments, along with the overall absurdity of the case, construct the patient as
responsible for her infection due to her misinterpretation of contraceptive
devices.[64] Such moments break up the typical dramatic tone of these shows.
At the same time, these messages paint the patients as fools, possibly discouraging viewers from seeking medical care, for fear of the health professionals'
incessant mockery.

DOCTOR KNOWS BEST

Even with the rise of the active patient model, television paints the doctor-
patient relationship as paternalistic, in which physicians hold the ultimate
authority, advising their patients on healthy behaviors, necessary procedures,
and treatments. Little has changed since the days of *Marcus Welby, M.D.*,
when patients asked, "What seems to be the trouble, Doctor?" Under this
model, "good" patients trust their health professionals to work in their best
interests and know the answer. They do not propose diagnoses or treatments,

nor do they question their doctors or seek a second opinion. In fact, patients that do attempt to partake in the medical process are conveyed as burdensome pains who hinder their path to recovery.

When patients assert themselves, attempt to self-diagnose, or ask questions, they are criticized and face negative consequences for their actions. Dr. House repeatedly mocks patients who question his diagnoses or treatments. In "TB or Not TB," a woman with cat allergies tells House that she does not want to take antihistamines or use nasal spray.[65] House responds by telling her to kill the cat. In another episode, House ridicules a mother's amateur diagnosis of epilepsy for her daughter, informing her that the girl is actually masturbating.[66] Because of House's reactions, patients seem hesitant to question his authority—especially because he almost always cures his patients.

TV doctors criticize patients who argue with them or discuss research they had done about their health. These reactions convey the message that patients' questions irritate doctors. This finding is not unique to fictional television. In real life, many doctors believe patients' questions about online material wastes their time, and are therefore, unnecessary.[67] Such negative messages about patient participation contradict contemporary literature on improving patient care, discouraging people from taking active roles in their health care. In more positive portrayals, fictional doctors could be receptive to patient questions, indirectly informing viewers on deciphering between credible and false information.[68] These programs could also discuss online support groups or other resources for people seeking additional health knowledge.

THE HEALTH CARE SYSTEM

TV largely ignores the health care system. In an idealized version of medicine, patients hardly wait. No one asks for insurance cards or uses words like "out of network" and "co-pay." As other scholars have noted, money has little presence in medical dramas.[69] Doctors do not address the need of universal health care (even though these shows largely aired before the Patient Protection and Affordable Care Act was passed). So without these bureaucratic burdens, how does a world constructed by television writers and advised by physicians portray the hospital experience and the "system?"

With little paperwork, doctors treat patients, period. Absent is the admitting process, triage, in which nurses assess patients' well-being. Medical dramas focus on the doctor-patient interaction, meaning that the numerous roles played by other types of health professionals are ignored. These programs have been heavily criticized for minimalizing the role that nurses, physician assistants, and other care providers play, even with the roles of Nurse Hathaway and Physician

Assistant Jeanie Boulet on *ER*.[70] Assuming that the portrayals of nurses and other non-physician professionals in popular programs like *Grey's Anatomy* may shape viewers' perception, these portrayals may lead viewers to believe that patients should disregard medical advice conveyed by nurses because they are not portrayed as knowledgeable or important. And, since medical dramas regularly portray doctors performing nurses' duties, a patient may question a nurse's ability to do the procedure when she does perform one of those duties. Fictional doctors do not just perform the duties of other professionals, they also take over the duties of other physicians. In the fictitious bubble of medical dramas, there are no specialists, just the renaissance health professionals who serve as surgeons, cardiologists, OBGYNs, radiologists, and in other capacities. In *Chicago Hope*, neurosurgeon Aaron Schutt easily becomes a psychiatrist after an aneurysm impairs his ability to perform surgery. The diagnostics team in *House, M.D.* moves from the patient's bedside, to the lab, to the operating room, and to the morgue, often in a single episode.

Especially in *House, M.D.*, doctors freely order expensive diagnostic tests or perform the tests themselves. Nearly every patient undergoes an MRI and PET scan, as well as many other extensive and expensive tests. Since the doctors perform the tests themselves, results are available immediately. For example, in the episode "Unwritten," Dr. Chase and Dr. Christopher Taub take the patient's history, do her physical exam, and later perform her MRI scan.[71] And in "Humpty Dumpty," a house painter undergoes extensive testing, including a Mantoux test for tuberculosis, a cervical MRI, an echocardiogram, and numerous blood panels.[72] Despite these tests, Dr. House determines the diagnosis from the patient's work history. Since most episodes follow this pattern, this program has been criticized for its overuse of diagnostic testing, with the notion that these representations have created the expectation of such tests in real life, even when they are unnecessary.[73] Not only do the fictional diagnostic tests lead to the correct diagnosis, another false expectation is that all people go to the hospital to be cured. As part of protecting the physician heroes, medical dramas have very low mortality rates for their fictional patients, ignoring the fact that more people die in the hospital than anywhere else.[74] Representations ignore these statistics, rarely addressing palliative or hospice care. Without media coverage of such choices, viewers may not be aware they exist.

What is missing from medical dramas are the macro issues that hospitals and health care systems face on a daily basis. According to the American College of Healthcare Executives, financial concerns, patient safety, and the implementation of health care reform rank as the three most important issues of hospital CEOs.[75] While we may see an irresponsible patient character, patient safety issues, for example, are ignored in medical dramas. Without depictions of the macro issues that affect everyday patient care, it may be difficult to understand the significance of having a primary care physician, for example, instead of simply visiting the emergency room.

CONCLUSION: WHY DO WE WATCH?

Overall, a disconnect exists between the current status of American health care and its images in entertainment television. Since the beginning of television, AMA members and other physicians have questioned the accuracy of the genre.[76] Contemporary programs are no different. Countless blogs document the errors of these shows, from medical misinformation to story arc inconsistencies.[77] Obviously, in real life, this hero image does not quite translate. You would be hard-pressed to find a general practitioner to play checkers with you in the middle of the night (as in *Marcus Welby, M.D.*). It would be inappropriate for medical students and their supervisors to engage in sex (especially in a patient's bed). And doctors who routinely perform tests and procedures without consent (as in *House, M.D.*) would be quickly stripped of their medical licenses.

Despite their outdated and unrealistic portrayals of doctors, patients, and the health care system, medical dramas continue to dominate in television. So, with the skepticism toward the American health care system, why does the doctor-as-hero image persist? As in other genres, fictional television protects the protagonists. Television thrives on predictability and generic formulas. One would be hard-pressed to find an inept police detective as the main character of a cop show or a legal drama with no smooth talkers. Medical dramas are no different, except that the stakes are higher, given that these programs have been demonstrated to teach viewers about health issues, the hospital experience, and their role as patients, even if the producers' intention is pure entertainment.

From the production side, "doctor" dramas are cost-effective for television in that the sets are simple, storylines can be recycled, and like its real-life reflection, employees at a hospital change periodically, especially those who are in training. All of the original cast members of *ER* left long before the series' finale. For the last season of *Chicago Hope*, all but two original cast members were replaced. In the eight seasons of *House, M.D.*, the diagnostics team cycled out characters four times. *Grey's Anatomy* killed off several main characters, replacing them with trainees and seasoned surgeons. With each new group of characters, storylines of the learning process emerge, new doctors learn how to intubate, run a trauma, and work with the nurses. Like their predecessors, the resident characters face ethical decisions about treating "frequent fliers," informed consent, and the delicate challenge of obtaining permission for organ retrieval from a comatose loved one.

And, of course, medical dramas are not the only representations of doctors in television. With the popularity of crime dramas, we see doctors as the occasional villains. For example, the program *Criminal Minds* portrays physicians as sociopaths, with the killer psychiatrist who murders patients through their phobias, and, even more horrifying, the "doctor" who amputated his victims' limbs and then sewed them onto other victims.[78] And like *M*A*S*H*, physician characters also appear in sitcoms, such as the medical comedies *Scrubs* and the *Mindy Project*. With DVRs and online streaming sites, the future of medical dramas is difficult to predict. At the same time, the heroic doctors in their utopic hospitals have survived sixty years of technological changes, suggesting that this genre will find new audiences.

NOTES

1. Candace Cummins Gauthier, "Television Drama and Popular Film As Medical Narrative," *Journal of American Culture* 22, no. 3 (1999), 23–25; Solange, Davin, "Healthy Viewing: The Reception of Medical Narratives," in *Health and the Media*, ed. Clive Seale (Malden: Blackwell Press, 2004), 143–159.

2. Truls Østbye, Bill Miller, and Heather Keller, "Throw That Epidemiologist Out of the Emergency Room! Using the Television Series *ER* as a Vehicle for Teaching Methodologists About Medical Issues," *Journal of Clinical Epidemiology* 50, no. 10 (1997), 1183–1186; Michael M. O'Connor, "The Role of the Television Drama *ER* in Medical Student Life: Entertainment or Socialization?" *JAMA: The Journal of the American Medical Association* 280, no. 9 (1998), 854–855.

3. "Key News Audiences Now Blend Online and Traditional Sources," Pew Research Center, last modified August 17, 2008, http://people-press.org/2008/08/17/key-news-audiences-now-blend-online-and-traditional-sources; Arvind Singhal, Michael J. Cody, and Everett M. Rogers, *Entertainment-education and Social Change: History, Research, and Practice* (Mahwah, N.J.: Lawrence Erlbaum & Associates, 2004).

4. Jay A. Winsten, "Promoting Designated Drivers: The Harvard Alcohol Project," *American Journal of Preventive Medicine* 10, no. 3 Suppl (1994), 11; Deborah Glik et al., "Health Education Goes Hollywood: Working with Prime-Time and Daytime Entertainment Television for Immunization Promotion," *Journal of Health Communication* 3, no. 3 (1998), 263–282; Mollyann Brodie, Ursula Foehr, Vicky Rideout, Neal Baer, Carolyn Miller, Rebecca Flournoy, and Drew Altman, "Communicating Health Information Through the Entertainment Media," *Health Affairs* 20, no. 1 (2001), 192–199; Kate L. Folb, "'Don't Touch that Dial!' TV as a—What!—Positive Influence," *SIECUS REPORT* 28, no. 5 (2000), 16–18.

5. George Gerbner, Larry Gross, Michael Morgan, and Nancy Signorielli, "Health and Medicine on Television," *New England Journal of Medicine* 305 (1981), 15, 901–904.

6. Gerbner et al. "Health and Medicine," 901–904.

7. Michael Pfau, Lawrence J. Mullen, and Kirsten Garrow, "The Influence of Television Viewing on Public Perceptions of Physicians," *Journal of Broadcasting & Electronic Media* 39, no. 4 (1995), 441–458; Rebecca M. Chory-Assad and Ron Tamborini, "Television Exposure and the Public's Perceptions of Physicians," *Journal of Broadcasting & Electronic Media* 47, no. 2 (2003), 197–215.

8. Paul Starr, *The Social Transformation of American Medicine* (New York: Basic Books, 1982).

9. Jonathan Engel, *Poor People's Medicine: Medicaid and American Charity Care since 1965* (Durham: Duke University Press, 2006).

10. Gregg Vandekieft, "From *City Hospital* to *ER*: The Evolution of the Television Physician," in *Cultural Sutures: Medicine and Media*, ed. Lester D. Friedman (Durham: Duke University Press, 2004), 215–233.

11. Marc Cohen and Audrey Shafer, "Images and Healers: A Visual History of Scientific Medicine," in *Cultural Sutures: Medicine and Media*, ed. Lester D. Friedman (Durham: Duke University Press, 2004), 197–233.

12. Vandekieft, "From City Hospital to ER," 215–233; Joseph Turow, *Playing Doctor: Television, Storytelling, and Medical Power* (Ann Arbor: University of Michigan Press, 2010).

13. Turow, *Playing Doctor*.

14. David A. Shore, *The Trust Crisis in Health Care: Causes, Consequences, and Cures* (New York: Oxford University Press, 2006).

15. Shore, *Trust Crisis in Health Care*; Ezekiel J. Emanuel and Linda L. Emanuel, "Four Models of the Physician-patient Relationship, *JAMA* 267, no. 16 (1992), 2221–2226.

16. Meredith Minkler, "Personal Responsibility for Health? A Review of the Arguments and the Evidence at Century's End," *Health Education & Behavior* 26, no. 1 (1999), 121–141.

17. Shore, *Trust Crisis in Health Care*.

18. Turow, *Playing Doctor*; Vandekieft, "From *City Hospital* to *ER*."

19. Turow, *Playing Doctor*.

20. Gerbner et al., "Health and Medicine," 901–904; James McLaughlin, "The Doctor Shows," *Journal of Communication* 25, no. 3 (1975), 182–184.

21. Turow, *Playing Doctor*.

22. Linda T. Kohn, Janet M. Corrigan, and Molla S. Donaldson, *To Err Is Human: Building a Safer Health System* (Washington: National Academy Press, 2000).

23. Kohn, Corrigan, and Donaldson, *To Err Is Human*.

24. Sheldon P. Blau and Elaine Fantel Shimberg, *How to Get Out of the Hospital Alive: A Guide to Patient Power* (New York: Macmillan, 1997); Karen Keating McCann, *Take Charge of Your Hospital Stay: A "Start Smart" Guide for Patients and Care Partners* (New York: Plenum Press, 1994); Thomas A. Sharon, *Protect Yourself in the Hospital: Insider Tips for Avoiding Hospital Mistakes for Yourself or Someone You Love* (New York: McGraw-Hill 2004).

25. Ha T. Tu and Genna R. Cohen, *Striking Jump in Consumers Seeking Health Care Information* (Washington: Center for Studying Health System Change, 2008);

Elizabeth Murray, Bernard Lo, Lance Pollack, Karen Donelan, Joe Catania, Martha White, Kinga Zapert, and Rachel Turner, "The Impact of Health Information on the Internet on The Physician-Patient Relationship: Patient Perceptions," *Archives of Internal Medicine* 163, no. 14 (2003), 1727.

26. Murray et al. "The Impact of Health Information," 1727; Suzy A. Iverson, Kristin B. Howard, and Brian K. Penney, "Impact of Internet Use on Health-Related Behaviors and the Patient-Physician Relationship: A Survey-Based Study and Review," *JAOA: Journal of the American Osteopathic Association* 108, no. 12 (2008), 699–711; Ronald M. Epstein, Brian S. Alper, and Timothy E. Quill, "Communicating Evidence for Participatory Decision Making," *JAMA: The Journal of the American Medical Association* 291, no. 19 (2004), 2359–2366.

27. Farrah Ahmad, Pamela L. Hudak, Kim Bercovitz, Elisa Hollenberg, and Wendy Levinson, "Are Physicians Ready for Patients with Internet-based Health Information?" *Journal of Medical Internet Research* 8, no. 3 (2006), e22.

28. *Chicago Hope*, directed by David E. Kelley, 1994–2000 by Fox.

29. *ER*, directed by Michael Crichton, 1994–2009 by Fox.

30. Turow, *Playing Doctor*; Jason Jacobs, *Body Trauma TV: The New Hospital Dramas* (London: British Film Institute, 2003).

31. *House, M.D.*, directed by David Shore, 2004–2012 by Fox.

32. *Grey's Anatomy*, directed by Shonda Rimes, 2005–present by ABC.

33. Turow, *Playing Doctor*; Jacobs, *Body Trauma*.

34. *House, M.D.*, "Airborne," directed by Elodie Keene, first broadcast April 10, 2007, by Fox.

35. Turow, *Playing Doctor*.

36. *House, M.D.*,"Euphoria: Part 1," directed by Deran Sarafian, first broadcast May 2, 2006, by Fox.

37. *Grey's Anatomy*, "Flight," directed by Rob Corn, first broadcast May 17, 2012, by ABC.

38. *Grey's Anatomy*, "Flight."

39. *Grey's Anatomy*, "Flight."

40. *ER*, "John Carter, M.D.," directed by Christopher Chulack, first broadcast May 16, 1996, by NBC.

41. *ER*, "The Crossing," directed by Jonathan Kaplan, first broadcast February 22, 2001, by NBC.

42. *Chicago Hope*, "The Parent Rap," directed by Arvin Brown, first broadcast April 29, 1996, by Fox.

43. *ER*, "Of Past Regret and Future Fear," Directed by Anthony Edwards, first broadcast April 30, 1998 by NBC.

44. *ER*, "Try Carter," directed by Jonathan Kaplan, first broadcast October 14, 2004, by NBC.

45. *Grey's Anatomy*, "Deterioration of the Fight or Flight Response," directed by Rob Corn, first broadcast May 15, 2006, by ABC.

46. *Chicago Hope*, "Over the Rainbow," directed by Michael Dinner, first broadcast September 22, 1994, by Fox.

47. *Chicago Hope*, "Over the Rainbow."

48. Tara F. Bishop, Alex D. Federman, and Salomeh Keyhani, "Physicians Views on Defensive Medicine: A National Survey," *Archives of Internal Medicine* 170 (2010), 1081–1083.

49. *ER*, "Family Matter," directed by Anthony Edwards, first broadcast January 6, 2000, by NBC; *ER*, "Dr. Carter, I Presume," directed by Christopher Chulack, first broadcast September 26, 1996, by NBC; *ER*, "Survival of the Fittest," directed by Marita Grabiak, first broadcast March 29, 2001, by NBC; *ER*, "Truth & Consequences," directed by Steve De Jarnatt, first broadcast November 4, 1999, by NBC.

50. *ER*, "Into That Good Night," directed by Charles Haid, first broadcast October 13, 1994, by NBC; *ER*, "Out of Africa," directed by Jonathan Kaplan, first broadcast October 30, 2003, by NBC; *House, M.D.*, "Last Temptation," directed by Tim Southam, first broadcast April 18, 2011, by Fox.

51. *ER*, "Faith."

52. *House, M.D.*, "Que Sera Sera," directed by Deran Sarafian, first broadcast November 7, 2006, by Fox.

53. *Grey's Anatomy*, "Tell Me Sweet Little Lies," directed by Adam Davidson, first broadcast January 22, 2006, by ABC.

54. *Grey's Anatomy*, "What I Am," directed by Dan Lerner, first broadcast October 12, 2006, by ABC.

55. *Grey's Anatomy*, "What I Am."

56. *House, M.D.*, "Distractions," directed by Daniel Attias, first broadcast February 14, 2006, by Fox.

57. *House, M.D.*, "Need to Know," directed by David Semel, first broadcast February 7, 2006, by Fox.

58. *Chicago Hope*, "Broken Hearts," directed by Sandy Smolan, first broadcast January 7, 1998, by Fox; *House, M.D.*, "Meaning," directed by Deran Darafian, first broadcast September 5, 2006, by Fox.

59. *ER*, "Mars Attacks," directed by Paris Barclay, first broadcast October 26, 2000, by NBC.

60. *ER*, "Insurrection," directed by Charles Haid, first broadcast October 10, 2002, by NBC.

61. *Grey's Anatomy*, "Begin the Begin," directed by Jessica Yu, first broadcast January 15, 2006, by ABC.

62. *House, M.D.*, "Autopsy," directed by Deran Sarafian, first broadcast September 20, 2005, by Fox; *House, M.D.*, "Deception," directed by Deran Sarafian, first broadcast December 13, 2005, by Fox.

63. *House, M.D.*, "Deception."

64. *House, M.D.*, "Deception."

65. *House, M.D.*, "TB or Not TB," directed by Peter O'Fallon, first broadcast November 1, 2005, by Fox.

66. *House, M.D.*, "Euphoria: Part 2," directed by Deran Sarafian, first broadcast May 3, 2006, by Fox.

67. Ahmad et al. "Are Physicians Ready?", 22.

68. Anthony G. Crocco, Miguel Villasis-Keever, and Alejandro R. Jadad, "Analysis of Cases of Harm Associated with Use of Health Information on the

Internet," *JAMA: The Journal of the American Medical Association* 287, no. 21 (2002), 2869–2871.

69. George J. Annas, "Sex, Money, and Bioethics: Watching *ER* and *Chicago Hope*," *Hastings Center Report* 25, no. 5 (1995), 40–43; Joseph Turow, "Television Entertainment and the US Health-care Debate," *The Lancet* 347, no. 9010 (1996), 1240–1243.

70. Sandy Jacobs Summers and Harry Jacobs Summers, "Media 'Nursing': Retiring the Handmaiden: What Viewers See on *ER* Affects Our Profession," *AJN: The American Journal of Nursing* 104, no. 2 (2004), 13.

71. *House, M.D.*, "Unwritten," directed by Greg Yaitanes, first broadcast October 4, 2010, by Fox.

72. *House, M.D.*, "Humpty Dumpty," directed by Daniel Attias, first broadcast September 27, 2005 by Fox.

73. Kevin Pho, "How *House, M.D.* is Affecting Patients' Expectations of Medical Care," *KevinMD.com*, last modified October 6, 2009, http://www.kevinmd.com/blog/2009/10/house-md-affecting-patients-expectations-medical-care.html.

74. Andrea Gruneir, Vincent Mor, Sherry Weitzen, Rachael Truchil, Joan Teno, and Jason Roy, "Where People Die: A Multilevel Approach to Understanding Influences on Site of Death in America," *Medical Care Research and Review* 64, no. 4 (2007), 351–378.

75. "Top Issues Confronting Hospitals: 2012," *American College of Healthcare Executives*, last modified January 7, 2013, http://www.ache.org/Pubs/Releases/2013/Top-Issues-Confronting-Hospitals-2012.cfm.

76. "How Authentic Is Medicine on Television?" *Journal of the American Medical Association*, May 4, 1957, 49–51.

77. See: "House—Episode 14 (Season 8), 'Love is Blind,'" *Polite Dissent*, last modified March 19, 2012, http://www.politedissent.com/archives/8788.

78. *Criminal Minds*, "Scared to Death," directed by Felix Enriquez Alcala, first broadcast October 10, 2007, by CBS.; *Criminal Minds*, "God Complex," directed by Larry Teng, first broadcast October 24, 2012, by CBS.

Section V

THE VOICE

Chapter Fourteen

Made Impossible by Viewers Like You: The Politics and Poetics of Native American Voices in US Public Television

Leighton C. Peterson

Eric Michaels, a scholar and participant observer in the development of Aboriginal public television in Australia, noted that the cultural producers who control television are ultimately the authors of history.[1] That is, the historical narratives and stereotypes of indigenous peoples circulated by mainstream producers in a range of media, including television, contribute to the erasure of indigenous views and voices in history, perpetuating colonial narratives.[2] In the case of US mainstream media, indigenous Native American voices are rare, and Native perspectives have been long misrepresented by content producers captivated by mythologies of Indian resistance and exile, spiritual primitivism, and eventual extinction or assimilation.[3] Persistent media stereotypes and expectations about Native American peoples are often tied to assumptions of failure. These "failures" include the inability to thwart Manifest Destiny, to exist contemporaneously with non-Natives, to save themselves from devastating social ills—or in the case of Lone Ranger–sidekick Tonto, to speak English correctly.[4] Such themes continue to resonate in Western literature, films, television programs, and news coverage that influence contemporary perceptions about all Native American peoples.

In contrast, American public television, including the Public Broadcasting Service (PBS) network and its numerous affiliated strands and series, is perceived and intended to be a safe space for marginalized histories and voices outside of the mainstream. A staple of PBS and US public television is the documentary film, both as repository of history and window into exotic worlds. Documentary films are also a crucial genre for indigenous [post]colonial interventions. Indeed the number of documentaries by Native American filmmakers has proliferated in the last twenty years, reflecting a kind of "cultural activism," or indigenous producers' desire to intervene in mediated misrepresentations and to get their communities' stories to wider publics.[5] It also reflects renewed support and interest for indigenous content from PBS and public broadcasting entities, which are imbued with symbolic power for being an authoritative voice of history and contemporary social commentary. In fact, PBS is considered to be one of the nation's most trusted institutions.[6] As one Native documentarian posited, "If it's on PBS, it must be true. That's what people believe." Documentary programs from series like *American Experience* are often adopted for broad educational use, and based on my own observations and experience, are distributed with curricular and educational engagements in mind.[7]

Thus public television documentaries are important sites for the negotiation of Native American voices designed to counter wide-ranging misrepresentations including stubborn tropes of extinction, exoticism, and failure. This chapter draws primarily from public television documentaries with significant Native involvement, including *Return of Navajo Boy* (2000), *Weaving Worlds* (2008), *Geronimo* (2009), *Columbus Day Legacy* (2011), and the acclaimed documentary mini-series *We Shall Remain* (2009). I use these productions as case studies to illustrate the specific links between editorial choices, institutional structures, and perceived audience expectations involved in the negotiation of Native voices in public television. These links are integral to the "politics" of Native documentaries, or the ways in which indigenous cultural producers engage an array of multi-sited and transnational social, professional, and political-economic structures and choices that directly impact their own filmic voices. In doing so, I argue for concurrent examination of the "poetics" of Native documentaries. This includes exploring the phenomenon of "voice" in documentary film as both subject position and actual linguistic performance. My focus on voice echoes the call from Rosiland Morris who suggested, "it is legitimate to ask why the representational capacity of the film should be reduced to its visual dimension. . . . Why is voice the mere supplement of vision?"[8]

This examination of voice elucidates representational practices such as testimonial interviews and editing, and it links them to positionality. Inherent in representing voice is the process of entextualization in film, or creating discrete audiovisual recordings that can be removed from their interactional, historical, and sociocultural contexts. This includes negotiating which languages are considered appropriate for audiences, capturing and editing interviews, and debating whether specific discursive styles such as long oral narratives can keep audiences attentive. It also involves the recontextualization of these recordings, or the ways in which producers and audiences make meaning through edited, decontextualized snippets of entextualized filmic voices.[9] Here, the visual elements and the linguistic performances (i.e., the sounds, grammars, and words) of film subjects are re-presented in the filmmaker's vision and ultimately interpreted by viewers.

Thus filmmakers use on-screen voices to negotiate their own "voice" through the process of shooting and editing, and the representation of entextualized voices reflects filmmaker and subject positionalities, ultimately leading to the opinions, ideas, and histories expressed in public television. How are voice and positionality negotiated in indigenous film, and who determines which "voices" are heard? What kinds of films are Native producers expected to make? And how do ideologies and editorial decisions link to funding and audience expectations and the circulation of meanings about Native American peoples? Approaching "voice" in documentary programming in this way, with all of its heteroglossic and multifaceted connotations, provides insight into the ways in which many structural and structuring inequities become naturalized, recreated, and challenged through language and film.

STRUCTURES, INSTITUTIONS, AND NATIVE DOCUMENTARIES

Indigenous television is a significant phenomenon in settler nations such as Canada and Australia, where aboriginal peoples have created their own public television networks and distribution entities with tremendous financial and governmental support.[10] In the United States, the relative lack of indigenized televisual culture reflects substantially less support for indigenous programming. Nonetheless, the US public television system is among the few ways to secure financing and distribution for a "high impact" documentary film produced by or about Native American peoples.[11] Most programs with Native American content are produced with support from Vision Maker Media, Inc., a member of the Corporation for Public Broadcasting's "Minority Consortia," created to foster programming by and about racial and ethnic minorities in public broadcasting.[12]

Native American documentaries broadcast on public television reflect two of what Faye Ginsburg identifies as the most "central and enduring concerns" of indigenous media. The first is "cultural and political activism," discussed below, and the second is engagement with "ways in which both radical alterity . . . and rights to represent indigenous realities are negotiated through contemporary media worlds, both on and off screen."[13] That is, Native documentary producers often represent communities with historical affiliations to marked phenotypes (i.e., skin color), different languages (such as Navajo, Navajo English, or Apache), and alternate worldviews and ideas about what constitutes good or "authentic" documentary films. They also work within a host of stereotypes, historical misrepresentations, and the realities of a media industrial complex geared for the entertainment or education of mostly non-Native viewers. They must also compete with non-Native producers, who continue to create Native content, and amongst themselves for limited resources. On its most basic level, the lack of self-representation is due to historical structural inequities that have often denied Native peoples the means of production, as well as a relatively small population.[14] Vision Maker Media executive director Shirley Sneve (Sicangu Lakota) ruminated on the issue. "I think that there's several reasons why we're not being represented. We just don't have that many Indians to begin with. And then when half of our kids aren't graduating from high school or going onto college . . . the pool of talent is very, very limited."[15]

Thus the "rights" to represent indigenous realities are negotiated in broader contexts of colonial inequities. Native peoples and their stories have been entextualized, recontextualized, and circulated widely in documentary form since Thomas Edison's kinetescope recorded a Hopi snake dance for the Chicago World's Fair in 1893. Robert Flaherty's *Nanook of the North* (1922), about life in a small Inuit community, is often considered to be the first "documentary" film ever made and was widely released and critically acclaimed. Navajo filmmakers were also the subjects of the foundational experiment in subject-as-filmmaker documentaries, 1966's Navajo Film Project.[16] Outside of documentaries there is a long tradition of savage and "noble savage" stereotypes in countless Hollywood westerns, as well as caricatures in television including Tonto in ABC's first serial hit *The Lone Ranger* (1949–1957) or Iron Eyes Cody's portrayal of the "crying Indian" in the 1970s anti-pollution campaigns, which solidified the trope of the "ecological Indian" in the American imagination.[17] In *Nanook*, the recurrent trope is that of a simple people, isolated and separate from modernity.[18] These are the kinds of stereotypes indigenous producers are attempting to counter, as with Cree filmmaker Neil Diamond's 2010 documentary *Reel Injun*, which aired on PBS's *Independent Lens* in the United States.

Ginsburg's second critical concern addressed here is "the uptake of media practices as an extension of cultural and political activism to establish the presence of indigenous lives within their own communities, in nation-states, and on the world stage."[19] Representing the historical perspectives, lived realities, and sociopolitical concerns of Native American peoples to a wider audience is one major reason cited by producers in wanting to engage the public television system. Renowned Native filmmaker Shelly Niro (Mohawk) noted, "You have to be filled with a powerful mission basically to right the wrongs that have been done to us."[20] Or, as Vision Maker's Sneve related, "If we talk about historical wrongs or historical trauma, we like to show solutions and answers to problems. Those are the kinds of films that we've been focusing on. We don't ignore the bad things that have happened but we like to think that there's hope for Native American people."[21]

Raheja's exposition of "visual sovereignty" rearticulates many of these concerns. Visual sovereignty is a broad concept encompassing specific acts of self-representation by indigenous media producers in a variety of political, economic, and cultural contexts, where contemporary media practices are in dialogue with the past, leading to cultural healing.[22] The concept transcends a focus on media stereotypes and embeds the indexical meanings such representations have for a range of indigenous media makers. That is, it puts the focus on acts of agency by indigenous producers, and the ways in which they entextualize and recontextualize a range of media texts and images. Native-produced documentaries broadcast on public television are most certainly acts of visual sovereignty. As Sneve related about Vision Maker's programs for the PBS system,

> I think they are interested in more of historic documentaries, *American Experience*-type documentaries about past Indians. We're interested in presenting contemporary Native American stories that show the people and issues of today, and perhaps how they are *related* to historical events in the past. So while we do a lot of history programs, they aren't buried in the past. They are told through the eyes of the relatives, the descendants who talk about their ancestors and historical events and how all of that translates to today.[23]

Sneve's statement is important. As a major funder and presenter of programming to the PBS system, Vision Maker Media's institutional mission as articulated here illustrates one unique way in which Native voices are integrated into the historical record. It also illustrates an alternate view of what constitutes an historical documentary.

Hence an understanding of the politics and poetics of indigenous documentary transcends the deconstruction of racial and ethnic stereotypes. It requires understanding the contexts, structures, and indexical understandings that make such [self]representations and expectations possible, and the ways that Native producers are challenging the system. Iliana Gershon and Joshua Malitsky advocate for analyses of "documentary ideologies," that is, the "set of beliefs, attitudes, and strategies about documentaries with which filmmakers, viewers, and critics explain or justify perceived film structure and meaning."[24] These sets of beliefs are tied to the idea of representational practice, that is, tied to an understanding of the culturally constructed and contextual ways in which particular images and texts are imbued with meaning. For example, what is it about the presentation of a Navajo elder speaking Navajo that may index authenticity and tradition for some filmmakers and viewers alike? How are indigenous histories rearticulated? What is it about the sound of the Apache language that becomes iconic for Apache audiences? The answers lie partly in voice, in the expectations that viewers and producers alike may have regarding the recontextualizations inherent in documentary films.

NEGOTIATING VOICE: GERONIMO AND COLUMBUS

Obfuscating and persistent stereotypes can lead audiences as well as public television producers and programmers—the ones who decide what makes it onto television—to have particular expectations about what constitutes Native documentary. But as Vision Maker Media's executive director further suggested, "Indians are so under the radar in so many parts of the country that sometimes I think that programmers and audiences have no expectations. Or maybe their expectations are that we still live in tipis."[25] Apart from very senior national programmers who select programs for major strands and major national broadcasts, individual station programmers ultimately select which documentaries are aired. Sneve continued to note that many Native-themed documentaries are "stories that are angry, sad, and mad and blaming of the White Man for all of the Native American's problems. And I think that programmers think that anything we're going to produce is going to be like that, because that's a stereotypical view that they have of Native American documentary film . . . but we're not."

Expectations about positionality, of course, can be deceiving. Navajo film-maker Bennie Klain's acclaimed *Columbus Day Legacy*, which premiered on many PBS stations in fall 2011, illustrates this negotiation of voice through the processes of entextualization and recontextualization.[26] The film portrays the issues of the freedom of speech, the ownership of history, and what it means to be an "American" through the lens of the annual Columbus Day parade and subsequent protests in Denver, Colorado (Figure 14.1). The structure of the film follows the thematic conflicts inherent in the holiday within the chronology of one parade day. The film visually and narratively pits local Italian-American organizations against indigenous rights groups led by the local chapter of the American Indian Movement (AIM). AIM members were protesting the legitimacy and appropriateness of a national holiday in honor of "an Indian killing slave trader," as leader Glen Morris bluntly states. Parade participant Miki Clayton, representing the Italian community, counters by recalling, "The thing I remember most about Columbus Day when it became a holiday, my father saying to me, 'Maybe now they'll like Italians.' I never forgot that. Because he had a hard life in America. He never found the American dream."

As the producer and unit II director of the film, I was involved with all aspects of research, production, and distribution. At first, members and leaders of AIM were much more reserved with the film crew and with Klain, especially upon learning we also were interviewing and following members of the parade organizers. Their expectation was that a Native American film-maker would and should automatically voice a singular opinion in media, and

Figure 14.1. Scene from *Columbus Day Legacy*. © 2007 TricksterFilms. Photo credit: Paul Abdoo.

in fact, "their side" was usually the one represented in media productions. The Italian American community was only briefly cautious, but then leader George Vendegnia told us, "We're just happy to have someone listen to our story." As Klain often notes in public discussions of the film, they invited us into their homes, fed us, and allowed us to shadow them in multiple vérité contexts.

The Native film participants were quite fluent in documentary media metapragmatics.[27] That is, they understood the "sound bite" and were well aware that any footage and interviews would be edited beyond their control, and they controlled their message accordingly. Noted Klain, who also edited the film, "They didn't give me much to humanize their story with." Well-known AIM activist Russell Means and others portrayed in the film were media professionals, and while they were gracious with their time, they were carefully following their own scripts in interview footage. They were also reluctant to allow access for unscripted vérité footage.

The film does have a distinctive, if subtle, point of view. I have seen a variety of audiences interact with the film, and they almost always comment on the "equal" portrayal of the competing issues and sides in the film. This editing structure easily allows for such interpretations. Klain said, "People and audiences always wonder about my politics with this film. But it's pretty clear. Look who gets screwed again at the end of the film." He is referring to the eighty Native protesters who got arrested. The film ends in front of the jail, with Native community members singing to a pow-wow drum, waiting for their loved-ones to be released.

Many audiences questioned us about why we weren't more directly involved in the anti–Columbus Day movement. The reality is that we were documenting a complex human story and were not immediately participating in an activist agenda. However, audiences are always confounded when the shooting context is explained; they invariably had expected us to receive full support from the Native community and resistance from the Italian Americans. They often also expect more "traditional" Native values to be displayed by the filmmaker. As one reviewer wrote, "Unfortunately, the documentary does not expand on the epistemological and spiritual depth of indigenous notions of territorial identity and the sense of place, nor does it dwell on traditional views . . . about the strong spiritual significance of indigenous ways of life."[28] This seemingly subtle expectation about what *should* be important—traditional beliefs and spirituality—illustrates how expectations of a Native filmmaker's voice affect both the production of a film and the indexical meanings audiences glean.

Columbus Day Legacy was a relatively low-budget independent film by public television standards, and involved a small team. Larger, big-budget, "high-impact" productions are inherently more complex. For example, in 2009, the groundbreaking multiple-episode documentary *We Shall Remain* was broadcast on PBS on the WGBH series *American Experience*. The 7.5–hour miniseries included five films, each exploring what producers at WGBH considered to be important turning points in the Native American historical experience.[29] The film *Geronimo*, discussed below, was the fourth of five segments. The ambitious series tagline was that it would establish "Native history as an essential part of American history." WGBH Boston, the public television station that has produced *American Experience* since 1988, is a major content producer for the PBS system, whose programs also include such acclaimed series as *Frontline, Antiques Roadshow*, and *NOVA*, shows that are imbued with an inherent symbolic power and authoritative voice.

We Shall Remain is seen by scholars and media professionals as a major step in representing Native voices on public television.[30] As with many other PBS programs, *We Shall Remain* was also an inherently collaborative, "transnational" cultural production in its institutional structure.[31] The series was supported by the federally funded Corporation for Public Broadcasting, global grant-making organizations, and Vision Maker Media; it was conceptualized and written by predominantly non-Native academics and public television professionals; and it involved Native American production personnel acting as "work for hire" in positions of director, co-directors, co-producers, and in one case co-writer. While the extent of Native involvement has been contested and defended numerous times to me by Native media professionals, the copyrights and editorial control were and are firmly in the hands of the WGBH production entity.[32]

One of the more popular programs in the series was *Geronimo*.[33] Geronimo was not originally included as a subject in the series of films. Dustinn Craig, a White Mountain Apache and Navajo filmmaker, was brought to WGBH to work on the series. He was hired originally to direct a project on Paiute educator and author Sarah Winnemuca, a relatively unknown figure in American history. According to Craig, "That was a great project. It worked on so many levels. But right away they did a bait and switch and wanted to do Geronimo." *American Experience* had produced another major film on Geronimo in 1988, albeit entirely in English and directed by a non-Native. During the research and development phase of the project, Craig, who ultimately acted as co-producer, director, and writer, instead suggested a portrait of the relatively unknown Navajo leader Manuelito. Manuelito is an important figure in Native history who guided many Navajo peoples from the trauma and transformations of capture and captivity to the confines of reservation life.[34] According to Craig, this idea was minimally entertained, and Geronimo was the decision handed down to the filmmakers. "Geronimo has cachet, man. It's all about Geronimo. Americans don't understand that Apaches don't think he's as great as they do."

Craig was at once surprised, annoyed, and intimidated by this choice. He related that "there are taboos on doing Geronimo. And so to trace down stories about a very scary individual, that was very intimidating for me. People weren't always willing to talk about it. And I had to get prayers done . . . But in the end, I had to fight to get our side of the story told, that Geronimo was not a good man for us."[35] To focus on Geronimo is a programming decision based upon the ultimate expectation of failure—resistance, yes, but ultimately a capture that led to the end of the Indian Wars. Geronimo is arguably the single most important Apache for *non*-Apache peoples. He is not idolized by all Apache, a view that Craig was able to impart. In instances like these, Native filmmakers actively negotiate their own positionality and their own communities' sociocultural norms in a broad process Ginsburg has called "embedded aesthetics."[36] These filmic sites of production—during research, casting, shooting, and editing—is where indigenous voices are actively negotiated at the nexus of embedded aesthetics and institutional structures.

VOICING NATIVE LANGUAGES

Amanda Weidman summarized multiple debates about "voice" in anthropology by noting "there is often a disjunction between the tendency to think about the voice in terms of representation—the metaphorical notion of 'having a voice'—and the study of actual voices or vocal practices."[37] Voice as sets of actual, audible, linguistic performances is directly linked to voice as positionality. This linkage is clearly illustrated in Aaron Fox's ethnographic work with rural Texas musicians, whose class position is expressed in the genre of country music, linked by the often iconic ways in which people talk about, and sing about, their lived experiences.[38] In documentary film, voice can be negotiated in the interview, shooting and editing, as well as the choice of style, such as the use of vérité or narration.[39] It can also be negotiated in choices of subtitling, translation, and voice-over, as well as all of the other representational choices filmmakers engage while recontextualizing imagery and entextualized voices.[40]

The work of Dell Hymes and Dennis Tedlock are important in understanding the idea of voice for those anthropologists who work in Native American communities. Their work, along with the scholarship of Jane Hill, reveals the ways that linguistic and social inequalities have been naturalized across time and space.[41] Although earlier studies of language often meant the grammatical structures of a language, this work concerns the interplay of grammar with actual ways of speaking and writing. This perspective takes into account how Native American peoples actually use languages, narratives, and sounds, as well as the ways outside institutions and practices misrecognize, marginalize, and silence those speakers and stories.[42] The persistent modernist Western ideology of language sees languages as abstract referential systems, largely homogenous and innocent in perpetuating social inequities. Words and sounds are presumed to be neutral, yet they are not.[43] For example, as Barbara Meek has shown, the child-like speech of adult Native American characters in Disney's (1953) classic *Peter Pan* juxtaposed against the perfect British English of the white children is a misrepresentation and erasure of Native ways of speaking in film that is complicit in the reproduction of social inequalities.[44]

Likewise, a kind of feelingful iconicity, or affective bonds and social intimacy that are created with audiences through the aesthetics of language, can be created or broken by [in]authentic linguistic portrayals of Native Americans. That is, Native audiences may relate to on-screen linguistic portrayals in different ways than other audiences.[45] For example, the use of Navajo and Navajo English in the acclaimed documentary *The Return of Navajo Boy* (2000) was a legitimizing aspect of representation for some Navajo audiences.[46] The film, which aired on PBS's *Independent Lens*, relates the story of Navajo matriarch Elsie Cly Begay and her family's relationship with old films and photos, uranium mining, and extratribal adoption. Initial cuts of the film were mainly in English, or more specifically, in the locally recognized variety called Navajo English with marked prosody and phonology stemming from its grammatical interplay with Navajo.[47] As Jeff Spitz, the director, related to me, "People were saying, 'she can't carry your story Jeff. You can barely understand the woman. She's old. You can't focus on her.'" "They" were professional film advisors who were referring to Elsie's use of Navajo English in the majority of scenes that were prominent before Bennie Klain's interventions as co-producer and translator involved in the editing. At once, there was misrecognition on the legitimacy of her literal voice, as well as a judgment on appropriate or comprehensible ways of speaking English in film—tied to the expectation of linguistic failure. Yet Navajo audiences related to the narrative voice, the Navajo English spoken by narrator Lorenzo Begay, Elsie's son, in the final version of the film.[48]

Spitz recounted on the production of *Return of Navajo Boy* that "the whole sensibility that Bennie brought to it was something that I didn't anticipate which is an irreverence and an insight and a deep sense of commitment to Elsie and Elsie's voice and her feelings." Note the link between Elsie's voice, feelings, and the narrative. Indeed, much of the final version of the film is in Navajo, due to the interventions of Klain, a fluent Navajo speaker. Sam Pack noted that one monolingual family matriarch in his study "particularly enjoyed this film because a large portion of the dialogue was spoken in the Navajo language, which bequeathed it with instant credibility in her eyes."[49] For the director, the use of Navajo was also a significant component in negotiating the voice of the film. The use of Navajo "opened up my eyes to nuances of language and their feelings, their sense of humor, friction, where they're speaking from. It's so much richer." Vision Maker executive director Sneve echoes these concerns about language.

> We try to show that Native Americans are hopeful and still very proud of their cultures and languages. Native languages are really important personally to me and to my board of directors. And so anytime that we can do the Native language with English subtitles we try to encourage that to show that people still speak these languages and that they're important to our connection to the world."[50]

In *Weaving Worlds*, which began airing on US public television in late 2008, audiences inevitably comment on the language used by characters. This film, which I produced and Bennie Klain directed, is an artistic and intimate portrait of contemporary Navajo weavers from an historical perspective. It was co-produced by ITVS in association with Vision Maker Media. The film illustrates the ties between the weavers, reservation traders and art dealers, and the global market for Navajo rugs, one of the most iconic and commodified symbols of Navajo culture. The film portrays numerous Navajo voices in the Navajo language, again due in part to the fact that the director is a Navajo speaker, and some of the participants were either monolingual or more comfortable—or more consciously aware of—speaking Navajo on film. Our intent was to include not only the figurative but the literal Navajo voices as well. As Klain related,

> Having learned from *Navajo Boy*, I know that using the language gives off a certain intimacy, a kind of kinship. But I didn't want to force any of the participants hands about, you know, "you have to speak Navajo." So one of the methods we used when we did our preinterviews, was to make a point to speak nothing but Navajo with them. So when it came to shooting they were very well aware that I could do that, but I didn't force them. And I guess that's what I was trying to do in all of my interviews in Navajo, I was trying to forge that kinship bond so they would be more open with me.[51]

In this case the filmmaker negotiated his own filmic voice reflexive of the embedded aesthetic, where Navajo sociocultural norms guided the selection of entextualized voices and the language of entextualization (Figure 14.2). The predominance of Navajo also allowed for a specific kind of filmic recontextualization in the editing process, one that figuratively and literally privileged Navajo voices. The Navajo voices provide intimacy and legitimization for a variety of audiences. As one prominent reviewer noted, "This film stands above most of the other films made by non-Navajo filmmakers because it allows the people to speak for themselves and to speak in their own language on film without the disgusting practice of having an English voice-over translation."[52] The Navajo language narratives and testimonies guide the structure of the film, which is a visual exploration of the Navajo concept of *k'e*, glossed as kinship, clanship, and reciprocity with the land, people, and animals. The term is never translated in the subtitles, but is inherent in the film. Here, linguistic performance guides positionality. The reviewer Gary Witherspoon noted this kind of recontextualization "brings the non-Navajo viewer into a more direct form of communication with the Navajo people and their experiences, struggles, and views. *Weaving Worlds* . . . avoids the distractions and distortions created by non-Navajo editors and narrators who attempt to 'guide' and 'translate' Navajo voices for non-Navajo consumption."[53]

Language was also a concern for the Native media professionals involved in *We Shall Remain*. Early on, Vision Maker Media was involved in the planning with WGBH producers. Vision Maker executives made sure to bring the issue of language to the forefront.

> One of the things that we had early conversations on with them was the fact that Native languages be included as much as possible. And I do believe that every single one of those movies had, at some point or another, the Native languages spoken with English subtitles. . . . We brought language to the conversation. And frankly *Weaving Worlds* is one of the reasons that I realized how important it was, because Bennie did that so well, with the back and forth between English and Navajo it just helped illustrate how important that language is.[54]

Figure 14.2. Director Bennie Klain with weaver Helen Bedonie on set for *Weaving Worlds.* © 2005 TricksterFilms. Photo Credit: Kathy M'Closkey.

As is often the case, Native languages are not a significant concern for non-Native media professionals. But language was ultimately and successfully brought to the forefront in the series, with some significant implications. For example, Cherokee actor Wes Studi, who starred in Chris Eyre's episode *The Trail of Tears*, related to me that this was "the first film I've ever done where I could speak my own Cherokee language. I'm usually speaking Lakota." For Studi, this was an emotional and significant moment, being able to represent his language.

Dustinn Craig, while working on *Geronimo*, noted, "it became obvious that in our Apache communities many of our elders are only predominantly fluent in their native tongue. So I knew early on that we definitely would be having some Apache language interviews." Therefore, his own filmic voice was determined by Apache language voices. The opening interview segment of *Geronimo*, in Apache from an Apache elder, challenges something as basic as his name, which in Apache is "Goyathle." This seemingly simple statement puts Goyathle into an alternate historical and cultural context, promptly distancing the American myth of "Geronimo" from the history that Craig explores. Yet there is something even more significant in this for Craig and his Apache audiences:

> Just the fact that America for the first time is properly hearing a real true version of one dialect of Apache language being spoken . . . for me, that's something that people outside of our small rural communities couldn't really understand. . . . To hear it spoken properly I think is a sign of validation and a form of respect. For so long we've had to wince when we hear bad Hollywood pronunciations of our languages.[55]

However, the inclusion of Native-language interviews in *Geronimo* was itself contested. This was not a unique experience for Craig; as a producer I have seen this kind of negotiation on numerous occasions. Based on my observations and experiences, programmers are often worried that American audiences don't like subtitles and have short attention spans. As seen in *The Return of Navajo Boy* examples above, Native elders may speak in alternate ways from unmarked forms of English that are considered incommensurate with non-Native expectations. Craig related his experience that "producers and programmers would say, 'They [Apache elders] talk so slow. Audiences are going to get bored. People don't like subtitles. . . . But if its 'history through Native eyes' . . . cut out those Native eyes, Native voices, Native language . . . what do we have?" This is indeed the ultimate question in the interplay between the politics and poetics of Native voices.

CONCLUSION: TOWARD COLLABORATIVE VOICES

As a service that is financially dependent upon donations by its audience, PBS makes it a point to proclaim that programming is "made possible by viewers like you." As such, the US public television system is reflexive of what programmers believe their viewers want. Ken Burns is considered by some to be "the U.S.'s foremost documentary filmmaker," and his works themselves are PBS staples. His 2009 epic miniseries *The National Parks: America's Best Idea*, is an homage to the honorable national project of democratizing the "wilderness" for all Americans to enjoy.[56] However, the miniseries essentially erases the re-appropriation of Indian lands and the physical displacement of Native peoples required to create the parks. The six episodes devote a mere fourteen seconds, for example, to Western Shoshone removal from Yellowstone, and "there is little suggestion at this moment or elsewhere in the series that what happened to the Shoshone in Yellowstone was part of a pattern that played itself out in other parks such as Yosemite, Glacier, or the Grand Canyon."[57] Thus public television has been complicit in the erasure and misrepresentation of Native voices. Yet, as I have illustrated, it also remains a productive space for dialectical engagement between Native and non-Native audiences, expectations, and lived experiences. This presents simultaneous challenges and opportunities for indigenous documentary producers in what remains a very televisual world. Despite increasing support for Native content, old paradigms, tropes, and expectations continue to reflect the kinds of voices Native producers are expected to have and the kinds of "voices" that are deemed appropriate.

Getting Native voices on public television is not quite "impossible." We continue to see Native American producers actively challenging and reframing received expectations through the filmic representations of their own voices and those of their communities. It is no small feat to represent, for example, Navajo or Apache voices within the structuring confines of the PBS system. Of course, even with a Native director, there is no one Native "voice," and it is virtually impossible to involve large numbers of community participants due to logistical and financial constraints of filmmaking. Likewise it is neither feasible nor warranted to exclude *all* non-Native filmmakers from indigenous topics. Deliberate and ongoing collaboration on all levels of production may be the most important tool in negotiating myriad voices in inherently heteroglossic documentary films. However, as Spitz stated about *The Return of Navajo Boy*, no matter the extent of collaboration one may have, "you have to understand what it means to get involved in the offline and online edit process. That's a very significant place for collaboration. If they're not in the editing room then they don't exist." This statement mirrors the experiences of Native filmmakers such as Klain and Craig discussed here. Without diligence, skill, and tenacity, their voices would be impossibly silent in the widely public and inherently authoritative voice of US public television.

NOTES

1. Eric Michaels, "Aboriginal Content: Who's Got It—Who Needs It?," *Visual Anthropology* 4, 3–4 (1991), 277–300.

2. I use the terms Native and Native American to refer to the indigenous peoples of the United States. I use the term "indigenous" to index global indigeneity, where the issues are not specific to the United States.

3. Bradley S. Greenberg, Dana Mastro, and Jeffrey E. Brand, "Minorities and the Mass Media: Television into the 21st Century," in *Media Effects: Advances in Theory and Research*, ed. Jennings Bryant and Dolf Zillmann (Mahwah: Lawrence Erlbaum Associates, 2002).

4. On the idea of "expectations" and failure, see Philip J. Deloria, *Indians in Unexpected Places* (Lawrence: University Press of Kansas, 2004); Anthony K. Webster and Leighton C. Peterson, "Introduction: American Indian Languages in Unexpected Places," *American Indian Culture and Research Journal* 35, 2 (2011), 1–18. For more on "Tontospeak" or "Hollywood Indian English," see Barbra A. Meek, "And the Injun Goes "How!" Representations of American Indian English in White Public Space," *Language in Society* 35, 1 (2006), 93–128.

5. On the notion of indigenous TV as "cultural activism," see Faye Ginsburg, "From Little Things, Big Things Grow: Indigenous Media and Cultural Activism," in *Between Resistance and Revolution*, ed. Dick Fox and Orin Starn (New Brunswick: Rutgers University Press, 1997), 118–44. On Native documentary productions, see for example, Beverly R. Singer, *Wiping the War Paint Off the Lens: Native American Film and Video* (Minneapolis: University of Minnesota Press, 2001); Steven Leuthold, "Historical Representation in Native American Documentary," *Ethnohistory* 44, 4 (1997), 727–739; Randolph Lewis, *Alanis Obomsawin: The Vision of a Native Filmmaker* (Lincoln: University of Nebraska Press, 2006); M. Elise Marubbio and Eric L. Buffalohead, eds., *Native Americans on Film: Conversations, Teaching, and Theory* (Lexington: University Press of Kentucky, 2012).

6. "In public trust for the sixth consecutive year, according to a national Roper survey," PBS, accessed July 15, 2013, http://www.pbs.org/aboutpbs/news/20090213_pbsropersurvey.html.

7. This is due to the mission of public television in the US and to the financial reality of educational ancillary markets.

8. Rosalind C. Morris, *New Worlds from Fragments: Film, Ethnography, and the Representation of Northwest Coast Cultures* (Boulder: Westview Press, 1994), 14.

9. On *entextualization, decontextualization,* and *recontextualization* as used in anthropology, see Richard Bauman and Charles L. Briggs, "Poetics and Performance as Critical Perspectives on Language and Social Life," *Annual Review of Anthropology* 19 (1990), 73. For more recent applications that link film studies and anthropology, see Iliana Gershon and Joshua Malitsky, "Documentary Studies and Linguistic Anthropology," *Culture, Theory and Critique* 52, 1 (2011), 46; Erin Debenport, "As the Rez Turns: Anomalies within and Beyond the Boundaries of a Pueblo Community " *American Indian Culture and Research Journal* 35, 2 (2011), 87–109.

10. See, for example, Jennifer Deger, *Shimmering Screens: Making Media in an Aboriginal Community* (Minneapolis: University of Minnesota Press, 2006); Faye Ginsburg, "Native Intelligence: A Short History of Debates on Indigenous Media and Ethnographic Film," in *Made to Be Seen: Perspectives on the History of Visual Anthropology*, ed. Marcus Banks and Jay Ruby (Chicago: University of Chicago Press, 2011). On the development of Aboriginal television in Australia, see Eric Michaels, *Bad Aboriginal Art: Tradition, Media, and Technological Horizons* (Minneapolis: University of Minnesota Press, 1994). Recent advances in Aboriginal media

representation have, however, been hindered by political turns. See Faye Ginsburg and Fred Myers, "A History of Aboriginal Futures," *Critique of Anthropology* 26, 1 (2006), 27–45.

11. By "high impact" I mean "professional" productions intended to reach large audiences beyond the reach of specialized film festivals or community venues. While YouTube and other online platforms can attain "high impact," this has yet to be the case for Native content, and many online video productions are much shorter than the standard PBS length of 56:40. For the impact of lower-scale productions and low-power public stations, see Jennifer A. Machiorlatti, "Video as Community Ally and Dakota Sense of Place: An Interview with Mona Smith," in *Native Americans on Film*, ed. M. Elise Marubbio and Eric L. Buffalohead (Lexington: University Press of Kentucky, 2013); Frank H. Tyro, "Localism and Low-Power Public Television on the Flathead Indian Reservation," *Wicazo Sa Review* 16, 2 (2001).

A note on the PBS structure: PBS is essentially a nonprofit television network made up of dues-paying member stations that are partially supported by another federally funded nonprofit, the Corporation for Public Broadcasting, and through corporate underwriters and public donations, i.e., the ubiquitous tagline "made possible by viewers like you." Content can be created and presented to the system in a variety of ways, including productions by member stations such as WGBH, by production entities such as ITVS (The Independent Television Service), series such as POV, or by independent producers who are commissioned or sell programs to the system. Major national strands such as ITVS's *Independent Lens* or WGBH's *American Experience* often air the nationally broadcast, "high impact" documentary programs that member stations are often required to air. "One-offs," or films that aren't carried by a major strand, can be presented to the system through a variety of organizations such as American Public Television (APT), National Education Television Association (NETA), or PBS Plus. Such programs can have "high impact" but are not necessarily supported by major national publicity campaigns and are not "hard feeds," i.e., required airings.

12. Vision Maker Media, Inc. was known until early 2013 as Native American Public Telecommunications, Inc. (NAPT). For consistency, I use the current names, Vision Maker or Vision Maker Media, for all references to the former NAPT. See http://www.visionmakermedia.org.

13. Ginsburg, "Native Intelligence," 256.

14. For more on early Native film producers, see Deloria, *Indians in Unexpected Places*, 53–108; Michelle H. Raheja, *Reservation Reelism: Redfacing, Visual Sovereignty, and Representations of Native Americans in Film* (Lincoln: University of Nebraska Press, 2010).

15. Shirley K. Sneve, Interview with the Author, 2013.

16. Sol Worth and John Adair, *Through Navajo Eyes: An Exploration in Film Communication and Anthropology* (Bloomington: Indiana University Press, 1972). On the impact of the project and efforts to reclaim Navajo voices, see Leighton C. Peterson, "Reclaiming Diné Film: Visual Sovereignty and the Return of *Navajos Film Themselves*," *Visual Anthropology Review* 29, 1 (2013): 29–41.

17. On the "ecological Indian," see Shepard Krech, *The Ecological Indian: Myth and History* (New York: W. W. Norton & Co., 1999). For works on Native American

stereotypes in film, see Harald E. L. Prins, "Visual Media and the Primitivist Perplex: Colonial Fantasies, Indigenous Imagination, and Advocacy in North America," in *Media Worlds*, ed. Faye D. Ginsburg, Lila Abu-Lughod, and Brian Larkin (Berkeley: University of California Press, 2002), 58–74; M. Elise Marubbio, *Killing the Indian Maiden: Images of Native American Women in Film* (Lexington: University Press of Kentucky, 2006); Peter C. Rollins and John E. O'Connor, eds., *Hollywood's Indian: The Portrayal of the Native American in Film* (Lexington: University Press of Kentucky, 2003).

18. Raheja, "Reading Nanook's Smile"; Ann Fienup-Riordan, *Freeze Frame: Alaska Eskimos in the Movies* (Seattle: University of Washington Press, 1995).

19. Ginsburg, "Native Intelligence," 256.

20. Saza Osawa, "An Upstream Journey: An Interview with Sandra Osawa," in *Native Americans on Film*, ed. M. Elise Marubbio and Eric L. Buffalohead (Lexington: University Press of Kentucky, 2013), 321.

21. Sneve, Interview.

22. Raheja, *Reservation Reelism*.

23. Sneve, Interview.

24. Gershon and Malitsky, "Documentary Studies," 46.

25. Sneve, Interview.

26. *Columbus Day Legacy,* directed by Bennie Klan (USA: Vision Maker Media, 2011), DVD.

27. Gershon and Malitsky, "Documentary Studies."

28. Dina Fachin, "Film Review: *Columbus Day Legacy*," *Italian American Review* 2, 2 (2012), 128.

29. Access the *We Shall Remain* website and multiplatform components at "We Shall Remain," PBS, accessed July 15, 2013, http://www.pbs.org/wgbh/amex/weshallremain.

30. Ginsburg, "Native Intelligence."

31. For an analysis of the PBS series *Childhood* (1991) as both "multisited" and "transnational," see Barry Dornfeld, "Putting American Public Television Documentary in Its Places," in *Media Worlds*, ed. Faye D. Ginsburg, Lila Abu-Lughod, and Brian Larkin (Berkeley: University of California Press, 2002).

32. This is not to diminish the Native involvement, but to illustrate a point. While collaboration is an inherent aspect of documentary film production, and non-Natives (including anthropologists such as myself) work on Native documentaries, the political-economic and social structures in these larger institutions make the negotiation of voices much more complex.

33. "Geronimo," *We Shall Remain*, directed by Dustinn Craig and Sarah Colt (2009; Arlington: PBS Home Video, 2009), DVD.

34. See Jennifer Nez Denetdale, *Reclaiming Diné History: The Legacies of Navajo Chief Manuelito and Juanita* (Tucson: University of Arizona Press, 2007).

35. Dustinn Craig, Interview with the Author, 2012.

36. Faye Ginsburg, "Embedded Aesthetics: Creating a Discursive Space for Indigenous Media," *Cultural Anthropology* 9, 3 (1994), 365–382.

37. Amanda Weidman, "Anthropology and the Voice," *Anthropology News* 52, no 1 (2011), 13.

38. Aaron A. Fox, *Real Country: Music and Language in Working-Class Culture* (Durham: Duke University Press, 2004).

39. Bill Nichols, "The Voice of Documentary," *Film Quarterly* 36, 3 (1983), 17–30.

40. David MacDougall, "Subtitling Ethnographic Films: Archetypes into Individualities," *Visual Anthropology Review* 11, 1 (1995); Gershon and Malitsky, "Documentary Studies."

41. Dennis Tedlock, *The Spoken Word and the Work of Interpretation* (Philadelphia: University of Pennsylvania Press, 1983); Dell H. Hymes, *"In Vain I Tried to Tell You": Essays in Native American Ethnopoetics* (Philadelphia: University of Pennsylvania Press, 1981); Dell H. Hymes, *Ethnography, Linguistics, Narrative Inequality: Toward an Understanding of Voice* (London: Taylor & Francis, 1996); Jane H. Hill, *The Everyday Language of White Racism* (New York: Wiley-Blackwell, 2008).

42. These themes are further developed in Webster and Peterson, "Introduction: American Indian Languages in Unexpected Places."

43. Richard Bauman and Charles L. Briggs, *Voices of Modernity: Language Ideologies and the Politics of Inequality* (New York: Cambridge University Press, 2003).

44. Barbara A. Meek, "Failing American Indian Languages," *American Indian Culture and Research Journal* 35, 2 (2011), 43–60.

45. I develop this theme further in Leighton C. Peterson, "Reel Navajo: The Linguistic Creation of Indigenous Screen Memories," *American Indian Culture and Research Journal* 35, 2 (2011), 111–134. On feelingful iconicity and social intimacy in Apache music, see David W. Samuels, *Putting a Song on Top of It: Expression and Identity on the San Carlos Apache Reservation* (Tucson: University of Arizona Press, 2004); in Navajo poetry, see Anthony K. Webster, *Explorations in Navajo Poetry and Poetics* (Albuquerque: University of New Mexico Press, 2009).

46. Sam Pack, "Watching Navajos Watch Themselves," *Wicazo Sa Review* 22, 2 (2007), 111–27.

47. An expanded treatment of the film's production and linguistic aspects can be found in Peterson, "Reel Navajo." On Navajo English, see Anthony K. Webster, "'Please Read Loose': Intimate Grammars and Unexpected Languages in Contemporary Navajo Literature," *American Indian Culture and Research Journal* 35, 2 (2011), 62–87.

48. Pack, "Watching Navajos," 122.

49. Pack, "Watching Navajos," 123.

50. Sneve, Interview.

51. Bennie Klain, Interview with the Author, 2010.

52. Gary Witherspoon, "Film Review: *Weaving Worlds*," *American Anthropologist* 115, 2 (2013), 321.

53. Witherspoon, "Weaving Worlds," 322.

54. Sneve, Interview.

55. Craig, Interview.

56. Karl Jacoby, "Ken Burns Gone Wild: Naturalizing the Nation in *the National Parks: America's Best Idea*," *Public Historian* 33, 2 (2013), 19.

57. Jacoby, "Ken Burns Gone Wild," 21.

Chapter Fifteen

"Real" Black, "Real" Money: African American Audiences on *The Real Housewives of Atlanta*

Gretta Moody

In 1984, *The Cosby Show* introduced the televisual and real life "gold standard" for what it meant to be among Du Bois' "Talented Tenth," members of the black elite in America.[1] Today, the reality television genre offers a different take on what it means to be a member of the black upper-middle class in the United States. Bravo's *The Real Housewives of Atlanta* (*RHOA*) arguably leads the way in this effort.[2] Despite its position as one of the longest running and most popular showcases of the black elite lifestyle currently on-air,[3] *RHOA* has been berated in the popular press for its superficiality and what is perceived as an anti-*Cosby* value system.[4] While the Cosby family demonstrated restraint and offered only dignified displays of its status, the Atlanta housewives seem content with screaming matches and unending displays of conspicuous consumption. If what cultural critics suggest is true and *RHOA* simply perpetuates negative stereotypes about African Americans, what pleasure (if any) do black audiences get from watching the show?[5] Are there redeeming qualities or opportunities to "ferret out the beneficial," as Jacqueline Bobo suggests existed in black female audiences' readings of *The Color Purple*?[6] In an effort to explore these questions, this chapter uses focus group discourse to unpack the ways African American viewers relate to *RHOA* and negotiate the program's representation of (elite) Black America.

TO BE BLACK . . . AND NOT POOR . . .

"Black elite" is a slippery construct. When articulated with Du Bois's conceptualization of the "Talented Tenth" it refers to the "Best," who are the most educated of the "Negro race."[7] Blacks who attain college- and graduate-level degrees are not only considered among the upper echelons of black society, but Du Bois also charges this group with responsibility for uplifting the race as a whole.[8] When articulated with Lawrence Otis Graham's notion of "our kind of people," "black elite" takes on a more exclusive tone.[9] The upper strata of black society is narrowed to include only those with the "right" skin tone (nearly white), the "right" ancestry (multiple generations of economic success), and access to the "right" social groups (e.g., Jack and Jill, an invitation-only organization for black children from upper-middle class backgrounds). Education and self-presentation, while important for Graham, are secondary to factors associated with birthrights. One does not become but rather is born "our kind of people."[10] In *The Black Elite*, Lois Benjamin defines the group as comprised of those who have "achieved objective success—educationally, economically, and occupationally."[11] She interviews African Americans who followed the traditional Du Boisian path to the top and those who traveled more unconventional pathways, marked by fame or recognition in the community.[12] When considering these three examples alone—and there are many other voices contributing to this discussion—the porousness of the boundaries surrounding the black elite is evident. The elusiveness of the concept signals the need to cast a broad net when thinking about perspectives on the group.[13] For this analysis, it is also useful to consider, however briefly, the historical contingency of the term and the ways scholars discuss the relative positionality and sociocultural interactions of those said to belong to the group.

Existing literature identifies four key historical moments that relate directly to the dynamic definition of the black elite: (1) pre-emancipation, (2) segregation, (3) the post-civil rights era, and (4) the (alleged) post-racial era. Prior to the end of slavery, elitism among blacks was signaled largely by their statuses as free/slave and mulatto/black, where the former of each pairing suggested higher status.[14] These intra-racial distinctions existed even among enslaved Africans, whose relegation to either field or house duty—or relative proximity to whites—was used to mark their statuses within the slave community.[15] The segregation era later introduced a new meaning for the term "black elite" as a result of the complete separation of the races, most notably in the American South. As sociologist Bart Landry discusses, blacks' inability to access basic services (e.g., banking, funeral arrangements, and insurance) spurred the emergence of a "black business class," which soon defined black elite status.[16] During the pre-emancipation and segregation phases, laws prevented blacks from successfully competing with whites. In the years following the civil rights movement, however, greater access to "white collar" employment, housing outside of traditionally black communities, and education led to yet another shift in how one might define the black elite.[17] New characteristics or markers of the group emerged, including flight from urban black communities to the suburbs.[18] Some might insist we are now entering a new iteration of what it means to be black and of elite status in "post-racial" America. "Post-racial" is an umbrella term some use to describe the present state of the racial order. Conservatives, in particular, articulate the post-racial alongside the Obama election, which is heralded as "proof" that African Americans have won the hard-fought battle for political power in the United States.[19] Ebony Elizabeth Thomas and Shanesha R. F. Brooks-Tatum strongly position themselves against claims that America is post-race; they do argue, however, the potential for new ways of imagining and reconfiguring black subjectivities necessarily accompanies the "Obama era."[20] This reimagining most certainly includes reconsideration of the ways together race, class, and status work differently or remain the same given the presence of a black man in the highest seat of American political power and a black family living at the most famous address in the country, 1600 Pennsylvania Avenue. *RHOA* housewives and viewers who are identified or self-identify as black (upper-) middle class, among others, directly contribute to debates about how to define "black elite" in the contemporary moment.

Sociological examinations of the black elite range from E. Franklin Frazier's classic critique of the group as petty and insecure to Karyn Lacy's more recent assessment of its careful navigation of class, status, and racial boundaries.[21] Both recognize the unique position of the black elite as "betwixt and between," wedged in the middle of the "black masses" and the "mainstream" middle and upper classes and required to negotiate both racial and class differences daily.[22] Sociologist Ann Swidler usefully theorizes "culture as a repertoire" or a "toolkit" composed of skills, habits, and behaviors that people master at different levels and employ at different times.[23] Drawing on Swidler, Lacy extends Mary Pattillo's discussion of a uniquely "black cultural toolkit" to include class as an additional distinguishing factor.[24] With the *black middle-class toolkit* as an organizing framework, Lacy finds that middle-class blacks use varying elements of the toolkit to construct boundaries separating themselves from whites and lower-class blacks.[25] For example, Sherwood Park residents used their exclusive, predominately black subdivision to construct racial boundaries (their children were largely shielded from racism in neighborhood interactions; thus, the neighborhood itself was a "safe space" in which to promote positive racial identity development) and class/status boundaries (the exclusivity of the subdivision and home prices—over $275,000 in 1989—signaled residents' elite positionality within the black middle class).[26] Lacy also effectively theorizes the intersection of race and class, recognizing that at times one may take precedence over the other.[27] Her examination is, however, focused on neighborhoods, which serve as "construction sites" for a range of identities.[28] The present chapter builds upon

Lacy's understanding of racial, status-, and class-based identities by examining a different site of identity construction—discussions of the mass media.

(BLACK) MEDIA AUDIENCES
AND REALITY TELEVISION

The study of audiences as active and capable of using media to satisfy needs dates back to the earliest audience studies when female serials listeners were interviewed about listening habits and interests.[29] Media scholars who study today's audiences still seek to understand the ways in which people decode messages and apply the information gleaned to their everyday lives. S. Elizabeth Bird describes the "audience response" tradition as linked to a desire to work out how media representations relate to "people's sense of identity."[30] Television has been uniquely credited with exposing its viewers to the everyday realities of people from different walks of life.[31] This exposure aids in identity construction, as it offers a lens through which people can examine how they relate to others within society.[32] Similarities to and differences from others provide a framework for individuals to define themselves. Yet, despite traditional television's ability to increase women's awareness of men's lives outside of the home and children's knowledge of parents' private conversations,[33] it can be argued that television has not, and perhaps does not, expose Americans to the diversities of the African American community,[34] an issue that becomes more crucial when televisual representations stand in for human contact.[35]

Interestingly, reality television has emerged as a genre particularly apt for introducing new "slices of life" to mainstream America. The reliance on "truth" and "reality" in these programs is believed to offer unique freedom to tackle untried or taboo subjects, including those related to race and class.[36] Ji Hoon Park argues the "unscripted" nature of the genre—"ordinary" people speak for themselves and act without direction—potentially opens a space for critical discourses on race.[37] While each program claims to offer a realistic view of the lives of its cast members, viewers are aware of the role of television producers in constructing the storylines of each episode.[38] The nature of the genre as both "reality" and "fiction" produces "an unstable text," according to Laurie Ouellette and Susan Murray, thus requiring viewers to compare their own senses of real life with the representations offered on the screen.[39] A study of reality television audiences (*RHOA* audiences, more specifically) is, thus, a useful starting point for an examination of possible linkages between media representations of the black elite and identity construction.

Rich discussions of black middle classness and television audiences remain largely closeted. There is one noted exception: Sut Jhally and Justin Lewis examine issues of race and class in *Enlightened Racism*, their classic study of *The Cosby Show* audiences.[40] Rather than increasing the scope of black televisual representation, the researchers argue that despite admirable intentions, *Cosby* not only misleads blacks into believing the "American Dream" is easily attainable for everyone, but also excuses white Americans from responsibility for racial inequality.[41] Black viewers whose real lives resemble the Huxtables' upper-middle-class lifestyle are largely pushed to the margins of the conversation. Nearly twenty years later more frequent discussions of the fissures that exist within the black community have entered the academy and popular media, along with calls to analyze the unique aspects of elite black life.[42]

Programs like *RHOA*, which claim to offer a "real" peek into the lives of the black upper crust, have thrust the negotiation of race and class onto the ubiquitous television screen, adding to general discourses on what it means to be black and not poor in America. Annette Hill encourages scholars to examine the ways in which reality television presents learning opportunities for audiences.[43] Thinking with Hill, the housewives are, to some extent, teachers. *RHOA* viewers encounter multiple perspectives on what it means to be a black elite woman. Audiences, especially black audiences, must negotiate these narratives individually and within social groups to determine how they apply to their own senses of self. Rather than exploring black/white responses to racial conflict in reality television shows or auto-ethnographic understandings of black representation in reality TV, this chapter considers the ways African American viewers from different status groups understand the boundaries of (elite) blackness, as related to *RHOA*.[44] The analysis will connect *RHOA* (the text), African American viewers, and understandings of the black elite, thereby contributing to the body of work on race, status/class, and reality television.

READING *RHOA*

Bird suggests that people use discussions about the media as a "framing and organizing device" to tackle questions about their lives and society.[45] Despite the constructed nature of the research encounter, focus group methodology allows researchers to experience these discussions firsthand. Indeed, Tamar Liebes and Elihu Katz positively describe the focus group as "a catalyst for individual expression of latent opinions, for the generation of group consensus, for free-associating to life, and for analytic statements about art."[46] The successful use of focus groups in previous audience studies guided the methodological approach to this study.[47] A purposive sampling technique was used to identify African American viewers of the show from different educational and occupational backgrounds. Each participant was asked to suggest four to six friends (also *RHOA* viewers) to join his or her focus group. The decision to use primarily friendship groups was based on the likelihood that friends had already discussed the show and would be more comfortable expressing their feelings about sensitive issues (e.g., race and class) with one another.

Participants

Conducted in 2011, a total of eighteen participants engaged in six mini-focus groups, which ranged in size from two to five viewers per session. Individual sessions ranged in length from fifty minutes to over three hours and were semi-structured. Participants discussed twelve questions that covered the following key areas: (1) general thoughts about the program and its cast members; (2) elements of reality television programming; (3) major takeaways from the show; (4) understandings of the racialized aspects of the show; and (5) pleasure derived from watching. Responses focused primarily on Season 3 of the program, which ended just before the study began. All groups were encouraged to speak freely, and each session focused on the topics of most interest to participants. Groups convened in casual settings (including participants' homes, coffee shops, and student lounges) or via telephone conference call to facilitate informal talk about *RHOA* and simulate the environments in which most discussions about television viewing take place. The overwhelming majority of participants were black (17 of 18), with one participant who self-identified as mixed race (Black and Asian), and female (16 of 18).[48] Groups were naturally stratified by education, with four groups comprised of participants who had or were currently seeking bachelor's/advanced degrees ("educated elite") and two groups of participants with high school diplomas or some college ("core black middle class," hereafter "core BMC").[49] Occupation, a common status marker, also helped stratify the two cohorts.[50] For example, the "educated elite" included an attorney, clinical psychologist, and manager at a federal government agency, while the "core BMC" included a hairstylist and a clerk at a federal government agency. It is important to note that all participants are believed to be members of the black middle class in its broadest sense.[51] All sessions were recorded and transcribed in full. Following Robert Emerson, Rachel Fretz, and Linda Shaw, all data were analyzed using an "open," then "focused," coding process, which allowed for the identification and examination of significant themes.[52] To maintain anonymity, pseudonyms are used.

The Housewives

Episodes of *RHOA* begin with each "housewife" confidently stating a catch-phrase as her name dances across the bottom of the screen:

NeNe: When I walk into a room, I own it!

Kim: People call me a gold-digger, but they just want what I have.

Sheree: I like things that are elegant and sophisticated. Just like me!

Kandi: I have fame and fortune; and I've earned it!

Phaedra: I'm the ultimate Southern Belle; I get what I want!

Cynthia: I know how to work it and be seen![53]

These phrases ground the viewer in the lifestyles and personalities of the housewives. NeNe "owns" the room with her loud voice and willingness to confront anyone, at any time. She is better known for her brash personality than workplace successes (by Season 6, NeNe is lauded for her success as an actress). In fact, Season 3 focuses on NeNe's first attempts to enter the workforce, as the show chronicles the breakdown of her marriage. Kim, the only white housewife, was marked as a gold-digger in the first two seasons of the show because of her reliance on men, namely the anonymous "Big Poppa," to support her lavish lifestyle. Of course, Kim dismisses these attacks as jealousy—"[everyone] wants what she has"—revealing what seems to be an egotistical approach to life. Sheree's affinity for "elegance" and "sophistication" is a common theme on the show. Audiences witness an Aston Martin purchase and thousands of dollars in spending on designer furniture for her adult daughter's first apartment.[54] With footballer ex-husband, Bob, out of her life, Sheree uses her "elegance and sophistication" to try to land a man. In her search, she identifies money as the most important "quality" for a prospective partner. Season 3 also finds Sheree in the midst of her own identity-work, as she attempts to define herself first as a fashion designer and later, an actress. Unlike the previously described housewives, Kandi represents the "working woman." Her "fame and fortune" are the result of a longtime commitment to music. She was a member of Xscape, a popular R&B group in the 1990s, and has penned hit songs for many top artists, including "No Scrubs," TLC's 1999 chart-topper. She is often depicted as the most even-tempered of the housewives and spends more time focused on her career and family than engaged in petty squabbles with the other women. Phaedra, a respected entertainment lawyer in Atlanta, shares her journey to motherhood on Season 3 of the show. Her self-description as a "Southern Belle" foreshadows an obsession with "proper" decorum. One must note Phaedra does not always meet the standards she sets for others. Cynthia's "work it and be seen" description refers to her profession as a model. The show, however, does little to emphasize her success in the field, instead the audience finds Cynthia struggling to pay for her $1 million wedding, as she and her fiancé battle financial troubles. Characterizations of individual and overlapping aspects of these women's lives form the storylines for the series.

UNDERSTANDING "REAL" BLACK AND "REAL" MONEY

Focus group participants questioned the "authenticity" and "sincerity" of the everyday racial, status, and class performances exhibited by the Atlanta housewives and recognized that they "[could] not simply trust these performed doings and sayings," to quote John L. Jackson.[55] These tensions— between the real and the constructed, the sincere and the phony—served as a primary lens through which African American viewers interpreted the program.

ATL Housewives (Almost) Succeed at "Doing" Black[56]

Participants generally accepted *RHOA* as a representation of blackness. Still, questions of "authenticity" emerged in relation to norms—group discussions about religious practices and black masculinity are considered—and stereotypes.

Black Norms

Participants used their own understandings of norms within the black community to evaluate the show's "authenticity." This was particularly evident in focus group discussions about the role of spirituality on *RHOA*. When asked if spirituality was a theme on the show, all focus groups immediately began to converse about if any of the housewives were depicted as churchgoers:[57]

"Core BMC" Group A:

SANDRA: They don't go to church.

MICHELLE: No.

SANDRA: No, not housewives of Atlanta. I don't remember none of them going to no church.

Despite a lack of visual evidence—as Sandra implied, during Season 3 none of the housewives are shown attending church services—Leah believed most of the women were Christians, while Tiffany suggested a difference existed between "*church* church" and "somewhere else." With this distinction she signals the presence of vernacular traditions and shared performances within black religious services. Absent these aesthetic practices, "authenticity" is questioned:

"Educated Elite" Group A:

LEAH: Does anybody go to church?

NICOLE: Lisa, was a Christian I thought?

LEAH: Yea most of them are probably. I thought.

TIFFANY: But does she go to *church* church or somewhere else?

Mia further examined the idea by suggesting the lack of visual evidence was strange, given that we were discussing black Southerners:

"Educated Elite" Group B:

OLIVIA: Do they have spirit or soul? Did they ever go to church?

MIA: I don't think a single one of them did. And it's funny that you brought that up because these are black people and none of 'em went to church ever.

OLIVIA: That whole storyline with Phaedra and her mother . . . that was about spirituality. Indirectly.

MIA: But Phaedra even never went to church.

OLIVIA: You never saw her going, no.

MIA: Which is interesting because black people really are about church.

OLIVIA: In the South especially.

MIA: Especially

As shown by these examples, participants linked the question of spirituality to Christianity and the church, which were perceived as norms within the black community. Scholars have indeed identified the church as a central element of African American life.[58] Although visual proof is not present in the program, allusions to church membership are made throughout the season. Phaedra, for example, is shown having dinner with members of her church, who are assigned to help couples through the early stages of their marriages. She also makes frequent references to church practices in response to the other housewives' behaviors (e.g., "I need to get some holy oil!"). Despite these references, several participants viewed the fact that the Atlanta housewives were not shown attending religious services as a mark against the "authenticity" of the show's depiction of black life. Furthermore, participants explained the absence as linked to a producer's decision not to show certain, arguably important, aspects of the housewives' lives.

Black hypermasculinity and "cool pose" strategies formed another set of norms discussed across focus groups, often as related to Phaedra's husband, Apollo, and questions regarding his sexual orientation. Howard Stevenson defines "cool pose" strategies as "behaviors that prevent negative perceptions from devaluing the self-esteem of individuals."[59] While multiple participants made reference to what they called Apollo's "questionable status," the following exchange encapsulates the expected norm and Apollo's failure to meet that standard:

"Educated Elite" Group A:

LEAH: She's [Phaedra's] very sexual too. It's ok. But I don't want to see a straight (lowers voice) black man . . .

NICOLE: Yep! Especially, out of jail . . . do that

LEAH: Out of jail . . . exactly you got to put it in perspective.

The participants were responding to a scene in which Phaedra and Apollo have photographs taken prior to the birth of their first child. Pregnancy cravings serve as the theme for the photo shoot; and Apollo is shown inserting a pickle into his mouth. In the exchange above, participants expected Apollo to prevent speculations about his sexuality by exhibiting some form of "cool pose" and refusing to participate in the pickle scene. Leah and Nicole expressed their expectations for how a "straight black man" should act and thought Apollo's status as an ex-convict, which was believed to increase exposure to homosexual activity, should be used to contextualize the counterintuitive behavior. Interestingly, black hypermasculinity was a recurring theme on the show, frequently in reference to Apollo. As the other black housewives openly question his sexuality throughout the season, counterexamples of Apollo exhibiting the expected "cool pose" are also provided (e.g., his refusal to perform a ballroom-style dance with his wife during her baby shower—Dwight, Phaedra's friend, who is openly gay, steps in because, as Phaedra describes, her husband is "too macho" to participate). Questions of how (if at all) Apollo relates to the normative-mainstream image of the black male as hypermasculine affected participants' perceptions of the show as "authentic." Many participants—from both status cohorts—expected a "real" black man to fit the hypermasculine mold. Deviations from this norm were considered distasteful or demeaning; and participants singled out "the producers" as responsible for promoting such performances.

Black Stereotypes

As with other aspects of the show that participants rejected, the use of types was attributed to producers, who were thought to construct an image sanctioned by the mainstream. To paraphrase the sentiments expressed: *RHOA* can't be 100 percent "real" black when "they"—outsiders—are editing it. The following description from Candice, an "educated elite" participant, summarizes the most commonly mentioned types:

And it [race] also comes up when they sort of exemplify certain racial stereotypes. Like, obviously NeNe being very loud and boisterous. And Sheree being very driven; like, black women are seen as very independent and very driven.

No men. That's another thing I think also a lot of successful black women are also portrayed as being without men, because of their education or whatever qualifications make them threatening to other men. . . . Phaedra's husband being a convict, which is obviously another stereotype . . . that we don't have strong families. That our families are dysfunctional. Where you see Phaedra, Black women are so controlling . . . Kandi, the I want to be with a star or athlete. The thing where black men are kind of seen as commodities, a football player or something. ("educated elite" group D)

Discussion of perceived stereotypes—black women are angry, controlling, and gold digging, have no use for men, and contribute to dysfunction in families—emerged across focus groups. Similarly, issues with negative stereotyping form the crux of popular press arguments against the show.[60] While each mention of a stereotype was linked to participants' rejection of the show's portrayal as "authentic," stereotypes formed only one part of conversations about *RHOA* and did not keep participants from watching. Bobo argues negative assumptions about blacks "underlie the products of mainstream cultural production;" two options, therefore, exist for black media audiences: (1) refuse to engage with media or (2) "filter out that which is negative and select from the work elements we can relate to."[61] Despite its claim to "reality," participants in part identified *RHOA* as a stereotypical representation, in line with Bobo's description of mainstream cultural products. Black viewers of *RHOA* demonstrated Bobo's second option by "filtering" the negative when watching the show.

As they made sense of *RHOA*, participants brought their own "scripts" on how to "do" blackness to bear and rejected any depiction they felt was attributable to outsiders. Participants believed "authentic" black life stretched outside of the constructed box. Even still, there was a keen recognition of the tendency for media depictions of black life to somehow remain confined to stereotypical borders. Within these borders, the Atlanta housewives were largely accepted as "authentically" black. It is important to note that Mia, an "educated elite" participant, provided what I identified as a "colorblind" reading of *RHOA*, which opposed the interpretations of other participants: "I don't think of black people when I see that show. I don't see black people. I just see another *Housewives* show, with more drama." She later described a process by which she "matched" each of the Atlanta housewives with "their counterparts" from the other all-white *Housewives* series. Mia's ability to "match" each black housewife with a white housewife, whose "behaviors are the same," allowed her to eliminate race when evaluating the program. This perspective is wholly in line with Bravo's description of the show, as "an up-close and personal look at six fabulous women from Atlanta's social elite," a classed, but not racialized description.[62] The network chooses to focus on the women's Southern identities, rather than their racial identities, as the mark of distinction from other *Housewives* series. This alternate reading suggests that some African American viewers may not perceive the Atlanta housewives as representations (positive/negative, accurate/inaccurate, or otherwise) of black America, broadly or elite black America, more specifically. In Mia's case, however, she later commented on the ways she felt the show failed to accurately portray the housewives as black women.

ATL Housewives Fail at "Doing" (Black) Elite

While participants from both status cohorts remained largely aligned in their evaluations of the housewives as black, key differences between the two were identified in discussions of the housewives' elite status. Comparisons between *RHOA*, the "black housewives" and other *RH* series, the "other (white) housewives" fueled discussions in both status cohorts about the dominant class structure, the white standard. "Educated elites" also relied on their understandings of elite status within the black community—the black standard—to position the Atlanta housewives.

The White Standard

Both cohorts compared *RHOA* to other all-white *Housewives* series to support their claim that *RHOA* depicts "a class below" the others. As compared to the Beverly Hills housewives, who participants described as having "real money" or "old money," the Atlanta housewives were described as being in the "middle" or "peons." For a few "educated elite" participants, Phaedra was a noted exception—an educated lawyer with high-profile clientele and significant economic capital. Even still, she was considered among those with "straight money, no real passing down of wealth." Here, participants employed a strictly economically informed evaluation of the housewives' class position. In these comparisons, they paid little attention to common markers of status (e.g., education) and focused instead on "types of money." Benjamin Bowser compares class by race, similarly suggesting that the very top of the black class hierarchy is at best upper-middle in the white hierarchy.[63] Then, it seems participants appropriately located the positions of the black housewives, at least according to Bowser's conceptualization of the broader American class structure.

The Black Standard

While all participants recognized that the Atlanta housewives fell short of the economic benchmark set by the white elite, which for them was represented by the Beverly Hills, New York, and Orange County housewives, only "educated elite" participants took the discussion a step further to compare the black housewives to a decidedly "black" standard. Lacy finds that middle-class blacks often seamlessly use black cultural capital to navigate the black world, while drawing upon dominant cultural capital to navigate commonly class-dictated experiences in the white world.[64] In fact, a key goal among middle-class black parents is to ensure that their children are able to effortlessly shift between black and white worlds.[65] Then, Lacy's *black middle-class toolkit* is made up of an intricate mix of both dominant and nondominant cultural capital, black and white scripts.[66] "Educated elite" participants in this study were conversant in forms of black *elite* cultural capital and offered a nuanced understanding of why, in their opinions, the Atlanta housewives are not part of the status-determined black elite circle.[67] Responses fell largely into two categories: lack of (1) proper decorum and (2) legitimacy.

Based on the data, racial/class performance can be categorized along a spectrum from "bougie" to "ghetto." "Bougie" performance is correlated with Bourdieu's conceptualization of cultural capital, a set of actions that lead to economic and social benefits in the dominant culture.[68] Conversely, "ghetto" is more closely correlated with "the code of the streets," an intricate set of subcultural norms that permit survival in inner-city communities.[69] Kandi, one of the more respected housewives among participants, introduced the term "boughetto" on Season 3 of *RHOA*, which can serve as a mid-point or perhaps, a complicated hybrid on the decorum scale. In an interview with *Essence*, Kandi explains the term as follows:

> I thought it [Phaedra's baby shower] was boughetto . . . but we all know when you have the down home crowd and those that are known to be a little uppity, you look at them and think they trying to be bougie! They got ballerinas in here, they doing the waltz. That was the bougie part. The ghetto part was the roses in her hair, the rhinestones on her eyelashes . . . so it was boughetto. It's when a person who got a little hood in them and they trying to be all extra.[70]

The term reflects the idea that despite having achieved a certain class/status position some members of the black elite may still have "a little hood in them," residual attitudes or behaviors from their days in impoverished inner-city communities. The housewives' negotiations of these sets of behaviors—the "bougie," required to survive among the elite (e.g., the fine arts, including ballet) and the "ghetto," required to fit in with the "down home crowd" (e.g., blinged-out eyelashes)—was exhibited frequently on the show.

A comparison of how "educated elite" participants evaluated Phaedra's elite status versus NeNe's offers one example of the decorum requirement at work. Phaedra was much more readily accepted as an "authentic" member of the black elite, while NeNe was frequently questioned.[71] When describing NeNe, participants used the terms "ghetto" and "classless." Kandi's term, "boughetto," however, was used to describe Phaedra. Participants' acceptance of Phaedra as both "boughetto" and representative of the black elite suggests the term describes an identifiable aspect of black elite performance. Interestingly, multiple participants made comments equating their own personalities with the most flamboyant aspects of NeNe's, including, "I'm ready and willing to crank it up if necessary" (Patrice, "educated elite" group C). There seemed to be a sense among participants that there exists a time and space to employ what elites might consider a less desirable form of black cultural capital—"hood" behavior. There was not, however, an agreed upon moment. Thus, the in-betweeness of "boughetto" was accepted as "true" to elite black middle-class life, whereas the "ghetto" suggested standards for decorum were not met. One might equate the ideal position on this scale with Carter's notion of a *cultural straddler*, someone who is comfortable in both "bougie" and "ghetto" cultural situations.[72] The *cultural straddler* is able to seamlessly shift between cultural contexts and employ the "right" set of tools for each.[73] Participants did not believe that most of the housewives successfully navigated this terrain, given the perceived prominence of "ghetto" performance on the show.

The Cosby Show provided a point of comparison as "educated elite" focus groups grappled with the idea of what constituted the "legitimate route" to black elite status. Mia suggested education was the key difference between *Cosby* and *RHOA*:

> But the thing is you're looking at an educated upper-middle class when you're looking at the Cosbys versus the *Real Housewives* show. I think there's a significant difference between the two. What you value and the décor and how you carry yourself and the culture and what you think is important is significantly different between the two groups. . . . We saw that social climbing had to happen through education before or through being an athlete. Now, it's really just exclusively, you can do it through any route. As a result of that, there are so many more people who are wealthy, but they aren't necessarily representative of what we would consider the Black upper class. Because, black upper class, if they're made up of educated people, their houses are not going to look like what you see on *The Real Housewives*. ("educated elite" group A)

Patrice further stressed the importance of education for achieving elite status as an African American:

> I grew up in Atlanta; and I know Atlanta is one of the hubs for the black elite—judges, doctors, lawyers . . . and like [Kia] said a lot of them had to undergo some kind of professional training or graduate level training . . . and really work rigorously for what they had. ("educated elite" group C)

The fact that most of the housewives were not viewed as educated made "educated elite" participants uneasy about classifying them as elite. Beyond education, "educated elite" participants (with few exceptions) questioned the basic drive and motivation of the housewives. Discussions about "what they do" and "how they make their money" persisted across groups, an ironic focal point given the classic definition of a housewife. The lack of information about the "back story" was problematic for some, while others focused on the frivolity of the housewives' current projects, viewing them as "cookie cutter ambitions . . . as much in fashion as a Gucci bag" (Patrice, "educated elite" group C). Each of these elements, education and ambition, was thought to be fundamental to attainment and maintenance of status as an African American. The housewives' failure to produce the proper credentials led "educated elite" participants to question their elite status.

In a different comparison of the two shows, Leah described another theme that emerged across "educated elite" groups, one that is also echoed in the popular press: *Cosby* is a positive example of a black elite lifestyle, while *RHOA* is not.[74]

"Educated Elite" Group A:

LEAH: But I love *The Cosby Show* because it showed us . . . we don't have to be like the housewives of Atlanta. . . . We can aspire to have the doctor that's the father or the lawyer that's the mom. . . . We can aspire to do that. But as far as have we gotten there yet? I think our generation is working on it.

NICOLE: At the end of the day, I think *The Cosby Show* really focused on family. Granted they were perfect, but they loved each other so much.

LEAH: We [Blacks] love our family. We love you enough to, ah, bail you out. We love you . . . I'm just saying . . .

NICOLE: That we can be articulate.

LEAH: Well, yea.

NICOLE: We can . . . not be hoodlums, not walk around with our pants hanging down off our butts, not have children out of wedlock.

LEAH: That's a whole nother thing.

TIFFANY: It may be out of wedlock, but at least not at like 12 or 10.

NICOLE: We really needed that show, at that point, because the perception of black culture was just out of control. To the point they thought we were monkeys, apes, that we had the IQ of roaches. [pause] So we needed something to kind of bring us out of that hole.

LEAH: We need something like that now.

A tension between owning and fighting "negative" stereotypes clearly existed among "educated elite" participants, as evidenced by Leah's description of black families' responses to incarceration and Nicole's counter with a reference to articulation. The conversation is not a simple evaluation of good/bad or positive/negative televisual representations of blackness. Here, participants are actively engaged in a negotiation of how a rich, complex portrayal of black America should look. Participants in favor of the "legitimate route" exemplified by *Cosby* envisioned a churchgoing, strong-black-man-having, anti-stereotypical, protective of uniquely black social spaces, well-mannered, well-educated, highly driven, and financially savvy image. Strong identification with *Cosby* was linked to a desire to see elite black America (and perhaps black America more generally) through a lens of perfection. Conversely, *RHOA* was viewed as a lesson for blacks on what not to do or how not to act as members of the black upper-middle class and a lesson for whites on common black stereotypes.

"Core BMC" participants, on the other hand, signaled that the Atlanta housewives, if not comparable to the white elite, do offer some hope for African Americans. When asked what message *RHOA* sends about black people, Michelle stated the following:

"Core BMC" Group A:

MICHELLE: That we can succeed and have some money. And live in high-class places and go to the best restaurants, dress good, have cars, have a career, throw a party that can be catered. You know stuff they think we can't get.

SANDRA: That's true, Michelle! It's right on the head!

While the Atlanta housewives provided a list of "don'ts" for the "educated elite," they seemed to offer a more encouraging message for some "core BMC" participants.

ATL Housewives Affect Daily Living?

Although many "educated elite" participants closely identified with cast members on some levels, they rejected the housewives as lacking "authenticity" partly out of concern about outsiders' interpretations. When Olivia suggested "a lot of voices couldn't be heard" because *The Cosby Show* set such a high standard for black America and alluded to the idea that *RHOA* could be considered an alternative voice, others responded, "maybe we didn't need to hear 'em" and "those were the stereotypical voices." Anthony further described *RHOA* as "a direct attack on *Cosby* . . . it makes us settle for that stuff" or accept "negative" stereotypes as inherent to black culture. Debra Smith describes this tension in relation to African American producers of programs about black life; they feel obligated to uphold the positive while trying to "keep it real."[75] Is a "negative" characterization "keeping it real" or simply an attempt to degrade the group as a whole? And even if *RHOA* is "keeping it real," can we risk the "real life" repercussions of being associated with the housewives' performance of black upper-middle classness? These are the tensions "educated elite" viewers experienced when evaluating *RHOA*.

Tools developed over a lifetime allowed "educated elite" participants to identify "real" black culture and, more specifically, "real" elite black culture. As such, there was a level of discomfort attached to *RHOA* viewers who were assumed not to have a similar toolkit. Participants repeatedly mentioned the dangers of *RHOA* for "people who don't know" or "people without a lot of access to black people," a label applied most often to whites. It was believed that "people who don't know" would uncritically accept the housewives as accurate representations of members of the black upper-middle class. The idea that outsiders might apply the information taken away from the show about blacks as a group to them as individuals was a major concern for "educated elites." Evelyn Simien clearly defines "linked fate" among African Americans as "an acute sense of awareness that what happens to the group will also affect the individual member."[76] Michael C. Dawson argues lived experiences with racism fuels this awareness.[77] Throughout focus group sessions, "educated elite" participants connected the show's larger themes to their own lives, most frequently to experiences with outsiders who categorized them based on racial stereotypes. Even if participants themselves exhibited "proper" decorum, "real" money, and "genuine" ambition, they believed outsiders' lenses to be calibrated by media representations. Then, "educated elites" also understood treatment in the world as linked to these images, a discussion which was noticeably absent in "core BMC" groups.

(RE)DEFINING THE BOUNDARIES OF THE BLACK ELITE

This chapter has examined African American audiences' interpretations of *RHOA* in an effort to unpack how viewers understood the show and its conceptualization of (elite) black (upper-) middle-classness. African American viewers brought their own "scripts" to bear on the program and analyzed how the housewives employ dominant and nondominant forms of cultural capital on the show. Just as Lacy's participants utilized the *black middle-class toolkit* in their neighborhoods and public spaces,[78] black viewers in this study built racial boundaries to separate themselves and the housewives from producers, who were perceived as outsiders; class boundaries to separate the housewives from the white elite (both cohorts); and status boundaries to distinguish the housewives from themselves ("educated elite" only).

For all participants "the producers" represented an outside force that pushed the housewives beyond the "proper" boundaries of blackness. Despite its "fly-on-the-wall" potential, it seems black viewers still perceived reality television programming as confined to the same dominant scripts on blackness used for fictional shows. In spite of affronts to "authentic" blackness, participants maintained the ability to look beyond negative characterizations and discover something useful and enjoyable. Still, any claims for the potential of reality television to expose a broader audience to diverse aspects of African American culture must be tempered by concerns about the role of dominant culture in constructing storylines and the scripts/toolkits used by mainstream America to interpret programs. Future studies should consider looking at cross-racial audiences' responses to reality television programs with majority-black casts to fully test the "for people who don't know" phenomenon. For example, how do *RHOA* fans who do not identify as African American interpret the racial, status, and class dynamics in the show?

In evaluations of class/status, participants blamed the housewives directly for their inability to perform adequately. Among "educated elite" viewers, discussions of *RHOA* emerged as potential sites for the construction and confirmation of the boundaries of black elite identity. Their understanding of black elite culture suggested that there is a right and a wrong way to get to the top—*Cosby* is right; *RHOA* is wrong. While the representation caused uneasiness for many "educated elite" viewers, whose concerns about "linked fate" colored their evaluations of *RHOA*, a more hopeful outlook was present among some "core BMC" participants, who felt the show could teach about African American success. Interestingly, the positive discourse on *RHOA* as an example of black success among "core BMC" participants mimicked the conversations some "educated elites" had about the revered *Cosby*. Future studies should examine more closely these differing notions of success within the black community. For those who have already followed the "legitimate" path prescribed by *Cosby,* the approach to elite status detailed in *RHOA* is clearly unacceptable; but what about for teenagers or for working-class strivers?

The popularity of *RHOA* among black middle-class participants in this study can be explained, at least in part, by the enjoyment that accompanies viewers' negotiation of "authentic" versus "constructed" blackness and "real money" versus "posers." Conversations were not restricted to negative stereotyping, but included deeper negotiations of how the black elite should look and comparisons between insiders' and outsiders' constructions of the group. For "educated elite" viewers there existed pleasure in the foibles, especially when the housewives fell short of the expected ideal. Participants were able to "laugh with them" knowing that they themselves had not always embodied the ideal or that they knew people who still "had a little hood in them." They "love it" because it is "real" enough for identification—to recognize as black—yet, it allows for negotiations of and discussions about what it really means to be "real" black with "real" money, a member of the black elite in contemporary America.

NOTES

1. I thank Dr. John L. Jackson Jr. and Dr. Katherine Sender for their insightful comments on earlier drafts of this chapter. In May 2012, an earlier version of this chapter was presented at the International Communication Association Conference in Phoenix. Robin Givhan, "Echoes of TV's First Lady; Michelle Obama's Last True Cultural Antecedent Is *Cosby's* Clair Huxtable," *Washington Post*, June 19, 2009. Susan Fales-Hill, who served as an executive producer of *A Different World*, aptly notes in an interview with Givhan, the Huxtables "brought the dirty secret of America—the black bourgeoisie—out of the closet"; W. E. B. Du Bois, "Talented Tenth," in *The Negro Problem: A Series of Articles by Representative American Negroes of To-day*, ed. Booker T. Washington (New York: James Pott & Company, 1903); also, it should be noted that "Black," "black," and "African American" are used interchangeably throughout the chapter, reflecting the range of accepted labels for the group.

2. Other recent programs that feature the black upper-middle class include *Basketball Wives*, *What Chilli Wants*, and *Braxton Family Values*.

3. Derrick B. Taylor, "*RhoA*: Season Finale Breaks Ratings Records." *Essence*, February 1, 2011. Accessed July 31, 2011 http://www.essence.com/2011/02/01/rhoa-season-three-finale-breaks-bravo-ratings-record/. The Season 3 finale of *The Real Housewives of Atlanta* brought Bravo approximately 4.4 million viewers, breaking network records. The show began its sixth season in November 2013.

4. Ginia Bellafante, "Wealth (and Dior) on Their Minds," *New York Times*, July 30, 2009; Givhan, "Echoes of TV's First Lady."

5. For two critiques, see Givhan, "Echoes of TV's First Lady" and Bellafante, "Wealth (and Dior) on Their Minds."

6. Jacqueline Bobo, "*The Color Purple*: Black Women as Cultural Readers," in *Female Spectators: Looking at Film and Television*, ed. E. Deidre Pribram (London: Verso, 1988), 96.

7. Du Bois, "Talented Tenth."

8. Du Bois, "Talented Tenth."

9. Lawrence O. Graham, *Our Kind of People: Inside America's Black Upper Class* (New York: Harper Collins, 1999).

10. Graham, *Our Kind of People*; this statement echoes and is an inversion of Simone de Beauvoir's classic statement: "One is not born, but rather becomes, woman." [See Simone de Beauvoir, *The Second Sex*, trans. Constance Borde and Sheila Malovany-Chevallier (New York: Vintage Books, 2011), 283.]

Chapter Fifteen

11. Lois Benjamin, *The Black Elite: Still Facing the Color Line in the Twenty-first Century* (Lanham: Rowman & Littlefield Publishers, 2005), xix.

12. Benjamin, *Black Elite*; it is important to note some were considered "black elite" even if they lacked academic credentials and in some cases, economic resources.

13. Throughout the chapter, the terms "black elite" and "black (upper-) middle class" appear interchangeably and are meant to serve as a concise way to identify the group of interest. During focus group sessions, participants actively engaged with and (re-)defined these terms. The relative status/class positionality of the housewives was determined based on consumption patterns (e.g., Sheree's Aston Martin purchase or Cynthia's $1 million-plus wedding). The housewives also live in exclusive, luxury communities and attend upscale events throughout the season. Bravo also labels the housewives as among the Southern elite (see *"Real Housewives of Atlanta* Season Three," *BravoTV.com*, accessed May 1, 2011, http://www.bravotv.com/the-real-housewives-of-atlanta/season-3).

14. E. Franklin Frazier, *Black Bourgeoisie* (New York: The Free Press, 1957); Karyn Lacy, *Blue-chip Black: Race, Class, and Status in the New Black Middle Class* (Berkeley: University of California Press, 2007); Bart Landry, *The New Black Middle Class* (Berkeley: University of California Press, 1987).

15. Frazier, *Black Bourgeoisie*; Stephen Birmingham, *Certain People: America's Black Elite* (Boston: Little, Brown & Company, 1977).

16. Landry, *New Black Middle Class*.

17. Landry, *New Black Middle Class*; Lacy, *Blue-chip Black*.

18. Lacy, *Blue-chip Black*; Lacy identifies three key trends since the 1970s: (1) the percentage of African Americas choosing suburban neighborhoods has increased, (2) construction of and greater interest in black suburban enclaves, and (3) more variability in the quality of suburban neighborhoods where African Americans settle (e.g., distance from the poor and appreciation values) (see p. 41). For an early discussion of outmigration to the suburbs, see William J. Wilson, *The Declining Significance of Race: Blacks and Changing American Institutions* (Chicago: University of Chicago Press, 1978). For three ethnographic considerations of black middle-class life in urban black communities, see Mary Pattillo-McCoy, *Black Picket Fences: Privilege and Peril among the Black Middle Class* (Chicago: University of Chicago Press, 1999); John L. Jackson Jr., *Harlemworld: Doing Race and Class in Contemporary Black America* (Chicago: University of Chicago Press, 2001); and Mary Pattillo, *Black on the Block: The Politics of Race and Class in the City* (Chicago: University of Chicago Press, 2007). Pattillo's Chicago and Jackson's Harlem illustrate the ways the black middle class remains connected—physically and emotionally—to urban spaces, troubling claims that the black poor have been "abandoned" in urban "ghettos."

19. John McWhorter, "Racism in America Is Over," *Forbes,* December 30, 2008, http://www.forbes.com/2008/12/30/end-of-racism-oped-cx_jm_1230mcwhorter.html; many of these debates have occurred in the popular press. In *Forbes*, McWhorter argues the conservative position detailed in the main text. Lawrence Bobo provides a liberal counterargument in *The Root*: He argues not only was race a factor in Obama's (re)election, but Americans can also observe its continued influence in other sectors of life, including housing and interpersonal relationships. (See Lawrence

D. Bobo, "Are We 'Black No More'? Not Quite," *The Root,* January 2, 2013, http://www.theroot.com/views/are-we-black-no-more-not-quite).

20. Ebony Elizabeth Thomas and Shanesha R. F. Brooks-Tatum, eds., *Reading African American Experiences in the Obama Era: Theory, Advocacy, Activism* (New York: Peter Lang, 2012), see introduction. The authors also discuss the birth of an Obama generation—African Americans who have grown up amidst multiculturalism, diversity, and post-racial narratives and have witnessed the election of the nation's first black president early in their lives.

21. Frazier, *Black Bourgeoisie*; Lacy, *Blue-chip Black.*

22. Frazier, *Black Bourgeoisie*; Lacy, *Blue-chip Black*; Mary Pattillo, *Black on the Block*; Pattillo builds on Frazier's claim that the "black bourgeoisie" "serve two masters"—the "black masses" and the "white mainstream/elite"—with her detailed discussion of "middlemen" (especially chapter 3).

23. Ann Swidler, *Talk of Love: How Culture Matters* (Chicago: University of Chicago Press, 2001).

24. Lacy, *Blue-chip Black*, 14.

25. Lacy, *Blue-chip Black.*

26. Lacy, *Blue-chip Black*, see chapters 4 and 5.

27. Lacy, *Blue-chip Black.*

28. Lacy, *Blue-chip Black.*

29. Herta Herzog, "On Borrowed Experience," *Studies in Philosophy and Social Science* 11, no. 1 (1941), 65–69.

30. S. Elizabeth Bird, *The Audience in Everyday Life: Living in the Media World* (New York: Routledge, 2003), 90.

31. Joshua Meyrowitz, "We Liked to Watch: Television as Progenitor of the Surveillance Society," *The Annals of the American Academy of Political and Social Science* 625 (September 2009).

32. Kathryn Woodward, *Identity and Difference* (London: Sage, 1997).

33. Meyrowitz, "We Liked to Watch."

34. Jannette Dates and William Barlow, eds., *Split Image: African Americans in the Mass Media* (2nd ed.). (Washington, D.C.: Howard University Press, 1990).

35. Yuki Fujioka, "Television Portrayals and African-American Stereotypes: Examination of Television Effects When Direct Contact Is Lacking," *Journalism and Mass Communication Quarterly* 76, no. 1 (1999). Fujioka's findings suggest that absent direct experience televisual messages did influence respondents' perceptions of African Americans. Also see Sut Jhally and Justin Lewis, *Enlightened Racism: The Cosby Show, Audiences, and the Myth of the American Dream* (Boulder: Westview Press, 1992), chapter 1.

36. Ji Hoon Park, "The Uncomfortable Encounter between an Urban Black and a Rural White: The Ideological Implications of Racial Conflict on MTV's *The Real World,*" *Journal of communication* 59 (2009).

37. Park, "Uncomfortable Encounter"; In the case of *RHOA*, the unscripted nature of the program permits self-descriptions of racial difference and class/status boundaries.

38. Susan Murray and Laurie Ouellette, eds., *Reality TV: Remaking Television Culture* (2nd ed.) (New York: New York University Press, 2009).

39. Murray and Ouellette, *Reality TV*, 8.

40. Jhally and Lewis, *Enlightened Racism*; for another examination of class and African American media audiences, see Robin R. Means Coleman, *African American Viewers and the Black Situation Comedy: Situating Racial Humor* (New York: Garland Publishing, 1998).

41. Jhally and Lewis, *Enlightened Racism*.

42. Graham, *Our Kind of People*; Lacy, *Blue-chip Black*; Eugene Robinson, *Disintegration: The Splintering of Black America* (New York: Doubleday, 2010).

43. Annette Hill, *Reality Television: Audiences and Popular Factual Television* (London: Routledge, 2005).

44. For an example of black/white responses see Park, "Uncomfortable Encounter." For an example of the auto-ethnographic approach, see Robin M. Boylorn, "As Seen on TV: An Autoethnographic Reflection on Race and Reality Television," *Critical Studies in Media Communication* 25, no. 4 (October 2008), 413–433.

45. Bird, *Audience in Everyday Life*, 17.

46. Tamar Liebes and Elihu Katz, *The Export of Meaning: Cross-cultural Readings of Dallas* (New York: Oxford University Press, 1990), 28.

47. Jhally and Lewis, *Enlightened Racism*; Liebes and Katz, *Export of Meaning* offer two examples.

48. Participants fell into the following age categories: 20–29 (7 participants), 30–39 (6 participants), 40–49 (1 participant), and 50+ (4 participants). They lived in major cities and suburbs on the US East Coast.

49. Nina Angelique Johnson, "Talented Tenth or Black Bourgeoisie: The Black Educational Elites in the Twenty-First Century," (PhD diss., Northwestern University, 2011); Lacy, *Blue-chip Black*. The "educated elite" marker, which refers to African Americans who have ascended the educational attainment ladder, is borrowed from Johnson. While her research focuses on black Ivy League graduates, I include college graduates from any institution and those nearing graduation in this category. The "core black middle class" category—borrowed from Lacy—also takes on a slightly different meaning in this study. Lacy defines the "core black middle class" as comprised of individuals earning between $50,000 and $100,000. Lacking access to income data, I use it to refer to those participants who had not earned (and were not in the process of attaining) college degrees. If Lacy's salary specifications are applied, it is possible that some of the participants considered "core BMC" in this study would fall into the "lower middle class" category.

50. August Hollingshead, "Four Factor Index of Social Status" (Unpublished manuscript, Yale University, 1975).

51. See Lacy, *Blue-chip Black*. This assessment was made based on Lacy's stratification of the black middle class into lower, core, and elite subgroups. Estimates of participants' income based on their occupations would place them all within the middle class.

52. Robert M. Emerson, Rachel I. Fretz, and Linda L. Shaw, *Writing Ethnographic Fieldnotes* (Chicago: University of Chicago Press, 1995). In addition to focus groups, I analyzed eighteen episodes of *The Real Housewives of Atlanta* (Season 3), which appeared as part of *Bravo*'s Monday night lineup beginning October 4, 2010. The series

later moved to Sunday nights and continued through February 20, 2011. Emergent themes centered on the everyday experiences and norms of the black elite (as featured in the show). This information was used to prepare the focus group moderator guide. I also analyzed twenty-four newspaper articles about *RHOA* to better understand the discourse around the show. Emergent themes included frequent comparisons to other programs that feature African American casts (most often *The Cosby Show*), the discussion of race, and the level of taste and decorum exhibited by the cast members, among others. The data presented here is based primarily on the focus groups.

53. *The Real Housewives of Atlanta,* Season 3, directed by Glenda Hersh (New York: Bravo Media, 2010), DVD. "Housewife" appears in quotation marks to signal the fact that the women do not perform roles traditionally associated with the housewife. The quoted taglines are from Season 3 of the show. All descriptions are based on my reading of the third season of *RHOA*.

54. "Aston Martin DBS Review." *Edmunds*, accessed October 9, 2011, http://www.edmunds.com/aston-martin/dbs/. The MSRP was listed as $266,000.

55. John L. Jackson Jr., *Real Black: Adventures in Racial Sincerity* (Chicago: University of Chicago Press, 2005), 18. See Jackson, *Real Black* for a thorough discussion of racial sincerity as a productive lens through which scholars can interpret and understand questions of racial performance. Questions of "authenticity" and "sincerity" are intensified among reality television audiences who must actively seek "the fake" in a genre fixated with putting "the real" on display. This approach opposes the means many audiences use to engage with fictional programs, whereby suspension of disbelief reigns and audiences seek out "the real" or emotional elements of the show. For a cogent discussion of narrative structure, its link to realism, and more specifically emotional realism, see Ien Ang, *Watching Dallas: Soap Opera and the Melodramatic Imagination* (London: Methuen, 1985).

56. John L. Jackson Jr., *Harlemworld*; These section headings echo those of Jackson's ethnography on the performance of race and class in Harlem.

57. During focus group sessions, participants were asked to identify the major themes of the show. After discussing the themes generated during the session, I asked participants their opinions on some of the themes I identified in my textual analysis of Season 3. Spirituality was among the themes identified in my analysis of the show.

58. Mary Pattillo-McCoy, *Black Picket Fences*; for an earlier discussion of the black church as a central institution in Black America, see Frazier, *Black Bourgeoisie*.

59. Howard C. Stevenson, ed., *Playing with Anger: Teaching Coping Skills to African American Boys through Athletics and Culture* (Westport: Praeger, 2003), 137.

60. Givhan, "Echoes of TV's First Lady" offers one example.

61. Bobo, *Color Purple*, 101.

62. "*The Real Housewives of Atlanta* Season Three," *Bravo.com*, accessed May 1, 2011, http://www.bravotv.com/the-real-housewives-of-atlanta/season-3.

63. Benjamin P. Bowser, *The Black Middle Class: Social Mobility and Vulnerability.* (Boulder: Lynne Rienner, 2007). Graham would likely disagree with Bowser's claim given his insistence on the existence of a black upper class (see Graham, *Our Kind of People*).

64. Lacy, *Blue-chip Black*.

65. Lacy, *Blue-chip Black.*

66. Lacy, *Blue-chip Black.*

67. See Prudence L. Carter, *Keepin' It Real: School Success Beyond Black and White* (Oxford: Oxford University Press, 2005). *Elite* is added to distinguish this concept from Prudence Carter's original conceptualization of black cultural capital as tied to working class/folk ways of being.

68. Pierre Bourdieu, "The Forms of Capital," in *Education: Culture, Economy, and Society*, ed. A. H. Halsey et al. (Oxford: Oxford University Press, 1997); Carter, *Keepin' It Real*. "Bougie" is a shortened form of "bourgeoisie" common in black vernacular.

69. Elijah Anderson, "The code of the streets," *Atlantic*, May 1994. Accessed July 31, 2011. http://www.theatlantic.com/magazine/archive/1994/05/the-code-of-the-streets/6601/?single_page=true.

70. Derrick. B. Taylor, "*RhoA*: Kandi Burruss on 'boughetto' and Tiny and Toya," *Essence*, November 1, 2010, http://www.essence.com/entertainment/real_housewives_of_atlanta/kandi_burruss/rhoa_kandi_burruss_on_boughetto_and_tiny_and_ti.php.

71. Consider the following scenario: In the first episode of Season 3, Phaedra and Dwight discuss two other housewives, Sheree and NeNe, who allegedly owe Dwight money. After hearing the story, Phaedra encourages him not to "stoop to hood rat level." In this instance "hood rat level" is equivalent to "ghetto." Later in the episode NeNe demonstrates "hood rat level" with a full head-shaking, neck- and eye-rolling screaming match.

72. Carter, *Keepin' It Real.*

73. Carter, *Keepin' It Real.*

74. Givhan, "Echoes of TV's First Lady."

75. Debra C. Smith, "Critiquing Reality-based Televisual Black Fatherhood: A Critical Analysis of *Run's House* and *Snoop Dogg's Father Hood*," *Critical Studies in Media Communication* 25, 4 (October 2008), 409. Smith, thinking with cultural critic Kobena Mercer and communication scholars Nancy Cornwell and Mark Orbe, defines "keep it real" as an effort to craft rich, complex narratives—including the "positive" and the "negative"—about African American life. In their study of black middle-class viewers of *The Cosby Show*, Innis and Feagin found informants were reluctant to criticize a "positive" televisual representation of blackness, which also, to some degree, reflects the tension Smith describes. See Leslie B. Innis and Joe R. Feagin, "*The Cosby Show*: The View from the Black Middle Class," in *Say It Loud: African-American audiences, media, and identity*, ed. Robin Means Coleman (New York: Routledge, 2002).

76. Evelyn M. Simien, "Race, Gender, and Linked Fate," *Journal of Black Studies* 35, 5 (May 2005), 530.

77. Michael C. Dawson, *Behind the Mule: Race and Class in African-American Politics* (Princeton: Princeton University Press, 1994).

78. Lacy, *Blue-chip Black.*

Chapter Sixteen

He Who Has the Gold Makes the Rules: Tyler Perry Presents "The Tyler Perry Way"

Danielle E. Williams

Tyler Perry is one of the few African Americans in positions of power behind the scenes in television. He made this transition successfully because of his star power. This chapter is a star study of Perry as a public creative figure. I use the term "public creative figure" to describe his role as creator and co-executive producer of his television shows. Public creative figures are the official spokespeople for their shows. Perry—and other such individuals (e.g., Dick Wolf, Aaron Sorkin, J. J. Abrams, Matthew Weiner, Shonda Rhimes)—are perceived to be in control of the fate(s) of characters on their series, the narrative direction of the show, and other key decisions. In this role, they are often presented as responsible for a show's success or failure.[1] The label "public creative figure" adds a new contextual layer to the examination of stars and celebrities because it allows scholars to examine how perceived control and power during production is an important part of the construction of television personalities.

Most examinations of key creative figures come from non-academic sources such as industry trade publications or popular press books.[2] Further, most books on the subject consist of interviews with white executive producers. Coverage on black creative figures in prime-time television is extremely limited in the popular press and, even more so, in scholarly works.[3] This chapter provides a bridge between non-academic and academic examinations of the black public creative figure by examining how Perry is a very important black public creative figure in television. Examining his image as such is another means of examining race and representation on television. This approach goes beyond examining onscreen representation and provides insight into the individuals responsible for them. Looking at how Perry views himself as a black public creative figure reveals information about current ideologies and viewpoints in American culture as it relates to race, specifically blackness.

THE PUBLIC CREATIVE FIGURE

Over the past two decades, there has been a shift in the amount of coverage of individuals working behind the scenes. Roberta Pearson claims that authorship of a television program is now widely associated with the executive producer.[4] These figures are viewed in the same vein as film auteurs. The creative figure has carved a space for himself or herself in the public eye. This figure now often receives as much attention as the stars of the program.[5] The star image has long had a powerful role in society. Richard Dyer argues a star's image is a complex one that is industrially constructed through promotion, publicity, films, and commentary.[6] Through these discourses, stars present ideologies of race, class, gender, ethnicity, and sexuality.

Scholarship on this topic is as complex as the stars themselves, especially in terms of the use of terminology. The popular terms in the literature are "star," "personality," and "celebrity."[7] Sean Redmond and Su Holmes argue that it is difficult to make these distinctions because stars/celebrities/personalities are not limited to only one medium as they have inter-textual and cross-textual appeal.[8] James Bennett and Su Holmes make a distinction between the television star and the television personality.[9] For these authors, a "star" is an actor on a fictional program and a "personality" refers to presenters and other figures/actors in nonfictional programming. Perry qualifies as a star (he created and plays the character Madea, who is featured prominently in many of his television programs and film), but also as a personality because of his public image as creator and executive producer.

In acting as the public creative figure, Perry is an interesting case study because he is an "icon of intertextuality."[10] The creation of his first television series, *House of Payne* (*HOP*) added a new dimension to his fame and celebrity. Dyer argues stars have a market function; they are used to sell a film or television series.[11] P. David Marshall states that television celebrities are connected more to the economics of the television industry than their film counterparts.[12] This is especially true for Perry. He is now known for creating successful (i.e., profitable) shows on basic cable. As a public creative figure, his job is to promote his shows and continue delivering successful programs. He utilizes the Internet and social networking as well as media interviews to connect with his fans directly and sustain his image as a public creative figure. He is part of the industrial machine and responsible for creating stars on his shows as well as being a personality/celebrity himself.

As public creative figures, being in control behind the scenes is part of their image. However, Francesco Alberoni claims that in reality, stars have limited power.[13] They are part of the social elite but they do not have any authority behind the scenes. Dyer explores stars' battles over the lack of control of their images. He examines how Marilyn Monroe, Paul Robeson, and Judy Garland fought against their lack of power. These three were part of the studio system, in which their stardom was attached to a specific genre and personality type. Garland verbally spoke out, Monroe fought for better parts, and Robeson eventually quit making films. The issue of control continues today albeit in a different economic and industrial context. For example, Rebecca Williams explores how Drew Barrymore took control over her image and transformed it from "bad girl" roles to the leading lady in romantic comedies. Barrymore made the transition through the creation of her own production company, which provided her with control behind the scenes and onscreen. Williams claims that perceptions of control are just as important as control: "it is not that movie stars should be considered authors or auteurs, but rather the social and cultural patterns that stars embody should be worthy of study."[14] As a television personality, Perry exemplifies social and cultural patterns regarding race in his image as a public creative figure. Perry functions as a black creator/executive producer. Race is a significant part of his image. However in examining the role race plays in his image, it is necessary to examine the social and cultural significance of race in society.

Two terms often used to discuss race in contemporary American society are "colorblindness" and "post-racial." Using these labels to analyze racial representation in media is complicated because the terms have multiple meanings depending on the author or scholar.[15] According to the theory of colorblindness, the color of one's skin is not important and one will advance in society based on his or her merit.[16] A "post-racial" society is defined by Jennifer Esposito as one in which "we have moved beyond race and that race no longer structures our thinking or our actions . . . racial categories have no meaning."[17]

Ralina Joseph prefers the term post-racial over colorblindness because "it highlights the continued centrality of race in this ideology where race is ostensibly immaterial."[18] She maintains that this term makes race central to the discussion and acknowledges the very thing it denies. Joseph argues the media reinforces a post-racial ideology in which "racism no longer exist[s] . . . [and] race itself no longer matters."[19] Joseph argues that the post-racial identity is so deeply embedded in our society that deviations or ruptures are temporary. In addition, she finds the post-racial ideology problematic because of the racial inequalities present in our society. When stars of color reinforce a post-racial ideology they promote the idea that meritocracy and hard work equals success, while ignoring the structural, institutional, and historic forces that make a colorblind society impossible in the United States[20] Jennifer Esposito worries about the impact television shows that promote the post-racial myth have on viewers: "popular culture texts . . . are discursive practices that have material consequences on real bodies. These texts then contribute to current discourses about race and racism, which also struggle and shape the ways we live."[21]

Although these terms have been useful, a new term is needed to examine the place of race within current media industries. Mary Beltrán states that examining racial representation in the current media landscape "raise[s] the need for new methodological tools and theoretical frameworks . . . in this supposed post-racial era."[22] Ralph Banks suggests the term "neo-racial" to describe race in American society. He uses the term for legal analysis and scholarship, but it is also applicable for examining race and representation in television and other media. In a neo-racial society, racial inequities still exist but conditions for people of color are not as bad as they once were. Moreover, Banks states that racism is not the primary cause of these inequities:

> The neo-racial approach suggests that we should no longer accord racism and colorblindness the primacy that they have long enjoyed in analyses of racial inequality. We should resist the reflexive tendency to simplistically depict contemporary controversies as yet further evidence of racism. Racial inequality persists as a consequence of a complicated interplay of historical and contemporary factors, and our analyses should reflect that complexity.[23]

Banks prefers the term "neo-racial" because it removes discussions about race from the constrictions and fantasies of colorblindness and a post-racial America. The term neo-racial is valuable for scholarship on racial representation and is useful for this chapter because it acknowledges a shift in race and representation in television. Television's neo-racial phase is marked by the rise of a limited number of black creative figures. Using the term neo-racial acknowledges racial inequities as well as the need to examine the context surrounding these inequities.

Investigating Perry as a public creative figure thus presents another way to examine, understand, and situate media texts and paratexts especially in relation to race.[24] Perry is a valuable case study because he publicly negotiates race and his role as a black creator and executive producer in different and distinctive ways. Dyer's methodology remains a useful tool for examining current stardom/celebrity.[25] He notes that all star studies are limited; it is impossible to cover every aspect of a star's image in one study. This examination of Perry is limited to his role as a public creative figure for *HOP*. The people in control (or in this case publicly promoted as the ones in control) can reveal as much if not more than the actors about current ideologies about race in society.

To examine Perry's image, mainstream, niche, and trade publications are used. The mainstream publications include, but are not limited to, *TV Guide*, *Entertainment Weekly*, *USA Today*, and *The New York Times*. This analysis also includes African American targeted publications such as *Ebony*, *Jet*, and *Essence*. *Hollywood Reporter*, *Variety*, and *Broadcasting & Cable* are also used to provide an industry perspective on Perry as a public creative figure. I base the data accrued from how Perry represents himself (and is represented) in these publications. I also include social media forms such Tyler Perry's online message board on his website and his verified Twitter account.[26] He uses these technologies/platforms to promote *HOP* and reinforce his image as creator/executive producer. Cumulatively, the mainstream, niche, and trade publications as well as the online resources are the media texts that create Perry's image as a public creative figure.

THE TYLER PERRY WAY

Perry's image as a public creative figure is largely tied to his unprecedented entrée into television. He started as a playwright. From 1998–2004, Perry's plays generated over $50 million in ticket and merchandising sales.[27] Despite this, early television deals that Perry had with Fox and CBS fell through. Fox did not pick up his show, and Perry ended the CBS deal because the network wanted him to make too many changes.[28] Perry decided to focus on his film career. His first movie, *Diary of a Mad Black Woman* (2005), an adaptation of his play by the same name, was a financial success.[29]

For Perry, television was the next logical step: "I was onstage and the demand was so huge. I couldn't reach all the people so then I decided to do film and that demand was even larger so I said 'How can I get a Tyler Perry type story to a bigger audience?"[30] Although he had received media attention from his films, his transition to television received more attention because he did not follow the traditional routine of getting a television show on the air. Instead of pitching *HOP* to a broadcast network or cable channel, Perry used his own money to produce ten episodes, which he gave away for free to broadcast stations for a trial run in 2005 and 2006.[31] This unprecedented move is part of his image formation as a public creative figure. For Perry, the role of public creative figure goes beyond perceptions of being in control of the narrative direction of the show and key decisions behind the scenes. He was willing to take a financial risk in self-financing *HOP* because he believed that the show would be successful. Instead of waiting for a network or cable executive to green-light the show, he took the series directly to the audience. Perry received a lot of media attention because self-financing a television series for syndication was unheard of in the television industry at the time.[32] Perry's innovative strategy resulted in a deal with TBS, which has been described as groundbreaking and "one of the most unique business models in TV today."[33] Traditionally, cable and broadcast networks order thirteen to twenty-two episodes of a new series with the hopes that the show will be successful enough to make it several seasons and reach one hundred episodes, generally considered enough for syndication.[34] TBS paid Perry $200 million for an upfront commitment of one hundred episodes, and he delivered all of them in less than a year.[35] In addition, Perry's deal included complete ownership and creative control, which is a major component of his image as a public creative figure.[36]

"The Tyler Perry way" starts with all of his works beginning with the phrase "*Tyler Perry's.*" This practice started with his plays. He initiated it as a way to differentiate himself from other plays on the urban theater circuit and later turned it into a brand. Perry says that his name at the beginning of the title informs his fans that it is his work, with his seal of approval.[37] The Tyler Perry way can be seen in his work off-screen. Perry writes, directs, and produces most of his films and plays. For *HOP*, Perry directed the first 126 episodes and served as the executive producer.[38] Although he did not write the episodes, he retained control over the storylines and narrative direction of the series. Perry is one of the few television producers, white or black, with complete ownership and control.[39] This is emphasized throughout the discourse about him across all publications.[40]

Economics is also part of his persona as public creative figure. Throughout the discourse, Perry states that financial control enables him to have creative control. For years, Perry struggled financially before his first play was a success. He self-financed his play because he wanted to maintain his creative vision. Most articles about Perry talk about how he lived in his car at one point to finance his plays.[41] He figured out a way to create his works on a budget and maintain ownership and creative control. Perry has constructed an image of himself as a public creative figure in control. He regularly underscores the fact that he does not follow traditional business methods.[42] *HOP* was a great example. A traditional broadcast network sitcom shoots one episode a week. With *HOP* Perry shot three episodes a week. He describes how he has been able to do this:

> I can do it efficiently and at a fraction of what it costs in Hollywood because there are not 20 executives telling you 'Move the cup to the left' or 'I don't like the color of her sweater.' These are the kinds of notes they do on television shows. I go down, I look at everything. I like it. We shoot the show. I don't have all those people trying to justify their jobs.[43]

As previously discussed, CBS and Fox expressed interest in working with him but both wanted to make some changes to his series regarding religion. Religion has always been part of Perry's works, and getting rid of religious references made him uncomfortable: "Once they told me I couldn't say Jesus on television, I realized it wasn't going to work for me . . . had I compromised, whatever I did from that point forward always would have seemed like a failure to me."[44] He remained adamant about his creative vision for the series: "If it doesn't work, it's okay because I was still totally true to myself. That's what's important to me."[45] Perry's choice to put television on hold proved to be a smart decision. From 2007–2012, Perry completed 254 episodes of *HOP* and the series replaced *The Jeffersons* (1975–1985, 253 episodes) as the black-oriented sitcom with the greatest number of episodes that aired on television.[46] Its success resulted in a second series, *Meet the Browns*. TBS again ordered one hundred episodes for *MTB* after only airing ten episodes in 2009.[47]

Perry continuously reminds interviewers (and readers) that he is the one in charge of all of his projects. From 2005–2010, Perry acted in one film that was not his own; he had a cameo in *Star Trek* (2009). Perry claimed he took the acting job because the film's director, J. J. Abrams, asked him to do it. He also wanted to see if he could be on someone else's set. Perry's role was a two-day shoot, and he found it challenging not to be the one in charge: "(once) I yelled 'Cut!' on the set, and the whole room turned and looked at (Abrams). It was my fault. I was screwing up the line and I yelled 'Cut!' They all look at J. J. and J. J. has this big smile on his face."[48] This anecdote demonstrates how much control is part of Perry's image. Even Abrams knows that Perry cannot help himself; Perry is so used to being in control that it is difficult to step away from that role.

Yet one thing Perry cannot control is the color of his skin and how race is always a component of his image as a public creative figure. According to the National Association for the Advancement of Colored People (NAACP), "African Americans and other races are underrepresented in almost every aspect of the television . . . industry and have, for the most part, been denied access to any real positions of power in Hollywood."[49] The Writers Guild of America (WGA) states that as of 2009, "white males continue to dominate in both the film and television sectors."[50] Black writers make up 4.2 percent of the membership of the WGA though they are 13.1 percent of the US population.[51] In the 2007–2008 television season, only 7.1 percent of the executive producers, 6.4 percent of the co-executive producers, and 27.3 percent of staff writers were minorities.[52] African Americans make up only a portion of these small figures.[53] Also, the limited number of successful African Americans in

positions of power behind the scenes intensifies Perry's discourse as a black
public creative figure.

BLACK POWER

Perry's audience makes race a central component to his image as a black
public creative figure. His works are designed for an underserved audience: faith-based urban viewers. Audience demographics, specifically
black viewers, are tied more to Perry's image as a black public creative
figure than other black public creative figures.[54] This also means that Perry
receives more criticism about his works, especially regarding representations of African Americans.[55] Perry has been struggling with this line of
criticism since starting on the urban theater circuit. He defends himself by
saying that the characters he creates are based off people he has known.
Perry states that the critics "(don't) bother me. There's a clear division. . .
. Either you get it and understand the purpose of it or you don't. The intent
of the whole thing is to make someone feel better."[56] He also does not let
the critics change his vision. He tells interviewers (and notes in messages
on his website) that he is only accountable to his fans; they let him know
via his online message board how he is doing. For Perry, his goal as a public creative figure is to create works that speak to his very specific group
of dedicated fans. He acknowledges that his works are for his fans and
they respond well to his works, which can be seen by looking at audience
ratings, box office receipts, or merchandise sales.

Perry used his power as a black public creative figure to increase diversity
onscreen and off-screen. He openly discussed the lack of opportunity for African Americans in the industry: "black people can't get work now in Hollywood. You can't get a movie, can't get a television show."[57] As a key creative
figure, Perry's control behind the scenes allowed him to create *HOP* his way.
HOP is a black-oriented sitcom, but Perry calls it a dramedy. He said he had
to do this because "it's so difficult for African American people to have a
drama on television. It's rarely happened before, so where else do you put it?
Until I get into a position where I can have a complete drama, then I'll keep
mixing [the genres] together."[58] Perry also hired two actors from his plays,
LaVan Davis and Cassi Davis (no relation), to play Curtis and Ella Payne. His
discussion of both actors reinforces his image a black public creative figure:
"I really am especially happy for Cassi and LaVan who had been knocking
on doors for years trying to get a job in Hollywood. As talented as they are
nobody would hire them. Now look at them!"[59] The success of *HOP* resulted
in Perry creating a spin-off, *Meet the Browns*, which also features a mostly
African American cast.

In addition to increasing African American representation onscreen, Perry has been successful in adding diversity off-screen. In 2008, Perry opened Tyler Perry Studios (TPS) in Atlanta to accommodate his increasing number of film and television productions. TPS was the first African American–owned film and television studio in the United States and employs over 300 people in Atlanta, Georgia.[60] According to *Entertainment Weekly*, Perry's studio is the top employer of black actors in Hollywood.[61] Perry says he uses television to continue the work he has done in film in increasing diversity onscreen. He makes movies because:

> I look at movies where there are no African Americans at all and I go 'Where in the world is this place where there are no black people?' I want . . . people who have been ignored by Hollywood for years to get great entertainment that they can share with their families.[62]

For Perry, his job as a public creative figure always goes back to his fans, who he feels are the most important critics. He unabashedly creates projects that appeal to his loyal urban faith-based audience.

A MESSAGE FROM TYLER PERRY

On his website, Perry posts messages to fans, which they can also receive directly via e-mail. Although it impossible to know if Perry actually wrote these messages, they are constructed as if he is sending his fans a direct and personal message, which reinforces his persona as a public creative figure in control. In interviews and in messages sent to fans, Perry claims that he reads all of the messages that fans post on his website and their feedback is more important than any critic or executive.[63] In most messages, he thanks fans for their loyalty and mentions that he reads their messages. In his messages about *HOP*, he told fans to tune in because of the storylines. For example, on August 5, 2008, he warned fans about the intensity of the upcoming 100th episode: "You'll be blowing up the message boards. I know it. I'll be online tomorrow as I'm watching to see what you have to say about it."[64]

Perry makes sure his fans know that he is appreciative of their loyalty and he continues to deliver projects for them. For example, Perry wrote to fans before the release of *Madea Goes to Jail* (2009):

> Everyone who has seen this says it's the best "Madea" movie I've done. I'll let you be the judge of that. I'm sure you will be on the message board letting me know what you thought . . . Because you all have showed up in record numbers on the first weekend, I have been able to keep making movies our way- - the way we want to see them.[65]

Perry makes his fans feel as if they are part of the Tyler Perry team by using the words "we" and "our." The emphasis Perry places on reading his messages reinforces his image. He knows his fans have made him a success, which provided him with the financial resources to be a key creative figure with control. Perry emphasizes that he *is* the one reading his messages because his fans are too important to assign the task to an assistant or employee, which reinforces his persona as public creative figure who controls every detail. He talks about the loyalty of his audience, and he repays that loyalty by treating them as important people in his life in interviews and in messages on his website. He closes messages with phrases such as "Yo Boy," "Love ya," "Thanks again," "Talk to you soon," and "You know how to get me."[66]

Perry continues this intimacy and informality throughout all of the personal messages that he sends directly to his fans. He claims he sends such notes in order to show how he is like them. Perry overcame personal, emotional, physical, and financial challenges in his life. He uses these personal stories throughout his discourse to show that it is possible to overcome obstacles. For Perry, he has been able to thrive and succeed because of his faith in God. He uses his plays, films, television shows, and messages to fans to demonstrate his faith. For Perry, he has been a successful public creative figure because of his faith and his fans, who also share similar religious beliefs.

Perry started a Twitter account in August 2009, but most of the posts on Twitter refer to messages on his website or for posting information about upcoming radio and television interviews. However, he has slowly started to use Twitter to make more connections with his fans. Twitter provides fans with immediate access to Perry. This points to the limitations of his message board. Although fans know he constantly reads messages posted on the board, they do not know when or what time he will post. Also, although they can post messages, they cannot post replies to specific messages posted. As of October 2013, 1,886,488 people have posted messages to Perry.[67] Yet Perry continuously emphasizes in his discourse as public creative figure that he reads *all* of the messages posted on his website. He uses Twitter as an outlet to reinforce this as part of his persona: "I've been reading all of my messages. I'm glad you all love the movie! I do too."[68] Twitter provides Perry with the capability to send short, quick messages to fans to let them know personal details about his life (going to the gym or feeling ill) as well as information about his plays, television shows, and movies.

THE BLACK CREATIVE PUBLIC FIGURE

Although I have examined Perry's discourse as a black public creative figure, he does not operate in isolation. As the creator and executive producer, he has some control over the images and the narratives presented onscreen, but this is control that exists within larger institutional and cultural constraints. Rather, he works in an industry in which positions of power are dominated by whites. Perry's presence on basic cable, meanwhile, provides him with an image of having complete creative control. This is because basic cable is not held to the same scheduling pressures and business demands placed on the broadcast networks. An additional industrial limitation that is part of his persona is diversity. The lack of diversity within the television industry foregrounds race as part of Perry's image as public creative figure. Although it does not come up in every interview, blog, or Twitter posting, the topic is a constant in his discourse.

This also explains why there is a continued emphasis on onscreen representations. While the lack of representations of blackness onscreen is a topic of concern, it is part of a larger problem, which is the lack of African Americans in positions of power behind the scenes. This is why Perry is an important case study. The dominant ideology is a post-racial perspective in which race is not an issue or factor. Perry's discussions of inequities and advancements in the industry, meanwhile offer more to discussions and analyses of the role race plays in American society.[69] When it comes to race, Perry loses control in terms of the burden of representation—this is in spite of the fact that he regularly asserts his authority over his work. Because of the lack of African American public creative figures, Perry must represent the entire community. Because of the role race plays in our society and the lack of African Americans in the entertainment industry, race will continue to be a part of his images as a public creative figure. The fact that race is discussed in his discourse as a public creative figure demonstrates that we are not in a post-racial society and that race does matter when it comes to African Americans in power behind the scenes.

NOTES

1. Andy Meisler, "The Man Who Keeps 'E. R.'s' Heart Beating." *New York Times*, February 26, 1995.

2. For more information, see: Steven Prigge, *Created by . . . Inside the Minds of TV's Top Show Creators* (Los Angeles: Silman-James Press, 2005), and Alex Epstein, *Crafty TV Writing: Thinking inside the Box* (New York: Henry Holt & Co., 2006).

3. Steven Prigge interviewed Yvette Lee Bowser, creator and showrunner of *Living Single*, for his book. See Steven Prigge, *Created by . . ..* Darnell Hunt briefly discusses black showrunners and identifies Bill Cosby as the first showrunner in the conclusion of *Channeling Blackness: Studies on Television and Race in America* (New York: Oxford University Press, 2004). Kristal Zook does a great job of providing information about black creators and executive producers on Fox and UPN. See: Kristal Brent

Zook, *Color by Fox: The Fox Network and the Revolution in Black Television* (New York: Oxford University Press, 1999). Also see Gregory Adamo, *African Americans in Television Behind the Scenes* (New York: Peter Lang, 2010).

4. Roberta Pearson, "Lost in Transition: From Post-Network to Post-Television," in *Quality TV: Contemporary American Television and Beyond,* ed. Janet McCabe and Kim Akass (New York: I. B. Tauris, 2007), 239–256.

5. For more information, see: Jeremy Butler, *Star Texts: Image and Performance in Film and Television* (Detroit: Wayne State University Press,1991); Jeremy Butler, *Television: Critical Methods and Applications* (Mahwah: Lawrence Erlbaum Associates, 2002); and Steve Clements, *Showrunner: Producing Variety and Talk Shows for Television* (Los Angeles: Silman-James Press, 2004).

6. Richard Dyer, *Stars* (London: British Film Institute, 2008).

7. John Ellis, *Visible Fictions* (London: Routledge, 1982); Graeme Turner, *Understanding Celebrity* (London: Sage, 2004); and Jeremy Butler, *Star Texts.*

8. Sean Redmond and Su Holmes, *Stardom and Celebrity* (Los Angeles: Sage, 2007).

9. James Bennett and Su Holmes, "The 'Place' of Television in Celebrity Stories," *Celebrity Studies* 1–1 (2010), 65–80.

10. David Lusted, "The Glut of the Personality," in *Stardom: Industry of Desire,* Christine Gledhill, ed., (London: Routledge, 1991), 251–258.

11. Dyer, *Stars.*

12. P. David Marshall, *Celebrity and Power: Fame in Contemporary Culture* (Minneapolis: University of Minnesota Press, 1997).

13. Francesco Alberoni, "The Powerless 'Elite': Theory and Sociological Research on the Phenomenon of the Stars," in *Stardom and Celebrity: A Reader*, ed. Sean Redmond and Su Holmes (Los Angeles: Sage, 2005), 65–76.

14. Rebecca Williams, "From Beyond Control to In Control: Investigating Drew Barrymore's Feminist Agency/Authorship," in *Stardom and Celebrity: A Reader,* ed. Sean Redmond and Su Holmes (Los Angeles: Sage, 2005), 112.

15. Mary C. Beltrán, "What's at Stake in Claims of Post-Racial Media?" *Flow TV*, June 3, 2010, http://flowtv.org/2010/06/whats-at-stake-in-claims-of-post-racial-media/.

16. Michael Omi and Howard Winant, *Racial Formation in the United States from the 1960s to the 1990s* (New York: Routledge, 1994).

17. Jennifer Esposito, "What Does Race Have to Do With Ugly Betty? An Analysis of Privilege and Postracial(?) Representations on a Television Sitcom," *Television & New Media* 10, 6 (2009), 526.

18. Ralina L. Joseph, "'Tyra Banks Is Fat' Reading (Post-) Racism and (Post-) Feminism in the New Millennium," *Critical Studies in Media Communication* 26 (2009), 239.

19. Joseph, "Tyra Banks is Fat." 239.

20. Joseph, "Tyra Banks is Fat."

21. J. Esposito, "What Does Race Have to Do With Ugly Betty?"

22. Beltrán, "What's at Stake?"

23. Ralph Banks, "Beyond Colorblindness: Neo-Racialism and the Future of Race and Law Scholarship," *Harvard Blackletter Law Journal* 25 (2009), 42.

24. Jonathan Gray describes paratexts as materials that enhance our understanding of a text. Examples of paratexts include promos, DVD extras, fan videos, merchandising, and online resources (e.g., blogs and Twitter). See *Show Sold Separately: Promos, Spoilers, and Other Media Paratexts* (New York: New York University Press, 2010).

25. Su Holmes, "'Starring . . . Dyer?': Re-visiting Star Studies and Contemporary Celebrity Culture," *Westminster Papers in Communication and Culture* 2 (2005), 6–21.

26. Perry's website is http://www.tylerperry.com.

27. Jamie Foster Brown, "Tyler Perry on Another Level." *Sister 2 Sister*, April 2006.

28. Brown, "Tyler Perry." Although Perry does not mention Fox specifically, he does mention that a network picked Cedric the Entertainer's show over his. *Cedric the Entertainer Presents* (2002–2003), directed by John Bowman, Cedric the Entertainer, and Matt Wickline, first broadcast September 18, 2002, by Fox. Also, see Gerri Hirshey, "Tyler Perry's Brand New Day." *Best Life*, April 2008.

29. Perry made *Diary* for $5 million and the film made $20 million in its opening weekend. See Margena A. Christian, "Tyler Perry: Sky Is the Limit for 'Madea' Creator with New Movie, Upcoming Book, and TV Show." *Jet*, February 27, 2006, 32–38; Margena A. Christian, "Becoming Tyler," *Ebony*, October 2008, 72–83.

30. Dana Slagle, "Tyler Perry takes on TV with new sitcom 'House of Payne,'" *Jet,* June 11, 2007.

31. Perry paid for the production and a television distribution company, Debmar-Mercury, paid for the distribution costs ($300,000). During the summer of 2005, he did a two-week test run in Houston and New York. The show was not well received but Perry believed in his series. He did a second test run in the summer of 2006 in ten cities. Those audiences responded well to the show and TBS made a deal with Perry. For more information see Christopher Lisotta, "Easing the 'Payne,'" *TelevisionWeek*, April 17, 2006; Lacey Rose and Lauren Streib, "Cash for Trash," *Forbes,* March 16, 2009.

32. Jim Benson, "Debmar-Mercury Snags 'Feud,'" *Broadcasting & Cable*, November 20, 2006, 9; John Dempsey, "Syndies Rewrite Sitcom Script," *Variety,* August 28–September 3, 2006; "Essence 25 Most Influential of 2007," *Essence,* December, 2007; Cliff Hocker, "The Lawyer," *Black Enterprise*, March 2007; Lisotta, "Easing the 'Payne'"; Denene Millner, "Perry's House Party," *Essence*, July 2007; Rupal Parekh, "How Tyler Perry's House of Hits Was Built," *Advertising Age*, May 18, 2009; Rose and Streib. "Cash for Trash."

33. Quote from A. J. Frutkin, "Payne Breaks the Mold," *MediaWeek*, May 28, 2007, 10. Also see Albiniak, "Once He Got Going, Nothing Could Stop Him." *Broadcasting & Cable*, January 26, 2009; Alex B. Block, "Tyler Perry, Inc." *Hollywood Reporter*, February 19, 2009, 24–26; Millner, "Perry's House Party."

34. Dempsey, "Syndies rewrite sitcom script," *Variety,* August 28–September 3, 2006; Hocker, "The Lawyer."

35. Frutkin, "Payne Breaks the Mold"; Lisa Helem, "The King of All Media," *Essence*, July 2006; Tim Stack, "Tyler on Top," *Entertainment Weekly*, October 26, 2007.

36. Kimberly Nordyke. "No Payne No Gain," *Black Filmmaker*, November–December 2006.

37. Nicole LaPorte, "Diary of a Mad Niche Hit," *Variety*, March 7–13, 2007; Brown, "Tyler Perry on Another Level"; Christian, "Tyler Perry: Sky Is the Limit for 'Madea' Creator"; Neil Drumming, "The Gospel According to Tyler Perry," Entertainment Weekly, March 3, 2006; Millner, "Perry's House Party."

38. Perry brought in other African American directors to help with *HOP*. Perry's replacement directors were Kim Fields, Chip Hurd, and Roger Bobb. See: IMDB, "Tyler Perry's House of Payne," accessed December 22, 2013, http://www.imdb.com/title/tt0773264/?ref_=nm_flmg_dr_12.

39. Benson, "Debmar-Mercury Snags 'Feud,'" 9.

40. See: Slagle, "Tyler Perry Takes on TV"; Jim Benson, "Syndicated Sitcom to Cable First," 34; *Broadcasting & Cable*, August 28, 2006, 34; Nordyke, "No Payne No Gain"; LaPorte, "Diary of a Mad Niche Hit"; Drumming, "The Gospel According to Tyler Perry."

41. Zondra Hughes, "How Tyler Perry Rose from Homelessness to a $5 Million Mansion." *Ebony*, January 2004.

42. Nordyke, "No Payne No Gain."

43. Margena A. Christian, "Becoming Tyler."

44. Albiniak, "Once He Got Going, Nothing Could Stop Him."

45. Helem, "The King of All Media."

46. There were 215 episodes of *Family Matters* (1989–1998), directed by William Bickley and Michael Warren, first broadcast September 22, 1989, by CBS and 201 of *The Cosby Show* (1984–1992), directed by Bill Cosby, Micheal Leeson, and Ed Weinberger, first broadcast September 20, 1984, by NBC.

47. *Meet the Browns* (directed by Tyler Perry, first broadcast January 7, 2009, by TBS) ended its 140-episode run on TBS in November 2011.

48. Matthew Belloni and Stephen Galloway, "Q&A: Tyler Perry," *Hollywood Reporter*, 2009, http://www.hollywoodreporter.com.

49. NAACP, *Out of Focus–Out of Sync Take 4* (Hollywood: NAACP Hollywood Bureau, 2008), 38. In 2006, the minority population in the United States was 100.7 million. Hispanics are the largest minority group in the United States at 44.3 million; blacks are the second largest at 40.2 million. African Americans make up 13.4% of the US population. For more information see Robert Bernstein, "Minority Population Tops 100 Million," 2007, http://www.census.gov/Press-Release/www/releases/archives/population/010048.html; Dana Slagle, "Minority Population in U.S. Peaks at 100 Million," *Jet*, June 4, 2007.

50. "The 2009 Hollywood Writers Report," *WGA*, 2009, http://www.wga.org/uploadedFiles/who_we_are/HWR09.pdf.

51. The WGA found that number of black writers decreased 15.8 percent from 2003–2007. "USA Quick Facts," *United States Census Bureau*, http://quickfacts.census.gov/qfd/states/00000.html.

52. The WGA classifies African Americans, Hispanics, Asians, and Native Americans as minorities. For more information see: "The 2009 Hollywood Writers Report," *WGA, 2009*, http://www.wga.org/uploadedFiles/who_we_are/HWR09.pdf.

53. In the statistics provided, African Americans are only a portion of that small figure that also includes Asians, Latinos, and Native Americans.

54. For example, Shonda Rhimes does not receive the same amount of criticism as Perry for representations of African Americans in her television shows. See Danielle E. Williams, "Black Public Creative Figures in the Neo-Racial Moment: An Analysis of Tyra Banks, Tyler Perry and Shonda Rhimes, 2005–2010," *Communication Dissertations* (2012).

55. For more information see Robert Bianco, "House of Payne: It Hurts to Watch," *USA Today*, June 5, 2007; Brown, "Tyler Perry on Another Level"; Richard Corliss, "God and Tyler Perry vs. Hollywood," *Time*, March 20, 2008; Stanley Crouch, "Why We Line up for Tyler Perry," *Tulsa World*, April 12, 2008; Curt Holtman, "Tyler Perry Doesn't Need You," *Creative Loafing*, April 7–13, 2011; Hughes, "How Tyler Perry Rose From Homelessness"; Rose and Streib, "Cash for Trash"; Benjamin Svetkey, Margeaux Watson, and Alynda Wheat, "How Do You Solve a Problem Like Madea?" *Entertainment Weekly*, March 20, 2009.

56. Hirshey, "Tyler Perry's Brand New Day."

57. Belloni and Galloway, "Q&A: Tyler Perry."

58. Tim Stack, "Rocking the 'House." *Entertainment Weekly,* June 22, 2007.

59. Tyler Perry, "A Message from Tyler Perry," *Tylerperry.com*, September 23, 2008, http:www.tylerperry.com.

60. Cori Murray, "Oh What A Night," *Essence*, December 2008; Parekh, "How Tyler Perry's House of Hits Was Built." Perry was acknowledged as the first movie and television studio owned by an African American. Oprah Winfrey has a television studio but not a film studio. Harpo Studios is only for TV productions. Harpo Films is only a production company. Tim Reid used investors to build his New Millennium Studios in Virginia in 1997.

61. Svetkey, Watson, and Wheat, "How Do You Solve A Problem Like Madea?"

62. Stack, "Tyler on Top"; Felicia Lee, "Talking the Dream, Growing the Brand," *The New York Times*, June 6, 2007.

63. Hirshey, "Tyler Perry's Brand New Day"; Vicky Mabrey and Tarana Harris, "Perry Talks to 'Nightline' About His Past, Present, and Future," *Say It Black*, February 24, 2007; Stack, "Rocking the 'House; Svetkey, Watson, and Wheat, "How Do You Solve A Problem Like Madea?"

64. The number of messages Perry sends to his fans also increases for major occasions such as before and during the release of a film, opening of a play, etc. Tyler Perry, "A Message from Tyler Perry," *Twitter post*, August 5, 2008, http://www.twitter.com/tylerperry.

65. Tyler Perry, "A Message from Tyler Perry," *Twitter post,* February 18, 2009, http://www.twitter.com/tylerperry.

66. For examples see Tyler Perry, "A Message from Tyler Perry, " *Twitter post.* August 20, 2008, http://www.twitter.com/tylerperry; Tyler Perry, "A Message from

Tyler Perry," *Twitter post*, May 4, 2009; Tyler Perry," "Tour/Haiti/New Movie! A Message from Tyler Perry," *Twitter post*, February 2, 2010.

67. For more information see TylerPerry.com, accessed January 1, 2014, http:www.tylerperry.com/talk. As of this writing, I have been unsuccessful in finding out how many people subscribe to Perry's e-mailing list. The site administrator has not responded to my e-mails. However, in March 2005, Perry had 400,000 e-mail subscribers. Gregory Kirschling, "Mad Props." *Entertainment Weekly*, March 11, 2005.

68. Tyler Perry, comment on Twitter, "I've Been Reading All My Messages. I'm Glad You All Love the Movie! I Do Too."

69. He offers a more realistic point of view in his discussions about African Americans working in the media industries. Some critics believe that Perry's on-screen representations of African Americans do not provide a realistic perspective. For more information see Williams, "Black Public Creative Figures in the Neo-Racial Moment," 39.

Chapter Seventeen

Viewing *90210* from 12203: Affluent TV Teens Inspire a Cohort of Middle-Class Women

Michelle Napierski-Prancl

As the image on the television screen comes into focus, we see a group of teenagers in designer clothing, laughing and high-fiving each other; there's even an elaborate handshake and snap between two friends. The music introduction boasts a bold repeating guitar riff accented with two claps that synchronize to a close-up of the iconic boy next door Brandon Walsh faking a double punch to his bad-boy buddy Dylan McKay. We see Donna Martin's hot-pink spandex outfit complete with exposed midriff contrast with Andrea Zuckerman's more modest attire and intellectual-looking eyeglasses. This elaborate mock photo-shoot/music video signals to the women on the sofa that it's time to settle in to their "*90210* night."

"*90210* NIGHTS"

From *Beverly Hills, 90210*'s beginning in 1990 to its end in 2000, a cohort of friends from a high school in a more middle-class ZIP code in upstate New York, watched the television drama for special gatherings of "*90210* nights." Their commitment to the *90210* franchise lasted as they followed along with the new twenty-something characters in the 1992–1999 spin off *Melrose Place*, while their commitment to each other has spanned more than a quarter century. In fact, for two members of the cohort the bond of friendship began long ago in the early 1970s when they attended preschool together. This cohort is my cohort and in this chapter I employ what Leon Anderson terms analytic auto-ethnography. As a member of this cohort and author of this chapter, my objective is to analyze and report on the importance of watching *Beverly Hills, 90210* for my high school group of friends.[1] This methodology allows me to demonstrate how Cassie, Wendy, Carol, Samantha, Rebecca, Heather, Ariel,

Joanie, and I related to *90210* both in the past and today, despite the measurable difference between our social class standing and that of the wealthy characters on the show. This chapter also explores the group dynamics formulated through many years of friendship and a common enjoyment of a television show situated in Beverly Hills, California. For the women in my 12203 ZIP code cohort, *Beverly Hills, 90210* was more than just a television show: it was a community experience. Our ritual viewing of the show together resulted in a long-lasting connection to a shared popular culture phenomenon that continues to provide a frame of reference for our group.

As a sociologist, I was curious to explore the longitudinal effects that this type of community experience could have on its participants, including me. And, I wondered what would happen if my cohort gathered together once again to relive one of our old "*90210* nights." Twenty-one years after our first collective viewing, my cohort of friends from the 12203 ZIP code area reunited for a "*90210* brunch." The scheduling of a brunch instead of a "night" is indicative of our current positions in the lifecycle. We are all busy women. We have families with young children; some of us are also members of the sandwich generation, caring for both our children and our aging parents. We are all working; some of us are in the paid labor force, while others are stay-at-home mothers. Since our first "*90210* night" we have transformed from single college students to forty-something wives and mothers. As such, our schedules are more complex than a Dylan, Brandon, and Kelly love triangle. Many of us are experiencing role overload with too much to do, and some of us are experiencing role conflict where the expectation of our roles as mothers, wives, daughters, workers, and just plain human beings come in conflict with each other, as it is impossible to be in two places at once.

As a member of this 12203 cohort, and as the author of this chapter, I regularly find my roles overlapping and conflicting. For example, after leaving a printed copy of this chapter on the kitchen table so that I could edit it by hand, I returned to find it had been revised by my ten-year-old son who changed the topic of my paper from *Beverly Hills, 90210* to *Beverly Hills, Chihuahua* —a clear tribute to a popular culture reference for his generation. This is the point of our lives that we are currently immersed in, as we find that there is relatively no distinction between work and family; it's all mixed together. We try our best to balance it all, but ultimately, we could all use a little escape. Therefore, it's no surprise that despite our busy schedules, we found time to get together. However, it is quite interesting that the only common time we were able to schedule a gathering for a viewing of our all-time favorite television show, with our all-time favorite people, was on a Sunday morning for brunch. This is a time traditionally reserved in US culture for women to gather at women-centered events such as bridal and baby showers.

It was the summer of 2012 and Cassie had planned to travel to the 12203 region in August. Her current ZIP code is in a busy Boston suburb, and her son was looking forward to visiting his mother's hometown to attend the county fair. So this group of high school friends was able to coordinate a small reunion of six women from our cohort on the Sunday morning before Cassie set off on her return trip home. Cassie, Wendy, Carol, Samantha, Rebecca, and I reunited. Unfortunately, Heather and Joanie were on vacations with their families, and Ariel had relocated to a ZIP code in Florida and was unable to attend the brunch. This occasion allowed for the unique opportunity to reflect on what the show and the characters meant to us as young adults and again, what they mean to us today as forty-something "grown-ups."

One of the first findings that surfaced from this study was the acknowledgement that my friends from our 12203 cohort still hold a strong affection for *Beverly Hills, 90210.* And, so do many Americans: just consider the 2012 back-to-school advertising campaign for Old Navy that reunited four original cast members of *Beverly Hills, 90210.* The nostalgic commercial tributes to the show were fun and fashionable and included inside jokes that only the fans of *Beverly Hills, 90210* would recognize. Little did I know that right before I was to approach my cohort about this project, the Old Navy *Beverly Hills, 90210* commercials would start airing. With a simple text from another member of the cohort, enthusiastically alerting me to the Old Navy commercials, I knew I was on to something important.

Coincidentally, at the same time Old Navy was airing its commercials, Shannen Doherty, who played Brenda Walsh, began appearing in a much less prestigious ad campaign as a pitch woman for Education Connection. All of these advertisements helped to bring the cast back into the spotlight and it was not long before a classic *Beverly Hills, 90210* storyline developed. Pictures from behind the scenes at the filming of the Old Navy commercials emerged on the internet along with rumors that Kelly and Dylan were back together, because in real life Jennie Garth and Luke Perry were dating. The story was fabricated but it brought the *Beverly Hills, 90210* cast back into America's collective consciousness; only a few weeks later Jennie Garth appeared on the October 15, 2012, cover of *People Magazine* showcasing her new post-divorce body. All of this is evidence that points to the fact that *90210* is still relevant, even beyond my cohort of friends. In fact, a revival program with the same ZIP code but much younger stars premiered in 2008 on The CW Network and is further evidence that viewers are still interested in what happens at West Beverly High.

Like Jennie Garth and the other actors of *Beverly Hills, 90210,* the 12203 cohort of friends has endured many of the challenges and celebrations that life brings. Among the 12203 cohort there were dating dilemmas and then marriages, and there were babies, lots of babies. There have been health crises and special needs, and everyone has suffered loss. And of course, there been moves to other ZIP codes including ZIP codes in New York, Florida, Massachusetts, and Tennessee. Over time and place our friendships have endured. Occasionally, we have relived our connections to our favorite *Beverly Hills, 90210* stars when the actors end up on other programs or reality shows. At the beginning of the reunion brunch, Wendy asked if anyone had seen the new *American Girl* movie because Steve Sanders, aka Ian Ziering, played the father. Samantha revealed that she cheered on, and even phoned in votes for, Ziering and Garth when they competed on *Dancing with the Stars*. And admittedly, we all watched our fair share of the Lifetime and Hallmark Channel movies starring former *Beverly Hills, 90210* actors.

When we gathered, we began just like we did twenty-one years ago with food and conversation. Everyone checked in with each other, and then we settled down into the comfy couches and watched *Beverly Hills, 90210,* as a collective once more. We decided to watch one of our favorite episodes, "Something in the Air" from Season 3. This episode depicted the controversy that followed after Donna drank a couple of glasses of champagne at a pre-prom party hosted by David's father, Dr. Mel Silver. Donna's subsequent intoxicated behavior at the prom resulted in her being banned from graduation. Our episode began with Donna being reprimanded by the school administration and climaxes with her friends and classmates rallying behind her at the school board hearing and cheering: "Donna Martin Graduates!"[2]

Certainly the episode chosen influenced our responses and reactions. Had we watched an episode from Season 3 about gang violence at a neighboring school,[3] or from Season 4 depicting David as a crystal meth addict,[4] our conversations would have been very different. If we watched an episode from Season 5 depicting Donna's relationship with Ray, a working class guy, we would have talked extensively about the abuse that occurs towards the end of their relationship.[5] As a critical sociologist, I would have acknowledged the importance of the television series addressing intimate partner violence among young couples, but I would have also been critical of the decision to portray the working-class male as the perpetuator of the violence in this affluent ZIP code when the writers could have taken the opportunity to debunk stereotypes and show that domestic violence is perpetuated by the wealthy, as much as any other socioeconomic group. But the episode we seemed to hold most dear in our collective memories about *Beverly Hills, 90210* was the "Donna Martin Graduates!" episode.

The banter began the moment I unwrapped Disc 4 from the *Beverly Hills, 90210's* Season 3 DVD set. I put it in the DVD player and in an instant the anti-piracy warning popped up on the screen in Spanish. My friends began to laugh. "Did you totally buy a Spanish *90210*? That's hilarious!" teased Cassie. Wendy started laughing and said, "I'll never know what's going on." Samantha responded, "Yes, you will, this isn't rocket science, it's *90210*." Meanwhile, Rebecca and Carol sat quietly on each end of the couch laughing and shaking their heads. I, on the other hand, was worried that I had made a terrible error and purchased a DVD that would require subtitles. But then, I laughed at myself as well. Most importantly, I remembered that the whole point of the "*90210* nights" of the past was the same as it was today; it was about the people sitting on the sofa watching the program together, more than it was about the show itself.

To my relief, the DVD I purchased turned out to be an English language version after all. Soon after the program began, the conversation shifted from whether or not we should watch an episode in Spanish, to the ridiculous fashion, hairdos, and technology on the show that we once thought were trendy and cutting edge. Not surprising, much has changed in fashion and technology and it was fun to see how so many things we thought were symbolic of "the good life" are now the subject of the cohort's sarcasm. "Is that a cordless phone? Look at it, it's huge," said Wendy.

BEVERLY HILLS, 90210

At 9:00 p.m. on Thursday, October 4, 1990, America was first introduced to Brenda and Brandon Walsh, twins from Minnesota who relocated to Beverly Hills with their parents, Jim and Cindy. Through their fresh eyes we met the beautiful students of West Beverly High School. On the first day of school, Brenda befriends Kelly Taylor, who is best described as the popular girl and who we learn within the first few minutes of the show has returned from summer vacation with a new look, in fact, a new nose. This serendipitous encounter occurs in a classic popular girl avoids unpopular girl move. Seeing that an obviously less attractive, less popular student is about to approach her and ask to be her lab partner, Kelly Taylor calls to the new girl entering the classroom, Brenda Walsh. She invites Brenda to sit with her in science class, and the unpopular girl is forced to look for another lab partner. While Brenda is reaping the benefits of good timing, Brandon is making friends as well. It's not long before he meets over-achiever Andrea Zuckerman, the editor of the school paper, and party boy Steve Sanders, who drives a Corvette with the vanity license plate: I8A4RE (translation: I ate a Ferrari). Despite their best efforts to make their own friends, Brenda's and Brandon's new peer groups are instantly bonded when we learn Kelly Taylor and Steve Sanders used to be a couple. Donna Martin, a member of Kelly's popular crowd, and David

Silver, a freshman desperately trying to fit in, are also introduced to us in the first episode.[6] In the second episode we meet Dylan McKay, the beautiful bad boy.[7] And thus the stage is set for drama to play out among eight high school friends in Beverly Hills, California.

At four years old, Fox was a new television network looking for a way to compete with the big three networks: ABC, CBS, and NBC. At first, *Beverly Hills, 90210* made little impact. Adult viewers were not interested in watching the ways teenage angst played out at West Beverly High. However, American teenage viewers were very interested in the growing pains of affluent high school students. In fact, within the first season Fox found that 40 percent of twelve and seventeen year olds were watching *Beverly Hills, 90210* on Thursday nights.[8] As a young network, Fox was also well positioned to try fresh strategies, and one of their most innovative scheduling decisions involved airing new episodes of *Beverly Hills, 90210* during the summers of 1991 and 1992.[9] Fox took a gamble and won. The new summer episodes of *Beverly Hills, 90210* competed only with reruns on the three big networks, and as a result new viewers like us, tuned in.[10] How could we resist? The first episode of Season 2 airing on July 11, 1991, was titled "Beach Blanket Brandon." This episode was chock full of everything young female viewers craved: pregnancy scares, teenage break-ups, outraged parents, and a glamorous beach club setting.[11] In the following summer the episode titled "The Twins, the Trustee, and the Very Big Trip" revolved around Jim and Cindy Walsh's elaborate plan to send Brenda off to Paris with her friend Donna Martin, in an odd attempt to keep her from dating Dylan.[12] This unlikely scenario allowed the producers to transport us beyond even the glamour of Beverly Hills to the excitement of the City of Lights. However, there was more for us to love than the lavish location. The following week's episode revealed to us what happens when both Brenda's boyfriend and best friend miss her: they keep each other company. Brenda's absence sets the stage for a very juicy love triangle and along with millions of other viewers, we watched as a summer romance bloomed between Dylan and Kelly.[13]

Fox's summer episode strategy translated into ratings success. In 1991, the summer our cohort started watching together, an estimated ten million other households were also doing the same thing.[14] At the height of its popularity, *Beverly Hills, 90210* boasted an audience as large as thirteen million households.[15] Unfortunately, the success of the show also had real-life consequences and in the summer of 1991 more than twenty young people were hospitalized after a mob of 10,000 screaming fans stormed a shopping mall in Florida for a glimpse of Luke Perry, aka Dylan McKay.[16]

Beverly Hills, 90210 was a relatively well-received and recognized show. Not surprisingly, it won the 1992 People's Choice Award for favorite television series among young people, and Jennie Garth, who played Kelly Taylor, was nominated for a Teen Choice Award in 1999.[17] Early in the show's tenure, Jennie Garth and Brian Austin Green, who played David Silver, along with Douglas Emerson, who played Scott Scanlon, each won a Young Artist Award.[18] Tori Spelling and Shannen Doherty were also nominated for a Young Artist Award for their portrayals of Donna Martin and Brenda Walsh.[19] The show has also been recognized beyond its teenage audience and youthful actors; both the show and Jason Priestly who played Brandon Walsh, were twice nominated for a Golden Globe: *Beverly Hills, 90210* for best television series drama, and Priestly, for best actor in a television series.[20] Milton Berle was nominated for an Emmy for Outstanding Guest Actor in a drama series for his 1995 portrayal of Saul Howard, a man suffering with Alzheimer's disease, in the episode "Sentenced to Life."[21] And since the series finale, *Beverly Hills, 90210* has been nominated for variety of fun TV Land Awards such as Favorite Teen Dream: Luke Perry, and Favorite Greasy Spoon: The Peach Pit.[22] The program was even recognized when the sideburns of *Beverly Hills, 90210* made it on *Entertainment Weekly's* 50 Pop Culture Moments that Rocked Fashion.[23] These accolades illustrate that the show is well situated in my cohort's popular culture history. When references to The Peach Pit or sideburns are made I feel nostalgic, but more importantly, I feel an appreciation for the time I spent watching the show with my friends.

The plots of *Beverly Hills, 90210* covered a plethora of topics including realistic and mundane storylines such as Brenda repeatedly failing her driver's license road test[24] and slumber parties gone awry.[25] However, the evening soap opera genre also allowed for some more far-fetched storylines. In Season 3, Dylan's father, Jack McKay, is killed in a mafia-orchestrated car bomb.[26] In Season 4, David played keyboards for R&B singer/songwriter Kenneth "Babyface" Edmunds and Brandon met President Clinton.[27] Several episodes in Season 5 were dedicated to following controversial cult-like psychology professor Patrick Finley.[28] During this same season, Kelly modeled for the cover of *Seventeen* magazine,[29] and Dylan learned of his past life in the Wild West through hypnotic regression.[30] In Season 6 Donna was on the Rose Bowl court,[31] NFL quarterback Steve Young stopped by the Walsh's house on Thanksgiving,[32] and a young woman from rehab attempted to assume Kelly's identity.[33] A standard storyline for many soap operas is amnesia and in this regard, *Beverly Hills, 90210* did not disappoint: in Season 8, Kelly suffered from this condition after being shot in a drive-by shooting.[34]

Although the program had its fair share of improbable storylines, *Beverly Hills, 90210* mostly addressed topics that were relevant to teenagers and young adults. I asked my friends what social issues they remembered from *Beverly Hills, 90210* and without hesitation, Carol, Rebecca, and Cassie said in unison, "sex." From the onset, the program addressed the one universal issue of importance to young people: sex. One of the very first episodes of the inaugural season was entitled "The First Time," and as such, dealt with teen sex.[35] Sheryl, Brandon's girlfriend from Minnesota, traveled to Beverly Hills for a visit, and although Cindy Walsh, Brandon's mother, arranged for Sheryl to sleep on a cot in Brenda's room, during the middle of the night Sheryl quietly made her way through the doors of the adjoining bathroom to Brandon's bedroom. Interestingly, this was not Sheryl's "first time," but it was Brandon's. During the course of the evening the viewer sees Brandon's mother lying awake in bed anxiously listening for signs of inappropriate behavior from her son's bedroom. In the morning, it is obvious to the entire family that Brandon is a "new man," as indicated by his robust disposition and Glenn Miller's "In the Mood" playing loudly on his stereo. Cindy is concerned and asks her husband, Jim, who seems to be approving of his son's actions more so than he is concerned with them, to have a talk with Brandon. The episode ends with father and son playing basketball in the driveway. Through jump shots and dribbling, Jim talks to Brandon about love and broken hearts. However, the storyline plays out very differently later on when Jim believes his daughter Brenda and her boyfriend Dylan are sexually active. The sexual double standard is clearly depicted over the course of several episodes, and Brenda's relationship with Dylan proves to be a source of great tension between her and her parents.

Beverly Hills, 90210 taught our cohort a lot about teen love and romance, but today the effect of the lessons learned have been informed with time and life experience. Rebecca told us that in the past she was attracted to Dylan because he was cool but today, "I'd probably go for Brandon, the good guy." This change in perspective and attraction is likely due to the fact that Rebecca chose to marry a "good guy." Dylan was cool because he challenged the status quo but Brandon was now appealing because he played by the rules. Dylan was more desirable to Rebecca when she was younger and childless but today, as a wife and mother, she would rather see herself with Brandon, who would likely have a stable job and coach Little League.

Beverly Hills, 90210 dealt with a variety of other difficult issues beyond sex, including but not limited to: animal rights, AIDS, cancer, drunk driving, drug addiction, gun control, homelessness, prostitution, racism, rape, stalking, and unplanned pregnancy, which all played out within the affluent 90210 ZIP code. It was not necessarily that *90210* taught us anything new, or that it sugarcoated issues with glitz and glamour; instead it legitimated the issues that were important to our cohort as young adults, and it validated our reality. The stories were not always perfect as one study critiqued *Beverly Hills, 90210* for its well-meaning but stereotypical representation of a character with AIDS.[36]

In the very least, the show superficially addressed topics relevant to the times, which would then help us to initiate our own deeper conversations when we gathered together for "*90210* nights."

COLLECTIVE VIEWING

Fox's strategy for summer programming clearly worked for its ratings, and the summer programming also worked for our 12203 cohort. The timing was right as our cohort spent the summers of 1991 and 1992 back in the 12203 area, home from college, and enjoying the summer. *Beverly Hills, 90210* aired at an important juncture in our lives; we were recent high school graduates on our own, taking new and different pathways, but still tied to one another through a shared high school experience and a common attraction to a Fox television show about affluent teenagers. It took just one member of the cohort to get the rest of the group hooked on the show. Wendy was the first to identify as a fan of the show, and she was the first to host a "*90210* night" in the summer of 1991. In fact, she hosted most nights. Wendy's house was *the* house we went to in high school: welcoming parents, comfy couches, pool table in the basement, swimming pool in the backyard, and of course endless bowls of fresh-popped popcorn. We gathered at Wendy's house throughout high school: before the homecoming game, after prom, for my sweet sixteen, and it was the location we all assembled to celebrate Wendy's marriage a decade later. The "*90210* nights" allowed our group to continue our high school tradition of gathering at Wendy's house for an extended period of time after we graduated from high school.

At about the same time that the women in my 12203 ZIP code cohort were gathering together to enjoy *Beverly Hills, 90210*, Andrea Press was conducting research on the very topic of women watching television. She knew that there was something important about the process and experiences of women watching television, especially when women watched it together, and she directed her scholarly attention to this phenomenon. Her research explored women's experiences with a variety of different programs from dramas such as *Dallas*, to situation comedies such as *The Cosby Show*, and many of her findings are applicable to this cohort of women from 12203. Specifically, Press found that for young women, television watching was a collective experience that allowed them the opportunity to connect with family and friends.[37] E. Graham McKinley studied young women and girls who specifically watched *Beverly Hills, 90210* and these results also highlight the importance of collective viewing. McKinley found that instead of watching the show alone or with just a roommate, women in college would gather in each other's dormitory room or common area to watch the show together. Similarly, it was not unusual for younger viewers to watch the program while talking on the telephone with a peer.[38]

Like the young women in Press's study, the women in my 12203 cohort were born and raised in homes where television sets were prominent fixtures. And for our cohort, the timing was also such that *The Love Boat* (1977–1987), *Charlie's Angels* (1976–1981), *Dynasty* (1981–1989), and other Aaron Spelling programs aired on the television screens in our living rooms when we were growing up. When *Charlie's Angels* premiered we were just six years old, but by the time *Dynasty* ended in 1989, we were nineteen years old. We were familiar with, and sometimes watched these shows, but it was clear that these were our parents' programs. What we did not anticipate at the time was that, like our parents, in a few years we too would make up the target audience for a similarly formatted Aaron Spelling evening soap opera that followed the lives of teenagers living in Beverly Hills, California. And like the women in Press's study, our cohort from the 12203 ZIP code would find ourselves building community as we gathered together for "*90210* nights."

Press and McKinley were not the first scholars to devote attention to women's consumption of media products. In fact, they, as well as Naomi Rockler built upon the earlier research of Janice Radway.[39] Radway argued that women's engagement with media could be construed as a political act. She found that women who read romance novels engaged in the activity as a form of escape. By reading romance novels women would not only lose themselves in a fantasy love story, but perhaps more importantly, they would escape from the pressures of the "real" world through the simple act of reading.[40] Both McKinley's[41] and Rockler's[42] research focused specifically on women and girls who watched *Beverly Hills, 90210*. The parallels between my 12203 cohort in this study and the viewers in McKinley's and Rockler's samples are plentiful. Like readers of romance fiction, the fans of *Beverly Hills, 90210* whether in McKinley's, Rockler's, or this 12203 cohort, tell us that *Beverly Hills, 90210*, served as a form of enjoyment and escape. For my cohort, *90210* provided a departure from what we thought was a mundane middle-class suburban life in Upstate New York. Carol said, "Watching *90210* was like taking a vacation to the beach." In Beverly Hills the temperature rarely dips below fifty degrees while in Albany, New York, one can expect monthly average low temperatures to be less than sixty degrees ten months out of the year.[43] Thus, the television program depicting affluence and sunshine had a strong appeal for those of us from the 12203 ZIP code. Cassie was enchanted by the architectural design of West Beverly High School. "We went to high school indoors; in a brick building. The kids at West Beverly spent most of their school day sitting outside in the courtyard. They ate lunch under palm trees on beautiful sunny days." In essence, we lived vicariously through the characters of Brenda and Brandon who left snowy Minnesota for the sunny 90210 ZIP code.

McKinley's respondents reported adjusting their work and school schedules, turning off the ringer on their telephones, and even renegotiating evening shower times with siblings in an effort to protect the timeslot dedicated to viewing *Beverly Hills, 90210*.[44] We did this too but for our cohort it was about more than just protecting our time to watch the program, it was also about preserving the luxury of being with each other. We could depend on *Beverly Hills, 90210* to physically bring us together for an hour once a week, and as a result we were able to stay engaged in one another's lives at a time when we were moving in many different directions. Paradoxically, watching *90210* simultaneously transported us away from our 12203 ZIP code while also firmly attaching us to our 12203 roots.

The college-aged women in Rockler's study identified themselves as frequent viewers of *Beverly Hills, 90210,* yet also reported that they were critical of the show.[45] They found the portrayal of beauty and wealth to be too unbelievable and indicated that they watched the show for entertainment purposes only. The women also stated that they were not concerned about the potential negative impact the images of unattainable wealth and beauty ideals could have because the show's portrayal was too unrealistic to be believed. However, a study by Anne E. Becker and her colleagues raised concerns for the possible link between Western televisions shows such as *Beverly Hills, 90210* and the introduction of eating disorders in Fiji.[46] My cohort recognized the level of fantasy portrayed in *90210,* but we were not critical of it because we enjoyed the glamour of it. Even though the show was unrealistic, we found it visually appealing and we delighted in viewing the indulgent lifestyles of the characters. *90210* provided a picture perfect postcard look at what life was like on the West Coast and we consumed it. We embraced *Beverly Hills, 90210* for being fashion forward and providing a glimpse into the trends that would be soon making their way to the East Coast. Samantha emphasized that it was fun to see the newest styles and even though there were discernible differences between her bank account and the characters' credit lines, she said she enjoyed it because "it was like a fashion show." *Beverly Hills, 90210* incorporated many symbols of affluence into the episodes and as a group we admitted that we wanted to dress like Kelly and Donna, and own the same cars as Steve and Dylan. In some ways, we were able to mimic their style but we could never afford to do so completely; while we may have had cordless phones in our homes, none of us owned a Corvette in high school.

We could not imitate all the trends but we could purchase less expensive versions of the clothing and accessories we saw on the program. In this way we could relate to *Beverly Hills, 90210* because it was similar to a place where we spent much of our free time when we were younger: the shopping mall. Cassie said "watching the show was like watching high school play out in a mall. Everyone was pretty, the clothes were all new, and price was no object." For my cohort, the shopping mall in our town served as an active community space for young adults. We spent our leisure time and even our work time in the mall. Samantha, Joanie, Wendy, and I each worked at the shopping mall in our town at one time or another. And on our days off, we would go back to the mall to see a movie, to try on clothes, to eat in the food court, and of course, to shop. Kelly and Donna may have had Rodeo Drive, but we had the mall.

THE *90210* EFFECT

The effect of *90210* on my cohort was twofold. The most obvious effect was that we could relate to, envy, and even show empathy for the characters on the television program. We each had our own favorite characters and during our "*90210* brunch" I ask a general question: "who was your favorite character?" Without hesitation, Cassie replied, "Dylan." But Carol indicated that she liked Brandon and thought Dylan was too sulky and overacted. Carol also revealed that she did not like Andrea and thought she was annoying, which caused me to interject and defend Andrea, because I always liked her and identified a bit with her myself. Samantha liked Steve, and Carol thought David was cute. Wendy liked Brandon and Kelly, and Cassie boasted that she hated Brenda even before it was cool to hate Brenda. These comments are important because they show that even though we were watching the same show together our experiences were not necessarily the same: we found different meanings, and we identified with and liked or disliked different characters.

Interestingly, I was surprised to learn, as were my friends, that the characters that had the greatest effect on us were not the most central characters in the ensemble. It was not Dylan, Brandon, or Kelly. The characters most revered by my cohort were Jim and Cindy Walsh and Donna Martin. Jim and Cindy were not admired for their upward social mobility climb and Donna, while fashionable, was not respected for her style. These characters were most appreciated for their values and their relationships with others. Jim and Cindy Walsh were active and present in the lives of their children. Most importantly, they talked to their kids. They were also involved in the lives of their children's friends and supported them as illustrated by their attendance at Donna Martin's school board hearing. Thus, despite Jim and Cindy's traditional views about gender and their perpetuation of a sexual double standard on their twins, the members of my 12203 cohort wished their own parents were more like the Walshes.

> Rebecca: I had always wished my parents were more like Jim and Cindy. The thought of talking about sex or birth control with my parents is unimaginable.

> Samantha: I'm still waiting for my sex talk from my mom, and I've had three kids.

> Cassie: What's another show where the parents are present? In most other teen shows parents are absent from the story. I'm addicted to *The Vampire Diaries* and I noticed that very slowly the adults—parents, role models, care givers have all been killed off so literally, there are no parents. These kids are graduating from high school without parents. Of course they are vampires so they can fend for themselves . . . But I can't think of a show where the parents are such a big part the show as Jim and Cindy. You know, they're sitting on the couch, the kids come home from school and throw their keys in the bowl and say 'Dad I have to tell you about the condoms I bought yesterday.' I mean, they would, they would tell their parents everything, maybe begrudgingly, but eventually they would tell Jim and Cindy everything. You don't see that on any other show.

The fact that my cohort so endearingly reflects upon the show's portrayal of Jim and Cindy Walsh is equally interesting in terms of the past, as it is in terms of the present. In the past, we were young adults pushing for independence while our parents did their best to nurture and guide us through an awkward and often tension-filled time. Today, we are on the other side of the relationship as parents of soon-to-be adolescent children with only an inkling of what is to come. While we recognize the fictional depiction and the unlikelihood that we will be able to engage in such well-scripted dialog with our own children, we also see that the Walshes offer our cohort one model from which we can draw upon as we navigate parenthood today, and in the years to come.

In the same way Jim and Cindy portrayed a positive depiction of parents, Donna Martin represented an affirming image of a teenage girl. Donna will be perpetually remembered for her virginity. Some of my friends in our cohort did not remember that Donna was on the Rose Bowl Court or that she had a learning disability, but everyone remembered that Donna Martin was the "good girl," as the only self-proclaimed virgin on the show. Donna Martin was vocal about remaining chaste until marriage, but she was not oblivious to the fact that her friends were having sex. "I always liked that Donna was a virgin. She was a good example" said Rebecca, who went on to say,

> I still relate strongly to the episode where Donna stands up in front of the group of parents—at a PTA meeting I think. The issue was about sex ed or condoms

in school. Donna stood up and said, sex ed is like swim lessons, you might not want your kid to go swimming but if they're going to be hanging around a pool, you better teach them to swim.

"That episode always stood out for me, too," said Carol. In a teen drama with so much coupling of characters, Donna stands out because she gives credibility to the argument that not everybody is "doing it." Consider the following abbreviated inventory of couplings (See Table 17.1) that developed among the main characters over the course of the program's ten seasons:

Table 17.1.   Couples from *90210*

Kelly and Steve	Brandon and Jill	Brandon and Tracy
Brandon and Sheryl	Andrea and Dan	Donna and Cliff
Brenda and Dylan	Kelly and John	Kelly and Mark
Brandon and Melissa	Brenda and Stuart	Kelly and Tom
Brandon and Lydia	Brandon and Lucinda	David and Chloe
Brandon and Emily	Andrea and Jessie	David and Valerie
David and Donna	Steve and Laura	Steve and Carly
Kelly and Kyle	Kelly and Brandon	Brandon and Emma
Steve and Christine	Brandon and Clare	Steve and Sarah
Kelly and Jake	David and Ariel	Donna and Noah
Kelly and Dylan	Dylan and Valerie	David and Sophie
Andrea and Jay	Donna and Griffin	Kelly and Matt
Brandon and Brooke	David and Clare	Steve and Janet
Brenda and Rick	Donna and Ray	Dylan and Gina
David and Nikki	Andrea and Peter	David and Robyn
Brandon and Nikki	Kelly and Colin	Donna and Jerry
Andrea and Jordan	Dylan and Toni	David and Chrissy
Steve and Celeste	Brandon and Susan	David and Camille
Brenda and Tony	Steve and Clare	David and Donna
Steve and Jill	Donna and Joe	

There was a lot of sex and romance going on in the 90210 ZIP code. Yet, Donna's choice to practice abstinence does not negatively affect her social standing on the show. She remains popular and enjoys her fair share of boyfriends, eventually marrying her high school sweetheart, David Silver, in the series finale.[47] The lessons learned from Donna go beyond sex and abstinence to lessons about acceptance of different values and valuing different perspectives particularly among our friends. Friends do not have to always agree or share the same values in order to remain friends, and certainly this is true for our cohort.

It was not nearly as important that Donna was a virgin as it was that she was the only virgin on *Beverly Hills, 90210*. Donna stood up against peer pressure and maintained her popularity when doing so. She made it clear that she could stay true to her beliefs in the face of enormous social pressure and for the most part, her friends respected her for it. While the storyline sometimes became irritating and tired, and admittedly from time to time even I would agree with Samantha who felt "David and Donna were annoying," in general, we liked Donna. We admired her sense of self and integrity and we were even happy for her when she eventually began a sexual relationship with David at the end of Season 7.[48]

It is very revealing that for my cohort, out of all the glitz and glamour and romance portrayed in *Beverly Hills, 90210*, the character that stood out the most among all other characters was Donna Martin, and the commodity portrayed that we desired most, was the relationship Brenda and Brandon had with their parents. These feelings offer insight into our cohort's teenage years and our relationships with our own parents. Very few of us acknowledge ever having a sex talk with our parents. Most of what we learned about sex we learned from each other, from health class, and from the media. The majority of us were raised in traditional Catholic households and we were all going through puberty during the conservative Reagan/Bush era, during which time HIV/AIDS were only just being identified. Needless to say, our home environments at that time were not conducive to open talks about sex. The Walshes provided a refreshing and enlightening model of parenthood that is just as relevant for us today as it was two decades ago. Rebecca said, "My kids aren't at that age yet, but this show impacted how I relate to my nieces. I told them that as uncomfortable as it made me, I was always there for them if they had any questions about sex or if they needed anything. And it worked, they came to me."

The second *90210* effect deals directly with our relationships with each other. The evenings of collective viewing acted as a significant factor in cementing the 12203 cohort's relationships to each other and in sustaining the longevity of the group's identity. Wendy demonstrates this point clearly when she says, "I can't remember nearly as many episodes as Michelle, but I do remember having fun hanging out together watching the show." For Wendy, the connection to the memory of the gathering was more significant than the content of the show itself. The members of the cohort are also cognizant of the unique nature of their long-term friendship. Cassie explains:

> My friends from Boston, maybe they have one friend from childhood they still keep in touch with, but we're a pretty big size group of friends. We've known each other forever. No kidding, just yesterday my sister and I were looking at old pictures with my mother. There was a picture of me from the first day of school in a yellow V-neck shirt and yellow shorts. And I'd like to note that I was wearing smoking-hot tube socks with that ensemble. Anyway, my mother said she was talking to one of you ladies about that outfit at my 40th birthday party.

That was my favorite outfit in 6th grade and one of you remembered it—now
that's a long friendship.

Certainly, *90210* is not responsible for our enduring friendship but is a part
of our group's history. Watching *90210* together had an effect us. We connected with one another when we engage with the characters and the show.
We were active and collaborative viewers who would mock Brenda when
she spoke with a fake French accent while living in Paris.[49] And together, as
savvy viewers, we accurately predicted that the love connection she made in
Paris with Rick, an American citizen, would result in their path's awkwardly
crossing again, back in Beverly Hills.[50]

We were anything but passive viewers of the show, and it is clear that
Beverly Hills, 90210 was an active participant in the development of our cohort's bond. It is unlikely that we would have stayed committed to our "*90210*
nights" routine had we been watching any other show. As Samantha suggests,

> We were young when we watched the show and could relate to the trends; it
> was fun to see the West Coast trends, the clothing, the music—everything was
> trendy. There was nothing else geared toward our age group at the time; there
> were no other teen prime-time shows—it had to be the first. There's nothing
> like it today either.

Samantha is probably right, and that few other shows simultaneously targeted
a young-adult demographic and promoted collective viewing at the same
time. However, Carol posed an interesting question: "The closest show is
probably *Glee*; I wonder if there are groups of friends watching *Glee* like we
watched *90210*?" Undoubtedly, the answer is yes, and scholars are starting to
take notice. Times have changed, and the emerging research on the television
show *Glee* explores the role that social media plays in fostering collective
viewing of the program.[51]

Ironically, our 12203 cohort began watching the television drama about
high school life a couple of years after we had graduated from high school
ourselves, but that may be the very factor for why the show has had such a
firm hold on our group. The show served as a social gathering space where
we could reminisce about our high school years and argue about whether or
not something we saw on *Beverly Hills, 90210* would ever have happened at
our high school. The stories and the characters provided an opportunity for
us as young women to discuss the old days through the lens of the fictional
high school characters on the television screen. It worked to cement our connections to one another after taking our first steps on different pathways to
adulthood. We had new college friends and new interests, yet we bonded like
an early version of *American Idol* judges while we watched the characters on

Beverly Hills, 90210. McKinley's work supports this, arguing that the commentary about a character's outfit or hairstyle is more than trivial chitchat, but in fact, a type of talk which adheres together a panel of experts. McKinley also argued that it is not necessary for viewers to agree with each other in their critiques of characters' appearances or actions so much as it is that they share in a status as an expert looking in on the characters.[52] From the moment I turned on the DVD, my cohort began to judge our dear friends from West Beverly High School.

> Samantha: Look at Andrea's outfit; who is she, their mother?
>
> Cassie: I never liked Miss High-waist Jeans, No Belt, Brenda.
>
> Carol: Look at the shorts with belts.
>
> Wendy: I love the hair!
>
> Rebecca: I was going to wear a banana clip today but I couldn't find one.
>
> Cassie: 'Want to change the world? Start with the school,' said handsome, tight jeans, floppy-haired teacher. No wonder we watched the show; that teacher is cute.

Just like the women in McKinley's study, everyone in our cohort had something to say about just about everything and everyone in the show. Given the focus of the episode, Donna's mother, Felice Martin, took the brunt of negative commentary ranging from her overbearing personality, to overstuffed shoulder pads, to what Cassie termed a "shellac hair-do." Of course, looking at a television show twenty-one years later also lends itself to nostalgic and "I forgot about mock turtlenecks" type of comments, in addition to our normal commentary about characters and storylines. This type of discussion empowered the viewers in McKinley's study and for my 12203 cohort as well, particularly when our insight and predictions came true such as when we accurately predicted that Rick would eventually end up in Beverly Hills.[53]

As in the past, the episode we watched pushed our group toward a discussion about an important social issue: underage drinking. The majority of our cohort sympathized with Donna's situation. Cassie and Carol agreed that the offense was not severe enough to warrant the school's sanction of keeping her from graduating, and mandating that she enter an alcohol rehab program. Cassie went even further in her critique and argued, "I don't even think this topic warrants a sixty-minute episode. She had a glass of champagne that was served to her by an adult in a celebratory manner, and she hadn't eaten all day. If she went out and got someone to buy her alcohol, got wasted, had a history of drinking, it'd be different." Carol agreed, but Wendy on the other hand, said, "What is the message this show is sending? She broke the rules.

You're supposed to follow the rules, she should be penalized. She broke the law, it's not okay. Suffer the consequences." Within moments the whole group starts laughing because it is clear to us that time and parenthood have changed Wendy's perception of the situation. So I asked, "Wendy would you have stood up for me?" "Yes, I would have stood up for you in 1988 but today, I'm a parent and I would have said, 'you broke the law, there are consequences.' And now, I'd say Dr. Silver should be going to jail too." And with that statement everyone, including Wendy, laughs.

"DONNA MARTIN GRADUATES!"

The episode reaches its conclusion and the school board reverses it decision, and allows Donna Martin to participate in graduation ceremonies. The show ends with the gang hanging out at The Peach Pit where Brandon gives Donna her graduation gown and, without warning, our cohort of friends sitting on the sofa break out in spontaneous applause. The group laughs as we realize we are all clapping for a television show.

In 2000 when *Beverly Hills, 90210* went off the air, Eleni Gage published a love letter of sorts to the finale of *Beverly Hills, 90210* in the *New York Times*.[54] In it, she too talks about her ritual gatherings with friends to watch the show and she thanks the program for an "emotion-packed decade." This is evidence that *Beverly Hills, 90210* had a reach beyond my 12203 cohort to groups of young viewers around the country. Clearly there was something significant about watching television together, especially *Beverly Hills, 90210*. The fundamental sharing of physical space worked to nourish the relationships of those watching and discussing the show together. Cassie summed it up best:

> You know what's the same now as it was twenty years ago? We can all be sitting around watching something and all that action can be going on across the room on your TV and whether you asked a question about your study or not, we'd all have side conversations and we wouldn't pause what was on TV, we'd all just go back to the show when we were done talking and then we'd have another side conversation and so on. That's the same, that kind of interaction, the TV is part of it, the story is part of it, the characters are part of it, but they're over there and we are over here chatting and then we look and say—did you see her belt? And then we continue to watch and chat and hang out. That's part of it. And when the show's over, we go home but we know we can come back and watch TV together again and we will pick up where we left off and do it all over again. It's about us as much as it is about *90210*. Actually, it's more about us than it is about *90210*.

For our 12203 cohort, the viewing of *Beverly Hills, 90210* served multiple purposes as it worked to maintain our bond to one another after graduating high school, but it also acted as a spring board for our group to discuss current social issues that were relevant in our own lives. Despite the improbability of some of the storylines, *Beverly Hills, 90210* allowed the group to work through important issues, especially relationships, while watching the show. Most of us did not have open discussions with our parents about sex or other difficult topics, but the characters on *Beverly Hills, 90210* did. As a result, those of us watching the show in Wendy's living room elaborated on the conversations we watched play out on television. As Press's research suggests, our watching and talking about the television show with each other served as an exercise in personal problem solving.[55] And like the women in Rockler's sample,[56] our 12203 cohort enjoyed the show the most when it dealt with real-life problems and solutions.

The effect of *90210* has been long term as it serves not only as a beloved symbol of our younger days and our bond of friendship, but also as a reference point for our current position in the lifecycle. In the past we thought it was cool that Brandon had a dad who would talk to him about sex while playing basketball in the driveway. Today, we are hoping that we can have similar conversations with our own children, and if we make a three-point shot at the same time, it will be a bonus.

NOTES

1. Leon Anderson, "Analytic Autoethnography," *Journal of Contemporary Ethnography* 35 (2006), 375, doi:10.1177/0891241605280449.

2. *Beverly Hills, 90210*, "Something in the Air," directed by James Whitemore, Jr, first broadcast May 12, 1993, by Fox.

3. *Beverly Hills, 90210*, "Home and Away," directed by Jack Bender, first broadcast October 7, 1992, by Fox.

4. *Beverly Hills, 90210*, "Crunch Time," directed by Les Landau first broadcast January 5, 1994, by Fox.

5. *Beverly Hills, 90210*, "P.S. I Love You: Part 1," directed by Victor Lobl, first broadcast May 24, 1995, by Fox.

6. *Beverly Hills, 90210*, "Class of Beverly Hills," directed by Tim Hunter, first broadcast October 4, 1990, by Fox.

7. *Beverly Hills, 90210*, "The Green Room," directed by Michael Toshiyuki Uno, first broadcast October 11, 1990, by Fox.

8. Daniel M. Kimmel, *The Fourth Network: How Fox Broke the Rules and Reinvented Television* (Chicago: Ivan R. Dee, Publisher, 2004): 109.

9. Kimmel, *The Fourth Network*, 112.

10. Kimmel, *The Fourth Network*, 112.

11. *Beverly Hills, 90210*, "Beach Blanket Brandon," directed by Charles Braverman, first broadcast July 11, 1991, by Fox.

12. *Beverly Hills, 90210*, "The Twins, the Trustee, and the Very Big Trip," directed by David Carson, first broadcast July 22, 1992, by Fox.

13. *Beverly Hills, 90210*, "Shooting Star/American in Paris," directed by Daniel Attias, first broadcast August 12, 1992, by Fox.

14. The BH90210 Directory, accessed October 11, 2012, http://www.bh90210 .co.uk/ratings.

15. The BH90210 Directory.

16. "Teen Crush: TVs Luke Perry Sets 10,000 Hearts Aflutter," *People Magazine*, August 26, 1991, http://www.people.com/people/archive/article./0,,20115774,00.html

17. "Beverly Hills, 90210—Awards," IMDb.com, accessed October 18, 2012, http://www.imdb.com/title/tt0098749/awards.

18. "Beverly Hills, 90210—Awards."

19. "Beverly Hills, 90210—Awards."

20. "Beverly Hills, 90210—Awards."

21. "Beverly Hills, 90210—Awards"; *Beverly Hills, 90210,* "Sentence to Life," directed by Jack Bender, first broadcast January 4, 1995, by Fox.

22. "Beverly Hills, 90210—Awards."

23. "50 Pop Culture Moments that Rocked Fashion," *Entertainment Weekly*, June 18, 2007, http://www.ew.com/we/article/0,,2,2,7369,00.html.

24. *Beverly Hills, 90210,* "Leading from the Heart," directed by Daniel Attias, first broadcast October 10, 1991, by Fox.

25. *Beverly Hills, 90210*, "Slumber Party," directed by Charles Braverman, first broadcast January 31, 1991, by Fox.

26. *Beverly Hills, 90210.* "The Child Is Father to the Man," directed by James Whitmore Jr., first broadcast February 17, 1993, by Fox.

27. *Beverly Hills, 90210*, "Mr. Walsh Goes to Washington," directed by Michael Lange, first broadcast May 25, 1994, by Fox.

28. *Beverly Hills, 90210*, "Sweating It Out," directed by Jason Priestly, first broadcast January 11, 1995, by Fox.

29. *Beverly Hills, 90210*, "Girls on the Side," directed by Victor Lobl, first broadcast May 3, 1995, by Fox.

30. *Beverly Hills, 90210*, "The Real McCoy," directed by Jason Priestly, first broadcast May 10, 1995, by Fox.

31. *Beverly Hills, 90210*, "Everything's Coming Up Roses," directed by Victor Lobl, first broadcast September 27, 1995, by Fox.

32. *Beverly Hills, 90210*, "Breast Side Up," directed by David Semel, first broadcast November 22, 1995, by Fox.

33. *Beverly Hills, 90210*, "Strike the Match," directed by James Darren, first broadcast April 10, 1996, by Fox.

34. *Beverly Hills, 90210*, "The Way We Weren't," directed by Frank Thackery, first broadcast September 24, 1997, by Fox.

35. *Beverly Hills, 90210*, "The First Time," directed by Bethany Rooney, first broadcast October 25, 1990, by Fox.

36. Kylo-Patrick R. Hart, "Retrograde Representation: The Lone Gay White Male Dying of AIDS on *Beverly Hills, 90210,*" *The Journal of Men's Studies* 7 no. 2 (1999), 201.

37. Andrea L. Press, *Women Watching Television: Gender, Class, and Generation in the American Television Experience* (Philadelphia: University of Pennsylvania Press, 1991), 56–61.

38. E. Graham McKinley, *Beverly Hills, 90210: Television, Gender and Identity* (Philadelphia: University of Pennsylvania Press, 1997), 1; 13–14.

39. McKinley, *Beverly Hills, 90210;* Naomi R. Rockler, "From Magic Bullets to Shooting Blanks: Reality, Criticism and *Beverly Hills, 90210*," *Western Journal of Communications.* 63 no. 1 (1999), 72–94; Janice A. Radway, *Reading the Romance: Women, Patriarchy and Popular Literature* (Chapel Hill: University of North Carolina Press, 1984).

40. Radway, *Reading the Romance*, 86–118.

41. McKinley, *Beverly Hills*, *90210*, 31–47.

42. Rockler, "Magic Bullets," 83.

43. "Average Weather for Beverly Hills, CA—Temperature and Precipitation," weather.com accessed July 12, 2013, http://www.weather.com/weather/wxclim atology/monthly/graph/90210; "Average Weather for Albany, NY—Temperature and Precipitation," weather.com, accessed July 12, 2013, http://www.weather.com/ weather/wxclimatology/monthly/graph/12203.

44. McKinley, *Beverly Hills, 90210*, 13–14.

45. Rockler, "Magic Bullets," 82–84.

46. Anne E. Becker et al. "Eating Behaviors and Attitudes Following Prolonged Exposure to Television Among Ethnic Fijian Adolescent Girls," *British Journal of Psychiatry* 180 (2002), 511–512, doi:10.1192/bjp.180.6.509.

47. *Beverly Hills, 90210*, "Ode to Joy," directed by Kevin Inch, first, broadcast May 17, 2000, by Fox.

48. *Beverly Hills, 90210*, "Graduation Day: Part 1," directed by Jason Priestley, first broadcast May 21, 1997, by Fox.

49. *Beverly Hills, 90210*, "Shooting Star/American in Paris," directed by Daniel Attias, first broadcast August 12, 1992, by Fox.

50. *Beverly Hills, 90210*, "Destiny Rides Again," directed by Christopher Hibler, first broadcast November 4, 1992, by Fox.

51. Alice Marwick, Mary L. Gray, and Mike Ananny, "'Dolphins are Just Gay Sharks': *Glee* and the Queer Case of Transmedia as Text and Object," *Television & New Media* (2013): 1–22, doi:10.1177/1527476413478493; Kimra McPherson et al. "Glitter: A Mixed Methods Study of Twitter use during *Glee* Broadcasts," *Proceedings of the ACM 2012 Conference on Computer Supported Cooperative Work Companion.*(2012): 167–170, doi:10:1145/2141512.2141569.

52. McKinley, *Beverly Hills, 90210*, 68–82.

53. *Beverly Hills, 90210*, "Destiny Rides Again," directed by Christopher Hibler, first broadcast November 4, 1992, by Fox.

54. Eleni Gage, "Thank You, ZIP Code of My Dreams, for an Emotion-Packed Decade," *New York Times*, ST2, May 14, 2000, http://www.partners.nytimes.com/ library/style/weekend/051400stl-90210.html.

55. Press, *Women Watching Television*, 99–110.

56. Rockler, "Magic Bullets," 84.

Section VI

FUTURAMA

Chapter Eighteen

The Construction of Taste: Television and American Home Décor

Stylés I. Akira and Larry Ossei-Mensah

Throughout the latter half of the twentieth century, television arose as the technological successor to print and radio, becoming the central platform for the distribution of information designed for mass public consumption. The manipulation and gatekeeping of that information has been a controversial issue for many scholars who proclaim that media (especially since the advent of television) has been the testing grounds for an elitist class of capitalists who seek to dominate the social order through the tacit dispensation of ideology preferential to their economic and political agendas.[1] While much attention has been given to the sociopolitical role that news has played in the fate of public opinion,[2] a substantial amount of the television content in question may be primarily regarded as entertainment, which has been noted for its influence on sociocultural standards.[3] This chapter will analyze the use of television as an influential medium in the evolution of home décor by investigating television's role in population shifts; its influence on the representation of race and class; and TV's culpability in the global economic crisis of 2008. The authors argue that television has been an integral component in the society-wide codification of commercial standards of visual aesthetics. Moreover, it is asserted here that the richness of television as a media format has been instrumental in the emergence of American consumer culture as the dominant social form dictating the stylistic values of ordinary citizens in ways unimaginable with print and radio.[4]

Studies have long demonstrated the ability of television to facilitate the construction of audiences' understandings of real-world phenomena. Perceptions of crime rates, court proceedings, and physical trauma have all been shown to be highly dependent upon information received from television (whether accurate or fabricated) in the minds of viewers unfamiliar with these actual processes.[5] Given what is known about how consumers of television interpret these presentations, it follows logically that viewers would also use television to construct their own generalizations about the appearance and layout of emergency rooms (as Katherine A. Foss discusses in this collection), court-rooms, and police precincts (as Susan H. Sarapin and Glenn G. Sparks discuss in this collection). The point is to suggest that if the appearance popularly applied to these fundamental parts of life is so easily incorporated into the con-scious thinking of television audiences regardless of accuracy, then the mean-ing and value of design styles implemented in home décor should be just as readily absorbed into the waking psyche of viewers. Thus, audiences develop a significant degree of their ability to discriminate between the status and value attributed to different brands, design schemes, and color palettes from televi-sion. Television programs continually use visual signifiers as tools to create symbolic value in the domestic space, which shapes the populist comprehen-sion of home décor aesthetics.[6] Home décor has been selected as the focus of this study because the domestic arena has served as the linchpin for the unrestricted exercise of individual taste, self-expression, and the articulation of personal aspirations in the lives of everyday people in the United States.[7] The first section of this chapter discusses programming ideology (e.g., what did TV viewers see and what did that mean for the development of style and taste within the home). The authors lay the foundation for their argument by examining television's relevance in postwar American culture. Subsequently, they explore how television served as a catalyst for the emergence of middle-class idealism, which became one of the ideological benchmarks for achiev-ing the "American Dream." In the second section of this chapter, the authors investigate how the programming ideologies found on television have shaped the evolutions of style and design philosophies on television. Furthermore, this chapter examines how these shifts in ideological and philosophical paradigms informed how urban and suburban residences constructed the spatial environ-ment within the home in response to the stimuli they received via television shows.

TELEVISION'S EMERGING
RELEVANCE IN AMERICAN CULTURE

As television surpassed print and radio as the most popular means of social instruction there emerged a more modernized, integrated media industrial complex that brought about an abundance of contextual factors that must be taken into consideration.[8] The transition from the "Silent Generation" to the "Baby Boomers" played a significant role in the evolution of home décor. The recovery period post–World War II sparked an ideological evolution that was reflected in all aspects of the American social conscience. This created a quixotic atmosphere of hope, a desire for the "finer things in life," and the inception of a revisionist tone toward the "American Dream."[9] The symbolism emoted by the "house with the white picket fence" became real with the emergence of suburban enclaves outside of metropolitan cities across the United States.[10] The desire for affluence and "a piece of the pie" became the rallying call of the late 1950s and early 1960s.[11] These aspirations became part of the DNA of a populist dialogue present in television programming and advertising.[12]

Television programs such as *I Love Lucy* (1951–1957*)* and *Leave It to Beaver* (1957–1963) played a significant role in defining domestic aesthetics during the 1950s.[13] Programs such as these were hallmarks of the modern culture of their time, illustrating the inner anatomy of family values and domestic spaces to American audiences. This family-oriented perspective perpetuated the "homemaker" archetype as the defining role of the American woman. This was one of the many variables that helped shape the American middle-class ideal. The establishment of social order within the television household in the mid-twentieth century initiated a status-conscious perspective for the incipient generation of "Baby Boomers."[14] Television began indoctrinating the next generation of Americans into a mode of consumption dictated by the psycho-social hegemony of media producers.[15] Advertisers aggressively sought to take advantage of this new rich media format.[16] Therein, preferences assumed to be the product of individual agency were guided by visual paradigms paraded in the weekly broadcasts of programs aimed at conditioning audiences to embrace the lifestyles of their mediated counterparts.[17] One of the best illustrations of this tactic in television advertising would be the "Maytag Repairman." The figure first appeared in the late 1960s serving as the de facto "pitch man" for the brand. Maytag leveraged design elements, innovation, and aesthetic placement of their product within the home with the "homemakers" as the target. In *Sit-coms and Suburbs: Positioning the 1950s Homemaker*, Mary Beth Haralovich states, "Like housing design and suburban development, the consumer product industry built its economy on defining the social class and self-identity of women as homemakers."[18]

By the end of the twentieth century, consumers had begun purchasing replacements for goods—which were neither worn-out nor functionally outmoded—at an accelerated pace. Rather, they were buying new products because the old ones had fallen "out of fashion."[19] This presented a marked contrast to the historical notion that many durable items were essentially a once-in-a-lifetime purchase. This tendency toward unnecessary replacement facilitated the intentional incorporation of design obsolescence in the durable goods industry. The rapid-paced evolution of aesthetic sensibilities, dictated to audiences by television, replaced the emphasis on function with an ostentatious preoccupation with form.[20]

Television's American Infusion

The post-World War II climate in American society during the 1950s was one of transition, where the country sought to assert itself as a superpower and heal from the trauma of war. In an effort to acculturate a nation, media and entertainment served as the go-to tactic for socialization in the United States. Television significantly impacted not only the American psyche, but it also served as an aesthetic compass shaping the taste of American society. Television's programming not only influenced how Americans viewed the world, but these shows also cultivated the lens that Americans saw themselves through within the larger global context. Serving as a key variable in the spread of middle-class suburban ideals, television projected a stylized perspective of American living.[21] Furthermore, television's ability to seed aspirational tropes via mediated experiences enabled the medium to permeate every aspect of popular culture into the twenty-first century. By manufacturing an insatiable infatuation with cultural materialism, particularly amongst the middle and working classes, a socio-economic divide emerged that positioned these social groups to strive to maintain pace with the "haves." Paul Adams asserts in his book *Television a Gathering Place*:

> Television can be seen and heard by virtually any member of modern society; it allows people to rise above the chaos of daily life and survey the world from a position of omniscience; it separates one class of people—politicians, entertainers, and public figures—from the rest of people, and puts them in a privileged position where they can be seen and emulated and yet remain separate from society.[22]

The evolution of a bifurcated social hierarchy (e.g., upper and working class) served as the catalyst for the emergence of the middle-class citizen seeking to reside in the suburbs and achieve "upward mobility." Television programs like *The Honeymooners* (1955–1956), which featured the Kramdens, a working-class couple, illustrated a familial desire to migrate from the harsh realities of residing in cramped urban dwellings into the wide-open spaces of the suburbs. The post-World War II return of military veterans and the expansion of the American highway system were significant catalysts in the mass migration from the cities to the suburbs, as were governmental social welfare programs enacted by the New Deal and subsequently the Great Society. For many Americans, having the ability to physically remove themselves and enjoy the trappings of middle-class living fundamentally shifted the perspective of who were the "haves and have-nots." In her book *Make Room for TV: Television and the Family Ideal in Postwar America*, Lynn Spigel asserts, "The illustrations of domestic bliss and consumer prosperity presented a soothing alternative to the tensions of postwar life."[23] With this domestic bliss came the benefits of privacy, space, and property ownership: three things that were difficult to achieve in the urban centers of America.[24]

The emergence of family television programs like *My Three Sons* (1960–1972) and *The Brady Brunch* (1969–1974) laid the foundation for a cultural shift in values and consumption habits. Presenting tangible examples of what a family home should look like, family television programs now began to function as the new meeting place within the home, usurping the role of gathering around the dinner table or congregating in front of the radio.[25] Brands and networks relished the opportunity to leverage the new role that television played in our daily lives via advertisements and TV programming, which seeped into the consciousness of American families. Spigel notes, "The family circle ads, like suburbia itself, were only a temporary consumer solution to a set of complicated political, economic, and social problems."[26] In her recent work, *The Citizen Machine*, Anna McCarthy states that television broadcasting functioned as a tool for enlightenment and evoking stability into the minds of the American people.[27] Television also stimulated a shift of psychographic consumer behavior and social etiquette. The cultivation of this new social normative that celebrated individualism and its association with the ideals of consumerism and democracy enabled television to have comprehensive influence on the aesthetic taste of individuals and the family unit. The impact of television on the aesthetic taste of consumers, specifically with females who were the key decision makers and curators of the spatial dynamics within the home, was palpable from the perspective of television networks and advertisers who utilized visually seductive tactics in order to exploit the middle-class suburban aspiration to be amongst the bourgeois class.[28]

Middle-Class Idealism

Emerging as one of the leading voices in television research and its influence on how consumers see the world, Spigel identifies several key insights that have proved important to note in this research, including: the emergence of the white middle class, the cultivation of the suburban ideal, home as theater, and upward social mobility.[29] Each of these variables, reflecting the cultural mood of America during the 1950s and 1960s, encapsulates how television became such a powerful medium that influenced consumer preference, judgment, decision making, and what they aspired to acquire for their homes via the promotion of futurism through the desire for the "new."

The emergence of the middle class was a significant milestone in a country that believes everyone can achieve the "American Dream." Many white Americans who felt entitled to this dream sought to actively align their lives with this perceived "American Dream." Moreover, the postwar trend of bringing the family unit together in an effort to evoke domestic cohesion triggered an appetite for a change in the social environment propagated via television.[30] Television programs like *Father Knows Best* (1954–1960) and *The Guiding Light* (1952–2009) were shows that provided a blueprint of sorts to American families. The momentary escapism these programs provided enabled viewers to have a snapshot into the fabricated world of suburban living. From floral curtains to elegant vases and flatware, television during this period served as an "instructional video" for the middle class on how to decorate their homes and comport themselves within these domestic spaces. This pictorial analog of domestic life was amplified by seducing the viewer with tantalizing advertisements of how the television could fit into their daily lives. [31]

Many advertisers sought to sell consumers a fantasy of home life that aligned with the other cultural signifiers that complemented the cultivation of the suburban ideal.[32] By becoming an essential component to the domestic space in suburbia, owning a TV became a status symbol for middle-class families seeking to enjoy the accouterments of the "good life." Possession of this status symbol was deemed as a progressive step toward aesthetic expression. Although this aesthetic expression and perceived affluence was filtered via the prism of a mediated experience, it contributed to the development of the self-concept for many Americans who fancied themselves sophisticated.[33] The ability to express their aesthetic tastes empowered many middle-class families with the feeling of "making it" and fully participating in the "American Dream."

In a country obsessed with image construction, what better stage to craft a utopian environment that represents hope and aspiration than the home? The home becomes conflated with theater: "architects, planbook writers, religious leaders, domestic engineers, women's magazines, and books on interior décor variously imagined the bourgeois home as a stage on which a set of highly conventionalized social roles were played by family members alike."[34] Consumer aesthetic tastes tend to revolve around the performative nature of daily life in relation to the visual pleasure garnered via beautiful design.[35] From a mundane task like house cleaning to "sexier" activities such as purchasing new furniture for the home, networks and advertisers tapped into the aspirational desires of consumers. The desired migration of certain social groups also redefined the concept of upward mobility. The ability to physically and metaphorically be mobile complemented the middle-class suburban ideal.

The Working-Class Voice

Many in the working and lower classes had a different perspective of mobility due to the fact that they lacked the ability to be mobile as a result of social and economic challenges. Television programs like *The Honeymooners* (1955–1956), *All in the Family* (1971–1979), *Sanford and Son* (1972–1977), *Chico and the Man* (1974–1978), and *Good Times* (1975–1979) chronicled the challenges for working and lower classes struggling for,[36] as *The Jeffersons* (1975–1985) put it, their "piece of the pie." This last program offers one of the best expressions of this image of upward mobility. The Jeffersons were spinoff characters from *All in the Family*. Characters George and Louise Jefferson migrated from their working-class enclave of Queens, New York, where they lived next door to the Bunkers of *All in the Family*, into a luxury apartment on Manhattan's swanky Upper East Side. The shift in presentation of the domestic space on *The Jeffersons* featured floral wallpaper, landscape paintings, China cabinets, and a sky blue dining area exhibiting a high color contrast verses the mundane color palette found on *All in the Family*. The use of high color contrast in the case of the Jeffersons functioned as a visual signifier of their upward mobility.

By reinforcing the plight of the working class on television (or their potential mobility as is the case with the Jefferson's; even though the Jeffersons moved to a wealthier neighborhood and had a maid, their behavior indicated that culturally they were working class and didn't "fit" in their wealthy environs), these programs further cultivated division between the "haves and have nots."[37] These programs showcased the perspective of working-class families living in cramped and potentially volatile living spaces with aspirations of enjoying life in "greener pastures." A prime example would be the program *Good Times*. The characters on this show lived in a dilapidated tenement building featuring tarnished walls, worn doors, and mismatched dining furniture. The constant portrayal of these characters struggling against "the man" propagated an unpleasant picture of what inner-city life in these domestic spaces was like, further romanticizing middle-class idealism.

Beth Bailey and David Faber assert, "During the 1970s, Americans wrestled with fundamental questions of identity, particularly those related to gender, race, ethnicity, and sexuality. The social movements of the 1960s broke down many of the legal and political barriers that made people of color and women second-class citizens in the United States."[38] The emergence of a variety of social movements toward the end of the 1960s into the 1970s created a dramatic ripple effect in the public consciousness of the United States. Jeffery Cowie states,

> In 1970, the most popular television shows included the traditional escapism of *Marcus Welby, Flip Wilson, Here's Lucy, Ironside*, and, of course *Gunsmoke*.

By the middle of the decade, in contrast, the list of the top shows was a multi-cultural working-class ghetto in all its complexities: *All in the Family*, (backlash worker versus the new politics); *The Waltons* (return of the Great Depression); *Good Times*, *Welcome Back, Kotter*, and *Sanford and Son* (life and poverty in the inner city); *The Jeffersons* (black upward mobility); *Laverne and Shirley* (working girls in the classless fifties); and *One Day at a Time* and *Alice* (working women face life after divorce).[39]

Television networks during this period aimed to create programs that reflected the mood in America via sitcoms. Led by savvy television producers like Norman Lear, who created iconic programs like *All in the Family*, *Sanford and Son*, *The Jeffersons*, and *Good Times*, these shows sought to put their fingers on the pulse of a variety of social issues grappling the nation. These shows provided a rare look into the worlds of working-class families seeking the "American Dream." By providing insights into these worlds, the programs marked a role reversal from the conservative modernist ethos of the 1950s and 1960s to a more liberal and at times eccentric point of view. The characters on Lear's shows cobbled together an aesthetic that reflected a lack of tonal differences that devoid the domestic space of "rhythm," relegating the interior décor to be more a matter of function verses form or design.[40] When you examine the blue-collar aesthetic of *All in the Family*, the composition of the domestic space lacked "presence"[41] and was organized out of necessity (function) verses design (form).[42] Set in Queens, the aesthetics on *All in the Family* were drab and featured such items as pea-green flatware, plastic water pitchers, an open-planned living/dining room that was wallpapered verses painted, and capped with decorated plates that functioned as "art work" on the walls. Contrast this with the program *Leave It to Beaver*, where the home reflected a conscious effort to illustrate the benefits of middle-class life: numerous small rooms, which evoked a sense of space. This stood in opposition to a home space where all family activities occurred in one open room as illustrated on programs like *The Honeymooners*, where the kitchen, dining room, and living room were all in the same space.

Television's New Money

By the 1980s and 1990s, a new consumer emerged, temporally and ideologically removed from the postwar Western consciousness prevalent between the 1950s and 1970s. This resulted in "an increasing orientation toward questions of lifestyle" that is cemented in the dialogue around culture.[43] Television programs like *Lifestyles of the Rich and Famous* (1984–1995) and MTV's *Cribs* (2000–present) perpetuated the fabrication of "pseudo-worlds" and "pseudo-places," igniting a yearning from the viewer to replicate these experiences.[44] The opportunity to engage these "worlds and places" through viewership, or by emulating these experiences through interior design, exemplifies television as a byproduct of capitalism, functioning as a tool for the promotion of consumerist culture.[45] Watching television creates a platform for viewers to form parasocial relationships[46] with TV characters who traverse these pseudo-worlds. The admiration of the characters' movements through these spaces serves as a coping mechanism allowing individuals to escape the mundane rituals of daily life.

Sonia Livingstone notes, "The social trends of the twentieth century combined to transform the Victorian family, a model of domestic life that prioritized a culture of stability, hard work, security, duty, and respect into the democratic family that prizes role flexibility, gender, and generational equality, and a culture of self-fulfillment and individual rights."[47] Guided by the assumption that to be on TV one must possess a certain level of social status, consumers often correlated items "as seen on TV" as having a higher value proposition than those that are not. When this correlation is made it becomes the genesis of aspiring individuals seeking to acquire items that are deemed to possess high symbolic value.

The reintroduction of family programming in the 1980s as one of the key viewing options on television seemed like an attempt by Baby Boomers to reset family values as demonstrated in shows of the 1950s.[48] The one wrinkle in this situation is that these programs began to reflect the idiosyncrasies of American life. This was expressed in a variety of ways all with the aim of providing an authentic point of view to the world around us. Shows like *The Cosby Show* (1984–1992) fundamentally reframed how television audiences understood the function of the family unit, especially an African American family who were actively participating in the middle-class ideal while living in New York City. *The Cosby Show* resonated with families from various cultural backgrounds seeking to achieve social status. The show provided a look into a brownstone in Brooklyn featuring the accouterments of upper-middle-class living. By reframing the visual discourse, family programming in the 1980s, 1990s, and into the 2000s expanded the dialogue around who was allowed to participate in the "American Dream."

THE EVOLUTION OF STYLE

Interior design and home decoration have continuously served as passive benchmarks for the chronological progress of human civilization. Home furnishings, like all consumer products, follow design motifs that embrace the aesthetic sensibilities of the cultural era in which they were produced.

However, the expensive, stationary, and semi-conspicuous nature of home décor plays a significant role in the inability of its design trends to spread as swiftly as trends in other product classes. Television has been integral as a catalyst for overcoming this inherent resistance to rapid mass diffusion and adoption[49] by facilitating the mimetic distribution of design motifs[50] in household flooring, window treatments, furniture, and appliances. However, these transitions are also informed by other forms of design, especially fashion. For instance, when the shag haircut fell out of style, its demise was soon followed by the shag carpet. Similarly, during the 1970s mid-hue earth tones such as chocolate brown, burnt orange, sunflower yellow, and split-pea green fell in and out of vogue in fashion apparel. Likewise, these dated color schemes also followed the same trends in minor durable goods, such as dining sets, vacuum cleaners, toasters, blenders, and lamps. These in turn led the way for the transition of more expensive and difficult to replace items such as sofas, floor rugs, curtains, wallpaper, and large stationary appliances.

Consequently, many elaborate, ornamental, and meandering line patterns of traditional décor also fell from prominence in lieu of more neutral, stable, and streamlined contemporary designs during the onset of the postmodern era, only to be later reinstated around the turn of the millennium with praise as vintage artifacts of superior quality. During the late twentieth century real estate bubble, vegetative motifs found in patterns such as floral, paisley, damask, and ogee became too idiosyncratic for the massive expansion of the US housing market. Check patterns such as plaid, argyle, gingham, and hounds tooth became too folksy for use in establishing universal appeal for the hopeful American home-buyer. By the 1990s neutral off-white and ivory walls were the standard format for open residential listings. This layout was a reference to the white cube aesthetic, popularized in fine art galleries and museums,[51] which became idealized with the affluent middle-class lifestyles portrayed on television shows such as *Frasier* (1993–2004) and *The Fresh Prince of Bel-Air* (1990–1996). Meanwhile the vestiges of substantive, articulate design schemes became denigrated to their associations with the mass produced, low-culture, post-industrial kitsch on display in shows like *Roseanne* (1988–1997) and *Married with Children* (1987–1997), with interiors featuring dingy, low-contrast earth tones used in flooring, walls, counters, and cabinets. These household sets included mismatches of outdated designs such as gaudy floral and plaid patterns on sofas, pillows, throws, wallpaper, and carpet. Designs appear to be notably constructed from synthetic materials such as linoleum, polyester, ceramic, and acrylic in contrast to natural materials used in the ideal middle-class households today like granite, marble, steel, and wool.

The intention of the postmodern white cube's use in the home for sale or rent was to present a blank space for occupation as an empty canvas, pristine, and bearing no traces of its previous inhabitants. In this way it needed no purification from the pollution of their dwelling, their habits, and their subjective tastes.[52] Likewise, in this way the home is fully prepared for complete possession by a new resident. The potential residents can imagine themselves in the home when its mood and appearance is dictated by their own personal tastes, making them "master of the domain" in question.[53] The clean neutral palette is to be ornamented by easily exchanged accents in window treatments, wall hangings, flooring, lighting, and well-placed decorations. These trends can be noted not only for their status-based occurrence across the social hierarchy, but also for their tendency to shift temporally across generations, as noted below.

One might make note of these temporal trends within media, as the aesthetic values of the middle-class American household have undergone constant transition on television from the time of TV's explosion until the present day. The televised household became a paradigm for the construction of self and social identity, serving as a source of expectation and inspiration for generations of middle-class (and aspiring middle-class) consumers in the interior decoration of their homes.[54] Studies have noted the disproportionate representation of social affluence on television.[55] However, not only has television played a vital role in the dissemination of visual directives for middle-class home decoration, it has also given the viewer strong indications of the idealized arrangement of poor, working-class, and upper-class homes. In doing so, television has provided cues for both avoidance and aspiration in the pursuit of increased social status.

Design Philosophies on Television

Many televised representations of the home stem from the authentic folk Americana reminiscent of that depicted in the commercial portraiture of Norman Rockwell's *Saturday Evening Post* paintings, now often criticized as kitsch.[56] With the rich media format of television, and its hypnotic illusion of animated life, these images became more definitive and convincing as depicted in the televised stories of family-oriented dramas and situational comedies based in domestic settings,[57] and their accompanying advertisements.[58] In early shows first filmed in black and white like *I Love Lucy* (1951–1957), *Leave It to Beaver* (1957–1963), and *The Donna Reed Show* (1958–1966), one might note visual attestations of traditional middle-class values in decorative features such as molded trimming along the living room walls, dark mahogany accent furniture heavily ornamented with curved legs and beaded woodwork, wall-to-wall carpeting, floral-patterned sofa sets with ruffled leg skirts, brass candleholders and wall lamps, and wooden framed canvas paintings of countryside landscapes.[59] Moreover, the narrow range of available programming and the immense popularity of television in general, made its influence over the public perception of the ideal home even more potent during this early period. In this sense, in its incipient stages, network television had a dramatically homogenizing effect over the public consciousness when compared to the communicative limitations and specialized interest targeting of many radio and print publications offering similar sociocultural perspectives, because viewers had little choice but to watch the same limited selection of television programs at this time.

During the 1960s and early 1970s these middle-class aesthetics evolved, influenced by design philosophies rooted in the psychedelic, and other burgeoning reactions to the conservative ideologies of 1950s traditionalism.[60] These evolutions came to the public view under the new perspective of color television, which received widespread distribution in the US market in 1965. Shows such as *Bewitched* (1964–1972), *I Dream of Jeannie* (1965–1970), and *The Brady Bunch* (1969–1974) exhibited these changes with the introduction of vivid color palettes, including rich greens, oranges, yellows, and browns, in piled and shag carpets and floor rugs, curtains, and woolen sofa sets. Decorative accents introduced more eclectic tastes like Chinese character paintings, bonsai trees, and sofa pillows with re-stitched bricolage print patterns, countered by daisy, damask, and cornflower wallpaper patterns; soft pastel orange, green, or blue painted walls; or exposed brick and stone walls. During this era sofas began to appear with lower, narrower profiles, and sharper, streamlined edges, while tall-shaded ornamental table lamps became a popular trend. Floor plans began to approach less spatially congested non-conventional designs with more sparse furnishing layouts, open area room designs, and exposed staircases.

Later shows such as *Family Ties* (1982–1989), *Mr. Belvedere* (1985–1990), and *Who's the Boss?* (1984–1992), brought forth continued testimonies of ideal middle-class American life with signifiers of its proper domestic presentation. These included hardwood floors and doors with white walls suggesting early iterations of the white cube within the home, or walls plastered with sheets of gingham print, oak leaf patterns, stripes, or flower print wallpaper. Walls continued to include old-fashioned features like molded trimming and elaborate hangings such as regulator clocks and framed coats of arms. Spangled rivet patterns appear on microfiber sofas or accent pillows in beige and navy. Sofas and armchairs are also subject to carry gaudy floral prints, as are stair runners and Turkish rugs. These floral motifs were epitomized in the large green leaves of Dieffenbachia, and Chinese Evergreen houseplants. Meanwhile ornamentally curved and beaded woodwork continued its prominence in decorative furniture and railings. This era was typified by its modest shift toward the white cube in some aspects, while maintaining a heavy reliance on traditionalist design forms in others.

Similar but somewhat more modern home interiors were found in other shows overlapping the same time period like *Growing Pains* (1985–1992), *Charles in Charge* (1987–1990), *Full House* (1987–1995), and *Home Improvement* (1991–1999). In these shows features like recessed lighting, vaulted ceilings, spiral staircases, and white on white walls became legitimate middle-class aspirations. Rear kitchens included window walls and greenhouses. Ornamental woodwork was still common, but less prevalent than the cleaner lines of more modern cabinets, tables, chairs, and staircase railings. Lighter-colored spruce and beech wood began gaining popularity in lieu of darker mahogany stains. Green carpet and seating upholstery took on undertones of blue as a departure from the deep hunter greens of the 1960s and 1970s. Wall paintings now included maritime themes in addition to rustic countryside landscapes. Although they were in the process of being phased out of the middle-class paradigm of domestic aspiration, traditional designs such as lower-third wall paneling, floral vases and flatware decoratively set on open-faced cabinet shelves, check patterns, and gaudy golden chandeliers maintained their presence in the houses of American sitcoms. However, by this point these designs were becoming emerged within the symbolism of the white cube as older-styled woodwork was often painted over in light tones, or antique artifacts like mahogany caned settees became isolated points of focus within the clean lines of the postmodern household.

By the late 1990s the notion of aspiration had become more prominent as public policy began to strip the middle class of its access to legitimate social affluence at an accelerated pace—reducing its ranks to a fraction of its one-time glory as the cornerstone upon which the American economy rested. Increasingly, real wages were driven down against inflation and the rising income of a class of uber-wealthy plutocrats.[61] In an effort to maintain the "American Dream"[62] being sold to them on television, a host of Americans took on credit debt[63] in order to drive new cars, eat at the local Applebee's, keep their premium cable subscriptions, and furnish their marble-laden McMansions with imitation designer furniture.[64] Retailers like Ikea, Target, and Bed Bath & Beyond cashed in heavily on the opportunity[65] to exploit the pocketbooks of a waning middle class now on the edge of financial ruin. Thanks to television, these same individuals had developed an unhealthy affinity for a wasteful lifestyle of over-consumption.[66] Centuries of functional design rationale would fly out the window as American consumers flocked to big box home furnishing retailers to decorate the walls of their postmodern "cubes" with mass-produced hallmarks of artifice in the form of faux antique, Mediterranean, and country home-styled housewares.[67] Lifestyle-based programming found on shows like *The Martha Stewart Show* (2005–2012) and programs on the Home & Garden Television network have been critical to the popularization of this growing obsession with material comfort.

Location, Location, Location

Eventually there arose a divide between town and country[68] with the coming of the postmodern abode of the city-slicking professional featured on shows like *Seinfeld* (1989–1998), *Frasier* (1993–2004), and *Friends* (1994–2004). These homes portrayed the new-age design philosophy that is ubiquitous to the public and private spaces frequented by progressive, coastal, metropolitan city dwellers who are often employed by glamour industries, and rank amongst the intelligentsia.[69] Apple Stores, trendy bars and eateries, corporate offices, and creative spaces all share the central motifs of this sleek, minimalist, postmodern aesthetic. Current programs including *The Big Bang Theory* (2007–present) and *New Girl* (2011–present) remain true to this paradigm, which has rapidly changed the face of home décor since the 1970s.

In these households beech-stained wooden floors meet deep earth-toned, or soft neutral-colored living room sets. Walls are white and light neutral shades or painted in pastels such as teal, peach, pink, or periwinkle. Art deco dining sets and halogen lamps are contrasted with old-world artifacts such as antique telescopes and vases. The stage of these apartments has been set for the display of tasteful possessions. Glass-framed or open-faced kitchen cabinets expose stacks of flatware, dry food products, and kitchen utensils, complementing the glimmer of granite countertops. Square-compartmented bookshelves are filled with books and decorative works of contemporary art. The floor plans of these units are also highly expository with open or loft-style arrangements. Black and white framed photography hangs on the walls, while woodwork has been stripped of its ornamental traits and painted to contrast with the room in a way that is cold and technical rather than the natural way stained wood blends into a room.

Modernized remnants of vintage and traditional American folk culture endured on the set designs of suburban sitcom series such as *Hope & Faith* (2003–2006), *According to* Jim (2001–2009), and *Everybody Loves Raymond* (1996–2005), while *Modern Family* (2009–present) and *Last Man Standing* (2001–present) have updated the folk-inspired trends into the present. Within the confines of these middle-American McMansions, there are similar features in glass cabinetwork and granite countertops found in the city but with more olive, stained wood, and neutral ivory earth tones, or more saturated colors, or soft combinations of pastels serving as a quiet backdrop accented by vintage stripe, check, or floral patterns. In this way the classic—which one might argue to be indicative of the real—has become objectified as the central attraction in an environment dominated by artifice and imitation,[70] in many cases being little more than an imitation itself.[71] Both town and country postmodern style and postmodern re-framings of traditionalism became effective tools for marketing cookie-cutter residences to the mass public, in open houses and on television. Because these programs promoted if not initiated many of the ideas constituting a particular aspirational standard of American living, in a sense the inspiration drawn from these contemporary television shows made it somewhat easier for an army of real estate agents to sell homes to middle-class Americans as they took the nation by storm with their infamous hypnotic mantra of "location, location, location."

As such, location became the imagined justification for the multiplying of the market prices of homes whose essential value could be easily deduced to the much lower cost of materials plus labor and development and marketing expenses. Yet, in many ways it was not the structures themselves that served as the point of interest in the sale of housing, or even the location per se. Rather, it was the idea of the American household, which was being sold to the public under the false assumption of indefinite growth.[72] That is to say, as Americans began to crave the affluence they were witnessing daily in their televised entertainment, the acquisition of that lifestyle at all costs became a central preoccupation. It became feasible to pay unreasonable sums for houses similar to the ones on TV as the market value appeared to be growing without end. Though no one was for certain exactly where this value was actually being produced, or how it was to be accounted for, housing prices continued to soar throughout the 1990s and early 2000s, and this unsubstantiated production of value, underscored by inflation, was eating what would become an irreparable hole into the global economy.[73] What happened next bears elaboration.

THE TELEVISION ECONOMY

With urban sprawl in full swing,[74] and the Glass-Steagall Act[75] under repeal by 1999, a swarm of predatory mortgage lenders took to arms against working and middle-class US citizens with adjustable mortgages that often held the unwary consumer at an immense disadvantage.[76] This allowed bankers to devise subprime contracts with many under-qualified borrowers for, what amounted to, unsustainable access to the "American Dream" portrayed on television at unjustifiably high prices and interest rates.[77] Essentially this created debt that would never be reconciled. Ordinary consumers were widely misguided by the false assumption that houses were the ultimate asset of personal investment, and that their values would continue to rise as they had for decades, without restraint. Desperate for their chance at a quality life, millions of ambitious Americans bought-in to some of the most extensive schemes of fraud and corruption the world has ever seen.[78] It soon became apparent that a large number of home buyers could not afford to maintain the fantasies sold to them on the sitcoms they had used as a guide to prosperity. It turned out that the price of prosperity was grossly inflated, as were the interest rates on the loans used to secure its benefits. In this way television served as an accomplice of sorts to the 2008 global economic meltdown, which initiated in the US housing market. The main point to be noted is that city apartments and suburban McMansions became the point of entry into this fantasy of middle-class socioeconomic affluence. The ideal image of those dwellings had been largely programmed into the public via staged representations of domestic spaces.

The housing market crisis was marked by the common symptoms of irrational exuberance,[79] mass hysteria,[80] and herd-like imitation[81] as it passed through the bubble-panic-crash cycle typical of economic fall-out.[82] Part of this imitative behavior of crowd-oriented contagion[83] involved the long-term consumption of images that provided a nation of viewers with a particular understanding of the world, including their own homes. To be certain, television had informed viewers of the normative standards of what their everyday lives should look like given their social status and the cultural climate.[84] In so doing, it planted within the population the idea that the overpriced postmodern styled apartments and McMansions—being hocked by developers and realtors across the country—were the quintessential high-notes of modern middle-class living.

Not only this, but it also raised the demands[85] of self-presentation placed on ordinary people in several aspects.[86] Suddenly, under the influence of shows like *Sex and the City* (1998–2004) there was a hyper-accelerated desire for Louis Vuitton bags and Manolo Blahnik stilettos within the fashion repertoires of ordinary middle- and even working-class Americans. Where they could not afford these, they "traded up"[87] with Coach and Dooney & Bourke or they wore luxury knock-offs or counterfeit goods. In a similar way, granite countertops, marble floors, and sub-zero refrigerators became designer standards for the interior of the middle-class American home. Likewise, where these could not be afforded they were also heavily imitated with synthetic vinyl countertops and ceramic tiles bearing marble prints, and large-framed, silver aluminum refrigerators similar in appearance to sub-zero units.

In the same sense, the McMansion itself is imitative of the actual provincial or country estate—its brick façade and drywall interior intended to mimic the mason work and plaster of the large elaborate homes of society's old-guard. In many contemporary homes artificial painted patinas and lightweight aluminum plumbing fixtures imitate the authenticity of oxidized bronze and tarnished heavy brass. Since the turn of the millennium, these aesthetic sensibilities have increasingly been exploited through the aspirational overtones regularly conveyed in the segments and advertisements presented within lifestyle genre programs based in home improvement and domestic arts. From celebrity lifestyle gurus like Martha Stewart to reality programming such as *Extreme Makeover: Home Edition* (2003–2012), *House Hunters* (1999–present) and its series of spin-offs, *Celebrity House Hunting* (2012–present), MTV's *Cribs*, and even *This Old House* (1979–present), the home lifestyle marketers have relentlessly promoted a set of aesthetic standards of domestic organization and presentation that has catered to the broadening of faux antique Mediterranean and country house decoration motifs now prominent in modern middle-class homes.

By serving as aesthetic barometer via much of its programming, television fortifies the aspirations that reflect the essence of American culture. It has become one of the key benchmarks in how consumers measure their aesthetic taste. From the 1950s to present day, the television has shaped the way Americans see the world and themselves. By fostering a consumerist ideology steeped in the concepts of image construction, middle-class suburban ideals, and the pursuit of the "American Dream," television serves as a tool that continues to mold the public consciousness.

Trends in interior décor have depended heavily on television programming for the current rate of accelerated diffusion, which has enabled faster transitions in the prevailing paradigm of domestic presentation. Over a half-century of network and cable sitcoms have ingrained the general public with a specific understanding of social status and personal identity based upon design features found in the home environment. Moreover, the turn of the millennium witnessed the rise of reality-based genres of television, which produced an unmitigated pressure on audiences to engage materialistic fantasies pursuant to the agendas of the capitalist class and its directors of media. The establishment of this worldview and its preferential standards has profoundly impacted many aspects of our society including: a single-minded interpretation of superficial symbolism as an indicator of status and quality, the progressive displacement of the real in lieu of imitative artifice, and an inadvertent contribution to the meltdown of the global economy.

NOTES

1. Anna McCarthy, *The Citizen Machine: Governing By Television in 1950s America* (New York: The New Press, 2010), 2–3.

2. George Gerbner and Larry Gross, "Living With Television: The Violence Profile," *Journal of Communication* 26, no. 2 (1976): 172–199.

3. Mary Beth Haralovich, "Sit-coms and Suburbs: Positioning the 1950s Homemaker," in *Private Screenings: Television and the Female Consumer*, ed. Lynn Spigel and Denise Mann (Minneapolis: University of Minnesota Press, 1992), 114–115.

4. Haralovich, "Sitcoms and Suburbs," 128.

5. Michael Morgan, James Shanahan, and Nancy Signorielli, "Growing Up With Television: Cultivation Processes," in *Media Effects: Advances in Theory and Research 3rd ed.*, ed. Jennings Bryant and Mary Beth Oliver (New York: Routledge, 2009), 43–45.

6. Jean Baudrillard, *The System of Objects (Radical Thinkers)* (New York City: Verso, 2005), 13–19.

7. Henri Lefebvre, *Everyday Life In the Modern World* (New Brunswick: Transaction Publishers, 1984), 55.

8. Jean Baudrillard, *Simulacra and Simulation* (Ann Arbor: University of Michigan Press, 1995), 81–82.

9. Stewart Ewen, *Captains of Consciousness: Advertising and the Social Roots of Consumer Culture* (New York: McGraw-Hill Book Company, 1976), 139–140.

10. Jane Jacobs, *The Death and Life of Great American Cities* (New York: Random House, 1961), 122.

11. Lefebvre, *Everyday Life*, 122.

12. Ewen, *Captains of Consciousness*, 113.

13. Haralovich, "Sitcoms and Suburbs," 111.

14. Lynn Spigel, *Make Room for TV: Television and the Family Ideal in Postwar America* (Chicago: The University of Chicago Press, 1992), 32–33.

15. Lefebvre, *Everyday Life*, 91.

16. McCarthy, *The Citizen Machine*, 243.

17. Haralovich, "Sitcoms and Suburbs," 112.

18. Haralovich, "Sitcoms and Suburbs," 120.

19. Lefebvre, *Everyday Life*, 165–167.

20. Baudrillard, *The System of Objects*, 67.

21. Lynn Spigel, *Make Room for TV: Television and the Family Ideal in Postwar America* (Chicago: The University of Chicago Press, 1992), 42.

22. Paul C. Adams, "Television as Gathering Place," *Annals of the Association of American Geographers,* 82, no. 1 (1992): 126.

23. Spigel, *Make Room for TV*, 43.

24. Jane Jacobs, *The Death and Life*, 123.

25. Spigel, *Make Room for TV*, 39.

26. Spigel, *Make Room for TV*, 43.

27. McCarthy, *The Citizen Machine*, 2.

28. Lynn Spigel, *TV By Design: Modern Art and the Rise of Network Television* (Chicago: The University of Chicago Press, 2008), 13.

29. Lynn Spigel, *Welcome to the Dreamhouse: Popular Media and Postwar Suburbs* (Durham: Duke University Press, 2001), 64–65, 92.

30. S. Robert Lichter, Linda S. Lichter, and Stanley Rothman, *Prime Time: How TV Portrays American Culture* (Washington, D.C.: Regnery Publishing, 1994), 150.

31. Spigel, *Make Room for TV*, 36.

32. Spigel, *Welcome to the Dreamhouse*, 60.

33. Baudrillard, *The System of Objects*, 14–15.

34. Spigel, *Welcome to the Dreamhouse*, 64–65.

35. Spigel, *Welcome to the Dreamhouse*, 65.

36. Lichter, Lichter, and Rothman, *Prime Time*, 189.

37. Lichter, Lichter, and Rothman, *Prime Time*, 186.

38. Beth Bailey and David Farber, *America in the 70s* (Lawrence: University Press of Kansas 2004), 4.

39. Jefferson Cowie, "Vigorously Left, Right, and Center at the Same Time: The Crosscurrents of Working-Class America in the 1970s," in *America in the Seventies*, ed. Beth Bailey and David Farber. (Lawrence: University Press of Kansas, 2004), 90.

40. Baudrillard, *The System of Objects*, 35.

41. Baudrillard, *The System of Objects*, 19.

42. Pierre Bourdieu, "Distinction & The Aristocracy of Culture" in *Cultural Theory and Popular Culture*, ed. John Storey. (Athens: University of Georgia Press, 1998), 434–435.

43. Sonia Livingstone, "Half a Century of Television in the Lives of Our Children," *Annals of the Association of American Academy of Political and Social Sciences*, vol. 625 (2009): 155.

44. Adams, "Television as Gathering Place," 121.

45. Adams, "Television as Gathering Place," 122.

46. Tim Cole and Laura Leets, "Attachment Styles and Intimate Television Viewing. Insecurely Forming Relationships in a Parasocial Way," *Journal of Social and Personal Relationships* 16, (1999): 495–511.

47. Livingstone, "Half a Century of Television in the Lives of Our Children," 157.

48. Lichter, Lichter, and Rothman, *Prime Time,* 161.

49. Everett Rogers, *Diffusion of Innovations* (New York: The Free Press, 2003), 247–250.

50. Richard Brodie, *Virus of the Mind: The New Science of the Meme* (Carlsbad: Hay House, Inc., 2009), 28–39.

51. Olav Velthuis, *Talking Prices: Symbolic Meanings of Prices on the Market for Contemporary Art* (Princeton: Princeton University Press, 2005), 4, 30–32.

52. Russell W. Belk, "Possessions and the Extended Self," *Journal of Consumer Research* 15, no. 2 (1988): 151.

53. Belk, "Possessions and the Extended Self," 146.

54. Grant D. McCracken, "Culture and Consumption: A Theoretical Account of the Structure and Movement of the Cultural Meaning of Consumer Goods," *Journal of Consumer Research* 13, no. 1 (1986): 73.

55. Hyeseung Yang and Mary Beth Oliver, "Exploring the Effects of Television Viewing on Perceived Quality of Life: A Combined Perspective of Material Value and Upward Social Comparison," *Mass Communication and Society* 13, no. 2 (2010), 119–122.

56. Deborah Solomon, "In Praise of Bad Art," *New York Times*, January 24, 1999. Retrieved May 21, 2013, http://www.nytimes.com/1999/01/24/magazine/in-praise-of-bad-art.html.

57. Haralovich, "Sitcoms and Suburbs," 112.

58. Lefebvre, *Everyday Life in the Modern World*, 55.

59. Haralaovich, "Sitcoms and Suburbs," 114.

60. Reyner Banham, *Theory and Design in the First Machine Age* (New York: Praeger, 1978), 9–10.

61. Thomas Frank, *One Market Under God: Extreme Capitalism, Market Populism, and the End of Economic Democracy* (New York: Doubleday, 2000), 95–98.

62. James E. Burroughs, L. J. Shrum, and Aric Rindfleisch, "Does Television Viewing Promote Materialism? Cultivating American Perceptions of the Good Life," *Advances in Consumer Research* 29, no. 1 (2002): 442–443.

63. Steve Fraser, *Every Man a Speculator: A History of Wall Street in American Life* (New York: HarperCollins, 2005), 591.

64. Lefebvre, *Everyday Life*, 56.

65. Michael J. Silverstein, Neil Fiske, and John Butman, *Trading Up: Why Consumers Want New Luxury Goods—And How Companies Create Them* (New York: Portfolio, 2008), 15–51.

66. McCracken, "Culture and Consumption," 73.

67. Lefebvre, *Everyday Life*, 38.

68. Lefebvre, *Everyday Life*, 122.

69. Pierre Bourdieu, *Distinction*, 379.

70. Bourdieu, *Distinction*, 360–365.

71. Lefebvre, *Everyday Life*, 30, 89, 113.

72. Haralaovich, "Sitcoms and Suburbs," 119.

73. George A. Akerlof and Robert J. Shiller, *Animal Spirits: How Human Psychology Drives the Economy and Why It Matters for Global Capitalism* (Princeton: Princeton University Press, 2009), 47–50.

74. Jane Jacobs, *The Death and Life,* 20–22.

75. Glass-Steagall is the title summarily applied to the Banking Act of 1933. Its repeal meant the reunification of commercial and investment banking, allowing investors to leverage greater risk with ordinary the government-insured savings of ordinary customers as collateral.

76. Frederic S. Mishkin, "Over the Cliff: From the Subprime to the Global Financial Crisis," *Journal of Economic Perspectives* 25, no. 1 (2011): 50–51.

77. Akerlof, and Shiller, *Animal Spirits*, 36–38.

78. Akerlof, and Shiller, *Animal Spirits*, 36–38.

79. Edward Chancellor, *Devil Take the Hindmost: A History of Financial Speculation* (New York: Plume, 2000), 3–29.

80. Charles P. Kindleberger and Robert Z. Aliber, *Manias, Panics, and Crashes* (Hoboken: Wiley & Sons, Inc., 2005), 110–112.

81. Mark Pingle, "Imitation Versus Ration: An Experimental Perspective on Decision Making," *The Journal of Socio Economics* 24, no. 2 (1995), 282.

82. Kindleberger and Aliber, *Manias, Panics, and Crashes*, 110–112.

83. David A. Levy and Paul R. Nail, "Contagion: A Theoretical and Empirical Review and Reconceptualization," *Genetic, Social & General Psychology Monographs* 119, no. 2 (1993): 235–285.

84. Haralovich, "Sitcoms and Suburbs," 112.

85. Joseph M. Sirgy et al., "Does Television Viewership Play a Role in the Perception of Quality of Life?," *Journal of Advertising* 27, no. 1 (1998): 125–142.

86. Erving Goffman, *The Presentation of Self In Everyday Life* (Woodstock: The Overlook Press, 1956), 24.

87. Silverstein, Fiske, and Butman, *Trading Up*, 1–14.

Chapter Nineteen

Bordertown: Manufacturing Mexicanness in Reality Television

Ariadne Alejandra Gonzalez

Living between worlds. This is the best way I can describe what living on the US-Mexico border is like. It is as simple and as complicated as that and in good faith, my description does not give it justice. It is peculiar to attempt to describe something that can only be experienced first-hand and for that reason, I have a propensity to safeguard my own description to others that know nothing about my home—Laredo, Texas. On September 2, 2011, the A&E Television Network announced *Bordertown: Laredo* as a ten-episode original real-life series documenting the Laredo, Texas, Police Department's Narcotic Unit. The series chronicled the Unit's struggle with drug trafficking from Mexico to the United States and protecting the South Texas border. This chapter explores how Mexicanness is manufactured in the reality-crime series, *Bordertown: Laredo*. The first season of *Bordertown: Laredo*, along with the promotional ad that was nationally circulated, are analyzed to focus on three specific sites: music, space, and language. The three sites expose the perpetual (mis)representation of Laredo, Texas and frame the reinforcement of the border as a space of alterity, inhabited by residents who are marked as other in relation to the ideal citizen. These sites also reveal a precarious representation of Latinos. A closer analysis further demonstrates how each site works in conjunction with the others. They are not mutually exclusive but are interdependent of each other, creating otherness in Latinos and furthering the feelings and thoughts of uncertainty and threat that many in greater America presently have for Latinos in the United States.

CLIMATE SURROUNDING BORDER CITIES

Over the years, Laredo has kept such a low profile across the United States that when residents step out of the South Texas region many find themselves explaining where Laredo is geographically located. Laredo, located in the South Texas region bordering Nuevo Laredo, Tamaulipas, Mexico, has a population of 236,100 inhabitants of which 95.6 percent are Hispanic or of Latino origin.[1] However, three distinct events placed border cities and specifically Laredo, Texas, under the international spotlight. First, the September 11, 2001, terror attacks called for expeditious attention to border security. Second, the Secure Fence Act of 2006 drew nationwide scrutiny and attention as a call to support border security efforts in the aftermath of 9/11. Third, the Cartel Drug War playing out across Mexico yet specifically targeting US border cities rendered much concern and consternation. Suddenly, border cities across the 1,900-mile-long United States–Mexico border were on the front-page news and Laredo was no exception.

Equally important, however, is the anti-Mexican immigrant climate, which has set a firm foundation for the negative tone against Latinos living in the Unites States. For example, the English-only movement in this country that gained popularity since the 1980s often disregards and discredits the use of the Spanish language, even though it has sustained communities throughout the United States.[2] Continuous unsuccessful attempts in making English the official language demonstrate how some Americans feel threatened by the rise of the Latino population in the United States. According to the 2006 tabulation of Latinos, the Pew Hispanic Center reported that almost forty-two million Latinos live the United States.[3] As these numbers rise, so too does the continual sentiment of threat and fear of *illegals invading* the United States and taking over the land of the free. Because of this spurious threat, conservative groups have made it their mission to find ways to further marginalize Latinos, thus creating a recurring pattern to racialize language practices of Latinos.[4]

At the same time, rigorous immigration legislation surfaced in states like Alabama, Georgia, Indiana, Utah, and South Carolina calling for illegal immigration reform.[5] This recent upheaval stems from the initial anti-illegal immigration law, the Support Our Law Enforcement and Safe Neighborhoods Act (more commonly known as SB 1070) that passed in Arizona in 2010. Even though this law was met with legal challenges, in June 2012 the United States Supreme Court ruled in favor of SB 1070's most controversial provision: allowing local police to check residents' immigration status during law enforcements stops.[6] Mississippi's House of Representatives passed their version of the Support Our Law Enforcement and Safe Neighborhoods Act, requiring police to inspect the immigration status of those who are arrested as well as prohibiting business transactions such as renewing a driver's license or obtaining a business license.[7] These attempts to ratify immigration policies at the state level have caused a significant rift between the Obama administration and several independent states that believe the federal government has been standing idle on immigration reform. These discussions have led many to wonder which governmental body has the authority and duty to police the border between the United States and Mexico. Policing the border has become a contested political maneuver, bringing about questions of regulation and duty. In this case, the body functions as a site to represent the inspection, control, enforcement, and supervision of the border and the people who populate these border towns. This leads us to ask the tougher question of who decides the determining factors of what is deemed "illegal" and "alien."[8] In order to comprehend the meaning it produces, careful consideration of what is disseminated to the American people as informational, real life, and even as a form of entertainment must be scrutinized.[9]

LATINO PORTRAYALS IN MEDIA

For decades, Latinos have been historically (mis)represented and underrepresented in the media. Hollywood has played a principal role in stereotyping Latinos as inferior and typifying the white hero as "moral, resourceful, brave and intelligent—in a word, superior."[10] Charles Ramirez Berg argues that a distinct characteristic of Hollywood filmmakers is to make the "white, handsome, middle-aged, upper-middle-class, heterosexual, Protestant, Angle-Saxon male" the hero.[11] For more than a century six distinct stereotypes have been consistent in Hollywood's Latino imagery: el bandito, the harlot, the male buffoon, the female clown, the Latin lover, and the dark lady, where the object was to eroticize or ridicule the men and women that portray these roles.[12] Because the WASP "way of life is asserted as a norm worth fighting," people of color are deemed insignificant and marked as other.[13] While portraying the white hero as superior, Latinos have been represented as inferior and lawless. Beginning in the 1980s, however, the tide shifted and an increasing number of Latinos were being portrayed as struggling workers with strong family ties, since their own people directed many of the films.[14] Dana E. Mastro and Amanda L. Robinson argue that Latinos have been underrepresented in television as well.[15] Latinos represent 3–4 percent of primetime television characters, even though they are the largest ethnic minority in the country.[16] Latinos' roles are minor and often depicted as "criminal suspects" or "crooks, cops, or comic."[17] These ongoing deviant media (mis)representations have reduced Latinos to detrimental categorizations that carry dangerous and real implications for how viewers locate that which is inferior and unacceptable in this country.

Similarly, in their study on Latino representation during the 2002 prime-time television season, Dana E. Mastro and Elizabeth Behn-Morawitz found that even though there were some instances of diminishing Latino stereotypes, other categorical depictions were clearly present.[18] Latinos on television were portrayed as "unintelligent and least articulate" and depicted as the most "hot tempered men on television" alongside blacks; meanwhile, Latinas were depicted as "lazy, verbally aggressive, unintelligent, embodied the lowest work ethic, and were the most ridiculed."[19] Their study detailing the depiction of minority groups on television reveals that because of the impact of television exposure to social reality, fictional programming may very well lead to "associations of minorities with crime, victimization, and criminal justice themes" especially as laws are presently being created to criminalize Latinos.[20] The link is also problematic since this raised apprehension may be present as viewers interact with Latinos. These dangerous depictions reveal how stereotypes construct the real. Additionally, Mastro and Robinson claim that proponents for cultivation theory suggest "differences in perceptions about social reality emerge as a result of varying degrees of exposure to television, such that heavy viewers believe in a reality consistent with that found on television—regardless of the accuracy of these beliefs."[21] If this is the representation that America's viewership is afforded, it is unsurprising that stereotypical characterizations can construct the real, especially at a time where there is a continuing national discourse concerning immigration reform.

Media outlets frame the ongoing national discourse concerning immigration issues in the United States. Substantial negative news coverage of "immigration, in particular immigrant crime, and violent activities" adds to the blame media outlets have received.[22] Otto Santa Ana analyzed *The Los Angeles Times* news articles focusing on Latino immigration issues and found powerful metaphors published from the inception of the Proposition 187 campaign in 1992–1994. The dominant metaphor used was "dangerous waters" (e.g., floods, tide) and the secondary metaphor suggested a takeover or an "invasion" (e.g., alien, foreign invasion) was taking place in California. More importantly, the metaphors suggest that a sense of threat is felt and, therefore, action must take place in order to alleviate the "alien invasion."[23] Furthermore, this affects how individuals view their social environment and in particular shapes their understanding about immigrants in this country.[24] This is troublesome because it captures a racist and incendiary perception that is disseminated throughout this country. However, film, news media, and scripted television have not been isolated in their (mis)representation of Latinos.

REALITY TELEVISION, RACE, AND THE REAL

The fascination with reality television has taken these depictions to an elevated level. Bethany Ogdon argues that the most powerful human experience is one that is presented as "the reality of everyday life" and living in the "here and now."[25] The unscripted *reality* of reality television is packaged to represent the real and focused on *real* people, all "in the name of dramatic uncertainty, voyeurism, and popular pleasure."[26] However, careful consideration must be paid to what is considered real in reality television. According to Mark P. Orbe, reality television is considered "non-fictional programming in which the portrayal is presumed to present current or historical events or circumstances," yet he argues that varying definitions generate skeptical thoughts on what is considered reality.[27] For example, whereas one definition stresses that reality television involves "edited footage of unscripted interactions," a differing description characterizes it as a programming genre that "scripted or not, offers its viewers an ostensibly real depiction of both individuals and issues."[28] These varying definitions absolutely alter the meaning of what is packaged as real. Rather than obtaining a more concrete definition, various abstractions come to light. Therefore, the ambiguous meaning of what is considered reality television is never known and left to be open to a gaping interpretation.

As strikingly different as these definitions are, reality television in general has been instrumental to the much-needed diversity in television programming but at what cost? Much of the drama that unfolds is based from a clash of diversity—an unsuccessful attempt to bridge cultural paradigms.[29] (Mis)representations in film, scripted or fictional television, news coverage, and reality television have continuously victimized minorities and placed them as deviant and unaccepted. Reality-crime television has been made popular by past reality shows like *America's Most Wanted* (1988–2012), *Hard Copy* (1989–1999), *Inside Edition* (1989–present), and *Real Stories of the Highway Patrol* (1993–1999) that incorporated law enforcement.[30] According to Elayne Rapping these reality shows were low budget, shared a documentary approach, and did "actual police work."[31] However, none gained such popularity than *Cops* (1989–present).[32] This reality television show centers on the notion that crime meets ordinary life. While cameras follow law enforcement officers, viewers are taken into the trenches of police work while simultaneously glancing into the "key assumptions and implications of current political trends," often far outside of urban areas.[33] Criminality and deviance are now located in the borderlands—a representation of what is considered foreign and outside of the United States imagery.[34]

THEORIZING THE BORDER

Viviendo entre mundos . . . The border has been continuously conceptualized as *living between worlds* to the United States imaginary. Latino scholars have described the borderlands as a third space or hybridity.[35] This nuance gets lost when people attempt to represent the border. It is instantly marked as a foreign and strange space. It is an indication of Latinos being the insiders yet seen as the forever outsiders. Even though citizenship has been legally acquired, it has never been considered an "ultimate mark of privilege and status" to racial others.[36] This third space or what Gloria Anzaldúa refers to as the borderlands speaks to conflicting cultures coming into negotiation—a "struggle of borders" where there is ambivalence or an "emotional state of perplexity."[37] This is significant since Latinos are viewed as conflicted between these two worlds and seen as living in no man's land.

The same is true in films depicting the border as strange and different. US filmmakers have persistently marked the United States–Mexico border as a third space where degenerates and outlaws reside. In this space, the putative insider is clearly distinguished as the perpetual outsider, not quite belonging in this space, thus creating a demarcation line between what is recognized as worthy to what is regarded as unbecoming and discreditable. Rosa Linda Fregoso argues that US filmmakers and Mexico's film industry have become fixated with the border. She asserts that the "border figures as the trope for absolute alterity" in which a cultural imaginary of "no-man's land" is created.[38] The representation of the border is accepted and recognized as the absolute other that cannot find a place in the United States.

ANALYZING THE BORDER

This ongoing discourse regarding the history of Latino portrayals in media coupled with border security and its continual treatment of being atypical and on the outside of what is accepted is important because it naturalizes the meaning of what passes as "American" in this country, but more importantly what does not. *Bordertown: Laredo*'s (mis)representation of Laredo, Texas, suggests that Laredo is a city that embodies the Mexicanness of one country yet happens to be geographically placed in US territory. The city is depicted as yet another example of this third space where conflict and otherness reside. The following analysis examines the show's depiction of Laredo and the implications it transmits to its audience. The first season of *Bordertown: Laredo* was analyzed using a text-based methodology. A&E Television Network's nationally released promotional ad, which circulated prior to the premiere of the reality show, was also selected for analysis. Three specific sites emerged from the show depicting the (mis)representation of Latinos: music, space, and language. Analyzing these three specific sites evokes a detrimental representation of Latinos. A closer analysis further demonstrates how each site works in conjunction with the other. They are not mutually exclusive but are interdependent on each other, creating otherness in Latinos, specifically Laredo residents, and fueling notions of uncertainty and threat that many Americans presently have for Latinos in the United States.

Music, Mariachi, and Mexicanness

Music has the power to captivate and set the tone for an audience. During a television show, it is the opening song that allows us to be part of what is taking place in the moment; it transfixes our disposition by telling us what to think and how to feel about the story that is unfolding. For example, if the beat is rapidly increasing or is suspenseful, we can deduce that something is about to happen to modify or thicken the plot. At the same time, music can draw our attention to the actual television show. These moments enable an audience to pay particular attention to its surroundings. Furthermore, music has the ability to enable the audience to evoke certain ideas and emotions about a scene. It directs our attention to certain feelings and a state of mind that we didn't know existed and suddenly we are caught smiling, crying, or even becoming nostalgic.[39] Music is powerful and paints a particular picture of the television show and the people it depicts.

The same is true the opening song in *Bordertown: Laredo*: powerful and loud trumpets are accompanied by an ear-piercing guitar and vihuela (five-string guitar) in a style vividly recognized as mariachi. There are no lyrics, only the intense sounds of three instruments that showcase the cultural and traditional essence of mariachi music. The mariachi stems from Mexico and is considered part of its rich culture. The mariachi sounds capture the audience's attention since it is seen as incompatible to many forms of what is considered "American" music. Because of the close relationship between mariachi and Mexico, the choice of music in the opening song of *Bordertown: Laredo* depicts the US border city as part of a Mexican site. A strong opening statement is being made initially by launching such music in the opening scene. It is telling its audience that Laredo, Texas, is a foreign place—one that cannot be imagined as the all-American scene that is usually portrayed and accepted on television. The music represents otherness[40] by depicting it as something that communicates feelings and ideas of Laredo being on the outside of the United States. It is sending a clear message that even though Laredo may be part of the United States the "American" way of life is not practiced there, thus contributing to the discourse that Laredoans need state regulation and surveillance.

Regulation, in this sense, represents a need to control, enforce, and preserve what is recognized as acceptable and "American" in the United States. Furthermore, *Bordertown* tells the story of the people of Laredo; therefore, the Latino body is a site to be monitored, in this case by the Laredo Police Department's Narcotic Unit. This representation attests to being an insider but forever marked as an outsider, thus producing feelings and thoughts of what it means to belong in this country. While the music already displaces Laredoans as outsiders—Mexican rather than American—the content further criminalizes Laredoans as personas non grata in the United States.[41]

In the first scene of the premiere episode, Sergeant Robert Sifuentes, who is the head of Laredo Police Department's Narcotics Unit, opens up on certain assumptions about the city. "I think what people assume about Laredo is that it's the Wild West." The commentary is compelling since he reinforces the perception of the Old West as part of Laredo, and once the strong and distinct mariachi and flamenco music are disseminated, it firmly situates Laredo as an undistinguished constituent of the Old West—one that evokes an inkling of lawlessness. The music, which is part mariachi with an egregious flamenco and a feeble Old West flourish, helps to create and transmit the representation of unruliness and disorder.

At the same time, the music from the opening song is strategically manipulated throughout each episode and serves as background music in the show's website. Throughout each episode, specific scenes of car chases or plot resolutions employ the use of strong guitars and vihuelas that were previously listened to during the opening song. These two instruments are strategically placed in order for the viewer to be cognizant of the fact that even though they are watching a television show that depicts an American city, the signification of Mexico is part of Laredeons' fabric that cannot be separated from them. The same is true for the website. One cannot be detached from what the story is portraying: little Mexico. This powerful tie is what Stuart Hall refers to as placing oneself within the image that implicates the production of meaning.[42] In this case, there is no clear identification to the visual that the music represents; therefore, viewers cannot imagine or find any relation to the image and a certain (mis)representation of the border is made: unfamiliar, strange, and regarded as other. In effect, it is constitutive to its (mis)representation.

Space and Signifying Practices

The use of space in *Bordertown: Laredo* manufactures "Little Mexico" by employing strategic editing and sequencing. Numerous scenes throughout the episodes and especially in the opening song and the promotional video elevate the master plan of depicting the border as a suspect and strange site. Three specific shots in the opening theme song, which are seen as an introduction to each episode, foster the manufacturing of Laredo as "Little Mexico." The first shot is a grand shot of the Mexican flag overshadowing the clouds in the sky. Along with mariachi music, that is the first visualization and image that is captured in *Bordertown: Laredo*. It is the *tricolor* of the red, white, and green along with the Mexican coat of arms that is transfixed in the United States imagery. These signifying practices illustrated through the Mexican flag are involved in the production of meaning of what Laredo represents: a space that embodies the solidarity of Mexico through the use of color. The strategic use of the Mexican flag reinforces the manufacturing of Mexico in this US border town.

Moreover, seconds after each police officer is introduced during the opening song, screen shots of caged *gallos* (roosters) are vividly displayed. In Mexico, *gallos* are part of the culture and the well-known *pelea de gallos* or "cockfight" that is commonly seen in major arenas also known as *palenques*, are part of the vitality and spirit of what Mexico symbolizes. Using caged *gallos* in these introductory scenes inculcates the visualization of the city of Laredo as being a Mexican site, but it more importantly indicates the caged vitality and spirit of Mexicans living on the borderlands. This caged frame is a constant reminder and reaffirmation of the enclosed space surrounding Mexicans in Laredo. The perpetual manufacturing of Laredo as part of a foreign country identifies it as being on the outside and belonging in Mexico, thus creating this fixed meaning of what is considered an unacceptable representation of the United States.

Additional opening shots reveal colorful Mexican markets and exotic women working in local "beer runs." It must also be stated that the subsequent use of the opening shots stopped and can only be seen in the original videos. The removal of such shots seems to be a part of a concern by either the cable channel or producers over showcasing images of striking and unfamiliar beauty. In this case, the women become the object of the man's gaze, thus encapsulating the exotic harlot that continuously stereotypes Latina women in film.[43]

What is even more compelling is how the police are defined by the space. In each of the ten episodes the Narcotics Unit congregates in police headquarters to discuss the culprits and any leads gathered. The video shots always zero in on the expanding shot of Laredo Police Department's headquarters, capturing its towering proportions and then quickly centers on a discussion of the offenders. Even though they are there to examine different strategies and tactics, the dialogue among the officers is nevertheless light and even entertaining. However, once the raid, drug bust, or arrest has been made, they once again close in on its headquarters' dominating size, drawing attention to a more somber tone and professional attitude. The citizens, on the other hand, are rarely seen in this encapsulating or protected space. The citizens are affiliated with the streets of Laredo and not to a secure or enclosed space. The police, defined by their prominent headquarters, are seen as regulating and monitoring a protected space.

At the same time, the promotional advertisement that ran for several months on the A&E Television Network before the show premiered was violent and disturbing. Even though this material ran before the show premiered, it is important to examine how it was utilized and the implications it produced. One of Laredo's local television networks even stated that "residents were not happy with the negative portrayal of the city."[44] Here, strategic screen shots show numerous bloodied bodies on the streets and a substantial amount of drugs. However, the promotional advertisement was later removed because it was revealed that the screen shots were inaccurate. Before it was removed from the air, Al Roker, executive Producer of *Bordertown: Laredo* and NBC's television weather forecaster, said he had absolutely no control of the promotional advertisement and that "promo departments get a little worked up," admitting to the sensationalization that the promo produces.[45] This unmindful response by the use of such promotional material continues the manufacturing of criminality that equates it with "Little Mexico" on US soil and furthers the rationalization to regulate and supervise the border since it has become unhinged, unmanageable, and reckless. In other words, Laredo has yet again become suspect and detached of the Americana way of life. It also draws our attention to the effects of the negative news portrayals of immigrants. According to Yuki Fujioka, images of out-group members "inform people about how other group members look and act and contribute to how people feel about others."[46] This is undeniably problematic since promo ads certainly add value to the negative portrayal of Latinos and construct the real for greater America. Furthermore, (mis)representing Laredo through the use of strategic space allows the viewer to create Laredo as a Mexican site where there is no need to cross the border since all that is Mexico can be attained in this Mexican town. These (mis) representations attempt to fix or naturalize the meaning of the border as a site that is strange, unfamiliar, and even suspect. As a result, it creates the need to inspect, control, enforce, and supervise the border.

Locating Words and Language Use

The power of words is paramount to the meaning we attach to them. This third site, the control and influence of word usage and language, skews our understanding of Laredo, furthering the marginalization and racialization of the Laredoans and the border in *Bordertown: Laredo*.

First, the promotional advertisement claimed that "ninety percent of the cocaine in the United States comes from one city—welcome to Laredo!" After its initial run though, the promo ad was removed and the Laredo Police Department rapidly removed itself from that ad, claiming that they did not know where the information stemmed from or who was responsible for the particular false statistic.[47] Such a dangerous claim suggests that Laredo is ground zero for drugs and therefore a dangerous and significant threat. Furthermore, accompanied with the language used, a picture of the US map with countless geographic lines zeroing in on Laredo produces the (mis)representation that Laredo is the hub of instability and risk. The specific words that are used together with the image of the map pointing directly to Laredo, creates and reinforces Laredo to be (mis)represented as degenerate and criminal.[48]

Additionally, some of the text on the show's website changed. Originally, Laredo was described as being "under siege" yet was modified to read, "Laredo is besieged by drugs." The first description tells the story of a city that is surrounded in a fortress of criminality and trouble. However, after promotional ads were released I returned to the website and realized the language had been altered to now read "besieged," yet Laredo is still portrayed as a city that is encircled by wrongful activities. What does this play on words signify? No matter the change, the word usage still produces feelings and thoughts of a national threat. It is portrayed as abnormal and isolated—away from the untarnished American way, a modality presented as free, as long as one adheres to what is considered "American" by hegemonic forces.

Lastly, throughout the opening song and the episodes, most of the video shots taken display Spanish billboards. Laredo is a Spanglish community that welcomes both English and Spanish into many of its homes, businesses, and advertisement materials, but to disregard most of the English language usage in its billboards is problematic. For example, in two back-to-back shots, a red and black billboard of a gun ammunition store reads, "Armería" (armory). This again (mis)represents Laredo as a Mexican site where Spanish is embraced and as a threat to the United States imaginary—a disposition of the social world that can have real ramifications. A second example is even more present and powerful since it shows a large sign for a Mexican themed restaurant that reads "Super Tortas—Taquitos Ravi" (super sandwiches—mini tacos) in red, white, and green color (colors of the Mexican flag). This signifying practice produces a meaning of confusion and detachment to the greater United States as well as an attempt to manufacture the Mexicanness of color and language. The use of displaying a majority of Spanish language billboards generates thoughts of what is accepted as American, especially when there is a discourse of the Spanish language represented as the "language of foreigners."[49] However, throughout the series, almost no English signage is shot, underlining the Mexicanness of this town even though there are plenty to showcase in English. The need to negatively mark the Spanish language speaker as other began to emerge when the number of Spanish-speaking immigrants arose in the United States. The Spanish language became a dirty word and as Samuel Huntington stated, it placed Spanish-speaking immigrants "outside of U.S. society."[50] Huntington, who in 2004 stressed, "There is no *Americano* dream. There is only the American dream created by an Anglo-Protestant society. Mexican Americans will share in that dream and in that society only if they dream in English."[51] This play on words extends the idea of the other whose opinions and choices are unwanted and unsolicited. If Spanish-speaking immigrants want to share the American dream, according to Huntington and his followers, it can become a reality if and when we play by their rules. This implies that Spanish-speaking or bilingual immigrants should only speak English since it is the only language that is desired, warranted, and privileged in this country. This dominating opinion that an English-only dream is possible if we follow their rules is an example of what Joe R. Feagin calls the "view of white superiority, virtue, and moral goodness" that has been the dominant racial frame for hundreds of years.[52] Their form of indoctrinating direct discriminatory action against those who are Spanish speakers extends the viewpoint of othering those who do not play into their paradigm. At the same time, it reinforces societal fears of what is outside the norm and places it as menacing and destructive. Once again, the (mis)representation of Laredo creates a threat to national security and bears the question: what is to be done in order to regulate this city back to what fits as normal, established . . . American?

CONCLUSION

This chapter explored how Mexicanness is manufactured in the (mis)representation of the reality-crime series *Bordertown: Laredo*. Three sites uncover the perpetual (mis)representation of Laredo and frame the reinforcement of the border as a space of alterity. Through the manipulation of music, space, and language, these three sites work in conjunction, creating an ideology to naturalize the meaning of what it means to be on the outside of what is viewed as American. An attempt to close the meaning and stop the flow of difference evokes feelings of forever being marked other. In effect, the television show's message of crime in the city and fighting the war on drugs is somewhat lost. The viewer becomes preoccupied with the (mis)representation of the music, space, and language employed throughout the series. This television show attempts to depict the city of Laredo and the people of Laredo as part of Mexico, without ever leaving the United States. It creates a message that those who populate the city are different and separate from the American norm. Angharad N. Valdivia says it best when she describes how "mainstream media help to naturalize the superiority of white people and justify a system of racial inequalities."[53] This is the exact representation of what *Bordertown: Laredo* offers the city of Laredo and even more dangerously what it declares to greater America.

NOTES

1. "United States Census Bureau: Laredo, Texas," United States Census Bureau, accessed April 22, 2013, http://quickfacts.census.gov/qfd/states/48/4841464.html.

2. Ofelia Garcia, "Racializing the Language Practices of U.S. Latinos," in *How the United States Racializes Latinos: White Hegemony and its Consequences*, ed. José A. Cobas, Jorge Duany, and Joe R. Feagin (Boulder: Paradigm Publishers, 2009), 101–115.

3. Garcia, "Racializing the Language Practices," 101–115.

4. Garcia, "Racializing the Language Practices," 101–115.

5. Tim Gaynor, "California Senate Passes 'Anti-Arizona' Immigration Bill," *Reuters*, July 6, 2012, http://www.reuters.com/article/2012/07/06/us-usa-california-immigration-idUSBRE86502720120706.

6. Tom Cohen and Bill Mears, "Supreme Court Mostly Rejects Arizona Immigration Law; Gov Says 'Heart' Remains," *CNN,* June 25, 2012, http://edition.cnn.com/2012/06/25/politics/scotus-arizona-law/index.html.

7. Joe Sutton, "Mississippi Lawmakers Pass Controversial Immigration Bill," *CNN*, March 16, 2012, http://edition.cnn.com/2012/03/16/us/mississippi-immigration-law/index.html.

8. Arlene Dávila, *Latino Spin: Public Image and the Whitewashing of Race* (New York: New York University Press, 2008).

9. Stuart Hall, "The Work of Representation," in *Representation: Cultural Representations and Signifying Practices,* ed. Stuart Hall,(London: Sage, 1997), 14–74.

10. Charles Ramirez-Berg, *Latino Images in Film: Stereotypes, Subversion, and Resistance* (Austin: University of Texas Press, 2002), 67.

11. Ramirez-Berg, *Latino Images in Film*, 67.

12. Ramirez-Berg, *Latino Images in Film*, 66.

13. Ramirez-Berg, *Latino Images in Film*, 66.

14. John L. Marambio, and Tew Chad, "The Promised Land: Resonance and Dissonance of Hollywood's Portrayals of Latin Americans in Film," *Studies in Latin American Popular Culture* 25 (2010), 119–139.

15. Dana E. Mastro and Amanda L. Robinson, "Cops and Crooks: Images of Minorities on Primetime Television," *Journal of Criminal Justice* 28, (2000), 385–396.

16. Dana E. Mastro, Elizabeth Behm-Morawitz, and Maria E. Kopacz, "Exposure to Television Portrayals of Latinos: The Implications of Aversive Racism and Social Identity Theory," *Human Communication Research* 34, (2008), 2; Dana E. Mastro and Elizabeth Behn-Morawitz, "Latino Representation of Primetime Television," *Journalism & Mass Communication Quarterly* 82, no. 1, (2005), 110–130.

17. Mastro and Robinson, "Cops and Crooks," 388.

18. Mastro and Behn-Morawitz, "Latino Representation of Primetime Television."

19. Mastro and Behn-Morawitz, "Latino Representation of Primetime Television,"126.

20. Mastro and Robinson, "Cops and Crooks," 394.

21. Mastro and Robinson, "Cops and Crooks," 386.

22. Yuki Fujioka, "Perceived Threats and Latino Immigrant Attitudes: How White and African American College Students Respond to News Coverage of Latino Immigrants," *The Howard Journal of Communication* 22, (2011), 47.

23. Otto Santa Ana, *Brown Tide Rising: Metaphors of Latinos in Contemporary American Public Discourse* (Austin: The University of Texas Press, 2002).

24. Fujioka, "Perceived Threats and Latino Immigrant Attitudes," 47.

25. Bethany Ogdon, "The Psycho-Economy of Reality Television in the Tabloid Decade," in *Essays on Representation and Truth: How Real is Reality TV*, ed. David S. Escoffery (Jefferson: Macfarland and Company, Inc., 2006), 30.

26. Laurie Oullette and Susan Murray, "Introduction," in *Reality TV: Remaking Television Culture*, ed. Susan Murray and Laurie Oullette (New York: New York Press, 2004), 2.

27. Mark P. Orbe, "Representations of Race," *Critical Studies in Media Communication* 25, no. 4 (2008), 346.

28. Orbe, "Representations of Race," 346.

29. Orbe, "Representations of Race," 349.

30. Elayne Rapping, "Aliens, Nomads, Mad Dogs, and Road Warriors," in *Reality TV: Remaking Television Culture*, ed. Susan Murray and Laurie Ouellette (New York: New York Press, 2004). 214–230; Sarah Escholz, Brenda Sims-Blackwell, Marc Gertz, and Ted Chiricos, "Race and Attitudes Toward the Police: Assessing the Effects of Watching 'Reality' Police Programs," *Journal of Criminal Justice* 30 (2002), 327–341.

31. Rapping, "Aliens, Nomads, Mad Dogs, and Road Warriors," 217.

32. Rapping, "Aliens, Nomads, Mad Dogs, and Road Warriors"; Escholz, Sims-Blackwell, and Chiricos, "Race and Attitudes."

33. Rapping,"Aliens, Nomads, Mad Dogs, and Road Warriors," 217.

34. Rapping, "Aliens, Nomads, Mad Dogs, and Road Warriors," 217.

35. Gloria E. Anzaldúa, *Borderlands: The New Mestiza* (San Francisco: Aunt Lute Books, 2007); Rosa L. Fregoso, *MeXicana Encounters: The Making of Social Identities on the Borderlands* (Los Angeles: University of California Press, 2003).

36. Dávila, *Latino Spin*, 170.

37. Anzaldúa, *Borderlands*.

38. Fregoso, *MeXicana Encounters*, 53.

39. Krystine I. Batcho, "Nostalgia: A Psychological Perspective," *Perceptual and Motor Skills* 80 (1995), 131–143.

40. Hall, "The Work of Representation."

41. Dávila, *Latino Spin*, 38.

42. Hall, "The Spectacle of the 'Other,'" in *Representation: Cultural Representations and Signifying Practices*, ed. Stuart Hall (London: Sage, 1997), 223–290.

43. Ramirez-Berg, *Latino Images in Film.*

44. "Al Roker Visits Gateway City to Discuss 'Bordertown Laredo,'" *Pro8News*, September 30, 2011, http://www.pro8news.com/news/Al-Roker-Visits-the-Gateway-City-to-Discuss-Bordertown-Laredo-130893313.html.

45. "Al Roker Visits."

46. Fujioka, "Perceived Threats," 59.

47. "Bordertown Laredo Preview," *Pro8News*, October 2, 2011, http://www.pro8news.com /news/blog/Border-Town-Laredo-130953393.html.

48. Fregoso, *MeXicana Encounters.*

49. Ofelia Garcia, "Racializing the Language Practices," in *How the United States Racializes Latinos: White Hegemony and its Consequences*, ed. José A. Cobas, Jorge Duany, and Joe R. Feagin (Boulder: Paradigm Publishers, 2009),104.

50. Garcia, "Racializing the Language Practices," 104.

51. Garcia, "Racializing the Language Practices," 104–105.

52. Joe R. Feagin, *The White Racial Frame: Centuries of Racial Framing and Counter Framing.* (New York: Routledge, 2009), 11.

53. Anghaard N. Valdivia, *Latina/os and the Media*, (Cambridge: Polity Press, 2010), 6.

Chapter Twenty

Cyborgs in the Newsroom: Databases, Cynicism, and Political Irony in *The Daily Show*

Noah J. Springer

The Daily Show with Jon Stewart (*TDS*) has proved to be an influential political force over the last decade. From interviewing President Obama to throwing a rally on the mall in Washington, DC, Stewart and company have contributed a new, humorous voice into the public sphere. However, the show has also come under scrutiny, specifically for supposedly fostering cynicism in its audience.[1] These accusations rely on comparisons between *TDS* and traditional televised news and assume that *TDS* shares the same epistemological position as traditional journalism, which in fact it does not. Through the use of technology to redact video clips of politicians and other media outlets, *TDS* constructs ironic critiques of contemporary society and deconstructs the traditional binary between information and entertainment. This deconstruction is the work of a cyborg interpretation of information that shows its audience the false binary established between "hard" and "soft" news; the same binary on which the accusations of cynicism are based. In this chapter, I argue that *TDS* should be considered in the same framework as new media products (i.e., social media, streaming services, blogs), rather than compared with traditional media (i.e., televised news, newspapers, radio). Under the framework of new media, *TDS* engages its audience in "cyborg citizenship,"[2] a postmodern metaphor of an embodied politic, relying on interaction between humans and technology to provide new modes of engagement with a participatory democracy.

I first establish how *TDS* has been considered in prior research, specifically focusing on accusations of cynicism about the program. I next show how, if *TDS* is considered as a new media phenomenon, the accusations of cynicism become dubious. Following this, I look at three segments of *TDS* during the presidential campaign of 2012, using each as an example of a technique used in *TDS* that corresponds with notions of new media technologies. I then conclude that rather than cynicism, Stewart fosters a new form of cyborg citizenship in his viewers.

NEW MEDIA AND THE LANGUAGE OF THE CYBORG

Early understandings of politics and late-night comedy began as examinations of how these programs were a "new" media, differing from traditional notions of televised entertainment and news.[3] However, as soon as focus began to shift away from programs like *The Late Show with David Letterman* and *The Tonight Show with Jay Leno* to *TDS* as a primary site of analysis (somewhere around 2004), theories of new media were quickly forgotten for questions surrounding political ideologies and activism,[4] humor as politics,[5] and comparisons with other news programs.[6] While these are certainly important issues, the loss of emphasis on "new" media has led to discussions of *TDS* in contexts of traditional, narratively based media, rather than in the context which it belongs: the context of the cyborg.

Donna Haraway famously argued that the continuing erosion of the binary between human and technology has given way to a new epistemological stance of the "cyborg," which emphasizes interactions between humans and machines as a new understanding of the world.[7] Through a feminist stance, Haraway lists a variety of dichotomies that form "informatics of domination."[8] These dichotomies are deconstructed and put under critical scrutiny through the new logic of a cyborg.[9] Often called "infotainment," various scholars have blamed *TDS* for corrupting traditional "hard" news with humor and entertainment ("soft" news).[10] I want to add the traditional binary between "hard" and "soft" news into Haraway's list as yet another informatic of domination. *TDS* is not a corruption of traditional television news. It is a cyborg newsroom that deconstructs the binary between information and entertainment, participating in the cyborg politics of new media.

Despite claims that *TDS* is sexist,[11] this deconstruction of the hard/soft dichotomy is an inherently feminist act. The division between hard and soft news is a socially constructed binary that reflects the gendered politics of the newsroom. Monika Djerf-Pierre and Monica Löfgren-Nilsson argue that as women entered the public sphere and the newsroom, changes in the genre were often described in terms of *"feminization."*[12] Male anchors and correspondents were often associated with detachment, neutrality, and the public sphere, while female anchors and correspondents were more often aligned as private, empathetic, and personal. The authors argue that the distinction between hard and soft news falls down a strictly gendered binary, because of two driving logics: "the first logic is derived from the view that women and men have different beliefs about what are important and therefore newsworthy public issues," and "the second logic assumes that women and men are interested in and derive pleasure from different subjects and topics."[13] *TDS* places both of these logics under scrutiny through the logic of the cyborg, combining the traditionally separate worlds of hard and soft news (information and entertainment) to create a hybrid that relies exclusively on a new logic mediated through technology.

CYNICISM IN *THE DAILY SHOW*

The feminist deconstruction performed by *TDS* is important because it points to certain fundamental problems in the article "*The Daily Show* Effect: Candidate Evaluations, Efficacy, and American Youth." In this article Jody Baumgartner and Jonathan S. Morris argue two primary points. First, they propose that young viewers will have negative opinions about the presidential candidates (George W. Bush and John Kerry). Secondly, they argue "young viewers' cynicism toward the electoral system will increase with exposure to campaign coverage on *The Daily Show*," and "young viewers' cynicism toward the news media will increase with exposure to campaign coverage on *The Daily Show*."[14] To test these hypotheses, the authors conducted an experiment where 732 students were assigned to watch either election coverage by *TDS*, segments of the *CBS Evening News* for similar periods of time and with similar content, or nothing at all. They determined that participants had more negative associations with candidates after exposure to *TDS*, while those watching *CBS Evening News* showed no negative association.[15] Furthermore, they argued *TDS* has a "negative influence on trust and overall ratings of the news media" and "exposure to *The Daily Show* does indeed seem to generate increased cynicism toward the news media. Again, this relationship did not exist among participants exposed to *CBS Evening News*."[16]

Baumgartner and Morris concluded that the cynicism encouraged by *TDS* could result in a lack of political voting and action rather than encouraging political engagement and participatory democracy as others had suggested.[17] However, with youth voting in record numbers during the 2008 presidential campaign, it seems that the cynicism of *TDS* had not affected the audience as much as anticipated.[18] The underlying assumption of Baumgartner and Morris's work that *TDS* is analogous to the traditional newsroom of *CBS Evening News* is specious. The reality is that *TDS* behaves much more like an object of new media. Stewart and company do not weave traditional journalistic narratives. Instead, they rely on the vast databases of Internet to expose the hypocrisies and irony of contemporary political life and media. *TDS* acts as an interface to the database whereas traditional news systems focus on the construction of narrative from traditional journalistic news gathering practices. Lev Manovich stated, the "database and narrative are natural enemies" and comparisons between the two prove unfruitful.[19]

The rest of this chapter demonstrates how *TDS* implements the database logic throughout the program. Through examinations of the role of irony, "redactive editing,"[20] and "discursive integration"[21] on *TDS* during the 2012 presidential election, I show that Stewart is not in fact encouraging cynicism, but promoting negotiated readings in his audience and encouraging them to understand the world as "cyborg citizens."[22] It is not cynicism that is fostered by *TDS*, but critical engagement with political and media discourse through logics generated through databases and structures of new media.

IRONY

Haraway introduces her concept of the cyborg as an epistemology based in irony. She begins:

> this essay is an effort to build an ironic political myth faithful to feminism, socialism, and materialism. . . . Irony is about humor and serious play. It is also a rhetorical strategy and a political method, one I would like to see more honoured within socialist-feminism. At the centre of my ironic faith, my blasphemy, is the image of the cyborg.[23]

Previously, I have argued that "serious play" is a primary organizing factor of *TDS*, as well as *The Colbert Report* and *South Park*.[24] However, considering Stewart's show under the new epistemological underpinnings of the cyborg provides a new avenue for understanding the role of irony in the program.[25] Previous scholars have examined the role of irony on *TDS*,[26] but considering it as part of cyborg politics can help explain how the politics of irony informs *TDS*'s politics.

Stewart and his team of correspondents travelled to both the Democratic and Republican National Conventions (DNC and RNC) during August and September 2012.[27] The *TDS* crew spent time interviewing participants, local residents, and officials at both events. During the DNC, Stewart opened a segment by questioning the inclusiveness of the Democratic "big tent" mentality, and throws to his correspondents, Jason Jones and Samantha Bee, as "the best f#@cking news team ever." Jones's voiceover states, "There's one key message at the Democratic National Convention that's just not in dispute," and after a quick cut, a lady speaks into the microphone: "We are the big tent party. We represent everyone." Quick cuts follow showing various people speaking to Jones and Bee, and extolling the virtues of open acceptance by their party. Various people claim that their party is "the arms wide open party" or "the party of inclusion." A white man states, "We're Latinos, Hispanics, we're Blacks, we're the LGBT community, we're women, we're poor [. . .] Everyone's welcome." Jones butts in: "except." The man continues, "except, unless you own a corporation, or if you're a hunter, a gun-owner, white males." Within fifty-five seconds Jones and Bee have successfully exposed the irony of the "big tent" philosophy of the Democratic Party.

The rest of the segment focuses on this irony through a montage of people declaring how open the Democratic Party is, and then immediately denying entrance to the party for anybody who fits stereotypes of Republicans. One interviewee states, "The Democratic Party, we don't stereotype and we don't generalize." Another claims, "We don't judge." Meanwhile, members of the Republican Party are called: "gun-toting, hillbilly, tea-partiers," "beer-toting, fakers down in Florida," "anti-science," "narrow-minded," and "whack-job, evangelical gun nuts," "nazis," "evil," "red-neck freaks," among various other derogatory terms. This irony is nicely summed up by one interviewee.

Jones: "What don't they get about intolerance?"

Interviewee: "I would never call a redneck a name."

Another participant ironically states, "The teabagger's generalize because they are very narrow-minded people."

Interviewee: "The world would be very beautiful if we could just accept everybody's differences."

Jones: "Exactly, accept everyone's differences."

Interviewee: "Yes." *nods*

Jones: "We need to accept EVERYONE."

Interviewee: "You mean I should accept them. Is that what you're saying?"

Jones: *shrugs*

This quick segment exposes several important points about the logic of *TDS* as a cyborg. Jones deconstructs the ideology of the Democratic Party as a "big tent" through the ironic statements of party members. This interaction with technology is the important building block of Haraway's claims about cyborgs. She argues that interaction with technology has produced a new type of ontology, and that this new cyborg ontology provides a form of ironic politics. Consequently, cyborgs do not fall down party lines, but engage in the political struggle "to see from both perspectives at once because each reveals both domination and possibilities unimaginable from the other vantage point."[28] Jones and Bee are exposing the Democratic view of themselves, and how they are viewed from the Republican side of the aisle. This is even more important as it explains how Stewart himself is self-admittedly on the left of the aisle (a former socialist even),[29] but still constructs important criticism about the blue branches of government and the Democratic Party as a whole. *TDS* does not choose sides but is based on the logic of a cyborg whose politics rely on exposing irony, and deconstructing the ideologies on which hypocrisies are based.

REDACTIVE JOURNALISM

So far, this chapter has focused on *TDS* in the notion of Haraway's cyborg. However, others may argue that every news station is a cyborg, because they all interact with technology and media on a daily basis. The difference between *TDS* and traditional news stations then lies in the logic. Traditional notions of journalism are based on constructions of narratives.[30] Instead, *TDS* constructs its programming from the logic of new media: the logic of a database. Instead of going out and practicing traditional news gathering techniques and constructing a narrative surrounding events witnessed, Stewart engages with databases to dip into the archive and expose the hypocrisy of those in power. Manovich argues that both database and narrative try to occupy the same space by providing methods to "make meanings out of the world."[31] The narrative structure of traditional television news sources is not compatible with the epistemological standpoints of *TDS*.

This can most readily be seen, again, at the technological level. Jeffrey Jones, author of *Entertaining Politics: Satiric Television and Political Engagement*, argues that "redactive journalism"[32] is a primary tool in Stewart's critiques of media and politics. John Hartley defines redaction as "the action or process of preparing for publication; reduction to literary form; revision, rearrangement. The result of such a process; a new edition; an adaptation; a shortened form, an abridged version. The action of bringing or putting into a definite form."[33] Jones adapts this idea and suggests that various editing techniques employed on *TDS* function as redactive journalism. Jones points to "four sets of redactive techniques" through which "Stewart is able to construct evidence in ways that resemble the behaviors of a criminal prosecutor, yet also stand in contrast to that which television does (or fails to do) in its usage of video materials at its disposal."[34] Specifically, he points to methods of interrogation, cross-examination, summarization, and conclusion as results of an editorial process that relies on a database of information. Geoffrey

Baym makes a similar claim, stating that "it is possible, *The Daily Show* suggests, to construct a newscast simply by mining the raw material available on the average cable television system."[35] The vision of a narratively structured newscast does not apply to *TDS*. It is based in the new media epistemology of the database.

Although all of these redactive techniques are important, Jones explains them well and, for the sake of space, this chapter will focus primarily on the use of redaction as cross-examination. During the Republican primaries of 2012, Stewart kept careful track of the results from the various states.[36] During the Michigan primaries, candidate Rick Santorum released a statewide, automated phone call to encourage liberals to vote against Romney during the Republican primary (Michigan's primary is open to voters of all parties.) Later, on Fox News, Romney declared Santorum's tactics "outrageous, and disgusting. A terrible dirty trick." Stewart quickly began to ask questions: "What are the odds of a tape existing of Mitt Romney endorsing that very same practice?" He pulls out a large, red button (the "Mitt Romney Flip-Flop Finder"), hits the button, and a clip of Romney speaking with George Stephanopoulos in 2007 immediately appears on the screen. Romney states that when there was little competition in the Republican primary, he would vote for the weakest Democratic candidate in the open Massachusetts primary election. By redactively editing the two clips, *TDS* exposes the irony behind Romney's recent stand against Santorum. This editing is a product of the database logic that undergirds *TDS* through which the producers can access any recorded file of the candidate and cross-reference it against what the candidate is currently saying.

Stewart is unwilling to even leave this issue standing though. He continues to mine the archive, pulling up a clip of Romney from later in 2007 saying the same sentiment in a "twelve-year-old gleeful girly voice." Again, Stewart relies on the cyborg politics of irony to deconstruct current narratives constructed by a presidential campaign. This clip also exposes that through redactive editing, Stewart and company are engaging with the database in a manner not used by traditional news journalism. By diving into the archive, *TDS* provides historical contextualization to the current narratives of power being represented by other news outlets.

DISCURSIVE INTEGRATION

Until now, I have shown how *TDS* acts under the politics of a cyborg and the logic of the database. However, I have not shown how this new conception undermines the argument that Stewart fosters a cynical audience. Baumgart-ner and Morris begin their essay by discussing soft news, including tabloid newsmagazine shows, network and news cable shows, and

> daytime talk shows (e.g., *The Oprah Winfrey Show, Dr. Phil*) [that] tend to take more of a human interest approach to entertainment, late-night talk shows (e.g., *The Tonight Show with Jay Leno, The Late Show with David Letterman*), es-pecially in the monologue segments of the programs, are more humor oriented. *The Daily Show with Jon Stewart* fits into this subcategory.[37]

Again, their claims are based on a traditional binary of journalism: hard and soft news. A problem arises because *TDS* does not actually belong in either of those categories and actively deconstructs the established dichotomy. A primary method used by Stewart to deconstruct this binary is what Geoffrey Baym calls "discursive integration," or an alternative journalism that pro-vides "a way of speaking about, understanding, and acting within the world defined by the permeability of form and the fluidity of content."[38] *TDS* defies traditional genres of journalism, entertainment, comedy, and news to inter-rogate power and media through satire and parody, creating a new way for its audience to receive information and be entertained.

The binaries established through traditional newsrooms no longer apply to the cyborg newsroom of *TDS*. Traditional news outlets (and traditional schol-ars) "have so far failed to grasp the deeper insight that in an age of discursive integration, it is possible to be entertaining in the sense of both amusement and serious thought, and that each one may have the ability to enhance the other."[39] This new method of journalism, as Baym sees it, does not replace the traditional newsroom, but allows for experimental journalism.

Baym places particular emphasis on satire as an active part of discursively integrated journalism. Baym points to the rejection of both standard quote selection practices and ideas of objective journalism in favor of a *dialogic* discourse that juxtaposes multiple voices against each other.[40] This juxta-position and engagement of a dialogical voice is the root of satire, which "represents searching for truth through the process of dialogical interaction. Unlike traditional news, which claims an epistemological certainty, satire is a discourse of *inquiry*, a rhetoric of challenge that seeks through the asking of unanswered questions to clarify the underlying morality of a situation."[41] Thus, satire helps translate the monologic narrative established through tra-ditional power structures and media institutions into a dialogic attack on the foundations of that power.

Stewart's special segment, "Chaos on Bulls**t Mountain," performs pre-cisely this task through discursively integrated journalism.[42] He starts the segment, "I think if there's one thing everybody can agree on, in the entire country, it's that Barack Obama is . . ." and points directly at the camera, which cuts to a montage of Fox News personalities saying variations of "Barack Obama is the worst president in history." Here we see another instance of the redactive editing discussed previously. However, as opposed to going across time and digging into the database, this time Stewart edits clips from across four programs on Fox News to expose the consistent talking point for the entire network, rather than just specific programs. Having seen all these pundits calling Obama the worst president ever, Stewart assumes that Obama is losing in the polls, until he reveals (with the help of NBC News) that in fact, Obama is five points ahead of Romney.

The Romney campaign had initiated a "reboot" earlier that week, but it was primarily thwarted by the release of a video from a private fundraising dinner, which soon became notorious for Romney's attitude regarding 47 percent of Americans: "There are 47 percent of the people who will vote for the president no matter what . . . who are dependent upon government, who believe that they are victims . . . who believe they are entitled to health care, to food, to housing." This video proved to be a major roadblock for the Romney campaign, but the video itself is not the subject of the segment. Stewart states that this video "touched off a firestorm everywhere, but nowhere more acutely than Romney campaign headquarters [Fox News]," resulting in "CHAOS ON BULLSHIT MOUNTAIN." He starts deconstructing the narrative of Fox News by letting the pundits speak for themselves. Although this may appear as another narrative in itself, in fact Stewart acts more as an interface that "provides access to the underlying database."[43] Stewart acts as a guide into the database. Clearly any citizen with Internet access can find these same contradictions directly from these pundits themselves, but Stewart acts as a humorous guide through the ironic deconstruction.

Clips of Sean Hannity, Bill O'Reilly, and Brian Killmeade all emphasize the "left-wing website" (*Mother Jones*), and Neil Cavuto implies that Jimmy Carter's grandson had something to do with the release of this video. Stewart summarizes: "Yeah, he said it, but you only found out about it because of people we don't like."[44] He then jumps to the second talking point on Fox News, where the pundits try to defend Romney's statements in the video: "It was not the best way of saying something"; "He confused a lot of things"; "It's not the most ideal language." Stewart again summarizes, "You're looking and hearing the cynical, condescending plutocratic words that he [Romney] was saying, not the aspirational optimistic message he, in retrospect, should have been meaning. It's like Romney jazz. It's the words you don't hear that's the [message] [*sic*]." Stewart concludes that the discourse on Fox News surrounding the 47 percent video boiled down to "inartful words from a dubious source. Oh, and one other thing." Again, producers cut to the database to reveal Hannity stating, "This is factually accurate, what Romney is saying." O'Reilly follows: "If I'm Governor Romney, I run with this all day long." Others follow: "It was the truth"; "He's a boss who says the truth"; "I think this will be seen as a win for Romney." Stewart stares at the camera, dumfounded: "You don't summit Bullshit Mountain unless you know your way around a turd or two."

The next set of talking points Stewart exposes relates to the discourse of the campaign. Various Fox News contributors state that, in effect, liberals are using this video to distract from the important topics of discussion, such as the national debt, oil dependence, and the wars in Iraq and Afghanistan. Ann Coulter states, "You can't actually discuss serious issues today in the campaign. You have to move on to secretly recorded videos." Stewart invites the pundits to discuss said issues of import. Immediately, the screen cuts to Greta van Susteren discussing a recently released video of Obama discussing redistributing wealth in 1998. Stewart: "The Obama video is pertinent, but the Romney video is a distraction. Why?" A quick clip of Hannity defending Romney's video plays, stating that it was no longer relevant because it happened "way back in May." Stewart (after a quick bit about how far away May is), concludes that although May is far enough away for Romney to "radically change positions," Obama's video is from more than "fourteen Mays ago."

Using the redacted footage from Fox News, Stewart cuts across programming and traditional notions of narrative structure to expose the redundant, cynical, and uncritical discourse of Fox News. He discursively integrates elements from various texts (in this case programs on Fox News) to expose the monologic discourse on the channel, and opens it up for dialogical satire. The narrative of the 47 percent video is actively deconstructed by integrating various voices from Fox News into *TDS* broadcast but exposes that, in fact, those multiple voices are only saying one thing. Through satire redactive editing, Stewart adeptly challenges the notions promoted on Fox News by discursively integrating not only footage, but himself. He adopts multiple identities: sometimes the fool, sometimes the avid Fox News viewer, sometimes the critical cyborg. He actively crafts a dialogical discourse with the database of Fox News clips. In Manovich's terminology, he acts as the algorithm through which the audiences engage in the database: in this case, a set of clips from Fox News.

CYBORG CITIZENSHIP

The previous three sections have focused on how *TDS* functions as a product of new media. Stewart engages in the ironic politics of the cyborg, functions through the logic of a database to critique discourses of power, and engages in discursive integration to construct dialogic criticisms of the monological talking points of Fox News. All this was to show that if scholars understand *TDS* as a new media phenomenon, accusations of cynicism become suspect. If the underlying epistemologies of the two programs under examination (in Baumgartner and Morris's case *TDS* and *CBS Evening News*) are contradictory, surely the results are questionable at least.

But if *TDS* does not foster cynicism, what kind of politics does it instill in its audience? I argue that *TDS* focuses on encouraging what Chris H. Gray calls "cyborg citizenship." Like Haraway, he argues that the interaction between human and technology has generated a new epistemology, one that is capable of destroying master narratives of power and marginalization. He hopes the cyborg can help lead us to a more democratic government based on participatory citizenship. For this argument, however, his words regarding power hold the most weight. He argues that cyborg politics is all about power, and that if knowledge is power, then the cyborg has power because the cyborg can access the database. Gray states, "To be empowered, the cyborg citizen has to have specific information that govern our technical and political situation, and we need to understand information theory, which lays out the limits of knowledge . . . its formative rules . . . and its promises."[45] Stewart and everyone involved with *TDS* actively pursues and promotes the engagement of his audience with technology to discover these rules, limits, and promises of the knowledge provided by new media (every episode streams free at www.dailyshow.com). Rather than cynicism, *TDS* promotes a new form of politics that takes power out of the hands of politicians and media outlets, and encourages cyborg citizens to interrogate their traditionally established binaries of the separation between entertainment and information. This was best seen at the 2010 *Rally to Restore Sanity and/or Fear* on the Washington Mall. With the help of Stephen Colbert, Stewart drew approximately 215,000 people to the Mall as a rebuttal to Glenn Beck's "Rally to Restore Honor" earlier that year.[46] Various musical and comedic acts performed at the rally, but it became clear that Stewart was also calling for his audience to become politically engaged as they enjoyed the music and humor. Gray acknowledges that these new, cyborg politics

> will have its horrifying moments, and the reaction of those who fear change will be more horrifying still. But reaching towards greater democracy, stronger citizenship, and a proliferation of human and posthuman possibilities is our only choice besides a turn to the past that, since it would be in the context of postmodern technoscience, would make the Holocaust and the Gulag look like rehearsals.[47]

The new cyborg politic appears dangerous and unsettling, and often the new form of citizenship is met with disdain and aggression. However, as shown by *The Rally to Restore Sanity and/or Fear*, these new politics are in fact engaging citizens in a participatory democracy and encouraging political engagement.

CONCLUSION

The goal of this chapter was twofold. First, I intended to show how *The Daily Show with Jon Stewart* is a new media phenomenon as opposed to the traditional view that it was more of a hybrid between traditional media genres. I established this by showing how irony, redactive journalism, and discursive integration (all acknowledged traits of the program) are in fact based on the logic of databases and the ironic politics of the cyborg. Secondly, I wanted to defend *TDS* from Baumgartner and Morris's accusation that Stewart fosters cynicism in his audience. They based their experiment on two faulty premises: understanding *TDS* as "soft news" and comparing it with traditional media outlets. Ultimately, *TDS* actively deconstructs the gendered hard/soft dichotomy that underscores their experiment and establishes a cyborg logic and politics that makes comparison with traditional televised news questionable.

The concept that a television program could be seen as new media product presents several complications, including concepts of distribution (*TDS* is still on television), satire (does Stewart's satire undercut the ironic commentary), and audience (does the *TDS* audience understand the cyborg politic). However, the idea of a television program as a new media product also provides a variety of avenues for future research. Scholars should begin to look at what other television programs adapt the logics of new media to drive their cultural critique and where new media discourse enters traditional media. Other research ought to begin to look empirically at the ways through which *TDS* functions as a cyborg, and whether the audience understands this notion, or whether the accusations of cynicism maintain despite *TDS*'s database logic and cyborg politics.

NOTES

1. Jody Baumgartner and Jonathan S. Morris, "*The Daily Show* Effect: Candidate Evaluations, Efficacy, and American Youth," *American Politics Research* 34, no. 3 (2006), 341–367; *The Colbert Report*, Stephen Colbert's spin-off from *TDS*, has also faced similar charges of cynicism and exhibits many of the same qualities as *TDS*. However, Baumgartner and Morris's article was only related to Stewart's program, and so this study will also only discuss *TDS*. Future research should focus on *The Colbert Report* as an arbiter of the cultural logics of new media in the television format.

2. Chris H. Gray, *Cyborg Citizen: Politics in the Posthuman Age* (New York: Routledge, 2001).

3. Josh Compton, "Introduction: Surveying Scholarship on *The Daily Show* and *The Colbert Report*," in *The Stewart/Colbert Effect: Essays on the Real Impacts of Fake News*, ed. Amarnath Amarasingam (Jefferson: McFarLand & Company, Inc., Publishers, 2011), 9.

4. Heather L. LaMarre, Kristen D. Landreville, and Michael A. Beam, "The Irony of Satire: Political Ideology and the Motivation to See What You Want to See in *The Colbert Report*," *The International Journal of Press/Politics* 14, no. 2 (2009), 212–231; Lance R. Holbert, Jennifer L. Lambe, Anthony D. Dudo, and Kristin A. Carlton, "Primacy Effects of *The Daily Show* and National TV News Viewing: Young Viewers, Political Gratifications, and Internal Political Self-Efficacy," *Journal of Broadcasting & Electronic Media* 51, no. 1 (2007), 20–38; Lindsay H. Hoffman and Tiffany L. Thomson, "The Effect of Television Viewing on Adolescents' Civic Participation: Political Efficacy as a Mediating Mechanism," *Journal of Broadcasting & Electronic Media* 53, no. 1 (2009), 3–21.

5. Lauren Feldman, "The News about Comedy: Young Audiences, *The Daily Show,* and Evolving Notions of Journalism," *Journalism* 8, no. 4 (2007), 406–427; Jamie Warner, "Political Culture Jamming: The Dissident Humor of *The Daily Show With Jon Stewart*," *Popular Communication* 5, no. 1 (2007), 17–36; Jay D. Hmielowski, Lance R. Holbert, and Jayeon Lee, "Predicting the Consumption of Political TV Satire: Affinity for Political Humor, *The Daily Show*, and *The Colbert Report*," *Communication Monographs* 78, no. 1 (2011), 96–114.

6. Kevin Coe, David Tewksbury, Bradley J. Bond, Kristin L. Drogos, Robert W. Porter, Ashley Yahn, and Yuanyuan Zhang, "Hostile News: Partisan Use and Perceptions of Cable News Programming," *Journal of Communication* 58, no. 2 (2008), 201–219; Jody Baumgartner and Jonathan S. Morris, "One 'Nation,' under Stephen? The Effects of *The Colbert Report* on American Youth", *Journal of Broadcasting & Electronic Media* 52, no. 4 (2008), 622–643.

7. Donna Haraway, "A Cyborg Manifesto," in *The Cultural Studies Reader*, ed. Simon During (New York & London: Routledge, 1993).

8. Haraway, "A Cyborg Manifesto," 281.

9. These dichotomies include representation/simulation, perfection/optimization, reproduction/replication

10. Baumgartner and Morris, "*The Daily Show* Effect," 342.

11. Irin Carmon, "*The Daily Show*'s Woman Problem," *Jezebel*, June 23, 2010, http://jezebel.com/5570545/comedy-of-errors-behind-the-scenes-of-the--daily-shows-lady-problem.

12. Monika Djerf-Pierre and Monica Löfgren-Nilsson, "Gender-Typing in the Newsroom: The Feminization of Swedish Television News Production, 1958–2000," in *Gender and Newsroom Cultures: Identities at Work*, ed. Marjan de Bruin and Karen Ross (Cresskill: Hampton Press, Inc., 2004), 79.

13. Djerf-Pierre and Löfgren-Nilsson, "Gender-Typing in the Newsroom," 82.

14. Baumgartner and Morris, "*The Daily Show* Effect," 346.

15. Baumgartner and Morris, "*The Daily Show* Effect," 349.

16. Baumgartner and Morris, "*The Daily Show* Effect," 352.

17. Geoffrey Baym, "*The Daily Show*: Discursive Integration and the Reinvention of Political Journalism," *Political Communication* 22, no. 3 (2005), 259–276.

18. Scott Keeter, Juliana Horowit, and Alec Tyson, "Young Voters in the 2008 Election," *Pew Research Center,* November 13, 2008, http://www.pewresearch.org/2008/11/13/young-voters-in-the-2008–election/.

19. Lev Manovich, *The Language of New Media* (Cambridge: The MIT Press, 2001), 225.

20. Jeffrey P. Jones, *Entertaining Politics: Satiric Television and Political Engagement* (Lanham: Rowman & Littlefield Publishers, Inc., 2010).

21. Baym, "*The Daily Show*: Discursive Integration and the Reinvention of Political Journalism."

22. Gray, *Cyborg Citizen.*

23. Haraway, "A Cyborg Manifesto," 272.

24. Noah Springer, "Serious Play: Evaluating the Comedic, Political and Religious Relationships between *The Daily Show*, *The Colbert Report*, and *South Park*" (master's thesis: Southern Illinois University, 2011).

25. Future research should also examine how *South Park* and *The Colbert Report* relate with theories of new media.

26. Lisa Colletta, "Political Satire and Postmodern Irony in the Age of Stephen Colbert and Jon Stewart," *The Journal of Popular Culture* 42, no. 5 (2009), 856–874; Richard van Heertrum, "Irony and the News: Speaking through Cool to American Youth," in *The Stewart/Colbert Effect: Essays on the Real Impacts of Fake News*, ed. Amarnath Amarasingam (Jefferson: McFarland & Company, Inc., Publishers, 2011), 117–135; Lamarre et al., "The Irony of Satire."

27. Until the next note, all quotes in text are from the following: *The Daily Show*, "Hope and Change 2—The Party of Inclusion," produced by Miles Kahn and Stuart Miller, edited by Einar Westerlund, first broadcast September 5, 2012, by Comedy Central, http://www.thedailyshow.com/watch/wed-september-5–2012/hope-and-change-2–--the-party-of-inclusion.

28. Haraway, "A Cyborg Manifesto," 275.

29. Gary Younge, "Such a Tease," *The Guardian,* September 30, 2005, http://www.guardian.co.uk/media/2005/oct/01/usa.television.

30. Itzhak Roeh, "Journalism as Storytelling, Coverage as Narrative," *American Behavioral Scientist* 33, no. 2 (1989), 162–168.

31. Manovich, *The Language of New Media*, 225.

32. Jones, *Entertaining Politics*, 75.

33. John Hartley, "Communicative Democracy in a Redactional Society: The Future of Journalism Studies," *Journalism* 1, no. 39 (2000), 44.

34. Jones, *Entertaining Politics*, 116.

35. Baym, "*The Daily Show*: Discursive Integration and the Reinvention of Political Journalism." 264

36. Until the next note, all quotes are from the following: *The Daily Show*, "Indecision 2012 – Mitt Romney's and Rick Santorum's Michigan Campaigns," feat. Jon Stewart, first broadcast February 28, 2012, by Comedy Central, http://www.thedailyshow.com/watch/tue-february-28–2012/indecision-2012–--mitt-romney-s--rick-santorum-s-michigan-campaigns.

37. Baumgartner and Morris, "*The Daily Show* Effect," 342.

38. Baym, "*The Daily Show*: Discursive Integration and the Reinvention of Political Journalism," 262.

39. Baym, "*The Daily Show*: Discursive Integration and the Reinvention of Political Journalism," 274.

40. See Bakhtin, *The Dialogic Imagination.*

41. Baym, "*The Daily Show*: Discursive Integration and the Reinvention of Political Journalism," 267.

42. Until the next note, all quotes are from the following: *The Daily Show*, "Chaos on Bulls**t Mountain," featuring Jon Stewart, first broadcast September 19, 2012, by Comedy Central, http://www.thedailyshow.com/watch/wed-september-19–2012/chaos-on-bulls--t-mountain.

43. Manovich, *The Language of New Media*, 226.

44. Until the next note, all quotes are from the following: *The Daily Show*, "Chaos on Bulls**t Mountain," featuring Jon Stewart, first broadcast September 19, 2012, by Comedy Central, http://www.thedailyshow.com/watch/wed-september-19–2012/chaos-on-bulls--t-mountain.

45. Gray, *Cyborg Citizen*, 198–199.

46. Brian Montopoli, "Jon Stewart Rally Attracts Approximately 215,000," *CBS News,* October 30, 2010, http://www.cbsnews.com/8301–503544_162–20021284–503544.html.

47. Gray, *Cyborg Citizen*, 200–201.

Bibliography

"50 Pop Culture Moments that Rocked Fashion." *Entertainment Weekly*, June 18, 2007. http://www.ew.com/ew/article/0,,20207369,00.html.

"A Nation at Risk." Washington, D.C.: U.S.A. Research, 1984.

Abelman, Robert, and David J. Atkin. *The Televiewing Audience: The Art and Science of Watching TV.* Cresskill: Hampton Press, 2002.

Adamo, Gregory. *African Americans in Television Behind the Scenes.* New York: Peter Lang, 2010.

Adams, Carol J. *The Sexual Politics of Meat: A Feminist-Vegetarian Critical Theory.* New York: Continuum, 1990.

——. *The Pornography of Meat.* New York: Continuum, 2003.

Adams, Paul C. "Television as Gathering Place." *Annals of the Association of American Geographers* 82, no. 1 (1992): 117–135.

Adz, King. *The Stuff You Can't Bottle: Advertising for the Global Youth Market.* London: Thames and Hudson, 2013.

Ahmad, Farah, Pamela L. Hudak, Kim Bercovitz, Elisa Hollenberg, and Wendy Levinson. "Are Physicians Ready for Patients with Internet-based Health Information?" *Journal of Medical Internet Research* 8, no. 3 (2006).

Akerlof, George A., and Robert J. Shiller. *Animal Spirits: How Human Psychology Drives the Economy and Why It Matters for Global Capitalism.* Princeton: Princeton University Press, 2009.

Alberoni, Francesco. "The Powerless 'Elite': Theory and Sociological Research on the Phenomenon of the Stars." In *Stardom and Celebrity: A Reader,* edited by Sean Redmond and Su Holmes. 65–76. Los Angeles: Sage, 2005.

Albiniak, Paige. "Once He Got Going, Nothing Could Stop Him." *Broadcasting & Cable*, January 26, 2009.

Allen, Mark S. "A Systematic Review of Content Themes in Sport Attribution Research: 1954–2011." *International Journal of Sport and Exercise Psychology* 10, no. 1 (March 2012): 1–8.

Almasy, Steve. "Glee' Star Cory Monteith Found Dead." CNN.com, July 15, 2013. http://www. cnn.com/2013/07/14/showbiz/glee-star-dead.

"Al Roker Visits Gateway City to Discuss 'Bordertown Laredo.'" *Pro8News.* September 30, 2011. http://www.pro8news.com/news/Al-Roker-Visits-the-Gateway-City-to-Discuss-Bordertown-Laredo-130893313.html.

Alston, Joshua. "The Bully Pulpit." *Newsweek,* October 21, 2010. http://www.thedailybeast. com/newsweek/2010/10/21/tv-isn-t-exactly-hurting-for-gay- teen-role-models.html.

Alterman, Eric. *What Liberal Media? The Truth About Bias and the News.* New York: Basic Books, 2003.

Armstrong, Jennifer. *Mary and Lou and Rhoda and Ted: And All the Brilliant Minds Who Made* The Mary Tyler Moore Show *a Classic.* New York: Simon and Schuster, 2013.

Anderson, Elijah. "The Code of the Streets." *Atlantic,* May 1994. Accessed July 31, 2011. http://www.theatlantic.com/magazine/archive/1994/05/the-code-of-the-streets/6601/?single_page=true.

Anderson, Leon. "Analytic Autoethnography," *Journal of Contemporary Ethnography* 35 (2006): 373–395, doi: 10.1177/0891241605280449.

Ang, Ien. *Watching* Dallas*: Soap Opera and the Melodramatic Imagination.* London: Methuen, 1985.

Ankersmit, F. R. "Historiography and Postmodernism." *History and Theory* 28:2 (May 1989): 137–153.

Annas, George J. "Sex, Money, and Bioethics Watching *ER* and *Chicago Hope.*" *Hastings Center Report* 25, no. 5 (1995): 40–43.

Anzaldúa, Gloria E. *Borderlands: The New Mestiza.* San Francisco: Aunt Lute Books, 2007.

Ariyanto, Amarina, Matthew J. Hornsey, and Cindy Gallois. "Group Allegiances and Perceptions of Media Bias: Taking Into Account Both the Perceiver and the Source." *Group Processes and Intergroup Relations* 10–2 (2007): 266–279.

Armstrong, Jennifer. "Gay Teens on TV." *Entertainment Weekly*, September 1, 2011. http://www.ew.com/ew/article/0,,20361194_20524710,00.html.

"Arreviderci, Arnold." *Welcome Back, Kotter.* DVD, directed by Bob LaHendro. Burbank, CA: Warner Home Video, 2007.

Association for Media Literacy. Accessed August 10, 2013. http://www.aml.ca/.

"Aston Martin DBS Review." *Edmunds.* Accessed October 9, 2011. http://www. edmunds. com/aston-martin/dbs/.

Ausiello, Michael. "Scoop: Darren Criss Joins 'Glee.'" *Entertainment Weekly,* September 26, 2010. http://insidetv.ew.com/2010/09/26/darren-criss-glee-kurt-boyfriend/.

Bailey, Beth, and David Farber. *America in the Seventies.* Lawrence: University Press of Kansas, 2004.

Bakhtin, M. M., and Michael Holquist. *The Dialogic Imagination: Four Essays.* Austin: University of Texas Press, 1981.

"Balanced Literacy Model." *English Language Arts Mapping Model.* Accessed August 14, 2013. http://www.methuen.k12.ma.us/images/ela_mapping/balanced%20 literacy%20m odel.pdf.

Ball-Rokeach, Sandra, and Melvin DeFleur. *Theories of Mass Communication*, 5th ed. White Plains: Longman, 1989.

Bandura, Albert. "Social Cognitive Theory of Mass Communication." *Media psychology* 3, no. 3 (2001): 265–299.

———. *Social Learning Theory*. New York: General Learning Press, 1971.

Bandura, Albert., Dorothea Ross, and Sheila A. Ross. "Vicarious Reinforcement and Imitative Learning." *The Journal of Abnormal and Social Psychology* 67, no. 6 (1963): 601.

———. "Imitation of Film-Mediated Aggressive Models." *Journal of Abnormal and Social Psychology* 66, (1963): 3–11.

Banham, Reyner. *Theory and Design in the First Machine Age*. New York: Praeger, 1978.

Banks, Ralph. "Beyond Colorblindness: Neo-Racialism and the Future of Race and Law Scholarship." *Harvard Blackletter Law Journal* 25 (2009): 41–56.

Barnosky, Anthony, Nicholas Matzke, Susumu Tomiya, Guinevere Wogan, Brian Swartz, Tiago Quental Tiago, Charles Marshall, Jenny McGuire, Emily Lindsey, Kaitlin Maguire, Ben Mersey, and Elizabeth Ferrer. "Has the Earth's Sixth Mass Extinction Already Arrived?" *Nature* 471 (2011): 51.

Barwind, Jack A., Philip J. Salem, and Robert D. Gratz. "All the News that's Fit to Invent." Paper presented to the Popular/American Culture Associations, SWTX PCA/ACA Joint Conference. San Antonio, TX. April 23, 2011.

Batcho, Krystine Irene. "Nostalgia: A Psychological Perspective." *Perceptual and Motor Skills* 80, (1995): 131–143.

Baudrillard, Jean. *The System of Objects (Radical Thinkers)*. New York: Verso, 2005.

———. *Simulacra and Simulation*. Ann Arbor: University of Michigan Press, 1995.

Bauer, Dale M. "Indecent Proposals: Teachers in the Movies." *College English 60,* no. 3. (1998): 301–317.

Bauman, Mattew A., and Tim Groeling. "New Media and the Polarization of American Political Discourse." *Political Communication* 25 (2008): 345–365.

Bauman, Richard. and Charles L. Briggs. *Voices of Modernity: Language Ideologies and the Politics of Inequality*. New York: Cambridge University Press, 2003.

———. "Poetics and Performance as Critical Perspectives on Language and Social Life." *Annual Review of Anthropology* 19 (1990): 59–88.

Baumgartner, Jody, and Jonathan S. Morris. "*The Daily Show* Effect: Candidate Evaluations, Efficacy, and American Youth." *American Politics Research* 34, no. 3 (2006): 341–367.

———. "One 'Nation,' under Stephen? The Effects of *The Colbert Report* on American Youth." *Journal of Broadcasting & Electronic Media* 52, no. 4 (2008): 622–643.

Baym, Geoffrey. "T*he Daily Show*: Discursive Integration and the Reinvention of Political Journalism." *Political Communication* 22, no. 3 (2005): 259–276.

Becker, Anne E., Rebecca A. Burwell, David B. Herzog, Paul Hamburg, and Stephen E. Gilman. "Eating Behaviors and Attitudes Following Prolonged Exposure to Television among Ethnic Fijian Adolescent Girls." *British Journal of Psychiatry* 180 (2002): 509–514, doi:10.1192/bjp.180.6.509.

Belk, Russell W. "Possessions and the Extended Self." *Journal of Consumer Research* 15, no. 2 (1988): 139–168.

Bellafante, Ginia. "Wealth (and Dior) on Their Minds." *New York Times*, July 30, 2009.

Belloni, Matthew, and Stephen Galloway. "Q&A: Tyler Perry." *Hollywood Reporter*, 2009. http://www.hollywoodreporter.com.

Beltrán, Mary C. "What's At stake in Claims of Post-racial Media?" *Flow TV*, June 3, 2010. http://flowtv.org/2010/06/whats-at-stake-in-claims-of-post-racial-media/

Benjamin, Lois. *The Black Elite: Still Facing the Color Line in the Twenty-first Century.* Lanham: Rowman & Littlefield Publishers, 2005.

Bennett, James, and Su Holmes. "The 'Place' of Television in Celebrity Stories." *Celebrity Studies* 1, no. 1 (2010): 65–80.

Benson, Jim. "Syndicated Sitcom to Cable First." *Broadcasting & Cable*, August 28, 2006, 34.

———. "Debmar-Mercury Snags 'Feud.'" *Broadcasting & Cable*, November 20, 2006, 9.

Bergson, Henri. "On Laughter." In *Comedy*, edited by Wylie Sypher, 61–103. Baltimore: Johns Hopkins University Press, 1956.

Berliner, David C., and Bruce J. Biddle. *The Manufactured Crisis: Myths, Fraud, and the Attack on America's Public Schools.* Cambridge: Perseus Books, 1995.

Berman, John. "Blown Call." *World News With Diane Sawyer*, ABC, originally aired June 3, 2010.

Bernstein, Robert. "Minority Population Tops 100 Million," 2007. http://www.census.gov/ Press-Release/www/releases/archives/population/010048.html

Bianco, Robert. "'House of Payne': It hurts to watch." *USA Today*, June 5, 2007.

Bilandzic, Helena. "The Perception of Distance in the Cultivation Process: A Theoretical Consideration of the Relationship Between Television Content, Processing Experience, and Perceived Distance." *Communication Theory* 16, no. 3 (2006): 333–355.

Bilandzic, Helena, and P. Rössler. "Life According to Television. Implications of Genre-specific Cultivation Effects: The Gratification/Cultivation Model." *Communications-Sankt Augustin then Berlin-* 29 (2004): 295–326.

Bird, Elizabeth S. *The Audience in Everyday Life: Living in the Media World.* New York: Routledge, 2003.

Bird, Elizabeth S. and Robert W. Dardenne. "Myth, Chronicle, and Story. Exploring the Narrative Quality of News." In *Media, Myths, and Narratives. Television and the Press*, edited by James W. Carey, 67–86. Newbury Park: Sage, 1988.

Birmingham, Stephen. *Certain People: America's Black Elite.* Boston: Little, Brown & Company, 1977.

Bishop, Bill. *The Big Sort: Why the Clustering of Like-minded America Is Tearing Us Apart.* Boston: Houghton Mifflin. 2008.

Bishop, Tara F., Alex D. Federman, and Salomeh Keyhani. "Physicians Views on Defensive Medicine: A National Survey." *Archives of Internal Medicine* 170 (2010): 1081–1083.

Blain, Neil. "Beyond 'Media Culture': Sport as Dispersed Symbolic Activity." In *Sport, Media, Culture: Global and Local Dimensions*, edited by Alina Bernstein and Neil Blain, 227–254. New York: Routledge, 2003.

Blau, Sheldon P., and Elaine Fantel Shimberg. *How to Get Out of the Hospital Alive: A Guide to Patient Power.* New York: Macmillan, 1997.

Block, Alex B. "Tyler Perry, Inc." *Hollywood Reporter*, February 19, 2009, 24–26.

Bobo, Jacqueline. "*The Color Purple*: Black Women as Cultural Readers."In *Female Spectators: Looking at Film and Television*, edited by. E. Deidre Pribram, 90–105. London: Verso, 1988.

Bobo, Lawrence D. "Are We 'Black No More'? Not Quite," *The Root*, January 2, 2013. http://www.theroot.com/views/are-we-black-no-more-not-quite.

Bourdieu, Pierre. *Distinction: A Social Critique of the Judgment of Taste.* Translated by Richard Nice. Cambridge: Harvard University Press, 1984.

———. "The Forms of Capital." In *Education: Culture, Economy, and Society*, edited by A. H. Halsey, Hugh Lauder, Phillip Brown, and Amy Stuart Wells, 46–58. Oxford: Oxford University Press, 1997.

———. "Distinction & The Aristocracy of Culture." In *Cultural Theory and Popular Culture*, edited by John Storey, 434–439. Athens: University of Georgia Press, 1998.

Bowser, Benjamin P. *The Black Middle Class: Social Mobility and Vulnerability.* Boulder: Lynne Rienner, 2007.

Boylorn, Robin M. "As Seen on TV: An Autoethnographic Reflection on Race and Reality Television." *Critical Studies in Media Communication* 25, no. 4 (October 2008): 413–433.

Briggs, James. "Detroit Tigers Pitcher Armando Galarraga Saves Jim Joyce from Steve Bartman's Curse." *The Oakland Press*, June 6, 2010.

Brodie, Richard. *Virus of the Mind: The New Science of Memetics.* Carlsbad: Hay House Inc, 2009.

Brodie, Mollyann, Ursula Foehr, Vicky Rideout, Neal Baer, Carolyn Miller, Rebecca Flournoy, and Drew Altman. "Communicating Health Information Through the Entertainment Media." *Health affairs* 20, no. 1 (2001): 192–199.

Brook, Vincent. *Something Aint Kosher Here: The Rise of the "Jewish" Sitcom.* New Brunswick: Rutgers University Press, 2003.

Brooks, Durryle. "Gay, Lesbian, Bisexual, Transgender and Questioning (GLBTQ) Youth: A Population in Need of Understanding and Support." *Advocates for Youth.* Last modified 2010. http://www.advocatesforyouth.org/storage/advfy/documents/glbtq_youth%20201 0.pdf.

Brown, Jamie Foster. "Tyler Perry on Another Level." *Sister 2 Sister*, April 2006.

Brown, Mary, and Carol Orsborn. *BOOM: Marketing to the Ultimate Power Consumer—the Baby Boomer Woman.* New York: AMACOM, 2006.

Bukow, Wolf-Dietrich, Claudia Nikodem, Erika Schulze, and Erol Yildiz. *Was heißt hier Parallelgesellschaft? Zum Umgang mit Differenzen.* Wiesbaden: VS Verlag für Sozialwissenschaften, 2007.

Bumiller, Elisabeth. "Videos From bin Laden's Hide-Out Released." *New York Times*, May 7, 2011. Accessed October 14, 2013, http://www.nytimes.com/2011/05/08 /world/asia/08intel.html?_r=1.

Burke, Kenneth. "Language as Action: Terministic Screens." In *On Symbols and Society*, edited by Joseph R. Gusfield, 114–125. Chicago: University of Chicago Press, 1989.

Burke, Kenneth. *Permanence and Change.* Berkley: University of California Press, 1954.

Burns, Eric. *Infamous Scribblers: The Founding Fathers and the Rowdy Beginnings of American Journalism.* New York: PublicAffairs, 2006.

Burroughs, James E., L. J. Shrum, and Aric Rindfleisch. "Does Television Viewing Promote Materialism? Cultivating American Perceptions of the Good Life." *Advances in Consumer Research* 29, no. 1 (2002): 442–443.

Butler, Daniel M., and Emily Schofield. "Were Newspapers More Interested in Pro-Obama Letters to the Editor in 2008? Evidence From a Field Experiment." *American Politics Research* 38–2 (2010): 356–371.

Butler, Jeremy. *Star Texts: Image and Performance in Film and Television.* Detroit: Wayne State University Press, 1991.

———. *Television: Critical Methods and Applications.* Mahwah: Lawrence Erlbaum Associates, 2002.

Butler, Judith. *Gender Trouble Tenth Anniversary Edition.* London: Routledge, 1999.

Butterworth, Trevor. "Speed Journalism: Some Stories Need Just a Tweet—Some Need Real Thought." *The Daily*, June 13, 2011.

Byock, Lila. "Talking 'Mad Men' with Matthew Weiner." *The New Yorker*, October 18, 2009. http://www.newyorker.com/online/blogs /festival/lila-byock.

Cael. "Exploring Gender: Trans Character on *Glee*." *Lezbelib*, May 6, 2012. http://www.lezb elib.com/tv-movies/exploring-gender-trans-character-on-glee.

Cantril, Hadley, Hazel Gaudet, and Herta Herzog. *The Invasion from Mars: A Study in the Psychology of Panic.* Princeton: Princeton University Press, 1940.

Cardwell, Sarah. "Is Quality Television Any Good? Generic Distinctions, Evaluations and the Troubling Matter of Critical Judgment." In *Quality TV; Contemporary American Television and Beyond,* edited by Janet McCabe and Kim Akass, 19–34. New York: I. B. Tauris, 2007.

Carey, James W. "American Journalism on, before, and after September 11." In *Journalism after September 11*, edited by Barbie Zelizer and Stuart Allan, 71–90. London: Routledge, 2003.

Carlson, James M. "Television Viewing: Cultivating Perceptions of Affluence and Support for Capitalist Values." *Political Communication* 10, no. 3 (1993): 243–257.

Carmon, Irin. "*The Daily Show*'s Woman Problem." *Jezebel*, June 23, 2010. http://jezebel.com/5570545/comedy-of-errors-behind-the-scenes-of-the--daily-shows-lady-problem.

Carr, David, and Tim Arango. "A Fox Chief at the Pinnacle of Media and Politics," *The New York Times*, January 10, 2010.

Carter, Bill. "Devoted to Politics, MSNBC Slips on Breaking News." *New York Times*,June 2, 2013. http://www.nytimes.com/2013/06/03/business/media/devoted-to-politics-msn bc-slips-on-breaking-news.html?hp&_r=4&pagewanted=all&.

Carter, Prudence L. *Keepin' It Real: School Success Beyond Black and White.* Oxford: Oxford University Press, 2005.

Cassirer, Ernst. *An Essay on Man.* New Haven: Yale University Press, 1944.

Chancellor, Edward. *Devil Take the Hindmost: A History of Financial Speculation.* New York: Plume, 2000.

Chory-Assad, Rebecca M., and Ron Tamborini. "Television Exposure and the Public's Perceptions of Physicians." *Journal of Broadcasting & Electronic Media* 47, no. 2 (2003): 197–215.

Christen, Cindy T., Prathana Kannaovakun, and Albert C. Gunther. "Hostile Media Perceptions: Partisan Assessment of the Press and Public During the 1997 United Parcel Service Strike." *Political Communication* 19–4 (2002): 423–436.

Christian, Margena A. "Tyler Perry: Sky Is the Limit for 'Madea' Creator with New Movie, Upcoming Book, and TV Show." *Jet*, February 27, 2006, 32–38.

———. "Becoming Tyler." *Ebony*, October 2008, 72–83.

Christopher, F. Scott, Richard A. Fabes, and Patricia M. Wilson. "Family Television Viewing: Implications for Family Life Education." *Family Relations* 38, no. 2 (1989): 210–214.

Chyi, Hsiang Iris, and Maxwell McCombs. "Media Salience and the Process of Framing: Coverage of the Columbine School Shootings." *Journalism & Mass Communication Quarterly* 81, no. 1 (Spring 2004): 22–35.

Clements, Steve. *Showrunner: Producing Variety and Talk Shows for Television.* Los Angeles: Silman-James Press, 2004.

Cochran, John K., and Beth A. Sanders. "The Gender Gap in Death Penalty Support: An Exploratory Study." *Journal of Criminal Justice* 37, no. 6 (2009): 525–533.

Coe, Kevin, David Tewksbury, Bradley J. Bond, Kristin L. Drogos, Robert W. Porter, Ashley Yahn, and Yuanyuan Zhang. "Hostile News: Partisan Use and Perceptions of Cable News Programming." *Journal of Communication* 58–2 (2008): 201–219.

Cohen, Jacob, Patricia Cohen, G. W. Stephen, and S. A. Leona. *Applied Multiple Regression/Correlation Analysis for the Behavioral Sciences.* Mahwah: Lawrence Erlbaum Assoc Incorporated, 2003.

Cohen, Lizbeth. *A Consumers' Republic: The Politics of Mass Consumption in Post-War America.* New York: Knopf, 2003.

Cohen, M., and Audrey Shafer. "Images and Healers: A Visual History of Scientific Medicine." In *Cultural Studies: Medicine and Media.* Edited by Lester D. Friedman. 197–233. Durham: Duke University Press, 2004.

Cohen, Tom, and Bill Mears. "Supreme Court Mostly Rejects Arizona Immigration Law; Gov Says 'Heart' Remains." *CNN,* June 25, 2012. http://edition.cnn.com /2012/06/25/politics/scotus-arizona-law/index.html.

Cole, Matthew, and Karen Morgan. "Vegaphobia: Derogatory Discourses of Veganism and the Reproduction of Speciesism in UK National Newspapers." *The British Journal of Sociology* 62, no. 1 (2011): 134–153.

Cole, Simon, and Rachel Dioso-Villa. "CSI and Its Effects: Media, Juries, and the Burden of Proof." *New England Law Review* 41, no. 3 (2007)

———. "Should Judges Worry about the 'CSI Effect'?." *Court Review* 47 (2011): 20–102.

Cole, Tim, and Laura Leets. "Attachment Styles and Intimate Television Viewing. Insecurely Forming Relationships in a Parasocial Way," *Journal of Social and Personal Relationships* 16, (1999): 495–511.

Coleman, Robin R. Means. *African American Viewers and the Black Situation Comedy: Situating Racial Humor.* New York: Garland Publishing, 1998.

Colletta, Lisa. "Political Satire and Postmodern Irony in the Age of Stephen Colbert and Jon Stewart." *The Journal of Popular Culture* 42, no. 5 (2009), 856–874.

Compton, Josh. "Introduction: Surveying Scholarship on *The Daily Show* and *The Colbert Report*." In *The Stewart/Colbert Effect: Essays on the Real Impacts of Fake News*, edited by Amarnath Amarasingam, 9–24. Jefferson: McFarLand and Company, Inc., Publishers, 2011.

Connor, Jacqueline, and Anne Endress Skove. "Dial 'M' for Misconduct: The Effect of Mass Media and Pop Culture on Juror Expectations." in *Future Trends in State Courts*. Williamsburg: National Center for State Courts, 2004.

Conroy, Pat. *The Water Is Wide*. New York: Dell Publishing, 1977.

Cooper, Howard. "Some Thoughts on 'Scapegoating' and its Origins in Leviticus 16." *European Judaism* 41, no. 2 (October 2008): 112–119.

Corliss, Richard. "Media Watch: Flashbacks in Black and White." *Time*, January 13, 2003. http://content.time.com/time/magazine/article/0,9171,1004 033,00.html.

———. "God and Tyler Perry vs. Hollywood." *Time*, March 20, 2008. http://content .time. com/time/magazine/article/0,9171,1724393,00.html.

Covert, Tawnya Adkins, and Philo C. Wasburn. "Information Sources and the Coverage of Social Issues in Partisan Publications: A Content Analysis of 25 Years of the Progressive and the National Review." *Mass Communication and Society* 10 (2007): 67–94.

Cowie, Jefferson. *Stayin' Alive: The 1970s and the Last Days of the Working Class*. New York: The New Press, 2012.

———. "Vigorously Left, Right, and Center at the Same Time: The Crosscurrents of Working-Class America in the 1970s." In *America in the Seventies*, edited by Beth Bailey and David Farber, 75–107. Lawrence: University Press of Kansas, 2004.

Crocco, Anthony G., Miguel Villasis-Keever, and Alejandro R. Jadad. "Analysis of Cases of Harm Associated with Use of Health Information on the Internet." *JAMA: the journal of the American Medical Association* 287, no. 21 (2002): 2869–2871.

Crouch, Stanley. "Why We line up for Tyler Perry." *Tulsa World*, April 12, 2008.

Crozier, Susan. "Making It After All: a Reparative Reading of *The Mary Tyler Moore Show*." *International Journal of Cultural Studies*, (2008): 51–67.

Curry, Kathleen. "Mediating Cops: An Analysis of Viewer Reaction to Reality TV." *Journal of Criminal Justice and Popular Culture* 8, no. 3 (2001): 169.

D'Alessio, Dave, and Mike Allen. "Media Bias in Presidential Elections: A Meta-Analysis." *Journal of Communication*, 50–4 (2000): 133–157.

Dalton, Mary M. *The Hollywood Curriculum: Teachers in the Movies*. New York: Peter Lang, 2010.

———. "Introduction," In *The Sitcom Reader: American Viewed and Skewed*, edited by Mary M. Dalton and Laura R. Linder, 2–14. Albany: State University of New York Press, 2005.

———. "Our Miss Brooks: Situating Gender in Teacher Sitcoms." In *The Sitcom Reader: America Viewed and Skewed*, edited by Mary M. Dalton and Laura R. Linder, 99–111. Albany: State University of New York Press, 2005.

Dalton, Mary M., and Laura R. Linder. *Teacher TV: Sixty Years of Teachers on Television*. New York: Peter Lang, 2008.

Danesi, Marcel. *Understanding Media Semiotics*. New York: Oxford Press, 2002.

Dates, Jannette, and William Barlow. *Split Image: African Americans in the Mass Media*. Washington, D. C.: Howard University Press, 1990.

Dautrich, Kenneth, and Thomas M. Hartley. *How the News Media Fail American Voters*. New York: Columbia University Press, 1999.

Davenport, Thomas. H., and John C. Beck. *The Attention Economy: Understanding the New Currency of Business*. Boston: Harvard Business School Press, 2001.

Dávila, Arlene. *Latino Spin: Public Image and the Whitewashing of Race*. New York: New York University Press, 2008.

Davin, Solange. "Healthy Viewing: The Reception of Medical Narratives." In *Health and the Media*, edited by Clive Seale, 143–159. Malden: Blackwell Press, 2004.

Davis, Hazel. "The Process of Scapegoating." *Journal Of Analytical Psychology* 32, no. 3 (July 1987): 286.

Dawson, Michael C. *Behind the Mule: Race and Class in African-American Politics*. Princeton: Princeton University Press, 1994.

de Beauvoir, Simone. *The Second Sex*, translated by Constance Borde and Sheila Malovany-Chevallier. New York: Vintage Books, 2011.

Debenport, Erin. "As the Rez Turns: Anomalies within and Beyond the Boundaries of a Pueblo Community," *American Indian Culture and Research Journal* 35, no. 2 (2011): 87–109.

Debord, Guy. *The Society of the Spectacle*. Detroit: Black & Red, 1995.

Deger, Jennifer. *Shimmering Screens: Making Media in an Aboriginal Community*. Minneapolis: University of Minnesota Press, 2006.

De Grazia, Victoria. *Irresistible Empire: America's Advance through Twentieth-Century Europe*. Cambridge: Belknap Press of Harvard University Press, 2006.

Deloria, Philip J. *Indians in Unexpected Places*. Lawrence: University Press of Kansas, 2004.

Deltombe, Thomas. *L'islam imaginaire. La construction médiatique de l'islamophobie en France: 1975–2005*. Paris: La Découverte, 2005.

Dempsey, John. "Syndies Rewrite Sitcom Script." *Variety,* August 28–September 3, 2006.

Denetdale, Jennifer Nez. *Reclaiming Diné History: The Legacies of Navajo Chief Manuelito and Juanita*. Tucson: University of Arizona Press, 2007.

DePaulo, Bella. *Singled Out: How Singles Are Stereotyped, Stigmatized, and Ignored, and Still Live Happily Ever After*. New York: St. Martin's, 2007.

Dewey, John. *How We Think*. Boston: D. C. Heath and Company, 1910.

De Zengotita, Thomas. *Mediated*. New York: Bloomsbury, 2005.

DiFonzo, J. Herbie, and Ruth C. Stern. "Devil in a White Coat: The Temptation of Forensic Evidence in the Age of CSI." *New England Law Review* 41 (2007): 503–532.

Djerf-Pierre, Monika, and Monica Löfgren-Nilsson. "Gender-Typing in the Newsroom: The Feminization of Swedish Television News Production, 1958–2000." In *Gender and Newsroom Cultures: Identities at Work*, edited by Marjan de Bruin and Karen Ross, 79–104. Cresskill: Hampton Press, Inc., 2004.

Dornfeld, Barry. "Putting American Public Television Documentary in Its Places." In *Media Worlds*, edited by Ginsburg, Faye D., Lila Abu-Lughod and Brian Larkin, 247–263. Berkeley: University of California Press, 2002.

Douglas, Susan J. *Enlightened Sexism: The Seductive Message that Feminism's Work Is Done*. New York: Henry Holt and Company, 2010.

Douglas, Susan. *Where the Girls Are: Growing Up Female with the Mass Media*. New York: Three Rivers Press, 1995.

Dow, Bonnie. "Ellen, Television, and the Politics of Gay and Lesbian Visibility." *Critical Studies in Media Communication* vol 18 no 2. June (2001): 123–140.

———. *Prime-time Feminism: Television, Media Culture, and the Women's Movement Since 1970*. Philadelphia: University of Pennsylvania Press, 1996.

Drew, Emily M. "Pretending to be "Postracial": The Spectacularization of Race in Reality TV's Survivor." *Television New Media* 12, (2011): 326–346.

Druckman, James N. "The Implications of Framing Effects for Citizen Competence." *Political Behavior* 23, no. 3 (September 2001): 225–256.

Drumming, Neil. "The Gospel According to Tyler Perry." *Entertainment Weekly*, March 3, 2006.

Du Bois, W. E. B. "Talented Tenth," in *The Negro Problem: A Series of Articles by Representative American Negroes of To-day*, edited by Booker T. Washington, 31–75. New York: James Pott & Company, 1903.

Duncan, Hugh Dalziel. *Communication and Social Order*. London: Oxford University Press, 1962.

Dunlap, Railey, Kent VanLiere, Angela Mertig, and Robert Jones. "Measuring Endorsement of the New Ecological Paradigm: A Revised NEP Scale." *Journal of Social Issues* 56, 3 (2000): 425–442.

Dyer, Richard. *Stars*. London: British Film Institute, 2008.

Dykes, Ashley. "Situation Comedies and the Single Woman on Television." PhD diss., Louisiana State University and Agricultural and Mechanical College, 2011.

EEOC. "Milestones in the History of the U.S. Equal Employment Opportunity Commission." Accessed May 2, 2012. http://www.eeoc.gov/eeoc/history/35th/milestones/index.html.

Eisinger, Robert M., Loring R. Veenstra, and John P. Koehn. "What Media Bias? Conservative and Liberal Labeling in Major U.S. Newspapers." *Harvard International Journal of Press/Politics* 12–1 (2007): 17–36.

Emanuel, Ezekiel J., and Linda L. Emanuel. "Four Models of the Physician-Patient Relationship." *JAMA: The Journal of the American Medical Association* 267, no. 16 (1992): 2221–2226.

Emerson, Robert M., Rachel I. Fretz, and Linda L. Shaw. *Writing Ethnographic Fieldnotes*. Chicago: University of Chicago Press, 1995.

Engel, Jonathan. *Poor People's Medicine: Medicaid and American Charity Care since 1965*. Durham: Duke University Press Books, 2006.

Elliott, Richard, and Kritsadarat Wattanasuwan. "Brands as Symbolic Resources for the Construction of Identity." *International Journal of Advertising* 17, no. 2 (1998): 131–144.

Ellis, Donald, and Ifat Maoz. "Online Argument Between Palestinians and Jews." *Human Communication Research*, 33, no. 3 (2007): 291–309.

Ellis, John. *Visible Fictions: Cinema:Television:Video*. London: Routledge, 1982.

Entman, Robert. "Framing: Toward Clarification of a Fractured Paradigm." *Journal of Communication* 43 (1993): 51–60.

Epstein, Alex. *Crafty TV Writing: Thinking Inside the Box*. New York: Henry Holt & Co., 2006.

Epstein, Ronald M., Brian S. Alper, and Timothy E. Quill. "Communicating Evidence for Participatory Decision Making." *JAMA: The Journal of the American Medical Association* 291, no. 19 (2004): 2359–2366.

Eschholz, Sarah, Brenda Sims-Blackwell, Marc Gertz, and Ted Chiricos. "Race and Attitudes Toward the Police: Assessing the Effects of Watching 'Reality' Police Programs." *Journal of Criminal Justice* 30 (2002): 327–341.

Escoffery, David S. "Introduction" in *Essays on Representation and Truth: How Real is Reality TV?*, edited by David S. Escoffery, 1–3. Jefferson: Macfarland and Company, Inc., 2006.

ESPN. "Cubs Will Have to Wait Another Year." Accessed August 15, 2013, http://scores.espn. go.com/mlb/recap?gameId=231015116.

———. "Umpire: 'I Just Cost that Kid a Perfect Game.'" Accessed August 15, 2013, http://scores.espn.go.com/mlb/recap?gameId=300602106.

Esposito, Jennifer. "What Does Race Have to Do With *Ugly Betty*?: An Analysis of Privilege and Postracial(?) Representations on a Television Sitcom." *Television & New Media* 10, no. 6 (2009): 521–535.

"Essence 25 Most Influential of 2007." *Essence*, December, 2007.

Ewen, Stewart. *Captains of Consciousness: Advertising and the Social Roots of Consumer Culture*. New York: McGraw-Hill Book Company, 1976.

Fachin, Dina. "Film Review: Columbus Day Legacy." *Italian American Review* 2, no. 2 (2012): 135–139.

Fairclough, Norman. "Political Correctness: The Politics of Culture and Language." *Discourse & Society* 14:17 (2003): 17–28.

Faludi, Susan. *Backlash: The Undeclared War against American Women*. New York: Crown Publishers, 1991.

"Farmed Animal Indicators: HumaneTrends.com." *Humane Research Council*, August 15, 2011, http://www.humanetrends.org/farmed-animal-indicators/.

Fateh-Moghadam, Bijan. "Religiös-weltanschauliche Neutralität und Geschlechterordnung: Strafrechtliche Burka-Verbote zwischen Paternalismus und Moralismus," in *'Als Mann und Frau schuf er sie.' Religion und Geschlecht*, edited by Barbara Stollberg-Rilinger. Würzburg: Ergon Verlag, forthcoming.

Feagin, Joe R. *The White Racial Frame: Centuries of Racial Framing and Counter Framing*. New York: Routledge, 2009.

Feld, Rob, Jean Oppenheimer, and Ian Stasukevich. "Tantalizing Television." *American Cinematographer*, March 2008. Accessed March 23, 2012. http://www.theasc.com/ac_magazine/March2008/Television/page1.php.

Feldman, Lauren. "The News about Comedy: Young Audiences, *The Daily Show*, and Evolving Notions of Journalism." *Journalism* 8, no. 4 (2007): 406–427.

Ferguson, Christopher J. "Violent Crime Research." In *Violent Crime: Clinical and Social Implications*, edited by Christopher J. Ferguson, 3–18. London: Sage, 2010.

Fernandez, Maria Elena. "Chris Colfer's Journey from Small Town to 'Glee.'" *Los Angeles Times,* September 8, 2009. http://latimesblogs.latimes.com/showtracker/2009/09/glee-creator-and-executive-producer-ryan-murphy-discovered-chris-colfer-but-dont-tell-the-young-actor-that-it-makes-him-feel.html.

Feuer, Jane. *Seeing Through the Eighties: Television and Reaganism. Console-ing passions.* Durham: Duke University Press, 1995.

———. "HBO and the Concept of Quality TV." In *Quality TV: Contemporary American Television and Beyond*, edited by Janet McCabe and Kim Akass, 145–157. New York: I. B. Tauris, 2007.

Fico, Frederick, and Eric Freedman. "Biasing Influence on Balance in Election News Coverage: An Assessment of Newspaper Coverage of the 2006 U.S. Senate Elections." *Journalism & Mass Communication Quarterly* 85 (2008): 499–514.

Fienup-Riordan, Ann. *Freeze Frame: Alaska Eskimos in the Movies*. Seattle: University of Washington Press, 1995.

Fisher, Luchina. "'Glee' Sparks Controversy with First Time Episode." *ABC News*, November 9, 2011, http://abcnews.go.com/blogs/entertainment/2011/11/glee-sparks-controversy-with-first-time-episode/.

Fisherkeller, JoEllen. *Growing Up with Television: Everyday Learning Among Young Adolescents*. Philadelphia: Temple University Press, 2002.

Fiske, John. *Television Culture*. London: Routledge, 1987.

Fiske, John, and John Hartley. *Reading Television*. London: Routledge, 1990.

Fitzgerald, Michael R. "Evolutionary Stages of Minorities in the Mass Media: An Application of Clark's Model to American Indian Television Representations." *Howard Journal of Communication* 21 (2010): 367–384.

Flesch, Rudolf. *Why Johnny Can't Read And What You Can Do About It*. New York: Perennial Books, 1966.

Folger, Joseph P., Marshall Scott Poole, and Randall. K. Stutman. *Working Through Conflict: Strategies, Relationships, Groups, and Organizations*, 6th ed. New York: Pearson, Allyn and Bacon. 2009.

Folb, Kate L. "Don't Touch that Dial! TV as a—What!—Positive Influence." *SIECUS REPORT* 28, no. 5 (2000): 16–18.

Foster, John Bellamy. *Ecology Against Capitalism*. New York: Monthly Review Press, 2002.

Foucault, Michel. *Discipline and Punish: The Birth of the Prison*. Vintage: 1995.

Fox, Aaron A. *Real Country: Music and Language in Working-Class Culture.* Durham: Duke University Press, 2004.

Fox, Charity. "Manifest Mercenaries: Mercenary Narratives in American Popular Culture, 1850–1990." PhD diss., The George Washington University, 2010. ProQuest (AAT 3413647).

Francione, Gary L. *Rain Without Thunder: The Ideology of the Animal Rights Movement*. Philadelphia: Temple University Press, 1996.

Frank, Thomas. *One Market Under God: Extreme Capitalism, Market Populism, and the End of Economic Democracy*. New York: Doubleday, 2000.

Fraser, Steve. *Every Man a Speculator: A History of Wall Street in American Life.* New York: HarperCollins, 2005.

Frazier, E. Franklin. *Black Bourgeoisie.* New York: The Free Press, 1957.

Freeman, Carrie Packwood. "This Little Piggy Went to Press: The American News Media's Construction of Animals in Agriculture." *Communication Review* 12, no. 1 (March 2009): 78–103, doi:10.1080/10714420902717764.

Freeman, Carrie Packwood, and Debra Merskin, "Having It His Way: The Construction of Masculinity in Fast Food TV Advertising." in *Food for Thought: Essays on Eating and Culture,* edited by Lawrence C. Rubin, 277–293. Jefferson: McFarland, 2008.

Fregoso, Rosa L. *MeXicana Encounters: The Making of Social Identities on the Borderlands.* Los Angeles: University of California Press, 2003.

Friedan, Betty. *"It Changed My Life": Writings on the Women's Movement.* New York: Dell, 1991.

———. *The Feminine Mystique.* New York: Dell, 1964.

Friedman, Diana. *Sitcom Style: Inside America's Favorite TV Homes.* New York: Clarkson Potter, 2005.

Frosh, Paul. "The Face of Television." *Annals of the Association of American Academy of Political and Social Sciences* 625, no. 1 (2009): 87–102.

Frum, David. "After Boston, Nothing Will Change." *CNN,* April 23, 2013. http://www.cnn. com/2013/04/23/opinion/frum-boston-change.

Frum, David, and Celeste Headlee. "Why Can't Traumatic Events Bring Politicians Together?" *NPR,* April 26, 2013. http://www.npr.org/2013/04/26/179240478/why-cant-traumatic-events-bring-politicians-together.

Frutkin, A. J. "Payne Breaks the Mold." *MediaWeek,* May 28, 2007.

Fujioka, Yuki. "Television Portrayals and African-American Stereotypes: Examination of Television Effects When Direct Contact Is Lacking." *Journalism and Mass Communication Quarterly* 76, no. 1 (1999): 52–75.

———. "Perceived Threats and Latino Immigrant Attitudes: How White and African American College Students Respond to News Coverage of Latino Immigrants." *The Howard Journal of Communication* 22 (2011): 43–63.

Gage, Eleni N. "Thank You, ZIP Code of My Dreams, for an Emotion-Packed Decade." *New York Times,* May 14, 2000. http://partners.nytimes.com/library/style/weekend/051400stl -90210.html.

Galarraga, Armando, Jim Joyce, and Daniel Paisner. *Nobody's Perfect: Two Men, One Call, and a Game for Baseball History.* New York: Atlantic Monthly Press, 2011.

Gallup. "Supreme Court: Gallup Historical Trends." Retrieved May 22, 2012. http://www.gal lup.com/poll/4732/supreme-court.aspx.

Garcia, Ofelia. "Racializing the Language Practices of U.S. Latinos." In *How the United States Racializes Latinos: White Hegemony and Its Consequences,* edited by José A. Cobas, Jorge Duany, and Joe R. Feagin, 101–115. Boulder: Paradigm Publishers, 2009.

Gardner, Frank. "Osama bin Laden's Abbottabad House 'Was Al-Qaeda-Hub'," *BBC,* May 8, 2011, accessed October 14, 2013. http://www.bbc.co.uk/news/world-us-canada-13325595.

Garrett, R. Kelly. "Troubling Consequences of Online Political Rumoring." *Human Communication Research,* 37, (2011): 255–274.

Gauthier, Candace Cummins. "Television Drama and Popular Film as Medical Narrative." *Journal of American Culture* 22, no. 3 (1999): 23–25.

Gaynor, Tim. "California Senate Passes "Anti-Arizona" Immigration Bill." *Reuters.* July 6, 2012, http://www.reuters.com/article/2012/07/06/us-usa-california-immigration-idUSB RE86502720120706.

Gerbner, George. "The 'Mainstreaming' of America: Violence Profile No. 11." *The Journal of Communication,* no. 3 (1980): 10–29.

———. "Cultivation Analysis: An Overview." *Mass Communication & Society* 3/4 (1998): 180.

Gerbner, George, and Larry Gross. "Living with Television: The Violence Profile." *Journal of Communication* 26, no. 2 (1976): 172–199.

Gerbner, George, Larry Gross, Michael Morgan, and Nancy Signorielli. "Political Correlates of Television Viewing." *Public Opinion Quarterly* 48, no. 1B (1984): 283–300.

———. "Health and Medicine on Television." *New England Journal of Medicine,* 305 (1981): 15, 901–904.

Gerbner, George, Larry Gross, Michael Morgan, Nancy Signorielli, and James Shanahan. "Growing Up with Television: Cultivation Processes." *Media effects: Advances in theory and research* 2 (2002): 47.

Gerbner, George, Michael Morgan, and Nancy Signorielli. "Living with Television: The Dynamics of the Cultivation Process." In *Perspectives on Media Effects.* Edited by Jennings Bryant and Dolf Zillmann. 17–40. Hillsdale: L. Erlbaum Associates, 1986.

Gergen, Kenneth. *The Saturated Self: Dilemmas of Identity in Contemporary Life.* New York: Basic Books. 1991.

Gershon, Iliana, and Joshua Malitsky. "Documentary Studies and Linguistic Anthropology." *Culture, Theory and Critique* 52, no. 1 (2011): 45–63.

Gibney, Alex. *Catching Hell.* Directed by Alex Gibney. Bristol, CT: ESPN Films, 2011.

Gibson, James William. *Warrior Dreams: Paramilitary Culture in Post-Vietnam America.* New York: Hill and Wang, 1994.

Gill, Rosalind. *Gender and the Media.* Malden: Policy Press, 2007.

Ginsburg, Faye. "Embedded Aesthetics: Creating a Discursive Space for Indigenous Media." *Cultural Anthropology* 9, no. 3 (1994): 365–382.

———. "From Little Things, Big Things Grow: Indigenous Media and Cultural Activism." In *Between Resistance and Revolution,* edited by Dick Fox and Orin Starn, 118–144. New Brunswick: Rutgers University Press, 1997.

———. "Screen Memories: Resignifying the Traditional in Indigenous Media." In *Media Worlds,* edited by Faye D. Ginsburg, Lila Abu-Lughod and Brian Larkin, 39–57. Berkeley: University of California Press, 2002.

———. "Native Intelligence: A Short History of Debates on Indigenous Media and Ethnographic Film." In *Made to Be Seen: Perspectives on the History of Visual Anthropology,* edited by Marcus Banks and Jay Ruby, 234–255. Chicago: University of Chicago Press, 2011.

Ginsburg, Faye, and Fred Myers. "A History of Aboriginal Futures." *Critique of Anthropology* 26, no. 1 (2006): 27–45.

Gitlin, Todd. *Inside Prime Time*. London: Routledge, 1994.

Givhan, Robin. "Echoes of TV's First Lady; Michelle Obama's Last True Cultural Antecedent Is Cosby's Clair Huxtable." *Washington Post*, June 19, 2009.

Glee Equality Project. "GEP Mission Statement." Accessed July 1, 2013. http://glee-equality-project.tumblr.com/missionstatement.

Glik, Deborah, Emil Berkanovic, Kathleen Stone, Leticia Ibarra, Marcy Connell Jones, Bob Rosen, Myrl Schreibman, Lisa Gordon, Laura Minassian, and Darcy Richardes. "Health Education Goes Hollywood: Working with Prime-Time and Daytime Entertainment Television for Immunization Promotion." *Journal of Health Communication* 3, no. 3 (1998): 263–282.

Godsey, Mark, and Marie Alou. "She Blinded Me with Science: Wrongful convictions and the 'reverse CSI-effect'." *Texas Wesleyan Law Review* 17, no. 4 (2011): 481–498.

Goffman, Erving. *The Presentation of Self in Everyday Life*. Woodstock: The Overlook Press, 1956.

Gold, Elizabeth. "Headwraps and All, Rhoda Morgenstern Is a Misfit Girl's Dream: A Lonely Teenager Discovers Mary Tyler Moore's Wise-Cracking, Insecure Sidekick and Derives Inspiration." *Forward,* February 2, 2000.

Goltz, Dustin Bradley. *Queer Temporalities in Gay Male Representation: Tragedy, Normativity, and Futurity*. New York: Routledge, 2010.

Goncalo, Jack A., and Michelle M. Duguid. "Hidden Consequences of the Group-Serving Bias: Causal Attributions and the Quality of Group Decision Making." *Organizational Behavior and Human Decision Processes* 107 (2008): 219–233.

Good, Jennifer. "Shop 'til We Drop? Television, Materialism and Attitudes About the Natural Environment." *Mass Communication & Society* 10, no. 3 (2007): 365–383.

———. "The Cultivation, Mainstreaming and Cognitive Processing of Environmentalists Watching Television," *Environmental Communication: The Journal of Nature and Culture* 3, no. 3 (2009): 279–297.

———. *Television and the Earth: Not a Love Story*. Halifax: Fernwood, 2013.

Goodman, Tim. "*Mad Men*: TV Review." The HollywoodReporter, March 14, 2012. Accessed March 30, 2012. http://www.hollywoodreporter.com/review/mad-men-review-season-5-300109

Gorman, Bill. "Broadcast Finals Tuesday: Dancing, Lost Adjusted Up; V Adjusted Down." *TV by the Numbers*, April 14, 2010. http://tvbythenumbers.zap2it.com/2010/04/14/ broadcast- finals-tuesday-dancing-lost-adjusted-up-v-adjusted-down/48563/.

Gottlieb, Lori. "Marry Him!: The Case for Settling for Mr. Good Enough." *The Atlantic*, March 1, 2008.

Graber, Doris. *Mass Media and American Politics*. Washington, D. C.: CQ Press, 1993.

Graham, Lawrence O. *Our Kind of People: Inside America's Black Upper Class.* New York: Harper Collins, 1999.

Grauerholz, Liz. "Cute Enough to Eat: The Transformation of Animals into Meat for Human Consumption in Commercialized Images." *Humanity & Society* 31, no. 4 (November 2007): 334–354.

Gray, Chris H. *Cyborg Citizen: Politics in the Posthuman Age*. New York: Routledge, 2001.

Gray, Herman. "Remembering Civil Rights: Television, Memory, and the 1960s." In *The Revolution Wasn't Televised: Television and Social Conflict*, edited by Lynn Spigel and Michael Curtin, 349–359. New York: Routledge, 1997.

Gray, Jonathan. *Show Sold Separately: Promos, Spoilers, and Other Media Paratexts*. New York: New York University Press, 2010.

Green, Justin. "A Brief Mediation on Blogging." *Daily Beast*, May 21, 2013. http://www.thedailybeast.com/articles/2013/05/21/a-brief-meditation-onblogging.html.

Greenberg, Bradley S., Dana Mastro, and Jeffrey E. Brand. "Minorities and the Mass Media: Television into the 21st Century." In *Media Effects: Advances in Theory and Research*, edited by Jennings Bryant and Dolf Zillmann, 333–351. Mahwah: Lawrence Erlbaum Associates, Inc., 2002.

Grief, Mark. "You'll Love the Way It Makes You Feel." *London Review of Books*, October 2008. Accessed October 4, 2011. http://www.lrb.co.uk/v30/n20/mark-greif/youll-love-the-way-it-makes-you-feel.

Gross, Larry. *Up from Invisibility: Lesbians, Gay Men, and the Media in America*. New York: Columbia University Press, 2001.

Gross, Terry. "For *Mad Men* It's All About the Hard Sell." Fresh Air on NPR, August 9, 2007. Accessed by November 10, 2013. http://www.npr.org/templates/story/story.php?storyId =12626662.Gruneir, Andrea, Vincent Mor, Sherry Weitzen, Rachael Truchil, Joan Teno, and Jason Roy. "Where People Die: A Multilevel Approach to Understanding Influences on Site of Death in America." *Medical Care Research and Review* 64, no. 4 (2007): 351–378.

Habib, Daniel G. "You Gotta Believe." *Sports Illustrated*, October 31, 2003.

Hafez, Kai. *Die politische Dimension der Auslandsberichterstattung*. Baden-Baden: Nomos, 2002.

Hall, Jacquelyn Dowd. "The Long Civil Rights Movement and the Political Uses of the Past." *Journal of American History* 91, 4 (2005): 1233–1263.

Hall, Stuart. "The Work of Representation." In *Representation: Cultural Representations and Signifying Practices*, edited by Stuart Hall, 13–74. London: Sage, 1997.

———. "The Spectacle of the 'Other.'" In *Representation: Cultural Representations and Signifying Practices*, edited by Stuart Hall, 223–290. London: Sage, 1997.

Han, Young Ji., Joseph C. Nunes, and Xavier Drèze. "Signaling Status with Luxury Goods: The Role of Brand Prominence." *Journal of Marketing* 7, no.4 (2010): 15–30.

Hans, Valerie P., and Juliet L. Dee. "Media Coverage of Law: Its Impact on Juries and the Public." *American Behavioral Scientist* (1991), 136–149.

Haralovich, Mary Beth. "Sit-coms and Suburbs: Positioning the 1950s Homemaker." In *Private Screenings: Television and the Female Consumer*, edited by Lynn Spigel and Denise Mann, 111–142. Minneapolis: University of Minnesota Press,1992.

Haraway, Donna. "A Cyborg Manifesto." In *The Cultural Studies Reader*, edited by Simon During, 271–291. New York & London: Routledge, 1993.

Harmon, Mark D. "Affluenza: Television Use and Cultivation of Materialism." *Mass Communication & Society* 4, no. 4 (2001): 405–418.

Harris, Paul. "Bin Laden Videos Give a Remarkable Insight into Life in His Lair." *The Guardian*, May 7, 2011. Accessed October 14, 2013, http://www.guardian .co.uk/world /2011/may/07/bin-laden-video-abbottobad-seals-death.

Hart, Kylo-Patrick. "Retrograde Representation: The Lone Gay White Male Dying of AIDS on *Beverly Hills, 90210*." *Journal of Men's Studies* 7(2) (1999): 201–213.

Hartley, John. *Communication, Cultural and Media Studies: The Key Concepts*. London: Routledge, Taylor & Francis Group, 2002.

Hawkins, Jim. "Nobody's Perfect." *The Oakland Press* (Pontiac, MI), June 3, 2010.

Heitmeyer, Wilhelm. "Für türkische Jugendliche in Deutschland spielt der Islam eine wichtige Rolle." *Die Zeit*, August 23, 1996 Accessed October 25, 2013, http://www.zeit. de/1996/35/heitmey.txt.19960823.xml.

Helem, Lisa. "The King of All Media." *Essence*, July, 2006.

Henshel, Richard L., and Robert A. Silverman. "Perception and Criminal Process," *Canadian Journal of Sociology/Cahiers canadiens de sociologie* (1975): 39.

Herman, David. "Introduction." In *The Cambridge Companion to Narrative*, edited by David Herman, 3–21. Cambridge: Cambridge University Press, 2007.

Herman, Edward S., and Noam Chomsky. *Manufacturing Consent: The Political Economy of the Mass Media*. New York: Pantheon, 1988.

Herzog, Herta. "On Borrowed Experience." *Studies in Philosophy and Social Science* 11, no. 1 (1941): 65–69.

"He's Coming to Get You: The Day Osama bin Ladenbin Laden Sat Glued Watching TV of Barack Obama, the Man Who Had Him Killed." *Daily Mail*, May 8, 2011. Accessed October 14, 2013. http://www.dailymail.co.uk/news/article-1384573/ Osama-Bin-Laden-sat-glued-watching-TV-pictures-Barack-Obama.html.

Hickethier, Knut. "Narrative Navigation durchs Weltgeschehen. Erzählstrukturen in Fernsehnachrichten." In *Fernsehnachrichten. Prozesse, Strukturen, Funktionen,* edited by Klaus Kamps and Miriam Meckel, 185–202. Wiesbaden: Westdeutscher Verlag, 1998.

Hill, Annette. *Reality Television: Audiences and Popular Factual Television*. London: Routledge, 2005.

Hirshey, Gerri. "Tyler Perry's Brand New Day." *Best Life*, April 2008.

Hmielowski, Jay D., Lance R. Holbert, and Jayeon Lee. "Predicting the Consumption of Political TV Satire: Affinity for Political Humor, *The Daily Show*, and *The Colbert Report*." *Communication Monographs* 78, no. 1 (2011): 96–114.

Hocker, Cliff. "The Lawyer." *Black Enterprise*, March 2007.

Hoffman, Lindsay H., and Tiffany L. Thomson. "The Effect of Television Viewing on Adolescents' Civic Participation: Political Efficacy as a Mediating Mechanism." *Journal of Broadcasting & Electronic Media* 53, no. 1 (2009): 3–21.

Hogan, Heather. "Is Ryan Murphy Trolling 'Glee's' Lesbian Fandom?" *AfterEllen. com*, November 7, 2012. http://www.afterellen.com/is-ryan-murphy-trolling-glees-lesbian-fandom/11/2012/.

Holbert, Lance R., Jennifer L. Lambe, Anthony D. Dudo, and Kristin A. Carlton. "Primacy Effects of The Daily Show and National TV News Viewing: Young Viewers, Political Gratifications, and Internal Political Self-Efficacy." *Journal of Broadcasting & Electronic Media* 51, no. 1 (2007): 20–38.

Hollingshead, August. "Four Factor Index of Social Status." Unpublished manuscript, Yale University, 1975.

Holmes, Su. "'Starring . . . Dyer?': Re-visiting Star Studies and Contemporary Celebrity Culture." *Westminster Papers in Communication and Culture* 2 (2005):6–21.

Holtman, Curt. "Tyler Perry Doesn't Need You Because God Has His Back." *Creative Loafing*, April 7–13, 2011.

Hooper, Rowan. "Television Shows Scramble Forensic Evidence." *New Scientist* (2005):1

Hopkins, Nancy M., and Ann. K Mullis. "Family Perceptions of Television." *Family Relations* 34, no. 2 (1985): 177–181.

Horowitz, Daniel. *Jimmy Carter and the Energy Crisis of the 1970s: The "Crisis of Confidence" Speech of July 15, 1979*. New York: Bedford/St. Martin's, 2004.

Horton, Donald, and R. Richard Wohl. "Mass Communication and Para-social Interaction: Observations on Intimacy at a Distance." *Psychiatry* (2010): 215–29.

"How Authentic is Medicine on Television?" *Journal of the American Medical Association*, May 4, 1957: 49–51.

Howard-Williams, Rowan. "Consumers, Crazies and Killer Whales: The Environment on New Zealand Television." *International Communication Gazette* 73 (2011): 27–43.

Howden, Lindsay M., and Julie A. Meyer. "Age and Sex Composition: 2010." *2010 Census Briefs* (2011): 1–15.

Huey, Laura. "'I've Seen this on CSI': Criminal investigators' perceptions about the management of public expectations in the field." *Crime, Media, Culture* 6, no. 1 (2010): 49–68.

Hughes, Zondra. "How Tyler Perry Rose From Homelessness to a $5 Million Mansion." *Ebony,* January 2004.

Hulse, Carl. "In Lawmakers Outburst, a Rare Breach of Protocol." *The New York Times*, September 10, 2009, A26.

Hunt, Darnell. *Channeling Blackness: Studies on Television and Race in America*. New York: Oxford University Press, 2004.

Huston, Aletha C., Diana Zuckerman, Brian L. Wilcox, and Ed Donnerstein. *Big World, Small Screen: The Role of Television in American Society*. Lincoln: University of Nebraska Press, 1992.

Hymes, Dell H. *"In Vain I Tried to Tell You": Essays in Native American Ethnopoetics*. Philadelphia: University of Pennsylvania Press, 1981.

———. *Ethnography, Linguistics, Narrative Inequality: Toward an Understanding of Voice*. London: Taylor & Francis, 1996.

Hymowitz, Carol, and Michaela Weissman. *A History of Women in America*. New York: Bantam, 1984.

Ibrahim, Dina. "The Middle East in American Media. A 20th-Century Overview." *The International Communication Gazette* 71 (2009): 511–524.

Ignatius, David. "Writing the Middle East's New Narrative," *Washington Post*, May 19, 2011. Accessed October 14, 2013. http://www.washingtonpost.com/opinions/writing-the-middle-easts-new-narrative/2011/05/17/AFTmAm6G_story.html.

IMDb. *"Beverly Hills, 90210*–Awards." Accessed October 18, 2012. http://www.imdb.com/title/tt0098749/awards.

———. *"The Simpsons* (TV Series 1989–)." Accessed July 20, 2013. http://www. imdb. com/title/tt0096697/.

———. *"Tyler Perry's House of Payne."* Accessed December 22, 2013. http://www.i mdb.com/title/tt0773264/?ref_=nm_flmg_dr_12

———. *"Friends* (TV Series 1994–2004)." Accessed July 20, 2013. http://www.imdb. com /title/tt0108778/?ref_=sr_1.

———. "Lisa Kudrow–Awards." Accessed July 20, 2013, http://www.imdb.com/ name /nm0001435/awards.

Innis, Leslie B., and Joe R. Feagin, "The Cosby Show: The View from the Black Middle Class," in *Say it loud: African-American audiences, media, and identity*, edited by Robin Means Coleman. 187–204. New York: Routledge, 2002.

"In the States." Common Core State Standards Initiative. Accessed August 14, 2013. http://www.corestandards.org/in-the-states.

Israel, Betsy. *Bachelor Girl: The Secret History of Single Women in the Twentieth Century*. New York: HarperCollins, 2002.

It Gets Better Project. Accessed July 1, 2013. http://www.itgetsbetter.org.

———. "Chris Colfer for the Trevor Project." Accessed July 1, 2013. http://www. itgetsbetter. org/video/entry/733/.

———. *"Glee's* Max Adler." Accessed July 1, 2013. http://www.itgetsbetter.org/ video/entry/ah fm_iv-554/.

Ito, Robert. "'Glee' Actress Naya Rivera's Santana Comes out to Applause." *Los Angeles Times,* May 24, 2011. http://articles.latimes.com/2011/may/24/entertainment/ la-et-naya-rivera-20110524.

Itzkoff, Dave. "Teenage Dreams and Nightmares." *The New York Times Arts Beat*, November 11, 2010. http://artsbeat.blogs.nytimes.com/2010/11/10/teenage-dreams-and-nightmares -talking-never-been-kissed-with-ryan-murphy-of-glee/.

———. "Matthew Weiner Closes the Book on Season 4 of 'Mad Men'." *New York Times Arts Beat*, October 17, 2010. Accessed October 6, 2011. http://artsbeat. blogs.nytimes.com /2010/10/17/matthew-weiner-closes-the-books-on-season-4– of-mad-men/?_r=0.

Iverson, Suzy A., Kristin B. Howard, and Brian K. Penney. "Impact of Internet Use on Health-Related Behaviors and the Patient-Physician Relationship: A Survey-Based Study and Review." *JAOA: Journal of the American Osteopathic Association* 108, no. 12 (2008): 699–711.

Jackson Jr., John L. *Harlemworld: Doing Race and Class in Contemporary Black America*. Chicago: University of Chicago Press, 2001.

———. *Real Black: Adventures in Racial Sincerity*. Chicago: University of Chicago Press, 2005.

Jacobs, Jane. *The Death and Life of Great American Cities*. New York: Random House, 1961.

Jacobs, Jason. *Body Trauma TV: The New Hospital Dramas*. London: British Film institute, 2003.

Jacoby, Karl. "Ken Burns Gone Wild: Naturalizing the Nation in the National Parks: America's Best Idea." *Public Historian*, 33, 2 (2013): 19–23.

Jane H. Hill. *The Everyday Language of White Racism*. New York: Wiley-Blackwell, 2008.

Japp, Phyliss. "Gender and Work in the 1980s: Television's Working Women as Displaced Persons." *Women's Studies in Communication* 14, no. 1 (1991): 49–74.

Jefferson, Thomas. *Master Thoughts of Thomas Jefferson*. Edited by Benjamin S. Catchings. New York: The Nation Press, 1907.

Jeffords, Susan. *Hard Bodies: Hollywood Masculinity in the Reagan Era*. New Brunswick: Rutgers University Press, 1994.

Jensen, Aaron, Edward Janak, and Timothy Slater. "Changing Course: Exploring Impacts of Waiting for Superman on Future Teachers' Perspectives on the State of Education." *Contemporary Issues in Educational Research* 5, no. 1 (2012): 23–31.

Jhally, Sut, and Justin Lewis. *Enlightened Racism:* The Cosby Show, *Audiences, and the Myth of the American Dream*. Boulder: Westview Press, 1992.

Johnson, Nina Angelique. "Talented Tenth or Black Bourgeoisie: The Black Educational Elites in the Twenty-First Century." PhD diss., Northwestern University, 2011.

Jones, Gerard. *Honey, I'm Home: Sitcoms: Selling the American Dream*. New York: St. Martin's, 1993.

Jones, Jeffrey P. *Entertaining Politics: Satiric Television and Political Engagement*. Lanham: Rowman & Littlefield Publishers, Inc., 2010.

Joseph, Ralina L. "'Tyra Banks Is Fat:' Reading (Post-) Racism and (Post-) Feminism in the New Millennium." *Critical Studies in Media Communication* 26 (2009): 237–254.

Joy, Melanie. *Why We Love Dogs, Eat Pigs, and Wear Cows: An Introduction to Carnism*. San Francisco: Conari Press, 2010.

Juffer, Jane. *Single Mother: The Emergence of the Domestic Intellectual*. New York: New York University Press, 2006.

Jule, Allyson. "Using *The Mary Tyler Moore Show* as a Feminist Teaching Tool." *Gender & Education*. no. 1 (2010): 123–130.

Kane, Matt. "*Glee* Episode Hits the Wrong Note." *GLAAD*, October 29, 2010. http://www. glaad.org/2010/10/29/glee-episode-hits-the-wrong-note.

Kane, Matt. "*Glee* Gives Fans the Kiss They've Been Waiting For." *GLAAD,* March 16, 2011. http://www.glaad.org/2011/03/16/glee-gives-fans-the-kiss-theyve-been-waiting-for.

Kane, Paul. "'Tea Party' Protestors Accused of Spitting on Lawmaker, Using Slurs." *Washington Post*, March 20, 2010. http://www.washingtonpost.com/wpdyn/content /article/2010/03/20/AR2010032002556.html.

Karis, Tim. "Postmodernes Feindbild und aufgeklärte Islamophobie? Grenzen der Analysekategorie ‚Feindbild' in der Islambildforschung." In *Vom Ketzer bis zum Terroristen: Interdisziplinäre Studien zur Konstruktion und Rezeption von Feindbildern,* edited by Alfons Fürst, Harutyun Harutyunyan, Eva-Maria Schrage, and Verena Voigt, 179–190. Münster: Aschendorff Verlag, 2012.

———. *Mediendiskurs Islam: Narrative in der Berichterstattung der Tagesthemen 1979–2010*. Wiesbaden: Springer VS, 2013.

Keeter, Scott, Juliana Horowitz, and Alec Tyson. "Young Voters in the 2008 Election." Pew Research Center, November 13, 2008. http://www.pewresearch.org/2008/11/13/young-voters-in-the-2008–election/.

Kelley, Christopher. "Will & Grace Changed Nothing." *Salon,* October 2, 2012. http://www. salon.com/2012/10/03/will_grace_changed_nothing/.

Kellner, Douglas. *Media Culture: Cultural Studies, Identity and Politics between the Modern and the Postmodern.* New York: Routledge, 1995.

Kelly, Walt. *Pogo: We Have Met the Enemy and He Is Us.* New York: Simon & Schuster, 1987.

Kifner, John. "Poverty Pickets Get Paper-Bag Dousing on Madison Avenue." *New York Times*, May 28, 1966. Accessed May 2, 2012. http://select.nytimes.com/gst/ abstract. html?res=FB0B12F83D55117B93CAAB178ED85F428685F9.

Kim, Kyun Soo and Yorgo Pasadeos. "Study of Partisan News Readers Reveals Hostile Media Perceptions of Balanced Stories." *Newspaper Research Journal* 28–2 (2007): 99–106.

Kimmel, Daniel M. *The Fourth Network: How Fox Broke the Rules and Reinvented Television.* Chicago: Ivan R. Dee, Publisher, 2004.

Kimple, Dan. "A Gift of 'Glee' from Lima, Ohio." *The Huffington Post*, April 23, 2012. http://www.huffingtonpost.com/dan-kimpel/a-gift-of-glee-from-limaohio_b_1447646. html.

Kindleberger, Charles P., and Robert Z. Aliber. *Manias, Panics, and Crashes.* Hoboken: Wiley & Sons Inc, 2005.

Kirby, David. "Making It Work; Sitcom City.*" New York Times*. October 26, 1997.

Kirschling, Gregory. "Mad Props." *Entertainment Weekly*, March 11, 2005.

Kirst, Michael W. "Who's in Charge? Federal, State, and Local Control." In *Learning From the Past: What History Teaches Us About School Reform*, edited by Diane Ravitch and Maris Vinovskis, 25–51. Baltimore: Johns Hopkins University Press, 1995.

Klain, Bennie. *Columbus Day Legacy*, DVD. Directed by Bennie Klain. Lincoln, NE: Vision Maker Media, 2011.

Klein, Allison. *What Would Murphy Brown Do? How the Women of Prime Time Changed Our Lives.* New York: Seal Press, 2006.

Klein, Hugh and Kenneth Shiffman. "Underrepresentation and Symbolic Annihilation of Socially Disenfranchised Groups ('Out Groups') in Animated Cartoons." *The Howard Journal of Communications* 20 (2009): 55–72.

Klosterman, Chuck. "Bad Decisions." *Grantland*, July 12, 2011. Accessed January 26, 2012. http://www.grantland.com/story/_/id/6763000/bad-decisions.

Kohn, Linda T., Janet M. Corrigan and Molla S. Donaldson. *To Err is Human: Building a Safer Health System.* Vol. 627. Washington: National Academies Press, 2000.

Konigsberg, Eric. "Inside 'Mad Men': A Fine Madness." *Rolling Stone*, September 16, 2010. Accessed March 13, 2012. http://www.rollingstone.com/movies/news/ inside-mad-men-a-fine-madness-20100916.

Kooijaman, Jaap. *Fabricating the Absolute Fake.* Amsterdam: University Press, 2005.

Kosar, Kevin. *Failing Grades: The Federal Politics of Education Standards.* Boulder: Lynee Reinner Publishers, 2005.

Kozol, Jonathan. *Savage Inequalities: Children in America's Schools.* New York: Crown Publishing, 1991.

Kuhn, Sarah. "Life Stages." *Backstage*, September 3, 2009. http://www.backstage.com/inter view/life-stages/.

Kutulas, Judy. "Liberated Women and New Sensitive Men: Reconstructing Gender in the 1970s Workplace Comedies." In *The Sitcom Reader: America Viewed and Skewed*, edited by Mary M. Dalton and Laura R. Linder, 217–227. Albany: State University of New York Press, 2005.

Lacy, Karyn. *Blue-chip Black: Race, Class, and Status in the New Black Middle Class.* Berkeley: University of California Press, 2007.

LaMarre, Heather L., Kristen D. Landreville, and Michael A. Beam. "The Irony of Satire: Political Ideology and the Motivation to See What You Want to See in The Colbert Report." *The International Journal of Press/Politics* 14, no. 2 (2009): 212–231.

Landay, Lori. *Madcaps, Screwballs, and Con Women: The Female Trickster in American Culture.* Philadelphia: University of Pennsylvania Press, 1998.

Landry, Bart. *The New Black Middle Class.* Berkeley: University of California Press, 1987.

Landsberg, Alison. "Memory, Empathy, and the Politics of Identification." *International Journal of Politics, Culture and Society* 22(2009): 221–229.

LaPorte, Nicole. "Diary of a Mad Niche Hit." *Variety*, March 7–March 13, 2007.

Latham, Richard A. *The Economics of Attention: Style and Substance in the Age of Information.* Chicago: The University of Chicago Press. 2006.

Lee, Felicia R. "Talking the Dream, Growing the brand." *New York Times*, June 6, 2007.

Lee, Tien-Tsung. "The Liberal Media Myth Revisited: An Examination of Factors Influencing Perceptions of Media Bias." Lefebvre, Henri. *Everyday Life in the Modern World.* New Brunswick: Transaction Publishers, 1984.

Lehman, Katherine. *Those Girls: Single Women in Sixties and Seventies Popular Culture.* Lawrence: University Press of Kansas, 2011.

Leuthold, Steven. "Historical Representation in Native American Documentary." *Ethnohistory,* 44, no. 4 (1997): 727–739.

Levy, David A. and Paul R. Nail. "Contagion: A Theoretical and Empirical Review and Reconceptualization." *Genetic, Social & General Psychology Monographs* 119, no. 2 (1993): 235–285.

Lewicki, Roy J., David. M. Saunders, John. W. Minton, and Bruce Barry. *Negotiation*, 5th ed. Boston: McGraw-Hill Irwin, 2006.

Lewine, Edward. "Matthew Weiner's 'Mad' House." *New York Times*, September 29, 2011. Accessed October 6, 2011. http://www.nytimes.com/2011/10/02/magazine/domains-matthew-weiners-mad-house.html.

Lewis, Randolph. *Alanis Obomsawin: The Vision of a Native Filmmaker.* Lincoln: University of Nebraska Press, 2006.

Lewis-Beck, Michael S. "Election Forecasts in 1984: How Accurate Were They?" *PS: Political Science and Politics* 18–1 (1985): 53–62.

Lichter, S. Robert. "Election Watch: Campaign 2008 Final: How TV News Covered the General Election." *Media Monitor XXIII-1* (2009).

Lichter, S. Robert, Linda S. Lichter, and Stanley Rothman. *Prime Time: How TV Portrays American Culture.* Washington, DC: Regnery, 1994.

Lichter, S. Robert, and Richard Noyes. *Good Intentions Make Bad News. Why Americans Hate Campaign Journalism.* New York: Rowman & Littlefield, 1988.

Liebes, Tamar, and Elihu Katz. *The Export of Meaning: Cross-cultural Readings of Dallas,* New York: Oxford University Press, 1990.

Link, Michael W., and Jennie W. Lai. "Cell-phone-only Households and Problems of Differential Nonresponse Using an Address-based Sampling Design." *Public Opinion Quarterly* 75, no. 4 (2011): 613–635.

Lisotta, Christopher. "Easing the 'Payne'." *TelevisionWeek,* April 17, 2006.

Littlejohn, Stephen W. ,and Karen A. Foss. *Theories of Human Communication.* Long Grove: Waveland Press Inc., 2011.

"Livestock a Major Threat to Environment." *Food and Agriculture Organization of the United Nations,* November 29, 2006. http://www.fao.org/newsroom/en/news/2006/ 1000448/index.html.

Livingstone, Sonia. "Half a Century of Television in the Lives of our Children." *Annals of the Association of American Academy of Political and Social Sciences* 625, no. 1 (2009): 151–163.

Lotz, Amanda Dyanne. *Redesigning Women: Television after the Network Era.* Champaign: University of Illinois Press, 2006.

Louv, Richard. *Last Child in the Woods: Saving Our Children from Nature-Deficit Disorder.* Chapel Hill: Algonquin Books, 2005.

Lovgren, Stefan. "'CSI effect' Is Mixed Blessing for Real Crime Labs." *National Geographic News,* September 23, 2004. Accessed December 16, 2013. http://news.nationalgeo graphic.com/news/2004/09/0923_040923_csi.html.

Lowe, Robert. "Teachers as Saviors, Teachers Who Care." In *Images of Schoolteachers in America,* edited by Pamela Bolotin Joseph and Gail E. Burnaford, 211–228. Mahwah: Lawrence Erlbaum Associates, 2001.

Lusted, David. "The Glut of the Personality." In *Stardom: Industry of Desire,* edited by Christine Gledhill, 251–258. London: Routledge, 1991.

Luyendijk, Joris. "Beyond Orientalism." *The International Communication Gazette* 72 (2010): 9–20.

Mabrey, Vicki, and Tarana Harris. "Perry Talks to 'Nightline' About His Past, Present, and Future." *Say It Black,* February 24, 2007. http://sayitblack.blogspot.kr/search?q =Perry+Talks+to+'Nightline'+About+His+Past,+Present.

MacDougall, David. "Subtitling Ethnographic Films: Archetypes into Individualities." *Visual Anthropology Review* 11, no. 1 (1995): 83–91.

Machiorlatti, Jennifer A. "Video as Community Ally and Dakota Sense of Place: An Interview with Mona Smith." In *Native Americans on Film,* edited by M. Elise Marubbio and Eric L. Buffalohead, 322–336. Lexington: University Press of Kentucky, 2013.

Maerz, Melissa. "Longing for a Time When Bad Was Good." *Los Angeles Times,* May 22, 2011. Accessed October 4, 2011. http://articles.latimes.com/2011/may/22/entertainment/la-ca-fall-TV-mad-men-influence-20110522.

Mann, Thomas E., and Norman. J. Ornstein. *It's Even Worse Than It Looks: How the American Constitutional System Collided with the New Politics of Extremism.* New York: Basic Books. 2012.

Manovich, Lev. *The Language of New Media.* Cambridge: The MIT Press, 2001.

Marambio, John L., and Tew Chad. "The Promised Land: Resonance and Dissonance of Hollywood's Portrayals of Latin Americans in Film." *Studies in Latin American Popular Culture* 25 (2010): 119–139.

Marques, Angela C. S., and Rousley C. M. Maia. "Everyday Conversations in the Deliberative Process: An Analysis of Communication Exchanges in Discussion Groups and Their Contributions to Civic Discourse." *Journal of Communication,* 60, no. 4 (2011), 611–635.

Marshall, P. David. *Celebrity and Power: Fame in Contemporary Culture.* Minneapolis: University of Minnesota Press, 1997.

Marubbio, M. Elise. *Killing the Indian Maiden: Images of Native American Women in Film.* Lexington: University Press of Kentucky, 2006.

Marubbio, M. Elise, and Eric L. Buffalohead. *Native Americans on Film: Conversations, Teaching, and Theory.* Lexington: University Press of Kentucky, 2012.

Marwick, Alice, Mary L. Gray and Mike Ananny. "'Dolphins Are Just Gay Sharks': *Glee* and the Queer Case of Transmedia As Text and Object." *Television and New Media* 20 (2013): 1–21, doi:10.1177/1527476413478493.

"Mary Tyler Moore." *CNN.* July 1, 2005. http://transcripts.cnn.com/TRAN-SCRIPTS/05 07/01/lkl.01.html.

Mastro, Dana E., and Amanda L. Robinson. "Cops and Crooks: Images of Minorities on Primetime Television." *Journal of Criminal Justice* 28 (2000): 385–396.

Mastro, Dana E., and Elizabeth Behm-Morawitz. "Latino Representation of Primetime Television." *Journalism & Mass Communication Quarterly* 82, no. 1, (2005): 110–130.

Mastro, Dana E., Elizabeth Behm-Morawitz, and Michelle Ortiz. "The Cultivation of Social Perceptions of Latinos: A Mental Models Approach." *Media Psychology* 9, (2007): 347–365.

Mastro, Dana E., Elizabeth Behm-Morawitz, and Maria A. Kopacz. "Exposure to Television Portrayals of Latinos: The Implications of Aversive Racism and Social Identity Theory." *Human Communication Research* 34, (2008): 1–27.

Mauer, Mark. "Why Are Tough on Crime Policies So Popular." *Stanford Law & Policy Review* 11 (1999): 9–17.

Maurer, Donna. *Vegetarianism: Movement or Moment?* Philadelphia: Temple University Press, 2002.

McAlister, Melani. *Epic Encounters: Culture, Media, and U.S. Interests in the Middle East since 1945.* Berkeley: University of California Press, 2001.

McCann, Karen Keating. *Take Charge of Your Hospital Stay: A "Start Smart" Guide for Patients and Care Partners.* New York: Plenum Press, 1994.

McCarthy, Anna. *The Citizen Machine: Governing By Television in 1950s America.* New York: The New Press, 2010.

McChesney, Robert Waterman. *Rich Media, Poor Democracy: Communication Politics in Dubious Times.* Urbana: University of Illinois Press, 1999.

McComas, Katherine, James Shanahan, and Jessica Butler. "Environmental Content in Prime-Time Network and TV's Non-news Entertainment and Fictional Programs." *Society and Natural Resources* 14 (2001): 533–542.

McCombs, Maxwell E., and Donald R. Shaw. "The Agenda-Setting Function of the Mass Media." *Public Opinion Quarterly* 36 (1972): 176–187.

McCracken, Grant, D. "Culture and Consumption: A Theoretical Account for the Structure and Movement of the Cultural Meaning of Consumer Goods." *Journal of Consumer Research* 13, no. 1 (1986): 71–84.

McCutcheon, Lynn E., Mara Aruguete, Jennifer S. Parker, John A. Calicchia, F. Stephen Bridges, and D. D. Ashe. "Nearly the Greatest: Psychological Profiles of Professional Baseball Players Who Almost Became Famous." *North American Journal of Psychology* (2007): 21–34.

McKinley, E. Graham. Beverly Hills, 90210: *Television, Gender and Identity.* Philadelphia: University of Pennsylvania Press, 1997.

McLaughlin, James. "The Doctor Shows." *Journal of Communication* 25, no. 3 (1975): 182–184.

McNamara, Mary. "Back When Men Were Mad Men." *Los Angeles Times*, July 19, 2007. Accessed October 4, 2011. http://archive.is/aAp5D.

McPherson, Kimra, Kai Huotari, F. Yo-Shang Sheng, David Humphrey, Coye Cheshire, and Andrew L. Brooks. "Glitter: A Mixed Methods Study of Twitter Use during *Glee* Broadcasts." *Proceedings of the ACM 2012 Conference on Computer Supported Cooperative Work Companion.*(2012): 167–170, doi: 0:1145/2141512.2141569.

McWhorter, John. "Racism in America Is Over." *Forbes*, December 30, 2008. http://www.forbes.com/2008/12/30/end-of-racism-oped-cx_jm_1230mcwhorter.html.

Meacham, Jon. "What an Umpire Could Teach BP." *Newsweek*, June 14, 2010.

Meadow, Robert G. "Cross-Media Comparison of Coverage of the 1972 Presidential Campaign." *Journalism Quarterly* 50 (1973): 482–488.

Meek, Barbara A. "Failing American Indian Languages." *American Indian Culture and Research Journal* 35, no. 2 (2011): 43–60.

———. "And the Injun Goes 'How!' Representations of American Indian English in White Public Space." *Language in Society* 35, no. 1 (2006): 93–128.

Media Literacy Project. Accessed August 10, 2013. http://medialiteracyproject.org/.

Meisler, Andy. "The Man Who Keeps *E.R*'s Heart Beating," *New York Times*, February 26, 1995.

Mellencamp, Patricia. "Situation Comedy, Feminism, and Freud: Discourses of Gracie and Lucy." In *Feminist Television Criticism*, edited by Charlotte Brunsdon, Julie D'Acci, and Lynn Spigel, 60–74. Oxford: Clarendon Press, 1997.

Mendelsohn, Daniel. "The Mad Men Account." *The New York Review of Books*, February 24, 2011. Accessed October 4, 2011. http://www.nybooks.com/articles/archives/2011/feb /24/ mad-men-account/.

Meyrowitz, Joshua. "We Liked to Watch: Television as Progenitor of the Surveillance Society." *The Annals of the American Academy of Political and Social Science* 625 (September 2009): 32–48.

Michaels, Eric. "Aboriginal Content: Who's Got It—Who Needs It?" *Visual Anthropology* 4, no. 3–4 (1991): 277–300.

————. *Bad Aboriginal Art: Tradition, Media, and Technological Horizons.* Minneapolis: University of Minnesota Press, 1994.

Michie, Gregory. *Holler If You Hear Me: The Education of a Teacher and His Students.* New York: Teachers College Press, 1999.

Milicia, Joe. "Criminals taking tips from TV crime shows." *USA Today*, January 30, 2006.

Miller, Taylor Cole. "Performing *Glee*: Gay Resistance to Gay Representations and a New Slumpy Class." *Flow,* July 6, 2011. http://flowtv.org/2011/07/performing-glee/.

Millner, Denene. "Perry's House Party." *Essence*, July 2007.

Mills, Carol J. "Juror Characteristics: To what Extent are they Related to Jury Verdicts?" *Judicature* 8, no. 22 (1980): 23.

Mineart, Steph. "Ryan Murphy Does Hate Lesbians, Apparently." *Commonplacebook*, December 7, 2012. http://commonplacebook.com/current-events/glbt-issues/ryan-murphy-does-hate-lesbians-apparently/.

Miner, Barbara. "Ultimate $uperpower: Supersized Dollars Drive Waiting for Superman Agenda." *Not Waiting for Superman.* Accessed August 14, 2013. http://www.notwaiting forsuperman.org/Articles/20101020–MinerUltimateSuperpower.

Minkler, Meredith. "Personal Responsibility for Health? A Review of the Arguments and the Evidence at Century's Ed." *Health Education & Behavior* 26, no. 1 (1999): 121–141.

Mishkin, Frederic S. "Over the Cliff: From the Subprime to the Global Financial Crisis." *Journal of Economic Perspectives* 25, no. 1 (2011): 49–70.

Mlodinow, Leonard. *Subliminal: How Your Unconscious Mind Rules Your Behavior.* New York: Random House, 2012.

Montopoli, Brian. "Jon Stewart Rally Attracts Approximately 215,000." *CBS News*, October 30, 2010. http://www.cbsnews.com/8301–503544_162–20021284–503544.html.

Moore, Mary Tyler. "Interview with Mary Tyler Moore." By Larry King. *Larry King Live*, CNN, July 1, 2005. http://transcripts.cnn.com/TRANSCRIPTS/0507/01/lkl.01.html.

Morales, Mark, and Bev Ford. "Boston Marathon Spectator Salah Barhoum, Who was Interviewed by Authorities Following the Bombings, Swears He 'Didn't Do It'." *New York Daily News*, April 18, 2013. http://www.nydailynews.com/news/national/hs-track-star-speaks-didn-article-1.1320766?print.

Morgan, Michael, James Shanahan, and Nancy Signorielli. "Growing Up With Television: Cultivation Processes." In *Media Effects: Advances in Theory and Research*, 3rd ed. Edited by Jennings Bryant and Mary Beth Oliver, 34–49. New York: Routledge, 2009.

————. *Living with Television Now: Advances in Cultivation Theory and Research.* New York: Peter Lang, 2012.

Morris, Jonathan. "Slanted Objectivity? Perceived Media Bias, Cable News Exposure and Political Attitudes." *Social Science Quarterly* 88–3 (2007): 707–728.

Morris, Rosalind C. *New Worlds from Fragments: Film, Ethnography, and the Representation of Northwest Coast Cultures.* Boulder: Westview Press, 1994.

Moses, Michele, and Mitchell J. Chang. "Toward a Deeper Understanding of the Diversity Rationale." *Educational Researcher* 35, no. 1: 7–9.

Moyer-Guse, Emily, and Robin Nabi. "Explaining the Effects of Narrative in an Entertainment Television Program: Overcoming Resistance to Persuasion." *Human Communication Research* no. 1 (2010): 26–52.

Muder, Craig. "Baseball Doubles as a Symbol of the Country." *Phi Kappa Phi Forum* 89, no. 2 (2009): 16–18.

Mullen, Brian, David Futrell, Debbie Stairs, Dianne M. Tice, Roy F. Baumeister, Kathryn E. Dawson, Catherine A. Riordan, Christine E. Radloff, George R. Goethals, John G. Kennedy, and Paul Rosenfeld. "Newscasters' Facial Expressions and Voting Behavior of Viewers. Can a Smile Elect a President?" *Journal of Personality and Social Psychology* 51–2 (1986): 291–295.

Mumford, Laura Stempel. "Feminist Theory and Television Studies." In *The Television Studies Book*, edited by Christine Geraghty and David Lusted, 114–130. London: Arnold, 1998.

Murphy, Ryan, and Tim Wollaston. "The Rocky Horror Glee Show." *Glee*, directed by Adam Shankman, first broadcast October 26, 2010, by Fox.

Murray, Cori. "Oh, What A Night!" *Essence*, December 2008.

Murray, Elizabeth, Bernard Lo, Lance Pollack, Karen Donelan, Joe Catania, Martha White, Kinga Zapert, and Rachel Turner. "The impact of Health Information on the Internet on the Physician-patient Relationship: Patient Perceptions." *Archives of Internal Medicine* 163, no. 14 (2003): 1727.

Murray, Susan, and Laurie Ouellette. *Reality TV: Remaking Television Culture*. New York: New York University Press, 2009.

NAACP, *Out of Focus—out of Sync Take 4*. Hollywood: NAACP Hollywood Bureau, 2008.

"New Cross Platform Report Says Fewer People Have Multichannel Subscriptions." *Broadcasting & Cable*, August 10, 2013. http://www.broadcastingcable.com/article /print/493938–Nielsen_Time_Spent_Watching_Traditional_TV_Up.php.

Newman, Michael. "Turning Creative Success into Business is Your Work!" *zigzagger*, July 26, 2010. Accessed March 22, 2012. http://zigzigger.blogspot.com/2010/07/turning-creative-success-into-business_26.html.

Nichols, Bill. "The Voice of Documentary." *Film Quarterly*, 36, no. 3 (1983): 17–30.

Nordyke, Kimberly. "No Payne No Gain." *Black Filmmaker*, November–December 2006.

Noske, Barbara. *Humans and Other Animals: Beyond the Boundaries of Anthropology*. London: Pluto Press, 1989.

Nowak, Joey. "Players Tab Joyce MLB's Best Umpire." *MLB.com*. August 18, 2011. http://mlb.mlb.com/news/article.jsp?ymd=20110818&content_id=23386260&vkey=news_mlb&c_id=mlb.

Noyes, Richard. "No Doubt About It: All but Fox News Tipping Obama's Way." *Newsbusters*, accessed September 6, 2010. http://newsbusters.org/blogs/rich-noyes/2008/11/01/no-doubt-about-it-all-fox-news-tipping-obama-s-way

Obama, Barack. "Obama: Bin Laden Will Not Walk this Earth Again." By Steve Kroft. 60 Minutes. CBS News, May 4, 2011. http://www.cbsnews.com/stories/2011/05/04/60mi nutes/main20059768.shtml.

O'Connor, Michael M. "The Role of the Television Drama *ER* in Medical Student Life: Entertainment or Socialization?." *JAMA: The Journal of the American Medical Association* 280, no. 9 (1998): 854–855.

Ogdon, Bethany. "The Psycho-Economy of Reality Television in the Tabloid Decade." In *Essays on Representation and Truth: How Real is Reality TV*, edited by David S. Escoffery, 26–41. Jefferson: McFarland and Company, Inc., 2006.

Oliver, Mary Beth. "Portrayals of Crime, Race, and Aggression in 'Reality-Based' Police Shows: A Content Analysis." *Journal of Broadcasting & Electronic Media* 38, no. 2 (1994): 179–192.

Omi, Michael, and Howard Winant. *Racial Formation in the United States from the 1960s to the 1990s*. New York: Routledge, 1994.

Orbe, Mark P. "Representations of Race in Reality TV: Watch and Discuss." *Critical Studies in Media Communication* 25, no. 4, (2008): 345–352.

Oregma, Dirk, Jan Kleinnijenhuis, Koos Anderson, and Anita van Hoof. "Flaming and Blaming: The Influence of Mass Media Content on Interactions in Online Discussions." In *Mediated Interpersonal Communication*, edited by Elly A. Konijin, Sonjia Utz, Martin Tanis, and Susan B. Barnes, 331–358. New York: Routledge. 2008.

Orr, Bob. "Videos Demystify the Osama bin Ladenbin Laden Legend." *CBS News*, May 7, 2011. Accessed October 14, 2013. http://www.cbsnews.com/stories/2011/05/07/even ingnews/main20060808.shtml.

Osawa, Saza. "An Upstream Journey: An Interview with Sandra Osawa." In *Native Americans on Film,* edited by M. Elise Marubbio and Eric L. Buffalohead, 303–321. Lexington: University Press of Kentucky, 2013.

Ostbye, Truls, Bill Miller, and Heather Keller. "Throw That Epidemiologist Out of the Emergency Room! Using the Television Series *ER* as a Vehicle for Teaching Methodologists about Medical Iissues." *Journal of Clinical Epidemiology* 50, no. 10 (1997): 1183–1186.

Oullette, Laurie, and Susan Murray. "Introduction." In *Reality TV: Remaking Television Culture*, edited by Susan Murray and Laurie Oullette, 1–15. New York: New York Press, 2004.

Oxoby, Mark. *The 1990's*. Westport: Greenwood Press, 2003.

Pack, Sam. "Watching Navajos Watch Themselves." *Wicazo Sa Review*, 22, no. 2 (2007): 111–127.

Packer, George. "What's So Good About 'Mad Men'?" *The New Yorker*, November 2, 2009. Accessed December 28, 2012. http://www.newyorker.com/online/blogs/georgepacker/ 2009/11/mad-men.html.

Parekh, Rupal. "How Tyler Perry's House of Hits Was Built." *Advertising Age*, May 18, 2009.

Pariser, Eli. *The Filter Bubble: What the Internet Is Hiding from You*. New York: The Penguin Press, 2011.

Park, Chan Wang, Bernard J. Jaworski, and Deborah J. MacInnis. "Strategic Brand Concept-Image Management." *Journal of Marketing* 50, no. 4 (1986): 135–145.

Park, Ji Hoon. "The Uncomfortable Encounter between an Urban Black and a Rural White: The Ideological Implications of Racial Conflict on MTV's *The Real World*," *Journal of communication* 59 (2009): 152–171.

Park, Rolla E. "The Growth of Cable TV and Its Probable Impact on Over-the-Air Broadcasting." *The America Economic Review*, 61, no. 2 (1971): 69–73.

Pattillo, Mary. *Black on the Block: The Politics of Race and Class in the City*. Chicago: University of Chicago Press, 2007.

Pattillo-McCoy, Mary. *Black Picket Fences: Privilege and Peril among the Black Middle Class*. Chicago: University of Chicago Press, 1999.

Paulus, Stanislawa. "Einblicke in fremde Welten. Orientalische Selbst/Fremdkonstruktionen in TV-Dokumentationen über Muslime in Deutschland." In *Orient- und IslamBilder. Interdisziplinäre Beiträge zu Orientalismus und antimuslimischem Rassismus,* edited by Iman Attia, 279–89. Münster: Unrast, 2007.

Pearson, Roberta. "Lost in Transition: From Post-Network to Post-Television." In *Quality TV: contemporary American television and beyond,* edited by Janet McCabe and Kim Akass, 239–256. New York: I. B. Tauris, 2007.

"Percent of Households with Cable and Satellite Television." *Free By 50.* February 14, 2010. http://www.freeby50.com/2010/02/percent-of-households-with-cable-and. html.

Perlman, Allison. "The Strange Career of Mad Men: Race, Paratexts and Civil Rights Memory." In *Mad Men*, edited by Gary R. Edgerton, 209–206. New York: I.B. Tauris, 2011.

Perry, Tyler. "A Message from Tyler Perry," *Tylerperry.com.* September 23, 2008. http:www.tylerperry.com.

Peterson, Leighton C. "Reel Navajo: The Linguistic Creation of Indigenous Screen Memories." *American Indian Culture and Research Journal*, 35, no. 2 (2011): 111–34.

———. "Reclaiming Diné Film: Visual Sovereignty and the Return of Navajos Film Themselves." *Visual Anthropology Review*, 29, no. 1 (2013): 29–41.

Pew Research Center for People and the Press. "Americans Spending More Time Following the News. Ideological News Sources: Who Watches the News and Why." Last modified September 12, 2010. http://www.people-press.org /2010/09/12/section-1-watching-reading-and-listening-to-the-news.

———. "Internet News Audience Highly Critical of News Organizations." Accessed August 31, 2010. http://people-press.org/report/348/internet-news-audience-highly-critical-of-news-organizations.

———. "Key News Audiences Now Blend Online and Traditional Sources." Accessed June 28, 2013. http://people-press.org/2008/08/17/key-news-audiences-now-blend-online-and-traditional-sources/.———. "Most Voters Say News Media Wants Obama to Win." Accessed August 31, 2010. http://pewresearch.org/pubs/1003/joe-the-plumber.

Pew Research Center's Project for Excellence in Journalism. "State of the News Media 2013." Accessed March 18, 2013. http://stateofthemedia.org.

———. "Winning the Media Campaign." Accessed September 6, 2010. http://www. journalism. org/node/13312.

———. "The Color of News: How Different Media Have Covered the General Election." Project for Excellence in Journalism. Accessed September 6, 2010. http:// www.journa lism.org/node/13436.

Pew Research Journalism Project. "Journalism, Satire, or Just Laughs: 'The Daily Show with John Stewart' Examined." Last modified May 8, 2008. http://www .journalism.org/ files/Dail y%20Show%20PDF _3.pdf.

Pfau, Michael, Lawrence J. Mullen, and Kirsten Garrow. "The Influence of Television Viewing on Public Perceptions of Physicians." *Journal of Broadcasting & Electronic Media* 39, no. 4 (1995): 441–458.

Pho, Kevin. "How *House, M.D.* Is Affecting Patients' Expectations of Medical Care," KevinMD.com, Last modified October 6, 2009. http://www.kevinmd.com/blog/2009/10/house-md-affecting-patients-expectations-medical-care.html.

Pingle, Mark. "Imitation Versus Rationality: An Experimental Perspective on Decision Making." *Journal of Socio-Economics* 24, no. 2 (1995): 281–315.

Pitts, Leonard, Jr. "Facts Might Be Stupid Things, But They Are Still Facts." *Austin American-Statesman,* March 21, 2011, A9.

———. "Lies, Lies and More Lies." *Austin American-Statesman*, April 14, 2011, A7.

Pludowski, Tomasz. *Journal of Media Sociology Special Issue: How the World's News Media Reacted to 9/11. Essays from around the Globe.* Spokane: Marquette Books, 2010.

Podlas, Kimberlianne. "CSI Effect: Exposing the Media Myth, The." *Fordham Intellectual Property, Media & Entertainment Law Journal* 16 (2005): 429–465.

Polsby, Nelson W. *How Congress Evolves: Social Bases of Institutional Change.* New York: Oxford University Press, 2004.

Pomerantz, Dorothy. "TV's Biggest Moneymakers." *Forbes*, April 10, 2012. http://www. forbes.com/pictures/mfl45jigd/tvs-top-moneymakers/.

Poole, Elizabeth, and John E. Richardson. *Muslims and the News Media.* London: Tauris, 2006.

"Position Paper on Vegetarian Diets." *Academy of Nutrition & Dietetics*, July 2009. http://www.eatright.org/about/content.aspx?id=8357.

Postman, Neil. *Amusing Ourselves to Death.* New York: Penguin Books. 1985.

Postman, Neil, and Charles Weingartner. *Teaching as a Subversive Activity.* New York: Delta Books, 1971.

Potter, W. James. *Media Literacy,* 5th ed. Los Angeles: Sage. 2011.

Press, Andrea L. *Women Watching Television: Gender, Class, and Generation in the American Television Experience.* Philadelphia: University of Pennsylvania Press, 1991.

Preston, Julia. "Immigration Decreases, but Tensions Remain High." *New York Times*, March 10, 2012.

Prigge, Steven. *Created by . . . Inside the Minds of TV's Top Show Creators.* Los Angeles: Silman-James Press, 2005.

Prins, Harald E. L. "Visual Media and the Primitivist Perplex: Colonial Fantasies, Indigenous Imagination, and Advocacy in North America." In *Media Worlds,* edited by Faye D. Ginsburg, Lila Abu-Lughod and Brian Larkin, 58–74. Berkeley: University of California Press, 2002.

"Protecting Life in the Sea." *Pew Enviornmental Group*, 2007. http://www.pewtrusts. org/ uploadedFiles/wwwpewtrustsorg/TaxonomyCopy/Enviroment/oceans_final_ web.pdf.

Public Law 107–110, The No Child Left Behind Act of 2001. Accessed October 9, 2013. http://www2.ed.gov/policy/elsec/leg/esea02/index.html.

Putnam, Robert. *Bowling Alone: The Collapse and Revival of American Community.* New York: Touchstone, 2001.

Rabinovitz, Lauren. "Sitcoms and Single Moms: Representations of Feminism on American TV." *Cinema Journal*, no. 1 (1989): 3–19.

Radio Television Digital News Association. "RTNDA Code of Ethics and Professional Conduct." Accessed August 31, 2010. http://www.rtdna.org/pages/media_items/code-of-ethics-and-professional-conduct48.php.

Radway, Janice A. *Reading the Romance: Women, Patriarchy and Popular Literature.* Chapel Hill: University of North Carolina Press, 1984.

Raheja, Michelle H. *Reservation Reelism: Redfacing, Visual Sovereignty, and Representations of Native Americans in Film.* Lincoln: University of Nebraska Press, 2010.

Ramirez Bérg, Charles. *Latino Images in Film: Stereotypes, Subversion, and Resistance.* Austin: University of Texas Press, 2002.

Rapping, Elayne. "Aliens, Nomads, Mad Dogs, and Road Warriors: The Changing Face of Criminal Violence on TV." In *Reality TV: Remaking Television Culture*, edited by Susan Murray and Laurie Ouellette, 214–230. New York: New York Press, 2004.

Ravitch, Diane. *The Death and Life of the Great American School System.* New York: Perseus Books, 2010.

Redmond, Sean, and Su Holmes. *Stardom and Celebrity: A Reader.* Los Angeles: Sage, 2007.

Rees, Tim, David K. Ingledew, and Lew Hardy. "Attribution in Sport Psychology: Seeking Congruence Between Theory, Research, and Practice." *Psychology of Sport and Exercise* 6 (2005): 189–204.

Regan, Tom. *The Case for Animal Rights.* Berkeley: University of California Press, 1983.

Reich, Robert. "American Bile." *New York Times*, September 23, 2013, http://opinion tor.blogs.nytimes.com/2013/09/21/american-bile.

Resnik, Eric. "Two Miami U. Students Beaten in Possible Hate Crime," Gay People's Chronicle.com, June 4, 2010, http://www.gaypeopleschronicle.com/stories10/june /0604104.htm.

Reston, Maeve. "Republican Candidates Face Big Latino Problem." *Los Angeles Times*, March 15, 2012.

"Rhoda and Mary: Love and Laughs." *Time*, October 28, 1974.

Richardson, John G., and Brenda Wooden Hatcher. "The Feminization of Public School Teaching: 1890–1920." *Work and Occupations* 10, no. 1. (1983): 81–99.

Richins, Marsha L. "Valuing Things: The Public and Private Meanings of Possessions." *Journal of Consumer Research* 21, no. 3 (1994): 504–521.

Richins, Marsha, and Scott Dawson. "A Consumer Values Orientation for Materialism and its Measurement: Scale Development and Validation." *Journal of Consumer Research* 19 (1992): 303–316.

Roane, Kit R., and Dan Morrison. "The CSI Effect." *US News & World Report* 138 (2005): 48–54.

Roberts, Julian V., and Anthony N. Doob. "News Media Influences on Public Views of Sentencing." *Law and Human Behavior* 14, no. 5 (1990): 451–468.

Robinson, Eugene. *Disintegration: The Splintering of Black America.* New York: Doubleday, 2010.

Robinson, Michael J. T., and Margaret A. Sheehan. *Over the Wire and on TV: CBS and UPI in Campaign '80*. New York: Russell Sage, 1983.

Rockler, Naomi R. "From Magic Bullets to Shooting Blanks: Reality, Criticism, and *Beverly Hills, 90210" Western Journal of Communications* 63(1) (1999): 72–94.

———. "'Be Your Own Windkeeper': 'Friends,' Feminism, and Rhetorical Strategies of Depoliticization." *Women's Studies in Communication* 29, no. 2 (2006): 260.

Rodriguez, César. G. "Congressman Discusses Border." *Laredo Morning Times*, March 16, 2012.

Roeh, Itzhak. "Journalism as Storytelling, Coverage as Narrative." *American Behavioral Scientist* 33, no. 2 (1989): 162–168.

Rogers, Everett. *Diffusion of Innovations*. New York: The Free Press, 2003.

Rogers, Richard A. "Beasts, Burgers, and Hummers: Meat and the Crisis of Masculinity in Contemporary Television Advertisements." *Environmental Communication* 2, no. 3 (November 2008): 281–301.

Rollins, Peter C., and John E. O'Connor. *Hollywood's Indian: The Portrayal of the Native American in Film*. Lexington: University Press of Kentucky, 2003.

Rose, Charlie. "Charlie Rose – William J. Fallon/Mad Men." *Charlie Rose*, directed by Charlie rose, first broadcast July 28, 2008 by Charlie Rose, Inc.

Rose, Lacey, and Lauren Streib. "Cash for Trash." *Forbes,* March 16, 2009.

Rosenberg, Debra. "The 'Will & Grace' Effect." *Newsweek,* May 23, 2004. http://www. thedailybeast.com/newsweek/2004/05/23/the-will-amp-grace-effect.html.

Rosenberg, Emily. *A Date Which Will Live: Pearl Harbor in American Memory*. Durham: Duke University Press, 2003.

Rosin, Hanna. "The End of Men." *The Atlantic*, July 2010.

Ross, Brian, and Avni Patel. "Bin Laden Tapes Show 'Pathetic' Side of Al Qaeda Leader." *ABC News*, May 9, 2011. Accessed October 14, 2013, http://abcnews.go.com/Blotter/ osama-bin-laden-tapes-show-pathetic-side- al/story?id=13559652#.TtZbjfKVpdO.

Rowe, Kathleen. *The Unruly Woman: Gender and Genres of Laughter*. Austin: University of Texas Press, 1995.

Russell, Gordon W. "Sport Riots: A Social-Psychological Review." *Aggression and Violent Behavior* 9 (2004): 353–378.

Rutecki, Jared W., and Gregory W. Rutecki. "A Study of Media Impact on Public Opinion Regarding Performance Enhancement in Major League Baseball." *The Open Sports Sciences Journal* 3 (2010): 140–148.

Ruva, Christine L., and Cathy McEvoy. "Negative and Positive Pretrial Publicity Affect Juror Memory and Decision Making." *Journal of Experimental Psychology: Applied* 14, no. 3 (2008): 226–235.

Said, Edward W. *Covering Islam. How the Media and the Experts Determine How We See the Rest of the World*. New York: Vintage Books, 1997.

———. *Orientalism: 25th Anniversary Edition*. New York: Vintage Books, 2003.

"Sample Math Block Schedules." *Palm Beach Schools*. Accessed August 14, 2013. http://www.palmbeachschools.org/qa/documents/SampleMathBlockSchedules .pdf.

Samuels, David W. *Putting a Song on Top of It: Expression and Identity on the San Carlos Apache Reservation*. Tucson: University of Arizona Press, 2004.

Sandman, Peter M., David M. Rubin, and David B. Sachsman. *Media: An Introductory Analysis of American Mass Communications.* Englewood Cliffs: Prentice-Hall, 1976.

Santa Ana, Otto. *Brown Tide Rising: Metaphors of Latinos in Contemporary American Public Discourse.* Austin: The University of Texas Press, 2002.

Sarapin, Susan H., and Glenn G. Sparks. "The Viewing of TV Crime Drama and the 'CSI effect': There's a Verdict Hanging in the Balance." Paper presented at the NCA 96th Annual Convention, Hilton San Francisco, California, November 13, 2010.

Schaap, Jeremy. "Bill Buckner: Behind the Bag." ESPN, October 25, 2011.

Schenk, Susan. *Das Islambild im internationalen Fernsehen. Ein Vergleich der Nachrichtensender Al Jazeera English, BBC World und CNN International.* Berlin: Frank & Timme, 2009.

Schiappa, Edward. *Beyond Representational Correctness: Rethinking Criticism of Popular Media.* Albany: State University of New York Press, 2008.

Schiappa, Edward, Peter B. Gregg, and Dean E. Hewes. "Can One TV Show Make a Difference? Will & Grace and the Parasocial Contact Hypothesis." *Journal of Homosexuality* 51 (2006): 15–37. doi:10.1300/J082v51n04_02.

———. "The Parasocial Contact Hypothesis." *Communication Monographs.* no. 1 (2005): 92–115.

"School to Work Opportunities Act." *United States Department of Education.* Accessed August 12, 2013. http://www2.ed.gov/pubs/Biennial/95–96/eval/410–97.pdf.

Schulman, Bruce. *The Seventies: The Great Shift in American Culture, Society, and Politics.* New York: Free Press, 2001.

Schulman, Bruce, and Julian Zelizer. *Rightward Bound: Making America Conservative in the 1970s.* Cambridge: Harvard University Press, 2008.

Schumacher, E. F. *Small Is Beautiful: Economics as if People Mattered.* New York: Harper & Row, 1975.

Schwarz, Benjamin. "Mad About Mad Men." *The Atlantic*, November 2009. Accessed December 28, 2012. http://www.theatlantic.com/magazine/archive/2009/11/mad-about-mad-men/307709/.

Schwartzbaum, Lisa. "Love Is on the Air." *Entertainment Weekly*, February 14, 1992. Accessed November 10, 2013. http://www.ew.com/ew/article/0,,309552,00.html.

Schweitzer, Nicholas J., and Michael J. Saks. "The CSI effect: Popular fiction about forensic science affects the public's expectations about real forensic science." *Jurimetrics* 47 (2006): 357–364.

Screening the Past. "Prosthetic memory/traumatic memory: *Forrest Gump* (1994)." Accessed by November 10, 2013. http://tlweb.latrobe.edu.au/humanities/screeningthepast/firstre lease/fr0499/rbfr6a.htm.

Seate, Anita Atwell, Jake Harwood, and Erin Blecha. "'He was Framed!' Framing Criminal Behavior in Sports News." *Communication Research Reports* 27, no. 4 (October/ December 2010): 343–354.

Segura, Melissa, and Tom Verducci. "A Different Kind of Perfect." *Sports Illustrated*, June 14, 2010.

"Selected Occupational Projections Data: Search by Education." *United States Department of Labor—Bureau of Labor Statistics.* Accessed August 13, 2013. http://data.bls.gov/oep/noeted.

Shanahan, James, and Katherine McComas. *Nature Stories: Depictions of the Environment and Their Effects.* Cresskill: Hampton Press, 1999.

Shanahan, James and Michael Morgan Shanahan. *Television and its Viewers: Cultivation Theory and Research.* Cambridge: Cambridge University Press, 1999.

Shanahan, James, Michael Morgan, and Mads Stenbjerre. "Green or Brown? Television and the Cultivation of Environmental Concern, *Journal of Broadcasting & Electronic Media* 41, no. 3 (1997): 305–323.

Sharon, Thomas A. *Protect Yourself in the Hospital: Insider Tips for Avoiding Hospital Mistakes for Yourself or Someone You Love.* New York: McGraw-Hill 2004.

Shelton, Hon. Donald E., Gregg Barak, and Young S. Kim. "A Study of Juror Expectations and Demands Concerning Scientific Evidence: Does the 'CSI Effect' Exist?" *Vanderbilt Journal of Entertainment & Technology Law* 9, no. 2 (2007): 331–368.

Shepard, Krech. *The Ecological Indian: Myth and History.* New York: W. W. Norton & Co., 1999.

Shore, David A. *The Trust Crisis in Healthcare: Causes, Consequences, and Cures.* New York: Oxford University Press, 2006.

Shrum, Larry J. "Media Consumption and Perceptions of Social Reality: Effects and Underlying Processes." *Media Effects: Advances in theory and research* 2 (2002): 69–95.

——. "Assessing the Social Influence of Television: A Social Cognition Perspective on Cultivation Effects." *Communication Research 22*, no. 4 (1995): 402–429.

Shrum, Larry J., Jaehoon Lee, James Burroughs, and Aric Rindfleisch. "An Online Process Model of Second-Order Cultivation Effects: How Television Cultivates Materialism and Its Consequences for Life Satisfaction." *Human Communication Research* 37 (2011): 34–57.

Shrum, Larry J., Robert S. Wyer Jr., and Thomas C. O'Guinn. "The Effects of Television Consumption on Social Perceptions: The Use of Priming Procedures to Investigate Psychological Processes." *Journal of Consumer Research* 24, no. 4 (1998): 447–458.

Silverstein, Michael J., Neil Fiske, and John Butman. *Trading Up: Why Consumers Want New Luxury Goods—And How Companies Create Them.* New York: Portfolio, 2008.

Simien, Evelyn M. "Race, Gender, and Linked Fate." *Journal of Black Studies* 35, no. 5 (May 2005): 529–550.

Singer, Beverly R. *Wiping the War Paint Off the Lens: Native American Film and Video.* Minneapolis: University of Minnesota Press, 2001.

Singer, Peter, and Jim Mason. *The Ethics of What We Eat: Why Our Food Choices Matter.* New York: Rodale, 2006.

Singer, Peter. *Animal Liberation*, 2nd ed. New York: Random House, 1990.

Singhal, Arvind., Michael J. Cody, and Everett M. Rogers. *Entertainment-education and Social Change: History, Research, and Practice.* New York: Routledge, 2004.

Sirgy, Joseph M., Dong-Jin Lee, Rustan Kosenko, H. Lee Meadow, Don Rahtz, Muris Cicic, Guang Xi Jin, Duygan Yarsuvat, David L. Blenkhorn, and Newell Wright.

"Does Television Viewership Play a Role in the Perception of Quality of Life?" *Journal of Advertising* 27, no. 1 (1998): 125–142.

Slagle, Dana. "Tyler Perry Takes on TV with New Sitcom 'House of Payne'." *Jet,* June 11, 2007.

———. "Minority Population in U.S. Peaks at 100 Million," *Jet,* June 4, 2007.

Slotkin, Richard. *Gunfighter Nation: The Myth of the Frontier in Twentieth-Century America.* Norman: University of Oklahoma Press, 1998.

Smith, Debra C. "Critiquing Reality-based Televisual Black Fatherhood: A Critical Analysis of Run's House and Snoop Dogg's Father Hood." *Critical Studies in Media Communication* 25, no. 4 (October 2008): 393–412.

Society of Professional Journalists. "Code of Ethics." Accessed October 29, 2011. http://www.spj.org/ethicscode.asp.

Solomon, Deborah. "In Praise of Bad Art." *New York Times*, January 24, 1999. Accessed May 21, 2013. http://www.nytimes.com/1999/01/24/magazine/in-praise-of-bad-art.html.

Soulliere, Danielle M. "Prime-time Murder: Presentations of Murder on Popular Television Justice Programs." *Journal of Criminal Justice and Popular Culture* 10, no. 1 (2003): 12–38.

Spangler, Lynn C. *Television Women from Lucy to Friends: Fifty Years of Sitcoms and Feminism.* Westport: Praeger, 2003.

Spigel, Lynn. "Object Lessons for the Media Home: From Storagewall to Invisible Design." *Public Culture* 24, no. 3 (2012): 535–576.

———. "Designing the Smart House: Posthuman Domesticity and Conspicuous Production." *European Journal of Cultural Studies* 8, no. 4 (2009): 403–426.

———. *Welcome to the Dreamhouse: Popular Media and Postwar Suburbs.* Durham: Duke University Press, 2001.

———. *TV By Design: Modern Art and the Rise of Network Television.* Chicago: The University of Chicago Press, 2008.

———. *Make Room for TV: Television and the Family Ideal in Postwar America.* Chicago: The University of Chicago Press, 1992.

Springer, Noah. "Serious Play: Evaluating the Comedic, Political and Religious Relationships between *The Daily Show*, *The Colbert Report*, and *South Park*." Master's Thesis, Southern Illinois University, 2011.

Squires, Catherine. "Race and Reality TV: Tryin' to Make it Real—but Real Compared to What?" *Critical Studies in Media Communication* 25, no. 4 (2008): 434–440.

Stack, Tim. "*Glee*: Ryan Murphy Defends Tonight's Controversial Teen Sex Episode." *Entertainment Weekly*, November 8, 2011. http://insidetv.ew.com/2011/11/08/glee-ryan-murphy-the-first-time-exclusive/.

———. "Rocking the 'House'." *Entertainment Weekly,* June 22, 2007.

———. "Tyler on Top." *Entertainment Weekly*, October 26, 2007.

Stahler, Charles. "How Often Do Americans Eat Vegetarian Meals?" *The Vegetarian Resource Group*, 2011. http://www.vrg.org/journal/vj2011issue4/vj2011issue-4poll.php.

Starr, Paul. *The Social Transformation of American Medicine*. New York: Basic Books, 1982.

Steinberg, Jacques. "In Act 2, the TV Hit Man Becomes a Pitch Man." *New York Times*, July 18, 2007. Accessed March 12, 2012. http://www.nytimes.com/2007/07/18/arts/tele vision/18madm.html.

Stelter, Brian. "Media Decoder: The End of MSNBC's Experiment." New York Times, September 7, 2008. http://mediadecoder.blogs.nytimes.com/2008/09/07/the-end-of-msnbcs-experiment/.

Stephens, Sheila L. "The CSI Effect on Real Crime Labs." *New England Law Review* 41 (2006): 591.

Stevenson, Howard C. *Playing with Anger: Teaching Coping Skills to African American Boys through Athletics and Culture*. Westport: Praeger, 2003.

Stinson, Veronica., Marc W. Patry, and Steven M. Smith. "The CSI Effect: Reflections from Police and Forensic Investigators." *The Canadian Journal of Police and Security Services* 5, no. 3 (2007): 1–9.

Students Last. "Stoning Teachers Raises Some Eyebrows." Accessed October 9, 2013. http://studentslast.blogspot.com/2012/08/stoning-teachers-raises-some-eyebrows.html?spref=fb.

Sugrue, Thomas. "Racial Romanticism." *Democracy,* Summer 2009. Accessed by November 10, 2013. http://www.democracyjournal.org/13/6694.php?page=all

Summers, Sandy Jacobs, and Harry Jacobs Summers. "Media 'Nursing': Retiring the Handmaiden: What viewers see on ER affects our profession." *AJN The American Journal of Nursing* 104, no. 2 (2004): 13.

Sundar, S. Shyam. "Self as Source: Agency and Customization in Interactive Media." In *Mediated Interpersonal Communication*, edited by Elly A. Konijin, Sonjia Utz, Martin Tanis, and Susan B. Barnes. 58–74. New York: Routledge. 2008.

Sutter, Daniel. "Can the Media be so Liberal? The Economics of Media Bias," *Cato Journal* 20–3 (2001): 431–451.

Sutton, Joe. "Mississippi Lawmakers Pass Controversial Immigration Bill." *CNN,* March 16, 2012. http://edition.cnn.com/2012/03/16/us/mississippi-immigration-law/index.html.

Svensson, Peter. "Pay TV Industry Loses Record Number of Subscribers." *ABCNews,* August 10, 2011. http://abcnews.go.com/Technology/wireStory?id=14271831#. T7ub247v3v9.

Svetkey, Benjamin, Margeaux Watson, and Alynda Wheat. "How Do You Solve A Problem Like Madea?" *Entertainment Weekly*, March 20, 2009.

Swidler, Ann. *Talk of Love: How Culture Matters*. Chicago: University of Chicago Press, 2001.

Szalai, Georg. "Cable Shows with the Wealthiest Viewers." *The Hollywood Reporter*, October 14, 2010. Accessed January 11, 2012. http://www.hollywoodreporter.com/news/cable-shows-wealthiest-viewers-25905.

Tan, Yue, and David H. Weaver. "Media Bias, Public Opinion, and Policy Liberalism from 1956 to 2004: A Second-Level Agenda Setting Study." *Mass Communication and Society* 13–4 (2007): 412–434.

Taylor, Derrick. B. "RhoA: Season Finale Breaks Ratings Records." *Essence*, February 1, 2011. Accessed July 31, 2011. http://www.essence.com/2011/02/01/rhoa-season-three-finale-breaks-bravo-ratings-record/

———. "RhoA: Kandi Burruss on 'boughetto' and Tiny and Toya," *Essence*, November 1, 2010.http://www.essence.com/entertainment/real_housewives_of_atlanta/kandi_burruss/rhoa_kandi_burruss_on_boughetto_and_tiny_and_ti.php.

Taylor, Ella. *Prime-Time Families: Television Culture in Post-War America*. Berkeley: University of California Press, 1989.

Tedlock, Dennis. *The Spoken Word and the Work of Interpretation*. Philadelphia: University of Pennsylvania Press, 1983.

———. *Finding the Center: The Art of the Zuni Storyteller*. Lincoln: University of Nebraska Press, 1999.

"Teen Crush: TVs Luke Perry Sets 10,000 Hearts Aflutter." *People Magazine* 36(7), August 26, 1991. http://www.people.com/people/ achive/article/0,,20115774,00.html

"The 2009 Hollywood Writers Report," *WGA*, 2009. http://www.wga.org/uploaded-Files /who_we_are/HWR09.pdf

The American Presidency Project. "Remarks on Signing the Bill Making the Birthday of Martin Luther King, Jr. a National Holiday." November 2, 1983. Accessed November 10, 2013. http://www.presidency.ucsb.edu/ws/?pid=40708

The BH90210 Directory. Accessed October 11, 2012. http://www.bh90210.co.uk/ratings.

The Board of the Millennium Ecosystem Assessment. *Living Beyond Our Means: Natural Assets and Human Well-being*. Washington: Millennium Ecosystem Assessment, 2005.

"The Making of *Mad Men*." http://www.amctv.com/ mad-men/videos/the-making-of-mad-men-part-1

"The Nielsen Company Historical Daily Viewing Activity Among Households and Persons 2+." *Nielsen*. August 10, 2013. http://www.nielsen.com/content/dam/corporate/us/en/ newswire/uploads/2009/11/historicalviewing.pdf

TheTVAddict.com. "The Ugly Truth About the TV Ratings Game." Accessed January 4, 2011. http://www.thetvaddict.com/2011/01/04/one-program-executive-attempts-to-use-jedi-mind-manipulation-to-convince-us-that-these-are-not-the-tv-shows-we-are-looking-for/

The U.S Department of Defense. "Background Briefing with Senior Intelligence Official at the Pentagon on Intelligence Aspects of the U.S. Operation Involving Osama Bin Laden." Accessed October 14, 2013, http://www.defense.gov/transcripts/transcript. aspx?transcriptid=4820

The Weather Channel. "Average Weather for Albany, NY." Accessed July 11, 2013. http://www.weather.com/weather/wxclimatology/monthly/graph/12203.

———. "Average Weather for Beverly Hills, CA." Accessed July 11, 2013. http://www. weather.com/weather/wxclimatology/monthly/graph/90210.

The White House. "Remarks by the President on the Middle East and North Africa." Accessed October 14, 2013, http://www.whitehouse.gov/the-press-office/2011/05/19/ remarks-president-middle-east-and-north-africa.

Thomas, Ebony Elizabeth, and Shanesha R. F. Brooks-Tatum. *Reading African American Experiences in the Obama Era: Theory, Advocacy, Activism*. New York: Peter Lang, 2012.

Todd, Anne Marie. "Prime-time Subversion: The Environmental Rhetoric of 'The Simpsons'," in *Environmental Sociology: From Analysis to Action*, edited by Leslie King, 230–247. Lanham: Rowman & Littlefield, 2009.

Tooby, John. "Rivaling Gutenberg." In *Is the Internet Changing the Way You Think?*, edited by John Brockman, 60–65. New York: Harper Perennial. 2012.

"Top Issues Confronting Hospitals: 2012." *American College of Healthcare Excecutive*. Last modified January 7, 2013. http://www.ache.org/Pubs/Releases/2013/Top-IssuesConfron ting-Hospitals-2012.cfm

Torres, Bob. *Making a Killing: The Political Economy of Animal Rights*. Oakland: AK Press, 2008.

Travers, Scott D. "Pundits in Muckrakers' Clothing: Political Blogs and the 2004 Presidential Election," in *Blogging, Citizenship and the Future of Media,* edited by. Mark Tremayne, 39–58. New York: Routledge, 2006.

Trimberger, Ellen Kay. *The New Single Woman*. Boston: Beacon Press, 2006.

Tu, Ha T., and Genna R. Cohen. *Striking jump in consumers seeking health care information*. Washington: Center for Studying Health System Change, 2008.

Turner, Graeme. *Understanding Celebrity*. London: Sage, 2004.

Turner, Joel. "The Messenger Overwhelming the Message: Ideological Cues and Perceptions of Bias in Television News." *Political Behavior* 29 (2007): 441–464.

Turow, Joseph. "Television entertainment and the US health-care debate." *The Lancet* 347, no. 9010 (1996): 1240–1243.

———. *Playing Doctor: Television, Storytelling, and Medical Power*. Ann Arbor: University of Michigan Press, 2010.

Turvey, Brent E. "The Role of Criminal Profiling in the Development of Trial Strategy." *Knowledge Solutions Library*, November 1997, accessed December 16, 2013. http://www.corpus-delicti.com/Trial_Strategy.html.

TylerPerry.com. Accessed January 1, 2014, http:www.tylerperry.com/talk.

Tyler, Tom R. "Public mistrust of the law: A political perspective." *University of Cincinnati Law Review 66* (1997): 847–875.

———. "Viewing CSI and the threshold of guilt: Managing truth and justice in reality and fiction." *The Yale Law Journal* (2006): 1050–1085.

Tyro, Frank H. "Localism and Low-Power Public Television on the Flathead Indian Reservation" *Wicazo Sa Review*, 16, no. 2 (2001): 19–28.

"United States Census Bureau: Laredo, Texas." *United States Census Bureau*. 2013. http://quickfacts.census.gov/qfd/states/48/4841464.html

Unnever, James D., Francis T. Cullen, and Bonnie S. Fisher. "'A Liberal is Someone Who Has Not Been Mugged': Criminal victimization and political beliefs." *Justice Quarterly* 24, no. 2 (2007): 309–334.

"USA Quick Facts." *United States Census Bureau*, http://quickfacts.census.gov/qfd/states/00000.html

Valdivia, Angharad N. *Latina/os and the Media.* Cambridge: Polity Press, 2010.

Vandekieft, Gregg. "From *City Hospital* to *ER*: The Evolution of the Television Physician." In *Cultural Sutures: Medicine and Media,* edited by Lester D. Friedman L. D. Friedman, 215–233. Durham: Duke University Press, 2004.

van Heertrum, Richard. "Irony and the News: Speaking through Cool to American Youth." In *The Stewart/Colbert Effect: Essays on the Real Impacts of Fake News*, edited by Amarnath Amarasingam, 117–135. Jefferson: McFarLand & Company, Inc., Publishers: 2011.

Vargas-Cooper, Natasha. "Murphy's Honor." *Out*, April 11, 2013. http://www.out.com/enter tainment/television/2013/04/11/ryan-murphy-glee-american-horror-story?page=full.

Veith, Robin, and Christopher Manley. *Mad Men, Season Three*, DVD. Directed by Matthew Weiner. Santa Monica, CA: Lionsgate Home Entertainment.

Velthuis, Olav. *Talking Prices: Symbolic Meanings of Prices on the Market for Contemporary Art.* Princeton: Princeton University Press, 2005.

Vena, Jocelyn. "Will Cory Monteith's Finn Die from 'Accidental Drug Overdose' on 'Glee'?" MTV.com, August 15, 2013. http://www.mtv.com/news/articles/1712413/cory-monteith-glee-death-ryan-murphy.jhtml

Viehöver, Willy. "Diskurse als Narrationen." In *Handbuch Sozialwissenschaftliche Diskursanalyse Bd. I: Theorien und Methoden,* edited by Reiner Keller, Andreas Hirseland, Werner Schneider, and Willy Viehöver, 179–208. Wiesbaden: VS Verlag für Sozialwissenschaften, 2006.

Williams, Rebecca. "From Beyond Control to in Control: Investigating Drew Barrymore's Feminist Agency/Authorship." In *Stardom and Celebrity: A Reader, edited by Sean Redmond and Su Holmes,* 111–125. Los Angeles: Sage, 2005.

Votta, Rae. "'Glee' Q&A: Alex Newell on Unique's Future." *Billboard,* November 21, 2012. http://www.billboard.com/articles/columns/pop-shop/474063/glee-qa-alex-newell-on-uniques-future-his-beyonce-obsession-frank.

———. "Glee Season Finale," *Billboard,* May 10, 2013.http://www.billboard.com/articles /news/1561269/glee-season-finale-all-or-nothing-delivers-regionals-a-surprisewedding-and/

Waldinger, Roger. *Still the Promised City?: African-Americans and New Immigrants in Postindustrial New York.* Cambridge: Harvard University Press, 1996.

Waldron, Vince, and Dick Van Dyke. *The Official Dick Van Dyke Show Book: The Definitive History and Ultimate Viewer's Guide to Television's Most Enduring Comedy.* New York: Applause, 2001.

Wann, Daniel L., and Michael P. Schrader. "Controllability and Stability in the Self-Serving Attributions of Sport Spectators." *The Journal of Social Psychology* 140, no. 2 (2000): 160–168.

Warner, Jamie. "Political Culture Jamming: The Dissident Humor of 'The Daily Show With Jon Stewart.'" *Popular Communication* 5, no. 1 (2007): 17–36.

Webster, Anthony K. *Explorations in Navajo Poetry and Poetics.* Albuquerque: University of New Mexico Press, 2009.

———. ""Please Read Loose": Intimate Grammars and Unexpected Languages in Contemporary Navajo Literature." *American Indian Culture and Research Journal*, 35, no. 2 (2011): 61–86.

Webster, Anthony K., and Leighton C. Peterson. "Introduction: American Indian Languages in Unexpected Places." *American Indian Culture and Research Journal*, 35, no. 2 (2011): 1–18.

Weidman, Amanda. "Anthropology and the Voice." *Anthropology News*, 52, no. 1 (2011): 13.

Weiner, Juli. "Dr. Lyle Evans, We Presume?" *Vanity Fair*, August 23, 2010. Accessed March 9, 2012. http://www.vanityfair.com/online/daily/2010/08/mad-meme-dr-lyle-evans-we-presume

White, Hayden. *Figural Realism: Studies in the Mimesis Effect.* Baltimore: John Hopkins University Press, 1999.

White, Randy, and Vicki Stoecklin. "Nurturing Children's Biophilia: Developmentally Appropriate Environmental Education for Young Children." *White Hutinson Learning and Leisure Group,* 2008, accessed July 2, 2013. http://www.whitehutchinson.com/children/articles/nurturing.shtml

Will, George. "This Week," ABC, originally aired June 8, 2010.

Willens, Michele. "They've Come a Long Way; The Pioneer was Ethel, And Later on Came Rhoda. But Sitcom Sidekicks Of The '90s are neither Frumpy nor Frowzy. These Women Wear Their Libidos on Their Sleeves." *Los Angeles Times*, May 26, 1996. Accessed by November 10, 2013. http://articles.latimes.com/1996–05–26/ entertainment /ca-8432_1_female-sidekick

Williams, Danielle E. "Black Public Creative Figures in the Neo-Racial Moment: An Analysis of Tyra Banks, Tyler Perry and Shonda Rhimes, 2005–2010" *Communication Dissertations* (2012).

Wilson, Michael. "On 'Mad Men,' an Opening Scene Straight From Page 1." *New York Times,* March 28, 2012. Accessed May 2, 2012. http://cityroom.blogs.nytimes.com/2012 /03/28/on-mad-men-an-opening-scene-straight-from-page-1/

Wilson, William J. *The Declining Significance of Race: Blacks and Changing American Institutions.* Chicago: University of Chicago Press, 1978.

Winsten, Jay A. "Promoting designated drivers: The Harvard Alcohol Project." *American Journal of Preventive Medicine* 10, no. 3 Suppl (1994): 11.

Witchel, Alex. ""Mad Men' Has Its Moment." *New York Times*, June 22, 2008. Accessed March 13, 2012, http://www.nytimes.com/2008/06/22/magazine/22madmen-t .html? pagewanted=all.

Witherspoon, Gary. "Film Review: *Weaving Worlds.*" *American Anthropologist*, 115, no. 2 (2013): 321–22.

Wolf, Michelle. "Trans as 'Personal Truth'? Thanks for the Screw Over, *Glee.*" *Pinkessence Transgender Social Network,* March 24, 2013. http://pinkessence.com/profiles/blogs/trans-as-personal-truth-thanks-for-the-screw-over-glee.

Wolfenden, Katherine J. "Challenging Stereotypes in Glee, Or Not?" *Student Pulse* 5 (2013). http://www.studentpulse.com/articles/724/challenging-stereotypes-in-glee-or-not-exploring-masculinity-and-neoliberal-flexibility.

Woodward, Kathryn. *Identity and Difference.* London: Sage, 1997.

Worth, Sol, and John Adair. *Through Navajo Eyes: An Exploration in Film Communication and Anthropology.* Bloomington: Indiana University Press, 1972.

Wright, Lawrence. *The Looming Tower. Al-Qaeda and the Road to 9/11.* New York: Knopf, 2006.

Yang, Hyeseung, and Mary Beth Oliver. "Exploring the Effects of Television Viewing on Perceived Quality of Life: A Combined Perspective of Material Value and Upward Social Comparison." *Mass Communication and Society* 13, no. 2 (2010): 118–138.

Younge, Gary. "Such a Tease." *The Guardian*, September 30, 2005. http://www.guar dian.co.uk/media/2005/oct/01/usa.television

Zaharopoulos, Thimios. "The News Framing of the 2004 Olympic Games." *Mass Communication & Society* 10, no. 2 (2007): 235–249.

Zeldes, Geri Alumit, Frederick Fico, Serena Carpenter, and Arvind Diddi. "Partisan Balance and Bias in Network Coverage of the 2000 and 2004 Presidential Elections," *Journal of Broadcasting & Electronic Media* 52 (2008): 563–580.

Zook, Kristal Brent. *Color by Fox: The Fox Network and the Revolution in Black Television.* New York: Oxford University Press, 1999.

Zuckerman, Miron. "Attribution of Success and Failure Revisited, or The Motivational Bias is Alive and Well in Attribution Theory." *Journal of Personality* 47, no. 2 (June 1979): 245–287.

Zultan, R., Gerstenberg T., and David A. Lagnado, "Finding Fault: Causality and Counterfactuals in Group Attributions." *Cognition* 125 (2012): 429–440.

Zurawik, David. *The Jews of Primetime. Brandeis Series in American Jewish History, Culture, and Life.* Hanover: Brandeis University Press, 2003.

Index

About the Contributors

Stylés Akira received his B.A. from Pace University, Manhattan, in Applied Psychology & Human Relations, and earned his M.A. in Liberal Studies with a concentration in Sociology from St. John's University in May 2009. Akira worked in the recording industry in New York City for a decade prior to pursuing a doctoral degree in Communication at the University of Southern California, Annenberg School of Communication. He is interested in advertising, strategic branding, mass media effects, behavioral economics, and consumer culture.

Jack A. Barwind lived for four years in the United Arab Emirates and became increasingly aware of the impact technology has on the transformation of a culture. He began writing extensively about the role of cell phones in the secularization of an Islamic traditional culture. It was at that point he published (along with James Picowye) "Your Media, My Literacy: A Curriculum Model Considered," in a 2002 edition of *Technos Quarterly*; it was an early attempt to view the development of a curriculum in Media Literacy as a response to the onslaught of technology. Subsequently his interests evolved into views concerning a more generalized view of media ecology. Recently Dr. Barwind focused on media and incivility. Courses that he has taught pertinent to these current interests are "The Frontiers of Communication" and "The Psychology of Communication." During the final preparation of this chapter, on May 16, 2013, Dr. Barwind passed away.

Cindy Conaway is an assistant professor and area coordinator of Media Studies and Communications at SUNY Empire State College's Center for Distance Learning. She earned her doctorate in American Culture Studies with an emphasis on Media, Film, and Culture from Bowling Green State

University. Her primary research concerns teen television and representations of "brainy girls." She also studies race, television, and new media, and is working on a book, *Girls Who (Don't) Wear Glasses: The Smart Teenage Girl on TV in the 1990s.*

Lane C. Clegg is a founding faculty member at the Tulsa Lighthouse Charter School in Tulsa, Oklahoma, after teaching in the Teach For America Oklahoma Corps for two years. Her B.A. from Miami University is in Political Science and Journalism. She first began work on the study in "Media Bias in the 2008 Presidential Election" during her junior and senior years, at Miami, under the supervision of Dr. Kathleen Ryan.

Ashley Donnelly is currently an Assistant Professor of Telecommunications at Ball State University in Muncie, Indiana. She received her Ph.D. from the University of South Florida in English with a concentration in Film in 2008 and her M.A. from Birkbeck College at the University of London in cultural and critical studies in 2003. Her research focuses on mainstream US culture and gender studies.

Jennifer Good, Ph.D., is an associate professor in the Communication, Popular Culture and Film department at Brock University in St. Catherine, Ontario. Good's research and teaching interests sit at the intersection of mass media, materialism, and our relationship with the natural environment. Her current work includes looking at the mass communication of climate change, investigating how parents' television viewing relates to their willingness to let their children play in the outdoors.

Ariadne A. Gonzales is a Ph.D. candidate in Organizational and Intercultural Communication at Texas A&M University. Her research centers on issues of difference within work-life experiences and occupational identity among Mexican immigrant workers and Hispanic leadership. She is currently working on her dissertation that examines the lived experiences of domestic work on the South Texas border of Laredo, Texas, and Nuevo Laredo, Mexico, as well as how identity work can help us understand domestic workers' occupational identity in relation to other occupational influences. She is also an instructor at Texas A&M International University.

Robert D. Gratz, Ph.D., is currently the Special Assistant to the President and a professor of Communication Studies at Texas State University–San Marcos. He previously served as the vice president for Academic Affairs from 1990–2004. Gratz has co-authored several articles on organizational communication and on the social impacts of emerging technologies.

Katharine Foss is an assistant professor of Mass Communication at Middle Tennessee State University. She earned her Ph.D. from the University of Minnesota in 2008. Her current research focuses on media discourse surrounding breastfeeding (from advertising to entertainment television), constructions of health responsibility, and representations of deafness and hearing loss. Her past research projects have examined gender and victimization in television forensics programs, the discourse of television theme songs, pioneer medicine in television, and portrayals of journalists in comic book films.

Charity Fox, Ph.D., is an assistant professor in the School of Communications Design at the University of Baltimore. She teaches popular culture studies, media studies, literature, and writing in an interdisciplinary department that combines studies of English, communications, media, and design. Her research and teaching explore cultural, social, and artistic reactions to historical moments; masculinity and gender studies; war and conflict broadly defined; and narratives of America in the world that circulate within the cultures of everyday life and contribute to cultural constructions of identity.

Chandler Harris holds a B.S. in Broadcast Journalism and an M.A. in Communication from Abilene Christian University. During his undergraduate career, he completed internships with both ESPN in New York City and KTVT-CBS 11 in Dallas/Ft. Worth, Texas. These experiences, combined with his lifelong love of America's pastime, led him to examine the topic of failure in baseball for his master's thesis. He now works as a program analyst for PFSweb, a global end-to-end eCommerce solution corporation headquartered in Allen, Texas.

Edward Janak is an associate professor in Educational Studies at the University of Wyoming. He earned his B.A. from SUNY Fredonia and M.Ed. and Ph.D. from the University of South Carolina–Columbia. His research interests lie in the foundations of education and how they can be used to inform and interpret present practice in education. He is beginning a new line of research examining philanthropic funding in public education.

Tim Karis is a postdoctoral research fellow at the Center for Islamic Theology (CIT), which is located at the University of Münster, Germany. At CIT, he coordinates an interdisciplinary research group called "Religious Pluralism as a Challenge for Societies and Religious Communities." Before joining CIT, Karis was a Ph.D. student at the Cluster of Excellence "Religion and Politics in Pre-Modern and Modern Cultures" located at the University of Münster.

Katherine J. Lehman is the author of the book *Those Girls: Single Women in Sixties and Seventies Popular Culture*. She is an associate professor of Communications at Albright College in Pennsylvania, where she also co-directs the Women's and Gender Studies program. Her other publications include articles on Rosie O'Donnell and *The View*, contemporary motherhood and postfeminism on television, and *Mad Men*'s portrayals of working women.

Lauren Lemley is an assistant professor of Communication and director of the Speaking Center at Abilene Christian University. She received her Ph.D. in communication with an emphasis in rhetoric from Texas A&M University. Her dissertation focused on understanding and analyzing the rhetoric of the Salem witchcraft crisis, and her current research and teaching fall primarily in the fields of argumentation, public address, and public memory studies.

Joy Chavez Mapaye is an assistant professor in the Department of Journalism and Public Communications at the University of Alaska Anchorage. Her dissertation was honored with the Broadcast Education Association's Kenneth Harwood Outstanding Dissertation Award in 2011. Her research interests include television, new media/digital culture, marketing communication, and health communication. She received her Ph.D. from the University of Oregon's School of Journalism and Communication, and her M.A. and B.A. degrees from Washington State University.

Gretta Moody is a doctoral student in the Annenberg School for Communication at the University of Pennsylvania. Her research interests include media audiences, black subjectivities, and racial/class performance.

Michelle Napierski-Prancl is an associate professor of Sociology and Director of the Sociology and Criminal Justice programs in the Department of History and Society at Russell Sage College for Women in Troy, New York. Napierski-Prancl's research interests focus on gender, work, family, media, and popular culture. Her publications include essays on the portrayal of gender in popular literature and articles on teaching pedagogy. She lives with her husband and three children in upstate New York and is currently working on a project about "The Mommy Wars."

Larry Ossei-Mensah earned his B.A. from Clark University, Worcester in Business Management and his M.B.A from Les Roches, Switzerland, in Hospitality Management and Marketing in 2007. He is an advertising and entertainment veteran whose stints at Sony Music, ClearChannel, Fox TV, and Carat Media have been the catalyst for his scholastic interest in digital and media studies. He seeks to aggregate his work experience in media with his scholastic interests in order to contribute to the production of innovative research that will bring diverse intellectual perspectives to the scholarly body of knowledge.

Carrie Packwood Freeman, Ph.D., is a critical/cultural studies scholar whose research interests include media ethics, communication strategies for social justice movements, and the media's coverage of nonhuman animal and environmental issues (specifically, animal agribusiness and veganism). In addition to a previous career in public relations and HR/training, she's been active in the animal rights and vegetarian movement for almost two decades and has served as a volunteer director for local grassroots groups in three states.

Leighton C. Peterson is an assistant professor of Anthropology at Miami University and a producer for Vision Maker Media, Inc. He is the author of numerous articles on Native American media and indigenous languages and the co-editor of "American Indian Languages in Unexpected Places," a special issue of *American Indian Culture & Research Journal*. His documentary works include *Columbus Day Legacy* (2011), *Weaving Worlds* (2008), and the forthcoming *Apache Scouts*.

Philip J. Salem, Ph.D., is a professor in the Department of Communication Studies at Texas State University–San Marcos. He has been writing about communication and technology since the late 1970s. His primary concerns have been how changing communication technology might alter emerging psychological and social processes and how the development of communication technology networks might constrain those processes. His work about these topics and organizational communication has been recognized by national and international associations. He is the author of *The Complexity of Human Communication*, a book describing communication as a nonlinear emergent social process.

Susan H. Sarapin earned a Bachelor of Science degree in medical illustration from the University of Illinois Medical Center, and earned her M.A. and Ph.D. in mass communication from Purdue University's Brian Lamb School of Communication in West Lafayette, Indiana. Sarapin's emphasis is in media, technology, and society. She is an assistant professor of Journalism and Communication at Troy University in the Hall School of Journalism and Communication. Her research focuses on the effects of the media on the public's perceptions of the law.

Glenn Sparks has been a professor of Communication at Purdue University since 1986. He served as the associate head of what is now the Brian Lamb School of Communication for twelve years (2001–2013). He conducts research and teaches courses in communication theory, mass media effects, relationships in the electronic era, and research methods.

Margaret Tally is the chair of the Master of Arts in Social Policy program at Empire State College in New York. Her article "Television Women from Lucy to *Friends*: Fifty Years of Sitcoms and Feminism" appeared in the *Journal of American Culture*. Her research interests include cultural sociology, class, gender, race, sex/gender, and work and labor.

Danielle E. Williams is an assistant professor of Film at Georgia Gwinnett College. She completed her Ph.D. in Communication from Georgia State University. She also works as a researcher for Internet Decisions, LLC and the Georgia Technology Authority. She holds a B.A. in Mass Communication and an M.A. in Communication from Auburn University. Her research specializations are African American Media Studies, Television Studies, and Media Industries Studies.

About the Editors

Deborah A. Macey received her Ph.D. in Communication and Society from the University of Oregon's School of Journalism and Communication. She is a visiting assistant professor at Saint Louis University, her alma mater, where she earned a B.S. of Business Administration with a major in Marketing and an M.A. in Communication. She teaches courses in human communication and media studies. Her research interests focus on the intersections of gender, race, and class in popular culture representations, particularly television. As a lifetime member of the Organization for the Study of Communication, Language, and Gender, she frequently presents at its annual conference, among others including Women and Society, National Communication Association, and International Communication Association. Her work has appeared in *Media Depictions of Brides, Wives, and Mothers* (Lexington), *International Encyclopedia of Communication* (Blackwell) and *Human Studies: A Journal for Philosophy and the Social Sciences*.

Kathleen M. Ryan spent more than twenty years in network and local news production, and she continues to work as an active multimedia director and producer. Ryan's research interests include news labor and content, as well as oral history and visual communication. She has been recognized for excellence in both her professional and academic work, including an award of merit from the Broadcast Education Association for the film *Backstretch*; research honors from the International Communication Association and Association for Education in Journalism and Mass Communication, a Chris Award as co-producer for *Saving Faces*, and numerous other national and regional broadcast awards including a New England Emmy nomination. Her research has appeared in several edited collections and numerous journals, including

Visual Studies, *Electronic News*, and *Journal for Cultural Inquiry.* Ryan holds a Ph.D. in Communication and Society from University of Oregon, an M.A. in broadcast journalism from University of Southern California, and a B.A. in political science from University of California, Santa Barbara.

Noah J. Springer is a Ph.D. student at the University of Colorado, Boulder. Springer's areas of research interest include televised news and satire, digital culture, and political economy of information distribution systems. He holds an M.A. in media theory and research from Southern Illinois University, Carbondale. His thesis examined the critical, comedic, and political connections between *The Daily Show with Jon Stewart, The Colbert Report* and *South Park.* He received his B.A. in Art History from Southern Illinois University, Edwardsville.

0 1341 1661429 5